THE ADVANCED DICTIONARY
OF MARKETING

This book is due for return on or before the last date shown below.

The Advanced Dictionary of
Marketing

PUTTING THEORY TO USE

Scott G. Dacko

OXFORD
UNIVERSITY PRESS

*This book has been printed digitally and produced in a standard specification
in order to ensure its continuing availability*

OXFORD
UNIVERSITY PRESS

Great Clarendon Street, Oxford OX2 6DP
Oxford University Press is a department of the University of Oxford.
It furthers the University's objective of excellence in research, scholarship,
and education by publishing worldwide in

Oxford New York

Auckland Cape Town Dar es Salaam Hong Kong Karachi
Kuala Lumpur Madrid Melbourne Mexico City Nairobi
New Delhi Shanghai Taipei Toronto
With offices in
Argentina Austria Brazil Chile Czech Republic France Greece
Guatemala Hungary Italy Japan South Korea Poland Portugal
Singapore Switzerland Thailand Turkey Ukraine Vietnam

Oxford is a registered trade mark of Oxford University Press
in the UK and in certain other countries
Published in the United States
by Oxford University Press Inc., New York

ISBN 978-0-19-928600-3

Acknowledgments

Special thanks go to all who have contributed to the wealth of knowledge contained within this advanced dictionary. In assisting with its production, many thanks go to: Janet Biddle for the typing of some earlier background material; Marwa Gad for conducting background research on many of the terms as well as consolidating research material and formatting many entries, and all members of staff at Warwick Business School, University of Warwick, who have reviewed the entries in this dictionary, including David Arnott, Sue Bridgewater, Simon Collinson, and Philip Stern, among others. At (and for) Oxford University Press, many people are also to be praised for making this advanced dictionary possible, including David Musson, Matthew Derbyshire, Tanya Dean, Edwin Pritchard, and Andrew Hawkey. Finally, very special thanks go to Gala, Alex, and my parents for their patience, love, and support during the preparation of this work.

SGD

Contents

Thematic Index 1: Table of Applications

This table provides an index of dictionary entries with direct relevance and application to particular key areas of marketing. For further information, please see the 'How to Use this Dictionary' section of the Introduction.

Term	Marketing Strategy	Marketing Management	Consumer Behavior	Marketing Research	Marketing Modeling	Services Marketing	Retail Marketing	Online Marketing	Business-to-Business Marketing	International Marketing	Other Application Areas
above-the-line marketing	•					•					new product development
absolute cost advantage	•										
absorptive capacity	•										
accelerator principle					•					•	mergers and acquistions
achievement motivation theory		•									
acquiescence response set				•							
actor–observer difference		•	•			•				•	
adaptation										•	
adaptation-level theory	•		•	•							marketing education
adaptive strategy	•										
adopter categories	•				•						
adoption process			•		•						
adoption theory	•		•								
adverse selection	•					•		•			
advertising theory			•								advertising
advertising wearout effect											advertising
affect	•		•								
affiliate marketing								•			

Term	Marketing Strategy	Marketing Management	Consumer Behavior	Marketing Research	Marketing Modeling	Services Marketing	Retail Marketing	Online Marketing	Business-to-Business Marketing	International Marketing	Other Application Areas
affinity marketing	•		•								non-profit marketing
agency theory	•										franchising
agglomeration economies	•										
ambush marketing	•										marketing ethics, sponsorship marketing
anchoring and adjustment			•								
anchoring effect			•								
ancient mariner effect								•			
announcement effect	•						•				
antimarketing	•					•					
approach–avoidance conflict	•	•	•								
arbitrage pricing theory	•										pricing
Asch phenomenon		•									
assimilation–contrast theory			•								
attitudes, functional theory of	•						•				
attribution theory			•			•					advertising
audience effect									•		
averages, law of	•	•	•								
Averch–Johnson effect	•										
backwash effects										•	

Term	Marketing Strategy	Marketing Management	Consumer Behavior	Marketing Research	Marketing Modeling	Services Marketing	Retail Marketing	Online Marketing	Business-to-Business Marketing	International Marketing	Other Application Areas
buyer influence/readiness		•		•		•					advertising, sales
bystander effect	•							•			boycotts
cannibalization											new product introductions, product portfolios
capture theory						•					product regulation
carry over effect	•		•		•	•					
catastrophe theory							•	•			
category killer											
cause-related marketing	•		•								
ceiling effect				•							
celebrity marketing	•										advertising
central place theory							•				
certainty effect			•								pricing
channel arrangement	•	•			•						
channel conflict	•	•		•						•	
chaos theory	•			•						•	
characteristics theory				•	•						
Churchill's paradigm		•									
clubs, theory of			•			•					

Term	Marketing Strategy	Marketing Management	Consumer Behavior	Marketing Research	Marketing Modeling	Services Marketing	Retail Marketing	Online Marketing	Business-to-Business Marketing	International Marketing	Other Application Areas
consumer marketing								•			pricing
consumer satisfaction theory	•		•		•						
consumer sovereignty		•									
consumer-to-business				•		•		•			
consumer-to-consumer				•		•		•			
consumerism	•										
context effect			•								
contingency theory	•	•	•								
contingency theory of management accounting		•									
contrast effect			•								
convergence marketing	•										
cooperative marketing	•	•								•	tourism marketing
corporate marketing	•	•				•				•	
cost	•										
counter-marketing	•		•								
country of origin effect	•	•	•								advertising
cross-cultural marketing	•	•		•		•				•	
customer equity	•	•		•							
customer-oriented marketing	•	•				•					

Term	Marketing Strategy	Marketing Management	Consumer Behavior	Marketing Research	Marketing Modeling	Services Marketing	Retail Marketing	Online Marketing	Business-to-Business Marketing	International Marketing	Other Application Areas
door-in-the-face technique	•										promotions
double jeopardy effect				•	•						marketing communications
drive theory of social facilitation						•					
dynamic capabilities	•									•	new product development
E and O theories of change	•									•	
eclectic paradigm										•	
economies of growth	•										
economies of scale		•									
economies of scope	•					•					
effect, law of			•								
efficient market hypothesis	•			•							
elaboration likelihood model			•								relationship marketing, advertising
elasticity of demand	•				•						pricing
elation effect		•									
e-marketing	•	•						•		•	marketing education
endowment effect			•								
Engel's law						•					forecasting
enlightened marketing	•										

Term	Marketing Strategy	Marketing Management	Consumer Behavior	Marketing Research	Marketing Modeling	Services Marketing	Retail Marketing	Online Marketing	Business-to-Business Marketing	International Marketing	Other Application Areas
forecasting methods		●		●							
forgetting curve	●		●								advertising
framing effect	●		●	●							
free rider effect			●								green marketing
frequency marketing	●		●								
fundamental attribution error			●								
fusion marketing								●		●	
fuzzy set theory											
gain–loss effect			●			●					decision making
gambler's fallacy			●		●						decision making
game theory	●				●						
generalizability theory	●			●							
generational marketing	●			●							advertising
gestalt theory			●	●					●		marketing ethics
global marketing	●	●									advertising
glocal marketing	●										
Goodhart's law	●										
goods	●	●		●	●	●	●	●		●	advertising
government marketing	●	●				●				●	
gravity theory					●					●	

Term	Marketing Strategy	Marketing Management	Consumer Behavior	Marketing Research	Marketing Modeling	Services Marketing	Retail Marketing	Online Marketing	Business-to-Business Marketing	International Marketing	Other Application Areas
institutional marketing	•										marketing education, marketing ethics
integrated marketing communications	•	•									advertising
integration	•										
intellectual property	•										
internal marketing	•										
internalization theory						•					
international marketing	•	•						•			
intertemporal substitution		•	•	•						•	
intrusive marketing	•	•		•						•	mobile marketing
isolation effect	•		•	•							
item response theory				•							
job characteristics theory		•									
John Henry effect											marketing education
just world hypothesis											social marketing
key success factors	•			•			•		•		mobile marketing
laddering	•			•							
lagged effect					•						advertising
large numbers, law of					•			•			

Term	Marketing Strategy	Marketing Management	Consumer Behavior	Marketing Research	Marketing Modeling	Services Marketing	Retail Marketing	Online Marketing	Business-to-Business Marketing	International Marketing	Other Application Areas
Pollyanna effect	•	•									
population ecology theory	•	•									
portfolio theory	•	•									
positioning	•	•				•					
power law of forgetting	•	•	•								
precision marketing		•	•						•		
preference reversal			•						•		
price discrimination	•	•	•							•	
price effect	•	•	•	•			•	•			
price theory					•						pricing
pricing strategies											pricing
primacy, law of											marketing communications
primacy effect			•	•				•			
private label	•	•	•	•			•				
product classifications, consumer	•	•				•					
product levels	•			•							
product life cycle	•	•		•	•				•	•	
product line	•	•		•	•						

Term	Marketing Strategy	Marketing Management	Consumer Behavior	Marketing Research	Marketing Modeling	Services Marketing	Retail Marketing	Online Marketing	Business-to-Business Marketing	International Marketing	Other Application Areas
resource-based view	•	•		•		•		•	•	•	global marketing
resource dependency theory	•	•		•					•		government marketing
retail accordion theory							•				
retail gravitation, law of							•				
retail marketing	•	•	•			•	•	•			marketing education
retro-marketing	•	•	•				•				advertising
ripple effect	•										
satisficing	•			•							
scale				•		•					
segment-of-one marketing	•	•		•	•						
segmentation	•	•		•	•						
segmentation viability	•	•					•				advertising
selective exposure			•						•		
self-fulfilling prophecy	•		•	•							
self-perception theory	•			•							
selling process	•	•							•	•	
serial position effect								•			advertising
service, laws of						•					
service characteristics	•	•				•					
services marketing	•	•	•					•			

Term	Marketing Strategy	Marketing Management	Consumer Behavior	Marketing Research	Marketing Modelling	Services Marketing	Retail Marketing	Online Marketing	Business-to-Business Marketing	International Marketing	Other Application Areas
strategic options	•	•			•		•	•	•	•	
strategic window	•										
strategies, generic	•	•							•	•	small businesses
strategy	•	•									
subcultural theory			•	•							
subjective expected utility theory				•							
subliminal advertising			•								advertising
substitute awareness effect	•			•	•						
substitute product	•	•		•		•					
substitution effect			•								
sunk cost fallacy	•										
supply, law of	•				•						
supply and demand, law of	•						•	•			decision making
survey research				•							
sustainable competitive advantage	•										
SWOT analysis	•			•							
symbolic interaction theory	•		•								
synergy	•										new product development

Term	Marketing Strategy	Marketing Management	Consumer Behavior	Marketing Research	Marketing Modeling	Services Marketing	Retail Marketing	Online Marketing	Business-to-Business Marketing	International Marketing	Other Application Areas
value-based marketing	•	•									
value chain analysis	•							•	•	•	marketing education
value proposition	•	•									
variety effect	•										
viral marketing	•		•								
von Restorff effect			•								
Wal-Mart effect								•			
Walras' law					•						
want	•		•			•					social marketing
warm/cold effect											marketing education
Web marketing	•							•			
Weber–Fechner law											pricing, promotion
wheel of retailing theory				•			•				
wholesale marketing		•		•			•				
willingness to pay			•			•	•				
winner's curse											auctions
word-of-mouth communication				•		•					
word-of-mouth effect	•				•	•					

Thematic Index 2: Searching for Marketing Terms Using Key Words

This list of descriptive key words provides a means of identifying relevant advanced marketing terms. For further information, please see the 'How to Use this Dictionary' section of the Introduction.

abstractions   fallacy of misplaced concreteness
accountability   diffusion of responsibility
accuracy   reliability
achievement   achievement motivation theory
acquisition(s)   integration, utility
action(s)   actor–observer difference, bandwagon effect, conative, domino effect, escalation of commitment
activities   sponsorship marketing, sports marketing
actors   microenvironment
adaptability   adaptive strategy
adaptation   adaptation-level theory, Darwinian evolution theory
added value   value
adoption   adoption theory, diffusion of innovation, innovation effect
adoption stages   adoption process
advertising   above-the-line marketing, advertising wearout effect, out-of-home marketing, pull marketing, ratchet effect, recency principle, ripple effect, share of voice, subliminal advertising
advertising agencies   below-the-line marketing
advertising effectiveness   advertising theory, hierarchy of effects
advertising effects   advertising theory
advice   opinion leader
affective state   mood effect
age   generational marketing
agents   agency theory
aggregate data   iceberg principle
agreements   moral hazard
alternative evaluation   isolation effect, rational choice theory
alternative products   substitute product
analysis   generalizability theory, scale, shareholder value analysis

areas   place marketing
arguments   inoculation theory, primacy, law of
asset valuation   efficient market hypothesis
assets   marketing strategy, resource-based view
asymmetric response functions   ratchet effect
athletics   sports marketing
attack strategies   offensive marketing
attention   cocktail party phenomenon
attitude formation   self-perception theory
attitudes   actor–observer difference, antimarketing, attitudes,
    functional theory of, boomerang effect, comparative judgment, law of,
    elaboration likelihood model, mere exposure effect, mood effect,
    opinion leader, planned behavior, theory of, reasoned action, theory
    of, reference group, selective exposure, subcultural theory
attributes   positioning
attributions   actor–observer difference, blaming the victim, just world
    hypothesis
auctions   winner's curse
audiences   audience effect, drive theory of social facilitation
authoritative marketing statements   marketing, rules of
background characteristics   upper echelons theory
balanced offerings   product portfolio analysis
basic marketing generalizations   marketing, principles of
behavior   announcement effect, antimarketing, consumer behavior,
    theory of, elation effect, ERG theory, exercise, law of, expectancy
    theory, field theory, Hawthorne effect, illusion of control, least effort,
    principle of, mood effect, opinion leader, planned behavior, theory of,
    reasoned action, theory of, reference group, reinforcement,
    self-perception theory, small group theory, social cognitive theory,
    temperament theory
behavioral consequences   effect, law of
behavioral explanations   attribution theory, fundamental attribution
    error
behavioral intentions   reasoned action, theory of
behavioral modeling   social learning theory
belief popularity   bandwagon effect
beliefs   expectancy theory, fallacy of composition, overconfidence
    effect, Pygmalion effect, reference group, selective exposure
benefits   agglomeration economies, free rider effect, positioning,
    product levels, social exchange theory, value proposition
bias   acquiescence response set, anchoring and adjustment,
    confirmation bias, conjunction fallacy, demand characteristics,
    experimenter effect, experimenter expectancy effect, halo effect,
    hindsight bias, sunk cost fallacy, testing effect, unrealistic optimism
bidding   winner's curse
brand choice   Dirichlet model
brand distinctiveness   brand positioning

brand preference   brand loyalty
brand quality   reputation effect
brand superiority   brand positioning
brand value   brand equity
brand variety   variety effect
branding   private label
brands   double jeopardy effect
broad appeal   mass marketing
broadened marketing concept   megamarketing
budget-setting   promotion budget setting methods
bureaucracy   skunkworks
business relationships   resource dependency theory
buyer readiness   buyer influence/readiness
buying behavior   industrial buyer behavior
buying cycle   hockey stick effect
buying decision behavior   consumer buyer behavior
buying decision process   evoked set
bygone marketing practices   retro-marketing
capabilities   E and O theories of change, top-down marketing
capital   Averch–Johnson effect
causality   attribution theory, fundamental attribution error
cause   Pareto principle, placebo effect, ratchet effect
certainty   overconfidence effect
chance   illusion of control
change   Darwinian evolution theory, dialectic process theory, domino
   effect
channels   hybrid marketing, transaction cost theory
channels of distribution   gray markets
choice   common ratio effect, expected utility theory, framing effect,
   group polarization, Hick's law, isolation effect, options theory, utility
   theory
circumstances   fundamental attribution error
cities   local marketing, retail gravitation, law of
clustering   agglomeration economies
cognition(s)   cognitive consistency theory, cognitive dissonance, context
   effect, social cognitive theory
cognitive arousal   Yerkes–Dodson law
cognitive bias   false consensus effect
cognitive consistency   balance theory
cohorts   generational marketing
collective behavior   clubs, theory of
combined offerings   bundling
commission-free   below-the-line marketing
commissions   above-the-line marketing
commitment   escalation of commitment
commodities   commodification, one price, law of

communication   boomerang effect, communication-information
   processing theory, consumer-to-consumer, information processing
   theory, primacy, law of, sleeper effect
communication technology   e-marketing
communications integration   integrated marketing communications
community   tribal marketing
community behavior   brand community
comparisons   comparative judgment, law of
competence   Peter principle
competencies   marketing strategy, resource-based view
competition   game theory
competitive advantage   absolute cost advantage, cluster theory, dynamic
   capabilities, resource-based view, strategic marketing, strategic
   options, sustainable competitive advantage, loyalty marketing
competitive analysis   strategic group
competitive dynamics   red queen effect
competitive environment   competition
competitive position   market share
competitive positioning   positioning
competitive strategy   decline strategies, leapfrogging
competitiveness   key success factors
complex systems   butterfly effect, complexity theory
complexity   systems theory
compliance   door-in-the-face technique, foot-in-the-door technique,
   low-ball technique
computer network   online marketing
concepts   fallacy of misplaced concreteness
confidence   overconfidence effect
confirmation   consumer satisfaction theory
conformity   Asch phenomenon
confounding influences   Hawthorne effect
confusion   confusion marketing
connecting   tribal marketing
connectivity   network theory
consensus   false consensus effect
consistency   reliability
consumer activities   lifestyle marketing
consumer advocacy   consumerism
consumer awareness   substitute awareness effect
consumer behavior   cognitive dissonance, income effect
consumer benefit   variety effect
consumer characteristics   segmentation
consumer demand   pull marketing
consumer deprivation   need
consumer groups   segmentation
consumer influence   opinion leader

customer interests   affinity marketing
customer needs   house of quality
customer relationships   customer equity, marketing
customer retention   frequency marketing, relationship marketing
customer value   customer equity
customization   micromarketing
customized marketing plans   bespoke marketing
data   information systems theory
data analysis   iceberg principle, outlier effect
data collection   order effect
data collection methods   marketing research
data gathering   survey research
decision making   Asch phenomenon, Bayesian decision theory,
   behavioral decision theory, bounded rationality, buyer decision
   process, certainty effect, common ratio effect, confirmation bias,
   decision theory, expected utility theory, fallacy of composition,
   framing effect, gain–loss effect, game theory, group polarization,
   groupthink, locality, principle of, organization theory, prospect
   theory, rational choice theory, satisficing, subjective expected utility
   theory, sunk cost fallacy, utility theory
decreasing returns   diminishing returns, law of
delay   lagged effect
demand   consumer demand theory, demand, law of, elasticity of
   demand, supply and demand, law of
demand creation   pull marketing
demand elimination   counter-marketing
demand reduction   demarketing
design   organization theory
desire   want
detectable change   Weber–Fechner law
development   dialectic process theory
diffusion   imitation effect, innovation effect, trickle down theory
direct communication   direct-to-consumer marketing
direct sales   retail marketing
discriminatory pricing   price discrimination
disorder   chaos theory
disproportional influence   Pareto principle
dissonance reduction   cognitive consistency theory
distance   gravity theory, retail gravitation, law of
distinctive capabilities   strategic competency
distinctiveness   von Restorff effect
distribution   gray markets, hybrid marketing
distribution intensity   distribution strategies
distribution systems   channel arrangement, network marketing
distributor conflict   channel conflict
distributor interaction   field marketing
drive   achievement motivation theory

expectations   customer satisfaction, expectation-disconfirmation model, experimenter expectancy effect, Pygmalion effect
experience   experience curve effect
experimental research   demand characteristics
experiments   experimenter effect, Hawthorne effect, John Henry effect
explanation   parsimony, law of
exporting   comparative advantage, law of
exposure   mere exposure effect, recency principle
external information   absorptive capacity
failure   Icarus paradox
fairness   equity theory
fallacy   conjunction fallacy
false belief   better mousetrap fallacy
fashion   trickle down theory
features   product levels
feeling   affect
financial assets   arbitrage pricing theory
financial return   portfolio theory
firm   key success factors
firm concentrations   cluster theory
firm-initiated marketing   outbound marketing
firm investment   accelerator principle
firm orientations   marketing management orientation
firm performance   market share effect, reputation effect, ten percent, rule of
firm resource   strategic asset
firm share price   random-walk theory
fiscal performance   hockey stick effect
fixed-fee   below-the-line marketing
focus   strategies, generic
focused marketing   niche marketing
food   Engel's law
forecast   self-fulfilling prophecy
forecasting   accelerator principle, Engel's law
foreign direct investment   eclectic paradigm
foreign market entry   psychic distance
forgetting   forgetting curve, power law of forgetting
forms   gestalt theory
framing   prospect theory
freedom of choice   options theory
functional integration   total integrated marketing
functional strategies   marketing strategy
gains   gain–loss effect, prospect theory
games   game theory
gaps   unmet need
general equilibrium   Walras' law
generalizability   generalizability theory

informal communication   word-of-mouth communication, word-of-mouth marketing
informal communication effects   word-of-mouth effect
information   communication-information processing theory, data types, direct marketing, iceberg principle, information processing theory, information systems theory, opinion leader, primacy effect, recency effect, selective exposure, survey research
information complexity   bounded rationality
information processing   Pollyanna effect
information processing capacity   magical number seven
information technologies   database marketing
information transfer   boundary spanning
innovation   absorptive capacity, diffusion of innovation, disruptive technology, innovation effect, skunkworks
innovators   adopter categories
inputs   diminishing returns, law of
institutional change   wheel of retailing theory
institutions   corporate marketing
intangible offerings   services marketing
integration   integrated marketing communications, total integrated marketing
intended measurement   validity
interactivity   experiential marketing, online marketing
intermediaries   disintermediation, indirect marketing
international markets   one price, law of
international operations   eclectic paradigm, internalization theory
internationalization   eclectic paradigm, psychic distance
internet   online marketing
interorganizational bargaining   bargaining theory
interorganizational relationships   network theory, resource dependency theory, transaction cost theory
interpersonal relationships   personal construct theory
interpretation   reader-response theory
interviewing   laddering
investment(s)   escalation of commitment, greater fool theory, portfolio theory, product-market investment strategies
items   item response theory
items of commerce   product marketing
job design   job characteristics theory
judgment(s)   anchoring effect, base-rate fallacy, behavioral decision theory, comparative judgment, law of, confirmation bias, congruity theory, conjunction fallacy, halo effect, majority fallacy, overconfidence effect, reference group, sunk cost fallacy, utility theory
justice   blaming the victim, just world hypothesis
knowledge   absorptive capacity
lag time   lagged effect
laggards   adopter categories

large markets   mass marketing
large organizations   institutional marketing
late majority   adopter categories
learning   absorptive capacity, effect, law of, fan effect, learning curve
  effect, overlearning, primacy effect, recency effect
learning processes   learning theory
legal protection   intellectual property
life cycle   product life cycle
liking   mere exposure effect
limited information   Bayesian decision theory
line   product line
literature   reader-response theory
local marketing   glocal marketing
local needs   local marketing
location   agglomeration economies, cluster theory
location analysis   gravity theory
location preference   central place theory
location tendencies   central place theory
long-term benefits   societal classification of products
long-term horizon   strategic marketing
long-term plans   strategy
long-term relationships   relationship marketing
losses   gain–loss effect, prospect theory
loyalty   Dirichlet model, double jeopardy effect, frequency marketing,
  loyalty effect, loyalty marketing, loyalty ripple effect
luxury goods   snob effect
management   management theory, Parkinson's law
management approaches   contingency theory of management
  accounting
management guidance   ten percent, rule of
management objectives   firm, theory of the
management practice   X, theory, Y, theory, Z, theory
market decline   decline strategies
market efficiency   efficient market hypothesis
market entry   entry barriers, megamarketing
market equilibrium   supply and demand, law of
market introduction process   new product development
market needs   demand
market operations   megamarketing
market position   defensive marketing
market practice   Gresham's law
market segmentation   differentiated marketing
market segments   niche marketing
market share   market share effect
market testing   test marketing
market transformation   disruptive technology
marketing   exchange theory

mergers   integration
message acceptance   assimilation–contrast theory
message rejection   assimilation–contrast theory
message repetition   repetition effect
misfortunes   blaming the victim
misleading conclusions   spurious correlation
misrepresentation   bias
mission   non-profit marketing
mobile consumers   mobile marketing
modeling   demand, law of, supply, law of
models   fuzzy set theory, hierarchy of effects
monitoring   balanced scorecard
moral conduct   ethical marketing
motivation   achievement motivation theory, drive theory of social
   facilitation, elaboration likelihood model, expectancy theory,
   Herzberg's theory of motivation, job characteristics theory
multinational enterprise(s)   eclectic paradigm, internalization theory
multiple marketing approaches   fusion marketing, hybrid marketing
myth   better mousetrap fallacy
national marketing systems   comparative marketing
nature of marketing   marketing, theories of
need categories   hierarchy of needs theory
need hierarchy   hierarchy of needs theory
need(s)   attitudes, functional theory of, ERG theory, exchange, law of,
   field theory, hierarchy of needs theory, unmet need
negotiation   bargaining theory, door-in-the-face technique,
   foot-in-the-door technique, low-ball technique
neighborhoods   local marketing
networks   Metcalfe's law, network effect, network theory
new product development   skunkworks
new product introduction(s)   takeoff, test marketing
new products   cannibalization
non-profit organizations   cause-related marketing
non-traditional marketing   unconventional marketing
nostalgic offerings   retro-marketing
numerical data   outlier effect
objects   set theory
observation   audience effect, Hawthorne effect, social learning theory
observers   actor–observer difference
offering attractiveness   adverse selection
ongoing analysis   value-based marketing
online marketing   Web marketing
operational innovation   Wal-Mart effect
operationalization   tactic, tactical marketing
opinions   opinion leader
opportunism   strategic approaches
opportunities   SWOT analysis

optimal decisions   decision theory
optimism   unrealistic optimism
order of entry   market entry timing
organization   adaptive strategy, gestalt theory, organization theory,
    Parkinson's law, Peter principle, red queen effect
organizational activities   value chain analysis
organizational behavior   firm, theory of the
organizational buy-in   internal marketing
organizational change   E and O theories of change, population ecology
    theory, retail accordion theory
organizational communication   boundary spanning
organizational design   contingency theory
organizational evolution   dialectic process theory
organizational function   marketing
organizational marketing   business-to-business marketing
organizational mission   non-profit marketing
organizational performance   upper echelons theory
organizational performance evaluation   balanced scorecard
organizational philosophies   marketing management orientation
organizational processes   benchmarking
organizational relationships   microenvironment
organizational stakeholders   stakeholder theory
organizational structure   population ecology theory
organizational support   sponsorship marketing
organizational teaming   affinity marketing
organizations   complexity theory, industrial buyer behavior, learning
    curve effect
original products   new product
outcomes   averages, law of, preference reversal, Pygmalion effect
outdoors   out-of-home marketing
outputs   diminishing returns, law of
ownership   endowment effect
partnerships   cooperative marketing
pattern recognition   Bayesian decision theory
pay-for-performance   affiliate marketing
payoffs   preference reversal
perceived value   value, willingness to pay
perception(s)   adaptation-level theory, cocktail party phenomenon,
    context effect, contrast effect, country of origin effect, even price
    effect, halo effect, hindsight bias, income effect, odd price effect,
    reputation effect, Weber–Fechner law
performance   audience effect, averages, law of, customer satisfaction,
    drive theory of social facilitation, expectation-disconfirmation model,
    honeymoon effect, job characteristics theory, learning curve effect,
    Little's law, overlearning, Pygmalion effect
performance evaluation   benchmarking
performance improvement   benchmarking

performance measures Goodhart's law
personal disclosure ancient mariner effect
personal selling push marketing
personal websites blog marketing
personal welfare social marketing
personality attribution theory, personal construct theory,
  psychoanalytic theory, temperament theory, warm/cold effect,
personality assessment Barnum effect
persuasion assimilation–contrast theory, boomerang effect,
  door-in-the-face technique, elaboration likelihood model,
  foot-in-the-door technique, hierarchy of effects, inoculation theory,
  low-ball technique, primacy, law of, sleeper effect
persuasive messages subliminal advertising
physical locations location theory, place marketing
physical objects product marketing
planning Murphy's law, strategic marketing
planning process STP marketing
plans strategy, tactic
point-of-sale below-the-line marketing
policy Goodhart's law
portfolios portfolio theory
positioning STP marketing
positive information Pollyanna effect
power least interest, principle of
pre-announcements announcement effect
prediction(s) forecasting methods, regression towards the mean,
  self-fulfilling prophecy
preference preference reversal, reference group, utility theory
prestige snob effect
price(s) demand, law of, elasticity of demand, price theory, supply, law
  of, supply and demand, law of, x-inefficiency
price changes price effect, substitution effect
price comparison reference price
price competition commodification
price sensitivity shared-cost effect, substitute awareness effect, unique
  value effect
price setting pricing strategies
pricing even price effect, odd price effect, one price, law of, price effect,
  price theory
pricing approaches pricing strategies
primacy primacy effect, primacy, law of
principals agency theory
proactive marketing outbound marketing
proactive marketing strategy offensive marketing
probabilities averages, law of, base-rate fallacy, certainty effect,
  common ratio effect, conjunction fallacy, gambler's fallacy, large
  numbers, law of, preference reversal

rewards elation effect, reinforcement
risk arbitrage pricing theory, expected utility theory, group polarization, moral hazard, portfolio theory, preference reversal, prospect theory
risk-seeking prospect theory
risk-taking prospect theory
sales achievement motivation theory, cannibalization, product life cycle, selling process
sales force selling process
sales locations point-of-sale marketing
sales promotion(s) below-the-line marketing, pull marketing, ratchet effect
salience von Restorff effect
sampling bias, large numbers, law of
satisfaction diminishing marginal utility, law of, effect, law of, expectation–disconfirmation model, Herzberg's theory of motivation, job characteristics theory, utility
satisfactory outcomes satisficing
scale diseconomies of scale, economies of scale
scale development acquiescence response set, Churchill's paradigm
segment attractiveness target marketing
segment selection targeting
segmentation STP marketing
segmentation feasibility segmentation viability
segmentation implementation segmentation viability
self-fulfillment self-fulfilling prophecy
self-interest behavior moral hazard
self-observation self-perception theory
selling achievement motivation theory, door-in-the-face technique, foot-in-the-door technique, low-ball technique
sensemaking actor–observer difference
senses experiential marketing
sensory communication experiential marketing
sensory experience event marketing
serial position serial position effect
service(s) goods, Little's law
service advantages benefits
service development house of quality
service factors service characteristics
service offerings service, laws of
service production costs Baumol's cost disease
service productivity Baumol's cost disease
sets fuzzy set theory, set theory
share market share
shareholders shareholder value analysis
short-sightedness marketing myopia
short-term benefits societal classification of products

short-term performance   random-walk theory
short-term plans   tactical marketing
significance   snowball effect
simplicity   parsimony, law of
single offering   undifferentiated marketing
size   double jeopardy effect, Metcalfe's law
small firms   entrepreneurial marketing
small groups   small group theory
social categorizations   social identity theory
social class   trickle down theory
social comparison   social identity theory
social context   social learning theory
social facilitation   drive theory of social facilitation
social identification   social identity theory
social indicators   Goodhart's law
social influence   imitation effect, conspicuous consumption
social interaction   social exchange theory, symbolic interaction theory
social justice   equity theory
social learning   social cognitive theory
social networks   viral marketing
social pressure   Asch phenomenon
social responsibility   enlightened marketing
societal forces   macroenvironment
societal needs   macromarketing
societal welfare   social marketing
spatial distance   construal-level theory
spatial locations   location theory
specialization   division of labor effect
spending   Engel's law
sponsorship   ambush marketing, sports marketing
sports organizations   sports marketing
spreading effect   ripple effect
staffing   Parkinson's law
stages   hierarchy of effects
stakeholders   marketing
standards of conduct   ethical marketing
statistical analysis   ceiling effect, cohort effect, floor effect, large
    numbers, law of, spurious correlation
stimuli   adaptation-level theory, contrast effect, primacy effect, recency
    effect, Weber–Fechner law
stimulus   exercise, law of, reinforcement, repetition effect
strategic action   strategic window
strategic analysis   value chain analysis
strategic frameworks   strategies, generic
strategic moves   leapfrogging
strategic positioning   positioning
strategy   game theory, marketing strategy, red queen effect

Introduction

The Motivation for this Dictionary

No book or dictionary currently compiles, explains, and discusses the topics to be covered in this advanced marketing dictionary. Although there have been dozens of marketing dictionaries written over the decades, what is lacking in each is an emphasis on laws, theories, concepts, and effects. More often than not, marketing dictionaries emphasize definitions of basic marketing terms (e.g. copy, logo, advertisement). The aim of this dictionary is to assume the reader is familiar with such basic terms and, rather than include any here, exclusively focus on advanced and more conceptual marketing terminology. By *advanced*, we mean an emphasis on terminology that is relatively higher level and more complex than basic marketing terminology. By *conceptual*, we mean an emphasis on marketing terminology that is either abstract or involves a central or unifying idea. In marketing, and disciplines closely related to marketing, much peer-reviewed journal research has been performed in support of the identification and development of advanced conceptual terminology, yet little work seems to find its way into marketing dictionaries, perhaps due to the complex nature of the ideas involved. In particular, there are many insightful areas of marketing and marketing-related research that have ultimately been given the label of a law, principle, theory, concept, or effect—clearly suggesting their centrality and importance—yet scant mention of these terms are found in marketing dictionaries. For example, in one international marketing dictionary having over 2,500 entries, there are only two entries found on theories. This is peculiar, since it is said, 'There is nothing more practical than a good theory.' For the serious marketing researcher, practitioner, academician, and/or student, most marketing dictionaries are, therefore, clearly inadequate, especially when understanding, explaining, and applying advanced marketing terminology is increasingly imperative in the marketing discipline.

This dictionary presents hundreds and hundreds of advanced marketing terms, including laws, theories, concepts, and effects. Going beyond mere introductory descriptions, the dictionary includes key insights as well as implications and applications for marketers. As such, the dictionary will appeal to individuals who are concerned with the relevance and usefulness of advanced marketing terms. Marketing academics will find the dictionary to be a useful resource for more effective teaching as well as research development. MBA students can use this dictionary an essential resource for dissertations and coursework related to marketing. Advanced undergraduate students can use the dictionary as an essential resource for marketing essays and exams. In all cases, the dictionary helps in knowing how and where advanced conceptual terminology can be used to simplify the complexities of marketing. Practitioners can use the dictionary to bridge the gap between theory and practice and potentially gain an edge over the competition by being more effective in marketing management or strategy development and implementation. Finally, individuals either currently pursuing a Ph.D. in marketing or considering the pursuit of a marketing Ph.D. will benefit from the knowledge contained in this dictionary to support their current research and to provide a source of ideas for studying any particular marketing phenomenon.

It should be clear by now that this compilation is by no means a dictionary of general marketing or business terms (i.e. including definitions of simple terms such as artwork, coupon, and credit); these are widely discussed in textbooks and other marketing and business dictionaries. Although some foundational terms are included as they are deemed central to marketing, any such terminology is also described and explained in terms of their key insights and implications. For all terms included in this dictionary, advanced marketing research is drawn upon. Furthermore, knowledge generated and applied to marketing from multiple academic disciplines including management, psychology, economics, and sociology is also drawn upon to ensure completeness and comprehensiveness.

At the same time, although this dictionary emphasizes advanced conceptual marketing terms, there will be many models and frameworks applicable to marketing that will not be found in this dictionary. That is because many such models and frameworks tend to be relatively specialized and are perhaps better covered by an academic journal article or a textbook section. Furthermore, as each issue of each major journal in the field contains new sets of models and frameworks with which to reflect upon, no dictionary would ever be complete in its coverage of models and frameworks. In this dictionary, the emphasis is on advanced conceptual terms that tend to be concisely labeled as particular laws, theories, concepts, and effects in the academic literature. Although one may debate whether any given term labeled as a theory actually meets a rigorous definition of a theory, or whether a term labeled as a law is actually unbreakable as to be most appropriately termed a law, such conceptual labels nevertheless signify a level of importance and potential for impact in and across the broad field of marketing as to warrant their inclusion.

Structure for Each Term

Each term covered in this dictionary includes six elements:

- Description—how is the term defined?
- Key insights—what insights are provided by an understanding of the term?
- Key words—what words can assist the reader in further understanding the nature of the term?
- Implications—what does knowledge of the term mean to marketers?
- Application areas and further readings—what are key areas where such knowledge is being put to use?
- Bibliography—what articles or books are referenced?

In addition to the above six-element structure, the astute reader will observe that the referenced materials (i.e. journal articles and books) are intentionally not listed in alphabetical order. In keeping with the spirit of an advanced dictionary, the materials referenced in both the application areas and further readings and bibliography sections are presented in order of their relative importance, where the most influential and/or highly cited materials are presented first.

How to Use this Dictionary

Readers can use this dictionary in many ways. First, a reader may come across a term in use that is not clearly defined or understood. The dictionary entry for this term can then provide the reader with a far better understanding of its meaning, background, scope, and application.

Secondly, a reader may find browsing the dictionary to be a means for understanding and appreciating far more fully the scope and richness of the field of marketing itself. Never before have so many laws, theories, concepts, and effects been compiled and discussed in a single marketing dictionary. Browsing this dictionary enables the reader to recognize immediately that the field of marketing is far more advanced than that which is—or will ever be—presented in any single marketing text or in any set of marketing textbooks.

Thirdly, a reader interested in examining a particular marketing problem, issue, or phenomenon (say, for example, understanding what influences marketing communication effectiveness) may find, through the descriptions and discussions of the advanced conceptual terms included, that much more is known about such issues than the reader may initially realize. As such, the dictionary provides the reader with a source of inspiration as well as means to understand better those terms providing advanced insights into practical issues deemed important to the reader for either further marketing study (e.g. dissertation or essay preparation) or application in marketing practice.

Fourthly, a reader interested in a particular area of marketing that is still relatively broad, such as marketing strategy or consumer behavior, may find perusing the dictionary as well as the Table of Applications thematic index at the beginning of dictionary to be a useful way of learning about the richness of these sub-areas of marketing as well as identifying understudied conceptual perspectives for further study.

Finally, the reader also can choose to locate relevant—yet unfamiliar—marketing laws, theories, concepts, and effects with greater ease by using the 'Searching for Marketing Terms Using Key Words' thematic index at the beginning of the dictionary. For example, many marketers are concerned with 'loyalty' and may therefore wish to know more about advanced topics related to loyalty. Using the key word thematic index, the reader will find that several loyalty-related topics are presented in this dictionary including three effects: the 'double jeopardy effect,' the 'loyalty effect,' and the 'loyalty ripple effect.'

What is a Law?

There are dozens of useful laws presented in this dictionary. They are called 'laws' in this dictionary because they are referred to as such within the marketing discipline. Yet, unlike laws of nature which are widely accepted as a result of extensive empirical observation and scientific investigation, it must be accepted that, with very few exceptions (e.g. Little's Law), marketing related laws are often more along the lines of broad generalizations which appear to have considerable merit based on empirical observation and scientific investigation. As such, one may reasonably question whether many such terms should be referred to as 'laws' at all. While it is up to the reader to evaluate each law presented on its own merits and evidence, we should begin our evaluations by nevertheless acknowledging that the very fact that they are called laws suggests their importance should not be underestimated!

What is a Theory?

> Grey are all theories
> And green alone Life's golden tree.
>
> *Johann Wolfgang von Goethe, 1749–1832, Faust, I, iv.*

There are well over 100 useful theories presented in this dictionary. Theory, of course, is a term with many meanings, broad and specific. It can, for example, refer to an organized body of knowledge. At the other end of the spectrum, a theory can refer to 'a systematically related set of statements, including some law-like generalizations, that is empirically testable' (Hunt 1991). The many terms used in marketing which are referred to as 'theories' are found to span this spectrum. It is not the purpose of this dictionary to debate where such terms may sit specifically along such a spectrum, however, nor is it the purpose of the dictionary to evaluate evidence acting in their support or refutation. Rather, this dictionary accepts the fact that marketing researchers refer to certain terms as 'theories' even though such terms vary in the extent they might meet certain rigorous criteria that would enable them to be referred to as theories without hesitation. A major benefit of their inclusion in this dictionary is that it provides the reader with a sense of where there are organized bodies of knowledge that are influential to marketing. A greater knowledge of such areas can provide marketers with the opportunity to approach the study of a wide range of marketing phenomena in a way that draws upon substantial pools of scientific research. As such, their appropriate application can potentially provide the marketer with a better understanding, explanation, and/or prediction of any number of marketing phenomena.

What is a Concept?

There are many hundreds of useful concepts presented in this dictionary. They are concepts in the sense that they are ideas or abstractions of reality. As with theories, concepts also provide the marketer with the potential to understand better any number of marketing phenomena with an abstract lens, lenses capable of providing fresh insights that may otherwise be missed by relying on first-hand observation alone. Marketing, for example, is characterized by an extremely wide range of approaches. By understanding better the many different ways marketers within a firm can approach marketing conceptually, strategically, and tactically, one immediately has the ability to understand, evaluate, and critique any particular marketing effort either planned or in process.

What is an Effect?

Effects are phenomena that are caused by other phenomena. Marketing is concerned with the creation of a wide range of desirable effects, ranging from increased profitability to increased consumer satisfaction. There are, however, a great many effects that can influence any marketing effort, including those associated with consumer behavior and competitive actions. This dictionary presents well over 100 useful effects that are all potentially influential to marketing success, whether it is success in the area of marketing research, marketing strategy, or marketing management. As with theories and concepts, a greater working knowledge of the many different effects that have received attention in academic marketing research provides any marketer with an opportunity to benefit from a wealth of accumulated marketing knowledge.

REFERENCE
Hunt, Shelby D. (1991). *Modern Marketing Theory: Critical Issues in the Philosophy of Marketing Science*. Cincinnati: South-Western Publishing Co.

The Advanced Dictionary of Marketing Terms

A

☐ a priori validity *see* validity

■ above-the-line marketing

DESCRIPTION
Marketing comprised of activity that, traditionally, entails commission charges by advertising agencies which, mainly, comprises mass media advertising.

KEY INSIGHTS
Above-the-line activity in marketing refers to marketing practices making use of the mass media where, given a firm's use of an advertising agency, the agency would make a commission on advertisements which are placed in media including television, newspapers, billboards, radio, magazines, and cinema, and where the commission charged by the advertising agency typically appears 'above-the-line' on the ad agency's bill to the firm. Above-the-line marketing activity can be contrasted with 'below-the-line' marketing activity, which typically is that where an ad agency would charge a firm a fixed fee. (See **below-the-line marketing**.) *Through-the-line marketing* refers to a marketing approach that makes use of both above-the-line marketing and below-the-line marketing. Above-the-line marketing is generally associated with classic and traditional approaches to marketing where advertising is used to build a brand's image. As such, to some marketers, the approach has been considered one of marketing's 'necessary evils,' but, in some industries (e.g. tobacco), below-the-line marketing approaches have gained momentum, or even overtaken above-the-line marketing in importance, particularly as a result of increased regulatory scrutiny of mass media advertising.

KEY WORDS Advertising, mass media advertising, commissions

IMPLICATIONS
In order to be in a position to evaluate the potential benefits and costs of above-the-line marketing approaches, marketers should seek to understand carefully their competitive and regulatory environments in addition to consumer buying behavior. While there may be clear benefits to above-the-line approaches including that of brand image building, below-the-line approaches may also be beneficial (as when there is considerable advertising clutter in the marketplace), either alone or in being selectively integrated with above-the-line marketing approaches.

APPLICATION AREAS AND FURTHER READINGS
Marketing Strategy
Kim, W. Chan, and Mauborgne, Renee (2005). *Blue Ocean Strategy: How to Create Uncontested Market Space and Make the Competition Irrelevant.* Cambridge, Mass.: Harvard Business School Press.

Services Marketing
Clark, R. (1997). 'Looking after Business: Linking Existing Customers to Profitability,' *Managing Service Quality*, 7(3), 146–149.

BIBLIOGRAPHY
Carter S. M. (2003). 'Going below the Line: Creating Transportable Brands for Australia's Dark Market,' *Tobacco Control*, 2 (suppl III), 87–94.
Smith, P. R., and Taylor, Jonathan (2002). *Marketing Communications: An Integrated Approach.* London: Kogan Page.

■ absolute cost advantage

DESCRIPTION
A concept referring to the beneficial state where an incumbent firm is able to achieve and sustain lower average total costs for its products or services relative to that achievable by newer entrants.

KEY INSIGHTS
Influential early research on the concept by Bain (1956) suggests that an absolute cost advantage can be achieved as a result of certain actions of the firm including, but not limited to: obtaining access to lower costs of capital, securing exclusive access to scarce raw materials or other inputs, implementing low-cost production techniques through experience, and/or superior management skills. Once obtained, an absolute cost advantage can create a form of entry barrier to the extent that new firms will experience higher costs in comparison to the firm with the absolute cost advantage.

KEY WORDS **Entry barriers**, competitive advantage

IMPLICATIONS
While the concept of this type of firm advantage is ultimately linked to costs achievable by newer entrant firms, research on the concept suggests that an absolute cost advantage does not automatically accrue to an incumbent firm but rather is a result of the firm successfully acting upon opportunities to achieve such an advantage. Firms must also consider the extent that changes in the macroenvironment and microenvironment may lead to the lessening of any absolute cost advantage over time, for example, as a result of a new, lower-cost production technology available for adoption by newer entrants that may be costlier for incumbent firms to adopt due to their previous investment in an existing technology.

APPLICATION AREAS AND FURTHER READINGS
Marketing Strategy
Schmalensee, Richard (1974). 'Brand Loyalty and Barriers to Entry,' *Southern Economic Journal*, 40(4), April, 579–588.

Agarwal, Rajshree, and Gort, Michael (2001). 'First-Mover Advantage and the Speed of Competitive Entry, 1887–1986,' *Journal of Law and Economics*, 44, 161–177.

Kerin, Roger A., Varadarajan, P. Rajan, and Peterson, Robert A. (1992). 'First-Mover Advantage: A Synthesis, Conceptual Framework, and Research Propositions,' *Journal of Marketing*, 56(4), October, 33–52.

New Product Development
Golder, Peter N., and Tellis, Gerard J. (1997). 'Will It Ever Fly? Modeling the Takeoff of Really New Consumer Durables,' *Marketing Science*, 16(3), 256–270.

BIBLIOGRAPHY
Bain, Joe Staten (1956). *Barriers to New Competition: Their Character and Consequences in Manufacturing Industries*. Cambridge, Mass.: Harvard University Press.

■ absorptive capacity

DESCRIPTION

A conceptual term characterizing a firm's ability to recognize value in information arising outside the firm, internalize and assimilate such information, and apply it for commercial purposes.

KEY INSIGHTS

According to research on the concept of absorptive capacity by Cohen and Levinthal (1990), absorptive capacity as a capability is critical in supporting firms' innovation capabilities and successful innovation processes within firms. In terms of explaining what determines the extent of a firm's absorptive capacity, Cohen and Levinthal (1990) argue the capability is driven to a large extent by the firm's level of related prior knowledge.

KEY WORDS External information, knowledge, innovation, learning

IMPLICATIONS

For those managing innovation within firms, a major implication of the concept is that a greater absorptive capacity capability will lead to strengthened innovation capabilities and a higher likelihood of successfully developing innovations. As such, individuals throughout a firm should strive to develop essential skills and a shared language of related knowledge to be able to more readily identify and comprehend developments outside the firm and assimilate such knowledge with the aim of establishing and pursuing appropriate commercial applications. Having a strong internal R&D capability and conducting the firm's R&D internally can, for example, help to prepare a firm to make better use of external information as part of strengthening the firm's absorptive capacity.

APPLICATION AREAS AND FURTHER READINGS

Marketing Strategy
Johnson, Jean L., Sohi, Raviprect S., and Grewal, Rajdeep (2004). 'The Role of Relational Knowledge Stores in Interfirm Partnering,' *Journal of Marketing*, 68(3), July, 21–36.
Hurley, Robert F., and Hult, G. Tomas M. (1998). 'Innovation, Market Orientation, and Organizational Learning: An Integration and Empirical Examination,' *Journal of Marketing*, 62, July, 42–54.

Van den Bosch, Frans A. J., Volberda, Henk W., and de Boer, Michiel (1999). 'Coevolution of Firm Absorptive Capacity and Knowledge Environment: Organizational Forms and Combinative Capabilities,' *Organization Science*, 10(5), September-October, 551-568.

Lane, Peter J., and Lubatkin, Michael (1998). 'Relative Absorptive Capacity and Interorganizational Learning,' *Strategic Management Journal*, 19(5), 461-477.

International Marketing
Lane, Peter J., Salk, Jane E., and Lyles, Marjorie A. (2001). 'Absorptive Capacity, Learning, and Performance in International Joint Ventures,' *Strategic Management Journal*, 22(12), 1139-1161.

BIBLIOGRAPHY
Cohen, Wesley M., and Levinthal, Daniel A. (1990). 'Absorptive Capacity: A New Perspective on Learning and Innovation,' *Administrative Science Quarterly*, 35, 128-152.

■ accelerator principle

(also called the accelerator effect, acceleration principle, or acceleration effect)

DESCRIPTION
The idea or theory that aggregate net investment by firms in an industry is dependent on firms' expectations about changes in outputs such as sales, profits, and/or cash flow, and where such a relationship has the effect of amplifying further the magnitude of changes in firms' demands on suppliers.

KEY INSIGHTS
Research on the accelerator principle finds that the principle or effect can and does operate within industries. While the actual extent of the acceleration effect certainly varies among industries, the principle nevertheless suggests that firms' investment practices are influenced at least to some extent by their expectations of their future prospects, where such expectations are shaped by changes in the growth of the economy, for example, and where such investment practices has the potential to accelerate (or decelerate) further industry (and broader economic) growth. Thus, firms will tend to adjust inventories in response to expected changes in consumer demand, for example, where such inventory adjustments are positive when the expected change in demand is positive and negative when the expected change in demand is negative. Such changes to firm inventories and other investments will not only have corresponding influences on suppliers but also further stimulate (or impede) industry growth and also potentially accelerate (or decelerate) broader economic growth or decline.

KEY WORDS Firm investment, economic growth, forecasting

IMPLICATIONS
Decisions to increase/decrease inventory levels, build factories, and invest in plant and equipment, for example, will be influenced by profit and

sales expectations and business confidence. Firms must therefore not only strive to accurately forecast expected changes in their outputs (e.g. sales) but also be sensitized to how associated changes to planned investments by the firm or other firms in the industry may potentially accelerate (or decelerate) favorable or unfavorable economic prospects for the industry and the broader economy.

APPLICATION AREAS AND FURTHER READINGS

Marketing Modeling
Fousekis, Panos, and Stefanou, Spiro E. (1996). 'Capacity Utilization under Dynamic Profit Maximization,' *Empirical Economics*, 21(3), September, 335–359.

Mergers and Acquisitions
Weston, J. Fred (2001). 'Mergers and Acquisitions as Adjustment Processes,' *Journal of Industry, Competition, and Trade*, 1(4), December, 395–410.

BIBLIOGRAPHY
Kuehn, Alfred A., and Day, Ralph L. (1963). 'The Acceleration Effect in Forecasting Industrial Shipments,' *Journal of Marketing*, 27(1), January, 25–28.

☐ accessibility *see* segmentation viability

☐ accordion theory *see* retail accordion theory

■ achievement motivation theory

DESCRIPTION
Theory or theories relating personal characteristics and background to a need for achievement and the associated competitive drive to meet standards of excellence.

KEY INSIGHTS
According to theoretical research by Murray (1938), McClelland, Atkinson, Clark, and Lowel (1953), and McClelland (1961), achievement motivation or need for achievement is influenced by a combination of internal factors including personal drives and external or environmental factors including pressures and expectations of relevant organizations and society. Related to an individual's need for achievement and overall motivation is the individual's need for power and need for affiliation.

KEY WORDS Drive, achievement, motivation, goals, sales, selling

IMPLICATIONS
Understanding and explaining individuals' achievement motivation is important within organizations where such characteristics are strongly associated with ongoing organizational success, most notably in the sales function. Staffing the organization with individuals having backgrounds and personal characteristics that are suggestive of a high need for achievement becomes an important consideration. While many factors are potentially influential and interact, e.g. an individual's values (e.g. valuing the accomplishment of tasks over personal relationships), culture

and educational background, providing appropriate external support in the form of organizational systems, structures, and culture (e.g. including opportunities for promotion, recognizing and rewarding successes, ensuring performance feedback, and matching individual control with role responsibilities and role importance) becomes just as important as the organization's assessing and nurturing an individual's personal drives.

APPLICATION AREAS AND FURTHER READINGS
Marketing Management
Chowdhury, Jhinuk (1993). 'The Motivational Impact of Sales Quotas on Effort,' *Journal of Marketing Research*, 30(1), February, 28–41.
Silver, Lawrence S., Dwyer, Sean, and Alford, Bruce (2006). 'Learning and Performance Orientation of Salespeople Revisited: The Role of Performance-Approach and Performance-Avoidance Orientations,' *Journal of Personal Selling and Sales Management*, 26(1), Winter, 27–38.

BIBLIOGRAPHY
McClelland, D. C. (1961). *The Achieving Society*. Princeton: Van Nostrand.
McClelland, D. C., Atkinson, J. W., Clark, R. A., and Lowell, E. L. (1953). *The Achievement Motive*. Princeton: Van Nostrand.
Murray, H. A. (1938). *Explorations in Personality*. New York: Oxford University Press.

■ acquiescence response set

DESCRIPTION
A form of bias involving a consistent individual tendency to agree with statements such as attitude statements regardless of the content or to consistently answer yes/no questions either in the affirmative (yes) or in the negative (no) irrespective of a question's content.

KEY INSIGHTS
Research on acquiescence response set as a form of bias finds the tendency varies in prevalence in responses to questionnaires and surveys (where, for example, cross-cultural differences in its prevalence are clearly observed). Nevertheless, the potential for its occurrence (with similarly worded questions in particular) is of sufficient concern to experienced researchers including survey researchers and developers of question or statement-based scales and that methods for controlling for and/or compensating for the bias are typically implemented with the aim of obtaining more meaningful responses.

KEY WORDS **Bias**, questionnaires, surveys, scale development

IMPLICATIONS
When acquiescence response set as a form of bias is a potential concern in survey research or in scale development, a common approach for attempting to control or compensate for it when providing multiple statements or asking multiple questions is to have some statements or questions positively worded and others negatively worded in a sense that the two types of questions are far more opposite than similar. In doing so, responding in agreement to all or in responding with a consistent

affirmative or negative answer to all would be found to be contradictory and, as such, would require respondents to potentially engage more fully with the statements or questions given.

APPLICATION AREAS AND FURTHER READINGS

Marketing Research
Podsakoff, P. M., MacKenzie, S. B., Lee, J. Y., and Podsakoff, N. P. (2003). 'Common Method Biases in Behavioral Research: A Critical Review of the Literature and Recommended Remedies,' *Journal of Applied Psychology*, 88(5), 879–903.

International Marketing
Baumgartner, Hans, and Steenkamp, Jan-Benedict E. M. (2001). 'Response Styles in Marketing Research: A Cross-National Investigation,' *Journal of Marketing Research*, 38, May, 143–156.
Malhotra, Naresh K., Agarwal, James, and Peterson, Mark (1996). 'Methodological Issues in Cross-Cultural Research: A State of the Art Review,' *International Marketing Review*, 13(5), 7–43.

BIBLIOGRAPHY
Winkler, J. D., Kanouse, D. E., and Ware, J. E., Jr. (1982). 'Controlling for Acquiescence Response Set in Scale Development,' *Journal of Applied Psychology*, 67, 555–561.

☐ **action** *see* buyer influence/readiness

☐ **actionability** *see* segmentation viability

■ actor–observer difference

DESCRIPTION
The phenomenon where the attributed causes of an individual's action(s) tend to systematically differ depending on whether one is the actor or an observer. More specifically, an observer tends to attribute an actor's behavior to the actor's inherent personality, whereas the actor tends to attribute his/her behavior to situational factors.

KEY INSIGHTS
Based on pioneering research by Jones and Nisbett (1972), explanations for this observable phenomenon include the general fact that actors tend to have more action-related information available than observers; actors and observers have different motives in producing explanations for actions; and a tendency for actors and observers to differ in where they ultimately selectively attend to information concerning actions.

KEY WORDS Observers, actions, attitudes, attributions, sense making

IMPLICATIONS
As the actions of marketing managers and sales staff can sometimes be very visible to customers or others outside an organization (e.g. suppliers, business partners) as well as within the organization, the marketer should not assume that individuals observing his/her (or the company's) action(s) will attribute the action(s) to the same causes as does the marketer him/herself. For example, a bystander at an airport observing a man being told by a ticketing agent that he is unable to check in for

a scheduled airline flight because he is thirty seconds late in checking in relative to the airline's policy of requiring check-ins a minimum of thirty minutes before departure may attribute the refusal in being allowed to check in to the ticketing agent's insensitive, stubborn, and unsympathetic personality, whereas the ticketing agent may attribute the service encounter outcome to that of being told to enforce his company's policy. While such an example illustrates the actor–observer difference on a relatively small scale, such difference may certainly be amplified on larger scales as when actions are strategic in nature (e.g. in interpreting motivations of an entire salesforce or in crucial negotiations with a potential business partner). Marketers should therefore seek to understand and perhaps even anticipate possible interpretations of marketing actions from stakeholding observer perspectives and reconcile them with their own perspectives in efforts to reduce misunderstandings that may lead to undesirable marketing outcomes (e.g. customer dissatisfaction, marketer mistrust).

APPLICATION AREAS AND FURTHER READINGS
Consumer Behavior
Folkes, Valerie S. (1988). 'Recent Attribution Research in Consumer Behavior: A Review and New Directions,' *Journal of Consumer Research*, 14(4), March, 548–565.

Marketing Management
Balakrishnan, P. V. (Sundar), Patton, Charles, and Lewis, Philip A. (1993). 'Toward a Theory of Agenda Setting in Negotiations,' *Journal of Consumer Research*, 19(4), March, 637–654.
Teas, R. Kenneth, and McElroy, James C. (1986). 'Causal Attributions and Expectancy Estimates: A Framework for Understanding the Dynamics of Salesforce Motivation,' *Journal of Marketing*, 50(1), January, 75–86.

Services Marketing
Van Raaij, Fred, and Pruyn, Ad Th. H. (1998). 'Customer Control and Evaluation of Service Validity and Reliability,' *Psychology and Marketing*, 15(8), 811–832.

BIBLIOGRAPHY
Jones, Edward E., and Nisbett, Richard E. (1972). 'The Actor and the Observer: Divergent Perceptions of the Causes of Behavior,' in Edward E. Jones et al. (eds.), *Attribution: Perceiving the Causes of Behavior*, Morristown, NJ: General Learning Press, 79–84.
Wagner, J. A., III, and Gooding, R. Z. (1997). 'Equivocal Information and Attribution: An Investigation of Patterns of Managerial Sensemaking,' *Strategic Management Journal*, 18(4), 275–286.

☐ **actual product** *see* product levels

■ **adaptation**

DESCRIPTION
The process or strategy of adapting or tailoring an otherwise standardized product or service offering to meet the needs and preferences of a particular market or set of consumers, where such markets and consumers are typically examined and managed within an international marketing context.

KEY INSIGHTS
The subject of marketing strategy and marketing mix element adaptation versus standardization has been the subject of much marketing research and debate. Since there are many potential factors influencing the appropriateness of such a strategy, it is difficult to say when it is best relative to a standardization approach. In international marketing, adaptation is an essential consideration when marketing to multiple countries or cultures where there are likely to be significant differences in consumer wants and needs relative to a particular product or service offering. While adapting marketing strategies and marketing mix elements often takes more time and effort to develop and implement and is often costlier than standardized approaches which benefit from larger economies of scale, the potentially greater market receptivity to adapted offerings may make such a costlier approach worthwhile over the longer term. Ultimately, however, the desirability, extent, and type of adaptation, whether in marketing communications, product packaging, or positioning, will invariably be highly dependent on characteristics of the company, product, industry, and market.

KEY WORDS Marketing mix adaptation

IMPLICATIONS
Marketing managers involved in international or regional marketing should consider the potential for adapted marketing strategies or marketing mix elements. As the decision to adapt such offerings is highly context dependent, research assessing the market, industry, and competition will be essential. Company resources and skills will also be an important consideration to determine whether the assets and competencies of the firm can accommodate and support an adaptation approach for possible competitive advantage. Even highly standardized firms such as McDonald's still find it is strategically desirable to engage in limited adaptations to local tastes for their sandwich offerings, for example.

APPLICATION AREAS AND FURTHER READINGS
International Marketing
Theodosiou, M., and Leonidou, L. C. (2002). 'Standardization vs. Adaptation of International Marketing Strategy: An Integrative Assessment of the Empirical Research,' *International Business Review*, 12(2), April, 141–171.
Solberg, Carl R. (2002). 'The Perennial Issue of Adaptation or Standardization of International Marketing Communication: Organizational Contingencies and Performance,' *Journal of International Marketing*, 10(3), Fall, 1–21.
Johnson, Jean L., and Arunthanes, Wiboone (1995). 'Ideal and Actual Product Adaptation in US Exporting Firms: Market-Related Determinants and Impact on Performance,' *International Marketing Review*, 12(3), June, 31–46.

BIBLIOGRAPHY
Cavusgil, S. Tamer, Zou, Shaoming, and Naidu, G. M. (1993). 'Product and Promotion Adapatation in Export Ventures: An Empirical Investigation,' *Journal of International Business Studies*, 24(3), 476–506.

Szymanski, David M., Bharadwaj, Sundhar G., and Varadarajan, P. Rajan (1993). 'Standardization vs. Adaptation of International Marketing Strategy: An Empirical Investigation,' *Journal of Marketing*, 57(4), October, 1–17.

■ adaptation-level theory

(also called AL theory or the theory of adaptation level)

DESCRIPTION

A theory positing that an individual's reference point for subjective judgments regarding particular classes of stimuli is determined by the individual's prior exposure to such stimuli as well as recollections of past judgments of similar stimuli.

KEY INSIGHTS

Put forth in pioneering research by Helson (1947), adaptation-level theory posits that one's judgment or evaluation of an outcome is a function of all the previously experienced outcomes. In particular, the theory expresses the relationship mathematically by proposing that one's adaptation level, or reference point for subjective judgments, is the logarithm of the mean of relevant stimuli, where individuals weight such stimuli based on their recency and salience among other criteria. In this sense, adaptation-level theory is a psychological theory of relativity based on the general principle of perceptual contrast where any subjective judgment is influenced by the prevailing norm or adaptation level. The theory also suggests that individuals continually adapt to label the existing level of any stimulus as the norm.

KEY WORDS Adaptation, perception, stimuli

IMPLICATIONS

While adaptation-level theory has been formulated in precise mathematical terms, it also provides a basis for non-mathematical application. For example, the theory can be used to explain why an individual may see a new car model of a particular size and consider it to be 'big,' as it would be judged in relation to the individual's perception of the prevailing norm for new car model size, yet, given a case where most new car models become bigger over time, the individual's reference point for car size judgments will shift to that of a bigger size. Marketers should therefore seek to understand how a consumer's judgment is influenced by his or her prior exposures to related stimuli in order to explain and predict better such judgments. Such knowledge can therefore provide the marketer with insights into appropriate marketing communications or persuasive messages that may be aimed at altering or influencing such consumer judgments.

APPLICATION AREAS AND FURTHER READINGS

Marketing Strategy

Bearden, William O., and Teel, Jesse E. (1983). 'Selected Determinants of Consumer Satisfaction and Complaint Reports,' *Journal of Marketing Research*, 20(1), February, 21–28.

Anderson, Eugene W., and Sullivan, Mary W. (1993). 'The Antecedents and Consequences of Customer Satisfaction for Firms,' *Marketing Science*, 12(2), Spring,
125–143.

Marketing Research
Oliver, Richard L. (1980). 'A Cognitive Model of the Antecedents and Consequences
of Satisfaction Decisions,' *Journal of Marketing Research*, 17(4), November, 460–469.

Consumer Behavior
Brickman P., Coates D., and Janoff-Bulman, R. (1978). 'Lottery Winners and Acci-
dent Victims: Is Happiness Relative?' *Journal of Personality and Social Psychology*,
36(8), August, 917–927.

Marketing Education
Goldman, Roy D., and Hewitt, Barbara Newlin (1975). 'Adaptation-Level as an
Explanation for Differential Standards in College Grading,' *Journal of Educational
Measurement*, 12(3), Autumn, 149–161.

BIBLIOGRAPHY
Helson, Harry (1947). 'Adaptation-Level as Frame of Reference for Prediction of
Psychophysical Data,' *American Journal of Psychology*, 60(1), January, 1–29.
Helson, Harry (1964). *Adaptation-Level Theory: An Experimental and Systematic Approach
to Behavior.* New York: Harper Row.
Sarris, Viktor (1967). 'Adaptation-Level Theory: Two Critical Experiments on
Helson's Weighted-Average Model,' *American Journal of Psychology*, 80(3), Septem-
ber, 331–344.
Brickman, Philip, and Campbell, Donald T. (1971). 'Hedonic Relativism and the
Good Society,' in Appley, M. H. (ed.), *Adaptation-Level Theory: A Symposium.* New
York: Academic Press.

■ adaptive strategy

DESCRIPTION
Strategy or strategies that involve making adjustments based on new environmental conditions.

KEY INSIGHTS
While business and marketing strategies are often characterized by consistency in direction and approach over the longer term, the notion of
an adaptive strategy incorporates the view that the strategic approach
is to some significant extent dependent on environmental conditions
encountered by a firm.

KEY WORDS Organization, adaptability

IMPLICATIONS
As strategy development and implementation is an essential part of
marketing over the long term, marketers must critically examine the
essential characteristics of business and marketing strategies pursued
to assess how and to what extent such strategies should be adaptive in
nature.

APPLICATION AREAS AND FURTHER READINGS
Marketing Strategy
Achrol, Ravi S. (1991). 'Evolution of the Marketing Organization: New Forms for
Turbulent Environments,' *Journal of Marketing*, 55(4), October, 77–93.

McKee, Daryl O., Varadarajan, P. Rajan, and Pride, William M. (1989). 'Strategic Adaptability and Firm Performance: A Market-Contingent Perspective,' *Journal of Marketing*, 53(3), July, 21–35.

BIBLIOGRAPHY
Miles, Raymond E., and Snow, Charles C. (1978). *Organizational Strategy, Structure, and Process*. Stanford, Calif.: Stanford University Press.
Chaffee, Ellen Earle (1985). 'Three Models of Strategy,' *Academy of Management Review*, 10(1), January, 89–98.

☐ **administered VMS** *see* channel arrangement

■ adopter categories

DESCRIPTION
Categorical classifications of individuals or organizations according to when they adopt new product(s) in comparison to others.

KEY INSIGHTS
One of the most commonly used approaches for categorizing adopters is that of Rogers (1995) where he proposes five categories and percentages for each and where the non-cumulative adopter distribution of such individuals forms a bell-shaped curve: (1) innovators (2.5%), (2) early adopters (13.5%), (3) early majority (34%), (4) late majority (34%), and (5) laggards (16%). While the number of categories, the percentages of each, and the method of categorical determination are in many ways somewhat arbitrary, the adopter categories nevertheless provide a means to evaluate new product adoption behavior among individuals (or organizations in the case of business-to-business marketing).

KEY WORDS Innovators, early adopters, early majority, late majority, laggards

IMPLICATIONS
Marketers must be sensitive to differences in adoption timing tendencies among potential customers for products and services and strive to strategically manage marketing efforts to ensure appropriate receptivity among targeted categories. Marketers of really new products, for example, tend to target innovators early on in marketing efforts because receptivity among innovators can lead to favorable follow-on influences in subsequent adopter categories.

APPLICATION AREAS AND FURTHER READINGS
Marketing Modeling
Mahajan, V., Muller, E., and Srivastava, R. K. (1990). 'Determination of Adopter Categories by Using Innovation Diffusion Models,' *Journal of Marketing Research*, 27(1), February, 37–50.

Marketing Strategy
Mahajan, V., and Muller, E. (1998). 'When is it Worthwhile Targeting the Majority Instead of the Innovators in a New Product Launch?' *Journal of Marketing Research*, 35(4), November, 488–495.

BIBLIOGRAPHY
Rogers, E. M. (1995). *Diffusion of Innovations*, 4th edn. New York: Free Press.
Peterson, Robert A. (1973). 'A Note on Optimal Adopter Category Determination,' *Journal of Marketing Research*, 10(3), August, 325–329.

☐ **adoption** *see* adoption process

■ adoption process

DESCRIPTION
The process by which a consumer adopts a new product or service.

KEY INSIGHTS
Before adopting, or purchasing, a new product or service, it is generally recognized that a consumer typically moves through different stages of a process of adoption. Commonly recognized stages before *adoption* (actually regularly purchasing the offering) include that of *awareness* (being cognizant of the offering), *interest and information search* (having some receptivity in the offering and seeking information about it), *evaluation* (assessing the offering in relation to adoption aims), and *trial* (using the offering on a temporary basis). While the adoption process is often described as a series of stages that are followed in a non-repeating sequence, it can also be far from such as some consumers may skip certain stages of the process, while others may revisit certain stages in one or more iterations. The process may end with rejection, rather than adoption, and in other versions of the modeled process there is a stage of *symbolic adoption*, where the product is embraced as a notion, following the initial evaluation stage.

KEY WORDS Adoption stages, purchase

IMPLICATIONS
A key task of marketers is to understand what is involved in the psychological adoption process of consumers for particular product and service offerings in order to be able to positively influence such consumers at appropriate stages, thereby encouraging them to successfully complete the adoption process and purchase the offering. For example, product trial may be an important stage to be completed before adopting some new products such as newly flavored soft drinks, prompting marketers to offer free samples of the products in supermarkets. Similarly, marketers may give away to consumers small trial-sized packages of products such as shampoos or laundry detergents to encourage adoption. Yet, in adopting other products such as mobile phones, awareness, interest, and evaluation become more essential, leading marketers to emphasize marketing communications and other means to move consumers successfully through these stages of the adoption process. Finally, it is important for marketers to understand the time and effort consumers take within each stage of the adoption process and the nature of actual succession of adoption stages through consumer research. For example, the fact that *evaluation* and *symbolic adoption* may, in reality, not take place early

in a consumer's adoption process, but later after *trial*, can change the dynamics of the marketing communication plans marketers set in relation to commonly held assumptions about the typical consumer adoption process. (See also **buyer influence/readiness**.)

APPLICATION AREAS AND FURTHER READINGS

Consumer Behavior

Manning, Kenneth C., Bearden, William O., and Madden, Thomas J. (1995). 'Consumer Innovativeness and the Adoption Process,' *Journal of Consumer Psychology*, 4(4), 329–345.

Klonglan, Gerald E., and Coward, E. Walter (1970), 'The Concept of Symbolic Adoption: A Suggested Interpretation,' *Rural Sociology*, 35(1), 77–83.

Labay, Duncan G., and Kinnear, Thomas C. (1981). 'Exploring the Consumer Decision Process in the Adoption of Solar Energy Systems,' *Journal of Consumer Research*, 8(3), December, 271–278.

Marketing Modeling

Norton, John A., and Bass, Frank M. (1987). 'A Diffusion Theory Model of Adoption and Substitution for Successive Generations of High-Technology Products,' *Management Science*, 33(9), September, 1069–1086.

BIBLIOGRAPHY

Ozanne, Urban B., and Churchill, Jr., Gilbert A. (1971). 'Five Dimensions of the Industrial Adoption Process,' *Journal of Marketing Research*, 8(3), August, 322–328.

Huff, Sid L., and Munro, Malcolm C. (1985). 'Information Technology Assessment and Adoption: A Field Study,' *MIS Quarterly*, 9(4), December, 327–340.

■ adoption theory

DESCRIPTION

Theory or theories aimed at understanding, explaining, or predicting how, why, and to what extent individuals or organizations will adopt or purchase new offerings.

KEY INSIGHTS

Theories of adoption recognize the role of multiple factors in influencing product or service adoption by an individual or organization. The extent that a potential adopter values innovativeness, the degree of innovation that is communicated by a new product or service offering, and the knowledge and experience of the prospective adopter are just some examples of potentially influential factors in determining the rate and extent of adoption.

KEY WORDS Adoption, readiness

IMPLICATIONS

While understanding, explaining, and predicting individual or organizational adoption of a new offering is often complex, it behooves marketers to research the drivers and impediments of adoption in an effort to facilitate new product adoption and make appropriate plans for the expected rate of adoption by individuals or organizations in a given market. Knowledge of the adoption process (see **adoption process**) as well as buyer influences and readiness (see **buyer influence/readiness**) can be highly beneficial in this regard.

APPLICATION AREAS AND FURTHER READINGS
Marketing Strategy
Foxall, Gordon R., and Bhate, Seema (1993). 'Cognitive Styles and Personal Involve-
    ment of Market Initiators for "Healthy" Food Brands: Implications for Adoption
    Theory,' *Journal of Economic Psychology*, 14(1), March, 33–56.
Kimberly, John R., and Evanisko, Michael J. (1981). 'Organizational Innovation:
    The Influence of Individual, Organizational, and Contextual Factors on Hospital
    Adoption of Technological and Administrative Innovations,' *Academy of Manage-
    ment Journal*, 24(4), December, 689–713.
Jensen, R. (1982). 'Adoption and Diffusion of an Innovation of Uncertain Profitabil-
    ity,' *Journal of Economic Theory*, 27(1), 182–193.
O'Callaghan, Ramon, Kaufmann, Patrick J., and Konsynski, Benn R. (1992). 'Adop-
    tion Correlates and Share Effects of Electronic Data Interchange Systems in
    Marketing Channels,' *Journal of Marketing*, 56(2), April, 45–56.

Consumer Behavior
Fisher, Robert J., and Price, Linda L. (1992). 'An Investigation into the Social Context
    of Early Adoption Behavior,' *Journal of Consumer Research*, 19(3), December, 477–
    486.

BIBLIOGRAPHY
Alavi, M., and Henderson, J. C. (1981). 'An Evolutionary Strategy for Implementing
    a Decision Support System,' *Management Science*, 27(11), 1309–1323.
Venkatraman, M. P. (1991). 'The Impact of Innovativeness and Innovation Type on
    Adoption,' *Journal of Retailing*, 67, 51–67.

■ adverse selection

DESCRIPTION
The tendency for any offering to a market to be most attractive to those most
likely to benefit from it.

KEY INSIGHTS
The concept of adverse selection suggests that, when a firm's offering is
non-selective, as when health insurance can be obtained by any individual without a medical examination, one should expect that those most
likely to benefit from it will accept it (e.g. those in poor health), whereas
others that will benefit from it less will be more likely to seek alternative
offerings (e.g. those in better health accepting a more selective insurer).

KEY WORDS Offering attractiveness, customer benefit

IMPLICATIONS
Marketers should recognize how, in trying to be non-selective with an
offering, adverse selection leads customers posing the greatest risk to
the firm to select themselves. To the extent such self-selected high-risk
customers lead to higher costs for the firm, marketers should seek to
understand such risks and develop strategies and policies for their more
effective management. Marketers may also benefit from learning from
competitors' introduction of new product and service offerings to understand better the nature and extent of adverse selection relative to the
competitor's offerings and customers.

APPLICATION AREAS AND FURTHER READINGS
Services Marketing
Browne, Mark J. (1992). 'Evidence of Adverse Selection in the Individual Health
   Insurance Market,' *Journal of Risk and Insurance*, 59(1), March, 13–33.
Puelz, Robert, and Snow, Arthur (1994). 'Evidence on Adverse Selection: Equi-
   librium Signaling and Cross-Subsidization in the Insurance Market,' *Journal of
   Political Economy*, 102(2), April, 236–257.
Ausubel, Lawrence M. (1999). 'Adverse Selection in the Credit Card Market.' Work-
   ing Paper, Department of Economics, University of Maryland, June.

Online Marketing
Fabel, Oliver, and Lehmann, Erik E. (2002). 'Adverse Selection and Market Substi-
   tution by Electronic Trade,' *International Journal of the Economics of Business*, 9(2),
   175–194.
Steckbeck, Mark, and Boettke, Peter (2001). 'Turning Lemons into Lemonade:
   Entrepreneurial Solutions to Selection Problems in E-Commerce,' Third Annual
   Conference of the Association of Historians of the Austrian Tradition in Eco-
   nomic Thought, Pisa—Lucca, 24–26 May 2001.

Marketing Strategy
Ong, S.-E. (1999). 'Caveat Emptor, Adverse Selection in Buying Properties under
   Construction,' *Property Management*, 17(1), 49–64.
Cao, Y., and Gruca, T. S. (2005). 'Reducing Adverse Selection through Customer
   Relationship Management,' *Journal of Marketing*, 69(4), 219–229.
Guasch, J. Luis, and Weiss, Andrew (1980). 'Adverse Selection by Markets and the
   Advantage of Being Late,' *Quarterly Journal of Economics*, 94(3), May, 453–466.

BIBLIOGRAPHY
Eckbo, B., and Masulis, R. (1992). 'Adverse Selection and the Rights Offer Paradox,'
   Journal of Financial Economics, 32, 293–332.
Garella, Paolo G. (1987). *Adverse Selection and Intermediation*. Florence: European
   University Institute, Department of Economics.

■ advertising theory

DESCRIPTION
Theory or theories attempting to explain how and why advertising is effective
in influencing behaviors and accomplishing its objectives which may include
communicating with potential customers and persuading them to adopt a
particular attitude or preference toward products or brands and ultimately
purchase them.

KEY INSIGHTS
While there are numerous individual theories of advertising and considerable scope and complexity in the large body of knowledge which
comprises advertising theory, most theories of advertising implicitly or
explicitly adopt a view that advertising's effectiveness is dependent on
principles and practices including mere exposure and/or repetition. That
is, simply exposing a consumer to a product or brand's advertising can
result in increased liking of the product or brand, while repeatedly exposing the consumer to the product or brand's advertising over time can lead
to the consumer being, in a sense, conditioned to a potentially greater
extent to like a product or brand or to associate particular thoughts
or feelings with the product or brand. At the same time, advertising's

effectiveness can be highly context specific and dependent on numerous other principles and theory associated with message and media characteristics, consumer characteristics, product/service characteristics, and competitive actions.

KEY WORDS Advertising effectiveness, advertising effects

IMPLICATIONS

As it is often said that 'half of all advertising doesn't work,' aiming to understand and apply the many general and specific principles forming advertising theory may potentially do much to increase the likelihood that any particular advertising campaign or advertising strategy will be effective and accomplish its intended objectives. Marketers must therefore seek to understand the factors that influence advertising's effectiveness and ineffectiveness relative to intended objectives and particular contexts to be able to judiciously apply such knowledge. Even experienced firms can make advertising missteps, such as allowing the firm's ad agency to create an advertisement that is memorable and consistent with some elements of advertising theory (e.g. persuading with emotion for a low-involvement purchase) but not fully realizing until after it has aired that the ad runs counter to other principles associated with advertising theory (e.g. emphasizing those emotions that are desired to be positively associated with the brand).

APPLICATION AREAS AND FURTHER READINGS

Advertising
Tellis, Gerard J., Chandy, Rajesh K., and Thaivanich, Pattana (2000). 'Which Ad Works, When, Where, and How Often? Modeling the Effects of Direct Television Advertising,' *Journal of Marketing Research*, 37(1), February, 32–46.

Consumer Behaviour
Mick, David Glen (1992). 'Levels of Subjective Comprehension in Advertising Processing and their Relations to Ad Perceptions, Attitudes, and Memory,' *Journal of Consumer Research*, 18(4), March, 411–424.

BIBLIOGRAPHY
Tellis, Gerard J. (2005). *Advertising and Sales Promotions*. New York: Addison-Wesley.
Vakratsas, Demetrios, and Ambler, Tim (1999). 'How Advertising Works: What Do We Really Know?' *Journal of Marketing*, 63(1), January, 26–43.

■ advertising wearout effect

DESCRIPTION
The resulting effect when a particular ad is presented to consumers with such frequency and/or duration that the consumers begin to ignore it to a large extent or become tired of it and no longer react favorably to it.

KEY INSIGHTS
The advertising wearout effect is in many ways an acknowledgment that there will be diminishing returns to any form of advertising that is presented to consumers on an ongoing basis. While marketers must consider the possibility of such an effect in determining the exposure

characteristics and lifespan of a particular ad, especially with regards to cost effectiveness of advertising, it may not be easy to predict when such an effect will become evident to a large extent, if at all, in the life of an advertising campaign due to the many factors of influence including the ad's likeability and consumer attitudes toward the subject of the ad.

KEY WORDS Advertising, effectiveness, wearout

IMPLICATIONS
Periodic market research studies on consumer reactions to an ad over time is one way in which consumer sentiment can be established to determine if the advertising wearout effect is becoming or has become a significant issue in the life of an ad within a broader advertising campaign.

APPLICATION AREAS AND FURTHER READINGS
Advertising
Tellis, Gerard J. (1988). 'Advertising Exposure, Loyalty, and Brand Purchase: A Two-Stage Model of Choice,' *Journal of Marketing Research*, 25(2), May, 134–144.
Calder, Bobby J., and Sternthal, Brian (1980). 'Television Commercial Wearout: An Information Processing View,' *Journal of Marketing Research*, 17(2), May, 173–186.
Simon, Hermann (1982). 'ADPULS: An Advertising Model with Wearout and Pulsation,' *Journal of Marketing Research*, 19(3), August, 352–363.

BIBLIOGRAPHY
Craig, C. Samuel, Sternthal, Brian, and Leavitt, Clark (1976). 'Advertising Wearout: An Experimental Analysis,' *Journal of Marketing Research*, 13(4), November, 365–372.

■ affect

DESCRIPTION
Subjectively experienced feeling or emotion.

KEY INSIGHTS
While there are numerous subjectively experienced feelings or emotions, such as happiness, anger, sadness, and fear, it is also clearly recognized that individuals may also experience emotions in varying intensity. For example, some individuals may experience particular emotions with reduced intensity while still others may demonstrate a complete or near-absence of emotional expression altogether. Among others and under certain conditions, experienced emotions may also be unstable and fluctuate.

KEY WORDS Emotion, feeling

IMPLICATIONS
As there are many product and service offerings that have a strong emotional appeal to consumers, e.g. the brand of a sports car to be considered for purchase or the particular music that the individual considers for purchase, marketers should seek to know how and to what extent consumers relate to particular product and service offerings through their

feelings and emotions. Seemingly tame improvements to products, such as the attempt by Coca-Cola to introduce New Coke to consumers as a better-tasting cola beverage, may ultimately lead to unexpected and even severe emotional responses by consumers if such emotional relationships and attachments to products are not fully understood or appreciated by the marketer.

APPLICATION AREAS AND FURTHER READINGS

Marketing Strategy
Baker, Julie (1996). 'The Effects of the Service Environment on Affect and Consumer Perception of Waiting Time: An Integrative Review and Research Propositions,' *Journal of the Academy of Marketing Science*, 24(4), 338–349.
Chaudhuri, Arjun, and Holbrook, Morris B. (2001). 'The Chain of Effects from Brand Trust and Brand Affect to Brand Performance: The Role of Brand Loyalty,' *Journal of Marketing*, 65(2), 81–93.
Westbrook, Robert A. (1987). 'Product/Consumption-Based Affective Responses and Postpurchase Processes,' *Journal of Marketing Research*, 24(3), August, 258–270.

Consumer Behavior
Oliver, Richard L. (1993). 'Cognitive, Affective, and Attribute Bases of the Satisfaction Response,' *Journal of Consumer Research*, 20(3), December, 418–430.

BIBLIOGRAPHY
Bagozzi, Richard P. (1999). 'The Role of Emotions in Marketing,' *Journal of the Academy of Marketing Science*, 27(2), 184–206.

■ affiliate marketing

(also called referral marketing, many-to-many marketing, partner marketing, pay-for-performance marketing, performance-based marketing, or revenue-sharing marketing)

DESCRIPTION
The use of a revenue sharing partnership between a merchant and one or more affiliated or partner firms where the affiliates are paid for referring or leading consumers to the merchant and/or when consumers subsequently purchase from the merchant.

KEY INSIGHTS
Affiliate marketing is a form of marketing that is based on a pay-for-performance approach. While the approach often involves a complex process of tracking, monitoring, and payments, the process has become easier as a result of many organizations now providing such support services to firms seeking to engage in affiliate marketing. Affiliate marketing has become an increasingly common practice among Web-based businesses in particular, where compensation may be on a pay-per-click, pay-per-lead, or pay-per-sale basis. Many organizations with websites containing advertising, for example, use *pay-per-click marketing*, which is where an advertiser compensates the affiliated organization based on the number of times website visitors click on an ad that takes them to the website of the advertiser.

KEY WORDS Revenue sharing, pay-for-performance

IMPLICATIONS

Affiliate marketing provides a firm with a relatively efficient means to promote its offerings in a way where the firm pays for the results obtained. As many marketers view affiliate marketing as an approach that will become increasingly mainstream in e-commerce, marketers may benefit from a greater understanding of how and to what extent the approach may have strategic value to the firm as a means of cost effectively exposing potential customers to the firms' offerings with the aim of encouraging subsequent purchase.

APPLICATION AREAS AND FURTHER READINGS

Online Marketing
Hoffman, D. L., and Novak, T. P. (2000). 'How to Acquire Customers on the Web,' *Harvard Business Review*, 78, May–June, 179–183.
Duffy, Dennis L. (2005). 'Affiliate Marketing and its Impact on E-commerce,' *Journal of Consumer Marketing*, 22(3), 161–163.
Libai, Barak, Biyalogorsky, Eyal, and Gerstner, Eitan (2003). 'Setting Referral Fees in Affiliate Marketing,' *Journal of Service Research*, 5(4), 303–315.
Gummesson, E. (2004). *Many to Many Marketing*. Malmo: Liber.

BIBLIOGRAPHY
Goldschmidt, Simon, Junghagen, Sven, and Harris, Uri (2003). *Strategic Affiliate Marketing*. Northampton, Mass.: Edward Elgar.

■ affinity marketing

DESCRIPTION

An approach to marketing that involves the teaming together of organizations to attract customers with particular interests.

KEY INSIGHTS

As part of affinity programs, firms aim to find customers of particular products or services who also have an interest in, or affinity to, certain other areas or topics to allow such customers to be presented with products or services associated with those areas. While affinity marketing originated in the credit card industry, its scope and application now extends well beyond the area to markets ranging from financial services to charities and other non-profit organizations.

KEY WORDS Organizational teaming, customer interests

IMPLICATIONS

Affinity marketing provides a means for marketers to cost effectively leverage their brand and customer base assets by providing an expanded set of offerings to customers through strategic partnerships with other firms rather than through potentially more costly internal development. Marketers seeking to reach new customers with current products as well as current customers with new products may potentially benefit from strategic use of an affinity marketing approach to the extent there exists a common consumer interest on which organizations can build and partner to provide a set of offerings of increased value to consumers identified as sharing common interests.

APPLICATION AREAS AND FURTHER READINGS

Marketing Strategy
Worthington, Steve (2001). 'Affinity Credit Cards: A Critical Review,' *International Journal of Retail and Distribution Management*, 29(11), 485–512.

Consumer Behavior
Laing, Angus, Harris, Fiona, and Mekonnen, Aster (2004). 'Deconstructing Affinity Relationships: Consumers and Affinity Marketing,' *Journal of Customer Behavior*, 3(2), July, 215–228.

Non-Profit Marketing
Cowton, C. J., and Gunn, C. J. (2000). 'The Affinity Credit Card as a Fundraising Tool for Charities,' *International Journal of Nonprofit and Voluntary Sector Marketing*, 5(1), 11–18.

BIBLIOGRAPHY
Macchiette, B., and Abhijit, R. (1993). 'Affinity Marketing: What is it and How Does it Work?' *Journal of Product and Brand Management*, 2(1), 55–67.

☐ affordable method *see* promotion budget setting methods

☐ age segmentation *see* segmentation

■ agency theory

DESCRIPTION
Theory aimed at explaining how and why organizations or individuals are best empowered to act as representatives or agents for other organizations or individuals as principals given that the principals have incomplete information regarding the agents and where the agents may have different motives than the principals.

KEY INSIGHTS
Agency theory is concerned with the problems associated with motivating one party (an agent) to act on behalf of another (a principal). Specifically, under conditions where an agent is compensated by a principal for performing certain tasks which are useful to the principal and costly to the agent, and where there are elements of the performance which are costly to observe, the principal often does not know enough about the extent that an agent's performance is in accord with the principal's demands or expectations. The theory is therefore concerned with ways to align better the interests of the agent with those of the principal. Examples of mechanisms for doing so include certain financial incentives such as profit sharing, commissions, and piece-rate compensation. On the other hand, disincentives for an agent acting counter to a principal's interest may include a fear of firing. While agency theory research is considerable, the concepts and issues involved can provide important guidance for contract design and related activities in terms of characteristics including the nature of information involved and used as well as the intensity of incentives and monitoring and the equality of compensation.

KEY WORDS Agents, principals, empowerment, incentives

IMPLICATIONS

Agency theory's broad scope means it may help us to understand, explain, or predict better principal–agent actions in widely varying contexts including between firms as well as within firms. For example, agent firms or individuals may interact with the firm as employee, supplier, subcontractor, selling agent, franchisee, or other distributor. Beyond its benefits for identifying and evaluating the desirability of various agent incentives, the principles and practices suggested by agency theory may find strategic use by marketers in shaping planning efforts involving any form of agent role for, or on behalf of, the marketer's organization.

APPLICATION AREAS AND FURTHER READINGS

Marketing Strategy

Anderson, Paul F. (1982). 'Marketing, Strategic Planning and the Theory of the Firm,' *Journal of Marketing*, 46(2), Spring, 15–26.

Heide, Jan B. (1994). 'Interorganizational Governance in Marketing Channels,' *Journal of Marketing*, 58(1), January, 71–85.

Bergen, Mark, Dutta, Shantanu, and Walker, Orville C., Jr. (1992). 'Agency Relationships in Marketing: A Review of the Implications and Applications of Agency and Related Theories,' *Journal of Marketing*, 56(3), July, 1–24.

Franchising

Lafontaine, Francine (1992). 'Agency Theory and Franchising: Some Empirical Results,' *RAND Journal of Economics*, 23(2), Summer, 263–283.

BIBLIOGRAPHY

Eisenhardt, Kathleen M. (1989). 'Agency Theory: An Assessment and Review,' *Academy of Management Review*, 14(1), 57–74.

Sappington, David E. M. (1991). 'Incentives in Principal–Agent Relationships,' *Journal of Economic Perspectives*, 5(2), Spring, 45–66.

Milgrom, Paul, and Roberts, John (1992). *Economics, Organization and Management*. London: Prentice-Hall.

■ agglomeration economies

DESCRIPTION

Cost savings or benefits realized as a result of firms clustering together.

KEY INSIGHTS

By locating near one another, some firms and consumers can achieve desirable cost savings and benefits. For example, when retail outlets cluster together, it is easier for consumers to make price and product comparisons with less travel, thereby reducing consumers' acquisition costs and increasing the likelihood of product purchase. In other instances, cost savings can be achieved by firms through the sharing of infrastructure including that for communications and other support services. A characteristic of agglomeration economies is that the activities of any one firm also result in benefits to the other firms in the agglomeration.

KEY WORDS Clustering, location, cost savings, **benefits**

IMPLICATIONS

In deciding where to locate an organization, marketers should evaluate the nature and extent of agglomeration economies in both lowering costs and providing added benefits to the organization. The sharing of infrastructure may reduce operating costs or facilitate mutually beneficial communication in some instances, while in other instances, co-locating with complementary or even similar outlets may increase consumer traffic as well as make it easier for consumers to purchase by lowering their product search and acquisition costs.

APPLICATION AREAS AND FURTHER READINGS

Retail Marketing
Gautschi, David A. (1981). 'Specification of Patronage Models for Retail Center Choice,' *Journal of Marketing Research*, 18(2), May, 162–174.

Marketing Strategy
Pouder, Richard, and St. John, Caron H. (1996). 'Hot Spots and Blind Spots: Geographical Clusters of Firms and Innovation,' *Academy of Management Review*, 21(4), October, 1192–1225.
Dwyer, F. Robert, and Welsh, M. Ann (1985). 'Environmental Relationships of the Internal Political Economy of Marketing Channels,' *Journal of Marketing Research*, 22(4), November, 397–414.
Lyons, D. (1995). 'Agglomeration Economies among High Technology Firms in Advanced Production Areas: The Case of Denver/Boulder,' *Regional Studies*, 29, 265–278.
Karlsson, C. (1997). 'Product Development, Innovation Networks, Infrastructure and Agglomeration Economies,' *Annals of Regional Science*, 31(3), 235–258.

BIBLIOGRAPHY
Rosenthal, Stuart S., and Strange, William C. (2004). 'Evidence on the Nature and Sources of Agglomeration Economies,' in Vernon Henderson and Jacques-François Thisse (eds.), *Handbook of Regional and Urban Economics*, 4, Amsterdam: North-Holland.
Lambooy, J. G. (1997). 'Knowledge Production, Organisation and Agglomeration Economies,' *Geojournal*, 41(4), 293–300.

☐ AIDA *see* buyer influence/readiness

☐ AIDCA *see* buyer influence/readiness

☐ AL theory *see* adaptation-level theory

☐ alternative evaluation *see* buyer decision process

☐ ambient marketing *see* out-of-home marketing

■ ambush marketing

DESCRIPTION
Marketing intending to give an impression to consumers that a firm or brand is officially associated with an event or cause when, in fact, it is not.

KEY INSIGHTS
The aim of ambush marketing is to obtain more of the gains associated with an official or formal association, as through event sponsorship, but without incurring the same extent of its costs. While another organization may own the legal right to be the official sponsor of an event, for

example, a firm engaged in ambush marketing may locate or promote itself in ways that give consumers the impression that it, too, is a sponsor of the event.

KEY WORDS Sponsorship, events

IMPLICATIONS
While the ethics of the ambush marketing approach may be debated, it nevertheless is an approach that firms can and do use in their marketing efforts to associate with events and causes without incurring the full cost of a formal association with them. Marketers must therefore evaluate carefully the benefits and risks of its use by the firm and, should the firm choose to be formally associated with events or causes through means such as official sponsorship, marketers must then seek to identify and implement means to deter other firms from using an ambush marketing approach.

APPLICATION AREAS AND FURTHER READINGS
Marketing Ethics
Meenaghan, T. (1994). 'Point of View: Ambush Marketing—Immoral or Imaginative Practice?' *Journal of Advertising Research*, 34 (3), 77–88.

Sponsorship Marketing
Meenaghan, T. (1996). 'Ambush Marketing—A Threat to Corporate Sponsorship,' *Sloan Management Review*, 38, 103–113.

Marketing Strategy
Meenaghan, T. (1998). 'Ambush Marketing: Corporate Strategy and Consumers Reaction,' *Psychology and Marketing*, 15(4), 305–322.

BIBLIOGRAPHY
Sandler, Dennis M., and Shani, David (1989). 'Olympic Sponsorship vs. "Ambush" Marketing: Who Gets the Gold,' *Journal of Advertising Research*, 29, 9–14.

■ anchoring and adjustment

DESCRIPTION
An effect relating to the heuristic or commonsensical approach to problem solving that involves making an initial judgment and then adjusting the judgment to arriving at a final judgment, but where the final judgment tends to be biased by the value of the initial judgment.

KEY INSIGHTS
The anchoring and adjustment heuristic effect is a phenomenon of individual problem solving which shows how final judgments can be influenced—and potentially inaccurate—as a result of an individual's tendency to anchor on the initial judgment and subsequently make adjustments which are ultimately insufficient when arriving at a final judgment. First studied by Slovic and Lichtenstein (1971), the heuristic effect has been shown to lead to significantly different final judgments when substantially different values for initial judgments are also suggested in the formulation of the problem. Thus, if consumers are asked how many hours of television they watch in a year where they are first asked to

indicate whether an initial number suggested by an interviewer is too low (e.g. 20) or too high (e.g. 2000), and where they are subsequently asked to estimate a final number, those consumers given a low initial number will tend to provide significantly lower final estimates than consumers given a high initial number.

KEY WORDS Problem-solving heuristic, **bias**

IMPLICATIONS

As is suggested by the above example, the anchoring and adjustment effect is a phenomenon that may potentially lead to inaccurate or biased responses by consumers in research including survey research where individuals' initial judgments are given or suggested by others. Alternatively, consumer judgments may be biased when they themselves use the heuristic and make estimates which are too low or too high initially. As such, marketers must be aware of, and attempt to compensate for, the possibility of biased judgments when individuals may be applying an anchoring and adjustment approach in problem solving.

APPLICATION AREAS AND FURTHER READINGS

Consumer Behavior
Wansink, Brian, Kent, Robert J., and Hoch, Stephen J. (1998). 'An Anchoring and Adjustment Model of Purchase Quantity Decisions,' *Journal of Marketing Research*, 35(1), February, 71–81.
Davis, Harry L., Hoch, Stephen J., and Easton Ragsdale, E. K. (1986). 'An Anchoring and Adjustment Model of Spousal Predictions,' *Journal of Consumer Research*, 13(1), June, 25–37.
Yadav, Manjit S. (1994). 'How Buyers Evaluate Product Bundles: A Model of Anchoring and Adjustment,' *Journal of Consumer Research*, 21(2), September, 342–353.

BIBLIOGRAPHY

Tversky, A., and Kahneman, D. (1974). 'Judgment under Uncertainty: Heuristics and Biases,' *Science*, 185, 1124–1130.
Lichtenstein, Sarah, and Slovic, Paul (1971). 'Reversals of Preference between Bids and Choices in Gambling Decisions,' *Journal of Experimental Psychology*, 89, 46–55.

■ anchoring effect

DESCRIPTION

Any effect on judgment resulting from consideration of a reference point or anchoring position of judgment.

KEY INSIGHTS

The anchoring effect may be present when individuals make evaluations or comparisons based on a reference point or frame. Thus, consumer evaluations of a new product's overall quality may be influenced by judgments resulting from their knowledge of particular existing products which may be of worse or better quality than that of the new product.

KEY WORDS Judgment, reference points

IMPLICATIONS

As it may be common for individual judgments of product and service offerings to be influenced by earlier points of reference, marketers must recognize how individuals may perceive new information as a result of prior information and current views on which they are anchoring. Price comparisons, features, and benefit comparisons are but a few examples of areas where marketers must aim to understand how and why consumers may systematically respond to particular offerings as a result of anchoring effects.

APPLICATION AREAS AND FURTHER READINGS

Consumer Behavior

Simonson, Itamar, and Drolet, Aimee (2004). 'Anchoring Effects on Consumer's Willingness-to-Pay and Willingness-to-Accept,' *Journal of Consumer Research*, 31, December, 681–690.

Chapman, G. B., and Johnson, E. J. (2002). 'Incorporating the Irrelevant: Anchors in Judgments of Belief and Value,' in T. Gilovich, D. W. Griffin, and D. Kahneman (eds.), *Heuristics and Biases: The Psychology of Intuitive Judgment*. New York: Cambridge University Press, 120–138.

BIBLIOGRAPHY

Leefland, P. S. H., and Wittink, Dick R. (2000). *Building Models for Marketing Decisions: Past, Present, and Future*. Rijksuniversiteit te Groningen: Research School Systems, Organization and Management.

Strack, F., and Mussweiler, T. (1997). 'Explaining the Enigmatic Anchoring Effect: Mechanisms of Selective Accessibility,' *Journal of Personality and Social Psychology*, 73(3), 437–446.

■ ancient mariner effect

(also called the passing stranger effect)

DESCRIPTION

The tendency for individuals to disclose personal information more freely or openly to strangers than to closer acquaintances.

KEY INSIGHTS

While the psychology behind the effect may be quite involved, believing that one is unlikely to relate to an individual on an ongoing basis may potentially lead one to be more open to such an individual as a result of the situation contributing to the belief that one is immune to confrontations of long-term judgment by the individual and that the likelihood that personal information will be disclosed inappropriately will be minimal.

KEY WORDS Personal disclosure

IMPLICATIONS

Such an effect may be useful by a marketing researcher seeking personal and sensitive information from an individual consumer to the extent that the consumer views the researcher as a non-judgmental stranger whom he or she will not be acquainted with over the longer term. At the same time, marketers must be aware of the possibility that an organizations' employees may, particularly while traveling to infrequent destinations, inadvertently disclose sensitive information to passing strangers who just might be associated with a competing organization.

APPLICATION AREAS AND FURTHER READINGS
Online Marketing
Ellison, N., Heino, R., and Gibbs, J. (2006). 'Managing Impressions Online: Self-Presentation Processes in the Online Dating Environment,' *Journal of Computer-Mediated Communication*, 11(2), article 2.
Resnick, P., and Zeckhauser, R. (2002). 'Trust among Strangers in Internet Transactions: Empirical Analysis of eBay's Reputation System,' in M. R. Baye (ed.), *Advances in Applied Microeconomics: The Economics of the Internet and E-commerce*, 11, 127–157. Amsterdam: Elsevier Science.

BIBLIOGRAPHY
Rubin, Z. (1975). 'Disclosing Oneself to a Stranger: Reciprocity and its Limits,' *Journal of Experimental Social Psychology*, 11(3), 233–260.

■ announcement effect

DESCRIPTION
Any effect on consumer, market, or firm behavior resulting from an announcement by an organization where effects are evident before the action indicated by the announcement actually takes place.

KEY INSIGHTS
Effects stemming from announcements, whether by firms, industry organizations, or governmental institutions, can be immediate and influential to consumer, firm, and market behaviors to the extent that the individual or organization making the announcement has credibility. For example, a new product pre-announcement, where a firm announces its intention to introduce a particular new product on a particular date, sends signals to both potential customers and current competitors, where the announcement encourages potential customers to wait for the new product to be available and where the announcement also acts to discourage current competitors from entering with a similar new product by signaling that they will be pre-empted. Credibility of the organization making the announcement is often key in determining the extent of its effect.

KEY WORDS Pre-announcements, behavior

IMPLICATIONS
Marketers must be ready to respond to immediate, significant changes in market conditions and consumer behavior that may result from announcement effects. At the same time, marketers may be able to use announcements to create immediate consumer and market effects as well as provide strategic signals to deter or encourage certain competitive actions. Marketers must also recognize how the announcement effect may work against the firm as well, as when announcing the date for a planned introduction of the firm's next-generation product can lead to a dramatic slowing, or even halt, in sales of its current product and produce an excess current product inventory for the firm having immediately reduced resale value.

APPLICATION AREAS AND FURTHER READINGS
Marketing Strategy

Chen, S. S., Ho, K. W., and Ik, K. H. (2005). 'The Wealth Effect of New Product Introductions on Industry Rivals,' *Journal of Business*, 78, 969–996.

Mishra, Debi Prasad, and Bhabra, Harjeet S. (2001). 'Assessing the Economic Worth of New Product Pre-Announcement Signals: Theory and Empirical Evidence,' *Journal of Product and Brand Management*, 10(2), 75–93.

Rosenfeld, James D. (1984). 'Additional Evidence on the Relation between Divestiture Announcements and Shareholder Wealth,' *Journal of Finance*, 39(5), December, 1437–1448.

DeFusco, Richard A., Johnson, Robert R., and Zorn, Thomas S. (1990). 'The Effect of Executive Stock Option Plans on Stockholders and Bondholders,' *Journal of Finance*, 45(2), June, 617–627.

BIBLIOGRAPHY

Waud, Roger N. (1970). 'Public Interpretation of Federal Reserve Discount Rate Changes: Evidence on the "Announcement Effect," ' *Econometrica*, 38(2), March, 231–250.

Thornton, Daniel L. (1994). *The Information Content of Discount Rate Announcements: What's Behind the Announcement Effect?* St Louis: Federal Reserve Bank of St Louis.

Demiralp, Selva, and Jordá, Oscar (2002). 'The Announcement Effect: Evidence from Open Market Desk Data,' *Economic Policy Review*, Federal Reserve Bank of New York, May, 29–48.

Palmer, Clephan M. (1996). 'A Week that Shook the Meat Industry: The Effects on the UK beef Industry of the BSE Crisis,' *British Food Journal*, 98(11), 17–25.

☐ **Ansoff matrix** *see* product-market investment strategies

■ antimarketing

DESCRIPTION

Behaviors or attitudes reflecting the view that a person or organization rejects advocating or using any of an array of practices or principles perceived to be part of marketing.

KEY INSIGHTS

Among the possible reasons for why some individuals and organizations adopt an antimarketing view is that they are unable to see how a marketing approach would be beneficial in helping them to achieve their goals over the short or long term. Understanding how, why, and to what extent such beliefs have been developed in individuals or organizations is the first step in the development of strategies, programs, and practices intended to facilitate individual or organizational recognition of the value of marketing practices and principles in achieving both individual and collective goals.

KEY WORDS Marketing rejection, attitudes, behavior

IMPLICATIONS

The belief that an apparently sound marketing approach has positive value should not be assumed by marketers when developing and implementing organizational marketing strategies. More than just not being enthusiastic about a marketing approach, some individuals and organizations may go so far as to display behaviors that communicate a complete rejection of the view that a marketing approach can be beneficial. Adopting an internal marketing approach is one way that a marketer may attempt to influence internal organizational views of particular marketing strategies or practices as well as encourage the appreciation of the value of any particular marketing approach.

APPLICATION AREAS AND FURTHER READINGS
Services Marketing
Shontz, M. L., Parker, J. C., and Parker, R. (2004). 'What Do Librarians Think about Marketing? A Survey of Public Librarians' Attitudes toward the Marketing of Library Services,' *Library Quarterly*, 74(1), 63–84.
Roberts, J., and Roberts, T. (1985). 'Taking the Center to Market,' *Community Mental Health Journal*, 21, 264–281.

Marketing Strategy
Klein, Naomi (2000). *No Logo*. London: Harper Collins Publishers.

BIBLIOGRAPHY
Steiner, Robert L. (1976). 'The Prejudice against Marketing,' *Journal of Marketing*, 40(3), July, 2–9.

☐ **approach** *see* selling process

■ approach–avoidance conflict

DESCRIPTION
A tension experienced by an individual who is simultaneously attracted to and repulsed by the same goal.

KEY INSIGHTS
Approach–avoidance, a form of conflict initially examined in research by Lewin (1931), involves ambivalence toward a goal as a result of the goal containing both positive and negative elements. In such situations, an individual may exhibit vacillating behavior as he/she nears the goal, where approach behaviors predominate far from the goal but where avoidance behaviors predominate close to the goal.

A particular type of approach–avoidance conflict is known as the *Rosencrantz and Guildenstern effect*, which is a form of entrapment where a person is kept waiting while attempting to achieve a particular goal. Individuals in such situations experience increasing conflict with the passage of time since time is both an investment that increases the chance that a goal will be attained as well as an expense that may lead the individual to fail to attain the goal. An example is when an individual who waits at a town's empty taxi stand for a taxi to arrive to take him to his nearby destination faces a choice of waiting or walking to his destination but increasingly feels compelled to wait because of the increasing likelihood that a taxi will arrive.

KEY WORDS Goal conflict, tension

IMPLICATIONS

Marketers must consider how consumers attracted to particular goals associated with the marketer's offerings (e.g. the satisfaction of driving a luxury car) may simultaneously be repelled by the negative elements of goal achievement (e.g. anxiety over insurance costs, possible theft, the threat of not being able to make repayments, etc.) and as a result exhibit vacillating behaviors. Marketers must seek to identify such approach-avoidance conflicts facing particular consumers and facilitate in their resolution through appropriate marketing communications in order to achieve satisfaction in both the consumer decision-making process as well as the consumer's buying decision.

APPLICATION AREAS AND FURTHER READINGS

Consumer Behavior

Ridgway, Nancy M., Dawson, Scott A., and Bloch, Peter H. (1990). 'Pleasure and Arousal in the Marketplace: Interpersonal Differences in Approach–Avoidance Responses,' *Marketing Letters*, 1(2), June, 139-147.

Moye, L. N., and Giddings, V. L. (2002). 'An Examination of the Retail Approach-Avoidance Behavior of Older Apparel Consumers,' *Journal of Fashion Marketing and Management*, 6(3), 259-276.

Marketing Management

Rubin, J. Z., and Brockner, J. (1975). 'Factors Affecting Entrapment in Waiting Situations: The Rosencrantz and Guildenstern Effect,' *Journal of Personality and Social Psychology*, 31, 1054-1063.

Sweeney, J. C., and Wyber, F. (2002). 'The Role of Cognitions and Emotions in the Music-Approach-Avoidance Behavior Relationship,' *Journal of Services Marketing*, 16(1), 51-69.

Marketing Strategy

Lant, T. K., and Hurley, A. E. (1999). 'A Contingency Model of Response to Per-formance Feedback: Escalation of Commitment and Incremental Adaptation in Resource Investment Decisions,' *Group and Organization Management*, 24(4), 421-437.

BIBLIOGRAPHY

Lewin, Kurt (1931). 'The Conflict between Aristotelian and Galilean Modes of Thought in Contemporary Psychology,' *Journal of General Psychology*, 5, 141-177.

■ arbitrage pricing theory

DESCRIPTION

A theory holding that expected returns, and hence prices, for financial assets can be modeled as linear functions of multiple, generally macroeconomic factors.

KEY INSIGHTS

In contrast to a modeling approach involving a single systematic risk factor (i.e. the capital asset pricing model), the arbitrage pricing theory-based approach to modeling financial asset returns incorporates sensitivity to changes in multiple factors and, as such, incorporates multiple systematic risk factors. For example, risks related to inflation, interest rates, and industrial output may be appropriate for inclusion in a model of the expected return for a particular financial asset.

KEY WORDS Financial assets, returns, risk

IMPLICATIONS
While acceptance of the arbitrage pricing theory approach to financial asset return modeling is not completely without controversy in the domain of financial economics, the approach can nevertheless be insightful as a result of increased acknowledgment and incorporation of multiple factors of risk. Thus, whether marketing actions are funded by financial asset returns, or whether financial assets themselves are the subject of a firm's marketing efforts, giving modeling consideration to an arbitrage pricing theory-based approach provides an opportunity for an extensive, focused managerial and marketing understanding of multiple risk factors in the macroeconomic environment relative to any of an array of financial assets of importance to a firm.

APPLICATION AREAS AND FURTHER READINGS
Marketing Strategy
Jagpal, Sharan (1999). *Marketing Strategy and Uncertainty.* New York: Oxford University Press.
Devinney, Timothy M., and Stewart, David W. (1988). 'Rethinking the Product Portfolio: A Generalized Investment Model,' *Management Science*, 34(9), September, 1080–1095.

BIBLIOGRAPHY
Luttmer, Erzo G. J. (1996). 'Asset Pricing in Economies with Frictions,' *Econometrica*, 64(6), November, 1439–1467.
Allen, Franklin, and Gale, Douglas (1991). 'Arbitrage, Short Sales, and Financial Innovation,' *Econometrica*, 59(4), July, 1041–1068.

■ Asch phenomenon

DESCRIPTION
The tendency for individual decisions to be influenced by social pressures and forces of conformity stemming from reference groups and group norms.

KEY INSIGHTS
Named after psychologist S. E. Asch who pioneered work on understanding and explaining the phenomenon (Asch 1955), the phenomenon presents a view suggesting that individual decisions are, or can be, influenced by reference group or other group effects to a greater extent than individuals may actually be aware.

KEY WORDS Decision making, social pressure, conformity

IMPLICATIONS
Marketers aiming to understand and/or influence individual decision processes should acknowledge the Asch phenomenon as a relatively broad human decision-making tendency which may help to explain how, why, and to what extent individuals are, or can be, influenced by group actions, opinions, and norms. An individual's purchase decisions, for example, may be influenced by one of his or her reference groups to a large extent, suggesting a benefit to assessing the feasibility of marketing

activities focused on particular reference groups which may ultimately
hold influence over individual consumers.

APPLICATION AREAS AND FURTHER READINGS

Marketing Management

Laverty, Kevin J. (1996). 'Economic "Short-Termism": The Debate, the Unresolved
  Issues, and the Implications for Management Practice and Research,' *Academy of
  Management Review*, 21(3), July, 825–860.

BIBLIOGRAPHY

Asch, Solomon E. (1955). 'Opinions and Social Pressure,' *Scientific American*, 193(5),
  31–35.

☐ **asset** *see* strategic asset

■ assimilation–contrast theory

DESCRIPTION

A theory of judgments and attitudes holding that persuasion-related efforts
to change judgments or attitudes involve an individual's initial reference point
or anchor position and where new positions close to the reference point are
assimilated by the individual and positions discrepant from the reference point
are contrasted or rejected by the individual.

KEY INSIGHTS

Based on pioneering research by Sherif and Hovland (1961), the theory
offers an explanation for why particular items of information of persuasive communication are either accepted by individuals, rejected, or
similarly result in minimal change. The researchers relate information
not discrepant from an individual's anchor or reference position to falling
within a latitude of acceptance and leading to assimilation, whereas
information highly discrepant from the reference position falls within
either a latitude of neutrality (leading to minimal change) or a latitude
of rejection (leading to contrast with the individual's reference position).
Furthermore, the theory suggests that the level of ego involvement of
the individual is associated with the relative widths of the individual's
latitudes of acceptance and rejection where, more specifically, low ego
involvement is associated with wide latitudes of acceptance and narrow
latitudes of rejection and where high ego involvement is associated with
the opposite conditions.

KEY WORDS Persuasion, message acceptance, message rejection

IMPLICATIONS

Marketers involved in efforts to persuade or communicate with current
or potential customers should understand how marketing messages and
related elements of marketing communication aimed at changing attitudes or judgments may lead to acceptance, rejection, or little change
by individuals depending on the message position's distance or degree of
discrepancy from an individual's anchor positions or points of reference.
Particularly when individuals have a high degree of ego involvement,

marketers should be aware of the additional challenge of persuading such individuals to adopt positions which are highly discrepant from their initial positions of attitude or judgment. In contrast, it will be far easier for marketers to persuade individuals under conditions of low ego involvement to accept marketing messages which are less discrepant from individuals' initial points of reference. Evaluating how marketing messages are likely to be received in accordance with assimilation-contrast theory may therefore be a prudent task for marketers prior to implementing particular marketing communications.

APPLICATION AREAS AND FURTHER READINGS
Consumer Behavior
Anderson, Rolph E. (1973). 'Consumer Dissatisfaction: The Effect of Disconfirmed Expectancy on Perceived Product Performance,' *Journal of Marketing Research*, 10(1), February, 38–44.
Olshavsky, Richard W., and Miller, John A. (1972). 'Consumer Expectations, Product Performance, and Perceived Product Quality,' *Journal of Marketing Research*, 9(1), February, 19–21.

Pricing
Kalyanaram, Gurumurthy, and Winer, Russell S. (1995). 'Empirical Generalizations from Reference Price Research,' *Marketing Science*, 14(3), Part 2 of 2: Special Issue on Empirical Generalizations in Marketing, G161–G169.
Kalyanaram, Gurumurthy, and Little, John D. C. (1994). 'An Empirical Analysis of Latitude of Price Acceptance in Consumer Package Goods,' *Journal of Consumer Research*, 21(3), December, 408–418.

BIBLIOGRAPHY
Sherif, Muzafer, and Hovland, Carl Iver (1961). *Social Judgment: Assimilation and Contrast Effects in Communication and Attitude Change*. New Haven: Yale University Press.

☐ **attention** *see* buyer influence/readiness

■ attitudes, functional theory of

DESCRIPTION
A theoretical perspective holding that individual attitudes are developed to satisfy various functional needs or goals of the individual.

KEY INSIGHTS
According to the functional theory of attitudes, the attitudes of individuals are reflections of their underlying motivations. Such a motivational approach to attitudes provides focus on identifying, understanding, and explaining the way in which an individual's attitude helps the individual to satisfy certain individual needs or goals.

KEY WORDS Attitudes, goals, **need(s)**

IMPLICATIONS
The functional theory of attitudes can provide marketers with potential insights into how and why consumers may develop and maintain various attitudes, such as consumers' developing positive or negative attitudes toward the category of luxury goods, for example. Such a perspective

may assist marketers in inferring links between individuals' attitudes and their motivations or needs, such as a desire to either acquire or shun luxury goods. As such, marketers can understand the potential consequences, benefits, and limitations of marketing efforts occurring at the time individual attitudes are developing.

APPLICATION AREAS AND FURTHER READINGS

Marketing Strategy
Keller, Kevin Lane (1993). 'Conceptualizing, Measuring, and Managing Customer-Based Brand Equity,' *Journal of Marketing*, 57(1), January, 1-22.

Retail Marketing
Schlosser, A. E. (1998). 'Applying the Functional Theory of Attitudes to Understanding the Influence of Store Atmosphere on Store Inferences,' *Journal of Consumer Psychology*, 7(4), 345-370.

BIBLIOGRAPHY

Shavitt, Sharon (1989). 'Operationalizing Functional Theories of Attitude,' in Anthony R. Pratkanis, Steven J. Breckler, and Anthony G. Greenwald (eds.), *Attitude Structure and Function*, Hillsdale, NJ: Lawrence Erlbaum Associates, 311-337.
Locander, William B., and Spivey, W. Austin (1978). 'A Functional Approach to Attitude Measurement,' *Journal of Marketing Research*, 15(4), November, 576-587.

■ attribution theory

DESCRIPTION
Theory or theories concerned with explaining and predicting the ways in which individuals explain or attribute their own behavior and the behaviors of others, where attributions include both personality-related and situational variables.

KEY INSIGHTS
Based on pioneering and early research in social psychology by individuals such as Fritz Heider (1958), Harold Kelley (1967, 1972), Edward E. Jones (Jones and Harris 1967), and Lee Ross (1977), collective research in the area of attribution theory suggests that individuals attempt to logically explain causality in their environment, where inferences are made which may or may not be entirely accurate or without bias as a result of individual perspective and other factors including the extent to which events tend to vary across individuals, situations, and time. While the theoretical area is very broad and continues to encompass much social psychological research, insights from attribution theory include the views that individuals have a tendency to attribute the causes of other peoples' negative or undesirable behaviors relatively more to their personality than situational characteristics, whereas individuals tend to attribute similar behaviors for themselves relatively more to situational characteristics.

KEY WORDS Causality, personality, behavioral explanations

IMPLICATIONS
Implications of attribution theory include those associated with the actor–observer difference phenomenon (see **actor–observer difference**)

yet also extend beyond such specific implications since attribution theory encompasses an even broader body of knowledge. For example, certain attributional biases are observed through cross-cultural research to be more pervasive in individualistic cultures (e.g. northern European) than in collectivistic cultures. As such, international marketers should be sensitized to how and to what extent current and potential customers in different cultures may be likely to attribute the apparent causes of unexpected and/or undesirable service outcomes.

APPLICATION AREAS AND FURTHER READINGS
Consumer Behavior
Robertson, Thomas S., and Rossiter, John R. (1974). 'Children and Commercial Persuasion: An Attribution Theory Analysis,' *Journal of Consumer Research*, 1(1), June, 13–20.

Services Marketing
Bitner, Mary Jo, Booms, Bernard H., and Mohr, Lois A. (1994). 'Critical Service Encounters: The Employee's Viewpoint,' *Journal of Marketing*, 58(4), October, 95–106.
Bitner, Mary Jo (1990). 'Evaluating Service Encounters: The Effects of Physical Surroundings and Employee Responses,' *Journal of Marketing*, 54(2), April, 69–82.

BIBLIOGRAPHY
Heider, Fritz (1958). *The Psychology of Interpersonal Relations*. New York: John Wiley & Sons.
Kelley, Harold H. (1967). 'Attribution in Social Psychology,' in D. Levine (ed.), *Nebraska Symposium on Motivation*, vol. xv. Lincoln: University of Nebraska Press.
Kelley, Harold (1972). *Causal Schemata and the Attribution Process*. Morristown, NJ: General Learning Press.
Jones, E. E., and Harris, V. A. (1967). 'The Attribution of Attitudes,' *Journal of Experimental Social Psychology*, 3, 1–24.
Ross, Lee (1977). 'The Intuitive Psychologist and his Shortcomings: Distortions in the Attribution Process,' in L. Berkowitz (ed.), *Advances in Experimental Social Psychology*, vol. x. New York: Academic Press, 173–220.

■ audience effect

DESCRIPTION
Any effect of an audience on the behaviors or performance of an individual or individuals being observed.

KEY INSIGHTS
In the context of individual(s) engaged in tasks where performance is evaluated, the effect of an audience on task performance may be enhanced or diminished depending on the nature of the task and characteristics of the audience and individual(s) engaged in the task. For example, while live spectator audiences are clearly a motivator to professional sports team play and thus highly encouraged by marketers, an audience of onlookers may diminish the performance of a golfer used to secluded play at an exclusive course. More often than not, however, the audience effect is viewed as a form of social facilitation, whereby the mere presence of others in various capacities (e.g. active or passive, remote or co-located) can act to enhance the performance of individual(s)

who are the subject(s) of the audience as a result of the subject(s) feeling motivated to perform better given a desire to stand up to the greater scrutiny of an audience relative to the conditions of no scrutiny or lack of immediate observation.

KEY WORDS Performance, observation, audiences

IMPLICATIONS

Marketers can seek to harness the positive elements of the audience effect by understanding through experience, observation, and knowledge of communication-related theories when and how audiences, in various capacities, can facilitate individual or group performance on a limited or ongoing basis. As examples, enabling either the chefs in a restaurant or a health club's group fitness instructors to be observable behind glass windows to customers or spectators may motivate those performing the tasks to perform more professionally, energetically, and consistently than when their performance is not subject to audiences of spectators or observers.

APPLICATION AREAS AND FURTHER READINGS

Advertising

Webb, Peter H. (1979). 'Consumer Initial Processing in a Difficult Media Environment,' *Journal of Consumer Research*, 6(3), December, 225–236.

Business-to-Business Marketing

Levitt, Theodore (1965). *Industrial Purchasing Behavior: A Study of Communications Effects*. Boston: Harvard University.

BIBLIOGRAPHY

Zajonc, R. B. (1965). 'Social Facilitation,' *Science*, 149, 269–274.

□ augmented product *see* product levels

■ averages, law of

DESCRIPTION

A term expressing the view that, over the long run, probabilities will ultimately dictate and equalize the performance of repeated events.

KEY INSIGHTS

For events which are probabilistically determined, such as where the chance that the flip of a one-cent coin by an indecisive customer will be heads (to decide to buy product A) as opposed to tails (to decide to buy product B) is 50%, there is also the chance of skewed outcomes when events are repeated, such as in obtaining ten heads in ten flips of a similar coin by ten indecisive customers. However, the law of averages view of probabilistic outcomes holds that, in the long term, probabilities will dictate and equalize long-run performance, so that in 1,000 coin flips by 1,000 indecisive customers, for example, the number of heads and tails obtained will tend to equalize to a far greater extent in comparison to ten coin flips.

KEY WORDS Probabilities, events, outcomes, performance

IMPLICATIONS
Many areas of marketing are influenced directly or indirectly by the law of averages, where consumer behavior and marketing research are examples. When consumer behavior is dictated by probabilities, such as in selecting from two equally unknown brands of identical products, or in efforts to obtain equal marketing research samples of males and females, knowledge of the law of averages can guide the actions and estimates of marketers under conditions where events are repeated and long-run performance is a concern.

APPLICATION AREAS AND FURTHER READINGS
Consumer Behavior
Krishna, Aradhna (1994). 'The Effect of Deal Knowledge on Consumer Purchase Behavior,' *Journal of Marketing Research*, 31(1), February, 76–91.

Marketing Management
Alexander, Ralph S. (1965). 'The Marketing Manager's Dilemma,' *Journal of Marketing*, 29(2), April, 18–21.
Held, Gilbert (1998). 'Contract Renewal—Think Short Term,' *International Journal of Network Management*, 8(6), 323–324.

BIBLIOGRAPHY
Martin, Selden O. (1915). 'The Scientific Study of Marketing,' *Annals of the American Academy of Political and Social Science*, 59, The American Industrial Opportunity, May, 77–85.

■ Averch–Johnson effect

DESCRIPTION
Overcapitalization among regulated firms that results from their facing a given rate of return on capital.

KEY INSIGHTS
Identified and examined in research by Averch and Johnson (1962) on regulated firms, the Averch–Johnson effect refers to the profit-maximizing response of such firms to choose combinations of inputs that are more capital intensive than would otherwise be employed by the firms in the absence of an allowed rate of return on capital.

KEY WORDS Regulation, capital

IMPLICATIONS
Marketing strategists and public policy makers involved in firm regulation must consider the Averch–Johnson effect as a profit-maximizing response among regulated firms that can be anticipated and expected. To the extent that overcapitalization is inefficient and economically detrimental, firms and public policy makers must address the challenge of altering firm inputs in ways that lessen their capital intensity.

APPLICATION AREAS AND FURTHER READINGS
Marketing Strategy
Frank, Mark W. (2001). *The Impact of Rate-of-Return Regulation on Technological Innovation*. Aldershot: Ashgate Publishing Limited.

Kaserman, David L., and Mayo, John W. (1991). 'Regulation, Advertising, and Economic Welfare,' *Journal of Business*, 64(2), April, 255–267.
McKie, James W. (1970). 'Regulation and the Free Market: The Problem of Boundaries,' *Bell Journal of Economics and Management Science*, 1(1), Spring, 6–26.

BIBLIOGRAPHY
Averch, H., and Johnson, L. (1962). 'Behaviour of Firms under Regulatory Constraint,' *American Economic Review*, 52, 1052–1069.

☐ **awareness** *see* adoption process; buyer influence/readiness

B

■ backwash effects

DESCRIPTION
Adverse effects on the growth of a region or regions of an economy as a result of the growth of another region of the economy.

KEY INSIGHTS
Backwash effects, where the economic growth of certain region(s) of an economy are adversely affected by the growth of another region, typically arise from the movement of capital and skilled labor from lagging region(s) of an economy toward a more prosperous region. Backwash effects are also viewed as resulting from the increase in production efficiency that is associated with the geographic concentration of activity in the growing region.

KEY WORDS Regional economic growth

IMPLICATIONS
Marketers involved in international marketing or other areas of marketing where the economic growth of a region is an important consideration in a firm's activities may benefit from a greater understanding of the dynamics of backwash effects on regional economic growth. For retailers, manufacturers, and service firms alike, backwash effects may lead to either desirable or undesirable consequences for the firm, depending on the economic strength of the region in relation to the economic strength of surrounding areas.

APPLICATION AREAS AND FURTHER READINGS
International Marketing
Cater, E. (2002). 'Spread and Backwash Effects in Ecotourism,' *International Journal of Sustainable Development*, 5, 1–17.

Retail Marketing
Sullivan, Pauline, Savitt, Ronald, Zheng, Yi, and Cui, Yanli (2002). 'Rural Shoppers: Who Gets their Apparel Dollars?' *Journal of Fashion Marketing and Management*, 6(4), December, 363–380.

BIBLIOGRAPHY
Barkley, David L., Henry, Mark S., and Bao, Shuming (1996). 'Identifying "Spread" versus "Backwash" Effects in Regional Economic Areas: A Density Functions Approach,' *Land Economics*, 72(3), August, 336–357.

■ balance theory

DESCRIPTION
A motivational theory holding that people desire cognitive consistency in their drive to achieve psychological balance in their thoughts, feelings, and social relationships.

KEY INSIGHTS
Based on pioneering research by Fritz Heider (1946, 1958), balance theory provides a means to evaluate and explain how and why attitudes, values, and behaviors are developed and may or may not be stable and change given various states or degrees of balance/imbalance. The theory enables models to be constructed to explain and predict the outcomes of individual and interpersonal situations involving specified attitudes, beliefs, and relationships, where individuals' motives for cognitive consistency are instrumental.

KEY WORDS Cognitive consistency, psychological balance

IMPLICATIONS
Balance theory provides a rich framework with which to examine, assess, and manage many areas of marketing including customer satisfaction, sales forces, and supply chain relationships. In acknowledging and seeking to understand better individual desires for cognitive consistency and balance in interpersonal relationships, for example, marketers can establish stronger relationships with customers to the extent marketing actions (e.g. persuasive marketing communications) are consistent with such deep-rooted individual desires and personal motives.

APPLICATION AREAS AND FURTHER READINGS
Marketing Management
Bagozzi, Richard P. (1980). 'Performance and Satisfaction in an Industrial Sales Force: An Examination of their Antecedents and Simultaneity,' *Journal of Marketing*, 44(2), Spring, 65–77.

Marketing Communication
Perloff, Richard M. (1993). *The Dynamics of Persuasion Communication and Attitudes in the 21st Century*, 2nd edn. Mahwah, NJ: Lawrence Erlbaum Associates.

Business-to-Business Marketing
Phillips, J. M., Liu, B. S., and Costello, T. G. (1998). 'A Balance Theory Perspective of Triadic Supply Chain Relationships,' *Journal of Marketing Theory Practice*, 6(4), 78–91.

Consumer Behavior
Oliver, Richard L. (1993). 'Cognitive, Affective, and Attribute Bases of the Satisfaction Response,' *Journal of Consumer Research*, 20(3), December, 418–430.

BIBLIOGRAPHY
Scott, William A. (1963). 'Cognitive Complexity and Cognitive Balance,' *Sociometry*,
    26(1), March, 66–74.
Heider, Fritz (1946). 'Attitudes and Cognitive Organization.' *Journal of Psychology*, 21,
    107–112.
Heider, Fritz (1958). *The Psychology of Interpersonal Relations*. New York: John Wiley &
    Sons.

■ balanced scorecard

DESCRIPTION
An approach to organizational performance evaluation and monitoring that
involves using multiple measures including those based on financial, customer,
internal process, and employee learning and growth perspectives.

KEY INSIGHTS
Introduced by Kaplan and Norton (1992), the balanced scorecard aims to
provide managers with a comprehensive view of organizational performance rather than a view dominated by a financial perspective. As such,
the approach emphasizes balance with multiple areas inside and outside
the firm that are viewed as potentially influential in achieving successful
business performance over the longer term. While the specific measures
used in a balanced scorecard approach cannot be generalized but rather
are dependent on each organization's particular goals, the process of
implementing the approach within the firm is typically viewed as the
most beneficial means with which to arrive at useful measures as well as
derive strategic insights into their interrelated influences.

KEY WORDS Organizational performance evaluation, monitoring

IMPLICATIONS
While many firms use multiple indicators beyond measures of financial
performance as part of organizational performance evaluation and monitoring, the balanced scorecard approach aims to formalize and integrate
measures from multiple, important, and interrelated perspectives. As
such, marketing managers may benefit from undestanding what measures strategic decision makers consider to be important to the long-
term success of the firm to ensure marketing strategies are consistent
with such views. In addition, marketing managers may seek to influence
the nature of the balanced scorecard planning and evaluation approach
within a firm to the extent the approach itself may benefit from refinements drawing upon a stronger marketing perspective.

APPLICATION AREAS AND FURTHER READINGS
Marketing Strategy
Cravens, David W. (1998). 'Examining the Impact of Market-Based Strategy Para-
    digms on Marketing Strategy,' *Journal of Strategic Marketing*, 6(3), September, 197–
    208.
Thomas, M. J. (2000). 'Marketing Performance Measurement: Directions for Devel-
    opment,' *Journal of Targeting Measurement and Analysis for Marketing*, 9(1), 70–91.

Marketing Management
Kim, J., Suh, E., and Hwang, H. (2003). 'A Model for Evaluating the Effectiveness of CRM using the Balanced Scorecard,' *Journal of Interactive Marketing*, 17(2), 5–19.
Murphy, Brian, Maguiness, Paul, Pescott, Chris, Wislang, Soren, Ma, Jingwu, and Wang, Rongmei (2005). 'Stakeholder Perceptions Presage Holistic Stakeholder Relationship Marketing Performance,' *European Journal of Marketing*, 39(9/10), 1049–1059.

Marketing Research
Karmarkar, Uday S. (1996). 'Integrative Research in Marketing and Operations Management,' *Journal of Marketing Research*, 33(2), May, 125–133.

BIBLIOGRAPHY
Kaplan, R. S., and Norton, D. P. (1992). 'The Balanced Scorecard: Measures that Drive Performance,' *Harvard Business Review*, January–February, 71–80.
Kaplan, R. S., and Norton, D. P. (1993). 'Putting the Balanced Scorecard to Work,' *Harvard Business Review*, September–October, 2–16.

■ bandwagon effect

DESCRIPTION

The phenomenon or observation where individual actions or beliefs are positively influenced and whose adoption is considerably accelerated by the large-scale popularity of the actions or beliefs among individuals or groups.

KEY INSIGHTS

The bandwagon effect tends to occur when individuals or organizations believe that it is in their best interest to take action or adopt views on what has become or is increasingly becoming popular or fashionable.

KEY WORDS Action, belief popularity

IMPLICATIONS

In marketing terms, the bandwagon effect may translate into the view that 'success breeds success,' where popular products, brands, and services can become even more popular in the market as a result of their current state of popularity or fashion appeal. The challenge for marketers is therefore to create a critical level of popularity for a firm's offerings so the bandwagon effect may be realized and stimulate even greater popularity in the marketplace.

APPLICATION AREAS AND FURTHER READINGS

Marketing Strategy
Rohlfs, Jeffrey H. (2001). *Bandwagon Effects in High Technology Industries.* Cambridge, Mass.: MIT Press.
Hellofs, Linda L., and Jacobson, Robert (1999). 'Market Share and Customers' Perceptions of Quality: When Can Firms Grow their Way to Higher versus Lower Quality?' *Journal of Marketing*, 63(1), January, 16–25.

Technology Markets
John, George, Weiss, Allen M., and Dutta, Shantanu (1999). 'Marketing in Technology-Intensive Markets: Toward a Conceptual Framework,' *Journal of Marketing*, 63, Fundamental Issues and Directions for Marketing, 78–91.

BIBLIOGRAPHY
Robertson, Thomas S. (1967). 'The Process of Innovation and the Diffusion of Innovation,' *Journal of Marketing*, 31(1), January, 14–19.

■ bargaining theory

DESCRIPTION
Theory or theories aimed at understanding and explaining effective interorganizational bargaining in contexts including negotiations and policymaking.

KEY INSIGHTS
While bargaining theory encompasses a broad base of research and concepts grounded in game theory, much of bargaining theory emphasizes examination of the relative bargaining resources (e.g. assets) stakes of those involved in a given bargaining situation. The scope of entities which may be involved in a bargaining situation includes firms, governments, and countries. A focus on resources and stakes as well as corresponding interests and abilities of participants in a bargaining situation enables strategies and/or approaches to be developed and pursued that may increase the likelihood of successful bargaining outcomes (e.g. agreements) for situations having particular characteristics including those of one-time bargaining and time-constrained bargaining.

KEY WORDS Interorganizational bargaining, negotiation

IMPLICATIONS
Marketers involved in strategically important negotiations or policy development for interorganizational negotiations may potentially benefit from a greater knowledge of bargaining theory-based research to increase the effectiveness and/or efficiency of ongoing bargaining efforts of the firm and its management. For example, certain aspects of the theory can provide guidance to managers by helping them to understand better the expected outcomes for a bargaining situation rather than overly focusing on the processes of negotiation itself, whereas in other instances, certain bargaining theory-based approaches advocate specific bargaining procedures for effective outcomes.

APPLICATION AREAS AND FURTHER READINGS
Marketing Management
Dwyer, F. Robert, Schurr, Paul H., and Oh, Sejo (1987). 'Developing Buyer–Seller Relationships,' *Journal of Marketing*, 51(2), April, 11–27.
Iyer, Ganesh, and Villas-Boas, J. Miguel (2003). 'A Bargaining Theory of Distribution Channels,' *Journal of Marketing Research*, 40(1), February, 80–100.
Hirschman, Elizabeth C. (1987). 'People as Products: Analysis of a Complex Marketing Exchange,' *Journal of Marketing*, 51(1), January, 98–108.

Marketing Modeling
McGuire, Timothy W., and Staelin, Richard (1983). 'An Industry Equilibrium Analysis of Downstream Vertical Integration,' *Marketing Science*, 2(2), Spring, 161–191.

Consumer Behavior
Corfman, Kim P., and Lehmann, Donald R. (1993). 'The Importance of Others' Welfare in Evaluating Bargaining Outcomes,' *Journal of Consumer Research*, 20(1), June, 124–137.

BIBLIOGRAPHY
Muthoo, Abhinay (1999). *Bargaining Theory with Applications*. Cambridge: Cambridge University Press.
Sutton, John (1986). 'Non-Cooperative Bargaining Theory: An Introduction,' *Review of Economic Studies*, 53(5), October, 709–724.

■ Barnum effect

(also called the Forer effect)

DESCRIPTION
The tendency for individuals to accept as accurate statements describing their personality when led to believe such descriptions are tailored for them, when in fact such descriptions are vague, ambiguous, and general and may describe the personalities of a wide range of individuals.

KEY INSIGHTS
Pioneering empirical research by Bertram Forer (1949) quantifiably demonstrated the existence and prevalence of the effect, which includes a tendency to accept such statements as true or revealing the basic characteristics of one's personality.

KEY WORDS Personality assessment

IMPLICATIONS
As the Barnum (or Forer) effect as a phenomenon is pervasive among individuals, it offers a possible explanation for the popularity of certain pseudosciences among consumers, where individuals or organizations provide services to such consumers purporting to explain or predict personality-related characteristics by linking them to seemingly unrelated phenomena (e.g. planetary alignments). The effect may also provide a means for unscrupulous marketers to establish greater rapport with various individuals through claims of superior knowledge or understanding of their personalities.

APPLICATION AREAS AND FURTHER READINGS
Marketing Strategy
Mitchell, Vincent-Wayne, and Haggett, Sarah (1997). 'Sun-Sign Astrology in Market Segmentation: An Empirical Investigation,' *Journal of Consumer Marketing*, April, 14(2), 113–131.

Consumer Behavior
Mitchell, V.-W., and Tate, Elizabeth (1998). 'Do Consumers' Star Signs Influence What They Buy?' *Marketing Intelligence & Planning*, July, 249–259.
Sjöberg, Lennart, and Engelberg, Elisabeth (2005). 'Lifestyles, and Risk Perception Consumer Behavior,' *International Review of Sociology/Revue Internationale de Sociologie*, 15(2), July, 327–362.

BIBLIOGRAPHY
Dickson, D. H., and Kelly, I. W. (1985). 'The Barnum Effect in Personality Assessment: A Review of the Literature,' *Psychological Reports*, 57(2), 367–382.
Forer, B. R. (1949). 'The Fallacy of Personal Validation: A Clasroom Demonstration of Gullibility,' *Journal of Abnormal and Social Psychology*, 44, 118–123.

☐ barriers to entry *see* entry barriers

■ base-rate fallacy

DESCRIPTION
The failure of an individual to consider information about the effects of prior probabilities or base rates in making judgment of conditional probabilities, where instead the individual relies upon extraneous or irrelevant information.

KEY INSIGHTS
While information on prior probabilities may be readily available and highly relevant to a conditional probability judgment, such as in a consumer's estimate of the probability that a particular weekly airline flight will depart late when it departed late in 70 of 100 past instances, the consumer may ultimately overlook such information and focus instead on other factors such as the mood of the check-in staff. In doing so, the individual's judgment involves a logical fallacy in that it includes a view that the situation is insensitive to prior probabilities.

KEY WORDS Judgments, probabilities

IMPLICATIONS
When marketing actions or events are sensitive to prior probabilities (e.g. as when determining the probability that products will fail under warranty), marketers should strive to objectively consider and incorporate such information in their analyses, forecasts, and marketing plans. Otherwise, the result may be unwarranted optimism or an irresponsible marketing analysis.

APPLICATION AREAS AND FURTHER READINGS
Retail Marketing
Cox, Anthony D., and Summers, John O. (1987). 'Heuristics and Biases in the Intuitive Projection of Retail Sales,' *Journal of Marketing Research*, 24(3), August, 290–297.

Marketing Research
Hogarth, Robin M., and Makridakis, Spyros (1981). 'Forecasting and Planning: An Evaluation,' *Management Science*, 27(2), February, 115–138.

Consumer Behavior
Baumgartner, Hans (1995). 'On the Utility of Consumers' Theories in Judgments of Covariation,' *Journal of Consumer Research*, 21(4), March, 634–643.

BIBLIOGRAPHY
Novemsky, Nathan, and Kronzon, Shirit (1999). 'How are Base-Rates Used, When They are Used: A Comparison of Additive and Bayesian Models of Base-Rate Use,' *Journal of Behavioral Decision Making*, 12(1), 55–67.

☐ basement effect *see* floor effect
☐ basing-point pricing strategy *see* pricing strategies
☐ Baumol effect *see* Baumol's cost disease

■ Baumol's cost disease

(also called the Baumol effect)

DESCRIPTION
The phenomenon observed in certain primarily labor-intensive industries where there is little or no gain in productivity over time, resulting in rising production costs.

KEY INSIGHTS
Identified and developed in research by Baumol and Bowen (1966) on the performing arts sector, the phenomenon is generally attributed to conditions where labor intensiveness in the provision of services, combined with other constraints for the provision of services (e.g. desirable service provider-to-customer ratios) make it difficult for productivity gains to be achievable. As a result, increasing labor costs lead to increasing production costs within such industries which may include education, the performing arts, and certain public services such as public hospitals.

KEY WORDS Service productivity, service production costs

IMPLICATIONS
Marketing managers involved in the provision of service-related offerings that tend to be labor-intensive and which have demonstrated little or no gain in productivity over time may benefit from a greater understanding of the causes and consequences of Baumol's cost disease (or the Baumol effect) in order to develop and evaluate strategies for addressing the phenomenon. For example, marketing managers faced with such challenges may therefore need to consider actions and strategies including reductions in offering quality or supply, increases in offering price, complements or alternatives to wage compensation of service providers, or means of increasing productivity through outsourcing, etc., where possible.

APPLICATION AREAS AND FURTHER READINGS
Marketing Strategy
Heshmati, A. (2003). 'Productivity Growth, Efficiency and Outsourcing in Manufacturing and Service Industries,' *Journal of Economic Surveys*, 17(1), 79–112.
Nordhaus, W. D. (2002). 'Productivity Growth and the New Economy,' *Brookings Papers on Economic Activity*, 2, 211–265.

Services Marketing
Harker, Patrick T. (1995). *The Service Productivity and Quality Challenge*. Dordrecht: Kluwer Academic Publishers.
Blaug, M. (2001). 'Where Are We Now on Cultural Economics?' *Journal of Economic Surveys*, 15(2), 123–144.

BIBLIOGRAPHY
Baumol, W. J., and Bowen, W. (1966). *Performing Arts: The Economic Dilemma.*
    Cambridge, Mass.: MIT Press.
Baumol, W. J. (1997). 'Baumol's Cost Disease: The Arts and Other Victims,' in W. J.
    Baumol and R. Towse (eds.), *Baumol's Cost Disease.* Northampton, Mass.: Edward
    Elgar.

■ Bayesian decision theory

DESCRIPTION
Decision theory involving a fundamental statistical approach to pattern recognition, classification, and conditional probabilities.

KEY INSIGHTS
Bayesian decision theory is well-suited to marketing problems where a decision is required but where there is considerable uncertainty or limited information on which to base a decision. The theory involves the application of probabilities to each of the decision-related elements, where probabilities are typically established as a result of opinion rather than established by fact. The aim of the approach is to arrive at an understanding of an optimal outcome for a decision-making process.

KEY WORDS Decision making, uncertainty, limited information, pattern recognition

IMPLICATIONS
Marketers involved in strategic decision making where there is a high degree of uncertainty or limited information may draw upon Bayesian decision theory-based research to increase the robustness of the strategic decision-making process used as well as to obtain clearer insights into optimal outcomes. At the very least, the approach can be valuable to understand better the relationship between various outcomes and marketing actions involving varying degrees of risk.

APPLICATION AREAS AND FURTHER READINGS
Marketing Strategy
Anderson, Eugene W., and Sullivan, Mary W. (1993). 'The Antecedents and Consequences of Customer Satisfaction for Firms,' *Marketing Science*, 12(2), Spring, 125–143.

Pricing
Green, Paul E. (1963). 'Bayesian Decision Theory in Pricing Strategy,' *Journal of Marketing*, 27(1), January, 5–14.

Marketing Research
Rossi, Peter E., McCulloch, Robert E., and Allenby, Greg M. (1996). 'The Value of Purchase History Data in Target Marketing,' *Marketing Science*, 15(4), 321–340.
Carroll, J. Douglas, and Green, Paul E. (1995). 'Guest Editorial: Psychometric Methods in Marketing Research: Part I, Conjoint Analysis,' *Journal of Marketing Research*, 32(4), November, 385–391.

Marketing Modeling
Putler, Daniel S., Kalyanam, Kirthi, and Hodges, James S. (1996). 'A Bayesian Approach for Estimating Target Market Potential with Limited Geodemographic Information,' *Journal of Marketing Research*, 33(2), May, 134–149.

BIBLIOGRAPHY
Rossi, P. E., and Allenby, G. M. (2003). 'Bayesian Statistics and Marketing,' *Marketing Science*, 22(3), 304–328.
Berger, James O. (1985). *Statistical Decision Theory and Bayesian Analysis*. New York: Springer-Verlag.

□ **BCG growth-share matrix** *see* product portfolio analysis

■ behavioral decision theory

DESCRIPTION
Theory or theories for judgment and decision-making evaluation which emphasize individuals' subjective expected utilities, personal utility functions, and personal probability analyses.

KEY INSIGHTS
Behavior decision theory as pioneered by Edwards (1954) provides a systematic approach for describing how individual decision makers' values and beliefs are incorporated into their decisions as well as for prescribing courses of action which reflect closely the values and beliefs of decision makers. Explicit in the theoretical approach is the view that decision makers are able to express preferences given alternatives, where such preferences are able to be systematically evaluated with consideration of subjective expected utilities.

KEY WORDS Judgment, decision making, **utility**

IMPLICATIONS
Behavioral decision theory highlights the critical role of values and beliefs in the judgments and decision making of marketers as well as consumers. As such, marketing efforts aimed at understanding, explaining, and predicting strategically important decisions should consider analytical approaches grounded in behavioral decision theory. Many behavioral decision-based models have been developed by researchers with the purpose of providing ways to evaluate and explain successful marketing decisions and important consumer judgments.

APPLICATION AREAS AND FURTHER READINGS
Marketing Strategy
Glazer, Rashi, and Weiss, Alien M. (1993). 'Marketing in Turbulent Environments: Decision Processes and the Time-Sensitivity of Information,' *Journal of Marketing Research*, 30(4), November, 509–521.

Marketing Management
Curren, Mary T., Folkes, Valerie S., and Steckel, Joel H. (1992). 'Explanations for Successful and Unsuccessful Marketing Decisions: The Decision Maker's Perspective,' *Journal of Marketing*, 56(2), April, 18–31.

Consumer Behavior
Hoyer, W. D. (1984). 'An Examination of Consumer Decision Making for a Common Repeat Purchase Product,' *Journal of Consumer Research*, 11, December, 822–829.

BIBLIOGRAPHY
Slovic, P., Fischhoff, B., and Lichtenstein, S. (1977). 'Behavioral Decision Theory,' *Annual Review of Psychology*, 28, January, 1–39.
Edwards, Ward (1954). 'The Theory of Decision Making,' *Psychological Bulletin*, 51(4), July, 380–417.

☐ behavioral segmentation *see* segmentation
☐ behavioral theory of the firm *see* firm, theory of the

■ below-the-line marketing

DESCRIPTION
Marketing comprising of activity that, traditionally, is commission free or charged at a fixed fee by advertising agencies which, mainly, excludes mass media advertising.

KEY INSIGHTS
Below-the-line activity in marketing generally refers to marketing practices making use of forms of promotion that do not involve the use of mass media, where, in a firm's use of an advertising agency, there is usually no commission charged by the advertising agency, and thus the expense typically appears 'below-the-line' on the ad agency's bill to the firm. Below-the-line marketing activity can be contrasted with 'above-the-line' marketing activity, which typically is that where an ad agency would charge a firm a commission based on advertising placements in mass media such as television, newspaper, and radio. (See **above-the-line marketing**.) *Through-the-line marketing* refers to a marketing approach that makes use of both above-the-line marketing and below-the-line marketing. Below-the-line advertising can involve the use of any form of non-mass media promotion including sales promotions (e.g. premiums, price reductions, displays, and related point-of-sale activity), direct marketing, public relations activity, sponsorship, etc.

Firms may emphasize the use of below-the-line marketing activity for any number of reasons. For example, in the tobacco industry, such activity has been a way that firms in the industry have been able to conduct marketing that attracts less scrutiny from regulators in comparison to heavily regulated mass media advertising. Below-the-line marketing activity is also considered by some of its adopters to encounter a less cluttered communications environment in efforts to communicate with a target market, in contrast to the relatively more cluttered environment of mass media advertising.

KEY WORDS Advertising agencies, commission free, fixed-fee, point-of-sale, sales promotions

IMPLICATIONS
Marketers should seek to understand carefully their competitive and regulatory environments in addition to consumer buying behavior in order

to be in a position to evaluate the potential benefits and costs of below-the-line marketing approaches. In a marketplace filled with advertising clutter, for example, below-the-line marketing efforts may be potentially more cost effective and provide the marketer with opportunities to use more sophisticated marketing approaches in comparison to mass media-based approaches. In other instances, a marketing strategy involving the selective integration of below-the-line and above-the-line approaches may be more beneficial than those that rely on below-the-line approaches alone.

APPLICATION AREAS AND FURTHER READINGS
Marketing Strategy
Harper, T. (2001). 'Marketing Life after Advertising Bans,' *Tobacco Control*, 10(2), 196–198.

Retail Marketing
Carter, S. M. (2003). 'New Frontier, New Power: The Retail Environment in Australia's Dark Market,' *Tobacco Control*, 12 (suppl. III), iii. 95–110.

Promotions
Sepe, E., Ling, P. M., and Glantz, S. A. (2002). 'Smooth Moves: Bar and Nightclub Tobacco Promotions that Target Young Adults,'*American Journal of Public Health*, 92, 414–419.

BIBLIOGRAPHY
Carter S. M. (2003). 'Going Below the Line: Creating Transportable Brands for Australia's Dark Market,' *Tobacco Control*, 12 (suppl. III), iii. 87–94.

■ benchmarking

DESCRIPTION
A process involving organizational comparisons of processes or performance and particularly comparisons with organizations considered to be following best industry practices or setting the industry standard, with the aim of identifying and implementing process and performance improvements within the organization.

KEY INSIGHTS
The process of benchmarking involves examining how the organization or some part of the organization is performing in comparison to one or more organizations or parts of organizations of strategic interest to the firm and learning from the findings. Whether the comparisons are solely within the firm, with competing firms, or only with those firms or firms considered to have superior performance or that are implementing best practices within the industry for certain processes, the ultimate aim of benchmarking is to identify and adopt methods for improving the performance of the organization.

KEY WORDS Organizational processes, performance evaluation, performance improvement

IMPLICATIONS
Marketers have many opportunities to benchmark an organization's marketing processes and performance with similar or best-performing

organizations. Although the process is time consuming and not without development and maintenance costs, the benefits of benchmarking, particularly for organizations in search of new ideas for process and performance improvements, may be such that the gains exceed the costs involved. At the very least, marketers should recognize how their firm compares with others of strategic interest to assess the extent that actions should be pursued for further improvement.

APPLICATION AREAS AND FURTHER READINGS
Marketing Strategy
Gable, Myron, Fairhurst, Ann, and Dickinson, Roger (1993). 'The Use of Benchmarking to Enhance Marketing Decision Making,' *Journal of Consumer Marketing*, 10(1), March.
Vorhies, D. W., and Morgan, N. A. (2005). 'Benchmarking Marketing Capabilities for Sustainable Competitive Advantage,' *Journal of Marketing*, 69(1), 80–94.
Brownlie, D. (1999). 'Benchmarking your Marketing Process,' *Long Range Planning*, 32(1), 88–95.

Marketing Management
Horsky, Dan, and Nelson, Paul (1996). 'Evaluation of Salesforce Size and Productivity through Efficient Frontier Benchmarking,' *Marketing Science*, 15(4), 301–320.

BIBLIOGRAPHY
Zairi, Mohamed, and Leonard, Paul (1994). *Practical Benchmarking: The Complete Guide*. London: Chapman & Hall.
Drew, S. (1995). 'Strategic Benchmarking: Innovation Practices in Financial Institutions,' *International Journal of Bank Marketing*, 13(1), 4–16.

☐ **benefit segmentation** *see* segmentation

■ **benefits**

DESCRIPTION
The particular advantages or gains that are attained by an individual as a result of purchasing or using a particular product or service.

KEY INSIGHTS
While a product or service is commonly viewed as being able to provide one or more functional benefits to a consumer, such as a running shoe's ability to provide its wearer with good traction while running, the same product or service may also possess numerous other non-functional benefits to a consumer. For example, a running shoe's original styling can provide a self-expressive benefit in that it provides a means for allowing consumer self-expression. Similarly, a running shoe's reputable brand name can provide an emotional benefit to a consumer in that it can provide comfort, reassurance, and a sense of trust to the consumer who is new to running but who nevertheless recognizes the running shoe's brand name.

KEY WORDS Product advantages, service advantages

IMPLICATIONS

Marketers of new products and services must seek to understand and strategically manage the range and benefits provided by the offerings. In particular, astute marketers will recognize that, for some offerings, functional benefits can actually be less important to certain consumers than other non-functional benefits including emotional or self-expressive benefits.

APPLICATION AREAS AND FURTHER READINGS

Marketing Strategy
Haley, Russell I. (1968). 'Benefit Segmentation: A Decision-Oriented Research Tool,' *Journal of Marketing*, 32(3), July, 30–35.

Services Marketing
Gwinner, Kevin P., Gremler, Dwayne D., and Bitner, Mary Jo (1998). 'Relational Benefits in Services Industries: The Customer's Perspective,' *Journal of the Academy of Marketing Science*, 26(2), 101–114.

Promotions
Chandon, Pierre, Wansink, Brian, and Laurent Gilles (2000). 'A Benefit Congruency Framework of Sales Promotion Effectiveness,' *Journal of Marketing*, 64(4), October, 65–81.

Marketing Education
Easterling, D., and Rudell, F. (1997). 'Rationale, Benefits, and Methods of Service-Learning in Marketing Education,' *Journal of Education for Business*, 73(1), 58–61.

BIBLIOGRAPHY
Young, Shirley, and Feigin, Barbara (1975). 'Using the Benefit Chain for Improved Strategy Formulation,' *Journal of Marketing*, 39(3), July, 72–74.

■ bespoke marketing

DESCRIPTION

Marketing that is heavily customized or developed from scratch to meet customer requirements or needs.

KEY INSIGHTS

Bespoke marketing can be potentially beneficial when customer needs are highly distinctive and when more-routinized marketing approaches commonly employed as alternatives tend to lack impact. In developing bespoke marketing strategies and plans for an organizational customer, it is often essential to build a good relationship with the client in order to get a clear understanding of the client organizations' needs.

KEY WORDS Customized marketing plans

IMPLICATIONS

Whether in addressing the marketing needs of an organization or a consumer market, the development of bespoke marketing approaches provides a marketer with an opportunity to tailor and potentially optimize a marketing approach to be most suited to the client or customer.

APPLICATION AREAS AND FURTHER READINGS

Marketing Strategy
Dibb, S., Farhangmehr, M., and Simkin, L. (2001). 'The Marketing Planning Experience: A UK and Portuguese Comparison,' *Marketing Intelligence and Planning*, 19(6/7), 409–417.

Marketing Management
Dibb, S., and Simkin, L. (1997). 'A Program for Implementing Market Segmentation,' *Journal of Business and Industrial Marketing*, 12(1), 51–65.

Marketing Modeling
Doyle, Shaun (2004). 'Software Review: Which Part of my Marketing Spends Really Works? Marketing Mix Modelling may have an Answer,' *Journal of Database Marketing & Customer Strategy Management*, 11(4), July, 379–385.

BIBLIOGRAPHY
Goodman, M. R. V. (1999). 'The Pursuit of Value through Qualitative Market Research,' *Qualitative Market Research: International Journal*, 2(2), 111–120.

■ better mousetrap fallacy

DESCRIPTION
The myth or mistaken belief in the development and marketing of new products that any given market will more readily adopt technologically advanced or superior products should they ever be developed.

KEY INSIGHTS
While Ralph Waldo Emerson may have held this belief as he is quoted as saying, 'Build a better mousetrap and the world will beat a path to your door,' such a belief is clearly unjustified based on numerous marketing principles and practices. In most instances, superior product offerings do not automatically market themselves and drive consumers to seek them out and acquire them. Consumers may be resistant to change due to their investments in current products or they may view a superior product as overkill relative to their needs and have little or no need for them. The influential role of marketing strategy and functional area strategies of pricing, promotion, and distribution are neglected as well.

KEY WORDS Product development, product superiority, myth, false belief

IMPLICATIONS
When present, such a belief is a symptom that new product developers and/or marketers are so intent on developing products with superior attributes that they often end up making unwarranted assumptions regarding a market's true need for them and/or the marketing challenges associated with bringing such new products to market. While to some it may seem counter-intuitive that markets would not automatically welcome better products, such a view is simplistic given the richness of marketing knowledge regarding successful marketing strategies, new product development practices, consumer behavior, and competitive dynamics. Marketers should be on guard for individuals and organizations adopting such a mistaken belief.

APPLICATION AREAS AND FURTHER READINGS

New Product Development

Calantone, Roger, and Cooper, Robert G. (1981). 'New Product Scenarios: Prospects for Success,' *Journal of Marketing*, 45(2), Spring, 48–60.

Marketing Management

Griffin, Abbie, and Hauser, John R. (1992). 'Patterns of Communication among Marketing, Engineering and Manufacturing: A Comparison between Two New Product Teams,' *Management Science*, 38(3), March, 360–373.

Kohli, Ajay K., and Jaworski, Bernard J. (1990). 'Market Orientation: The Construct, Research Propositions, and Managerial Implications,' *Journal of Marketing*, 54(2), April, 1–18.

Business-to-Business Marketing

Hise, Richard T., O'Neal, Larry, McNeal, James U., and Parasuraman, A. (1989). 'The Effect of Product Design Activities on Commercial Success Levels of New Industrial Products,' *Journal of Product Innovation Management*, 6(1), March, 43.

BIBLIOGRAPHY

Hultink, Erik Jan, and Hart, Susan (1998). 'The World's Path to the Better Mousetrap: Myth or Reality? An Empirical Investigation into the Launch Strategies of High and Low Advantage New Products,' *European Journal of Innovation Management*, 1(3), December, 106–122.

■ bias

DESCRIPTION

In a measurement context, any situation where results or conclusions misrepresent what is being studied.

KEY INSIGHTS

Bias in measurement can take many forms. Aside from biases or errors in the choice or implementation of a sampling method (e.g. where a non-random sampling method is used as opposed to a random one), there may also be observation biases where results do not reflect what is observed or, alternatively, what is not observed. Bias from that which is not observed includes non-response bias, where results are skewed as a result of excessive non-response. In such an instance, results obtained are not representative of what is being studied as a result of responses obtained from respondents differing from that which would have been obtained from non-respondents. Another form of bias is late response bias which refers to bias in results due to responses of late respondents differing from responses of early respondents.

Biases may also be associated with particular measurement methods. In mail surveys, for example, respondents are able to see the entire survey before answering any question. Such a situation has the potential for what is referred to as sequence bias, where respondents' replies to certain questions are not independent but rather conditioned by knowledge of, or responses to, other questions and where the result may be distortions in the answers provided.

KEY WORDS Measurement, sampling, misrepresentation, error, surveys

IMPLICATIONS

Marketers should be wary of research designs that introduce bias into the study which ultimately lead to results which misrepresent that which is being studied. Marketers should employ methods of statistical analysis to prevent and identify the many forms of bias. An example is comparing the mean responses of early and late responders of a survey to determine if there is a statistically significant difference. Understanding the relationships among biases present may also provide useful insights, as in the case of research supporting the view that the later the responses of late responders, the more likely they will represent the views that would have been given by non-respondents (Armstrong and Overton 1971).

APPLICATION AREAS AND FURTHER READINGS

Marketing Research
Bradburn, Norman M., Sudman, Seymour, Blair, Ed, and Stocking, Carol (1978). 'Question Threat and Response Bias,' *Public Opinion Quarterly*, 42(2), Summer, 221–234.
Armstrong, J. Scott, and Overton, Terry S. (1977). 'Estimating Nonresponse Bias in Mail Surveys,' *Journal of Marketing Research*, 14(3), Special Issue: Recent Developments in Survey Research, August, 396–402.
Jones, Wesley H., and Lang, James R. (1980). 'Sample Composition Bias and Response Bias in a Mail Survey: A Comparison of Inducement Methods,' *Journal of Marketing Research*, 17(1), February, 69–76.
O'Dell, William F. (1962). 'Personal Interviews or Mail Panels?' *Journal of Marketing*, 26(4), October, 34–39.

BIBLIOGRAPHY
Kanuk, Leslie, and Berenson, Conrad (1975). 'Mail Surveys and Response Rates: A Literature Review,' *Journal of Marketing Research*, 12(4), November, 440–453.

■ blaming the victim

DESCRIPTION
Making the assumption that another person's misfortune is somehow deserved as a result of something they must have done.

KEY INSIGHTS
Individuals having a tendency to blame victims for their misfortunes are operating under the principle that the world is fair and just—that people will always get what they deserve. To the extent that there is a pervasive tendency for individuals to believe the world is just, there will be a tendency to place other people responsible for their mishaps or failures.

KEY WORDS Misfortunes, attributions, justice

IMPLICATIONS
While some marketers may believe that another person's problems are always in some way deserved or brought on by them (as when a customer's new product fails upon their first using it or when a customer is injured in using a product), such a view assumes a just

world, which isn't the case in reality. Marketers must strive to be objective and realistic in their assessments of and attributions for the causes of consumer misfortunes which may include the marketers themselves.

APPLICATION AREAS AND FURTHER READINGS
Social Marketing
Ling, J. C., Franklin, B. A. K., Lindsteadt, J. F., and Gearon, S. A. N. (1992). 'Social Marketing: Its Place in Public Health,' *Annual Review of Public Health*, 13, May, 341–362.
Yeo, Michael (1993). 'Toward an Ethic of Empowerment for Health Promotion,' Health Promotion International, 8(3), 225–235.

BIBLIOGRAPHY
Konovsky, Mary A., and Jaster, Frank (1989). ' "Blaming the Victim" and Other Ways Business Men and Women Account for Questionable Behavior,' *Journal of Business Ethics*, 8(5), May, 391–398.

■ bliss point

DESCRIPTION
A consumer equilibrium point where a consumer's total satiation for a good consumed is within the consumer's budget constraint.

KEY INSIGHTS
The concept of a bliss point most often refers to a point of consumer equilibrium and, as such, may refer to an individual consumer, a household, or the like. A bliss point is possible only when a consumer does not prefer an ever-increasing amount of a good.

KEY WORDS Consumption equilibrium

IMPLICATIONS
Marketers of consumer goods should seek to understand the nature of consumers' consumption of goods offered to determine to what extent it is possible or likely that consumption behavior, combined with consumer budget constraints, may result in a bliss point for the consumer. Such knowledge can provide the marketer with insight into subsequent consumer behavior as well as indications of a possible benefit to modifying or changing the offering (e.g. marketing mix elements) to enable future consumption of goods offered.

APPLICATION AREAS AND FURTHER READINGS
Marketing Modeling
Butler, David J., and Moffatt, Peter G. (2000). 'The Demand for Goods under Mixture Aversion,' *The Manchester School*, 68(3), June, 349.
Pollak, Robert A. (1970). 'Habit Formation and Dynamic Demand Functions,' *Journal of Political Economy*, 78(4), July–August, 745–763.
Haller, Hans (2000). 'Household Decisions and Equilibrium Efficiency,' *International Economic Review*, 41(4), 835–47.

BIBLIOGRAPHY
Ryan, A. J., and Pearce, D. W. (1977). *Price Theory*. Basingstoke: Macmillan.

■ blog marketing

DESCRIPTION

Marketing through the use of a website primarily composed of personal or professional observations and in journal or diary format.

KEY INSIGHTS

Blogs, short for weblogs, which are websites comprising of frequently updated personal or professional observations, can be used by individuals or organizations for marketing purposes. The typically informal journal style of an individual writer's blog can impart to its readers a sense of trust, honesty, credibility, or objectivity that may be somewhat more difficult to achieve through more polished or professionally prepared marketing communications material and media. Even though some blogs may actually be prepared by employees of organizations who are aiming to present their organization or its products or services in a positive light, the approach nevertheless has appeal to some readers as it is seen as communication that is not subject to as much organizational censorship or scrutiny as more mainstream marketing communications or public relations materials.

KEY WORDS Marketing communication, personal websites, professional websites

IMPLICATIONS

Marketers should recognize the growing power of blogs in the marketing of ideas, causes, products, services, brands, and organizations. While marketers can use blogs originating inside the organization to effectively communicate to the general public (or, at least to communicate to those who have discovered the blogger's website), marketers should also be aware of and learn from the growing number and power of independent bloggers' blogs who are informing, persuading, or at least partially influencing reader opinion or knowledge of timely issues that may be relevant to the marketer's organization.

APPLICATION AREAS AND FURTHER READINGS

Marketing Strategy
Lang, E. (2005). 'Would You, Could You, Should You Blog?' *Journal of Accountancy*, 199(6), 36–39.

Marketing Management
Lawson, J. (2004). 'Blogs as a Disruptive Technology,' *Law Practice*, 30(1), 41–45.
Gomez, J. (2005). 'Thinking outside the Blog: Navigating the Literary Blogosphere,' *Publishing Research Quarterly*, 21(3), 3–11.

BIBLIOGRAPHY
Wright, J. (2006). *Blog Marketing: The Revolutionary New Way to Increase Sales, Build your Brand, and Get Exceptional Results*. New York: McGraw-Hill.

■ boomerang effect

DESCRIPTION
A hypothesis or theoretical effect of persuasive communications where the end result is an attitude change by individuals in the direction opposite to that intended.

KEY INSIGHTS
When an individual views a particular form of persuasive communication as being highly discrepant from his/her original attitude, there is the possibility, consistent with assimilation–contrast theory, that such a discrepancy may lead the individual to change his/her attitude in the direction opposite to that intended by the message (see **assimilation-contrast theory**).

KEY WORDS Persuasion, communication, attitudes

IMPLICATIONS
While the boomerang effect may be a valid concern among marketers using persuasive communications, there is limited evidence that the effect occurs in practice. The area most concerned about its presence is social marketing, where marketers seek to persuade individuals in society that certain behaviors are bad (e.g. underage drinking) but are concerned that communications will have the opposite effect of that intended.

APPLICATION AREAS AND FURTHER READINGS
Social Marketing
Ringold, Debra Jones (2002). 'Boomerang Effects in Response to Public Health Interventions: Some Unintended Consequences in the Alcoholic Beverage Market,' *Journal of Consumer Policy*, 25(1), March, 27–63.
Kozup, John, Burton, Scot, and Creyer, Elizabeth (2001). 'A Comparison of Drinkers' and Nondrinkers' Responses to Health-Related Information Presented on Wine Beverage Labels,' *Journal of Consumer Policy*, 24(2), June, 209–230.

Marketing Communication
Bither, Stewart W., Dolich, Ira J., and Nell, Elaine B. (1971). 'The Application of Attitude Immunization Techniques in Marketing,' *Journal of Marketing Research*, 8(1), February, 56–61.

BIBLIOGRAPHY
MacKinnon, David P., and Lapin, Angela (1998). 'Effects of Alcohol Warnings and Advertisements: A Test of the Boomerang Hypothesis,' *Psychology and Marketing*, 15(7), 707–726.

☐ Boston Consulting Group matrix (or Boston matrix) *see* product portfolio analysis

■ bottom-up marketing

DESCRIPTION
The process of developing a marketing strategy within an organization by finding a workable tactic and then building on the tactic to create a powerful strategy.

KEY INSIGHTS
Conceptually developed by Ries and Trout (1989) in a popular book by
the same name, bottom-up marketing is advocated by the authors as an
alternative to traditional top-down marketing which involves deciding
what the firm wants to do (i.e. strategy) and then figuring out how to
do it (i.e. tactics) (see **top-down marketing**). In support of the approach,
the authors provide examples of organizations such as Federal Express,
Microsoft, and Little Caesars whose success is explained, according to
the author's research, by a bottom-up marketing approach. An example
of a tactic used by Domino's Pizza in the creation of its strategy is
'home delivery in 30 minutes, guaranteed.' In further conceptualizing the
approach, the authors consider tactics to be 'competitive mental angles'
and strategies as 'coherent marketing directions.'

KEY WORDS **Tactic(s)**, strategy development

IMPLICATIONS
Marketers involved in a firm's marketing strategy development should
recognize the potential for a bottom-up approach to provide the firm with
insights into ways the firm can develop and achieve a sustainable competitive advantage that may not be as evident with a top-down marketing
strategy development approach. While there are multiple approaches to
developing marketing strategies within an organization and arguably no
single best prescriptive approach, the bottom-up approach is certainly
consistent with the view that marketers should seek to understand
current and prospective customers, competitors, as well as the broader
marketing environment and identify ways it can provide customers with
offerings of value that are superior in some way relative to competitive offerings. The approach further suggests the need for marketers to
focus their efforts in identifying and meeting customer needs to avoid
diluting organizational resources which may include the firm's brand
itself.

APPLICATION AREAS AND FURTHER READINGS
Marketing Strategy
McDonald, M. (1992). 'Strategic Marketing Planning: A State-of-the-Art Review,'
   Marketing Intelligence & Planning, 10(4), 4–22.

Online Marketing
Wood, C. (2003). 'Marketing and E-commerce as Tools of Development in the
   Asia-Pacific Region: A Dual Path,' *International Marketing Review*, 21(3), 301–
   320.

International Marketing
Prendergast, Gerard, West, Douglas, and Shi, Yi-Zheng (2006). 'Advertising Budgeting Methods and Processes in China,' *Journal of Advertising*, 35(3), Fall, 165–
   176.

BIBLIOGRAPHY
Ries, A., and Trout, Jack (1989). *Bottom-Up Marketing*. New York: McGraw-Hill.

■ boundary spanning

DESCRIPTION
Effort within an organization that involves activity aimed at bridging one or more recognized organizational boundaries to facilitate the flow of information across such boundaries.

KEY INSIGHTS
Boundary spanning within an organization seeks to facilitate information transfer, frequently but not limited to information from outside the organization to inside the organization. The aim of such activity is to enhance communication and strategic decision-making effectiveness within the firm as a result of employees and managers being able to access and draw upon cross-boundary information that is both relevant and increasingly timely.

KEY WORDS Information transfer, organizational communication

IMPLICATIONS
Marketing managers and strategists should seek to recognize the benefits of organizational boundary spanning activity as a means of supporting effective strategic decision making. Given that such activity relies critically on the actions of key individuals who are routinely in a position to access information across organization boundaries, marketing managers should seek to ensure that systems and processes are in place to encourage and support sustained boundary spanning activity that frequently begins with information access by such individuals.

APPLICATION AREAS AND FURTHER READINGS
Marketing Strategy
Dollinger, Marc J. (1984). 'Environmental Boundary Spanning and Information Processing Effects on Organizational Performance,' *Academy of Management Journal*, 27(2), June, 351–368.

Marketing Management
Tushman, Michael L., and Scanlan, Thomas J. (1981). 'Boundary Spanning Individuals: Their Role in Information Transfer and their Antecedents,' *Academy of Management Journal*, 24(2), June, 289–305.
Singh, Jagdip (1998). 'Striking a Balance in Boundary-Spanning Positions: An Investigation of some Unconventional Influences of Role Stressors and Job Characteristics on Job Outcomes of Salespeople,' *Journal of Marketing*, 62(3), July, 69–86.

Services Marketing
Singh, Jagdip, Goolsby, Jerry R., and Rhoads, Gary K. (1994). 'Behavioral and Psychological Consequences of Boundary Spanning Burnout for Customer Service Representatives,' *Journal of Marketing Research*, 31(4), November, 558–569.

BIBLIOGRAPHY
Rosenkopf, L., and Nerkar, A. (2001). 'Beyond Local Search: Boundary-Spanning, Exploration, and Impact in the Optical Disc Industry,' *Strategic Management Journal*, 22(4), 287–306.

■ bounded rationality

DESCRIPTION

Partial rationality in individual decision-making behavior as a result of it being bounded by the limitations of individuals in their ability to handle the complexities of information available to them as well as limitations in the availability of information to such individuals.

KEY INSIGHTS

The concept of bounded rationality in relation to decision making suggests that individuals do not employ optimal decision-making approaches as a result of human limitations in the ability to comprehend and manage complex information as well as a result of challenges associated with limitations in information availability. Rather, the concept suggests that individuals adopt approaches that are more limited and which rely upon heuristics to ultimately make the decision-making process manageable, which includes the process of generating and evaluating alternatives for possible action.

KEY WORDS Decision making, information complexity

IMPLICATIONS

The concept of bounded rationality is far-reaching and is of influence in marketing decision making as much as consumer decision making. Recognizing the sub-optimality of much marketing decision making in marketing, marketers may therefore benefit from examining more critically the decision-making processes in use by the firm with the aim of understanding better the benefits and limitations involved. Similarly, marketers must strive to understand better how and to what extent consumer decision making is also characterized by bounded rationality in decision-making processes involved in their evaluations and, potentially, adoption of the firm's products or services.

APPLICATION AREAS AND FURTHER READINGS

Marketing Strategy
Taylor, Ronald N. (1976). 'Psychological Determinants of Bounded Rationality: Implications for Decision-Making Strategies,' *Decision Sciences*, 6, 409–429.

International Marketing
Shoham, A. (1999). 'Bounded Rationality, Planning, Standardization of International Strategy, and Export Performance: A Structural Model Examination,' *Journal of International Marketing*, 7(2), 24–50.

Marketing Modeling
Munier, B., Selten, R., Bouyssou, D., Bourgine, P., Day, R., Harvey, N., Hilton, D., Machina, M., Parker, P., and Sterman, J. (1999). 'Bounded Rationality Modeling,' *Report—Marketing Science Institute Cambridge Massachusetts*, 121, 21–24.

Consumer Behavior
Dyner, I., and Franco, C. J. (2004). 'Consumers' Bounded Rationality: The Case of Competitive Energy Markets,' *Systems Research and Behavioral Science*, 21(4), 373–390.

BIBLIOGRAPHY
Gigerenzer, G., and Goldstein, D. G. (1996). 'Reasoning the Fast and Frugal Way: Models of Bounded Rationality,' *Psychological Review* (New York), 103(4), 650–669.

Camerer, C. (1998). 'Bounded Rationality in Individual Decision Making,' *Experimental Economics*, 1(2), 163–183.

Gigerenzer, G., and Selten, R. (2002). *Bounded Rationality*. Cambridge, Mass.: MIT Press.

Simon, Herbert A. (1957). 'A Behavioral Model of Rational Choice,' in Herbert A. Simon (ed.), *Models of Man: Social and Rational*. New York: Wiley: 241-61.

■ brand community

DESCRIPTION

The sense of community developed, shared, and practiced by individuals using or having a common interest in a particular brand.

KEY INSIGHTS

The nature of some branded products and services has led to a following among certain consumers to the point where such individuals feel part of an active community of advocates or users of the brands. Harley-Davidson motorcycles, Saab automobiles, and Tide laundry detergent are just a few examples of branded products that have developed followings of users who are involved with the branded products to such a strong extent that they actively participate in discussions of the brands and their developments, whether via the internet or in person through clubs or associations.

KEY WORDS Community behavior

IMPLICATIONS

Marketers interested in developing a strong community (or community-like) following of consumers of the firm's brand(s) may benefit from understanding better the drivers and consequences of brand community-related research. In particular, recognizing the scope of consumer behaviors associated with brand communities can provide the marketer with insights into how and why particular marketing strategies may or may not be effective for brand community development.

APPLICATION AREAS AND FURTHER READINGS

Marketing Strategy

McAlexander, James H., Schouten, John W., and Koenig, Harold F. (2002). 'Building Brand Community,' *Journal of Marketing*, 66(1), January, 38–54.

McAlexander, J. H., Kim, S. K., and Roberts, S. D. (2003). 'Loyalty: The Influences of Satisfaction and Brand Community Integration,' *Journal of Marketing Theory and Practice*, 11(4), 1–11.

Consumer Behavior

Muniz, Albert M., Jr. and Schau, Hope Jensen (2005). 'Religiosity in the Abandoned Apple Newton Brand Community,' *Journal of Consumer Research*, 31, March, 737–747.

Algesheimer, R., Dholakia, U. M., and Herrmann, A. (2005). 'The Social Influence of Brand Community: Evidence from European Car Clubs,' *Journal of Marketing*, 69(3), 19–34.

BIBLIOGRAPHY
Muniz, Albert M., Jr., and O'Guinn, Thomas C. (2000). 'Brand Community,' *Journal of Consumer Research*, 27, 412–432.

■ brand equity

DESCRIPTION

The marketing and financial value that is built up and associated with a brand.

KEY INSIGHTS

The concept of brand equity captures the notion that marketing actions can lead to brands possessing equity in the sense that they become valuable strategic assets of a firm. Positive brand equity enables the firm to expect future revenues that are higher than that for an identical non-branded product as a result of the brand's positive influence on consumer purchase behavior. For example, a brand's association with perceived high quality can lead to trust and confidence in the firm's branded products that can increase product purchase likelihood among consumers.

KEY WORDS Brand value

IMPLICATIONS

Marketers should seek to understand and regularly monitor the level and nature of brand equity for each of their brands to determine and ensure their brands' strategic significance to the firm. The dynamic nature of many markets is such that brand equity will decline if not actively managed through coordinated marketing actions involving efforts to maintain or strengthen brand recognition and specific, positive brand associations.

APPLICATION AREAS AND FURTHER READINGS

Marketing Strategy
Keller, Kevin Lane (1993). 'Conceptualizing, Measuring, and Managing Customer-Based Brand Equity,' *Journal of Marketing*, 57(1), January, 1–22.

Marketing Management
Aaker, David A. (1991). *Managing Brand Equity: Capitalizing on the Value of a Brand Name*. New York: The Free Press.

Marketing Research
Krishnan, H. S. (1996). 'Characteristics of Memory Associations: A Consumer-Based Brand Equity Perspective,' *International Journal of Research in Marketing*, 3(4), October, 389–405.

BIBLIOGRAPHY
Aaker, David A. (1996). *Building Strong Brands*. New York: The Free Press.

■ brand loyalty

DESCRIPTION

The extent of consumer preference for a brand in comparison to close substitutes.

KEY INSIGHTS

Brand loyalty, as exemplified through consumer preference for the brand and an associated commitment to repurchasing the brand, is recognized by marketers as an important indicator of a brand's value. While repurchase behavior is clearly associated with brand loyalty, repurchase behavior does not in and of itself demonstrate brand loyalty, as a brand's repurchase may be due to convenience rather than loyalty, for example. In this context, many firms may have loyalty programs that encourage repurchase, but even frequent repurchases do not necessarily indicate that consumers are brand loyal to any degree.

KEY WORDS Consumer preference, brand preference

IMPLICATIONS
Marketers aiming to achieve strong brand loyalty among the firm's customers should seek to understand the extent of consumer preference for the firm's brand(s) in ways that go beyond examining repeat purchase behavior. Such an understanding can enable marketers to benefit from and make strategic use of brand loyalty in ways that include lowering the cost to serve loyal customers and leveraging loyalty to help attract new customers. (See **loyalty ripple effect**.)

APPLICATION AREAS AND FURTHER READINGS
Marketing Strategy
Raju, Jagmohan S., Srinivasan, V., and Lal, Rajiv (1990). 'The Effects of Brand Loyalty on Competitive Price Promotional Strategies,' *Management Science*, 36(3), March, 276-304.
Marketing Management
Bloemer, Jose M. M., and Kasper, Hans D. P. (1995). 'The Complex Relationship between Consumer Satisfaction and Brand Loyalty,' *Journal of Economic Psychology*, 16, 311-29.
Consumer Behavior
Jacoby, Jacob, and Kyner, David B. (1973). 'Brand Loyalty vs. Repeat Purchasing Behavior,' *Journal of Marketing Research*, 10(1), February, 1-9.
Baldinger, Allan L., and Rubinson, Joel (1996). 'Brand Loyalty: The Link between Attitude and Behavior,' *Journal of Advertising Research*, 36(6), 22-36.

BIBLIOGRAPHY
Jacoby, Jacob, and Chestnut, Robert W. (1978). *Brand Loyalty: Measurement and Management*. New York: Wiley.
Tucker, W. T. (1964). 'The Development of Brand Loyalty,' *Journal of Marketing Research*, 1(3), August, 32-35.

■ brand positioning

DESCRIPTION
The distinctive position adopted by a firm's brand in relation to competing brands.

KEY INSIGHTS
Effective brand positioning enables a firm's brand to be readily distinguishable from competing brands in the marketplace. Distinguishing the brand from other brands can be in terms of associated brand attributes, benefits to users, and/or market segment emphasis, among other factors. Effective brand positioning further emphasizes elements of superiority along one or more distinguishing dimensions which are valued by consumers. By adopting multiple brands, firms also have an opportunity to

strategically position brands with respect to each other and those of other competitors, such as when a firm chooses to introduce a *fighter brand* to protect one or more of its higher-priced brands. A fighter brand—a brand that is priced close to that of a competitor's lower-priced offering—can take pressure off the firm to lower the price of its higher-priced brand to compete with the competitor's brand in a market characterized by high price sensitivity.

KEY WORDS Brand distinctiveness, brand superiority

IMPLICATIONS
Marketers concerned with effective brand position for their firm's brands should seek to understand carefully the relevant dimensions along which their brands are able to be distinguishable and distinctive as a result of consumer evaluations of brands in the marketplace. Effective brand positioning is an important aim in a firm's marketing strategy development and associated marketing mix management.

APPLICATION AREAS AND FURTHER READINGS
International Marketing
Alden, Dana L., Steenkamp, Jan-Benedict E. M., and Batra, Rajeev (1999). 'Brand Positioning through Advertising in Asia, North America, and Europe: The Role of Global Consumer Culture,' *Journal of Marketing*, 63(1), January, 75–87.

Marketing Strategy
De Chernatony, Leslie, and Daniels, Kevin (1994). 'Developing a More Effective Brand Positioning,' *Journal of Brand Management*, 1(6), 373–379.

Marketing Research
Sujan, Mita, and Bettman, James R. (1989). 'The Effects of Brand Positioning Strategies on Consumers' Brand and Category Perceptions: Some Insights from Schema Research,' *Journal of Marketing Research*, 26(4), November, 454–467.

Marketing Modeling
Bronnenberg, Bart J., and Wathieu, Luc (1996). 'Asymmetric Promotion Effects and Brand Positioning,' *Marketing Science*, 15(4), 379–394.

BIBLIOGRAPHY
Sengupta, Subroto (2005). *Brand Positioning: Strategies for Competitive Advantage*. New Delhi: Tata McGraw-Hill.

□ **break-even pricing** *see* pricing strategies
□ **brick(s)-and-mortar marketing** *see entry at* online marketing
□ **brown goods** *see* goods

■ bundling

DESCRIPTION
The marketing strategy or practice that involves offering multiple products or services as a single combined product or service offering.

KEY INSIGHTS
A bundling strategy or practice can be potentially beneficial to a firm under conditions including those where products or services are

characterized by high volume and high margins. While the approach helps simplify consumer decision making and further enables consumers to benefit from possessing or consuming the combination offered, the firm may also benefit further from the approach as a result of economies of scale in production and/or economies of scope in distribution. The strategy or practice of bundling has variations including that of offering consumers an inseparable bundled offering (i.e. a pure bundling approach) or a separable bundled offering (i.e. a mixed bundling approach that allows the consumer to purchase one or more elements of the bundle).

KEY WORDS Combined offerings

IMPLICATIONS

Firms may benefit strategically from use of a bundling approach for their product or services to the extent the practice provides economic benefits to the firm and consumption-related benefits to consumers (e.g. financial, simplified decision making) in relation to benefits provided by unbundled offerings. Given the wide array of bundles that a firm may potentially offer its customers, marketing managers and strategists must seek to understand and manage carefully the characteristics of production, distribution, pricing, and promotion of its products and/or services that may make particular bundled offerings highly attractive to both the firm and its customers.

APPLICATION AREAS AND FURTHER READINGS

Marketing Strategy
Stremersch, Stefan, and Tellis, Gerard J. (2002). 'Strategic Bundling of Products and Prices: A New Synthesis for Marketing,' *Journal of Marketing*, 66(1), January, 55–72.

Services Marketing
Guiltinan, Joseph P. (1987). 'The Price Bundling of Services: A Normative Framework,' *Journal of Marketing*, 51(2), April, 74–85.

Online Marketing
Bakos, Yannis, and Brynjolfsson, Erik (2000). 'Bundling and Competition on the Internet,' *Marketing Science*, 19(1), Winter, 63–82.

Retail Marketing
Mulhern, Francis J., and Leone, Robert P. (1991). 'Implicit Price Bundling of Retail Products: A Multiproduct Approach to Maximizing Store Profitability,' *Journal of Marketing*, 55(4), October, 63–76.

Marketing Research
Soman, Dilip, and Gourville, John T. (2001). 'Transaction Decoupling: How Price Bundling Affects the Decision to Consume,' *Journal of Marketing Research*, 38(1), February, 30–44.
Yadav, Manjit S., and Monroe, Kent B. (1993). 'How Buyers Perceive Savings in a Bundle Price: An Examination of a Bundle's Transaction Value,' *Journal of Marketing Research*, 30(3), August, 350–358.

BIBLIOGRAPHY
Fuerderer, Ralph, Herrmann, Andreas, and Wuebker, Georg (1999). *Optimal Bundling: Marketing Strategies for Improving Economic Performance*. Berlin: Springer.

☐ business analysis *see* new product development
☐ business buyer behavior *see* industrial buyer behavior
☐ business buying process *see* industrial buyer behavior
☐ business marketing *see* business-to-business marketing

■ business-to-business marketing

(also called B2B marketing, business marketing, industrial marketing, organizational marketing, and trade marketing)

DESCRIPTION
The marketing of products and services by one organization to another and where such products and services are typically used in the production of other products for resale purposes or in support of service offerings provided to other customers.

KEY INSIGHTS
Business-to-business (B2B) marketing is often characterized by sophisticated buyers and complex products and constitutes a major proportion of all marketing activity. The scope of B2B marketing not only encompasses the marketing of products and services to other businesses, but to governments, institutions (e.g. hospitals) and other agencies, organizations, and authorities (e.g. those for airports) as well.

KEY WORDS Industrial marketing, organizational marketing

IMPLICATIONS
In many ways, B2B marketing approaches can be quite different than business-to-consumer marketing approaches, such as the frequently greater use of personal selling approaches in generating interest among potential customers. It is therefore imperative for B2B marketers to understand better the intricacies of business buyer behavior and the business buying process (see **industrial buyer behavior**) in order to accomplish the firm's B2B marketing objectives.

APPLICATION AREAS AND FURTHER READINGS
Services Marketing
Filiatrault, P., and Lapierre, J. (1997), 'Managing Business-to-Business Marketing Relationships in Consulting Engineering Firms', *Industrial Marketing Management*, 26(2), 213–222.

Online Marketing
Sharma, A. (2002). 'Trends in Internet-Based Business-to-Business Marketing,' *Industrial Marketing Management*, 31(2), February, 77–84.
Avlonitis, G. J., and Karayanni, D. A. (2000). 'The Impact of Internet Use on Business-to-Business Marketing: Examples from American and European Companies,' *Industrial Marketing Management*, 29(5), September, 441–459.

BIBLIOGRAPHY
Webster, F. E., Jr. (1995). *Industrial Marketing Strategy*, 3rd edn. New York: John Wiley & Sons.

☐ business-to-consumer marketing *see* consumer marketing

■ butterfly effect

DESCRIPTION
An effect in dynamic systems where small variations in the system can cause large variations over time.

KEY INSIGHTS
Examined and termed in pioneering research by Lorenz (1963), the butterfly effect has since been extended from the study of complex systems such as weather (e.g. where the breeze from a fluttering butterfly in China changes the weather in Chicago) to a wide range of phenomena also characterized by dynamic systems. The more technical term for the phrase in its relation to chaos theory is 'sensitive dependence on initial conditions'. (See **chaos theory**.)

KEY WORDS Dynamic systems, complex systems

IMPLICATIONS
Whether examined mathematically or conceptually, knowledge of the butterfly effect phenomenon can provide the marketer with potential insights into understanding and explaining the behavior of an array of complex, dynamic systems as well as a greater recognition of the limits of any such understanding. In particular, the phenomenon should be viewed by marketers as a contributing impediment to the marketer's ability to make reasonable or accurate predictions beyond a certain range of time for a given dynamic system (e.g. weather-dependent consumption behavior).

APPLICATION AREAS AND FURTHER READINGS
Consumer Behavior
Cannon L. (2003). 'The Butterfly Effect and the Virtues of the American Dream,' *Journal of Social Philosophy*, 34(4), December, 545–555.

Marketing Modeling
Schumacher, Norbert (2006). 'The Butterfly Effect: Estimating "Faux-New" Customers,' *Journal of Consumer Marketing*, 23(1), 43–46.

Online Marketing
Liang, T. Y. (2000). 'The e-Landscape: An Unexplored Goldmine of the New Millennium,' *Human Systems Management*, 19(4), 229–236.

BIBLIOGRAPHY
Lorenz, E. N. (2000). 'The Butterfly Effect,' in R. Abraham and Y. Ueda (eds.), *The Chaos Avant-Garde: Memories of the Early Days of Chaos Theory*. River Edge, NJ: World Scientific, 91–94.
Lorenz, E. N. (1963). 'Deterministic Nonperiodic Flow,' *Journal of the Atmospheric Sciences*, 20, 130–141.
Robert C. Hilborn (2004). 'Sea Gulls, Butterflies, and Grasshoppers: A Brief History of the Butterfly Effect in Nonlinear Dynamics,' *American Journal of Physics*, 72, 425–427.

☐ buyclass *see* industrial buyer behavior
☐ buyer concentration *see* competition

■ buyer decision process

DESCRIPTION
The decision-making process followed by a buyer of a good or service.

KEY INSIGHTS
The decision-making process of a buyer of a good or service can be characterized in many ways including a process involving the following elements: *problem recognition* (being cognizant of a problem that can be potentially solved by purchasing some offering); *information search* (the state of motivation to search for more information); *alternative evaluation* (using information to evaluate alternative offerings in one's choice set); *purchase decision* (deciding which offering to purchase); and *post-purchase behavior* (taking further action after purchase based on degree of satisfaction with the offering). While such elements may be common to many decision-making processes, it is widely accepted that buyer decision processes can vary considerably depending on characteristics of the decision maker as well as the nature of both the problem and the offering. The outlined process mostly reflects the purchase decision making of a consumer, whereas the industrial buyer's decision-making process, also known as the business buyer's (or the organizational buying) decision-making process, may somehow vary. This is clearly because the objectives and the players are both different in this case. (See **industrial buyer behavior.**)

KEY WORDS Decision making

IMPLICATIONS
A key task of marketers is to understand the elements of the decision-making process for the firm's offerings with the aim of successfully influencing the process. In addition, marketers need to draw upon empirical and offering-specific research on whether consumers actually follow a particular (e.g. standard) decision process, as this can influence the strategic timing of marketing communication approaches as well as that for other marketing actions. In some industrial buying situations, for example, efforts to establish a long-term supplier may involve extensive alternative evaluation, whereas in other buying situations where price is the only factor considered, alternative evaluation may be very simple. (See also **buyer influence/readiness.**)

APPLICATION AREAS AND FURTHER READINGS
Marketing Strategy
Dickson, Peter Reid (1992). 'Toward a General Theory of Competitive Rationality,' *Journal of Marketing*, 56(1), January, 69–83.
Bettman, James R. (1973). 'Perceived Risk and its Components: A Model and Empirical Test,' *Journal of Marketing Research*, 10(2), May, 184–190.

Marketing Management
Doney, Patricia M., and Cannon, Joseph P. (1997). 'An Examination of the Nature of Trust in Buyer-Seller Relationships,' *Journal of Marketing*, 61(2), April, 35-51.
Heide, Jan B., and Weiss, Allen M. (1995). 'Vendor Consideration and Switching Behavior for Buyers in High-Technology Markets,' *Journal of Marketing*, 59(3), July, 30-43.

Consumer Behavior
Kiel, Geoffrey C., and Layton, Roger A. (1981). 'Dimensions of Consumer Information Seeking Behavior,' *Journal of Marketing Research*, 18(2), May, 233-239.
Olshavsky, Richard W., and Granbois, Donald H. (1979). 'Consumer Decision Making—Fact or Fiction?' *Journal of Consumer Research*, 6(2), Special Issue on Consumer Decision Making, September, 93-100.
Newman, Joseph W., and Staelin, Richard (1972). 'Prepurchase Information Seeking for New Cars and Major Household Appliances,' *Journal of Marketing Research*, 9(3), August, 249-257.
Beatty, Sharon E., and Smith, Scott M. (1987). 'External Search Effort: An Investigation across Several Product Categories,' *Journal of Consumer Research*, 14(1), June, 83-95.
Bettman, James R., and Park, C. Whan (1980). 'Effects of Prior Knowledge and Experience and Phase of the Choice Process on Consumer Decision Processes: A Protocol Analysis,' *Journal of Consumer Research*, 7(3), December, 234-248.

Business-to-Business Marketing
Sheth, Jagdish N. (1973). 'A Model of Industrial Buyer Behavior,' *Journal of Marketing*, 37(4), October, 50-56.

Marketing Research
Green, Paul E., and Srinivasan, V. (1990). 'Conjoint Analysis in Marketing: New Developments with Implications for Research and Practice,' *Journal of Marketing*, 54(4), October, 3-19.

BIBLIOGRAPHY
Westbrook, Robert A., Newman, Joseph W., and Taylor, James R. (1978). 'Satisfaction/Dissatisfaction in the Purchase Decision Process,' *Journal of Marketing*, 42(4), October, 54-60.

■ buyer influence/readiness

DESCRIPTION

The general concept referring to the systematic understanding or characterization of the influence process on buyer behavior as well as the buyer's readiness to buy.

KEY INSIGHTS

One common characterization of the buyer influence process is a formulaic approach referred to as AIDA (*attention, interest, desire,* and *action*): getting the consumer's attention or awareness, generating interest, fostering desire, and encouraging action to buy the product or service. A common characterization of buyer readiness is referred to as AIDCA (*attention, interest, desire, conviction,* and *action*): being aware, being interested in buying, having a desire to buy, possessing conviction to buy, and taking action to buy. Similarly, buyer readiness can be characterized by the consumer's *awareness, knowledge, liking* of the offering, *preference* for the offering, *conviction* in the offering, and finally *purchase* of the offering.

KEY WORDS Influence process, buyer readiness

IMPLICATIONS

Understanding the buyer influence process and buyer readiness states is in many ways central to much of marketing theory and effective marketing practice. While there are numerous models of buyer influence and readiness, it is imperative for the astute marketer to be able to identify and manage the most relevant buyer influences and understand buyer readiness stages in establishing responsive marketing strategies, management processes, and marketing tactics. (See also **buyer decision process**; and **adoption process**.)

APPLICATION AREAS AND FURTHER READINGS

Marketing Management
Buvik, A., and Halskau, O. (2001). 'Relationship Duration and Buyer Influence in Just-in-Time Relationships,' *European Journal of Purchasing and Supply Management*, 7(2), 111–119.

Marketing Research
Parasuraman, A. (2000). 'Technology Readiness Index (TRI): A Multiple-Item Scale to Measure Readiness to Embrace New Technologies,' *Journal of Service Research*, 2(4), May, 307–20.

Services Marketing
Crosby, Lawrence A., Evans, Kenneth R., and Cowles, Deborah (1990). 'Relationship Quality in Services Selling: An Interpersonal Influence Perspective,' *Journal of Marketing*, 54(3), July, 68–81.

Advertising
Grewal, Dhruv, Monroe, Kent B., and Krishnan, R. (1998). 'The Effects of Price-Comparison Advertising on Buyers' Perceptions of Acquisition Value, Transaction Value, and Behavioral Intentions,' *Journal of Marketing*, 62(2), April, 46–59.

Sales
Siguaw, Judy A., Brown, Gene, and Widing, Robert E. (1994). 'The Influence of the Market Orientation of the Firm on Sales Force Behavior and Attitudes,' *Journal of Marketing Research*, 31(1), February, 106–116.

BIBLIOGRAPHY
Parasuraman, A., and Colby, Charles L. (2001). *Techno-Ready Marketing: How and Why your Customers Adopt Technology*. New York: Free Press.
Lengnick-Hall, C. A., Claycomb, V. C., and Inks, L. W. (2000). 'From Recipient to Contributor: Examining Customer Roles and Experienced Outcomes,' *European Journal of Marketing*, 34(3/4), 359–383.

☐ **buygrid** *see* industrial buyer behavior

☐ **buying center** *see* industrial buyer behavior

☐ **buyphase** *see* industrial buyer behavior

☐ **buzz marketing** *see* word-of-mouth marketing

☐ **by-product pricing** *see* pricing strategies

☐ **by-the-book marketing** *see* traditional marketing

■ bystander effect

(also known as the bystander apathy effect)

DESCRIPTION
The tendency for groups of bystanders to either not respond or respond more slowly to others' problems than individuals observing the same problem situations alone.

KEY INSIGHTS
Based on pioneering work by Latane and Darley (1968) where the bystander effect was empirically examined, research findings clearly show that the presence of others increases response times to problem situations as well as diminishing the likelihood that such individuals will choose to respond to problem situations at all. The bystander effect may be explained in part by the views that, even when facing emergencies, individuals have a dampened sense of personal responsibility when in groups than when alone and that there is a lesser perceived need for personal action as there are many others that can and will or should take action.

KEY WORDS Group behavior, helping behavior

IMPLICATIONS
When individuals face problem situations, help from bystanders may not always be as immediate or forthcoming as one would expect. Thus when marketers (or consumers) hope to rely on the helping behavior of groups of individuals to remedy problem situations of others, they may need to compensate for possible inaction or slowness through appropriate communications or other marketing initiatives. As an example, consumers are increasingly using the internet in requests for assistance in product selections and internet marketers are increasingly providing opportunities for consumers to do so more easily. As such, marketers should be aware of how consumer and market environments involving bystanders, live or virtual, may reduce helping behavior and attempt to compensate accordingly in their strategic and tactical actions.

APPLICATION AREAS AND FURTHER READINGS
Online Marketing
Lewis, C. E., Thompson, L. F., Wuensch, K. L., and Grossnickle W. F. (2004). 'The Impact of Recipient List Size and Priority Signs on Electronic Helping Behavior,' *Computers in Human Behavior*, 20, 633–644.
Blair, C. A., Thompson, L. F., and Wuensch, K. L. (2005). 'Electronic Helping Behavior: The Virtual Presence of Others Makes a Difference,' *Basic and Applied Social Psychology*, 27(2), 171–178.

Boycotts
Klein, Jill Gabrielle, Smith, N. Craig, and John, Andrew (2004). 'Why We Boycott: Consumer Motivations for Boycott Participation,' *Journal of Marketing*, 68(3), July, 92–109.

BIBLIOGRAPHY
Latane, B., and Darley, J. M. (1968). 'Group Inhibition of Bystander Intervention in Emergencies,' *Journal of Personality and Social Psychology*, 10, November, 215–221.

Darley, J. M., and Latane, B. (1968). 'Bystander Intervention in Emergencies: Diffusion of Responsibility,' *Journal of Personality and Social Psychology*, 8, April, 377–383.

Garcia S. M., Weaver, K., Moskowitz, G. B., Darley, J. M. (2002). 'Crowded Minds: The Implicit Bystander Effect,' *Journal of Personal Social Psychology*, 83(4), October, 843–53.

Chekroun, Peggy, and Brauer, Markus (2002). 'The Bystander Effect and Social Control Behavior: The Effect of the Presence of Others on People's Reactions to Norm Violations,' *European Journal of Social Psychology*, 32(6), 853–867.

C

☐ C2B *see* consumer-to-business
☐ C2C *see* consumer-to-consumer

■ cannibalization

DESCRIPTION

The situation where the result of a firm's new product introduction is a reduction in sales of its existing products.

KEY INSIGHTS

Ultimately, the extent of cannibalization depends on the extent that new products are substitutes for existing products. The cannibalization effect can be either intentional, as when a firm expects to replace its existing products with new ones, or unintentional, as when a firm only realizes after the introduction of a new product that sales for existing products are reduced.

KEY WORDS New products, existing products, sales

IMPLICATIONS

Marketers must aim to anticipate cannibalization effects of new product introductions in strategic marketing planning and implementation. Careful coordination of marketing strategies for new and existing products is needed to ensure that gains made with new products are not offset by losses in existing product sales and their value to the point where the firm is worse off as a result of introducing new products.

APPLICATION AREAS AND FURTHER READINGS

New Product Introductions
Moorthy, K. Sridhar, and Png, I. P. L. (1992). 'Market Segmentation, Cannibalization, and the Timing of Product Introductions,' *Management Science*, 38(3), March, 345–359.

Marketing Strategy
Desai, Preyas S. (2001). 'Quality Segmentation in Spatial Markets: When Does Cannibalization Affect Product Line Design?' *Marketing Science*, 20(3), Summer, 265–283.

Product Portfolios
Srinivasan, Sundara Raghavan, Ramakrishnan, Sreeram, and Grasman, Scott E. (2005). 'Identifying the Effects of Cannibalization on the Product Portfolio,' *Marketing Intelligence & Planning*, 23(4), June, 359–371.

BIBLIOGRAPHY
Lomax, Wendy, Hammond, Kathy, East, Robert, and Clemente, Maria (1997). 'The
   Measurement of Cannibalization,' *Journal of Product & Brand Management*, Febru-
   ary, 6(1), 27–39.

☐ **capital goods** *see* goods
☐ **captive-product pricing** *see* pricing strategies

■ **capture theory**

DESCRIPTION
A theory of regulation that posits a regulated industry can actually gain from
being regulated by 'capturing' the regulatory agency involved.

KEY INSIGHTS
Initially put forth by Stigler (1971), the capture theory of regulation suggests that regulated firms are able to benefit from regulation as a result of
actions that essentially capture, or encompass, the regulatory body. For
example, a regulatory body may be dependent on technical knowledge
found only within the industry. Other means of capture may be related
to general political influence or actions including the appointment of
regulatory body members which are selected from within the regulated
industry.

KEY WORDS Regulation, industry regulation

IMPLICATIONS
Marketers in regulated industries may benefit from a deeper knowledge
of capture theory to understand and explain better the nature of the
firm's—and industry's—relationship with a regulatory body. While the
extent of 'capture' may be a topic of debate and depend also on the perspective adopted, the theory may nevertheless be influential in shaping
regulatory policies of influence to the marketer's regulated organization.

APPLICATION AREAS AND FURTHER READINGS
Services Marketing
Bajtelsmit, V. L., and Bouzouita, R. (1998). 'Market Structure and Performance in
   Private Passenger Automobile Insurance,' *Journal of Risk and Insurance*, 65, 503–
   514.
Lueck, D., Olsen, R., and Ransom, M. (1995). 'Market and Regulatory Forces in the
   Pricing of Legal Services,' *Journal of Regulatory Economics*, 7, 63–83.

Product Regulation
Carpenter, D. P. (2004). 'Protection without Capture: Dynamic Product Approval
   by a Politically Responsive, Learning Regulator,' *American Political Science Review*,
   98(4), 613–631.

BIBLIOGRAPHY
Stigler, G. J. (1971). 'The Theory of Economic Regulation,' *Bell Journal of Economics
   and Management Science*, 2(1), 1–21.
Peltzman, Sam (1976). 'Toward a More General Theory of Regulation,' *Journal of Law
   and Economics*, 19(1), April, 109–148.

■ carry over effect

DESCRIPTION

Any effect of an action measured across multiple periods where the effect of the action extends beyond the initial period and has influence in subsequent periods.

KEY INSIGHTS

While there is certainly considerable scope for variation in the character-istics of carry over effects as they are of course context dependent, carry over effect considerations often occur when the effect of an action (e.g. remembering a product shown in an advertisement) is strong initially relative to a particular time frame or duration of interest and where the effects diminish over time yet are still present at the end of the period of measurement.

KEY WORDS Measurement, time frames

IMPLICATIONS

Carry over effects can be a consideration in planning and modeling the effects of many different marketing mix variables over time, as when the effect of reducing product prices to increase sales in a given year has the effect of decreasing demand for products in the subsequent year or when the effects of a safe winter driving campaign on consumer's driving behavior extend beyond the season and into subsequent winter seasons.

APPLICATION AREAS AND FURTHER READINGS

Marketing Strategy

Chintagunta, Pradeep K., and Jain, Dipak (1992). 'A Dynamic Model of Channel Member Strategies for Marketing Expenditures,' *Marketing Science*, 11(2), Spring, 168–188.

Consumer Behavior

Allenby, Greg M., and Lenk, Peter J. (1994). 'Modeling Household Purchase Behavior with Logistic Normal Regression,' *Journal of the American Statistical Association*, 89, 1218–1231.

BIBLIOGRAPHY

Tull, Donald S. (1965). 'The Carry-Over Effect of Advertising,' *Journal of Marketing*, 29(2), April, 46–53.

☐ cash cow *see* product portfolio analysis

■ catastrophe theory

DESCRIPTION

The area of mathematical theory or theories involving the study of dynamical systems where sudden, dramatic changes in system behavior are able to arise from small changes to the system.

KEY INSIGHTS

Based on pioneering mathematical research in the 1960s by Thom (1989), catastrophe theory has since been extended from the study of engineering phenomena to a wide range of phenomena including phenomena within marketing. Common to all areas of catastrophe theory study is the characteristic where small changes to a non-linear system are able to result in catastrophic change to the system. For example, the dramatic changes in the levels of tourism in particular cities and countries in Asia that resulted from a 2003 epidemic in the area has been examined and found to be consistent with the results predicted by catastrophe theory (Mao, Ding, and Lee 2006).

KEY WORDS Dynamical systems

IMPLICATIONS
Marketers involved in the study and modeling of any of a range of dynamical systems, whether involving consumer behavior, economic behavior (e.g. behavior within financial markets), or political behavior, may benefit from a deeper understanding of catastrophe theory if the aim of the marketer is to understand, explain, and predict the behavior of such systems. While catastrophe theory may not always apply to such systems, the theory is rich enough to enable a range of modeling approaches and thus may provide a means to break new ground in explaining and predicting complex system behavior.

APPLICATION AREAS AND FURTHER READINGS
Services Marketing
Oliva, Terence A., Oliver, Richard L., and MacMillan, Ian C. (1992). 'A Catastrophe Model for Developing Service Satisfaction Strategies,' *Journal of Marketing*, 56(3), July, 83–95.

Marketing Modeling
Kauffman, Ralph G., and Oliva, Terence A. (1994). 'Multivariate Catastrophe Model Estimation: Method and Application,' *Academy of Management Journal*, 37(1), February, 206–221.
Chidley, J. (1976). 'Catastrophe Theory in Consumer Attitude,' *Journal of Marketing Research Society*, 18, 64–92.
Mao, Chi-Kuo, Ding, Cherng G., and Lee, Hsiu-Yu (2006). 'Comparison of Post-SARS Arrival Recovery Patterns,' *InterJournal Complex Systems*, 1869, 1–8.

BIBLIOGRAPHY
Thom, René (1989). *Structural Stability and Morphogenesis: An Outline of a General Theory of Models*. Reading, Mass.: Addison-Wesley.
Poston, T., and Stewart, Ian (1998). *Catastrophe: Theory and its Applications*. New York: Dover.

■ category killer

DESCRIPTION
The term given to any generally large retail store that specializes in deep assortments of one or more product lines and which complements such offerings with a highly knowledgeable sales floor staff.

KEY INSIGHTS
The category killer term, of course, conveys the notion that smaller retail outlets—and particularly those with product lines of less depth— are likely to face a major challenge from larger stores with deep product

lines and equally knowledgeable employees. In particular, the danger to smaller retail outlets is that savvy consumers may forgo visits to their outlets if they view a larger store in reasonable proximity as being more of a one-stop shop for finding—or learning about—any, or many, products within a particular product category.

KEY WORDS Superstores, product line assortments

IMPLICATIONS

As category killer stores now exist for a tremendous range of product categories (e.g. from baby products to automotive supplies), marketers must seek to understand how and why particular customers may or may not be attracted to such offerings and emphasize appropriate value propositions in response. A baby supercenter, for example, may draw in customers (e.g. expectant parents) from a 100-mile radius if such customers wish to make in-depth examinations of possible products for purchase. On the other hand, a smaller store offering a limited selection of baby product may appeal to customers who are less willing to travel and who are far less selective about particular baby products.

APPLICATION AREAS AND FURTHER READINGS

Retail Marketing
Urban, D. J., and Hoffer, G. E. (1997). 'The Super Automotive Category Killer: Why Now? What Future?' *Journal of Consumer Marketing*, 14(1), 20–30.
Achrol, Ravi S., and Kotler, Philip (1999). 'Marketing in the Network Economy,' *Journal of Marketing*, 63, Fundamental Issues and Directions for Marketing, 146–163.
Merrilees, Bill, and Miller, Dale (2001). 'Superstore Interactivity: A New Self-Service Paradigm of Retail Service?' *International Journal of Retail & Distribution Management*, 29(8), 379–389.

Online Marketing
Siddiqui, Noreen, O'Malley, Antonia, McColl, Julie C., and Birtwistle, Grete (2003). 'Retailer and Consumer Perceptions of Online Fashion Retailers: Web Site Design Issues,' *Journal of Fashion Marketing and Management*, 7(4), December, 345–355.

BIBLIOGRAPHY
Michman, Ronald D., and Mazze, Edward M. (2001). *Specialty Retailers: Marketing Triumphs and Blunders*. Westport, Conn.: Quorum Books.

☐ causal marketing research *see* marketing research
☐ cause marketing *see* cause-related marketing

■ cause-related marketing

(also called cause marketing or social cause marketing)

DESCRIPTION

A marketing approach whereby an organization associates itself publicly with a particular cause, demonstrating support for it through activity that may include the donation of time, money, or expertise.

KEY INSIGHTS
Cause-related marketing in the broadest sense is when a firm's marketing strategy is co-aligned with corporate philanthropy. At the level of
implementation, the approach involves a firm supporting a particular
cause, often in conjunction with a non-profit organization, with some
of its own resources or some proportion of its revenues in exchange
for being allowed to publicize or commercialize the value from its
association with the cause. Firms can use the approach to enhance the
image of itself or its products or brands among current and potential
customers.

KEY WORDS Corporate philanthropy, non-profit organizations

IMPLICATIONS
Marketers may use cause-related marketing in many ways, ranging from
pure corporate philanthropy to the pursuit of pure commercial gain.
In contrast to the more overt approach of a sponsorship agreement,
cause-related marketing enables the organization to be perceived as
demonstrating corporate philanthropy to a greater extent. In considering
the benefit of the approach, marketers must therefore seek to understand how and to what extent associating with a cause may appeal to
and benefit stakeholders that are both inside as well as outside the
organization.

APPLICATION AREAS AND FURTHER READINGS
Marketing Strategy
Barone, Michael J., Miyazaki, Anthony D., and Taylor, Kimberly A. (2000). 'The
    Influence of Cause-Related Marketing on Consumer Choice: Does One Good Turn
    Deserve Another?' *Journal of the Academy of Marketing Science*, 28(2), 248–262.
Till, B. D., and Nowak, L. I. (2000). 'Toward Effective Use of Cause-Related Marketing
    Alliances,' *Journal of Product & Brand Management*, 9(7), 472–484.
File, K. M., and Prince, R. A. (1998). 'Cause Related Marketing and Corporate
    Philanthropy in the Privately Held Enterprise,' *Journal of Business Ethics*, 17, 1529–
    1539.

Consumer Behavior
Ross, John K., III, Patterson, Larry T., and Stutts, Mary Ann (1992). 'Consumer
    Perceptions of Organizations that Use Cause Related Marketing,' *Journal of the
    Academy of Marketing Science*, 20(1), 93–98.

BIBLIOGRAPHY
Varadarajan, P. Rajan, and Menon, Anil (1988). 'Cause-Related Marketing: A
    Coalignment of Marketing Strategy and Corporate Philanthropy,' *Journal of Mar-
    keting*, 52(3), July, 58–74.

■ ceiling effect

DESCRIPTION
Any effect on measurement or response where an upper limit to the range of
possible responses leads to a skewing of the distribution of responses.

KEY INSIGHTS

The ceiling effect becomes an issue in measurement and response when the imposition of an upper limit on possible responses impedes understanding the true nature of responses for a phenomenon as a result of its prominent effects on statistical analyses. Oftentimes, the existence of the ceiling effect in a set of measurements means only limited insights can be drawn about a phenomenon. For example, if consumers were surveyed to indicate the number of car brands they are able to name, where the range of choices given to them is, say, from five or fewer to ten or more, information from the survey would be lost if a relatively large proportion of respondents indicated an answer of ten or more.

KEY WORDS Measurement, response, statistical analysis

IMPLICATIONS

Marketers should be aware of the possibility of a ceiling effect in conducting marketing research when the upper limit to a range of possible responses to be collected or measured is essentially arbitrary.

APPLICATION AREAS AND FURTHER READINGS

Advertising

Singh, Surendra N., and Rothschild, Michael L. (1983). 'Recognition as a Measure of Learning from Television Commercials,' *Journal of Marketing Research*, 20(3), August, 235–248.

Kaul, Anil, and Wittink, Dick R. (1995). 'Empirical Generalizations about the Impact of Advertising on Price Sensitivity and Price,' *Marketing Science*, 14(3), Part 2 of 2, Special Issue on Empirical Generalizations in Marketing, G151–G160.

BIBLIOGRAPHY

Singh, Surendra N., Rothschild, Michael L., and Churchill, Jr., Gilbert A. (1988). 'Recognition versus Recall as Measures of Television Commercial Forgetting,' *Journal of Marketing Research*, 25(1), February, 72–80.

☐ celebrity endorsement *see* celebrity marketing

■ **celebrity marketing**

DESCRIPTION

Marketing involving the use of a widely known person.

KEY INSIGHTS

Celebrities, or well-known individuals, can be used in a firm's marketing efforts in many ways. The most common means, of course, is that of *celebrity endorsement*, where the firm establishes a contract with a relatively famous individual to have the individual give support or approval to one or more of the firm's offerings. The popularity of celebrity endorsements actually makes the term 'celebrity endorsement' much more widely used than that of 'celebrity marketing.' In using celebrity endorsement, there is the opportunity for the celebrity to associate his or her unique character and personality with that of the firm's offering which, assuming the celebrity is not endorsing competitors' offerings, allows the firm to market the offering in a way that cannot be imitated in that the individual imparts a unique meaning to the firm's offering in the minds of consumers.

While the bulk of celebrity marketing is in the context of endorsements of a firm's offerings, one should not forget that celebrities themselves are also engaged in their own marketing. In this sense, celebrity marketing can be viewed as a special case of *person marketing*, which involves marketing activity directed at creating a favorable attitude or impression of a particular individual and encouraging others (individuals or organizations) to act in ways that support the individual's marketing objectives.

KEY WORD Endorsements

IMPLICATIONS

Celebrity marketing, or celebrity endorsement more specifically, provides a marketer with an alternative to marketing involving the communication of emotional and/or logical appeals in the mass media. Since a firm has no real control over a celebrity's future status and perception, however, the marketer must give careful consideration to how and to what extent changes in the celebrity's public perception may positively, or negatively, influence the effective marketing of the firm's offerings. Marketers must also take care to consider the regulatory environment involving the use of celebrity endorsers, such as where advertisements cannot use celebrities to endorse products that they do not personally believe to be beneficial. Finally, marketers may also wish to consider the use of expert endorsers or lay endorsers as alternative to famous individuals for the endorsement of their offerings.

APPLICATION AREAS AND FURTHER READINGS

Marketing Strategy
Erdogan, Z., and Kitchen, P. (1998). 'Getting the Best Out of Celebrity Endorsers: Take Care Picking your Celebrity, but Don't Ignore the Bandwagon,' *Admap*, 33(4), 383, 17–20.
Erdogan, B. Z., and Baker, M. J. (2000). 'Towards a Practitioner-Based Model of Selecting Celebrity Endorsers,' *International Journal of Advertising*, 19(1), 25–42.

Marketing Research
Basil, M. D., and Brown, W. J. (1997). 'Marketing AIDS Prevention: The Differential Impact Hypothesis Versus Identification Effects,' *Journal of Consumer Psychology*, 6(4), 389–411.

BIBLIOGRAPHY
Rein, I., Kotler, P., and Stoller, M. (1990). *High Visibility: The Professional Guide to Celebrity Marketing*. Stoneham, Mass.: Butterworth-Heinemann.
Rein, Irving J. (2006). *High Visibility: The Making and Marketing of Professionals into Celebrities*. New York: McGraw-Hill.
McCracken, G. (1989). 'Who is the Celebrity Endorser? Cultural Foundation of the Endorsement Process,' *Journal of Consumer Research*, 16(3), 310–21.
Erdogan, B. Z. (1999). 'Celebrity Endorsement: A Literature Review,' *Journal of Marketing Management*, 15, 291–324.

☐ cell phone marketing *see* mobile marketing

■ **central place theory**

DESCRIPTION
Theory that aims to explain the spatial distribution of establishments, market areas, and settlements as well as their size and organization and further including the locational tendencies and preferences of businesses.

KEY INSIGHTS
Pioneering research by Christaller (1933) on city and town spacing provides a basis for essential elements of central place theory which suggests that located entities function as markets and are most effectively evaluated when they are viewed as part of competitive and interdependent systems. (See also **location theory**.)

KEY WORDS Location preference, location tendencies, retailing

IMPLICATIONS
Marketers involved in business location selection, whether for retailing or other purposes, can draw upon central place theory-based concepts to guide their analyses and evaluations. For example, it is recognized that consumers visiting shopping centers often have a preference for visiting multiple stores on a given shopping trip, so locating a business next to a popular retail outlet may increase the likelihood that one's store will be visited.

APPLICATION AREAS AND FURTHER READINGS
Retail Marketing
Clarkson, Richard M., Clarke-Hill, Colin M., and Robinson, Terry (1996). 'UK Supermarket Location Assessment,' *International Journal of Retail & Distribution Management*, 24(6), July, 22–33.
Gautschi, David A. (1981). 'Specification of Patronage Models for Retail Center Choice,' *Journal of Marketing Research*, 18(2), May, 162–174.
Applebaum, William (1965). 'Can Store Location Research be a Science?' *Economic Geography*, 41(3), July, 234–237.

BIBLIOGRAPHY
Eppli, Mark J., and Benjamin, John D. (1994). 'The Evolution of Shopping Center Research: A Review and Analysis,' *Journal of Real Estate Research*, 9(1), 5–32.
Christaller, W. (1993). *Central Places in Southern Germany*. Jena: Fischer.

■ **certainty effect**

DESCRIPTION
The tendency for individuals to underweight outcomes which are merely probable relative to outcomes which are certain.

KEY INSIGHTS
In comparing uncertain vs. certain outcomes, as in choosing between a certainty of receiving a $100 store gift certificate and a gamble involving a 50% chance of not receiving one at all and a 50% chance of receiving a gift

certificate of $110, the certainty effect predicts that most individuals will prefer the certain outcome rather than the uncertain one, even though the expected value of the uncertain one ($105) is more than the certain one ($100). The explanation for the certainty effect is based on a tendency for individuals to be risk averse, consistent with prospect theory. (See also **prospect theory**.)

KEY WORDS Decision making, probabilities

IMPLICATIONS
Marketers involved in the development of pricing strategies may benefit from a greater knowledge of the certainty effect in being able to understand, explain, and predict consumer behavior in relation to price evaluations and preferences to a greater extent.

APPLICATION AREAS AND FURTHER READINGS
Consumer Behavior
Tellis, Gerard J., and Gaeth, Gary J. (1990). 'Best Value, Price-Seeking, and Price Aversion: The Impact of Information and Learning on Consumer Choices,' *Journal of Marketing*, 54(2), April, 34–45.
Byrne, Kathleen (2005). 'How Do Consumers Evaluate Risk in Financial Products?' *Journal of Financial Services Marketing*, 10(1), September, 21–36.

Pricing
Tellis, Gerard J. (1986). 'Beyond the Many Faces of Price: An Integration of Pricing Strategies,' *Journal of Marketing*, 50(4), October, 146–160.

BIBLIOGRAPHY
Kahneman, Daniel, and Tversky, Amos (1979). 'Prospect Theory: An Analysis of Decision under Risk,' *Econometrica*, 47(2), March, 263–292.
Tversky, Amos, and Kahneman, Daniel (1992). 'Advances in Prospect Theory: Cumulative Representation of Uncertainty,' *Journal of Risk and Uncertainty*, 5(4), October, 297–323.

☐ change, E and O theories of *see* E and O theories of change

■ **channel arrangement**

DESCRIPTION
The general means by which a firm chooses to arrange the distribution of its offerings in conjunction with other intermediary firms.

KEY INSIGHTS
There are several different channel arrangements which marketers may use in the distribution of their offerings. Two common channel arrangements, or marketing systems, are the *horizontal marketing system* and the *vertical marketing system*. A *horizontal marketing system* is where multiple organizations collaborate in distribution to pursue market opportunities. In contrast, *vertical marketing systems* are where manufacturers and downstream distributors (e.g. wholesalers and retailers) coordinate distribution efforts for mutual benefit. Variations of the vertical marketing system (VMS) include: *contractual VMSs*, where firms at different levels of

the distribution system rely on contractual arrangements to coordinate efforts and where the aim is to achieve collective results that are superior in relation to when the same firms were to act independently; *corporate VMSs*, where multiple levels of the distribution system are under common ownership, thereby enabling the owner to lead the distribution effort for the distribution stages owned; and *administered VMSs*, where multiple levels of the distribution system are coordinated by the most influential firm(s) in the system (e.g. as a result of their size or power).

KEY WORDS Marketing system, distribution systems, supply chain management

IMPLICATIONS

The particular channel arrangement selected by a marketer is dependent on many factors including the characteristics of the product being distributed, the characteristics of the customer and market (e.g. geographic concentration), and the assets and competencies of other firms in the channel (e.g. proximity to the customer and relationships with other channel members). Marketers involved in the choice of channel arrangement must therefore weigh the advantages and disadvantages of the various approaches, recognizing as well that multiple approaches may also be an option for reaching particular segments of the market.

APPLICATION AREAS AND FURTHER READINGS

Marketing Management
Copacino, William C., and Byrnes, Jonathan L. S. (2001). 'How to Become a Supply Chain Master,' *Supply Chain Management Review*, September–October, 24–35.

International Marketing
Bello, Daniel C., and Williamson, Nicholas C. (1985). 'Contractual Arrangement and Marketing Practices in the Indirect Export Channel,' *Journal of International Business Studies*, 16(2), Summer, 65–82.
Frazier, Gary L., Gill, James D., and Kale, Sudhir H. (1989). 'Dealer Dependence Levels and Reciprocal Actions in a Channel of Distribution in a Developing Country,' *Journal of Marketing*, 53(1), January, 50–69.
Klein, Saul, Frazier, Gary L., and Roth, Victor J. (1990). 'A Transaction Cost Analysis Model of Channel Integration in International Markets,' *Journal of Marketing Research*, 27(2), May, 196–208.

Marketing Modeling
Zusman, Pinhas, and Etgar, Michael (1981). 'The Marketing Channel as an Equilibrium Set of Contracts,' *Management Science*, 27(3), March, 284–302.

Pricing Strategy
Lee, Enkyu, and Staelin, Richard (1997). 'Vertical Strategic Interaction: Implications for Channel Pricing Strategy,' *Marketing Science*, 16(3), 185–207.

BIBLIOGRAPHY

Kotler, Philip, and Armstrong, Gary (2006). *Principles of Marketing*, 11th edn. Upper Saddle River, NJ: Pearson Education, Inc.

■ channel conflict

DESCRIPTION
Discord or disagreement among member firms in a particular channel of distribution regarding distribution roles and goals.

KEY INSIGHTS
Channel conflict can potentially occur at any point in a channel of distribution. For example, there can be goal or role conflict among multiple firms at the same level of distribution (e.g. two retailers) or at different levels of the distribution channel (e.g. a wholesaler and a retailer). A common source of channel conflict is when the traditional channel of distribution becomes increasingly challenged by new, alternative channels of distribution, such as where a firm's products are made available to consumers through online retailers as well as traditional 'bricks and mortar' retailers. In such instances, it is essential that channel conflicts be addressed quickly to avoid disillusionment and dissatisfaction with the incentives to distribute a firm's offerings.

KEY WORDS Distributor conflict

IMPLICATIONS
Marketers involved in distribution channel management must recognize that channel conflict may not only be detrimental to a subset of firms in a distribution system but to the distribution system as a whole. Utimately, channel conflicts can jeopardize the effective and efficient distribution of a firm's offerings to current and/or prospective customers, such as where customers can be confused about what to expect in terms of pre-sale guidance or after-sales support from different distributors of a firm's products.

APPLICATION AREAS AND FURTHER READINGS

Marketing Strategy
Geyskens, Inge, Steenkamp, Jan-Benedict E. M., and Kumar, Nirmalya (1999). 'A Meta-Analysis of Satisfaction in Marketing Channel Relationships,' *Journal of Marketing Research*, 36(2), May, 223–238.
Gaski, John F. (1984). 'The Theory of Power and Conflict in Channels of Distribution,' *Journal of Marketing*, 48(3), Summer, 9–29.
Anderson, James C., and Narus, James A. (1990). 'Model of Distributor Firm and Manufacturer Firm Working Partnerships,' *Journal of Marketing*, 54(1), January, 42–58.
Mohr, Jakki, and Nevin, John R. (1990). 'Communication Strategies in Marketing Channels: A Theoretical Perspective,' *Journal of Marketing*, 54(4), October, 36–51.

Marketing Management
Gaski, John F., and Nevin, John R. (1985). 'The Differential Effects of Exercised and Unexercised Power Sources in a Marketing Channel,' *Journal of Marketing Research*, 22(2), May, 130–142.
Achrol, Ravi S., and Stern, Louis W. (1988). 'Environmental Determinants of Decision-Making Uncertainty in Marketing Channels,' *Journal of Marketing Research*, 25(1), February, 36–50.
Kumar, Nirmalya, Scheer, Lisa K., and Steenkamp, Jan-Benedict E. M. (1995). 'The Effects of Supplier Fairness on Vulnerable Resellers,' *Journal of Marketing Research*, 32(1), February, 54–65.

Marketing Research
Frazier, Gary L., and Summers, John O. (1986). 'Perceptions of Interfirm Power and Its Use within a Franchise Channel of Distribution,' *Journal of Marketing Research*, 23(2), May, 169–176.

International Marketing
Frazier, Gary L., Gill, James D., and Kale, Sudhir H. (1989). 'Dealer Dependence Levels and Reciprocal Actions in a Channel of Distribution in a Developing Country,' *Journal of Marketing*, 53(1), January, 50–69.

BIBLIOGRAPHY
Eliashberg, Jehoshua, and Michie, Donald A. (1984), 'Multiple Business Goal Sets as Determinants of Marketing Channel Conflict: An Empirical Study,' *Journal of Marketing Research*, 21, February, 75–88.

■ chaos theory

DESCRIPTION

Theory aimed at understanding the behavior of certain phenomena that appear random, but in fact have an element of underlying order, or regularity, which can be mathematically modelled.

KEY INSIGHTS

Building upon the research of early pioneers of chaos theory such as Lorenz (1963), chaos theory has subsequently expanded its scope from the study of phenomena such as the atmosphere and weather to a wide range of non-linear dynamical systems which may appear chaotic or random but are orderly to some degree. Numerous phenomena within the social sciences and marketing have since been studied from a chaos theory perspective, which has provided marketing researchers with a mathematics-based theoretical lens to study the behaviors of non-linear dynamical systems in contexts including marketing channel dynamics and the behavior of consumers.

KEY WORDS Dynamic systems, disorder

IMPLICATIONS

While chaos theory holds promise to provide fresh insights into the behavior of complex systems, particularly ones that appear to be characterized by complete disorder, the challenge remains to many marketers to model the precise relationships that can be found within complex systems. Still, chaos theory-based research and modeling is credited with benefits including spotting credit card fraud and facilitating consumer credit risk assessments by credit card issuers.

APPLICATION AREAS AND FURTHER READINGS

Marketing Strategy
Peters, Edgar E. (1994). *Fractal Market Analysis*. New York: John Wiley & Sons.
Hibbert, Brynn, and Wilkinson, Ian F. (1994). 'Chaos Theory and the Dynamics of Marketing Systems,' *Journal of the Academy of Marketing Science*, 22(3), 218–233.

Marketing Management
Wilkinson, Ian F. (1990). 'Toward a Theory of Structural Change and Evolution in Marketing Channels,' *Journal of Macromarketing*, 10(2), 18–46.

Marketing Research
Smith, A. (2002). 'Three Scenarios for Applying Chaos Theory in Consumer Research,' *Journal of Marketing Management*, 18(5), 517–531.

BIBLIOGRAPHY
Doherty, N., and Delener, N. (2001). 'Chaos Theory: Marketing and Management Implications,' *Journal of Marketing Theory and Practice*, 9(4), 66–76.
Elliot, Euel, and Kiel, Douglas (eds.) (1997). *Chaos Theory in the Social Sciences*. Ann Arbor: University of Michigan Press.
Lorenz, E. N. (1963). 'Deterministic Nonperiodic Flow,' *Journal of Atmospheric Sciences*, 20, 130–141.

■ characteristics theory

(also called Lancaster's characteristics theory, characteristics theory of consumer choice, characteristics theory of demand, characteristics theory of value, goods-characteristics theory, or product characteristics theory)

DESCRIPTION
A theory adopting the view that consumers do not demand products but rather the characteristics of products.

KEY INSIGHTS
Based on pioneering research by Lancaster (1966), characteristics theory adopts the view that the characteristics of products, as opposed to simple use of their broader categorical descriptions, provide a more beneficial means for understanding, explaining, and predicting consumer demand. Thus, in terms of the demand for detached houses, the theory suggests that the demand is not for detached houses but rather for privacy, quiet neighborhoods, spaces for children to play, gardens for outdoor relaxation, off-street parking for one's cars, etc.

While similar in terminology, Lancaster's goods-characteristics theory is not to be confused with job characterstics theory. (See **job characteristics theory**.)

KEY WORDS Product characteristics, good characteristics

IMPLICATIONS
A benefit of the characteristics theory approach to understanding, explaining, and predicting the demand for products is that it helps marketers to focus on the characteristics of products that are, and are not, being offered by existing products in the market. For new products in particular, where demand cannot be so easily assessed as with existing products, understanding the demand for various product characteristics (which may include undesirable characteristics as well) can assist marketers in determining overall product demand.

APPLICATION AREAS AND FURTHER READINGS
Marketing Strategy
Miracle, Gordon E. (1965). 'Product Characteristics and Marketing Strategy,' *Journal of Marketing*, 29(1), January, 18–24.

Shaw, R. (1982). 'Product Proliferation in Characteristics Space: The UK Fertiliser Industry', *Journal of Industrial Economics*, 31(1–2), 69–91.

Marketing Research
Hirschman, Elizabeth C. (1987). 'People as Products: Analysis of a Complex Marketing Exchange,' *Journal of Marketing*, 51(1), January, 98–108.
Hanley, N., Wright, R., and Adamowicz, W. (1998). 'Using Choice Experiments to Value the Environment,' *Environmental Resource Economics*, 11, 413–428.

Marketing Modeling
Vandenbosch, M., and Weinberg, C. (1995). 'Product and Price Competition in a Two-Dimensional Vertical Differentiation Model,' *Marketing Science*, 14(2), 224–249.
Reinhardt, P. G. (1976). 'Demand Analysis and Why the Poor May Pay More,' *Quarterly Journal of Economics*, 90(3), August, 509–513.

BIBLIOGRAPHY
Lancaster, K. (1966). 'A New Approach to Consumer Theory,' *Journal of Political Economy*, 74, 132–157.

□ **choice shift** *see* group polarization

■ Churchill's paradigm

DESCRIPTION
A paradigm for the measurement of marketing phenomena as developed and proposed by Gilbert Churchill.

KEY INSIGHTS
Paradigmatically developed by Churchill (1979) in what is now widely considered one of the seminal works in the measurement of marketing phenomena, Churchill's paradigm outlines an approach that marketing researchers are often advised to follow to ensure robustness in measurement. For any given construct in marketing (e.g. customer satisfaction, service quality) to be measured, Churchill's paradigm, as presented in his seminal journal article, provides an approach that has received widespread acknowledgment and praise among marketing researchers as a highly beneficial way in which marketing construct measurement should be understood and addressed.

KEY WORDS Scale development, marketing constructs, measurement

IMPLICATIONS
Churchill's paradigm provides marketers with both a means to develop potentially better measures of marketing constructs and a means with which to analyze and critique any given measure of a marketing construct that has been developed and applied in marketing research. While adoption of the paradigm for any given marketing scale development initiative is not entirely without difficulty (Smith 1999), it nevertheless provides essential guidance to marketers seeking to break new ground in scale development and measurement for use in any area of marketing research.

APPLICATION AREAS AND FURTHER READINGS

Marketing Research
Churchill, Gilbert A., Jr., and Surprenant, Carol (1982). 'An Investigation into the Determinants of Customer Satisfaction,' *Journal of Marketing Research*, 19(4), Special Issue on Causal Modeling, November, 491–504.

Menon, Anil, and Varadarajan, P. Rajan (1992). 'A Model of Marketing Knowledge Use within Firms,' *Journal of Marketing*, 56(4), October, 53–71.

Gerbing, David W., and Anderson, James C. (1988). 'An Updated Paradigm for Scale Development Incorporating Unidimensionality and its Assessment,' *Journal of Marketing Research*, 25(2), May, 186–192.

Peter, J. Paul, Churchill, Gilbert A., Jr., and Brown, Tom J. (1993). 'Caution in the Use of Difference Scores in Consumer Research,' *Journal of Consumer Research*, 19(4), March, 655–662.

Services Marketing
Smith, A. M. (1999). 'Some Problems when Adopting Churchill's Paradigm for the Development of Service Quality Measurement Scales,' *Journal of Business Research*, 46, 109–20.

BIBLIOGRAPHY
Churchill, Gilbert A., Jr. (1979). 'A Paradigm for Developing Better Measures of Marketing Constructs,' *Journal of Marketing Research*, 16(1), February, 64–73.

☐ click(s)-and-brick(s) marketing *see entry at* online marketing
☐ click(s)-and-mortar marketing *see entry at* online marketing
☐ closing *see* selling process

■ clubs, theory of

(also called the economic theory of clubs)

DESCRIPTION
A theory aimed at understanding, explaining, and predicting consumption-related club behavior including optimal club size and provision of goods within a club.

KEY INSIGHTS
Clubs are characterized by the ability to exclude whole groups of others from the consumption of goods within a club as well as the situation where the consumption of such goods by an individual does not substantially limit consumption by others within the club (e.g. health clubs, sporting clubs). For any given club offering, however, there is a point where excessive club membership leads to congestion in the consumption of club offerings. Club theory aims to determine optimal club membership in relation to the offerings of any particular club. Beyond such specific aims, club theory also seeks to understand and explain certain social and collective behaviors of consumers, such as when consumers adopt new fashions and later change fashions.

KEY WORDS Collective behavior, exclusive offerings

IMPLICATIONS

Marketers concerned with determining optimal club membership may benefit from a greater understanding of the economic principles of club theory. In addition, a deeper understanding of the considerable research on club theory can potentially provide marketers with an enhanced ability to understand and explain broad collective behaviors of consumers as well as specific consumption behaviors for particular club goods.

APPLICATION AREAS AND FURTHER READINGS

Consumer Behavior

Sandler, T., and Tschirhart, J. T. (1980). 'The Economic Theory of Clubs: An Evaluative Survey,' *Journal of Economic Literature*, 18, December, 1481–1521.

Adams, Roy D., and McCormick, Ken (1992). 'Fashion Dynamics and the Economic Theory of Clubs,' *Review of Social Economics*, 50(1), Spring, 24–39.

Landa, Janet T., and Carr, Jack L. (1983). 'The Economics of Symbols, Clan Names, and Religion,' *Journal of Legal Studies*, 12, 135–156.

Marketing Management

Carson, Stephen J., Devinney, Timothy M., Dowling, Grahame R., and John, George (1999). 'Understanding Institutional Designs within Marketing Value Systems,' *Journal of Marketing*, 63 (Special Issue), 115–130.

BIBLIOGRAPHY

Buchanan, J. M. (1965). 'An Economic Theory of Clubs,' *Economica*, 32, 1–14.

Cornes, R., and Sandler, T. (1996). *The Theory of Externalities Public Goods and Club Goods.* Cambridge: Cambridge University Press.

Ellickson, Robert C. (1991). *Order without Law: How Neighbors Settle Disputes.* Cambridge, Mass.: Harvard University Press.

■ cluster theory

DESCRIPTION

Theory or theories about geographic concentrations of interconnected companies, where such companies include specialized suppliers, service providers, firms in related industries, and associate institutions, and where the companies are in a particular field that competes but also cooperates.

KEY INSIGHTS

Research by Porter (2000) and others suggests that the study of company clusters reveals important insights about the microeconomics of competition and the role of location in competitive advantage and necessitates new roles for companies and governments to enhance competitiveness. In many ways, clusters can facilitate innovation, but in others they can retard innovation, as when they share a uniform approach to competing which creates rigidities impeding adoption of improvements or when threats to existing infrastructure impede radical innovation.

KEY WORDS Firm concentrations, location, competitive advantage

IMPLICATIONS

Marketers established or seeking to establish associations with organizational clusters could benefit from the insights of cluster theory as it raises ideas and issues that are potentially relevant to longer-term innovation and competitive advantage. For example, the nature of organization clusters suggests new roles for its members including interacting with government to promote and facilitate favorable microeconomic conditions for the cluster as well as conditions supporting its competitive advantages.

APPLICATION AREAS AND FURTHER READINGS

Technology Transfer
Singh, Robert P., and Jain, Ravi K. (2003). 'Improving Local Economies through Technology Transfer: Utilising Incubators to Facilitate Cluster Development,' *International Journal of Technology Transfer and Commercialisation*, 2(3), 249–262.

New Product Development
Ganesan, Shankar, Malter, Alan J., and Rindfleisch, Aric (2005). 'Does Distance Still Matter?' *Geographic Proximity and New Product Development*, 69(4), October, 44–60.

BIBLIOGRAPHY
Porter, Michael E. (2000). 'Location, Competition, and Economic Development: Local Clusters in a Global Economy,' *Economic Development Quarterly*, 14(1), 15–34.
Martin, Ron, and Sunley, Peter (2003). 'Deconstructing Clusters: Chaotic Concept or Policy Panacea?' *Journal of Economic Geography*, 3, 5–35.

■ cocktail party phenomenon

DESCRIPTION
The phenomenon of, and associated theories for, the situation where information not receiving primary attention by an individual is still attended to by the individual, though at a shallower level of processing.

KEY INSIGHTS
The phenomenon of being able to listen to, and follow, one speaker in the presence of others is one that is recognized as being common and essentially taken for granted, yet would stretch the capability of any automated system. Understanding and explaining ability to attend to sound under such conditions essentially involves the ability to filter and, more specifically, attenuate specific sounds.

KEY WORDS Attention, perception

IMPLICATIONS
Marketers concerned with the effectiveness of their communications, and advertising more specifically as it is often associated with a context of clutter and competing messages, may potentially benefit from understanding the mechanisms of, and abilities for, the cocktail party phenomenon at an individual level. For example, understanding the limits of individual abilities in this area may help marketers understand better when their communications become essentially ineffective in terms of reaching and influencing members of a target audience.

APPLICATION AREAS AND FURTHER READINGS

Advertising
Grunert, Klaus G. (1996). 'Automatic and Strategic Processes in Advertising Effects,' *Journal of Marketing*, 60(4), October, 88–101.

Consumer Behavior
Elliott, Emily M., Barrilleaux, Katie M., and Cowan, Nelson (2006). 'Individual Dif-
ferences in the Ability to Avoid Distracting Sounds,' *European Journal of Cognitive Psychology*, 8(1), January, 90–108.

BIBLIOGRAPHY
Davenport, Thomas H., and Beck, John C. (2001). *The Attention Economy*. Cambridge, Mass.: Harvard Business School Press.
Haykin, Simon (2005). 'The Cocktail Party Problem,' *Neural Computation*, 17, 1875–1902.

■ cognitive consistency theory

DESCRIPTION

Theory concerned with the effects of cognitions and inconsistent cognitions in particular, where cognitions are viewed as representing beliefs or items of knowledge, and where cognitions which are dissonant are viewed as motivating states of tension leading to dissonance-reducing behavior.

KEY INSIGHTS

Pioneering research by Festinger (1957) suggests that inconsistent cogni-
tions lead to behaviors to reduce cognitive tension. Such behaviors can include changing one of the cognitions, decreasing the perceived impor-
tance of the dissonance, and creating justifications through additional cognitions. Thus, cognitions including 'I gamble' and 'Gambling is bad for me as I seem to be addicted' may lead to changing the first cognition by giving up gambling; changing the second cognition by playing down the evidence; or adding justifying cognitions such as 'But some people say I am good at it and I can still pay my bills,' where the latter behavior in general is potentially the most common behavioral approach to reduce cognitive tension.

KEY WORDS Cognitions, dissonance reduction

IMPLICATIONS

Marketers concerned with developing communications and implement-
ing other actions aimed at changing consumers' dissonant cognitions, which may include, for example, consumers smoking and recognizing that smoking is bad for one's health or, alternatively, enabling consumers to more readily accept dissonant cognitions, should seek to understand how consumers may respond to such situations by drawing upon concepts stemming from cognitive consistency theory. Depending on the nature of the linkage between consumer cognitions and consumer behav-
ior, consumers may, for example, find it easier to alter cognitions than behavior and marketing actions may therefore focus on communications aimed at altering their cognitions.

APPLICATION AREAS AND FURTHER READINGS

International Marketing
Green, Robert T., and White, Phillip D. (1976). 'Methodological Considerations in Cross-National Consumer Research,' *Journal of International Business Studies*, 7(2), Autumn–Winter, 81–87.

Marketing Research
Anderson, Ronald D., Engledow, Jack L., and Becker, Helmut (1979). 'Evaluating the Relationships among Attitudes toward Business, Product Satisfaction, Experience, and Search Effort,' *Journal of Marketing Research*, 16(3), August, 394–400.
Hornik, Jacob (1981). 'Time Cue and Time Perception Effect on Response to Mail Surveys,' *Journal of Marketing Research*, 18(2), May, 243–248.

Services Marketing
Yen, Hsiu, Ju, Rebecca, Gwinner, Kevin P., and Su, Wanru (2004). 'The Impact of Customer Participation and Service Expectation on Locus Attributions Following Service Failure,' *International Journal of Service Industry Management*, February, 15(1), 7–26.

BIBLIOGRAPHY
Day, George S. (1972). 'Evaluating Models of Attitude Structure,' *Journal of Marketing Research*, 9(3), August, 279–286.
Festinger, Leon A. (1957). *A Theory of Cognitive Dissonance*. Stanford, Calif.: Stanford University Press.

■ cognitive dissonance

DESCRIPTION
A state of psychological discomfort where an individual has cognitions which are inconsistent.

KEY INSIGHTS
Cognitive dissonance is a key concept in Festinger's (1957) cognitive consistency theory and therefore is often examined and considered in the context of cognitive consistency. Cognitive dissonance is important in that it can ultimately lead to individuals changing their beliefs rather than behaviors which may have created or contributed to the inconsistency.

KEY WORDS Cognitions, inconsistency, consumer behavior

IMPLICATIONS
Marketers often speak of cognitive dissonance as a possible outcome of purchases that do not meet consumers' expectations. In this context, such consumers may decide not to purchase the same product again; they may convince themselves of the merits of the purchase by deciding to dismiss the problems or disappointments encountered; or they may add justifying cognitions (e.g. 'but the price was right.') In this context, marketers must consider how their communications and actions can potentially reduce cognitive dissonance occurring after a consumer's product purchase by, for example, providing appropriate messages of reassurance.

APPLICATION AREAS AND FURTHER READINGS
Consumer Behavior
Cardozo, Richard N. (1965). 'An Experimental Study of Customer Effort, Expectation, and Satisfaction,' *Journal of Marketing Research*, 2(3), August, 244–249.
Tse, David K., and Wilton, Peter C. (1988). 'Models of Consumer Satisfaction Formation: An Extension,' *Journal of Marketing Research*, 25(2), May, 204–212.

Buttle, Francis A. (1998). 'Word of Mouth: Understanding and Managing Referral Marketing,' *Journal of Strategic Marketing*, 6(3), September 1, 241-254.

BIBLIOGRAPHY
Anderson, Rolph E. (1973). 'Consumer Dissatisfaction: The Effect of Disconfirmed Expectancy on Perceived Product Performance,' *Journal of Marketing Research*, 10(1), February, 38-44.
Festinger, Leon A. (1957). *A Theory of Cognitive Dissonance*. Stanford, Calif.: Stanford University Press.
Akerlof, George A., and Dickens, William T. (1982). 'The Economic Consequences of Cognitive Dissonance,' *American Economic Review*, 72(3), June, 307-319.

■ cognitive theory

DESCRIPTION
Theory or theories aimed at understanding and explaining the relationship between mental processes and social behavior.

KEY INSIGHTS
Cognitive theory encompasses a broad range of theoretical perspectives, all of which are aimed at relating mental processes such as memory and perception to behavior. More specific theoretical perspectives include attribution theory (see **attribution theory**), cognitive balance theory (see **balance theory**), cognitive dissonance (see **cognitive dissonance**), and personal construct theory (see **personal construct theory**). Common to all such perspectives is the view that individuals engage in processes of actively making sense of their surroundings.

KEY WORDS Mental processes

IMPLICATIONS
While the body of theory referred to as cognitive theory is relatively large, the many theories within cognitive theory provide marketers with multiple perspectives with which to understand and explain better the drivers of social behaviors as well as the behavioral outcomes of the various mental processes of individuals.

APPLICATION AREAS AND FURTHER READINGS
Marketing Strategy
Peter, J. P., and Olson, J. C. (1987). 'Cognitive Theory and Marketing Strategy,' in G. A. Churchill Jr. (ed.), *Consumer Behavior: Marketing Strategy Perspectives*, Homewood, Ill: Irwin, 39-67.
Nooteboom, B. (1996). 'Towards A Cognitive Theory of the Firm: Issues and a Logic of Change,' *EIASM Conference on Organizational Cognition*, Stockholm.

Consumer Behavior
Hansen, Flemming (1972). *Consumer Choice Behavior: A Cognitive Theory*. New York: Free Press.
Ingwersen, Peter (1994). 'Polyrepresentation of Information Needs and Semantic Entities: Elements of a Cognitive Theory for Information Retrieval Interaction,' *ACM/SIGIR Conference Proceedings*, 101-110.

BIBLIOGRAPHY
Eiser, J. R. (1980). *Cognitive Social Psychology*. London: McGraw-Hill.

■ cohort effect

DESCRIPTION

An effect on the findings of a statistical study which is attributable to cohort membership, where cohorts are groups of individuals having certain meaningful characteristics in common.

KEY INSIGHTS

Cohort effects are a concern in statistical analyses; insufficient consideration of their effects may lead to inappropriate conclusions. For example, a study concluding that consumer attitudes to fast food become dramatically more negative with age after conducting a cross-sectional study comparing attitudes of multiple age cohorts may, in fact, be inaccurate in portraying such an attitudinal change with age and instead be a result of cohort membership characteristics.

KEY WORDS Groups, statistical analysis

IMPLICATIONS

In planning, implementing, and analyzing marketing research studies, marketers should be aware of the possibility of inaccurate or confounding results in studies where cohorts are a focus or essential element. In particular, studies of how consumer attitudes or behaviors change over time may be influenced by cohort effects and should therefore address how such effects can explicitly considered and controlled for.

APPLICATION AREAS AND FURTHER READINGS

Marketing Research

Rentz, Joseph O., and Reynolds, Fred D. (1991). 'Forecasting the Effects of an Aging Population on Product Consumption: An Age-Period-Cohort Framework,' *Journal of Marketing Research*, 28(3), August, 355–360.

Rentz, Joseph O., Reynolds, Fred D., and Stout, Roy G. (1983). 'Analyzing Changing Consumption Patterns with Cohort Analysis,' *Journal of Marketing Research*, 20(1), February, 12–20.

BIBLIOGRAPHY

Reynolds, Fred D., and Rentz, Joseph O. (1981). 'Cohort Analysis: An Aid to Strategic Planning,' *Journal of Marketing*, 45(3), Summer, 62–70.

■ collaborative marketing

DESCRIPTION

Generally, the process of working together with customers to create value in marketing exchanges and where customers may be an integral part of a firm's marketing activities.

KEY INSIGHTS

Collaborative marketing can be a viable and effective approach of firms in support of many areas of marketing and particularly new product development efforts. A collaborative marketing approach involves integrating the customer into the organization's marketing activities to a significant extent, thereby allowing the organization to understand customer needs and make use of customer knowledge to a far greater extent in comparison to an approach where there is a low-level relationship with customers. A motivation for customers to collaborate is the opportunity for them to receive firm-generated marketing offerings of significantly greater value in relation to that achievable with a more distant relationship with the firm.

KEY WORDS Customer alliances, customer integration

IMPLICATIONS

While some customers prefer more distant relationships with supplier organizations, marketers should recognize that there are some customers that may actually welcome an ongoing collaborative relationship with the marketer's firm if they believe they can receive offerings of superior value. Understanding better the nature, process, and benefits of collaborative marketing can enable marketers to initiate and manage collaborative relationships with customers to potentially obtain a sustainable competitive advantages over competitors who do not rely on such an approach, particularly in the area of new product or service development.

APPLICATION AREAS AND FURTHER READINGS

Retail Marketing
Corsten, D., and Kumar, N. (2005). 'Do Suppliers Benefit from Collaborative Relationships with Large Retailers? An Empirical Investigation of Efficient Consumer Response Adoption,' *Journal of Marketing*, 69(3), 80–94.

Non-profit Marketing
Abdy, M., and Barclay, J. (2001). 'Marketing Collaboration in the Voluntary Sector,' *International Journal of Non-profit and Voluntary Sector Marketing*, 6(3), September, 215–230.

Tourism Marketing
Fyall, A., and Garrod, B. (2005). *Tourism Marketing: A Collaborative Approach*. Clevedon: Channel View Publications.

Marketing Strategy
King, R., and DiGiacomo, G. (2000). *Collaborative Marketing: A Roadmap and Resource Guide for Farmers*. St Paul: University of Minnesota Extension Service.
Palmer, C. (1994). 'The Development of Collaborative Marketing: A Meat Industry Perspective,' *Agricultural Economics Society Conference Symposium on Collaborative Marketing: Farmer Driven or Retailer Led?*, University of Exeter.

BIBLIOGRAPHY
Magrath, A. J. (1991). 'Collaborative Marketing Comes of Age Again,' *Sales and Marketing Management*, 9, 61–64.

☐ comarketing *see* cooperative marketing

■ commercial marketing

(also called for-profit marketing or private sector marketing)

DESCRIPTION

Marketing by an organization engaged in commerce where the emphasis is primarily on organizational profit making.

KEY INSIGHTS

Commercial marketing encompasses the set of marketing approaches conducted by firms which are engaged in the buying and selling of goods and/or the provision of services and where one of the aims of such firms is to make a profit. The pervasiveness of such activity leads many individuals in the field of marketing to simply omit the term 'commercial' when referring to any number of marketing approaches. However, the distinction provided by the term is beneficial when comparing and contrasting such approaches with marketing approaches used in other contexts (particularly non-profit, or not-for-profit, firms) as well as when marketing approaches are not well understood in general.

KEY WORD Profit

IMPLICATIONS

In communicating with individuals unfamiliar with marketing practice, it may be beneficial for marketers to refer to the term 'commercial marketing' when describing or discussing 'marketing' to ensure the term's emphasis on a profit motive (e.g. profit maximization) is given appropriate emphasis. In addition, marketers concerned with the identification, evaluation, and implementation of marketing approaches for other contexts (e.g. non-profit marketing, social marketing) or for cross-contextual comparisons or applications (e.g. for-profit marketing practices applied to marketing in non-profit organizations), may benefit from a better understanding of the many marketing approaches that have greater firm profitability as a key aim.

APPLICATION AREAS AND FURTHER READINGS

Marketing Strategy

Kilbourne, W. E., and Marshall, K. P. (2005). 'The Transfer of For-Profit Marketing Technology to the Not-For-Profit Domain: Precautions from the Theory of Technology,' *Journal of Marketing Theory and Practice*, 13(1), 14–25.

Meade-D'Alisera, P., Merriweather, T., and Wentland, M. (2001). 'Impact of Commercial Marketing on Patient Demand,' *Urologic Nursing*, 21(6), December, 406–408.

Runyan, Jack L., Anthony, Joseph P., Kesecker, Kevin M., and Ricker, Harold S. (1986). 'Determining Commercial Marketing and Production Opportunities for Small Farm Vegetable Growers,' USDA, AMS, N. 1146, July, Washington, DC.

McKenna, J., Gutierrez, K., and McCall, K. (2000). 'Strategies for an Effective Youth Counter-Marketing Program: Recommendations from Commercial Marketing Experts,' *Journal of Public Health Management and Practice*, 6(3), 7–13.

Social Marketing

Peattie, S., and Peattie, K. (2003). 'Ready to Fly Solo? Reducing Social Marketing's Dependence on Commercial Marketing Theory,' *Marketing Theory*, 3(3), 365–386.

BIBLIOGRAPHY

Kotler, Philip, and Armstrong, Gary (2006). *Principles of Marketing*, 11th edn. Upper Saddle River, NJ: Pearson Education, Inc.

☐ commercialization *see* new product development

■ commodification

DESCRIPTION

The transformation of non-commodity offerings into ones that are generally regarded as commodities (also called commoditization).

KEY INSIGHTS

While commodities are goods that are almost solely bought and sold on the basis of price and not on the basis of quality or features, many other products are marketed in a way that differentiates them from competing offerings, as when a brand is used in conjunction with product features or qualities that are in some way different than competing offerings. Yet, over time, many non-commodity products (e.g. personal computers) are sought and bought by consumers increasingly on the basis of price, thereby making them quite commodity like. While such products may not be pure commodities, they nevertheless have lost some of their distinctiveness as perceived by consumers, making it increasingly challenging for the products to compete on characteristics other than price.

KEY WORDS Commodities, price competition

IMPLICATIONS

The challenge to marketers of offerings that are, or have become, commodity like (e.g. orange juice) is to either accept the commodity-like perception among consumers and compete accordingly or find ways to differentiate the offering from competing offerings in an effort to increase the perceived value of the offering. Orange juice, for example, can be differentiated in terms of source of the oranges, freshness, and even additives such as calcium.

APPLICATION AREAS AND FURTHER READINGS

Marketing Strategy

Holbrook, M. B. (1995). 'The Four Faces of Commodification,' *Journal of Marketing Management*, 11(3), 641–654.

Applbaum, Kalman (2000). 'Marketing and Commodification,' *Social Analysis*, 44, 106–28.

Marketing Management

Pasternack, Barry Alan (1985). 'Optimal Pricing and Return Policies for Perishable Commodities,' *Marketing Science*, 4(2), Spring, 166–176.

Marketing Education

Brownlie, D., and Saren, M. (1995). 'On the Commodification of Marketing Knowledge: Opening Theme,' *Journal of Marketing Management*, 11(7), 619–627.

BIBLIOGRAPHY

Manno, Jack (2000). *Privileged Goods: Commoditization and its Impact on Environment and Society*. Boca Raton, Fla.: Lewis Publishers.

☐ **commoditization** *see* commodification

■ common method bias

(also called common methods bias)

DESCRIPTION
A problem of research methodology leading to the outcome where data are related simply because they come from the same source, thereby making them subject to distortion.

KEY INSIGHTS
Common method bias, where the methodology employed by a researcher affects the measures being gathered, is essentially a methodological arte-fact. A solution to such a problem is to use multiple methods of data collection. For example, in the study of marketing strategy phenomena, methods including interviews, observation, and archival data could be used in combination, with the results triangulated to increase the robust-ness of the findings.

KEY WORDS Research method bias

IMPLICATIONS
Marketing researchers must be wary of developing and implementing research methodologies that ultimately suffer from common method bias, thereby leading to skewed, biased, questionable, or even useless findings. Experienced marketing researchers are much more likely to recognize the value and benefit of adopting multiple methods in studying any given marketing phenomenon, even though the approach clearly increases the complexity and scope of the research.

APPLICATION AREAS AND FURTHER READINGS
Marketing Research
Jap, S. D., and Anderson, E. (2004). 'Challenges and Advances in Marketing Strategy Field Research,' in C. Moorman and D. Lehmann (eds.) *Cool Tools for Assessing Marketing Strategy Performance.* Marketing Science Institute.
Doty, D. H., and Glick, W. H. (1998). 'Common Methods Bias: Does Common Methods Variance Really Bias Results?' *Organizational Research Methods*, 1(4), 374–406.

BIBLIOGRAPHY
Podsakoff, P. M., MacKenzie, S. B., Lee, J. Y., and Podsakoff, N. P. (2003). 'Common Method Biases in Behavioral Research: A Critical Review of the Literature and Recommended Remedies,' *Journal of Applied Psychology*, 88(5), 879–903.

■ common ratio effect

DESCRIPTION
The effect where an individual's choices change when the probabilities of a pair of gambles are scaled by a common factor.

KEY INSIGHTS

Pioneering research by Allais (1953) identified the effect as clearly indicating a systematic violation of expected utility theory since actual observed choices under the above conditions are inconsistent with expected utility theory's predictions. Such a difficulty gives rise to alternatives to the theory including Kahneman and Tversky's (1979) prospect theory. Also relevant in explaining the effect is the role of framing where identical items will result in different choices if presented differently (e.g. 80% chance of living vs. 20% chance of dying).

KEY WORDS Decision making, choice, probabilities

IMPLICATIONS

Marketers must recognize that a consumer's choice behavior will not always be governed by expected utilities. Anticipating how consumers will make choices may therefore not only consider the possible benefits of applying theoretical knowledge to identify systematic behavioral tendencies but also the results of earlier empirical research as well as applied marketing research.

APPLICATION AREAS AND FURTHER READINGS

Decision Making

Currim, Imran S., and Sarin, Rakesh K. (1989). 'Prospect versus Utility,' *Management Science*, 35(1), January, 22–41.

Barron, Greg, and Erev, Ido (2003). 'Small Feedback-Based Decisions and their Limited Correspondence to Description-Based Decisions,' *Journal of Behavioral Decision Making*, 16(3), May, 215–233.

BIBLIOGRAPHY

Camerer, Colin, and Weber, Martin (1992). 'Recent Developments in Modeling Preferences: Uncertainty and Ambiguity,' *Journal of Risk and Uncertainty*, 5(4), October, 325–370.

Allais, M. (1953). 'Le Comportement de l'homme rationnel devant le risque: critique des postulats et axiomes de l'école américaine,' *Econometrica*, 21, 503–546.

Kahneman, Daniel, and Tversky, Amos (1979). 'Prospect Theory: An Analysis of Decision under Risk,' *Econometrica*, 47, 263–292.

■ communication-information processing theory

(also called communication theory, information processing theory, or communication and information processing theory)

DESCRIPTION

Theory or theories related to how communication is transmitted and received relative to a sender and a receiver, respectively, and how characteristics of each as well as other factors can facilitate or hinder effective communication and information processing.

KEY INSIGHTS

Pioneers in communication-information processing theory include Shannon and Weaver (1948) who developed the theory and related concepts including transmitters, receivers, and noise. One of the most important principles of effective communications based on the theory is to try to eliminate or control for noise in the communication system since background noise can reduce the quality of communication through information distortion.

KEY WORDS Communication, information

IMPLICATIONS
Marketers are constantly seeking ways to communicate with current and potential customers more effectively. From a competitive standpoint, marketers are also interested in extracting information from the external environment (e.g. information on competitive developments) and to be in a position to respond to such information quickly and effectively. Principles of communication-information processing theory can be applied in both situations as the theory contributes elements of the communication process that can be examined individually or collectively to identify potentially weak information links in the process. For example, understanding why a firm may be slow to respond to competitive actions may be due to the stage of the communication process related to communicating external information up through the organization to key decision makers rather than sensing information from the market to begin with. As another example, ineffective marketing communications may be due to the firm's message not being received or understood by the firm's target market to a significant extent if there is considerable competing information being transmitted (e.g. advertising clutter) in the marketplace at the same time.

APPLICATION AREAS AND FURTHER READINGS
Market Entry Timing
Dacko, Scott G. (2002). 'Understanding Market Entry Timing Decisions: The Practitioner–Academic gap,' *Marketing Intelligence & Planning*, 20(2), April, 70–81.
Dacko, Scott G. (2000). 'Benchmarking Competitive Responses to Pioneering New Product Introductions,' *Benchmarking: An International Journal*, 7(5), December, 324–342.

Marketing Communications
O'Cass, Aron, and Grace, Debra (2004). 'Service Brands and Communication Effects,' *Journal of Marketing Communications*, 10(4), December, 241–254.

BIBLIOGRAPHY
Smith, Ken G., and Grimm, Curtis M. (1991). 'A Communication-Information Model of Competitive Response Timing,' *Journal of Management*, 17(1), 5–23.
Shannon, C., and Weaver, W. (1948). *A Mathematical Theory of Communcation*. Urbana, Ill.: University of Illinois Press.

■ comparative advantage, law of

(also called the theory of comparative advantage)

DESCRIPTION
An economic principle stating that people and countries should specialize in whatever leads them to give up the least, thereby providing their comparative advantage.

KEY INSIGHTS
Developed and advocated by economist David Ricardo, the law of comparative advantage is consistent with the observation that many countries tend to export those economic goods in the production of which they have a comparative advantage (e.g. ability to produce inexpensively) and import those economic goods in the production of which they have a comparative disadvantage (e.g. ability to produce but at high cost).

KEY WORDS Exporting, importing, production, trade policy

IMPLICATIONS
The law of comparative advantage clearly has implications for country export and import policies, including the views that a country should tend to produce those products for which it has the least comparative advantage even if it has no comparative advantage at all and additionally that a country is still able to gain from trade with other countries even if it has an absolute disadvantage in the production of all of its goods. Marketers should therefore seek to understand country trade and import/export policies and exploit advantages associated with international trade under these and other circumstances.

APPLICATION AREAS AND FURTHER READINGS
International Marketing
Ellis, Paul (2002). 'Macromarketing and International Trade: Comparative Advantage versus Cosmopolitan Considerations,' *Journal of Macromarketing*, 22(1), 32–56.
Howells, Jeremy, and Michie, Jonathan (1998). 'Technological Competitiveness in an International Arena,' *International Journal of the Economics of Business*, 5(3), November, 279–293.

BIBLIOGRAPHY
Buchholz, Todd G. (1990). *New Ideas from Dead Economists*. New York: Penguin Books.

■ comparative influence

DESCRIPTION
Influence on a consumer by a reference group where the consumer compares his or her attitudes, beliefs, and behaviors to those of the reference group.

KEY INSIGHTS
The greater the similarity between a consumer's attitudes, beliefs, and/or behaviors and those of a particular reference group, the greater the comparative influence of the reference group on the consumer.

KEY WORDS Reference groups, influence

IMPLICATIONS
Understanding the extent of comparative influence by reference groups can be critical in certain marketing situations, such as in a retail clothing store understanding and being able to anticipate what brands of clothing for skateboarding will likely be considered fashionable by individuals

closely associating with serious skateboarding. Brand attitudes and purchase intentions of many different consumer segments are potentially affected by reference groups' comparative influence.

APPLICATION AREAS AND FURTHER READINGS
Consumer Behavior
Park, C. Whan, and Lessig, V. Parker (1977). 'Students and Housewives: Differences in Susceptibility to Reference Group Influence,' *Journal of Consumer Research*, 4(2), September, 102–110.
Beaudoin, Pierre, and Lachance, Marie J. (2006). 'Determinants of Adolescents' Brand Sensitivity to Clothing,' *Family and Consumer Sciences Research Journal*, 34(4), 312–331.

BIBLIOGRAPHY
Cocanougher, A. Benton, and Bruce, Grady D. (1971). 'Socially Distant Reference Groups and Consumer Aspirations,' *Journal of Marketing Research*, 8(3), August, 379–381.

■ comparative judgment, law of

DESCRIPTION
A term referring to the specific mathematically represented conceptualization and measurement model of L. L. Thurstone for a particular process of judgment involving making comparisons and, more specifically, for such a process involving the judgment of noticeable differences on a continuum scale.

KEY INSIGHTS
Conceived by Thurstone (1927) as a way to mathematically model the process of making comparisons between pairs of a collection of entities, e.g. as in a consumer making comparisons between pairs of items of clothing in a collection of clothing in a retail store, the approach characterized by the law of comparative judgment (LCJ) enables pairwise comparisons to be used to scale the collection of entities along a continuum. The LCJ approach can be applied not only to physical entities but also psychological ones such as attitudes.

KEY WORDS Judgment, comparisons, attitudes

IMPLICATIONS
As marketing researchers are often concerned with discerning consumer attitudes, an LCJ-based approach could potentially be applied for this purpose. For example, an LCJ-based approach would be used by a researcher if he or she took a list of statements compiled from interviewing different consumers, where each statement in the list reflected an attitude of a particular intensity, and used a process involving making pairwise comparisons of statements in the list to create a list in the order of highest to lowest attitude intensity. As such, LCJ-based approaches can form the basis for an array of research methods aimed at modeling marketing or consumer phenomena.

APPLICATION AREAS AND FURTHER READINGS
Marketing Research
Droge, Cornelia, and Darmon, Rene Y. (1987). 'Associative Positioning Strategies through Comparative Advertising: Attribute versus Overall Similarity Approaches,' *Journal of Marketing Research*, 24(4), November, 377–388.
Sinha, Indrajit, and DeSarbo, Wayne S. (1998). 'An Integrated Approach toward the Spatial Modeling of Perceived Customer Value,' *Journal of Marketing Research*, 35(2), May, 236–249.
Rust, Roland T., Inman, J. Jeffrey, Jia, Jianmin, and Zahorik, Anthony (1999). 'What You Don't Know about Customer-Perceived Quality: The Role of Customer Expectation Distributions,' *Marketing Science*, 18(1), 77–92.

BIBLIOGRAPHY
Curry, David J. (1985). 'Measuring Price and Quality Competition,' *Journal of Marketing*, 49(2), Spring, 106–117.
Thurstone, L. L. (1927). 'A Law of Comparative Judgment,' *Psychological Review*, 34, July, 273–286.

■ comparative marketing

DESCRIPTION

Marketing that is focused on understanding how and why the marketing systems of different nations perform and interact.

KEY INSIGHTS

Comparative marketing entails the systematic study of similarities and differences between national marketing systems. As such, the area clearly has relevance to marketing strategists and managers within firms operating in international and global marketing contexts. The emphasis of research in the area is far broader than that which is typically conducted within an internationally operating business, however, as the area emphasizes the study of national marketing system similarities and differences across time, space, and industry sector for the purpose of building theory and applying theory. Comparative marketing thus encompasses research on areas ranging from marketing institutions and associated marketing activities to consumer behavior, where the aim is a better understanding and explanation of different nations' marketing systems and the way they interact for the provision of goods for public consumption. Methodologies for the study of comparative marketing systems include that of institutional analysis.

KEY WORDS National marketing systems, **global marketing**

IMPLICATIONS

Marketers seeking a deeper theoretical and conceptual understanding of global and international marketing issues may clearly benefit from a better understanding of comparative marketing as a result of the area's broad research emphasis. While the area consists of multiple research methodologies and theoretical perspectives, a greater knowledge of the area provides marketers with an opportunity to focus either broadly or more narrowly on particular elements of national marketing system similarities and differences such as distribution (e.g. wholesaling, retailing) or economic development.

APPLICATION AREAS AND FURTHER READINGS
Marketing Research
Iyer, G. R. (1997). 'Comparative Marketing: An Interdisciplinary Framework for Institutional Analysis,' *Journal of International Business Studies*, 28(3), 531–562.
Bartels, Robert (1963). *Comparative Marketing: Wholesaling in Fifteen Countries*. Homewood, Ill.: Irwin.

Global Marketing
Calantone, R. J., Lee, M. T., and Gross, A. C. (1990). 'Evaluating International Technology Transfer in a Comparative Marketing Framework,' *Journal of Global Marketing*, 3(3), 23–46.

BIBLIOGRAPHY
Boddewyn, J. J. (1981). 'Comparative Marketing: The First Twenty Five Years,' *Journal of International Business Studies*, Spring/Summer, 61–79.
Barksdale, Hiram C., and Anderson, L. McTier (1982). 'Comparative Marketing: A Review of the Literature,' *Journal of Macromarketing*, 2, Spring, 57–62.
Wright, R. W., and Ricks, D. A. (1994). 'Trends in International Business Research: Twenty-Five Years Later,' *Journal of International Business Studies*, 25, 687–701.

☐ competency *see* strategic competency

■ competition

DESCRIPTION
Rivalry in the provision of products and services to current and prospective customers.

KEY INSIGHTS
Competition can take many forms, as indicated by the many different competitive environments that a firm may face. Competitive environments can be characterized by terms including:

Buyer concentration—the extent to which a market is dominated by a small number of typically large buyers.
Duopoly—a market structure in which two suppliers of a product compete with each other, or, more generally, a market structure in which two suppliers of a product dominate competition in the market.
Monopolistic competition—a market structure where there are a large number of firms supplying similar but not identical products.
Monopoly—a market structure in which there is only one supplier of a product for which there are no real substitutes and where there are many buyers, or, more generally, a market structure in which one supplier substantially dominates competition in the market.
Monopoly power—the ability of a firm or a set of firms to substantially dictate the price or other attributes of a product or service in a market.
Monopsony—a market structure in which there is a single buyer for a product or service.

Non-price competition—the use of factors other than price (e.g. product quality, advertising) by a firm to compete in a given market.

Oligopolistic competition—a market structure in which only a few suppliers of a product compete with each other for a substantial share of the market.

Oligopoly—a market structure in which only a few suppliers of a product compete with each other and where such a small number of suppliers leads to mutual interdependencies in their production and sales as well as the anticipation of any single supplier's competitive actions on other suppliers and the market.

Oligopsony—a market structure in which a large number of suppliers compete with each other for the business of a relatively small number of buyers.

Perfect competition—a market structure characterized by conditions including: there are a large number of suppliers in a market; each supplier has a relatively insignificant share of the market; all suppliers produce the same product using the same production processes; and all suppliers possess perfect information (or complete knowledge and foresight) about the market.

Pure competition—a market structure where price is the dominant factor in the preference of a product by its customers and where the relatively insignificant share of the market by each supplier is such that each is relatively powerless to affect the product's market price.

Pure monopoly—a market structure where there is a single firm that is able to dictate completely the price and other attributes of a product or service in the market.

KEY WORDS Competitive environment

IMPLICATIONS
Given the considerable diversity in competitive environments facing firms involved in the marketing of their offerings, whether in competing locally, regionally, nationally, or worldwide, it is imperative that marketers understand the nature and composition of their competitive environments to enable realistic assessments of the challenges and opportunities for competing successfully over the long term. Futhermore, the dynamic nature of most competitive environments necessitates an ongoing assessment of the firm's broad competitive environment to ensure maximum responsiveness to changing competive demands.

APPLICATION AREAS AND FURTHER READINGS
Marketing Strategy

Weitz, Barton A. (1985). 'Introduction to Special Issue on Competition in Marketing,' *Journal of Marketing Research*, 22(3), August, 229–236.

Jayachandran, Satish, Gimeno, Javier, and Varadarajan, P. Rajan (1999). 'The Theory of Multimarket Competition: A Synthesis and Implications for Marketing Strategy,' *Journal of Marketing*, 63(3), July, 49–66.

Hunt, Shelby D., and Morgan, Robert M. (1995). 'The Comparative Advantage Theory of Competition,' *Journal of Marketing*, 59(2), April, 1–15.

Smith, Wendell R. (1956). 'Product Differentiation and Market Segmentation as Alternative Marketing Strategies,' *Journal of Marketing*, 21(1), July, 3–8.
Hunt, Shelby D., and Morgan, Robert M. (1996). 'The Resource-Advantage Theory of Competition: Dynamics, Path Dependencies, and Evolutionary Dimensions,' *Journal of Marketing*, 60(4), October, 107–114.
Dickson, Peter Reid (1992). 'Toward a General Theory of Competitive Rationality,' *Journal of Marketing*, 56(1), January, 69–83.

BIBLIOGRAPHY
Easton, G. (1988). 'Competition and Marketing Strategy,' *European Journal of Marketing*, 22(2), 31–69.

☐ competition-based pricing *see* pricing strategies
☐ competitive advantage *see* sustainable competitive advantage
☐ competitive parity method *see* promotion budget setting methods
☐ complex buying behavior *see* consumer buyer behavior

■ complexity theory

DESCRIPTION
Theory or theories concerned with the study of complex systems and their simplification.

KEY INSIGHTS
Complexity theory encompasses the study of a wide range of complex systems phenomena, ranging from biological, chemical, and atmospheric systems to those of complex organizations. In a marketing context, complexity theory is primarily concerned with the simplification of systems exhibiting, among other characteristics, relative complexity, non-linear interactions among elements in the system, self-organizing networks, and near-chaotic behavior. As such, complexity theory and chaos theory are related and sometimes either theory is referenced by the use of the other term. (See **chaos theory**.) Considerable marketing research focuses on how principles of complexity theory can provide insights into how organizations can become more effective and adaptive.

KEY WORDS Complex systems, organizations

IMPLICATIONS
At one level, a greater knowledge of complexity theory can provide marketers with a useful, albeit broad, metaphor for organizational analysis. At a deeper level, the theory can provide marketing strategists with a basis for a rigorous approach to extensive organizational analyses, recognizing, however, that the theoretical approach rests on assumptions (e.g. systems that are self-organizing) that may or may not be present in organizational systems examined and that organizational systems may possess characteristics that are not fully captured by complexity theory (e.g. organizational politics).

APPLICATION AREAS AND FURTHER READINGS
Marketing Strategy
White, M. C., Marin, D. B., Brazeal, D. V., and Friedman, W. H. (1997). 'The Evolution of Organizations: Suggestions from Complexity Theory about the Interplay between Natural Selection and Adaptation,' *Human Relations*, 50(11), 1383–1401.
Anderson, Philip (1999). 'Complexity Theory and Organization Science,' *Organization Science*, 10(3), Special Issue: Application of Complexity Theory to Organization Science, May–June, 216–232.
McKelvey, B. (1999). 'Complexity Theory in Organization Science: Seizing the Promise or Becoming a Fad?' *Emergence*, 1, 3–32.
Brown, S. L., and Eisenhardt, K. M. (1997). 'The Art of Continuous Change: Linking Complexity Theory and Time-Paced Evolution in Relentlessly Shifting Organizations,' *Administrative Science Quarterly*, 42(1), 1–34.

Marketing Management
Johnson, J. L., and Burton, B. K. (1994). 'Chaos and Complexity Theory for Management,' *Journal of Management Inquiry*, 3, 320–328.

BIBLIOGRAPHY
Byrne, David (1998). *Complexity Theory in the Social Sciences*. London: Routledge.

■ conative

DESCRIPTION
A term used to characterize the part of an individual's psychological processes that involves purposeful action.

KEY INSIGHTS
In contrast to cognitive (thinking, learning, processing information) and affective (feeling and emotion), the term conative is used in characterizing action that is inclined, attempted, or undertaken by an individual. Loyalty to a brand, for example, may be examined conatively as well as cognitively and affectively.

KEY WORDS Action, psychological processes

IMPLICATIONS
Marketers concerned with understanding consumer attitudes and preferences need to recognize how concepts or constructs such as brand loyalty may have multiple components, including a conative component, and not merely a cognitive or affective component. More generally, understanding consumers' psychological processes inclining them toward action is essential if the aim of the marketer is to influence consumer behavior.

APPLICATION AREAS AND FURTHER READINGS
Consumer Behavior
Back, K. J., and Parks, S. C. (2003). 'A Brand Loyalty Model Involving Cognitive, Affective, and Conative Brand Loyalty and Customer Satisfaction,' *Journal of Hospitality and Tourism Research* (Washington DC), 27(4), 419–435.
Dick, Alan S., and Basu, Kunal (1994). 'Customer Loyalty: Toward an Integrated Conceptual Framework,' *Journal of the Academy of Marketing Science*, 22(2), 99–113.

Marketing Strategy
Smith, Robert E., and Swinyard, William R. (1983). 'Attitude–Behavior Consistency: The Impact of Product Trial versus Advertising,' *Journal of Marketing Research*, 20(3), August, 257–267.

Marketing Education
Fritz, Robert L. (1991). 'The Association of Selected Conative Variables to Field-Dependence with Inferences for Reasoning Characteristics in Marketing Education,' Research Report No. ED341813, *Educational Resource Information Center*, 1–23.

BIBLIOGRAPHY
Kolbe, Kathy (1990). *The Conative Connection: Uncovering the Link between Who you Are and How you Perform*. Reading, Mass.: Addison-Wesley.

☐ concentrated marketing *see* niche marketing

☐ concept testing *see* new product development

☐ concorde fallacy *see* sunk cost fallacy

■ concurrent marketing

(also called integrated marketing)

DESCRIPTION
Marketing characterized by the systematic and simultaneous integration, planning, and development of marketing activities implemented by a firm over time.

KEY INSIGHTS
The major premise of concurrent marketing, as opposed to marketing efforts where the various steps and stages (e.g. new product development, production, new product introduction and promotion, and after-sales service) are viewed linearly, and planned sequentially and separately, is that the entire marketing process may be enhanced from the firm's as well as the customer's perspective if such steps or stages are planned simultaneously and systematically integrated. Similar to the notion of concurrent engineering which is aimed at reducing product development lead time and eliminating subsequent quality problems, current marketing, as advocated by Cespedes (1995), argues that marketing may also benefit in many ways by emphasizing simultaneous integration of marketing activities at the outset of, and throughout, marketing planning and implementation. When marketing activities and responsibilities are integrated throughout the organization and permeate every organizational function, the firm may be said to be adopting a total integrated marketing approach (see **total integrated marketing**).

KEY WORDS Marketing planning, marketing integration

IMPLICATIONS
Marketers should recognize that, while many marketing activities appear sequential, their effectiveness may be significantly enhanced by a concurrent marketing effort. Whether the emphasis is on new product

marketing or in analyzing existing marketing activities, a current marketing approach is becoming increasingly imperative to ensure both marketing effectiveness and efficiency.

APPLICATION AREAS AND FURTHER READINGS

Marketing Strategy

Schwartz, D. G. (2000). 'Concurrent Marketing Analysis: A Multi-agent Model for Product, Price, Place and Promotion,' *Marketing Intelligence and Planning*, 18(1), 24–29.

Kippenberger, T. (1998). 'Aligning Marketing Activities: Production, Sales and Service,' *The Antidote*, 3(5), 10–11.

Duncan, T., and Moriarty, S. (1997). *Driving Brand Value: Using Integrated Marketing to Manage Profitable Stakeholder Relationships*. New York: McGraw-Hill.

International Marketing

Sheth, J. N. (2001). 'From International to Integrated Marketing,' *Journal of Business Research*, 51, 5–9.

BIBLIOGRAPHY

Cespedes, Frank V. (1995). *Concurrent Marketing: Integrating Product, Sales, and Service*. Boston: Harvard Business School Press.

Hulbert, James M., Capon, Noel, and Piercy, Nigel (2003). *Total Integrated Marketing: Breaking the Bounds of the Function*. New York: Free Press.

☐ concurrent validity *see* validity

■ **confirmation bias**

DESCRIPTION

The tendency to seek out and select evidence in support of a belief, conjecture, or hypothesis and to ignore evidence or opportunities to gather evidence that could potentially work to disconfirm such views.

KEY INSIGHTS

Research on the confirmation bias suggests the tendency is one that is pervasive in human nature, where such a bias has the effect of maintaining one's beliefs, which may include views that are untrue (e.g. stereotypical views). As a result, approaches to compensate for the phenomenon have been developed, including the use of the scientific method which emphasizes efforts to disprove one's hypotheses.

KEY WORDS Decision making, judgment, **bias**, hypothesis testing

IMPLICATIONS

Marketers as well as consumers are equally prone to the human tendency to adopt the confirmation bias in their analyses and decision-making processes whenever beliefs, conjectures, or hypotheses (whether implicit or explicit) are evaluated or put to the test. For example, marketers that have developed an advertising campaign may seek out information that confirms the campaign is effective in creating excitement toward a particular brand and ignore information that suggests the campaign is largely ineffective or is even creating the opposite effect.

APPLICATION AREAS AND FURTHER READINGS
Consumer Behavior
Hoch, Stephen J., and Ha, Young-Won (1986). 'Consumer Learning: Advertising and the Ambiguity of Product Experience,' *Journal of Consumer Research*, 13(2), September, 221–233.

Marketing Management
Hoch, Stephen J., and Deighton, John (1989). 'Managing What Consumers Learn from Experience,' *Journal of Marketing*, 53(2), April, 1–20.
Wirtz, Jochen, and Mattila, Anna S. 'The Impact of Expected Variance in Performance on the Satisfaction Process,' *International Journal of Service Industry Management*, 12(4), October, 342–358.
McMillan, Jeffrey J., and White, Richard A. (1993). 'Auditors' Belief Revisions and Evidence Search: The Effect of Hypothesis Frame, Confirmation Bias, and Professional Skepticism,' *Accounting Review*, 68(3), July, 443–465.

BIBLIOGRAPHY
Fielder, Klaus (2000). 'On Mere Considering: The Subjective Exposure of Truth,' in Herbert Bless and Joseph P. Forgas (eds.), *The Message Within: The Role of Subjective Experience in Social Cognition and Behavior*. Philadelphia: Psychology Press, 13–36.
Klayman, Joshua, and Young-Won Ha (1987). 'Confimation, Disconfirmation, and Information in Hypothesis Testing,' *Psychological Review*, 94(2), 211–228.

■ confusion marketing

DESCRIPTION
A strategic marketing approach which involves making it difficult for consumers to make direct comparisons between a firm's and competitive offerings, thereby giving the firm a means of maintaining higher prices and profit margins than would otherwise be possible under conditions of easy comparisons of offerings.

KEY INSIGHTS
Research on the concept suggests that the concept of confusion marketing has been actively used by firms with offerings including credit cards, cellular (mobile) telephones, and banking products, with results that have had the effect of contributing to the maintenance of high product and service profit margins. When such conditions are present in a firm's marketing strategy, it may of course be questioned to what extent confusion marketing is actually intentional as opposed to an unintentional part of the strategy. Ultimately, negative consumer reactions may arise with such conditions to the extent consumers are dissatisfied or frustrated in their inability to make clear product comparisons on price and other important attributes given information provided by marketers. However, not all consumers are aware that such conditions may be the result of such an intentional marketing strategy.

KEY WORDS **Marketing strategy**, confusion, **value**

IMPLICATIONS
A strategic approach involving confusion marketing may be a completely viable approach to any firm operating in an industry characterized by wide arrays of niche offerings, for example. However, the approach is

ethically questionable as intentionally clouding transparency for product comparisons will ultimately work to a consumer's disadvantage in that the approach seeks to hide rather than expose the true value of various product offerings.

APPLICATION AREAS AND FURTHER READINGS
Marketing Strategy
Banyard, Peter (2001). 'Confusion Marketing,' *Credit Management*, April, 32–33.

Marketing Research
Drummond, Graeme, and Rule, Gordon (2005). 'Consumer Confusion in the UK Wine Industry,' *Journal of Wine Research*, 16(1), April, 55–64.

Marketing Education
Drummond, Graeme, (2004). 'Consumer Confusion: Reduction Strategies in Higher Education,' *International Journal of Educational Management*, 18(5), August, 317–323.

BIBLIOGRAPHY
Bond, Simon (2001). 'Brits in a Bristle Over Confusion Marketing,' *Media Life Magazine*, March 30. **http://www.medialifemagazine.com/news2001/mar01/mar26/ 5fri/ news6friday.html**. Accessed 20 July 2007.

■ congruity theory

DESCRIPTION
The name given to the quantitative model of Osgood and Tannenbaum (1955) of how a third-party observer might react, in terms of judgment, to a situation involving two contradicting parties or contradictory beliefs or behaviors.

KEY INSIGHTS
Congruity theory as formulated by Osgood and Tannenbaum (1955) proposes that an individual's observation of such a contradictory or inconsistent situation will lead to a motivation to reduce the associated dissonance by changing a judgment. If there were no incongruities, the individual would not experience any pressure to change a judgment but if there are incongruities, the level of pressure to change a judgment would be in relation to the level of incongruity.

KEY WORDS Judgment, contradictions, incongruity

IMPLICATIONS
As consumers are exposed to a tremendous amount of information about new and existing products, services, and brands, it is inevitable that consumers will at various points in time observe situations involving incongruities in behaviors, beliefs, or attitudes. For example, to the extent consumers believe that incongruities exist in a set of brand names, their evaluations of brand extensions may be influenced. Under such circumstances, concepts based on congruity theory may be useful to help understand the different ways in which consumers might react.

APPLICATION AREAS AND FURTHER READINGS
Consumer Behavior
Sirgy, M. Joseph (1982). 'Self-Concept in Consumer Behavior: A Critical Review,' *Journal of Consumer Research*, 9(3), December, 287–300.

Lorimor, E. S., and Dunn, S. Watson (1968). 'Reference Groups, Congruity Theory and Cross-Cultural Persuasion,' *Journal of Communication*, 18(4), 354.

Branding
Meyers-Levy, J., Louie, T. A., and Curren, M. T. (1994). 'How does the Congruity of Brand Names Affect Evaluations of Brand Name Extensions?' *Journal of Applied Psychology*, 79(1), 46–53.
Jamal, Ahmad, and Goode, Mark M. H. (2001). 'Consumers and Brands: A Study of the Impact of Self-Image Congruence on Brand Preference and Satisfaction,' *Marketing Intelligence & Planning*, 19(7), 482–492.

BIBLIOGRAPHY
Osgood, C., and Tannenbaum, P. (1955). 'The Principle of Congruity in the Prediction of Attitude Change,' *Psychology Review*, 62, 42–55.

■ conjunction fallacy

DESCRIPTION
A judgment bias where an individual overestimates the probability or likelihood for something involving two or more conditions relative to the probability or likelihood for something involving either condition alone.

KEY INSIGHTS
Pioneering research by Tversky and Kahneman (1982) identified and characterized the conjunction fallacy as a bias or judgment error that is a widespread human tendency. Specifically, the fallacy represents a violation of probability theory as the probability of two joined events A and B occurring can never exceed the probability of A or the probability of B. The conjunction fallacy is said to arise as a result of individuals using a representativeness heuristic in their judgment.

KEY WORDS Judgment, **bias**, fallacy, probabilities

IMPLICATIONS
Marketers must be aware of committing the conjunction fallacy in their judgments whenever they are involved in estimating probabilities associated with complex conditions. For example, the conjunction fallacy would occur in a manager's judging his or her young, professional customers as more likely to be people who read the *Financial Times* and own BMWs than individuals who own BMWs. Alternatively, in developing a new product, the conjunction fallacy would be committed if a marketer's estimate of the probability of successfully completing a multi-step new product development project was greater than the probabilities associated with successfully completing the project's individual steps.

APPLICATION AREAS AND FURTHER READINGS
New Product Development
Cooper, Lee G. (2000). 'Strategic Marketing Planning for Radically New Products,' *Journal of Marketing*, 64(1), January, 1–16.

BIBLIOGRAPHY
Tversky, A., and Kahneman, D. (1982). 'Judgments of and by Representativeness,' in D. Kahneman, P. Slovic, and A. Tversky (eds.), *Judgment under Uncertainty: Heuristics and Biases*. Cambridge: Cambridge University Press.

☐ **consensual validity** *see* validity

■ **conspicuous consumption**

DESCRIPTION

Purchasing or consuming goods for the purposes of displaying status or wealth and impressing others as opposed to satisfying a utilitarian need.

KEY INSIGHTS

Conceptually developed by economist Thorstein Veblen, conspicuous consumption captures the notion that some consumption behaviors are motivated fully by social factors. Originally examined in relation to the consumption behavior of upper-class society and supporting Veblen's theory of the leisure class (Veblen 1899), the term has since become used more broadly to refer to consumption behavior motivated strongly by the desire to display social status, prestige, or wealth.

KEY WORDS Social influences, consumption behavior

IMPLICATIONS

When a consumer's motivation to purchase or use a product or service is motivated more by social factors than need, conspicuous consumption can be said to be present in the consumer's buying and consumption behavior. An extreme example (based on fact) is when a consumer, in a highly social and mobile society, drives alone in a car and pretends to talk on his mobile phone, just to be seen by others doing so, but does so without having the telephone turned on! Marketers of products whose current and prospective consumers may potentially associate with status, prestige, and wealth should therefore seek to understand fully consumer motivations for purchase and consumption and leverage accordingly such knowledge in the development and implementation of such offerings as well as the associated strategies for their positioning, pricing, promotion, and distribution.

APPLICATION AREAS AND FURTHER READINGS

Marketing Strategy

Mason, R. (1998). *The Economics of Conspicuous Consumption.* Northampton, Mass.: Edward Elgar.

Bagwell, L. S., and Bernheim, B. D. (1996). 'Veblen Effects in a Theory of Conspicuous Consumption,' *American Economic Review*, 86, 349–373.

Consumer Behavior

Mason, R. (1981). *Conspicuous Consumption: A Study of Exceptional Consumer Behavior.* Farnborough: Gower.

O'Cass, A., and McEwen, H. (2004). 'Exploring Consumer Status and Conspicuous Consumption,' *Journal of Consumer Behaviour*, 4(1), 25–39.

Marketing Research

Mason, Roger S. (1982). 'Conspicuous Consumption: A Literature Review,' *European Journal of Marketing*, 18(3), 26–39.

BIBLIOGRAPHY

Veblen, Thorstein (1899). *Theory of the Leisure Class: An Economic Study in the Evolution of Institutions.* New York: Macmillan.

■ construal-level theory

DESCRIPTION

A theory proposing that individuals use more abstract and global mental models to represent information about distant future events and more concrete and local mental models to represent information about near future events.

KEY INSIGHTS

Construal-level theory (CLT), as developed in research by Trope and Liberman (2000, 2003), suggests that the spatial or temporal distance of social objects or events influences how individuals represent such objects or events. Specifically, when evaluating spatially distant events, CLT suggests that individuals will tend to use more central, abstract, and global features (i.e. high-level construals), and when evaluating near events, individuals will tend to use more peripheral, concrete, and local features (e.g. low-level construals). Supporting the theory is the view that removing an individual from the direct experience of an event makes information about the event less available and reliable, thereby leading individuals to rely more on prototypical information. When individuals use abstract mental models to characterize information concerning a distant event, they rely on general, superordinate, and essential features of the event. On the other hand, when individuals use concrete mental models to characterize information concerning a near event, they rely on contextual and incidental features of the event.

KEY WORDS Temporality, spatial distance

IMPLICATIONS

Marketers seeking to understand temporal influences on consumer behavior, such as how time can influence consumer evaluations of a new product for possible adoption, can benefit from a deeper knowledge of construal-level theory in that they may potentially be able to identify and predict systematic temporal influences on consumer behavior. In the context of consumer evaluation of new products or services, for example, it is found that, when thinking of using a new product in a distant future, consumers tend to put more weight on the benefits and less on the cost, or hassles, of using the new product. CLT, therefore, suggests important implications for marketers including the timing of market research and time-based advertising strategies.

APPLICATION AREAS AND FURTHER READINGS

Marketing Strategy

Ziamou, Paschalina, and Veryzer, Robert W. (2005). 'The Influence of Temporal Distance on Consumer Preferences for Technology-Based Innovations,' *Journal of Product Innovation Management*, 22(4), July, 336.

Lynch, John G., Jr., and Zauberman, Gal (2006). 'When Do You Want It? Time, Decisions, and Public Policy,' *Journal of Public Policy & Marketing*, 25, Spring, 67–78.

Marketing Research

Bonoma, Thomas V. (1985). 'Case Research in Marketing: Opportunities, Problems, and a Process,' *Journal of Marketing Research*, 22(2), May, 199–208.

Consumer Behavior
Kardes, Frank R., Cronley, Maria L., and Kim, John (2006). 'Construal-Level Effects on Preference Stability, Preference–Behavior Correspondence, and the Suppression of Competing Brands,' *Journal of Consumer Psychology*, 16(2), 135–144.

BIBLIOGRAPHY
Trope, Y., and Liberman, N. (2000). 'Temporal Construal and Time-Dependent Changes in Preference,' *Journal of Personality & Social Psychology*, 79, 876–889.
Trope, Y., and Liberman, N. (2003). 'Temporal Construal,' *Psychological Review*, 110, 403–421.

□ **construct validity** *see* validity

■ **consumer behavior, theory of**

DESCRIPTION
Theory or theories aimed at understanding, explaining, and predicting the behavior of consumers.

KEY INSIGHTS
As consumer behavior encompasses an extremely broad set of phenomena, consumer behavior theory is equally broad. While the aim of much consumer behavior theory is to provide a comprehensive theory for understanding, explaining, and predicting the bulk of consumer behavior, there have nevertheless been, and continue to be, many competing and complementary consumer behavior theories developed and advocated. Some economics-based consumer behavior theories, for example, adopt the view that consumers have utility functions which indicate their levels of satisfaction with any and all possible sets of goods and where such consumers then purchase goods to maximize those utilities within price and income constraints. Yet, it is also recognized in other theoretical perspectives on consumer behavior that consumers sometimes engage in satisficing behaviors (see **satisficing**), where they may use trial-and-error approaches in the purchase of goods, for example.

KEY WORDS Behavior, consumption

IMPLICATIONS
Marketers seeking a rigorous and critical understanding of consumer behavior may potentially benefit from a greater immersion in the rich body of consumer behavior theory-based research. Explaining and predicting consumer behavior is often very challenging, but adopting one or more theoretical perspectives provides the marketers with a means to test, evaluate, and compare actual behaviors with those suggested by particular consumer behavior theories.

APPLICATION AREAS AND FURTHER READINGS
Consumer Behavior
Assael, Henry (1997). 'Product Classification and the Theory of Consumer Behavior,' *Journal of the Academy of Marketing Science*, 2, 539–552.

Bettman, James R. (1979). *An Information Processing Theory of Consumer Behavior*. Reading, Mass.: Addison-Wesley.

Cohen, Joel B. (1968). 'Toward an Interpersonal Theory of Consumer Behavior.' *California Management Review*, 11, Spring, 73–80.

Duesenberry, James S. (1949). *Income, Saving, and the Theory of Consumer Behavior*. Cambridge, Mass.: Harvard University Press.

Georgescu-Roegen, Nicholas (1936). 'The Pure Theory of Consumer Behavior,' *Quarterly Journal of Economics*, 50, August, 545–593.

Michael, R. T., and Becker, G. S. (1973). 'On the New Theory of Consumer Behavior,' *Swedish Journal of Economics*, 75, 378–395.

Ratchford, B. T. (1975). 'The New Economic Theory of Consumer Behaviour: An Interpretive Essay,' *Journal of Consumer Research*, 2, 65–75.

BIBLIOGRAPHY
Blackwell, Roger D., Miniard, Paul W., and Engel, James F. (2001). *Consumer Behavior*, 9th edn. Fort Worth: Harcourt College Publishers.

■ consumer buyer behavior

DESCRIPTION
The purchase-related behavior of consumers.

KEY INSIGHTS
Consumer buyer behavior can be characterized in many ways, but primarily by the degree of consumer involvement and extent of perceived differences among brands. Common behavioral characterizations include: *complex buying behavior*, where consumer involvement in the purchase is high and where the consumer perceives many important differences among brands; *habitual buying behavior*, where consumer involvement in the purchase is low and where the consumer perceives few important differences among brands; *variety-seeking buyer behavior*, where consumer involvement in the purchase is low and where the consumer also perceives many important differences among brands, thereby leading to instances of brand switching for the purpose of experiencing variety; and *dissonance-reducing buyer behavior*, where consumer involvement in the purchase is high and where the consumer perceives few important differences among brands, thereby leading to instances where consumers are compelled to shop around for an expensive, infrequent, or risky purchase but then buy relatively quickly as a result of seeing little difference among brands.

KEY WORDS Buying decision behavior

IMPLICATIONS
Marketers must seek to understand the type of behavior involved in the consumer buying decision in order to be able to be effective in its timely influence. Recognizing the extent of buyer deliberation in the buying decision process can enable the marketer to provide appropriate marketing communications, such as where communications for toothpaste may be through a large shelf display denoting a good price but where

communications for a new electric toothbrush may be through print ads in health magazines where its benefits are able to be elaborated upon.

APPLICATION AREAS AND FURTHER READINGS

Online Marketing

Lohse, Gerald, Bellman, L. Steven, and Johnson, Eric J. (2000). 'Consumer Buying Behavior on the Internet: Findings from Panel Data,' *Journal of Interactive Marketing*, 14(1), February, 15–29.

Consumer Behavior

Belk, Russell W. (1975). 'Situational Variables and Consumer Behavior,' *Journal of Consumer Research*, 2(3), December, 157–164.

Burnkrant, Robert E., and Cousineau, Alain (1975). 'Informational and Normative Social Influence in Buyer Behavior,' *Journal of Consumer Research*, 2(3), December, 206–215.

Park, C. Whan, and Lessig, V. Parker (1981). 'Familiarity and its Impact on Consumer Decision Biases and Heuristics,' *Journal of Consumer Research*, 8(2), September, 223–231.

Marketing Strategy

Reddy, Allan C. (1997). *The Emerging High-Tech Consumer: A Market Profile and Marketing Strategy Implications*. Westport, Conn.: Quorum Books.

BIBLIOGRAPHY

Kotler, Philip, and Armstrong, Gary (2006). *Principles of Marketing*, 11th edn. Upper Saddle River, NJ: Pearson Education, Inc.

☐ **consumer choice, characteristics theory of** *see* characteristics theory

■ **consumer demand theory**

DESCRIPTION

Theory or theories aimed at understanding, explaining, and predicting how consumer demand changes in response to changes in related variables including the characteristics of goods and consumer purchasing ability.

KEY INSIGHTS

Consumer demand theory encompasses a broad base of theoretical research where the common aim is to understand, explain, and predict consumer demand in response to changes in one or more variables of influence including product price, competing product prices, and consumer income. While the foundation of consumer demand theory is based solidly in economics, application and extension of the theory now encompass a range of strategic marketing variables including branding and advertising.

KEY WORDS **Demand**, consumer response

IMPLICATIONS

An understanding of the basic principles of consumer demand theory as well as the associated methodological approaches involved can assist the marketer with performing a number of key tasks, namely, anticipating, stimulating, and meeting consumer demand for the firm's offerings. While there is a considerable body of theory on which to draw, marketers can rely on the particular chacteristics of their offerings to narrow their focus in putting relevant consumer demand theory to practical use.

APPLICATION AREAS AND FURTHER READINGS

Marketing Modeling
Banks, J., Blundell, R., and Lewbel, A. (1999). 'Quadratic Engel Curves and Consumer Demand,' *Review of Economics and Statistics*, 79, 527–39.
Arguea, N. M., Hsiao, C., and Taylor, G. A. (1994). 'Estimating Consumer Preferences using Market Data: An Application to US Automobile Demand,' *Journal of Applied Econometrics*, 9, 1–18.

Marketing Strategy
Brester, G. W., and Schroeder, T. C. (1995). 'The Impacts of Brand and Generic Advertising on Meat Demand,' *American Journal of Agricultural Economics*, 77, November, 969–979.

Marketing Research
Clements, W. K., Selvanathan, A., and Selvanathan, S. (1996). 'Applied Demand Analysis: A Survey,' *Economic Record*, 72, 63–81.

Marketing Management
Mark, John, Brown, Frank, and Pierson, B. J. (1981). 'Consumer Demand Theory, Goods and Characteristics: Breathing Empirical Content into the Lancastrian Approach,' *Managerial and Decision Economics*, 2(1), March, 32–39.

BIBLIOGRAPHY
Goldberger, Arthur S. (1987). *Functional Form & Utility: A Review of Consumer Demand Theory*. Boulder, Colo.: Westview Press Inc.

☐ **consumer goods** *see* goods

■ **consumer marketing**

(also called business-to-consumer marketing or B2C marketing)

DESCRIPTION
Marketing aimed at the consumers who are making marketplace decisions about a product or service and who are typically also users of the product or service.

KEY INSIGHTS
Consumer marketing encompasses all marketing activity where individuals, families, households, and the like—as opposed to businesses, governments, and other institutions—comprise the market for the organization's products or services and are the focus of its marketing efforts. In contrast to business-to-business marketing, where buyers tend to be sophisticated and products complex, consumer marketing may involve less critical customers and simpler products. Yet, the range of consumer offerings is so diverse and competition often so intense that marketers need to understand carefully consumer buyer behavior in order to develop marketing strategies that enable the firm to meet customer needs more effectively and profitably than competitors.

KEY WORDS Consumers, users

IMPLICATIONS

Marketing to consumers presents the marketer with many challenges and opportunities in terms of identifying, reaching, and meeting the needs of potential customers. It is therefore imperative for consumer marketers to understand better the intricacies of consumer buyer behavior (see **consumer buyer behavior**), the buyer decision process (see **buyer decision process**), and buyer readiness (see **buyer influence/readiness**) in order to achieve the firm's consumer marketing objectives.

APPLICATION AREAS AND FURTHER READINGS

Online Marketing

Peterson, Robert A., Balasubramanian, Sridhar, and Bronnenberg, Bart J. (1997). 'Exploring the Implications of the Internet for Consumer Marketing,' *Journal of the Academy of Marketing Science*, 25, Fall, 329–346.

Deighton, J. (1997). 'Commentary on Exploring the Implications of the Internet for Consumer Marketing,' *Journal of the Academy of Marketing Science*, 25, Fall, 347–351.

Lee, Matthew K. O., and Turban, Efraim (2001). 'A Trust Model for Consumer Internet Shopping,' *International Journal of Electronic Commerce*, 6(1), Fall, 75–91.

Smith, Michael D. (2002). 'The Impact of Shopbots on Electronic Markets,' *Journal of the Academy of Marketing Science*, 30(4), 446–454.

Pricing

Gijsbrechts, Els (1992). *Prices and Pricing Research in Consumer Marketing: Some Recent Developments*. Antwerp: Universitaire Faculteiten St Ignatius, Universiteit Antwerpen, Departement Economische Wetenschappen.

BIBLIOGRAPHY

Deshpande, R., and Zaltman, G. (1987). 'A Comparison of Factors Affecting Use of Marketing Information in Consumer and Industrial Firms,' *Journal of Marketing Research*, 24, February, 114–118.

Fern, Edward F., and Brown, James R. (1984). 'The Industrial/Consumer Marketing Dichotomy: A Case of Insufficient Justification,' *Journal of Marketing*, 48(2), Spring, 68–77.

☐ **consumer-oriented marketing** *see* enlightened marketing
☐ **consumer product classifications** *see* product classifications, consumer

■ consumer satisfaction theory

DESCRIPTION

Theory or theories aimed at understanding and explaining the satisfaction of consumers in terms of their evaluations of product performance or service use relative to pre-purchase expectations.

KEY INSIGHTS

Consumer satisfaction theories offer the view that satisfaction/dissatisfaction occurs in relation to the extent there is a case of confirmation or a certain type of disconfirmation. More specifically, confirmation occurs when the product or service conforms to exactly what was expected. In contrast, there may also be a form of disconfirmation, where disconfirmation is said to be negative when the product or service performance is worse than expected and positive when performance is better than expected. In addition to the development of broad theoretical perspectives on consumer satisfaction, there is also a considerable amount of attention by both researchers and practitioners on conceptual and practical issues associated with satisfaction management and measurement, where such efforts are often examined in terms of customer satisfaction. (See **customer satisfaction.**)

KEY WORDS Product evaluations, confirmation

IMPLICATIONS
Satisfaction of consumers is often a key consideration in evaluating the degree of success for a firm's marketing strategies and offerings. As such, marketers should not only seek to understand better how consumers make judgments about satisfaction but how to appropriately measure consumer satisfaction to obtain sufficiently strong insights regarding the process and state of consumer satisfaction for any of a firm's product or service offerings.

APPLICATION AREAS AND FURTHER READINGS
Marketing Modeling
Tse, David K., and Wilton, Peter C. (1988). 'Models of Consumer Satisfaction Formation: An Extension,' *Journal of Marketing Research*, 25(2), 204–12.

Consumer Behavior
Woodruff, Robert B. (1983). 'Modeling Consumer Satisfaction Processes Using Experience-Based Norms,' *Journal of Marketing Research*, 20, 296–304.
Stayman, Douglas M., Alden, Dana L., and Smith, Karen H. (1992). 'Some Effects of Schematic Processing on Consumer Expectations and Disconfirmation Judgments,' *Journal of Consumer Research*, 19(2), September, 240–255.

BIBLIOGRAPHY
Oliver, Richard L. (1997). *Satisfaction: A Behavioral Perspective on the Consumer*. New York: Irwin/McGraw-Hill.

■ consumer sovereignty

DESCRIPTION
The notion that consumers are the best judge of their own welfare.

KEY INSIGHTS
As most goods are produced to satisfy consumer wants, the concept of consumer sovereignty embraces the notion that consumers, as opposed to goods producers, are in the best position to dictate which goods producers are to provide. The principle is central in much of economic analysis where consumers are viewed as having power in directing market economies.

KEY WORDS Consumer welfare

IMPLICATIONS

As a common saying in marketing is 'the customer is king,' most marketers recognize and accept the power of the consumer in dictating the provision of offerings by a firm. Yet, astute marketers also recognize the power of marketing to influence consumer behavior through advertising and other means where consumer demands are driven to some extent by marketing efforts.

APPLICATION AREAS AND FURTHER READINGS

Marketing Strategy

Dixon, D. F. (1992). 'Consumer Sovereignty, Democracy and the Marketing Concept: A Macromarketing Perspective,' *Canadian Journal of Administrative Sciences*, 9(2), 116–125.

Firat, A. Fuat, Dholakia, Nikhilesh, and Venkatesh, Alladi (1995). 'Marketing in a Postmodern World,' *European Journal of Marketing*, 29(1), January, 40–56.

Knights, David, Sturdy, Andrew, and Morgan, Glenn (1994). 'The Consumer Rules? An Examination of the Rhetoric and "Reality" of Marketing in Financial Services,' *European Journal of Marketing*, 28(3), March, 42–54.

Holt, Douglas B. (2002). 'Why Do Brands Cause Trouble? A Dialectical Theory of Consumer Culture and Branding,' *Journal of Consumer Research*, 29, 70–90.

Marketing Research

Kroeber-Riel, Werner (1979). 'Activation Research: Psychobiological Approaches in Consumer Research,' *Journal of Consumer Research*, 5(4), March, 240–250.

Mazis, Michael B., Staelin, Richard, Beales, Howard, and Salop, Steven (1981). 'A Framework for Evaluating Consumer Information Regulation,' *Journal of Marketing*, 45(1), Winter, 11–21.

BIBLIOGRAPHY

Lowery, David (1998). 'Consumer Sovereignty and Quasi-Market Failure,' *Journal of Public Administration Research and Theory*, 8(2), 137–172.

Penz, Peter G. (1986). *Consumer Sovereignty and Human Interests*. Cambridge: Press Syndicate of the University of Cambridge.

■ consumer-to-business

(also called C2B)

DESCRIPTION

Transactional or other marketing activity originating from consumers and directed to business.

KEY INSIGHTS

While consumer-to-business (C2B) transactions occur in a wide range of marketing contexts, C2B mainly refers to transactions and marketing activity conducted online. In particular, the term builds upon the notion that the internet provides consumers with an enhanced ability to transact their business effectively and efficiently in comparison to that which is typically possible through traditional transaction channels (e.g. via retail or bricks-and-mortar firm transactions).

KEY WORD Transactions

IMPLICATIONS

Although the C2B concept is not entirely limited to application and relevance to online marketing, the term emphasizes the need for marketers to manage, facilitate, and respond effectively to consumer-to-business transactional activity. Whether by providing the consumer with an online means to submit new product ideas to the firm or offer suggestions for the incremental improvement of existing offerings, marketers may clearly benefit by balancing business-to-consumer marketing with a C2B approach as well.

APPLICATION AREAS AND FURTHER READINGS

Online Marketing

Neto, A., and Lucena, C. (2000). 'CommercePipe: Consumer to Business Commerce Channels on the Internet,' *SEA* (Software Engineering Applications), IASTED, Las Vegas, October.

Services Marketing

Shemwell, Donald J., Cronin, J. Joseph, and Bullard, William R. (1994). 'Relational Exchange in Services: An Empirical Investigation of Ongoing Customer Service-Provider Relationships,' *International Journal of Service Industry Management*, 5(3), August, 57–68.

Marketing Management

Law, Monica, Lau, Theresa, and Wong, Y. H. (2003). 'From Customer Relationship Management to Customer-Managed Relationship: Unraveling the Paradox with a Co-creative Perspective,' *Marketing Intelligence & Planning*, February, 21(1), 51–60.

BIBLIOGRAPHY

Eid, R., and Trueman, M. (2002). 'The Internet: New International Marketing Issues,' *Management Research News*, 25(12), 54–67.

■ consumer-to-consumer

(also called C2C)

DESCRIPTION

Transactional or other marketing-related activity originating from consumers and directed to other consumers.

KEY INSIGHTS

While consumer-to-consumer (C2C) transactions occur in a wide range of marketing contexts (as with C2B transactions), the main emphasis of the C2C concept is online transactional and marketing-related activity. In particular, the term builds on the notion that the internet provides consumers with an enhanced ability to articulate their views, needs, or wants regarding any marketing-related topic or general business transaction with other consumers relative to traditional or offline means (e.g. simple word-of-mouth communication).

KEY WORDS Transactions, communication

IMPLICATIONS

Although the C2C concept is not entirely limited to application and relevance to online marketing, the term clearly suggests an opportunity for marketers to incorporate consumer-to-consumer transactional activity into the firm's marketing processes. Whether by providing consumers with an online means to conduct business transactions with each other as an integral part of a firm's business model or by facilitating consumer-to-consumer communications regarding any marketing-related issue whatsoever, marketers clearly have an opportunity to integrate both traditional and online marketing approaches with a growing array of C2C approaches.

APPLICATION AREAS AND FURTHER READINGS

Marketing Research
Martin, C. L. (1996). 'Consumer-to-Consumer Relationships: Satisfaction with Other Consumers' Public Behaviours,' *Journal of Consumer Affairs*, 30(1), 146–169.

Services Marketing
Harris, Kim, and Baron, Steve (2004). 'Consumer-to-Consumer Conversations in Service Settings,' *Journal of Service Research*, 6(3), February, 287–303.

Online Marketing
Bailey, A. A. (2004). 'Thiscompanysucks.com: The Use of the Internet in Negative Consumer-to-Consumer Articulations,' *Journal of Marketing Communications*, 10(3), 169–182.

BIBLIOGRAPHY
Martin, C. L., and Clark, T. (1996). 'Networks of Customer-to-Customer Relationships in Marketing: Conceptual Foundations and Implications,' in Dawn Iacobucci (ed.), *Networks in Marketing*. Thousand Oaks, Calif.: Sage Publications, 342–366.

■ consumerism

DESCRIPTION
Activity advocating the rights and power of consumers in relation to sellers.

KEY INSIGHTS
The most commonly understood meaning of the concept of consumerism is that of a movement of organized advocacy of consumer rights and power relative to sellers, where the aim is to protect and improve consumer rights. Yet an alternate meaning of the term is that of equating personal happiness with the purchase and consumption of material goods. However, in the narrower marketing context, the term emphasizes activities by governments, independent organizations, or businesses to enhance consumer rights.

KEY WORDS Consumer rights, consumer advocacy

IMPLICATIONS
As most marketers face a dynamic external environment, it is essential that marketers ongoingly monitor, assess, anticipate, and respond effectively to general consumerism trends as well as specific externally led activities aimed at protecting or improving consumer rights. While the demands consumerism places upon marketers are clearly context specific, marketers should seek to continually understand the customer perspective as well as that of organizations involved in the advocacy of

consumer rights, whether independent or within the marketer's regulatory or legal environment.

APPLICATION AREAS AND FURTHER READINGS

Marketing Strategy
Firat, A. Fuat, Dholakia, Nikhilesh, and Venkatesh, Alladi (1995). 'Marketing in a Postmodern World,' *European Journal of Marketing*, 29(1), 40–56.
Kotler, P. (1972). 'What Consumerism Means for Marketers,' *Harvard Business Review*, 50, 48–57.

Consumer Behavior
Barksdale, Hiram C., and Darden, William R. (1972). 'Consumer Attitudes toward Marketing and Consumerism,' *Journal of Marketing*, 36(4), October, 28–35.

BIBLIOGRAPHY
Nicoulaud, B. M. M. (1987). 'Consumerism and Marketing Management's Responsibility,' *European Journal of Marketing*, 21(3), 7–15.
Miles, Steven (1998). *Consumerism—as a Way of Life*. London: Sage Publications.
Campbell, C. (1987). *The Romantic Ethic and the Spirit of Modern Consumerism*. Oxford: Blackwell.

☐ content validity *see* validity

■ context effect

DESCRIPTION
Any influence of circumstances, conditions, events, objects, or information surrounding an event or other stimulus on an individual's response to the stimulus, where responses include an individual's perceptions and cognitions.

KEY INSIGHTS
To the extent that an individual's response to a stimulus is influenced by its context, the ability to generalize how individuals will respond to the same stimuli given other contexts will be an issue. As such, a primary concern with context effects is that their presence may not be sufficiently recognized, considered, or controlled for when seeking to generalize beyond a particular context. For example, the effect of the ambience of an upscale restaurant may influence a consumer's perception of the food's taste to such a point that the same food may be perceived as less tasty when served at a very plain restaurant.

KEY WORDS Cognition, perception

IMPLICATIONS
As context may have an influence on the cognitions and perceptions of consumers for a variety of product and service evaluations, marketers should strive to be aware of the ways in which different contexts might affect consumer responses favorably and unfavorably. Where marketers have control over context, the context itself may be potentially manipulated to achieve a desired effect. Where there is little or no control over context, marketers may seek to consider how context effects may act to limit understanding, explaining, or predicting consumer responses to

particular marketing actions. For example, adverse weather at the time of a consumer survey on holiday travel planning may lead to different consumer views on desirable locations for travel.

APPLICATION AREAS AND FURTHER READINGS

Consumer Behavior

Levy, Joan Meyers, and Tybout, Alice M. (1997). 'Context Effects at Encoding and Judgment in Consumption Settings: The Role of Cognitive Resources,' *Journal of Consumer Research*, 24(1), June, 1-14.

Klein, Noreen M., and Yadav, Manjit S. (1989). 'Context Effects on Effort and Accuracy in Choice: An Enquiry into Adaptive Decision Making,' *Journal of Consumer Research*, 15(4), March, 411–421.

BIBLIOGRAPHY

Prelec, Drazen, Wernerfelt, Birger, and Zettelmeyer, Florian (1997). 'The Role of Inference in Context Effects: Inferring What You Want from What is Available,' *Journal of Consumer Research*, 24(1), June, 118-125.

■ contingency theory

DESCRIPTION

Theory or theories adopting the view that no single organizational structure or strategic approach is inherently more effective or efficient than all others.

KEY INSIGHTS

The contingency theory view of organization and strategy is that there is no one best way to devise a given organizational (or otherwise technical) process within the organization. Rather, appropriate structures and strategies to be adopted are viewed as contingent on a variety of contextual factors such as the nature of the technological environment in which the firm operates, the size of the organization, etc.

KEY WORDS Organizational design, strategy development

IMPLICATIONS

The widely varying nature of marketers' operating environments clearly suggests an appreciation by marketers for a contingency theory perspective to organizational process and strategy. While the approach recognizes the organizational and decision-making challenges facing a manager, knowledge of research adopting such a view can also provide managers with a basis for understanding better and evaluating different organizational and strategic options available to the firm.

APPLICATION AREAS AND FURTHER READINGS

Marketing Strategy

Ruekert, Robert W., Walker, Orville C., Jr., and Roering, Kenneth J. (1985). 'The Organization of Marketing Activities: A Contingency Theory of Structure and Performance,' *Journal of Marketing*, 49(1), Winter, 13-25.

Balkin, D. B., and Gomez-Mejia, L. R. (1987). 'Toward a Contingent Theory of Compensation Strategy,' *Strategic Management Journal*, 8, 169-182.

Hofer, C. W. (1975). 'Toward a Contingency Theory of Business Strategy,' *Academy of Management Journal*, 18, 784-810.

Marketing Management
Ferrell, O. C., and Gresham, Larry G. (1985). 'A Contingency Framework for Understanding Ethical Decision Making in Marketing,' *Journal of Marketing*, 49(3), Summer, 87–96.

BIBLIOGRAPHY
Donaldson, Lex (2001). *The Contingency Theory of Organizations*. Thousand Oaks, Calif.: Sage Publications.
Burns, T., and Stalker, G. M. (1961). *The Management of Innovation*. London: Tavistock.
Lawrence, P. R., and Lorsch, J. W. (1967). *Organization and Environment*. Cambridge, Mass.: Harvard University Press.

■ contingency theory of management accounting

DESCRIPTION

A theory in which many variables are considered to have a conceptual relationship with the design of appropriate management approaches, including approaches for performance measurement, thereby suggesting considerable room for the exercise of managerial judgment.

KEY INSIGHTS

Based on research by Otley (1980), the theory puts forth the view that there is no universally appropriate accounting system applicable to all organizations in all circumstances. As such, the theory's contingency-based view suggests an imperative for management accountants to identify and assess the impact of contingent variables on the design of a management control system. Contributions of the theory, however, are more along the lines of being able to identify better certain contingent variables than on increased ability to assess their impact.

KEY WORDS Management approaches, control, contingencies

IMPLICATIONS

The theory provides a broad basis for identifying and evaluating appropriate approaches for marketing as well as organizational management and control. For example, the theory may suggest that the effectiveness of managerial use of a directive, authoritarian leadership style is highest only under certain conditions, such as when leader–member relations are either very favorable or very unfavorable but not under intermediate conditions. Marketing managers and strategists may therefore benefit from understanding how various conditions suggested by theory can potentially influence the choice for and effective use of different managerial control approaches.

APPLICATION AREAS AND FURTHER READINGS

Marketing Management
Jaworski, Bernard J. (1988). 'Toward a Theory of Marketing Control: Environmental Context, Control Types, and Consequences,' *Journal of Marketing*, 52(3), July, 23–39.
Jaworski, Bernard J., Stathakopoulos, Vlasis, and Krishnan, H. Shanker (1993). 'Control Combinations in Marketing: Conceptual Framework and Empirical Evidence,' *Journal of Marketing*, 57(1), January, 57–69.

BIBLIOGRAPHY
Ginsberg, Ari, and Venkatraman, N. (1985). 'Contingency Perspectives of Organizational Strategy: A Critical Review of the Empirical Research,' *Academy of Management Review*, 10(3), July, 421-434.
Otley, D. (1980). 'The Contingency Theory of Management Accounting: Achievement and Prognosis,' *Accounting, Organizations and Society*, 5(4), 413-428.

☐ contractual VMS (vertical marketing system) *see* channel arrangement

☐ contrarian marketing *see* unconventional marketing

■ contrast effect

DESCRIPTION

Any effect of contrasting stimuli on individual perception, cognition, or resulting individual performance or action.

KEY INSIGHTS

In many ways, contrast effects are widely present in terms of their role in, and influence on, individual perception and cognition. The study and influence of contrast effects encompasses a wide range of consumer behavior research, although a primary aim of much contrast effect-related research is concerned with implications for consumer judgment.

KEY WORDS Stimuli, perception

IMPLICATIONS

Marketers seeking a deeper understanding of consumer behavior relative to their offerings may potentially benefit from a greater knowledge of contrast effect-related research by obtaining insights into more effective marketing strategies and/or tactical practices. For example, to the extent that marketer-controllable contrast effects are systematically related to elements of consumer behavior, such as in the use of a contrasting color to enhance awareness of a firm's product relative to those of competitors, marketers can develop communication approaches that not only use but seek to amplify such effects.

APPLICATION AREAS AND FURTHER READINGS

Consumer Behavior

Novemsky, Nathan, and Ratner, Rebecca (2003). 'The Time Course and Impact of Consumers' Erroneous Beliefs about Hedonic Contrast Effects,' *Journal of Consumer Research*, 29(4), 507-516.

Stapel, Diederik A., Koomen, Willem, and Velthuijsen, Aart S. (1998). 'Assimilation or Contrast? Comparison Relevance, Distinctness, and the Impact of Accessible Information on Consumer Judgments,' *Journal of Consumer Psychology*, 7(1), 1-24.

Meyers-Levy, Joan, and Sternthal, Brian (1993). 'A Two-Factor Explanation of Assimilation and Contrast Effects,' *Journal of Marketing Research*, 30(3), August, 359-368.

BIBLIOGRAPHY
Lynch, John G., Chakravarti, Dipankar, and Mitra, Anusree (1991). 'Contrast Effects in Consumer Judgments: Changes in Mental Representations or in the Anchoring of Rating Scales?' *Journal of Consumer Research*, 18, December, 284-297.

☐ convenience product *see* product classifications, consumer

■ convergence marketing

DESCRIPTION

Marketing emphasizing strategies for reaching 'the new hybrid' consumer who combines e-business and traditional business offerings to suit their tastes.

KEY INSIGHTS

Developed by Wind, Mahajan, and Gunther (2002) in a book by the same name, convergence marketing is characterized by five areas termed the 'five Cs': customerization, or convergence of customized and standardized offerings; community, or convergence of virtual and physical communities; channels, or seamless convergence of call, click, and visit; competitive value, or convergence of new and traditional competitive value equations and pricing models; and choice tools, or convergence of new search engines and decision tools for consumers and company-provided advice. In essence, convergence marketing advocates the view that marketers should develop marketing strategies to allow consumers to 'pick and choose' how they wish to receive and use information which, increasingly, involves online and offline approaches.

KEY WORDS Hybrid consumers

IMPLICATIONS

While many firms are increasingly engaging in online marketing activities, convergence marketing suggests that firms should find ways to seamlessly integrate their online and offline (e.g. traditional) marketing activities to satisfy the needs of the growing numbers of 'hybrid' consumers. To be sure, some offerings such as music are increasingly evaluated and purchased online and offline, while other traditional offerings such as toothpaste may have little need for online marketing support, but as the scope of the marketing effort increases to encompass information and value-added offerings surrounding basic product offerings (e.g. dental hygiene information in association with toothpaste), a convergence marketing approach is increasingly suggested. (See also **hybrid marketing** and **fusion marketing** for approaches conceptually similar to convergence marketing).

APPLICATION AREAS AND FURTHER READINGS

Marketing Strategy
Vaccaro, V., and Cohn, D. Y. (2004). 'The Evolution of Business Models and Marketing Strategies in the Music Industry,' *International Journal on Media Management*, 6(1&2), 46–58.
Dawson, R. (2003). *Living Networks: Leading your Company, Customers, and Partners in the Hyper-Connected Economy*. Upper Saddle River, NJ: Financial Times Prentice Hall.

BIBLIOGRAPHY
Wind, Yoram, Mahajan, Vijay, and Gunther, Robert E. (2002). Convergence Marketing: Strategies for Reaching the New Hybrid Consumer. Upper Saddle River, NJ: Financial Times Prentice Hall.

☐ **convergent validity** *see* validity

☐ **conviction** *see* buyer influence/readiness

☐ **cooperative game theory** *see* game theory

■ cooperative marketing

(also called comarketing, cross-marketing, joint marketing, partnership marketing, reciprocal marketing, or symbiotic marketing)

DESCRIPTION
Alliances between organizations for sharing in the responsibility of marketing their respective offerings with the aim of achieving a common objective.

KEY INSIGHTS
Firms engaging in cooperative or comarketing alliances and partnerships with other firms, whether in the same or different industries, may do so for any number of reasons including achieving greater marketing scale economies, pooling complementary assets or competencies, and more easily accessing new markets or market segments. Such marketing alliances among firms may be short or long term in duration, with the stability of the alliance often being dependent on the relative balance of power between the alliance partners as well as the ongoing strategic importance of the common marketing objectives to each.

Another meaning of cooperative marketing refers to the marketing efforts of cooperatives, or enterprises or organizations owned collectively by individual or organizational members and where it is operated for the benefit of its members (e.g. farm cooperatives, electrical cooperatives). While discussed less frequently in the marketing literature, the ambiguity associated with the term suggests it is essential to know the context in which the term is used in order to understand its intended meaning.

KEY WORDS Marketing alliances, partnerships

IMPLICATIONS
While it may be easy to view other firms in the same industry as competitors, or even fierce adversaries, marketers should also consider the possibility that marketing objectives may be able to be effectively pursued through a comarketing approach with one or more of such firms. An example is the case of two competing newspaper firms in Seattle that decided to engage in comarketing by sharing distribution resources (e.g. trucks) as a means to reduce their respective distribution costs while also making it easier to expand the distribution of their respective newspapers.

APPLICATION AREAS AND FURTHER READINGS
Marketing Strategy
Dowling, G., and Robinson, C. (1990). 'Strategic Partnership Marketing,' in *Gower Handbook of Logistics and Distribution Management*, 4th edn. Aldershot: Gower.
Adler L. (1966). 'Symbiotic Marketing,' *Harvard Business Review*, 44, November–December, 59–71.

Vardarajan, P. R., and Rajaratnam, D. (1986). 'Symbiotic Marketing Revisited,' *Journal of Marketing*, 50, January, 7–17.

International Marketing
McCutchen, W. W., and Swamidass, P. M. (1998). 'Explaining the Differences in Domestic and Cross-Boundary Strategic Alliances in the Pharmaceutical/Biotech Industry,' *International Journal of Technology Management*, 15(3–5), 490–506.

Tourism marketing
Standeven, J. (1997). 'Sport Tourism: Joint Marketing. A Starting Point for Beneficial Synergies,' *Journal of Vacation Marketing*, 4(1), 39–51.
Okoroafo, S. (1989). 'Cooperative Marketing,' in S. F. Witt and L. Moutinho (eds.), *Tourism Marketing and Management Handbook*. Hemel Hempstead: Prentice-Hall, 79–82.

BIBLIOGRAPHY
Bucklin, L. P., and Sengupta, S. (1993). 'Organizing Successful Co-marketing Alliances,' *Journal of Marketing*, 57, 32–46.

☐ copycat marketing *see* me-too marketing
☐ copyright *see* intellectual property
☐ core benefit *see* product levels

■ corporate marketing

DESCRIPTION
A marketing philosophy and function emphasizing an integrated approach to marketing at the institutional level.

KEY INSIGHTS
Corporate marketing is considered by its proponents including Balmer (1998) to be more of a philosophy of marketing than a marketing function. Its philosophical emphasis is a strong organizational concern with multiple past, present, and future exchange relationships of the organization with multiple stakeholders, where stakeholders may be individuals, groups, and/or networks. While the term suggests applicability to corporations defined in the narrow sense (i.e. registered legal entitities which are given similar legal rights to that of a natural person), the term adopts a broader definition of corporate (e.g. any group of individuals acting as a whole) and therefore suggests that the philosophical approach is applicable to a wide range of entities including non-profit organizations and business alliances. As there are a number of marketing concepts that are concerned with marketing activities at the corporate level (e.g. corporate branding, corporate identity, and corporate communications), corporate marketing can therefore be viewed as an 'umbrella' concept that seeks to synthesize multiple corporate-level concepts.

KEY WORDS Institutions, marketing integration

IMPLICATIONS
Marketers concerned with increased organizational effectiveness in exchange relationships with multiple stakeholders may benefit from a

greater understanding of the concept and principles of corporate marketing. Even though corporate marketing is much more of a philosophy than a function, increased adoption of the philosophy by marketers within the organization may ultimate lead marketers to become more effective at orchestrating multiple marketing elements at the corporate level and below.

APPLICATION AREAS AND FURTHER READINGS

Marketing Strategy
Wilson, M. A. (2001). 'Understanding Organizational Culture and Implications for Corporate Marketing,' *European Journal of Marketing*, 35(3–4), 353–367.

Marketing Management
Keller, K. L., and Aaker, D. A. (1997). 'Managing the Corporate Brand: The Effect of Corporate Marketing Activity on Consumer Evaluations of Brand Extensions,' Working Paper Report No. 97-106, May, Cambridge, Mass.: Marketing Science Institute.

Services Marketing
McDonald, M. H. D., De Chernatony, L., and Harris, F. (2001). 'Corporate Marketing and Service Brands: Moving beyond the Fast-Moving Consumer Goods Model,' *European Journal of Marketing*, 35(3–4), 335–352.

International Marketing
Farrelly, F. J., Quester, P. G., and Burton, R. (1997). 'Integrating Sports Sponsorship into the Corporate Marketing Function: An International Comparative Study,' *International Marketing Review*, 14(3), 170–182.

BIBLIOGRAPHY
Balmer, J. M. T. (1998). 'Corporate Identity and the Advent of Corporate Marketing,' *Journal of Marketing Management*, 14, 963–996.
Balmer, J. M. T. (2001). 'Corporate Identity, Corporate Branding and Corporate Marketing: Seeing through the Fog,' *European Journal of Marketing*, 35(3–4), 248–291.

☐ **corporate VMS (vertical marketing system)** *see* channel arrangement

■ cost

DESCRIPTION
Financial or other resources which are given up to obtain something via purchase, exchange, or production.

KEY INSIGHTS
Costs can be characterized many ways. Common characterizations of costs include: *fixed costs*—costs that remain the same regardless of a firm's production output or sales volume; *variable costs*—costs that vary in proportion to a firm's production output or sales volume; *sunk costs*—costs which cannot be recovered (as when a firm has unrecoverable costs when it withdraws a product from a market); *opportunity costs*—the value of forgone alternative actions (e.g. actions implemented at the expense of others); *transaction costs*—costs other than price (e.g. time) which are

incurred in the purchase or exchange of products or services; and *switching costs*—costs (e.g. financial, time) that are incurred by a consumer in the process of changing from one product to another.

KEY WORDS Purchase, exchange, production

IMPLICATIONS
As cost management is often part of a marketer's responsibility, a detailed knowledge of the nature of the various costs associated with marketing efforts is essential. In addition, beyond price, marketers need to understand and appreciate the extent of different types of costs that a consumer incurs or experiences in relation to the purchase of the firm's offerings. For example, consumers may pay a low ticket price when flying on a low-cost airline but the transaction may also involve experiencing extremely long queues and delays when checking in. In other instances, switching costs may be a deterrent to consumers, as in the case of banking, where consumers may experience significant switching costs (e.g. time and effort) to change from one bank to another.

APPLICATION AREAS AND FURTHER READINGS
Marketing Strategy
Sutton, J. (1991). *Sunk Cost and Market Structure: Pride Competition, Advertising, and the Evolution of Concentration.* Cambridge, Mass.: MIT Press.
Moorthy, K. S., and Srinivasan, K. (1995). 'Signaling Quality with a Money-Back Guarantee: The Role of Transaction Costs,' *Marketing Science*, 14(1), 442–466.
Phillips, Lynn W., Chang, Dae R., and Buzzell, Robert D. (1983). 'Product Quality, Cost Position and Business Performance: A Test of Some Key Hypotheses,' *Journal of Marketing*, 47(2), Spring, 26–43.

Marketing Management
Nilssen, Tore (1992). 'Two Kinds of Consumer Switching Costs,' *RAND Journal of Economics*, 23, 579–589.

BIBLIOGRAPHY
Buzzell, R. D., and Farris, P. W. (1977). 'Marketing Cost in Consumer Goods Industries,' in H. Thorelli (ed.), *Strategy, Structure, Performance.* Bloomington, Ind.: Indiana University Press, 122–145.

☐ **cost-plus pricing** *see* pricing strategies
☐ **cost strategy** *see* strategies, generic

■ counter-marketing

DESCRIPTION
Marketing that is aimed at nullifying the marketing efforts of another.

KEY INSIGHTS
In contrast to demarketing's emphasis on reducing demand (see **demarketing**), counter-marketing's aim is the elimination or reversal of demand created by the marketing efforts of another (e.g. firm, organization, industry). Thus, some public health organizations engage in counter-marketing to nullify the demand for cigarettes created by tobacco

industry marketing. In an effort to do so, a counter-marketing approach can involve drawing consumers' attention to the marketing strategies employed by the marketer(s) (e.g. using advertising that shows smokers as beautiful, popular, intelligent, and sophisticated) and then providing information demonstrating the inaccuracy of such images and messages. When consumers exposed to counter-marketing realize that marketing plans have been created specifically to influence their attitudes and consumption behaviors, they may realize they have been tricked or unfairly manipulated and subsequently change their attitudes and behaviors.

KEY WORDS Demand elimination

IMPLICATIONS
Marketers concerned with nullifying the demand created by other marketers may benefit from a greater understanding of counter-marketing strategies and tactics. At the same time, marketers must also recognize that responses to the firm's marketing efforts may include that of counter-marketing and, as such, marketers must evaluate carefully the firm's marketing strategies for susceptibility to nullification by various counter-marketing strategies.

APPLICATION AREAS AND FURTHER READINGS
Marketing Strategy
Zucker, D., Hopkins, R. S., Sly, D. F., Urich, J., Kershaw, J. M., and Solari, S. (2000). 'Florida's "Truth" Campaign: A Counter-Marketing, Anti-Tobacco Media Campaign,' *Journal of Public Health Management and Practice*, 6, 1–6.

Advertising
Siegel, M. (2002). 'Antismoking Advertising: Figuring out what Works,' *Journal of Health Communication*, 7, 157–162.
Sly, D. F., Hopkins, R. S., Trapido, E., and Ray, S. (2001). 'Influence of a Counteradvertising Media Campaign on Initiation of Smoking: The Florida "Truth" Campaign,' *American Journal of Public Health*, 91, 233–238.

Consumer Behavior
Kozlowski, L. T., Palmer, R., Stine, M. M., Strasser, A. A., and Yost, B. A. (2001). 'Persistent Effects of a Message Counter-Marketing Light Cigarettes,' *Addictive Behaviors*, 26(3), 447–452.

BIBLIOGRAPHY
McKenna, J., Gutierrez, K., and McCall, K. (2000). 'Strategies for an Effective Youth Counter-Marketing Program: Recommendations from Commercial Marketing Experts,' *Journal of Public Health Management and Practice*, 6, 7–13.

■ country of origin effect

DESCRIPTION
Any influence of knowledge of a product's country of origin, or where it was produced, manufactured, assembled, grown, or otherwise created, on an individual's perceptions and evaluations of the product's attributes.

KEY INSIGHTS
Because manufacturers usually disclose the country where a product is made, individuals evaluating the product may use such information to

infer product characteristics which are otherwise difficult to observe. More specifically, individuals may make associations between countries and product attributes including quality, reliability, durability, style, value, and cheapness. Associations between a product's country of origin and particular product attributes are sometimes justifiable; yet, in other instances, they may not be since location of manufacture may not have any relationship whatsoever with the expertise or quality of materials or manufacturing processes used for the product.

KEY WORDS Perceptions, evaluations, product quality

IMPLICATIONS
To the extent knowledge of a country of origin enhances product perceptions, the marketability of a product is enhanced. When there is a negative influence on product perceptions, the marketer's task is made more difficult, especially when negative perceptions do not correspond to a product's actual quality. Marketers should seek to understand how and to what extent a product's evaluation is influenced by consumer perceptions of its country of origin.

APPLICATION AREAS AND FURTHER READINGS
Consumer Behavior
Erickson, Gary M., Johansson, Johny K., and Chao, Paul (1984). 'Image Variables in Multi-Attribute Product Evaluations: Country-of-Origin Effects,' *Journal of Consumer Research*, 11(2), September, 694–699.
Johansson, Johny K., Douglas, Susan P., and Nonaka, Ikujiro (1985). 'Assessing the Impact of Country of Origin on Product Evaluations: A New Methodological Perspective,' *Journal of Marketing Research*, 22(4), November, 388–396.
Hong, Sung-Tai, and Wyer, Robert S., Jr. (1989). 'Effects of Country-of-Origin and Product-Attribute Information on Product Evaluation: An Information Processing Perspective,' *Journal of Consumer Research*, 16(2), September, 175–187.

BIBLIOGRAPHY
Al-Sulaiti, Khalid I., and Baker, Michael J. (1998). 'Country of Origin Effects: A Literature Review,' *Marketing Intelligence & Planning*, 16(3), June, 150–199.

☐ credence goods *see* goods
☐ Crespi effect *see* elation effect
☐ criterion validity *see* validity
☐ CRM *see* customer relationship management

■ cross-cultural marketing

DESCRIPTION
Marketing concerned with efforts to span cultural boundaries.

KEY INSIGHTS
Cross-cultural marketing's emphasis is on understanding and explaining cross-cultural differences along multiple dimensions (e.g. beliefs, attitudes, purchase behaviors) and using such knowledge to develop effective

marketing strategies, methods, and tactics that help an organization accomplish its marketing objectives. While cross-cultural marketing has much in common with international marketing (see **international marketing**) in its emphasis on spanning and/or bridging markets that differ in important broad respects, cross-cultural marketing may also be performed within a single domestic or country market where multiple cultures exist. Nevertheless, many cross-cultural differences exist across national borders. At the same time, there are also similarities with multicultural marketing in terms of the marketing emphasis on understanding cultural differences. (See **multicultural marketing**.) However, in contrast to multicultural marketing's emphasis on efforts to concurrently market to individuals situated within and among multiple cultures, cross-cultural marketing's emphasis is more on comparisons of differences that exist across cultures which are typically more geographically diverse or dispersed and which are more prevalent across national boundaries.

KEY WORDS Cultural differences

IMPLICATIONS

Marketers of firms with objectives to span cultural boundaries may benefit from a greater understanding of the many dimensions along which cultural differences can be assessed. Knowledge of cultural similarities and difference can therefore enable the marketer to develop effective marketing methods (e.g. research tools, communications strategies, channels of distribution) that are more closely aligned with the cultural characteristics of the firm's target markets.

APPLICATION AREAS AND FURTHER READINGS

Marketing Strategy
Herbig, P. A. (1998). *Handbook of Cross-Cultural Marketing*. New York: The Halworth Press, Inc.

Marketing Management
Jackson, T., and Artola, M. C. (1997). 'Ethical Beliefs and Management Behaviour: A Cross-Cultural Comparison,' *Journal of Business Ethics*, 16(12), 1163–1173.

Marketing Research
Malhotra, N. K., Agarwal, J., and Peterson, M. (1996). 'Methodological Issues in Cross-Cultural Marketing Research: A State-of-the-Art Review,' *International Marketing Review*, 13(5), 7–43.

Services Marketing
Smith, Anne M., and Reynolds, Nina L. (2001). 'Measuring Cross-Cultural Service Quality: A Framework for Assessment,' *International Marketing Review*, 19(5), 450–472.

International Marketing
Kaynak, Erdener (1999). 'Cross-National and Cross-Cultural Issues in Food Marketing: Past, Present and Future,' *Journal of International Food and Agribusiness Marketing*, 10(4), 1–11.

BIBLIOGRAPHY
Rugimbana, R., and Nwankwo, S. (2003). *Cross Cultural Marketing*. London: Thomson Learning.

Hofstede, Geert H. (1980). *Culture's Consequences: International Differences in Work-Related Values*. Beverly Hills, Calif.: Sage Publications.
Hofstede, G. (1991). *Cultures and Organizations: Software of the Mind*. New York: McGraw-Hill.

☐ cross-elasticity of demand *see* elasticity of demand
☐ cross-marketing *see* cooperative marketing
☐ cultural marketing *see* multicultural marketing
☐ custom marketing *see* one-to-one marketing
☐ customer-centric marketing *see* customer-oriented marketing

■ customer equity

DESCRIPTION
The value to a firm of its entire set of customers for the duration of their relationships with the firm.

KEY INSIGHTS
Customer equity equates to a firm's net ownership interest of its customers as indicated by their overall value to the firm. Given that each customer has a lifetime value, or *customer lifetime value*, where a firm is able to estimate a value to the stream of purchases the consumer is likely to make over the duration of their relationship with the firm, customer equity can be viewed as the summation of the customer lifetime values of individual customers. As such, an explicit or implicit objective of the firm may be to maximize customer equity, either at a very broad level or at a more detailed level by basing marketing efforts on a function of the customer lifetime value of each individual customer. With the latter approach, marketers seek to calculate and manage customer lifetime values by taking into account such factors as acquisition costs, retention costs, time period of customer relationship, revenue, and profit margins.

KEY WORDS Customer value, customer relationships

IMPLICATIONS
Customer equity and customer lifetime values are influenced by many factors which vary in the degree they are controllable by the marketer. Vibrant competition in some service industries, such as mobile telecommunication services, may be characterized by high churn rates, where customers frequently come and go, leading to short time periods for customer relationships. Nevertheless, operating on the assumption that it is usually less costly to keep a customer than to acquire a new one, many marketers recognize a benefit in pursuing marketing approaches aimed at customer retention as a way to extend customer lifetime values and, hence, enhance customer equity, where it is explicitly calculated or simply held as a strategic focus of the firm.

APPLICATION AREAS AND FURTHER READINGS

Marketing Management

Blattberg, R. C., and Deighton, J. (1996). 'Manage Marketing by the Customer Equity Test,' *Harvard Business Review*, 74(4), July–August, 136–144.

Dwyer, F. Robert (1997). 'Customer Lifetime Valuation to Support Marketing Decision Making,' *Journal of Direct Marketing*, 11(4), 6–13.

Marketing Strategy

Rust, Roland T., Lemon, Katherine N., and Zeithaml, Valarie A. (2004). 'Return on Marketing: Using Customer Equity to Focus Marketing Strategy,' *Journal of Marketing*, 68(1), January, 109–127.

Bayon, T., Gutsche, J., and Bauer, H. (2002). 'Customer Equity Marketing: Touching the Intangible,' *European Management Journal*, 20(3), June, 213–222.

Ulaga, W. (2001). 'Customer Value in Business Markets: An Agenda for Inquiry,' *Industrial Marketing Management*, 30(4), May, 315–319.

Berger, Paul D., and Nasr, Nada I. (1999). 'Customer Lifetime Value: Marketing Models and Applications,' *Journal of Interactive Marketing*, 12(1), March, 17–30.

Marketing Research

Jain, Dipak, and Singh, Siddhartha S. (2002). 'Customer Lifetime Value Research in Marketing: A Review and Future Directions,' *Journal of Interactive Marketing*, 16(2), March, 34–46.

BIBLIOGRAPHY

Reinartz, Werner, and Kumar, J. V. (2003). 'The Impact of Customer Relationship Characteristics on Profitable Lifetime Duration,' *Journal of Marketing*, 67(1), January, 77–99.

Hoekstra, Janny C., and Huizingh, Eelko K. R. E. (1999). 'The Lifetime Value Concept in Customer-Based Marketing,' *Journal of Market-Focused Management*, 3(3–4), September, 257–274.

☐ customer experience marketing *see* experiential marketing

☐ customer lifetime value *see* customer equity

■ customer-oriented marketing

(also called customer-centric marketing)

DESCRIPTION

Marketing based on a major organizational mission of developing and delivering offerings and associated marketing approaches that provide customers with unrivaled value and satisfaction.

KEY INSIGHTS

A customer-oriented marketing approach, where the customer is at the center of a firm's marketing efforts, ultimately requires the firm to be highly adept at understanding, anticipating, and responding to its customer's needs and wants on an ongoing basis. In many ways, customer-oriented marketing is the most common form of marketing pursued by organizations today. Even with the high commonality among firms in adopting such an emphasis, however, there remains, of course, considerable variation in firms' actual abilities in terms of identifying, predicting, and meeting customer needs and wants both effectively and efficiently.

KEY WORDS Customer focus

IMPLICATIONS

While customer-oriented marketing may seem to be an obvious emphasis in marketing practice, the extent of its achievement is another matter. Marketers may aim to keep the customer central in the firm's efforts but responding to customer wants and needs, even if they are well understood, usually involves tradeoffs and scarce resources. Anticipating changes in customer needs over the longer term also poses marketers with the challenge of both their timely understanding and profitable or otherwise effective accommodation.

APPLICATION AREAS AND FURTHER READINGS

Marketing Strategy
Gatignon, Hubert, and Xuereb, Jean-Marc (1997). 'Strategic Orientation of the Firm and New Product Performance,' *Journal of Marketing Research*, 34, February, 77–90.
Sheth, J. N., Sisodia, R. S., and Sharma, A. (2000). 'The Antecedents and Consequences of Customer-Centric Marketing,' *Journal of the Academy of Marketing Science*, 28(1), 55–66.

Services Marketing
Graham, P. (1995). 'Are Public Sector Organizations Becoming Customer Oriented?' *Marketing Intelligence and Planning*, 13(1), 35–47.

Marketing Management
Idassi, J. O., Young, T. M., Winistorfer, P. M., Ostermier, D. M., and Woodruff, R. B. (1994). 'A Customer-Oriented Marketing Method for Hardwood Lumber Companies,' *Forest Products Journal*, 44, July–August, 67–73.

BIBLIOGRAPHY
Votland, R. (1998). 'Customer-Oriented Marketing: Yesterday–Today–Tomorrow,' *POLIMERI–ZAGREB*, 19(6–7), 140–145.

■ customer relationship management

DESCRIPTION
Emphasis within a firm on developing, enhancing, and maintaining effective customer relationships.

KEY INSIGHTS
Customer relationship management (CRM) involves an emphasis on multiple, interdependent processes within the firm which support mutually beneficial relationships between firms and customers. Whether the processes are pre-sales, sales, service, or other processes directly or indirectly supporting marketing, CRM seeks to deepen and extend customer relationships with the firm through the development of processes which facilitate customer satisfaction and loyalty. By integrating customer-specific information into many of the firm's marketing processes, as opposed to making fragmented use of such information, the firm may not only increase its marketing effectiveness and efficiency but also enhance substantially the customer's experience with the firm. When the focus of the firm's marketing is based on CRM, the firm's approach

to marketing may be referred to as customer relationship marketing or simply relationship marketing. (See **relationship marketing**.)

KEY WORDS Relationships, customer integration

IMPLICATIONS

A firm's relationship with its customers may be short or long or close or distant. To the extent the firm sees a benefit in strengthening customer relationships by extending them and making them closer through integrating information on customer needs and wants into its processes, CRM can increasingly become a strategic focus of the firm. A greater knowledge of the many multidisciplinary processes supporting CRM can assist marketers in evaluating the benefits and costs associated with extensive or limited CRM adoption among current and future customers.

APPLICATION AREAS AND FURTHER READINGS

Marketing Strategy
Stone, M., Woodcock, N., and Wilson, M. (1996). 'Managing the Change from Marketing Planning to Customer Relationship Management,' *Long Range Planning*, 29(5), October, 675–683.

Marketing Management
Ryals, L., and Knox, S. (2001). 'Cross-Functional Issues in the Implementation of Relationship Marketing through Customer Relationship Management,' *European Management Journal*, 19(5), October, 534–542.
Goldsmith, Ronald E. (1997). 'Customer Relationship Management: Making Hard Decisions with Soft Numbers,' *Journal of Leisure Research*, 29, 355–357.
Wilson, Hugh, Daniel, Elizabeth, and McDonald, Malcolm (2002). 'Factors for Success in Customer Relationship Management (CRM) Systems,' *Journal of Marketing Management*, 18(1–2), February, 193–219.
Lemon, Katherine N., White, Tiffany Barnett, and Winer, Russell S. (2002). 'Dynamic Customer Relationship Management: Incorporating Future Considerations into the Service Retention Decision,' *Journal of Marketing*, 66(1), January, 1–14.

Online Marketing
Brown, S. A. (2000). *Customer Relationship Management: A Strategic Imperative in the World of E-business*. Toronto: Wiley.

BIBLIOGRAPHY
Winer, Russell (2001). 'A Framework for Customer Relationship Management,' *California Management Review*, 43, Summer, 89–105.

☐ customer relationship marketing *see* relationship marketing

■ **customer satisfaction**

DESCRIPTION
The extent to which a customer's perceived performance of an organization's offering matches the customer's expectations.

KEY INSIGHTS
Satisfying consumers by meeting their expectations is a key aspect of much of marketing practice. As such, there is considerable theoretical, conceptual, and empirical research aimed at understanding, explaining, and predicting the satisfaction of consumers generally (see **consumer satisfaction theory**) as well as an organization's existing customers more specifically. Satisfied customers can benefit a firm in many ways including higher levels of repeat buying by such customers as well as increased positive word-of-mouth communication regarding the firm's offerings.

KEY WORDS Expectations, performance

IMPLICATIONS
An imperative for marketers is satisfying customers. However, how and to what extent is a matter of debate among marketers. Some firms may adopt the view that customers should be 'barely satisfied' while others advocate efforts aimed at meeting or exceeding customer expectations. Either way, marketers also have an opportunity to influence customer expectations themselves, which may involve lowering expectations so that they are met more easily. Marketers should therefore seek to understand and appreciate the broad scope of customer satisfaction research to enable the identification and evaluation of multiple marketing strategies and tactics aimed at satisfying customers.

APPLICATION AREAS AND FURTHER READINGS

Marketing Research
Churchill, Gilbert A., Jr., and Surprenant, Carol (1982). 'An Investigation into the Determinants of Customer Satisfaction,' *Journal of Marketing Research*, 19(4), Special Issue on Causal Modeling, November, 491–504.
Fornell, Claes (1992). 'A National Customer Satisfaction Barometer: The Swedish Experience,' *Journal of Marketing*, 56(1), January, 6–21.
Anderson, Eugene W., Fornell, Claes, and Lehmann, Donald R. (1994). 'Customer Satisfaction, Market Share, and Profitability: Findings from Sweden,' *Journal of Marketing*, 58(3), July, 53–66.

Marketing Strategy
Anderson, Eugene W., and Sullivan, Mary W. (1993). 'The Antecedents and Consequences of Customer Satisfaction for Firms,' *Marketing Science*, 12(2), Spring, 125–143.
Anderson, Eugene W., Fornell, Claes, and Rust, Roland T. (1997). 'Customer Satisfaction, Productivity, and Profitability: Differences between Goods and Services,' *Marketing Science*, 16(2), 129–145.
Garbarino, Ellen, and Johnson, Mark S. (1999). 'The Different Roles of Satisfaction, Trust, and Commitment in Customer Relationships,' *Journal of Marketing*, 63(2), April, 70–87.
Crosby, Lawrence A., and Stephens, Nancy (1987). 'Effects of Relationship Marketing on Satisfaction, Retention, and Prices in the Life Insurance Industry,' *Journal of Marketing Research*, 24(4), November, 404–411.

Marketing Modeling
Smith, Amy K., Bolton, Ruth N., and Wagner, Janet (1999). 'A Model of Customer Satisfaction with Service Encounters Involving Failure and Recovery,' *Journal of Marketing Research*, 36(3), August, 356–372.

BIBLIOGRAPHY
Peterson, Robert A., and Wilson, William R. (1992). 'Measuring Customer Satisfaction: Fact and Artifact,' *Journal of the Academy of Marketing Science*, 20, Winter, 61–71.

☐ customer value marketing *see* value-based marketing
☐ customer volume effect *see* loyalty effect
☐ customized marketing *see* one-to-one marketing
☐ cybermarketing *see* online marketing
☐ cyberspace marketing *see* online marketing

D

■ Darwinian evolution theory

(also called natural selection theory)

DESCRIPTION
The theory that species evolve through a process of natural selection.

KEY INSIGHTS
Evolution commonly refers to the change in the traits of living organisms over generations as well as the emergence of new species. Darwinian evolution, as pioneered by Charles Darwin (1859), essentially adopts a 'survival of the fittest' perspective. The theory and the application of its insights have since extended well beyond the purely biological domain to that of organizations as living organisms as well as other areas including new products.

KEY WORDS Evolution, adaptation, change

IMPLICATIONS
In the context of organizations and products, the approach provides a basis for modeling how such entities may evolve over time, where, beyond the influence of natural forces (e.g. climate and natural resources), market forces provide a further or analogous basis for natural selection. Concepts drawing upon Darwinian evolution theory may therefore assist marketers in understanding and managing such dynamics in helping to ensure long-term success of the organization and its products.

APPLICATION AREAS AND FURTHER READINGS
Marketing Planning
Cooper, Lee G. (2000). 'Strategic Marketing Planning for Radically New Products,' *Journal of Marketing*, 64(1), January, 1–16.

Organizational Change
Jones, Colin (2004). 'An Alternative View of Small Firm Adaptation,' *Journal of Small Business and Enterprise Development*, 1(3), September, 362–370.

Consumer Behavior
Saad, Gad (2006). 'Applying Evolutionary Psychology in Understanding the Darwinian Roots of Consumption Phenomena,' *Managerial and Decision Economics*, 27(2–3), 189–201.

BIBLIOGRAPHY
Ziman, John (2000). *Technological Innovation as an Evolutionary Process*. Cambridge: Cambridge University Press.
Anderson, Paul F. (1983). 'Marketing, Scientific Progress, and Scientific Method,' *Journal of Marketing*, 47(4), Autumn, 18–31.

■ data types

DESCRIPTION
Particular categories of factual information.

KEY INSIGHTS
Factual information collected and used in marketing is frequently characterized as one of two types: *primary data* or *secondary data*. Primary data are those which are non-existent prior to the conduct of research and are collected specifically for the purpose of a particular research effort. Examples of primary data include those obtained in response to an interviewer's questioning of subjects in a research study and observations of subject's behaviors in an experiment. Secondary data are those which already exist and are in essence, second-hand in that they have already been collected or have become available as a result of a different purpose. Examples of secondary data include census data and company sales data collected or compiled prior to and independent from a research study in which they are put to use.

KEY WORD Information

IMPLICATIONS
Marketers conducting marketing research face tradeoffs in the collection and use of factual information. While secondary data is often inexpensive to obtain and readily available, it may not always provide the marketer with the insights desired. On the other hand, primary data can provide rich insight but often at a greater cost and/or effort relative to that for secondary data. Robust marketing research may involve a combination of both data types, where the research objectives and researcher's resources dictate the relative emphasis on each.

APPLICATION AREAS AND FURTHER READINGS
Marketing Research
Bonoma, Thomas V. (1985). 'Case Research in Marketing: Opportunities, Problems, and a Process,' *Journal of Marketing Research*, 22(2), May, 199–208.
Savitt, R. (1980). 'Historical Research in Marketing,' *Journal of Marketing*, 44, Fall, 52–58.
Wedel, M., Kamakura, W. A., and Böckenholt, U. (2000). 'Marketing Data, Models and Decisions,' *International Journal of Research in Marketing*, 17(2–3), 203–208.
Houston, Mark B. (2004). 'Assessing the Validity of Secondary Data Proxies for Marketing Constructs,' *Journal of Business Research*, 57, 154–161.
Crouch, S., and Housden, M. (1998). *Marketing Research for Managers*. Oxford: Butlernorth-Heinemann.

BIBLIOGRAPHY
Aaker, D. A., Kumar, V., and Day, G. S. (1998). *Marketing Research*, 6th edn. New York: Wiley.

■ database marketing

DESCRIPTION

A particular form of direct marketing where databases of customers and their profiles are used to generate tailored or personalized offerings as a central part of a firm's marketing efforts.

KEY INSIGHTS

Database marketing often takes advantage of flexible and efficient information technologies and its use for personalization may enable marketers to target customers with greater effectiveness relative to more traditional marketing approaches. An essential element of database marketing is the analysis of customer data to obtain insights useful to the marketer, which may include segmenting customers based on purchase behaviors such as purchase frequency, recency, or amount, thereby enabling the marketer to develop and implement marketing approaches that are more closely aligned with such behaviors.

KEY WORDS Information technologies

IMPLICATIONS

Advances in various information technologies make database marketing an increasingly attractive approach to marketers. Still, the effort can only be effective to the extent that analyses of customer data influence the development and implementation of personalized or other (e.g. direct) marketing practice. While much can potentially be gained from such an approach, database marketers must also ensure company practices conform to restrictions imposed by the firm's legal and regulatory environments regarding the appropriate use and retention of customer data.

APPLICATION AREAS AND FURTHER READINGS

Marketing Strategy

Cespedes, Frank V., and Smith, H. Jeff (1993). 'Database Marketing: New Rules for Policy and Practice,' *Sloan Management Review*, 34, Summer, 7–22.

Petrison, L. A., Blattberg, R. C., and Wang, P. (1997). 'Database Marketing: Past Present, and Future,' *Journal of Direct Marketing*, 11(4), 109–125.

Fletcher, K., Wheeler, C., and Wright, J. (1992). 'Success in Database Marketing: Some Critical Factors,' *Marketing Intelligence and Planning*, 10(6), 18–23.

Marketing Management

Kahan, H. (1998). 'Using Database Marketing Techniques to Enhance your One-to-One Marketing Initiatives,' *Journal of Consumer Marketing*, 15(5), 491–493.

BIBLIOGRAPHY

Hughes, Arthur M. (2000). *Strategic Database Marketing: The Masterplan for Starting and Managing a Profitable Customer-Based Marketing Program*, 2nd edn. New York: McGraw-Hill.

☐ **deciders** *see* industrial buyer behavior

■ decision theory

DESCRIPTION

Theory or theories concerned with understanding and explaining how decision makers make real decisions and with how optimal decisions can be reached.

KEY INSIGHTS

Choices under uncertainty, social decisions, choices where payoffs occur at different points in time, and complex decisions are just some areas where decision theories have been developed and applied to either prescribe approaches for identifying the best decision to take or to describe how such decisions are typically made. Much of decision theory makes the assumption that the decision taker is fully informed and fully rational.

KEY WORDS Decision making, optimal decisions

IMPLICATIONS

Decision theory is interdisciplinary and therefore has implications for marketing that draw upon economics, psychology, mathematics, statistics, and management. Knowledge of numerous decision theory-based models can be drawn upon to describe or explain how marketing decisions of various types are or should be made.

APPLICATION AREAS AND FURTHER READINGS

Managerial Decision Making

Curren, Mary T., Folkes, Valerie S., and Steckel, Joel H. (1992). 'Explanations for Successful and Unsuccessful Marketing Decisions: The Decision Maker's Perspective,' *Journal of Marketing*, 56(2), April, 18–31.

Gilboa, Itzhak, and Schmeidler, David (1995). 'Case-Based Decision Theory,' *Quarterly Journal of Economics*, 110(3), August, 605–639.

Hutchinson, J. Wesley, and Meyer, Robert J. (1994). 'Dynamic Decision Making: Optimal Policies and Actual Behavior in Sequential Choice Problems,' *Marketing Letters*, 5(4), October, 369–382.

BIBLIOGRAPHY

Resnik, Michael D. (1987). *Choices: An Introduction to Decision Theory*. Minneapolis: University of Minnesota Press.

☐ **decline stage** *see* product life cycle

■ decline strategies

DESCRIPTION

Organizational strategies for competing in a declining market.

KEY INSIGHTS

When there is a fall in demand in a market, perhaps as a result of a change in some technology, consumer preferences, or government policy, a firm competing in such a market must select a strategy that makes the best of the situation. Strategies that a firm may wish to consider in facing a declining market include a *leadership strategy*, where the firm pursues initiatives aimed at achieving or maintaining leadership in the market (e.g. by buying competitors) while the market is still profitable, even though it is in decline; a *niche strategy*, where the firm identifies and pursues the segment of the market that demonstrates the most favorable conditions for the firm (e.g. highest return, slowest rate of decline); a *harvest strategy* or *milking strategy*, where the firm cuts back on its costs and investments in the market, where the aim is to generate cash flow, even if a reduction in sales and market share results, since the cash generated could then be put to better use elsewhere; and a *divestment strategy*, where the firm opts to liquidate its position in the market, as a result of factors including expected extreme price pressure, rapid market decline, and dominant competitors with an irreversible advantage.

KEY WORDS Market decline, competitive strategy

IMPLICATIONS
Clearly, a firm has several strategies from which to choose when facing a declining market. Ultimately, in determining the most desirable (or least undesirable) strategy or strategies, marketing managers in a firm will need to assess carefully the strategic uncertainties facing the firm, including uncertainties associated with: the market, competitive intensity, firm performance and strengths, firm relationships with other businesses, and barriers to implementation including exit barriers and the firm's management ability.

APPLICATION AREAS AND FURTHER READINGS
Marketing Strategy
Anderson, Carl R., and Zeithaml, Carl P. (1984). 'Stage of the Product Life Cycle, Business Strategy, and Business Performance,' *Academy of Management Journal*, 27(1), March, 5–24.
Thietart, R. A., and Vivas, R. (1984). 'An Empirical Investigation of Success Strategies for Businesses along the Product Life Cycle,' *Management Science*, 30(12), December, 1405–1423.
McKee, P. R., and Varadarajan, W. M. (1989). 'Pride, Strategic Adaptability and Firm Performance: A Market-Conti,' *Journal of Marketing*, 53(3), 21–35.

BIBLIOGRAPHY
Aaker, David A. (2005). *Strategic Market Management*. New York: John Wiley & Sons, Inc.
Porter, Michael (1980). *Competitive Strategy*. New York: The Free Press.

■ defensive marketing

(also called status quo marketing)

DESCRIPTION
Marketing strategies aimed at protecting a company's status quo situation from change by competitors or other market forces.

KEY INSIGHTS
Companies may use any of an array of defensive marketing strategies, ranging from pre-emptive moves for keeping competitors out of its product-market segment to contraction moves for consolidating market

strength, in an attempt to maintain or stem erosion in its current market share, profitability, or positioning. A defensive marketing approach in which the firm chooses to redefine its business as a result of market or technological change, for example, involves the identification of new product markets that the firm moves into as a result of innovative activity within the firm. In contrast, one of the riskiest forms of defense is that of remaining stationary in terms of the firm's offerings, thereby leaving the firm vulnerable to competitors with more dynamic strategies.

KEY WORDS Market position

IMPLICATIONS
There are many unique options available to the marketer concerned with defending the firm's position, where each approach must be evaluated relative to the strengths and weaknesses of the firm in relation to competitors as well as assessments of opportunities and threats posed by the firm's external environment. Regardless of the need for a defensive marketing strategy, marketers must recognize that adopting a fortress-like approach to defending the firm—even if it is the current market leader—may ultimately be short-sighted in highly competitive markets.

APPLICATION AREAS AND FURTHER READINGS
Marketing Strategy
Roberts, John (2005). 'Defensive Marketing: How a Strong Incumbent can Protect its Position,' *Harvard Business Review*, 83(11), 150–157.
Fornell, C., and Wernerfet, B. (1987). 'Defensive Marketing Strategy by Customer Complaint Management: A Theoretical Analysis,' *Journal of Marketing Research*, 24, 337–346.
Boyd, Eric D. (1996). 'Defensive Marketing's Use of Post-Purchase Telecommunications to Create Competitive Advantages: A Strategic Analysis,' *Journal of Consumer Marketing*, 13(1), 26–34.

BIBLIOGRAPHY
Hauser, John R., and Shugan, Steven M. (1983). 'Defensive Marketing Strategies,' *Marketing Science*, 3, Fall, 327–351.

☐ deficient products *see* societal classification of products
☐ delayed response effect *see* lagged effect
☐ Delphi technique *see* forecasting methods

■ demand

DESCRIPTION
The amount of something that is sought after for purchase, use, or consumption.

KEY INSIGHTS
Demand, as it relates to the extent that products or services are needed or wanted by their markets, may be characterized any number of ways including primary, secondary, latent, incipient, derived, and negative.

Primary demand refers to instances where products are demanded by the customers themselves, as where canned soft drinks are purchased by consumers for their own consumption or for consumption by their families.

Secondary demand refers to the demand for a particular brand or product within a broader product category, as where, within demand for the product category of running shoes, there is secondary demand for Nike running shoes.

Latent demand refers to demand that is dormant, not observable, or not yet realized, as in the case where demand for a product exists but is constrained because of a lack of product supply or availability.

Incipient demand refers to demand which is emerging and only partly in existence as it is early in its development, as where new technologies have created an incipient demand for movies delivered directly via the World Wide Web.

Derived demand refers to instances where the demand for a product arises indirectly from some other downstream demand, as where demand for passenger jet fuel is derived from consumers' demand for air travel.

Negative demand refers to instances where consumers would prefer not to have a product in that they would go out of their way to avoid it and also pay more than its value to not have it, as would be the case for certain painful medical treatments.

Further characterizations of demand include those by Kotler (1973) which are: non-existent, irregular, faltering, full, overfull, and unwholesome demand.

KEY WORDS Market needs, **need(s)**, **want(s)**, consumption

IMPLICATIONS
Much of marketing is focused on meeting, stimulating, and creating demand in the marketplace. Additionally, where consumption of a product or service is to be societally discouraged (e.g. excessive water consumption or wastage), marketing's focus then becomes reducing demand. Understanding the many dimensional characteristics of demand for a marketer's product or service is essential in managing market demand effectively through appropriate marketing strategies.

APPLICATION AREAS AND FURTHER READINGS

Marketing Research
Allenby, G. M., Arora, N., and Ginter, J. L. (1998). 'On the Heterogeneity of Demand,' *Journal of Marketing Research*, 35(3), 384–389.
Hamilton-Gibbs, Derek, Esslemont, Don, and McGuinness, Dalton (1992), 'Predicting the Demand for Frequently Purchased Items,' *Marketing Bulletin*, 3, 18–23.
Wiser, R. H. (1998). 'Green Power Marketing: Increasing Customer Demand for Renewable Energy,' *Utilities Policy*, 7(2), 107–119.

Business-to-Business Marketing
Bishop, William S., Graham, John L., and Jones, Michael H. (1984). 'Volatility of Derived Demand in Industrial Markets and its Management Implications,' *Journal of Marketing*, 48(4), Autumn, 95–103.

Marketing Modeling

Arora, Neeraj, Allenby, Greg M., and Ginter, James L. (1998). 'A Hierarchical Bayes Model of Primary and Secondary Demand,' *Marketing Science*, 17(1), 29–44.

Kim, J., Allenby, G. M., and Rossi, P. E. (2002). 'Modeling Consumer Demand for Variety,' *Marketing Science*, 21(3), 229–250.

Jain, Dipak C., and Rao, Ram C. (1990). 'Effect of Price on the Demand for Durables: Modeling, Estimation, and Findings,' *Journal of Business & Economic Statistics*, 8(2), April, 163–170.

BIBLIOGRAPHY

Kotler, Philip (1973). 'The Major Tasks of Marketing Management,' *Journal of Marketing*, 37(4), October, 42–49.

☐ **demand, characteristics theory of** *see* **characteristics theory**

■ demand, law of

DESCRIPTION

The economic principle that states the amount of a product demanded increases with a fall in price and diminishes with a rise in price.

KEY INSIGHTS

Developed by economist Alfred Marshall, the law of demand suggests that the demand for most products will tend to vary inversely with their prices. Although since its inception, it has been recognized that there are other factors beside price that are able to influence demand, the general relationship suggested is consistent with the demand–price relationship observed for most products and services.

KEY WORDS **Demand**, price, modeling

IMPLICATIONS

All else equal, the law of demand predicts that consumers will typically buy more of a product at a low price than at a high price. Models based on the law of demand can thus be developed that enable further analyses of the sensitivity of product demand to changes in its price.

There are, of course, exceptions to the law of demand, where it is observed that demand for a product or service actually increases when price increases, as where demand for enrolling in a leading university's MBA program is observed to increase after the program announces an increase in its tuition fees. Exceptions to the law of demand can sometimes be explained by the signaling effect of price on quality, where a higher price suggests even higher quality, thereby attracting more quality-conscious consumers. Similarly, demand for a product may decrease when price decreases, if, for example, quality-conscious consumers suspect that the quality of an offering is being compromised.

APPLICATION AREAS AND FURTHER READINGS

Marketing Modeling

Bishop, William S., Graham, John L., and Jones, Michael H. (1984). 'Volatility of Derived Demand in Industrial Markets and its Management Implications,' *Journal of Marketing*, 48(4), Autumn, 95–103.

Song, Haiyan, and Wong, Kevin K. F. (2003). 'Tourism Demand Modeling: A Time-Varying Parameter Approach,' *Journal of Travel Research*, 42(1), 57–64.

BIBLIOGRAPHY
Buchholz, Todd G. (1990). *New Ideas from Dead Economists*. New York: Penguin Books.
Sraffa, Piero (1926). 'The Laws of Returns under Competitive Conditions,' *Economic Journal*, 36(144), December, 535–550.

■ demand characteristics

DESCRIPTION
Undesirable and unintended characteristics of an experimentally based research study where the outcome is influenced by conditions or cues which have assisted in leading subjects to perform certain behaviors, as in doing what was desired or expected of them.

KEY INSIGHTS
The actual or possible presence of demand characteristics presents a confounding influence in the interpretation of experimental research findings. Approaches for uncovering the extent of demand characteristics in a particular research design can be through methods including those aimed at assessing subjects' thoughts on an experiment's intent, as in interviewing subjects upon the experiment's completion or reenacting experimental procedures with new subjects from the population of subjects or using multiple, different methods for examining the phenomena in question to increase the robustness of experimental findings.

KEY WORDS Experimental research, **bias**

IMPLICATIONS
Marketers must be aware of the possibility of demand characteristics being present in experimental research designs and should consider evaluating and adopting recognized approaches for their elimination or control if the aim is to obtain robust research findings.

APPLICATION AREAS AND FURTHER READINGS
Consumer Behavior
Shimp, Terence A., Hyatt, Eva M., and Snyder, David J. (1991). 'A Critical Appraisal of Demand Artifacts in Consumer Research,' *Journal of Consumer Research*, 18(3), December, 273-283.

Experimental Research
Sawyer, Alan G. (1975). 'Demand Artifacts in Laboratory Experiments in Consumer Research,' *Journal of Consumer Research*, 1(4), March, 20–30.
Sawyer, A. G. (1975). 'Detecting Demand Characteristics in Laboratory Experiments in Consumer Research: The Case of Repetition-Affect Research,' in M. J. Schlinger (ed.), *Advances in Consumer Research*, 2. Ann Arbor: Association for Consumer Research, 712-723.
Sawyer, Alan G., Worthing, Parker M., and Sendak, Paul E. (1979). 'The Role of Laboratory Experiments to Test Marketing Strategies,' *Journal of Marketing*, 43(3), Summer, 60-67.

BIBLIOGRAPHY
Orne, M. T. (1969). 'Demand Characteristics and the Concept of Quasi-Controls,' in R. Rosenthal and R. L. Rosnow (eds.), *Artifact in Behavioral Research*. New York: Academic Press, 143-179.

McGuire, W. J. (1969). 'Suspiciousness of experiment's intent,' in R. Rosenthal and R. L. Rasnow (eds.), *Artifact in Behavioral Research*. New York: Academic Press, 13–57.

☐ **demand pull** *see* pull marketing

■ demarketing

DESCRIPTION
Marketing aimed at discouraging customer demand.

KEY INSIGHTS
While uncommon in mainstream marketing, demarketing involves the application of marketing principles and practices to curtail customer purchase and use of particular products and services which are typically considered undesirable from a societal perspective. Some products or services are sought to be demarketed out of scarcity in supply or a perceived need for rationing (e.g. water). For other products, however, the issue driving demarketing isn't product scarcity but rather the spillover effects of product consumption, such as the pollution caused by automobiles.

KEY WORDS Demand reduction

IMPLICATIONS
Whether a government agency is concerned with reducing the level of cigarette smoking by the general public out of concern for its burden on the public healthcare system, or whether a government-regulated water supplier is tasked by the government to encourage its customers to use less water during a drought, a demarketing approach, as with marketing itself, necessarily involves the development of a set of clear marketing objectives, a deep understanding of consumer behavior, and effective marketing strategy development and implementation. Marketers concerned with demarketing may not only benefit from understanding the many principles of effective marketing but also by examining effective and ineffective demarketing approaches for analogous products and services as developed and implemented by a range of organizations worldwide.

APPLICATION AREAS AND FURTHER READINGS
Marketing Strategy
Gerstner, E., Hess, J. D., and Chu, W. (1993). 'Demarketing as a Differentiation Strategy,' *Marketing Letters*, 4(1), 49–57.
Kindra, G. S., and Taylor, W. D. (1995). 'Demarketing Inappropriate Health Care Consumption,' *Journal of Health Care Marketing*, 15(2), 10–14.
Cullwick, D. (1975). 'Positioning Demarketing Strategy,' *Journal of Marketing*, 39(2), April, 51–57.

Marketing Management
Lawther, S., Hastings, G. B., and Lowry, R. (1997). 'Demarketing: Putting Kotler and Levy's Ideas into Practice,' *Journal of Marketing Management*, 13, 315–325.

BIBLIOGRAPHY
Kotler, Philip, and Levy, Sidney J. (1971). 'Demarketing, Yes, Demarketing,' *Harvard Business Review*, 49(6), November–December, 74–80.

☐ demographic segmentation *see* segmentation
☐ derived demand *see* demand
☐ descriptive marketing research *see* marketing research
☐ desirable products *see* societal classification of products
☐ desire *see* buyer influence/readiness
☐ destination marketing *see* place marketing

■ dialectic process theory

DESCRIPTION
A theory of organizational development and change whereby new organizational characteristics arise through the adoption of characteristics of other organizations.

KEY INSIGHTS
Dialectic process theory as developed by van de Ven and Poole (1995) is based on the premise that organizations evolve. Thus, new organizational formats as well as episodes of change within an organization can be explained in relation to characteristics adopted from other organizations.

KEY WORDS Organizational evolution, development, change

IMPLICATIONS
Marketers can seek to understand and explain change in their own organizations as well as those of competitors by drawing upon concepts found in dialectic process theory. The development of new specialty retail formats, for example, can be understood better in terms of their relationship to the formats of existing retailers and the adoption of characteristics from such retailers.

APPLICATION AREAS AND FURTHER READINGS
Strategic Change
Sminia, Harry (2003). 'The Failure of the Sport7 TV-Channel: Controversies in a Business Network,' *Journal of Management Studies*, 40(7), November, 1621.
Sminia, Harry (2002). 'Sector Process and Episodes of Change: An Analysis of Daily Newspapers in the Netherlands,' *Strategic Change*, 11(4), 215–223.

Retail Marketing
Michman, Ronald D., and Mazze, Edward M. (2001). *Specialty Retailers*. Westport, Conn.: Quorum/Greenwood.

BIBLIOGRAPHY
Van de Ven, Andrew H., and Poole, Marshall Scott (1995). 'Explaining Development and Change in Organizations,' *Academy of Management Review*, 20(3), July, 510–540.

☐ differential threshold *see* Weber–Fechner law

■ differentiated marketing

(also called segmented marketing or selective marketing)

DESCRIPTION
The strategic approach of focusing on two or more groups of consumers and using a different marketing approach for each.

KEY INSIGHTS
Differentiated marketing's scope ranges from the use of different retailing approaches for different consumer groups to the provision of different product or service offerings. The aim of differentiated marketing is to achieve a strong competitive position within each segment pursued, where the net result is superior individual and aggregate performance in relation to that achievable by an undifferentiated marketing approach reaching all segments in a market. Such an approach, however, does result in higher marketing costs relative to that for undifferentiated marketing since there is a need to develop and implement distinct marketing plans and strategies for each segment.

KEY WORDS Market segmentation

IMPLICATIONS
Many firms, particularly large consumer products firms, use a differentiated marketing approach by offering multiple products or services to carefully defined customer segments, as where a clothing manufacturer and retailer uses several retail store formats as a means for each to provide greater appeal to a specific customer segment. Ultimately, however, the relative emphasis a firm gives to differentiated marketing must depend on projections of its development and implementation costs versus the potential to increase sales in relation to an undifferentiated marketing approach.

APPLICATION AREAS AND FURTHER READINGS
Marketing Strategy
Cui, G., and Choudhury, P. (2002). 'Marketplace Diversity and Cost-Effective Marketing Strategies,' *Journal of Consumer Marketing*, 19(1), 24–74.
Dickson, Peter R., and Ginter, James L. (1987). 'Market Segmentation, Product Differentiation, and Marketing Strategy,' *Journal of Marketing*, 51(2), April, 1–10.
Biggadike, E. Ralph (1981). 'The Contributions of Marketing to Strategic Management,' *Academy of Management Review*, 6(4), October, 621–632.
Duffus, Lee R. (1981). *The Tourist Industry in Jamaica: Mass versus Differentiated Marketing*. Knoxville, Tenn.: College of Business Administration, University of Tennessee.

BIBLIOGRAPHY
Kotler, Philip, and Levy, Sidney J. (1969). 'Broadening the Concept of Marketing,' *Journal of Marketing*, 33(1), January, 10–15.

□ **differentiation strategy** *see* strategies, generic

■ diffusion of innovation

DESCRIPTION
The concept that adoption of innovations by individuals or other customers in a market is generally spread out over time as a result of, among other factors, variation in individuals' willingness and readiness to adopt innovations.

KEY INSIGHTS
The diffusion of innovation concept recognizes and highlights the importance of consumer readiness to adopt innovations. A common characterization of groupings of innovation adoption readiness in any given population is that of innovators (2.5%), early adopters (13.5%), early majority (34%), late majority (34%), and laggards (16%).

KEY WORDS Innovation, adoption, readiness

IMPLICATIONS
Marketers involved in new product development (NPD) efforts must seek to understand how, why, and to what extent new products are likely to diffuse in the market given their particular innovative characteristics when the aim is to maximize as well as accelerate diffusion in the market. To the extent that factors facilitating as well as hindering the diffusion of particular innovations are understood, models can be constructed which take into account a potentially rich set of factors, including that of variation in consumers' willingness and readiness to adopt innovations.

APPLICATION AREAS AND FURTHER READINGS
New Product Development
Mahajan, Vijay, and Muller, Eitan (1979). 'Innovation Diffusion and New Product Growth Models in Marketing,' *Journal of Marketing*, 43(4), Autumn, 55–68.
Mahajan, Vijay, Muller, Eitan, and Bass, Frank M. (1995). 'Diffusion of New Products: Empirical Generalizations and Managerial Uses,' *Marketing Science*, 14(3), Part 2 of 2: Special Issue on Empirical Generalizations in Marketing, G79–G88.
Gatignon, Hubert, and Robertson, Thomas S. (1985). 'A Propositional Inventory for New Diffusion Research,' *Journal of Consumer Research*, 11(4), March, 849–867.

BIBLIOGRAPHY
Robertson, Thomas S. (1967). 'The Process of Innovation and the Diffusion of Innovation,' *Journal of Marketing*, 31(1), January, 14–19.
Rogers, E. M. (1995). *Diffusion of Innovations*, 4th edn. New York: Free Press.

■ diffusion of responsibility

DESCRIPTION
A social phenomenon associated with groups where responsibility is not explicitly assigned, whereby individuals in the group perceive less personal responsibility and accountability for actions taken or to be taken.

KEY INSIGHTS
While the phenomenon of diffusion of responsibility does not occur in all groups, it nevertheless has the potential to manifest itself in groups of varying size and member composition in ways that include a mindset of reduced personal responsibility and accountability as well as group

actions or inactions that individuals would tend not to allow to occur on their own.

KEY WORDS Group behavior, responsibility, accountability

IMPLICATIONS

Marketers must be aware of, and strive to mitigate, potential dangers associated with diffusion of responsibility when part of larger groups where responsibility is not explicitly assigned. Dangers include prolonged inaction (e.g. a prolonged delay in publicly acknowledging and responding to a problem of product contamination) as well as taking inappropriate action (e.g. immediately denying publicly that there is a problem with product contamination).

APPLICATION AREAS AND FURTHER READINGS

Ethical Decision Making

Trevino, Linda Klebe (1986). 'Ethical Decision Making in Organizations: A Person-Situation Interactionist Model,' *Academy of Management Review*, 11(3), July, 601–617.

Dozier, Janelle Brinker, and Miceli, Marcia P. (1985). 'Potential Predictors of Whistle-Blowing: A Prosocial Behavior Perspective,'*Academy of Management Review*, 10(4), October, 823–836.

Trevino, Linda Klebe (1992). 'Behavioral Aspects of Business Ethics: Moral Reasoning and Business Ethics. Implications for Research, Education, and Management,' *Journal of Business Ethics*, 11(5–6), May, 445–459.

BIBLIOGRAPHY

Darley, J. M., and Latane, B. (1968). 'Bystander Intervention in Emergencies: Diffusion of Responsibility,' *Journal of Personality and Social Psychology*, 8(4), April 377–383.

☐ digital marketing *see* e-marketing

■ diminishing marginal utility, law of

DESCRIPTION

An economic principle summarizing the situation where, in each additional unit of a good consumed by an individual, less and less utility is derived from the consumption.

KEY INSIGHTS

As utility in the context of the consumption of goods is often associated with benefits including satisfaction, pleasure, enjoyment, and the like, the law of diminishing marginal utility essentially summarizes the frequent observation in human nature that individuals tend to perceive and obtain less incremental benefit from a good as more and more of it is consumed.

KEY WORDS Consumption, **utility**, satisfaction, **value**

IMPLICATIONS

Marketers should seek to understand how a consumer of a given product or user of a particular service is likely to experience decreased utility from increased consumption on any given occasion or over a longer period of time. In doing so, marketers can attempt to assign values to incremental and successive units of consumption over time, which may be of assistance in establishing the most appropriate quantities and prices for the offering, among other marketing mix elements.

APPLICATION AREAS AND FURTHER READINGS

Consumer Behavior
Monroe, Kent B., and Lee, Angela, Y. (1999). ' Remembering versus Knowing: Issues in Buyers' Processing of Price Information,' *Journal of the Academy of Marketing Science*, 27(2), 207–225.

Marketing Strategy
Heilbrun, James, and Gray, Charles M. (2001). *The Economics of Art and Culture*. Cambridge: Cambridge University Press.

Marketing Research
Yang, Ching-Chow (2003). 'Improvement Actions Based on the Customers' Satisfaction Survey,' *Total Quality Management and Business Excellence*, 14(8), October, 919–930.

BIBLIOGRAPHY
Lange, O. (1934). 'The Determinateness of the Utility Function,' *Review of Economic Studies*, 1(3), June, 218–225.
Latane, Henry Allen (1959). 'Criteria for Choice among Risky Ventures,' *Journal of Political Economy*, 67(2), April, 144–155.

■ diminishing returns, law of

(also called the law of increasing opportunity cost; sometimes referred to as the law of variable proportions)

DESCRIPTION
An economic principle summarizing the situation where the output for a given unit of input increases but at a decreasing rate with each additional unit of input.

KEY INSIGHTS
The law of diminishing returns is widely recognized outside of economics given the extent it appears to apply to a wide array of phenomena including consumption situations as described in the law of diminishing marginal utility. In its simplest form, the law refers to the effect on output when there is only one input involved. When there are multiple inputs involved, the effect generally refers to the situation where one input is increased but where all other inputs remain the same.

KEY WORDS Processes, decreasing returns, outputs, inputs

IMPLICATIONS
As marketers seek to make the best use of marketing resources in support of marketing strategies aimed at achieving particular objectives, marketers must seek to avoid a 'more is better' mentality of marketing resource use. Whether in efforts to establish appropriate advertising expenditures or an appropriate number of product options to present to consumers, the law of diminishing returns suggests marketers must attempt to establish what level of inputs is ultimately optimal given the effect on outputs such as consumer awareness or purchase interest.

APPLICATION AREAS AND FURTHER READINGS

Advertising
Simon, J. L., and Arndt, J. (1980). 'The Shape of the Advertising Response Function,' *Journal of Advertising Research*, 20(4), August, 11–28.

Direct Marketing
Thomas, J. S., Reinartz, W., and Kumar, V. (2004). 'Getting the Most out of All your Customers,' *Harvard Business Review*, 82(7–8), July–August, 116–123.

Consumer Behavior
Meyer, Robert, and Johnson, Eric J. (1995). 'Empirical Generalizations in the Modeling of Consumer Choice,' *Marketing Science*, 14(3), Part 2 of 2: Special Issue on Empirical Generalizations in Marketing, G180–G189.

BIBLIOGRAPHY
Sraffa, P. (1926). 'The Laws of Returns under Competitive Conditions,' *Economic Journal*, December, 535–550.

☐ **direct mail marketing** *see* direct marketing

■ direct marketing

(also called direct response marketing)

DESCRIPTION

Marketing that is aimed directly at a consumer at any location and which intends to elicit and obtain a measurable response from the consumer.

KEY INSIGHTS

As a result of the increasing use of specialized databases by marketers in the direct marketing industry, direct marketing applications involving brochures, letters, coupons, print ads, and the like continue to expand. Yet, direct marketing can involve virtually any medium provided it includes an element of communication asking the consumer to take some specific action (e.g. visit a website, call a telephone number, etc.). As such, in contrast to many other marketing efforts, a major appeal of direct marketing to a firm is the relatively greater ease by which the firm can measure directly the consumer response to any given direct marketing campaign. Firms can be said to use an *integrated direct marketing* approach when they explicity coordinate the use of multiple direct marketing methods to increase response rates in an effort to achieve even greater marketing effectiveness and firm profitability. Such methods may include: *e-mail marketing*—sending electronic messages containing marketing material from one computer to one or more consumer computers on a network; *fax marketing*—using facsimile equipment to electronically transfer written or graphic marketing material over telephone lines to consumer locations; *direct mail marketing, mail marketing,* or *postal marketing*—using the mail or postal system to send marketing material directly to one or more consumers; *telemarketing*—using the telephone as an interactive medium for communicating directly with consumers; *voice mail marketing*—using telecommunications equipment and telephone networks as a one-way medium for communicating indirectly with consumers by leaving voice messages on centralized voice mail systems or individual telephone answering machines; and *door-to-door marketing*—using marketing personnel to make in-person visits at consumers' residences.

KEY WORDS Consumer response, information

IMPLICATIONS
Marketers seeking greater measurability of the effectiveness of their marketing efforts may benefit from greater use of direct marketing approaches. While the use of direct marketing by a firm depends in part on the characteristics of the firms' offerings, marketers must also be sensitive to consumer preferences and attitudes to the approach, which may include negative attitudes if consumers perceive the approach as being both intrusive and wasteful as with some firms' large-scale direct mail campaigns.

APPLICATION AREAS AND FURTHER READINGS
Marketing Strategy
Nash, E. L., and Jackson, D. (2000). *Direct Marketing: Strategy, Planning, Execution*. New York: McGraw-Hill.
Roman, Ernan (1988). *Integrated Direct Marketing*. New York: McGraw-Hill Book Company.

Marketing Management
Nowak, G. J., and Phelps, J. (1997). 'Direct Marketing and the Use of Individual-Level Consumer Information: Determining How and When "Privacy" Matters,' *Journal of Direct Marketing*, 11(4), Fall, 94–109.
Stone, B. (1996). *Successful Direct Marketing Methods*. Chicago: NTC Business Books.

Marketing Research
Ling, C., and Li, C. (1998). 'Data Mining for Direct Marketing: Problems and Solutions,' in *Proceedings of the Fourth International Conference on Knowledge Discovery and Data Mining* (KDD-98). New York: AAAI Press.

Marketing Modeling
Allenby, G. M., Leone, R. P., and Jen, L. (1999). 'A Dynamic Model of Purchase Timing with Application to Direct Marketing,' *Journal of the American Statistical Association*, 94, 365–374.

Online Marketing
Walle, A. H. (1996). 'Tourism and the Internet: Opportunities for Direct Marketing,' *Journal of Travel Research*, 35(1), 72–77.

BIBLIOGRAPHY
Tapp, A. (1998). *Principles of Direct and Database Marketing*. London: Financial Times Pitman Publishing.

☐ direct response marketing *see* direct marketing

■ direct-to-consumer marketing

DESCRIPTION
Marketing by a manufacturer or other organization that involves direct communications with consumers, particularly in markets where the relationship between such organizations and consumers is typically indirect.

KEY INSIGHTS

While the scope of direct-to-consumer marketing is broad, manufacturers operating in markets where consumers traditionally rely on the advice of professional intermediaries in particular (e.g. physicians) may find benefit in using direct-to-consumer marketing methods to increase awareness, preference, purchase, and use of their offerings. Direct-to-consumer marketing is therefore able to educate consumers about the firm's offerings to a greater extent than is possible or likely through intermediaries. At the same time, the approach may involve oversight by legal or regulatory bodies concerned also with the net effect of its influence, such as where there may be concern that the approach may also lead to higher prices or over-prescription of certain medical devices, for example.

KEY WORDS Direct communication

IMPLICATIONS

In being able to communicate directly to consumers, direct-to-consumer marketing enables firms to increase awareness and interest in its branded offerings in relation to perceptions of the offering's benefits—something that may not be as effective or controllable when performed through intermediaries. Such knowledge may then lead consumers to enquire about, prefer, or specify directly the branded offerings when interacting with other intermediaries.

APPLICATION AREAS AND FURTHER READINGS

Marketing Strategy

Holmer, A. F. (1999). 'Direct-to-Consumer Prescription Drug Advertising Builds Bridges between Patients and Physicians,' *Journal of the American Medical Association*, 281(4), 380–381.

Hollon, M. F. (1999). 'Direct-to-Consumer Marketing of Prescription Drugs: Creating Consumer Demand,' *Journal of the American Medical Association*, 281(4), 382–384.

Wolfe, S. M. (2002). 'Direct-to-Consumer Advertising: Education or Emotion Promotion?' *New England Journal of Medicine*, 346(7), 524–525.

Lee, T. H., and Brennan, T. A. (2002). 'Direct-to-Consumer Marketing of High-Technology Screening Tests,' *New England Journal of Medicine*, 346, 529–531.

BIBLIOGRAPHY

Fintor, L. (200). 'Direct-to-Consumer Marketing: How Has It Fared?' *Journal of the National Cancer Institute*, 94(5), 329–331.

■ Dirichlet model

DESCRIPTION

A modeling approach for gaining insight into habitual, near-steady state consumer behaviors.

KEY INSIGHTS

A Dirichlet modeling approach (named after a prominent nineteenth-century German mathematician) describes and characterizes consumer buying behavior using five relatively simple assumptions regarding purchase incidence and brand choice for the market being examined:

(1) each buyer or buying unit has a steady as-if-random buying probability (i.e. these probabilities are Poisson distributed across the market); (2) there is a smooth (gamma) distribution of light, medium, and heavy buyers; (3) each buyer uses a portfolio of brands with steady probabilities and these probabilities are represented by a multinomial distribution across those in the market; (4) individuals' buying probabilities follow a smooth beta distribution across the market; and (5) brand choice is independent of purchase incidence. These assumptions enable analysis and prediction of a wide range of brand performance measures such as penetration, purchase frequency, and loyalty. There are a number of generalizations stemming from research involving the Dirichlet modeling approach, and one of the most notable is an effect termed 'double jeopardy.' (See **double jeopardy effect.**)

KEY WORDS Loyalty, brand choice

IMPLICATIONS
Marketers concerned with the study of loyalty and brand choice through the development and use of sophisticated marketing models may benefit from a greater understanding of the Dirichlet modeling approach as it can assist the marketer with identifying many buying patterns with minimal inputs. As its applicability has been demonstrated across a range of product markets, marketers wishing to adopt a modeling approach that is not only simple and easy to operationalize but relatively robust may find the Dirichlet modeling approach to be particularly beneficial.

APPLICATION AREAS AND FURTHER READINGS
Marketing Strategy
Stern, P., and Hammond, Kathy (2004). 'The Relationship between Customer Loyalty and Purchase Incidence,' *Marketing Letters*, 15(1), 5–19.

Marketing Modeling
Fader, Peter S., and Schmittlein, David C. (1993). 'Excess Behavioral Loyalty for High-Share Brands: Deviations from the Dirichlet Model for Repeat Purchasing,' *Journal of Marketing Research*, 30(4), November, 478–493.
Uncles, Mark, Ehrenberg, A. S. C., and Hammond, Kathy (1995). 'Patterns of Buyer Behavior: Regularities, Models, and Extensions,' *Marketing Science*, 14(3), G71–G78.

Marketing Research
Ehrenberg, A. S. C., Uncles, M. D., and Goodhardt, G. J. (2004). 'Understanding Brand Performance Measures: Using Dirichlet Benchmarks,' *Journal of Business Research*, 57(12), 1307–1325.

BIBLIOGRAPHY
Goodhardt, G. J., Ehrenberg, A. S. C., and Chatfield, C. (1984). 'The Dirichlet: A Comprehensive Model of Buying Behaviour,' *Journal of the Royal Statistical Society*, Series A (General), 147(5), 621–655.

☐ discriminant validity *see* validity

■ diseconomies of scale

DESCRIPTION
Increases in unit product costs resulting from an increase in production output.

KEY INSIGHTS

In contrast to economies of scale in a production process (see **economies of scale**), diseconomies of scale may arise when an organization's size and scale of output, perhaps beyond a certain point, result in inefficiencies rather than efficiencies that affect the firm's costs. As the scale of a firm's operations increases, factors leading to greater inefficiencies may be related to the increased cost and effort needed for effective communication and employee management as well as the decreased ability of the firm to respond quickly and flexibly to changes in the external environment.

KEY WORDS Production output, **cost(s)**, **scale**

IMPLICATIONS

Marketers seeking to reduce unit production costs for goods or services through economies of scale in any process, whether research and development or customer service operations, should be cognizant of how the increased scale of the firm's operations may also lead to increases in the firm's unit production costs. In particular, marketing managers should be aware of costs incurred as a result of the increased difficulty in organization-wide communication as well as effective and timely organizational decision making.

APPLICATION AREAS AND FURTHER READINGS

New Product Development
Zenger, Todd R. (1994). 'Explaining Organizational Diseconomies of Scale in R&D: Agency Problems and the Allocation of Engineering Talent, Ideas, and Effort by Firm Size,' *Management Science*, 40(6), June, 708–729.

Services Marketing
Katrishen, F. A., and Scordis, N. A. (1998). 'Economies of Scale in Services: A Study of Multinational Insurers,' *Journal of International Business Studies*, 29(2), S. 305–324.

BIBLIOGRAPHY
Stigler, George J. (1958). 'The Economies of Scale,' *Journal of Law and Economics*, 1, October, 54–71.

■ disintermediation

DESCRIPTION

The process of removing or eliminating intermediaries from a supply chain in the accomplishment of a transaction.

KEY INSIGHTS

In relation to traditional supply chains comprising distributors, wholesalers, brokers, or agents, the process of disintermediation enables the supplier of an offering to bypass such intermediaries and engage in transactions directly with the end-customer. Factors leading to disintermediation in many industries such as airline ticketing, where consumers can purchase airline tickets directly from an airline instead of having to buy from a travel agent, include decreases in the costs incurred by firms in providing services directly to consumers as well as increases in the transparency of markets (e.g. knowledge of supplier prices)—both of which are associated with advances in the use and scope of e-commerce, for example.

KEY WORDS Intermediaries, supply chain

IMPLICATIONS
While developments in many product markets (e.g. personal computers, travel services) include that of increased disintermediation activity, marketers should recognize that disintermediation is not an absolute and inevitable trend for every product market. In particular, marketers should seek to understand how and to what extent intermediaries add value in the exchange process and compare the costs and benefits of intermediary-based approaches with that of disintermediation as part of a critical evaluation of the firm's marketing strategies. Firms must recognize as well the limitations imposed by the legal and regulatory environments in some country markets, where such restrictions on disintermediation are in place to guard against possible adverse market competition even though there may be benefits of disintermediation to consumers.

APPLICATION AREAS AND FURTHER READINGS
Marketing Strategy
Achrol, Ravi S., and Kotler, Philip (1999). 'Marketing in the Network Economy,' *Journal of Marketing*, 63, Fundamental Issues and Directions for Marketing, 146–163.

International Marketing
Sheth, Jagdish N., and Sharma, Arun (2005). 'International E-marketing: Opportunities and Issues,' *International Marketing Review*, 22(6), 611–622.
Prasad, V. Kanti, Ramamurthy, K., and Naidu, G. M. (2001). 'The Influence of Internet-Marketing Integration on Marketing Competencies and Export Performance,' *Journal of International Marketing*, 9(4), Winter, 82–110.
Ritchie, B., and Brindley, C. S. (2001). 'Disintermediation, Disintegration and Risk in the Global Supply Chain,' *Management Decision*, 38(8), 575–583.

Online Marketing
Aldin, N., and Stahre, F. (2003). 'Electronic Commerce, Marketing Channels and Logistics Platforms: A Wholesaler Perspective,' *European Journal of Operational Research*, 144, 270–279.

BIBLIOGRAPHY
Ryan, C. (2000). 'How Disintermediation is Changing the Rules of Marketing, Sales and Distribution,' *Interactive Marketing* (London), 1(4), 368–374.

☐ disruptive innovation *see* disruptive technology

■ **disruptive technology**

(also known as disruptive innovation)

DESCRIPTION
A new technology or technological innovation that has the effect of radically transforming a market involving an existing or dominant technology.

While there may be few technologies that are intrinsically disruptive, there are certainly countless examples of markets that have been transformed by disruptive innovations (e.g. automobiles replacing the horse for transport; PCs replacing minicomputers; digital photography replacing chemically based photography). As such, disruptive innovations may be viewed as a narrower term capturing the same notion as disruptive technology but one that also recognizes how strategy is influential in its impact. It is also recognized that disruptive innovations can encroach on markets in different ways, such as where a disruption encroaches on a market from its low end or where a disruptive innovation transforms a market through its initial appeal to a new or emerging market segment.

KEY WORDS Technology, innovation, market transformation

IMPLICATIONS
Disruptive technologies and innovations can clearly have a dramatic effect on a product market, but marketers must acknowledge that such disruptions may be difficult to recognize given their significance takes time to become established. As such, marketers should continually scan the marketing environment for disruptive influences, where such efforts may involve proactive efforts (e.g. joint investments with innovative suppliers and/or customers) to understand better not only how various innovations are influencing the value provided by a firm's offerings to its customers but also how such innovations may be able to meet current and future customer wants and needs in ways that the firm's offerings do not.

APPLICATION AREAS AND FURTHER READINGS
Marketing Strategy
Newbert, S., Kirchhoff, B., and Walsh, S. (2002). 'Differentiating Market Strategies for Disruptive Technologies,' *IEEE Transactions on Engineering Management*, 49(4), 341–351.
Sandberg, B. (2002). 'Creating the Market for Disruptive Innovation: Market Proactiveness at the Launch Stage,' *Journal of Targeting, Measurement and Analysis for Marketing*, 11(2), 184–196.

Marketing Research
Danneels, E. (2004). 'Disruptive Technology Reconsidered: A Critique and Research Agenda,' *Journal of Product Innovation Management*, 21, 246–258.
Garcia, R., and Calantone, R. (2002). 'Critical Look at Technological Innovation Typology and Innovativeness Terminology: A Literature Review,' *Journal of Product Innovation Management*, 19(2), March, 110–132.

BIBLIOGRAPHY
Bower, Joseph L., and Christensen, Clayton M. (1995). 'Disruptive Technologies: Catching the Wave,' *Harvard Business Review*, 73(1), January–February, 43–53.
Christensen, C. (1997). *The Innovator's Dilemma*. Boston: Harvard Business School Press.
Christensen, C. M., and Rayor, M. E. (2003). *The Innovator's Solution: Creating and Sustaining Successful Growth*. Boston: Harvard Business School Press.

Tushman, M. L., and Anderson, P. (1986). 'Technological Discontinuities and Organizational Environments,' *Administrative Science Quarterly*, 31, 439–465.

☐ dissonance-reducing buyer behavior *see* consumer buyer behavior

☐ distinctiveness effect *see* von Restorff effect

■ distribution strategies

DESCRIPTION

Approaches to the distribution of a firm's offerings which are driven by strategic considerations and which have strategic implications for a firm.

KEY INSIGHTS

There are three general distribution approaches open to a firm. These are: *exclusive distribution*, where a firm gives a relatively small number of dealers an exclusive right to distribute the firm's offerings within the dealers' territories; *selective distribution*, where a firm chooses to distribute its offerings selectively through multiple (though not all possible) distributors; and *intensive distribution*, where a firm aims to distribute the firm's offerings in as many places or outlets as possible through an extremely wide range of distributors. The choice of a particular distribution strategy depends on many factors, of course, including the product characteristics. Exclusive distribution, for example, is consistent with the characteristics of exclusive products such as luxury watches. On the other hand, the distribution of Coca-Cola—a frequently purchased and relatively inexpensive product—clearly benefits from an intensive distribution strategy.

KEY WORDS Distribution intensity

IMPLICATIONS

Marketers must clearly understand the characteristics of their offerings (e.g. market segment appeal) as well as consumer buyer behavior to determine the most suitable distribution strategy. At the same time, marketers must give consideration to competitors' distribution strategies, which, for an increasing number of consumer products, involves intensive distribution through a combination of online retail distribution and traditional retail outlet distribution.

APPLICATION AREAS AND FURTHER READINGS

Marketing Strategy

Frazier, Gary L., and Lassar, Walfried M. (1996). 'Determinants of Distribution Intensity,' *Journal of Marketing*, 60, October, 39–51.

Premkumar, G. P. (2003). 'Alternate Distribution Strategies for Digital Music,' *Communications of the ACM*, 46(9), 89–95.

Relationship Marketing

Weitz, Barton E., and Jap, Sandy D. (1995). 'Relationship Marketing and Distribution Channels,' *Journal of the Academy of Marketing Science*, 23, 305–320.

Retail Marketing

Fernie, John (1992). 'Distribution Strategies of European Retailers,' *European Journal of Marketing*, 26(8–9), 35–47.

Online Marketing
Ranchhod, A., and Gurau, C. (1999). 'Internet-Enabled Distribution Strategies,' *Journal of Information Technology*, 14, 333–346.

BIBLIOGRAPHY
Kotler, Philip, and Armstrong, Gary (2006). *Principles of Marketing*. 11th edn. Upper Saddle River, NJ: Pearson Education, Inc.

☐ divergent validity *see* validity

☐ diversification *see* product-market investment strategies

☐ diversity marketing *see* multicultural marketing

☐ divestment *see* decline strategies

■ division of labor effect

DESCRIPTION
The tendency for increased efficiency and productivity as a result of decomposing the steps of a complex production process and dividing the tasks and responsibilities across multiple workers, where individual workers repeatedly engage in the same specialized tasks.

KEY INSIGHTS
A significant driver of increases in efficiency and productivity with a division of labor approach to production processes is the need for workers to only perfect particular sets of skills rather than many skills in the accomplishment of their tasks. Such an approach may lead to higher quality as specialized knowledge can be developed while at the same time a lower-cost workforce might be possible as a result of requiring workers with less overall skill. A recognized concern over the approach, however, is that overly simple and repetitive tasks may be detrimental to workers.

KEY WORDS Specialization, production processes

IMPLICATIONS
Marketers involved in establishing and managing complex marketing processes such as those supporting new product introductions may benefit in applying a division of labor approach to the extent that the approach leads to greater efficiencies as well as cost reductions and quality increases. Ultimately, marketers must consider how and to what extent division of labor within as well as outside the organization may lead to such benefits.

APPLICATION AREAS AND FURTHER READINGS

Innovation
Arora, Ashish, Fosfuri, Andrea, and Gambardella, Alfonso (2001). *Markets for Technology: The Economics of Innovation and Corporate Strategy*. Cambridge, Mass.: MIT Press.

Marketing Management
Achrol, Ravi S. (1991). 'Evolution of the Marketing Organization: New Forms for Turbulent Environments,' *Journal of Marketing*, 55(4), October, 77–93.

Relationship Marketing
Sheth, J. N., and Parvatiyar, A. (1995). 'The Evolution of Relationship Marketing,' *International Business Review*, 4(4), December, 397–418.

BIBLIOGRAPHY
Smith, Adam (1776). *An Inquiry into the Nature and Causes of the Wealth of Nations.* Boston: Adamant Media Corporation.

☐ **dog** *see* product portfolio analysis

■ domino effect

DESCRIPTION
The effect of an action or other change in state where it precipitates a sequence or chain of similar actions or changes.

KEY INSIGHTS
In a domino effect, the action or change precipitating subsequent changes may potentially be small in and of itself and thus have a potential for a much larger overall effect, as when the effect of one person's applause in the middle of a theatrical performance acts to initiate the applause of nearby individuals and subsequently most of the audience.

KEY WORDS Change, action, reaction

IMPLICATIONS
While anticipating possible domino effects in the marketing of products and services may be difficult, marketers should nevertheless not underestimate the potential for small actions to produce relatively large overall effects, either positive or negative. For example, a negative domino effect would be observed when one consumer's voice of dissatisfaction for waiting in a long check-out line in a supermarket leads to numerous consumers also in the line also voicing their dissatisfaction.

APPLICATION AREAS AND FURTHER READINGS
Services Marketing
Halstead, D., Morash E. A., and Ozment, J. (1996). 'Comparing Objective Service Failures and Subjective Complaints: An Investigation of Domino and Halo Effects,' *Journal of Business Research*, 36(2), June, 107–115.

Customer Satisfaction
Chong, Bessie, and Wong, Michael (2005). 'Crafting an Effective Customer Retention Strategy: A Review of Halo Effect on Customer Satisfaction in Online Auctions,' *International Journal of Management and Enterprise Development*, 2(1), 12–26.

Marketing Strategy
Tucker, James J., and Tucci, Louis A. (1994). 'Why Traditional Measures of Earnings Performance May Lead to Failed Strategic Marketing Decisions: A Focus on Core Operations,' *Journal of Consumer Marketing*, 11(3), 4–17.

BIBLIOGRAPHY
Byrne, N. M. (2004). 'The Domino Effect,' *Limras Marketfacts Quarterly*, 23(4), 68–70.

■ door-in-the-face technique

(also called the rejection-then-retreat technique)

DESCRIPTION

A technique for persuading an individual to accept or adopt a particular course of action where the individual is first presented with a request to accept a much larger course of action which the individual is almost certain to reject.

KEY INSIGHTS

Based on pioneering research by Cialdini et al. (1975), the door-in-the-face technique was observed to be more effective in obtaining volunteers for particular causes relative to the condition where volunteers were sought for the same causes without using the technique. The technique therefore involves presenting an option that is so extreme as to be unacceptable, thereby making lesser alternatives appear more acceptable in comparison.

KEY WORDS Persuasion, compliance, negotiation, selling

IMPLICATIONS

While the technique may certainly not be appropriate for use in all or even in most instances where marketers seek to persuade as it is one technique among many, it nevertheless may be an alternative, and marketers may wish to explore its viability in areas of persuasive communication including personal selling and negotiations.

APPLICATION AREAS AND FURTHER READINGS

Marketing Research

Groves, Robert M., Cialdini, Robert B., and Couper, Mick P. (1992). 'Understanding the Decision to Participate in a Survey,' *Public Opinion Quarterly*, 56(4), Winter, 475–495.

Marketing Strategy

Tybout, Alice M. (1978). 'Relative Effectiveness of Three Behavioral Influence Strategies as Supplements to Persuasion in a Marketing Context,' *Journal of Marketing Research*, 15(2), May, 229–242.

Fern, Edward F., Monroe, Kent B., and Avila, Ramon A. (1986). 'Effectiveness of Multiple Request Strategies: A Synthesis of Research Results,' *Journal of Marketing Research*, 23(2), May, 144–152.

Dillard, James P., Hunter, John E., and Burgoon, Michael (1984). 'Sequential-Request Persuasive Strategies: Meta-Analysis of Foot-in-the-Door and Door-in-the-Face,' *Human Communication Research*, 10(4), June, 461.

BIBLIOGRAPHY

Cialdini, R. B., Vincent, J. E., Lewis, S. K., Catalan, J., Wheeler, D., and Darby, B. L. (1975). 'Reciprocal Concessions Procedure for Inducing Compliance: The Door-in the-Face Technique,' *Journal of Personality and Social Psychology*, 31, 206–215.

□ door-to-door marketing *see* direct marketing

■ double jeopardy effect

DESCRIPTION

The phenomenon where big-share brands benefit in two ways when compared to small-share brands, namely, (1) having more buyers than small-share brands and (2) being bought slightly more frequently than small-share brands, where both effects occur within the same timeframe.

KEY INSIGHTS
The double jeopardy effect is present in a product category where it is observed that high market penetration tends to coincide with slightly higher purchase frequencies. Confirmed observations of the phenomenon make it an empirical generalization across a number of branded product categories, ranging from detergents to pet foods to pharmaceutical prescribing, in the UK, the USA, Europe and Japan.

KEY WORDS Brands, size, purchase frequency, loyalty

IMPLICATIONS
Marketers involved in brand management should strive to understand purchase behaviors for all brands in a particular product category and whether the double jeopardy pattern is visible. To the extent it is observed, marketers may be able to anticipate better how changes to encourage more buyers may also coincide with greater purchase frequency.

APPLICATION AREAS AND FURTHER READINGS
Promotions
Jones, J. P. (1990). 'The Double Jeopardy of Sales Promotions,' *Harvard Business Review*, 68(5), September–October, 145–152.

Marketing Modeling
Fader, Peter S., and Schmittlein, David C. (1993). 'Excess Behavioral Loyalty for High-Share Brands: Deviations from the Dirichlet Model for Repeat Purchasing,' *Journal of Marketing Research*, 30(4), November, 478–493.

Marketing Research
Ehrenberg, A. S. C. (1995). 'Empirical Generalisations, Theory, and Method,' *Marketing Science*, 14(3), Part 2 of 2: Special Issue on Empirical Generalizations in Marketing, G20–G28.

BIBLIOGRAPHY
Ehrenberg, Andrew S. C., Goodhardt, Gerald J., and Barwise, T. Patrick (1990). 'Double Jeopardy Revisited,' *Journal of Marketing*, 54(3), July, 82–91.
Ehrenberg, A., and Goodhardt, G. (2002). 'Double Jeopardy Revisited, Again,' *Marketing Research*, 14(1), 40–42.

■ drive theory of social facilitation

DESCRIPTION
A theory aimed at explaining how and why a social presence, such as that of a passive audience, may facilitate or hinder the performance of an individual's task.

KEY INSIGHTS
Based on pioneering research by Zajonc (1965), the theory suggests that the unpredictable nature of people leads one to be in a more alert or aroused state when performing a task. When an individual performs a task that is well learned or simple, a social presence may lead to enhanced performance as such a presence may facilitate eliciting dominant responses from the individual. On the other hand, performance

may be reduced by a social presence when an individual performs an inadequately learned or difficult task as a result of incorrect responses dominating.

KEY WORDS Audiences, social facilitiation, motivation, performance

IMPLICATIONS
Marketers should be sensitive to how audiences or other forms of social presence may facilitate or hinder the performance of particular individuals engaged in particular tasks, as when a marketing executive is interviewed before a live audience. In such a case, consideration should be given to not only the nature of the social presence (e.g. audience receptivity, friendliness) but also the abilities of the individual relative to the task (e.g. public speaking ability) and the relative simplicity or difficulty of the task (e.g. whether it is a well-known or difficult and controversial topic).

APPLICATION AREAS AND FURTHER READINGS
Marketing Communications
Sussman, Stephanie W., and Sproull, Lee (1999). 'Straight Talk: Delivering Bad News through Electronic Communication,' *Information Systems Research*, 10(2), June, 150–166.
Deaudelin, Colette, Dussault, Marc, and Brodeur, Monique (2003). 'Human-Computer Interaction: A Review of the Research on its Affective and Social Aspects,' *Canadian Journal of Learning and Technology*, 29(1), Winter.

Services Marketing
Sundaram, D. S., and Webster, Cynthia (2000). 'The Role of Nonverbal Communication in Service Encounters,' *Journal of Services Marketing*, 14(5), September, 378–391.

BIBLIOGRAPHY
Geen, R. G., and Gange, J. J. (1977). 'Drive Theory of Social Facilitation: Twelve Years of Theory and Research,' *Psychological Bulletin*, 84, 1267–88.
Zajonc, R. B. (1965). 'Social Facilitation,' *Science*, 149, 269–274.
Peskin, M. M. (1997). 'Drive Theory Revisited,' *Psychoanalytic Quarterly*, 66, 377–402.

☐ **Dunning's eclectic paradigm** *see* eclectic paradigm
☐ **durable good** *see* goods

■ dynamic capabilities

DESCRIPTION
Processes within a firm aimed at maintaining consistency with, or creating changes to, the firm's markets.

KEY INSIGHTS
As markets are rarely static, but rather are often in a state of constant change in terms of their evolution (e.g. they emerge, merge, divide, or die out), dynamic capabilities capture the notion that there are processes within a firm that assist it with maintaining compatibility with, or proactively changing, market conditions. In particular, firms can be viewed as having organizational and strategic routines that enable the

firm to harness, integrate, or reconfigure resources, as well as establish or release new resources, aimed at ensuring market consistency or its focused change, and where the ultimate aim is that of developing and achieving competitive advantages. While the term may be vaguely or generally applied in characterizations of the relative strength of the organization's overall capabilities, it can also be used in the identification of specific capabilities, such as those facilitating effective new product development efforts (e.g. via the presence and development of technological skills among workers) or effective strategic decision making (e.g. via the pooling of functional expertise among managers), for example.

KEY WORDS Competitive advantage, dynamic markets

IMPLICATIONS
As markets clearly vary in the nature and extent of their dynamic change, marketers must assess how and to what extent dynamic capabilities within the firm may contribute to maintaining consistency between the firm and its markets and/or influencing market change. At the extreme, a market may be so volatile that a firm's dynamic capabilities become unstable. At the very least, however, a firm may benefit from understanding, evaluating, and integrating 'best industry practices' as part of its efforts to develop and implement value-creating strategies given its specific resources.

APPLICATION AREAS AND FURTHER READINGS

Marketing Strategy
Teece, D. J., Pisano, G., and Shuen, A. (1997). 'Dynamic Capabilities and Strategic Management,' *Strategic Management Journal*, 18(7), 509–534.
Rindova, V., and Kotha, S. (2001). 'Continuous Morphing: Competing through Dynamic Capabilities, Form, and Function,' *Academy of Management Journal*, 44, 1263–1280.

International Marketing
Griffith, David A., and Harvey, Michael G. (2001). 'A Resource Perspective of Global Dynamic Capabilities,' *Journal of International Business Studies*, 32(3), 597–606.

New Product Development
Marsh, S. J., and Stock, G. N. (2003). 'Building Dynamic Capabilities in new Product Development through Intertemporal Integration,' *Journal of Product Innovation Management*, 20, 136–148.

BIBLIOGRAPHY
Eisenhardt, K., and Martin, J. (2000). 'Dynamic Capabilities: What are They?' *Strategic Management Journal*, 21, 1105–1121.

☐ **dynamic pricing** *see* pricing strategies

E

☐ **E, theory** *see* E and O theories of change

■ E and O theories of change

DESCRIPTION
A set of two dramatically different theories of organizational change, with
theory E focusing on the creation of economic value and with theory O focusing
on the development of the organization's human capabilities.

KEY INSIGHTS
Put forth and developed by Beer and Nohria (2000), the two different
approaches to organizational change emphasize differences in both the
purpose and means of organizational change. With theory E's purpose
being that of creating economic value (e.g. shareholder value), the means
of change associated with theory E is viewed as including, among other
factors, top-down leadership, an organizational emphasis on structure
and systems, and programmatic planning. In contrast, theory O's purpose
of developing human capabilities within the organization for effective
strategy implementation and learning from organizational change leads
the organization to adopt a cultural focus with participative leadership
and rely on an emergent approach to planning. Given that arguments
for both approaches to organizational change are equally legitimate and
plausible, each has shortcomings relative to the other, however. As such,
combining the two approaches, while somewhat paradoxical, may lead
to more effective organizational change in comparison to the adoption of
only one approach or the other. Still, the daunting challenge associated
with the effective integration of the two approaches (either by simultaneous or sequential means) suggests that firms lacking the overall skills
to integrate them may be better adopting only a single approach with
recognition of its particular costs and benefits.

KEY WORDS Organizational change, **value**, capabilities

IMPLICATIONS
Marketing managers and strategists involved in major efforts to develop
and implement organizational change may find a greater knowledge of
the E and O theories of change to understand and evaluate better the
change options and approaches open to the firm. In particular, managers must assess to what extent the firm may be able to integrate the

approaches or implement either in an effort to identify the most suitable means of pursuing particular organizational changes.

APPLICATION AREAS AND FURTHER READINGS

Marketing Strategy

Sturdy, A., and Grey, C. (2003). 'Beneath and beyond Organizational Change Management: Exploring Alternatives,' *Organization*, 10(4), 651–662.

Prastacos, G., Soderquist, K., Spanos, Y., and Van Wassenhov, L. (2002). 'An Integrated Framework for Managing Change in the New Competitive Landscape,' *European Management Journal*, 20(1), 55–71.

Lawson-Borders, G. (2003). 'Integrating New Media and Old Media: Seven Observations of Convergence as a Strategy for Best Practices in Media Organization,' *International Journal on Media Management*, 5(2), 91–99.

BIBLIOGRAPHY

Beer, M., and Nohria, N. (ed.) (2000). *Breaking the Code of Change*. Boston: Harvard Business School Press.

☐ **early adopters** *see* adopter categories

☐ **early follower** *see* market entry timing

☐ **early majority** *see* adopter categories

■ eclectic paradigm

(also called Dunning's eclectic paradigm or the OLI paradigm)

DESCRIPTION

A paradigmatic view for the consideration of foreign direct investment which suggests that ownership-specific advantages, location-specific advantages, and internalization advantages are three factors that are important in establishing whether a firm pursues direct investment in international operations.

KEY INSIGHTS

The eclectic paradigm as advanced by Dunning and developed in subsequent internationalization research suggests that the combination of ownership-specific advantages (i.e. advantages specific to the firm which enable them to compete against firms in the target country), location-specific advantages (advantages associated with the conditions prevailing in the target country), and internalization advantages (advantages associated with abilities to manage assets within the firm rather than license their use) often requires foreign direct investment, as in requiring a firm to establish production facilities where its foreign assets and resources are located.

KEY WORDS Internationalization, foreign direct investment, multinational enterprises, international operations

IMPLICATIONS

Marketers involved in international marketing strategy development and international marketing management may benefit from understanding mechanisms of internationalization which draw upon the eclectic paradigm when the aim of a firm is to ascertain the need for foreign direct investment given a firm's particular ownership, locational, and/or internalization advantages. Such knowledge may be beneficial, for example, in assisting marketers with decisions regarding the best way of meeting customer needs in different country markets (e.g. through a local presence versus a contractual arrangement with another organization).

APPLICATION AREAS AND FURTHER READINGS
International Marketing
Dawson, J. A. (1994). 'Internationalisation of Retail Operations,' *Journal of Marketing Management*, 10, 267–282.
Johansson, Jan, and Vahlne, Jan-Erik (1990). 'The Mechanism of Internationalisation,' *International Marketing Review*, 7(4), October.
Cantwell, John, and Narula, Rajneesh (2001). 'The Eclectic Paradigm in the Global Economy,' *International Journal of the Economics of Business*, 8(2), July, 155–172.

BIBLIOGRAPHY
Dunning, J. H. (1981). *International Production and the Multinational Enterprise*. London: Allen & Unwin.
Dunning, John H. (1995). 'Reappraising the Eclectic Paradigm in an Age of Alliance Capitalism,' *Journal of International Business Studies*, 26, 461.
Dunning, John H. (2001). 'The Eclectic (OLI) Paradigm of International Production: Past, Present and Future,' *International Journal of the Economics of Business*, 8(2), July, 173–190.
Williamson, O. E. (1979). 'Transaction-Cost Economics: The Governance of Contractual Relations,' *Journal of Law and Economics*, 22, October, 233–261.

☐ ecological validity *see* validity
☐ eco-centric marketing *see* green marketing
☐ eco-marketing *see* green marketing
☐ economic environment *see* macroenvironment
☐ economic theory of clubs *see* clubs, theory of

■ economies of growth

DESCRIPTION
Advantages accruing to a growing firm as a consequence of its current or earlier economic growth.

KEY INSIGHTS
Independent of other factors such as scale or scope, a growing firm may experience certain advantages relative to that experienced by a stationary firm. Beyond a certain rate of growth, a growing firm may find it is easier to retain and attract high-quality management, for example.

KEY WORD Growth

IMPLICATIONS
Depending on the current or past growth rate of their firm, marketers may find that such a measure of organizational performance provides the firm with certain advantages that are not achievable or evident in relation to other organizational performance indicators or strategies.

Given such favorable circumstances, marketing managers may wish to actively explore ways to put such advantages to use, such as in the area of recruitment of new management and related negotiations.

APPLICATION AREAS AND FURTHER READINGS

Marketing Strategy
Penrose, Edith T. (1960). 'The Growth of the Firm: A Case Study: The Hercules Powder Company?' *Business History Review*, 34(1), 1–23.
Pitelis, C. (ed.) (2002). *The Growth of the Firm: The Legacy of Edith Penrose*. Oxford: Oxford University Press.

BIBLIOGRAPHY
Penrose, E. (1958). *The Theory of the Growth of the Firm*. New York: Wiley.

■ economies of scale

DESCRIPTION
Reductions in unit production costs resulting from an increase in production output.

KEY INSIGHTS
Economies of scale in a production process can be achieved with higher output levels in a production process when the higher levels of output enable the use of more productive technologies, greater specialization of labor, lower per-unit material costs, more efficient equipment, better management utilization, and the like. In the context of economies of scale, production processes may include activities beyond the traditional manufacture of goods such as product distribution and services marketing and management. A benefit of economies of scale is that they enable a producer to offer products or services at more competitive prices or to obtain higher per-unit profit margins.

KEY WORDS Production output, **cost(s)**, **scale**

IMPLICATIONS
Marketers seeking to reduce unit production costs for goods or services in any process should consider how increasing output to specifically higher levels can provide opportunities to incorporate new or different approaches into the production process that could result in predictable cost reductions.

APPLICATION AREAS AND FURTHER READINGS

Marketing Management
Webster, Frederick E., Jr. (1992). 'The Changing Role of Marketing in the Corporation,' *Journal of Marketing*, 56(4), October, 1–17.
Srivastava, Rajendra K., Shervani, Tasadduq A., and Fahey, Liam (1999). 'Marketing, Business Processes, and Shareholder Value: An Organizationally Embedded View of Marketing Activities and the Discipline of Marketing,' *Journal of Marketing*, 63, Fundamental Issues and Directions for Marketing, 168–179.

International Marketing
Ayal, Igal, and Zif, Jehiel (1979). 'Market Expansion Strategies in Multinational Marketing,' *Journal of Marketing*, 43(2), Spring, 84–94.

Levitt, Theodore (1982). *The Globalization of Markets*. Boston: Soldiers Field, Division of Research, Graduate School of Business Administration, Harvard University.

BIBLIOGRAPHY
Stigler, George J. (1958). 'The Economies of Scale,' *Journal of Law and Economics*, 1, October, 54–71.

■ economies of scope

DESCRIPTION
Reductions in unit production costs resulting from an increase in the range of goods produced.

KEY INSIGHTS
Given that the production of goods can be broadly defined to include the provision of any product or service by a firm, economies of scope are present any time a change in the scope of the firm's offerings leads to a reduction in the unit costs associated with the provision of the offerings. Thus, an economy of scope is evident when it is more efficient for a salesperson to sell several of the firm's products rather than just one product. Typically, economies of scope arise when multiple activities of the firm are related and where common or shared resources such as equipment or personnel are involved.

KEY WORDS Product range, **cost(s)**

IMPLICATIONS
Marketing managers may benefit from examining the range of the firm's offerings for possible expansion if the aim is to manage and reduce such unit marketing costs. However, marketers should also seek to understand how and when there may be limits to the achievement of scope economies in certain marketing efforts (as when a salesperson is responsible for the sale of greater numbers of specialized products to the point where product knowledge suffers).

APPLICATION AREAS AND FURTHER READINGS
Marketing Strategy
Helfat, Constance E., and Eisenhardt, Kathleen M. (2004). 'Inter-temporal Economies of Scope, Organizational Modularity, and the Dynamics of Diversification,' *Strategic Management Journal*, 25(13), 1217–1232.
Nayyar, P., and Kazanjian, R. (1993). 'Organizing to Attain Potential Benefits from Information Asymmetries and Economies of Scope in Related Diversified Firms,' *Academy of Management Review*, 18, 735–759.

Services Marketing
Nayyar, Praveen R. (1993). 'Performance Effects of Information Asymmetry and Economies of Scope in Diversified Service Firms,' *Academy of Management Journal*, 36(1), February, 28–57.

BIBLIOGRAPHY
Gimeno, J., and Woo, C. Y. (1999). 'Multimarket Contact, Economies of Scope, and Firm Performance,' *Academy of Management Journal*, 43, 239–259.

☐ edge effect *see* serial position effect

■ effect, law of

DESCRIPTION

The psychological principle that states, of the several responses made to the same situation, that which is accompanied or closely followed by satisfaction, other things being equal, will more likely be repeated, and the connections learned, whereas those responses that are followed by punishment will be extinguished.

KEY INSIGHTS

Based on pioneering research by Thorndike (1927), the law of effect is a way to explain how people learn, which involves the selection of behaviors based on their consequences. According to this view, responses that lead to reward tend to increase in strength, whereas those that lead to punishment tend to decrease in strength. The first part of the law has been amply corroborated by empirical studies, while the second part of the law has received less corroboration.

KEY WORDS Learning, behavioral consequences, satisfaction

IMPLICATIONS

Based on the law of effect, marketers would expect consumers to be much more likely to repeatedly purchase a brand if they were satisfied with it and be much more likely to discontinue purchase if dissatisfied. In any offering, whether goods purchased or services used, future consumer behaviors may be dependent on consumers' views of the likely consequences of their particular consumption choice behaviors.

APPLICATION AREAS AND FURTHER READINGS

Consumer Behavior
Kahn, Barbara, Ratner, Rebecca, and Kahneman, Daniel (1997). 'Patterns of Hedonic Consumption over Time,' *Marketing Letters*, 8(1), January, 85–96.
Bennett, Peter D., and Mandell, Robert M. (1969). 'Prepurchase Information Seeking Behavior of New Car Purchasers: The Learning Hypothesis,' *Journal of Marketing Research*, 6(4), November, 430–433.
Heiner, Ronald A. (1983). 'The Origin of Predictable Behavior,' *American Economic Review*, 73(4), September, 560–595.

BIBLIOGRAPHY
Thorndike, Edward L. (1927). 'The Law of Effect,' *American Journal of Psychology*, 39(1–4), December, 212–222.
Herrnstein, R. J. (1970). 'On the Law of Effect,' *Journal of the Experimental Analysis of Behavior*, 13, 243–266.

■ efficient market hypothesis

DESCRIPTION

The view that asset prices in a market reflect fully all known information and therefore are the best available estimates of their real values.

KEY INSIGHTS

The efficient market hypothesis, largely examined in relation to the prices of securities in the stock market, provides a basis for economic assessments of market asset prices more generally. The hypothesis has both economic advocates and critics, with critics including many market analysts concerned with predicting share prices to identify those likely to achieve the best returns, for example. The hypothesis is further recognized as involving several forms (i.e. weak, semi-strong, and strong form efficiency), where weak form efficiency has received the broadest acceptance.

KEY WORDS Market efficiency, asset valuation

IMPLICATIONS

Marketers concerned with the accurate assessment (e.g. prediction or estimation) of asset prices may benefit from a greater understanding of the efficient market hypothesis in its various forms. While the overall hypothesis itself remains controversial, knowledge of its theoretical assumptions as well as its use in settings ranging from share price evaluations to currency exchange rate assessments may nevertheless provide the marketer with insights into alternative perspectives on asset valuations.

APPLICATION AREAS AND FURTHER READINGS

Marketing Research
Agrawal, Jagdish, and Kamakura, Wagner A. (1995). 'The Economic Worth of Celebrity Endorsers: An Event Study Analysis,' *Journal of Marketing*, 59(3), 56–62.

Marketing Strategy
Zulauf, C. R., and Irwin, S. H. (1998). 'Market Efficiency and Marketing to Enhance Income of Crop Producers,' *Review of Agricultural Economics*, 20, 308–331.
Dutt, S., and Ghosh, D. (1999). 'A Note on the Foreign Exchange Market Efficiency Hypothesis,' *Journal of Economics and Finance*, 23, 157–161.

BIBLIOGRAPHY
Fama, Eugene F. (1970). 'Efficient Capital Markets: A Review of Theory and Empirical Work,' *Journal of Finance*, 25, 383–417.

☐ **eighty-twenty principle** *see* Pareto principle

☐ **eighty-twenty rule** *see* Pareto principle

■ elaboration likelihood model

DESCRIPTION

A model of persuasion and attitude formation and change that proposes that an individual's process for attitude change is dependent on the individual's level of motivation.

KEY INSIGHTS

According to the elaboration likelihood model (ELM) as developed by Petty and Cacioppo (1983, 1986), a high level of individual motivation leads an individual to pay more attention to the quality of arguments presented in a persuasive message, whereas a low level of motivation leads an individual to be more likely to respond to peripheral elements of the message. Examples of peripheral elements in advertising include background music or spokesperson attractiveness. The model further suggests that individuals responding to peripheral elements of a message will experience attitude changes that are much more short-lived relative to the case of the individuals' focusing on, and responding positively to, the quality of a message's arguments which may lead to longer lasting attitude changes.

KEY WORDS Persuasion, attitudes, motivation

IMPLICATIONS
Marketers may benefit from understanding the extent that consumers are likely to have high or low motivations to process persuasive messages since such knowledge can enable marketers to adjust the content and composition of persuasive messages accordingly to achieve greater persuasive effectiveness.

APPLICATION AREAS AND FURTHER READINGS
Relationship Marketing
Gordon, M. E., McKeage, K., and Fox, M. A. (1998). 'Relationship Marketing Effectiveness: The Role of Involvement,' *Psychology and Marketing*, 15(5), 443–460.

Advertising
Droge, Cornelia (1989). 'Shaping the Route to Attitude Change: Central versus Peripheral Processing through Comparative versus Noncomparative Advertising,' *Journal of Marketing Research*, 26(2), May, 193–204.
Homer, Pamela M. (1990). 'The Mediating Role of Attitude toward the Ad: Some Additional Evidence,' *Journal of Marketing Research*, 27(1), February, 78–86.

BIBLIOGRAPHY
Bitner, M. J., and Obermiller, C. (1985). 'The Elaboration Likelihood Model: Limitations and Extensions in Marketing,' *Advances in Consumer Research*, 12, 420–425.
Petty, Richard E., Cacioppo, John T., and Schumann, David (1983). 'Central and Peripheral Routes to Advertising Effectiveness: The Moderating Role of Involvement,' *Journal of Consumer Research*, 10(2), September, 135–146.
Petty, Richard E., and Cacioppo, John T. (1986). *Communication and Persuasion: Central and Peripheral Routes to Attitude Change*. New York: Springer-Verlag.

□ elastic demand *see* elasticity of demand

■ elasticity of demand

DESCRIPTION
The change in demand for a good which results from a change in the price of the good itself or that of another related good.

KEY INSIGHTS
While elasticity of demand usually refers to the *price elasticity of demand* of a firm's own goods and thus is an indicator of the responsiveness of demand for the good relative to a change in its price, the term may also refer to *cross-elasticity of demand*, which is an indicator of the responsiveness of demand for the good relative to a change in the price of another related good. As such, users of the term may benefit from adopting greater specificity in terminology in avoiding any confusion or ambiguity.

Referring to price elasticity of demand, *elastic demand* is present when the elasticity of demand is greater than one (i.e. the percentage change in the quantity demanded is greater than that for its price), whereas *inelastic demand* is present when the elasticity of demand is less than one (i.e. the percentage change in the quantity demanded is less than that for its price). In assessing changes in demand attributable to the price change of another good, the relationship between goods (i.e. substitutes or complements) should be taken into account when determining cross-elasticity of demand.

KEY WORDS **Demand**, price

IMPLICATIONS

Marketers should clearly understand to what extent the demand for their goods is generally elastic or inelastic if the aim is to manage their current and future demand in response to price changes in the good or that of related goods. Relating the conceptual bases of elasticity of demand to that observed for a firm's good can provide the marketer with such insight. Beyond a general understanding, marketers should master the relatively straightforward methodologies required for their mathematical calculation to assist the firm in managing demand and price changes with even greater effectiveness.

APPLICATION AREAS AND FURTHER READINGS

Marketing Strategy
Hoch, J., Kim, B., Montgomery, A., and Rossi, P. (1995). 'Determinants of Store Level Price Elasticity,' *Journal of Marketing Research*, 32, February, 17–29.
Felton, M. V. (1992). 'On the Assumed Inelasticity of Demand for the Performing Arts,' *Journal of Cultural Economics*, 16, 1–12.

Pricing
Reibstein, D., and Gatignon, H. (1984). 'Optimal Product Line Pricing: The Influence of Elasticities and Cross-Elasticities,' *Journal of Marketing Research*, 21, 259–267.

Marketing Modeling
Tellis, Gerard J. (1988). 'The Price Elasticity of Selective Demand: A Meta-analysis of Econometric Models of Sales,' *Journal of Marketing Research*, 25(4), November, 331–341.
Forrest, D., Gulley, D., and Simmons, R. (2000), 'Elasticity of Demand for UK National Lottery Tickets,' *National Tax Journal*, 855–865.

BIBLIOGRAPHY
Case, Karl E., and Fair, Ray C. (1999). *Principles of Economics*, 5th edn. Upper Saddle River, NJ: Prentice-Hall.

■ elation effect

(also called the Crespi effect)

DESCRIPTION

The phenomenon whereby increasing the reward to an individual for a particular response leads to a greater rate of response by the individual.

KEY INSIGHTS
Based on pioneering research by Crespi (1942), a further characteristic of the elation effect is that, in comparison to responses obtained with a smaller reward, the rate of response to a larger reward is observed to increase to a greater extent than if the larger reward were given initially.

KEY WORDS Incentives, rewards, behavior

IMPLICATIONS
The phenomenon characterized as the elation effect has implications for the nature of incentives given to individuals as rewards for behaviors where the elicitation of similar future behaviors is also a consideration. The implications are therefore broad and may range from the nature of incentives given to salespeople to service staff as a means to encourage particularly desirable behaviors.

APPLICATION AREAS AND FURTHER READINGS
Marketing Management
Hines, George H. (1974). 'Sociocultural Influences on Employee Expectancy and Participative Management,' *Academy of Management Journal*, 17(2), June, 334–339.
Flaherty, C. F. (1995). 'Incentive Relativity,' *Problems in the Behavioural Sciences*, 15.

BIBLIOGRAPHY
Crespi, Leo P. (1942). 'Quantitative Variation of Incentive and Performance in the White Rat,' *American Journal of Psychology*, 55(4), October, 467–517.

☐ electronic marketing *see* e-marketing
☐ electronic word-of-mouth marketing *see* viral marketing
☐ e-mail marketing *see* e-marketing; direct marketing

■ e-marketing

(also known as digital marketing electronic marketing, or interactive marketing)

DESCRIPTION
Marketing that makes use of any interactive electronic communications technology or media in order to accomplish marketing objectives.

KEY INSIGHTS
In the broader context of e-commerce, e-marketing emphasizes the set of efforts by a firm that are focused on promoting its offerings and making them accessible to current and prospective customers by means involving electronic interactive communication. While e-marketing is often most closely associated with online marketing, as in marketing via the internet or Web (see **online marketing**; **Web marketing**), the scope of e-marketing and its applications continue to grow in areas including mobile communications (see **mobile marketing**), interactive television, and touch-screen electronic kiosks. As such, e-marketing approaches may include marketing approaches commonly associated with direct market-ing (see **direct marketing**) including *e-mail marketing*, which involves

sending electronic messages containing marketing material from one computer to one or more consumer computers on a network, and *fax marketing*, which involves using facsimile equipment to electronically transmit written or graphic marketing material over telephone lines to and from consumer and marketer locations.

KEY WORDS Communication technology

IMPLICATIONS
Marketers seeking to identify and evaluate e-marketing approaches as either a central or peripheral means by the firm to market its offerings should recognize the broad and growing scope of e-marketing. Since the key benefits of electronic communications technology include opportunities for cost-effectively expanding both the reach and richness of marketing communications relative to approaches not making use of such technology, a marketer's efforts may benefit from ongoing assessments of a wide array of the firm's marketing processes for possible e-marketing adoption and integration.

APPLICATION AREAS AND FURTHER READINGS
Marketing Strategy
De Kare-Silver, Michael (2000). *E-Shock 2000: The Electronic Shopping Revolution: Strategies for Retailers and Manufacturers.* Basingstoke: Macmillan.

Marketing Management
Turban, Ephraim (2006). *Electronic Commerce: A Managerial Perspective.* Upper Saddle River, NJ: Pearson Prentice Hall.

Online Marketing
Kalyanam, K., and McIntyre, S. (2002). 'The E-marketing Mix: A Contribution of the E-tailing Wars,' *Academy of Marketing Science,* 30(4), 487–499.
Smith, A. D. (2002). 'Loyalty and E-Marketing Issues: Customer Retention on the Web,' *Quarterly Journal of E-commerce,* 3(2), 149–61.

International Marketing
Adam, S., Mulye, R., Deans, K., and Palihawadana, D. (2002). 'E-marketing in Perspective: A Three Country Comparison of Business Use of the Internet,' *Marketing Intelligence & Planning,* 20(4), 243–251.

Marketing Education
Granitz, N., and Greene, C. (2003). 'Applying E-marketing Strategies to Online Distance Learning,' *Journal of Marketing Education,* 25(1), 16–30.

BIBLIOGRAPHY
Shapiro, Carl, and Varian, Hal R. (1999). *Information Rules.* Boston: Harvard Business School Press.
Chaston, Ian (2001). *E-marketing Strategy.* Maidenhead: McGraw-Hill.

☐ **end effect** *see* serial position effect

■ endowment effect

(also called status quo bias)

DESCRIPTION
The phenomenon whereby individuals tend to value objects more when they are owned than when not owned.

KEY INSIGHTS

Based on pioneering research by Thaler (1980), an individual's ownership of an object tends to lead the individual to demand more for the object to give it up in comparison to the amount that the individual is willing to pay to acquire it. The phenomenon suggests that evaluations of preferences should give consideration to reference points of the status quo.

KEY WORDS Ownership, valuation

IMPLICATIONS

Marketers seeking to understand and influence consumer choices and preferences for any number of objects or items of personal property should consider how the status quo situation of a consumer may ultimately be influential in product valuations and choices. For example, a marketer may find that consumers seeking to acquire prints created by a popular artist will be willing to pay lesser amounts for the prints in comparison to prices demanded by individuals who already own the prints and who are asked to sell them.

APPLICATION AREAS AND FURTHER READINGS

Consumer Behavior

Strahilevitz, Michal A., and Loewenstein, George (1998). 'The Effect of Ownership History on the Valuation of Objects,' *Journal of Consumer Research*, 25(3), December, 276–289.

Dhar, Ravi, and Simonson, Itamar (1992). 'The Effect of the Focus of Comparison on Consumer Preferences,' *Journal of Marketing Research*, 29(4), November, 430–440.

Simonson, Itamar, and Tversky, Amos (1992). 'Choice in Context: Tradeoff Contrast and Extremeness Aversion,' *Journal of Marketing Research*, 29(3), August, 281–295.

BIBLIOGRAPHY

Thaler, R. (1980). 'Towards a Positive Theory of Consumer Choice,' *Journal of Economic Behavior and Organization*, 1, 39–60.

■ Engel's law

DESCRIPTION

The economic observation that individuals tend to spend a lesser proportion of their income on food as their income rises.

KEY INSIGHTS

Originally formulated by Ernst Engel in 1857, the law or tendency is based on observations that lower-income individuals tend to spend a relatively greater proportion of their income on food in comparison to higher-income individuals whose incomes also tend to be spent across a wider range of goods and services.

KEY WORDS Income, spending, food, forecasting

IMPLICATIONS

The observation embodied in Engel's law provides one basis on which marketers may seek to establish predictions or forecasts of consumer food expenditures relative to consumer incomes.

APPLICATION AREAS AND FURTHER READINGS

Forecasting

Loeb, Benjamin S. (1955). 'The Use of Engel's Laws as a Basis for Predicting Consumer Expenditures,' *Journal of Marketing*, 20(1), July, 20–27.

Burk, Marguerite C. (1962). 'Ramifications of the Relationship between Income and Food,' *Journal of Farm Economics*, 44(1), February, 115–125.

BIBLIOGRAPHY

Engel, Ernst (1857). 'Die Productions- und Consumptionsverhaltnisse des Königreichs Sachsen,' *Zeitschrift des Statistischen Bureaus des Koeniglich Saechsischen Ministeriums des Inneren*, 8 and 9 (reprinted in: *Bulletin de l'Institut International des Statistiques*, 9, 1895).

■ enlightened marketing

DESCRIPTION

A marketing philosophy which holds that a company's marketing should optimally support the long-run performance of the overall marketing system.

KEY INSIGHTS

Enlightened marketing reflects business actions toward socially responsible marketing. In the pursuit of its broad aim, enlightened marketing advocates the adoption of five key principles or organizational philosophies: *consumer-oriented marketing*—where the firm is committed to viewing and organizing marketing activities from the consumer's perspective; *innovative marketing*—where the firm is committed to pursuing substantive product and marketing improvements; *sense-of-mission marketing*—where the firm emphasizes objectives having broad social implications as opposed to ones which are product focused; *societal marketing*—where the firm is committed to making marketing decisions which are based not only on interests of the firm but on the long-run interests of consumers and society; and *value marketing*—where the firm commits itself to actions and investments which create and build marketing value.

KEY WORDS Social responsibility

IMPLICATIONS

While much of marketing in many firms is clearly profit driven and market share focused over the short term, marketers should recognize how the adoption of an enlightened marketing philosophy may ultimately benefit the firm, consumers, and society over the long term. In particular, marketers should seek to understand and examine critically each of the philosophy's five supporting principles if the aim of the enlightened marketer is to move the firm's marketing efforts more in the direction of enlightened marketing.

APPLICATION AREAS AND FURTHER READINGS

Marketing Strategy

Laczniak, Gene R., and Murphy, Patrick E. (2006). 'Normative Perspectives for Ethical and Socially Responsible Marketing,' *Journal of Macromarketing*, 26, 154–177.

Abratt, R., and Sacks, D. (1988). 'The Marketing Challenge: Towards Profitable and
Socially, Responsible,' *Journal of Business Ethics*, 7(7), 497–507.

Services Marketing
Gronroos, Christian (1983). 'Innovative Marketing Strategies and Organization
Structures for Service Firms,' in Leonard L. Berry, G. Lynn Shostack, and Gre-
gory D. Upah (eds.), *Emerging Perspectives on Services Marketing*. Chicago: American
Marketing Association.

BIBLIOGRAPHY
Kotler, Philip, and Armstrong, Gary (2006). *Principles of Marketing*, 11th edn. Upper
Saddle River, NJ: Pearson Education, Inc.

■ entrepreneurial marketing

DESCRIPTION
Marketing adapted to small and medium-sized enterprises and particularly
where the entrepreneur has a pivotal role in the firm's marketing activities.

KEY INSIGHTS
In general terms, entrepreneurial marketing seeks to integrate the best
of entrepreneurial and marketing perspectives, e.g. entrepreneurship's
emphasis on opportunity identification and marketing's emphasis on
value creation. Thus, entrepreneurial marketing emphasizes the set of
approaches to marketing that acknowledge the resource-constrained
nature of small and medium-sized enterprises and additionally focuses
on the role of the entrepreneur in both marketing and entrepreneurial
success. For example, entrepreneurial marketing recognizes a need for
such firms to often pursue more creative and less sophisticated marketing
approaches relative to those of larger firms. In such a context, one area
which entrepreneurial marketing has focused on is that of the marketing
networks, where a firm's relationships with other firms enable it to partially overcome resource constraints in its pursuit and accomplishment
of marketing objectives.

KEY WORDS Small firms, medium-sized enterprises

IMPLICATIONS
Marketers concerned with the constraints faced by small and medium-
sized firms as well as the opportunities afforded entrepreneurs in such
firms may benefit from a deeper understanding of entrepreneurial marketing's scope and range of practices. In addition, to the extent marketers
in larger organizations have some degree of autonomy and are interested
in proactively pursuing marketing efforts that involve some degree of
innovation and risk taking, a greater knowledge of entrepreneurial marketing may also provide insights to actions and processes not previously
considered within the organization.

APPLICATION AREAS AND FURTHER READINGS
Marketing Strategy
Bjerke, B., and Hultman, C. M. (2002). *Entrepreneurial Marketing: The Growth of Small
Firms in the New Economic Era*. Cheltenham: Edward Elgar.

Gilmore, A., and Carson, D. (1999). 'Entrepreneurial Marketing by Networking, New England,' *Journal of Entrepreneurship*, 2(2), 31–38.

Morris, M., Schindehutte, M., and LaForge, R. (2002). 'Entrepreneurial Marketing: A Construct for Integrating Emerging Entrepreneurship and Marketing Perspectives,' *Journal of Marketing Theory and Practice*, 10(4), 1–20.

Stokes, David (2002). 'Entrepreneurial Marketing in the Public Sector: The Lessons of Headteachers as Entrepreneurs,' *Journal of Marketing Management*, 18, 397–414.

BIBLIOGRAPHY

Stokes, David (2000). 'Entrepreneurial Marketing: A Conceptualisation from Qualitative Research,' *Qualitative Market Research: An International Journal*, 3(1), 47–54.

Lodish, L., Morgan, H. L., and Kallianpur, A. (2001). *Entrepreneurial Marketing*. New York: John Wiley & Sons, Inc.

■ entry barriers

(also called barriers to entry)

DESCRIPTION

Factors which make it more difficult for a firm to begin operating in an industry or market.

KEY INSIGHTS

Entry barriers, whether natural or ones created by firms already operating in an industry or market, generally have the effect of putting new or would-be entrants at a cost disadvantage relative to an industry's or market's established firms. Large initial capital requirements and established firms' economies of scale (leading to lower costs) are examples of two common entry barriers that can put smaller firms desiring industry or market entry at a significant disadvantage. When such conditions are combined with an incumbent strategy of sufficiently low product pricing, for example, it can be very difficult for would-be entrants to profit from their entry.

KEY WORDS Industry entry, market entry

IMPLICATIONS

As part of an ongoing effort to assess the firm's competitive environment, marketers in incumbent firms should understand carefully how and to what extent natural entry barriers, as well as those created by strategic actions, can deter other firms from entering (or competing profitably in) an industry or market. The dynamic nature of many markets is such that entry barriers will change over time as well, leading marketers at both would-be entrant firms and incumbent firms to constantly look for barriers that are sufficiently low to provide an opportunity for firms' market entry. Advances in technology that decrease the investment required for industry entry, for example, as shown in the desktop publishing industry, may lead to relatively rapid changes in the levels of certain key entry barriers.

APPLICATION AREAS AND FURTHER READINGS
Marketing Strategy
Han, Jin K., Namwoon, Kim, and Hong-Bumm, Kim (2001). 'Entry Barriers: A
    Dull-, One, or Two Edged Sword for Incumbents? Unraveling the Paradox: A
    Contingency Perspective,' *Journal of Marketing*, 65, January, 1–14.
Baumol, William J., and Willig, Robert D. (1981). 'Fixed Costs, Sunk Costs, Entry
    Barriers, and Sustainability of Monopoly,' *Quarterly Journal of Economics*, 96(3),
    August, 405–431.
Caves, R. E., and Porter, M. E. (1977). 'From Entry Barriers to Mobility Barriers:
    Conjectural Decisions and Contrived Deterrence to New Competition,' *Quarterly
    Journal of Economics*, 91(2), May, 241–262.
Orr, Dale (1974). 'The Determinants of Entry: A Study of the Canadian Manufactur-
    ing Industries,' *Review of Economics and Statistics*, 56(1), February, 58–66.

BIBLIOGRAPHY
Karakaya, Fahri, and Stahl, Michael J. (1991). *Entry Barriers and Market Entry Decisions:
    A Guide for Marketing Executives*. New York: Quorum Books.

☐ environmental marketing *see* green marketing
☐ environmentally responsible marketing *see* green marketing

■ equity theory

DESCRIPTION
A theory of social justice suggesting that individuals strive toward social equity
where inputs and outputs are considered by individuals to be fair in relation to
those with whom they compare themselves.

KEY INSIGHTS
Based on pioneering research by Homans (1950) and developments by
subsequent researchers, equity theory includes the view that fairness is
perceived by individuals to the extent that the ratio of outcomes to inputs
for a social interaction or exchange is the same as others with whom they
are making comparisons. The theory further suggests that inequities felt
by individuals, even if in their favor, tend to lead individuals to behaviors
which try to restore equity.

KEY WORDS Fairness, social justice

IMPLICATIONS
As a key tenet of marketing involves the creation of mutually beneficial exchanges, equity theory principles and concepts can be applied by
marketers in an array of situations where a marketing aim is to create
mutually satisfying and equitable exchanges and exchange relationships
between specific buyers and sellers in a variety of contexts.

APPLICATION AREAS AND FURTHER READINGS
Marketing Research
Huppertz, John W., Arenson, Sidney J., and Evans, Richard H. (1978). 'An Applica-
    tion of Equity Theory to Buyer–Seller Exchange Situations,' *Journal of Marketing
    Research*, 15(2), May, 250–260.

Consumer Behavior
Oliver, Richard L., and Swan, John E. (1989). 'Consumer Perceptions of Interpersonal Equity and Satisfaction in Transactions: A Field Survey Approach,' *Journal of Marketing*, 53(2), April, 21–35.

Business-to-Business Marketing
Frazier, Gary L. (1983). 'Interorganizational Exchange Behavior in Marketing Channels: A Broadened Perspective,' *Journal of Marketing*, 47(4), Autumn, 68–78.

Marketing Strategy
Gundlach, Gregory T., and Murphy, Patrick E. (1993). 'Ethical and Legal Foundations of Relational Marketing Exchange,' *Journal of Marketing*, 57(4), October, 35–46.

BIBLIOGRAPHY
Homans, George (1950). *The Human Group*. New York: Harcourt, Brace & Company.
Homans, George C. (1968). *The Human Group*. London: Routledge & Kegan Paul.
Homans, George Casper (1961). *Social Behavior: Its Elementary Forms*. New York: Harcourt, Brace & World.
Adams, J. Stacy (1965). 'Inequity in Social Exchange,' in L. Berkovitz (ed.), *Advances in Experimental Psychology*, New York: Academic Press, 267–300.

■ ERG theory

DESCRIPTION

A theory or model of human needs involving the three categories of needs comprising existence, relatedness, and growth and their influence on individual behavior.

KEY INSIGHTS

Formulated by Clayton Aldefer in 1969, the model involves three non-stepped need categories of existence (e.g. physiological and safety needs such as hunger, thirst, and sex), relatedness (e.g. social and external esteem needs such as family and co-worker involvement), and growth (e.g. internal esteem and self-actualization such as the desire to be creative) where the relative importance of the three categories varies among individuals. According to the theory, an unfulfilled need may result in frustration and regression to attending to needs that appear easier to satisfy.

KEY WORDS **Need(s)**, behavior

IMPLICATIONS

Concepts from ERG theory may be potentially useful to marketers seeking to satisfy consumer needs as well as marketing managers involved in meeting the needs of employees as it provides a basis for systematic evaluations of individual needs and how such needs may impinge upon individual behaviors.

APPLICATION AREAS AND FURTHER READINGS

Consumer Behavior
Scherf, Gerhard W. H. (1977). 'Consumer Dissatisfaction: Search for Causes and Alleviation Outside the Marketplace,' *Journal of Consumer Policy*, 1(2), March, 101–108.

Services Marketing
Chiu, Hung-Chang, and Lin, Neng-Pai (2004). 'A Service Quality Measurement Derived from the Theory of Needs,' *Service Industries Journal*, 24(1), January, 187–204.

BIBLIOGRAPHY
Aldefer, Clayton P. (1969). 'An Empirical Test of a New Theory of Human Need,' *Organizational Behavior and Human Performance*, 4, 142–175.

■ escalation of commitment

DESCRIPTION
Becoming increasingly locked into a particular course of action where ever greater commitments of resources to the course of action are made in an effort to recoup past losses or investments.

KEY INSIGHTS
A cycle of escalating commitment can be produced when individuals or organizations make ongoing efforts to recoup some or all prior investment through increasing commitments of resources to a particular course of action irrespective of its likelihood of success. Explanations for escalations of commitment include the need for internal justification (e.g. protecting one's own self-image), external justification (e.g. proving to others that they were not wrong in an earlier decision), and possible norms of consistency, where, in the case of managers, those who are more consistent in their actions may be viewed as better managers than those switching from one line of behavior to another.

KEY WORDS Action, commitment, investment

IMPLICATIONS
Escalation of commitment may potentially occur in any area of marketing where resource commitments are required to accomplish objectives. One area particularly prone to escalation of commitment is that of new product development, where an individual or an organization may continue to pursue a development effort which has received considerable past investment to a point beyond economic desirability.

APPLICATION AREAS AND FURTHER READINGS
New Product Development
Boulding, William, Morgan, Ruskin, and Staelin, Richard (1997). 'Pulling the Plug to Stop the New Product Drain,' *Journal of Marketing Research*, 34(1), Special Issue on Innovation and New Products, 164–176.
Schmidt, Jeffrey B., and Calantone, Roger J. (2002). 'Escalation of Commitment during New Product Development,' *Journal of the Academy of Marketing Science*, 30(2), 103–118.

Marketing Management
Armstrong, J. S., Coviello, N., and Safrane, B. (1993). 'Escalation Bias: Does it Extend to Marketing?' *Journal of the Academy of Marketing Science*, 21(3), 247.

BIBLIOGRAPHY
Staw, Barry M. (1981). 'The Escalation of Commitment to a Course of Action,' *Academy of Management Review*, 6(4), October, 577–587.

Brockner, Joel (1992). 'The Escalation of Commitment to a Failing Course of Action: Toward Theoretical Progress,' *Academy of Management Review*, 17(1), January, 39–61.

■ ethical marketing

(also called responsible marketing or sociomarketing)

DESCRIPTION

Marketing concerned with conformance to morally acceptable standards of conduct.

KEY INSIGHTS

Even though marketing may adhere to laws and regulations governing its practice, certain practices of marketing that are within the law may nevertheless be questionable from an ethical perspective. Examples of such practices might include 'confusion marketing' (see **confusion marketing**) and the use of the 'lowball technique' (see **low-ball technique**). Ethical marketing is therefore concerned with making and implementing ethical marketing decisions. The values, attitudes, and beliefs of marketers that influence marketing decisions, the culture of a marketer's firm, the decision-making processes within the firm, the decision criteria, the marketing decisions themselves, the actions associated with marketing decisions, and the outcomes and consequences of marketing actions can all be evaluated from an ethical standpoint as opposed to one of simple legality.

KEY WORDS Ethics, marketing ethics, standards of conduct, moral conduct

IMPLICATIONS

The practice of marketing involves many ethical decisions. While consumers are tolerant of (or resigned to seeing) many marketing practices that present a firm's offering in a favorable light (e.g. packaging for bacon showing the meat but concealing the fat), ethical marketing recognizes that such practices and others may benefit from greater scrutiny to ensure they are morally acceptable. Marketers concerned with such evaluations, where the perspectives of multiple stakeholders (e.g. the firm's employees, consumers, broader society) and multiple timeframes (past, present, near future, distant future) are taken into account, may therefore benefit from a greater understanding of the growing body of research on ethical marketing. In addition, a greater knowledge of the ethical codes of professional marketers (e.g. the code of ethics of the American Marketing Association, available online at **marketingpower.com**) may also assist the marketer in making ethical decisions.

APPLICATION AREAS AND FURTHER READINGS

Marketing Strategy

Robin, Donald, and Reidenbach, Eric (1987). 'Social Responsibility, Ethics, and Marketing Strategy: Closing the Gap between Concept and Application,' *Journal of Marketing*, 51(1), 44–58.

Marketing Management
Robin, Donald P., Reidenbach, R. Eric, and Forrest, P. J. (1996). 'The Perceived
   Importance of an Ethical Issue as an Influence on the Ethical Decision-Making of
   Ad Managers,' *Journal of Business Research*, 35, 17–28.
Laczniak, Eugene R., and Murphy, Patrick E. (1993). *Ethical Marketing Decisions: The
   Higher Road*. Boston: Allyn & Bacon.

Online Marketing
Bush, Victoria S., Venable, Beverly T., and Bush, Alan J. (2000). 'Ethics and Market-
   ing on the Internet: Practitioners' Perceptions of Societal, Industry and Company
   Concerns,' *Journal of Business Ethics*, 23(3), 237–248.

Marketing Research
Sirgy, M. J. (2001). *Handbook of Quality-Of-Life Research: An Ethical Marketing Perspective*.
   Dordrecht: Kluwer.
Rao, S., and Quester, P. (2006).'Ethical Marketing in the Internet Era: A Research
   Agenda,' *International Journal of Internet Marketing and Advertising*, 3(1), 19–34.

Marketing Education
Lane, J. C. (1995). 'Ethics of Business Students: Some Marketing Perspectives,'
   Journal of Business Ethics, 14, 571–580.

BIBLIOGRAPHY
Murphy, P. E., Laczniak, G. R., Bowie, N. E., and Klein, T. A. (2005). *Ethical Marketing*.
   Upper Saddle River, NJ: Pearson Prentice-Hall.
Laczniak, Gene R., and Murphy, Patrick E. (1991). 'Fostering Ethical Marketing
   Decisions,' *Journal of Business Ethics*, 11, 259–271.
Reidenbach, R. Eric, and Robin, Donald P. (1995). 'A Response to "On Measuring
   Ethical Judgments,"' *Journal of Business Ethics*, 14, 159–162.
Sturdivant, Fredrick D., and Cocanougher, A. Benton (1973). 'What are Ethical
   Marketing Practices?' *Harvard Business Review*, November–December, 10–12.

☐ **ethnic marketing** *see* multicultural marketing

☐ **ethnomarketing** *see* multicultural marketing

☐ **evaluation** *see* adoption process

☐ **evangelism marketing** *see* word-of-mouth marketing

■ even price effect

DESCRIPTION
Any effect on product purchase amounts or purchase frequencies resulting
from a product's price ending in even-numbered digits.

KEY INSIGHTS
Pricing decisions involving setting product prices where even-numbered
prices are sought or avoided indicates that the pricing approach is a
form of psychological pricing, where there is an effort to manipulate consumers' perceptions of price desirability through the selection of a price's
ending digits. Research on the topic of price-setting behaviors for a wide
array of products clearly suggests that most managers believe that price
endings are important in influencing product sales as a result of believing
that most customers are more receptive to some price endings over
others. While some managers advocate the use of even pricing to increase
sales, particularly where endings of zero are used, other managers are

observed to advocate the use of odd pricing, especially where endings
of nine are used. Actual influences of price endings are observed to vary
among product categories and price amounts. Beyond operational considerations, explanations for managerial use of price endings to achieve
desired effects include the acknowledgment of consumer behaviors such
as tendencies for consumers to round prices down, limited consumer
memories, and consumers using price endings to draw conclusions about
whether or not a product is on sale.

KEY WORDS Pricing, perception

IMPLICATIONS
Marketers involved in price setting should seek to understand both
through prior research and experience how price endings can be used
as a means to influence subtly a consumer's perceptions of a product's
price or the product's attributes such as its value or quality.

APPLICATION AREAS AND FURTHER READINGS
Pricing
Estelami, H. (1999). 'The Computational Effect of Price Endings in Multi-
    dimensional Price Advertising,' *Journal of Product and Brand Management*, 8(2/3),
    244–256.
Gendall, P., Holdershaw, J., and Garland, R. (1997). 'The Effect of Odd Pricing on
    Demand,' *European Journal of Marketing*, 31(11–12), 799–813.
Naipaul, S., and Parsa, H. G. (2001). 'Menu Price Endings That Communicate Value
    and Quality,' *Cornell Hotel and Restaurant Administration Quarterly*, 42(1), 26–37.

BIBLIOGRAPHY
Stiving, Mark, and Winer, Russell S. (1997). 'An Empirical Analysis of Price Endings
    with Scanner Data,' *Journal of Consumer Research*, 24(1), June, 57–67.

■ event marketing

DESCRIPTION
Marketing aimed at consumers attending or similarly exposed to a particular
public or private event.

KEY INSIGHTS
While event marketing overlaps with sponsorship marketing to some
extent, sponsorship marketing does not necessarily need to involve an
event, whereas event marketing makes the event—that something which
happens at a particular place and time—focal to the firm's marketing
efforts. Events marketed may be large (e.g. a major charity concert) or
quite small (e.g. an in-store product tasting). Common to all events,
however, is their ability to provide consumers with positive experiences,
particularly ones that stimulate multiple senses, and an opportunity to
use personal contact with the consumer to communicate the organization's brand identity. Instead of learning about a new branded cola
product through a television advertisement, for example, an in-store
tasting enables consumers to see, taste, and smell the branded product.
In addition, when an event is associated with a single organization (e.g. a

charity run organized to raise funds for a specific charitable cause led by a specifically named charitable organization), the consumer's attention is relatively captive in that it is directed to, or at least connected to, the organization without interference from competing organizations.

KEY WORDS In-person communication, sensory experience

IMPLICATIONS
Whether an event is pre-communicated with controlled attendance or it merely 'happens' with any and all passers-by observing or taking part, event marketing provides the marketer with an opportunity to communicate in person the firm's brand identity. Marketers seeking to provide consumers with rich sensory experiences as an alternative or supplement to other marketing approaches may clearly benefit from a greater understanding of event marketing approaches spanning a wide range of events.

APPLICATION AREAS AND FURTHER READINGS
Marketing Management
Wohlfeil, M., and Whelan, S. (2005). 'Event-Marketing as Innovative Marketing Communications: Reviewing the German Experience,' *Journal of Customer Behavior*, 4(2), July, 181–207.

Marketing Strategy
Cunningham, M. H., and Taylor, S. F. (1995). 'Event Marketing: State of the Industry and Research Agenda,' *Festival Management and Event Tourism*, 2, 123–137.

BIBLIOGRAPHY
Hoyle, Leonard H. Jr., (2002). *Event Marketing: How to Successfully Promote Events, Festivals, Conventions, and Expositions.* New York: John Wiley & Sons, Inc.

■ evoked set

DESCRIPTION
The set of alternatives that are activated directly from consumer memory in response to some stimuli, where such alternatives are typically products or brands considered by the consumer in a buying decision process.

KEY INSIGHTS
In the context of a consumer's buying decision process, an evoked set can be viewed as a selected shortlist or top-of-mind set of alternatives that the consumer generates. In order for a firm's products or brands to have a chance of being evaluated by a consumer, such products or brands need to be in the consumer's evoked set.

KEY WORDS Buying decision process

IMPLICATIONS
Given the importance of evoked set inclusion in subsequent consumer evaluation of buying alternatives, marketers should seek to understand through marketing research to what extent their products or brands are likely to be found in consumers' evoked sets for the category (or categories) associated with the products or brands. Beyond influencing

their products' and brands' mere inclusion in such sets with marketing communications, however, marketers should additionally be concerned with understanding consumers' evoked set sizes and influencing the relative standing of their products and brands in such sets.

APPLICATION AREAS AND FURTHER READINGS

Marketing Strategy
Gronhaug, Kjell (1973-1974). 'Some Factors Influencing the Size of the Buyer's Evoked Set,' *European Journal of Marketing*, 7, 232-241.

Marketing Modeling
Roberts, John H., and Lattin, James M. (1991). 'Development and Testing of a Model of Consideration Set Composition,' *Journal of Marketing Research*, 28(4), November, 429-440.

Marketing Research
Alba, Joseph W., and Chattopadhyay, Amitava (1985). 'Effects of Context and Part-Category Cues on Recall of Competing Brands,' *Journal of Marketing Research*, 22(3), August, 340-349.

BIBLIOGRAPHY
Williams, T. G., and Etzel, M. J. (1976). 'An Investigation and Extension of the Evoked Set Concept Applied to Consumer Durables,' in Henry Nash and Donald Robin (eds.), *Proceedings of the Southern Marketing Association*. Starkville, Miss.: Southern Marketing Association, 237-239.

☐ **exchange** *see* exchange theory

■ exchange, law of

DESCRIPTION
A view that exchange can take place between two entities, under conditions where one entity holds assortment A and the other assortment B, with elements x and y within assortments A and B respectively when: (a) x is different than y, (b) the potency of assortment A is increased by dropping x and adding y, and (c) the potency of assortment B is increased by dropping y and adding x.

KEY INSIGHTS
Put forth by Alderson and Martin (1967), the law of exchange addresses the situation where two parties each give something of value to the other to satisfy needs. In broadly characterizing that which is exchanged, that which has value may include money, tangible goods, intangible services, or even an individual's support for a cause. While the law of exchange limits the exchange context to just two entities—even though more are possible—it is nevertheless considered influential to the field of marketing as marketing itself can be viewed as involving organized systems of exchange.

KEY WORDS **Value, need(s)**

IMPLICATIONS
To marketers, the law of exchange can be viewed as identifying conditions necessary for exchange to occur. However, the complexities of exchange in terms of that which has value and the number of entities

involved (e.g. individuals, organizations, or social actors more generally) also suggests that many exchange processes may involve dimensions which are not necessarily captured by the law of exchange. Nevertheless, given that exchange can be viewed as a fundamental 'building block' in marketing, the law of exchange provides marketers with one starting point on which to base further marketing theory and practice.

APPLICATION AREAS AND FURTHER READINGS
Marketing Strategy
Bagozzi, R. P. (1974). 'Marketing as an Organized Behavioral System of Exchanges,' *Journal of Marketing*, 38, October, 77–81.

Marketing Theory
Dixon, D. F. (1999). 'Some Late Nineteenth-Century Antecedents of Marketing Theory,' *Journal of Macromarketing*, 19(2), 115–125.

Non-profit Marketing
Clarke, P., and Mount, P. (2001). 'Nonprofit Marketing: The Key to Marketing's "Mid-Life Crisis"?' *International Journal of Nonprofit and Voluntary Sector Marketing*, 6(1), 78–91.

BIBLIOGRAPHY
Alderson, Wroe, and Martin, Miles W. (1967). 'Toward a Formal Theory of Transactions and Transvections,' in Bruce Mallen (ed.), *The Marketing Channel: A Conceptual Viewpoint*. New York: John Wiley & Sons, 50–51.

■ exchange theory

DESCRIPTION
Theory or theories aimed at understanding, explaining, and/or predicting exchange events and relationships.

KEY INSIGHTS
The concept of *exchange*, or the process of giving something in return for something received, is considered by many to be at the core of marketing. While much of marketing is focused on exchanges involving the direct transfer of tangible entities between two parties, there are also many exchanges in marketing that are indirect, intangible, or symbolic, and involve more than two parties. Exchange therefore exists in many forms and is not limited to simple money-for-product transactions, nor is it limited to marketing-related contexts. For example, exchange theory is also an alternative term for social exchange theory, a theory of human relationships and social interaction which also has tremendous significance to marketing. (See **social exchange theory**.) In a marketing context, elements of exchange theory can be considered to include understandings, explanations, and predictions for: prerequisites for exchange (e.g. there are at least two parties and where each party is free to accept or reject an exchange offer), forms that value can take (e.g. goods, services, ideas, places), assessments of value, and conditions that may turn exchange events into exchange relationships.

KEY WORDS Transactions, **marketing**

IMPLICATIONS

Given the centrality of exchange in marketing, marketers should seek to understand carefully the nature of exchanges the firm has not only with its customers but all others in the marketing system (e.g. distributors and suppliers). For example, marketers should not underestimate the significance to the firm of creating satisfying indirect exchanges and multi-party exchanges in support of accomplishing the firm's marketing objectives. While exchange theory embraces a relatively pervasive phenomenon, a better understanding of exchange theory elements and related research can potentially provide the marketer with insights into not only the many different types of exchanges but a greater knowledge of exchange characteristics useful for managing their effectiveness in a wide range of marketing contexts.

APPLICATION AREAS AND FURTHER READINGS

Marketing Strategy

Bagozzi, Richard P. (1975). 'Marketing as Exchange,' *Journal of Marketing*, 39(4), October, 32–39.

Frazier, Gary L. (1983). 'Interorganizational Exchange Behavior in Marketing Channels: A Broadened Perspective,' *Journal of Marketing*, 47(4), Autumn, 68–78.

Gundlach, Gregory T., Achrol, Ravi S., and Mentzer, John T. (1995). 'The Structure of Commitment in Exchange,' *Journal of Marketing*, 59(1), January, 78–92.

Marketing Research

Kaufmann, P. J., and Dant, R. P. (1992). 'The Dimensions of Commercial Exchange,' *Marketing Letters*, 3(2), 171–185.

Consumer Behavior

Brinberg, D., and Wood, R. (1983). 'A Resource Exchange Theory Analysis of Consumer Behavior,' *Journal of Consumer Behavior*, 10(3), 330–338.

BIBLIOGRAPHY

Houston, Franklin S., and Gassenheimer, Jule B. (1987). 'Marketing and Exchange,' *Journal of Marketing*, 51(4), October, 3–18.

■ exclusion principle

DESCRIPTION

A criterion used to distinguish a public good from a non-public good, where the ability of a producer to prevent others, particularly non-buyers, from consuming the product is indicative of a non-public good.

KEY INSIGHTS

Not to be confused with the physics-based exclusion principle, the principle provides one means of distinguishing between public goods and non-public (or private) goods, where public goods are those goods that, once supplied to one individual, can be consumed by others at no extra cost and where the individual's consumption precludes the consumption of the good by others.

KEY WORDS Public goods

IMPLICATIONS
Marketers concerned with the provision of goods that are of broader economic or social benefit may gain additional decision-making and policy insights from an understanding of the exclusion principle criterion. Of particular concern in evaluating the public/non-public good distinction is in identifying the extent to which individuals will have no incentive to pay for particular goods but will be able to benefit from them and where government action and intervention may be required.

APPLICATION AREAS AND FURTHER READINGS
Societal Marketing
Hansen, U., and Schrader, U. (1997). 'Modern Model of Consumption for a Sustainable Society,' *Journal of Consumer Policy*, 20(4), 443–468.
Peacock, Alan T. (1978). 'Preserving the Past: An International Economic Dilemma,' *Journal of Cultural Economics*, 2(2), 1–11.

BIBLIOGRAPHY
Plott, C. R., and Meyer, R. A. (1975). 'The Technology of Public Goods, Externalities, and the Exclusion Principle,' in E. S. Mills (ed.), *Economic Analysis of Environmental Problems*. New York: National Bureau of Economic Research, Columbia University Press, 65–90.

☐ **exclusive distribution** *see* distribution strategies

■ exercise, law of

DESCRIPTION
A principle stating that repetition tends to strengthen the association between a stimulus and a response, thereby making a response more likely to occur on the next presentation of a stimulus.

KEY INSIGHTS
Formulated by psychologist Edward Lee Thorndike, the law of exercise suggests that, as the association between a stimulus and a response is strengthened through repetition, presentation of the next stimulus will make the response increasingly likely to occur.

KEY WORDS Behavior, stimulus, response, education

IMPLICATIONS
The law of exercise clearly has many implications for marketing, where marketing stimuli (e.g. television commercials showing happy people eating a particular brand of ice cream) are intended by marketers to have the effect of responses such as a positive attitude toward a product, a desire to purchase the product, and/or associations with satisfaction as a result of consuming the product. Given that a consumer's initial response to a particular marketing initiative is favorable, the implication of the law of exercise is that further repetition of the marketing stimuli will be increasingly beneficial in that such a favorable response (e.g. desire to purchase the brand of ice cream) will become increasingly likely to occur upon subsequent presentation of the stimuli. Of course, a limitation to the strengthening effects of repetition is suggested with the law of

diminishing returns and the possibility of burnout occurring as a result of too much repetition.

APPLICATION AREAS AND FURTHER READINGS

Marketing Education

Brewer, Ernest W., DeJonge, Jacquelyn O., and Stout, Vickie J. (2001). *Moving to Online: Making the Transition From Traditional Instruction and Communication Strategies.* Thousand Oaks, Calif.: Corwin Press.

Mitchell, Garry (1998). *The Trainer's Handbook.* New York: AMACOM.

Tomlinson, Stephen (1997). 'Edward Lee Thorndike and John Dewey on the Science of Education,' *Oxford Review of Education*, 23(3), September, 365–383.

BIBLIOGRAPHY

Thorndike, Edward L. (1911). *Animal Intelligence.* New York: Macmillan.

■ expectancy theory

(also called expectancy-value theory)

DESCRIPTION

A theory of motivation aimed at explaining why individuals follow particular courses of action, where motivation is viewed as a function of an individual's beliefs characterized in terms of expectancy, valence, and instrumentality.

KEY INSIGHTS

Expectancy theory as developed by Victor Vroom in 1964 views a motivational force F to be equal to the products of Expectancy, Instrumentality, and Valence, that is, $F = E(I \times V)$. In the equation, Valence refers to the emotional orientations an individual holds about outcomes or rewards such as money or intrinsic satisfaction. Expectancy refers to expectations and levels of confidence about what one is capable of doing. Instrumentality refers to the expressed probability that a particular reward will actually be associated with a particular course of action.

KEY WORDS Motivation, behavior, beliefs

IMPLICATIONS

The expectancy theory of motivation has implications for understanding and explaining better many areas of employee management including an individual's view of job satisfaction, the likelihood of an individual staying in a particular job, and the level of effort that an individual may put into their job.

APPLICATION AREAS AND FURTHER READINGS

Sales

Oliver, Richard L. (1974). 'Expectancy Theory Predictions of Salesmen's Performance,' *Journal of Marketing Research*, 11(3), August, 243–253.

Business-to-Business Marketing

Walker, Orville C., Jr., Churchill, Gilbert A., Jr., and Ford, Neil M. (1977). 'Motivation and Performance in Industrial Selling: Present Knowledge and Needed Research,' *Journal of Marketing Research*, 14(2), May, 156–168.

Marketing Management

Chowdhury, Jhinuk (1993). 'The Motivational Impact of Sales Quotas on Effort,' *Journal of Marketing Research*, 30(1), February, 28–41.

Services Marketing
Solomon, Michael R., Surprenant, Carol, Czepiel, John A., and Gutman, Eve-
lyn G. (1985). 'A Role Theory Perspective on Dyadic Interactions: The Service
Encounter,' *Journal of Marketing*, 49(1), Winter, 99–111.

Ethics
Fudge, R. S., and Schlacter, J. L. (1999). 'Motivating Employees to Act Ethically: An
Expectancy Theory Approach,' *Journal of Business Ethics*, 18(3), 295–304.

BIBLIOGRAPHY
Vroom, Victor H. (1995). *Work and Motivation*, rev. edn. New York: Jossey-Bass
Classics.

☐ expectancy–value theory *see* expectancy theory

■ expectation–disconfirmation model

DESCRIPTION
A cognitive model of satisfaction involving the view that satisfaction depends
on the consistency between an individual's expectations regarding the performance of something (e.g. a product or a service) and actual performance.

KEY INSIGHTS
Cognitive models based on an expectation–disconfirmation view consider
satisfaction to be a consequence when actual performance equals or
exceeds an individual's expectations and dissatisfaction to be a consequence when performance is below the individual's expectations.

KEY WORDS Expectations, performance, satisfaction

IMPLICATIONS
Marketers can benefit from understanding the expectation-
disconfirmation modeling approach in knowing more about how
customer satisfaction may be determined. The model suggests that
customer expectations for product or service performance are just as
important as the actual product or service experience in establishing the
degree of a customer's satisfaction or dissatisfaction.

APPLICATION AREAS AND FURTHER READINGS
Customer Satisfaction
Churchill, Gilbert A., Jr., and Surprenant, Carol (1982). 'An Investigation into
the Determinants of Customer Satisfaction,' *Journal of Marketing Research*, 19(4),
Special Issue on Causal Modeling, November, 491–504.
Oliver, Richard L., and DeSarbo, Wayne S. (1988). 'Response Determinants in Satis-
faction Judgments,' *Journal of Consumer Research*, 14(4), March, 495–507.

International Marketing
Spreng, R. A., and Chiou, J.-S. (2002). 'A Cross-Cultural Assessment of the Satisfaction Formation Process,' *European Journal of Marketing*, 36(7/8), 829–839.

Customer Loyalty
Yoon, S.-J., and Kim, J.-H. (2000). 'An Empirical Validation of a Loyalty Model Based
on Expectation Disconfirmation,' *Journal of Consumer Marketing*, 17(2/3), 120–136.

BIBLIOGRAPHY
Oliver, Richard L. (1980). 'A Cognitive Model of the Antecedents and Consequences
of Satisfaction Decisions,' *Journal of Marketing Research*, 17(4), November, 460–469.

■ expected utility theory

DESCRIPTION

An economic theory of individual choice for situations involving uncertainty, risk, and/or ambiguity whereby an individual's utility for a situation is calculated by considering the individual's utility in each possible state and arriving at a weighted average.

KEY INSIGHTS

The expected utility theory (EUT) view of decision making is that a decision maker chooses between risky or uncertain prospects by comparing their expected utility values. Quantitatively, such expected utility values are weighted sums obtained by adding the utility values of outcomes multiplied by their respective probabilities. EUT is accepted as the standard theory of individual decision making in economics and, as such, constitutes a key building block of a vast range of other economic theories.

KEY WORDS Choice, decision making, risk, uncertainty

IMPLICATIONS

Expected utility theory provides a basis for many different models of decision making under risk or uncertainty. Marketers involved in the development of any such model, as when seeking to model possible consumer purchase behavior, may therefore benefit from understanding EUT's assumptions, variable relationships, and associated concepts in establishing explanations or forecasts of individual choice.

APPLICATION AREAS AND FURTHER READINGS

Consumer Behavior
Simonson, Itamar (1990). 'The Effect of Purchase Quantity and Timing on Variety-Seeking Behavior,' *Journal of Marketing Research*, 27(2), May, 150–162.

Decision Making
Schoemaker, Paul J. H. (1982). 'The Expected Utility Model: Its Variants, Purposes, Evidence and Limitations,' *Journal of Economic Literature*, 20(2), June, 529–563.
Machina, Mark J. (1989). 'Dynamic Consistency and Non-Expected Utility Models of Choice under Uncertainty,' *Journal of Economic Literature*, 27(4), December, 1622–1668.
Kahn, Barbara E., and Sarin, Rakesh K. (1988). 'Modeling Ambiguity in Decisions under Uncertainty,' *Journal of Consumer Research*, 15(2), September, 265–272.

BIBLIOGRAPHY

Von Neumann, John, and Morgenstern, Oskar (1944). *Theory of Games and Economic Behavior*. Princeton: Princeton University Press. 2nd edn. 1947; 3rd edn. 1953. Section 3, chapter I reprinted in Alfred N. Page, *Utility Theory: A Book of Readings*. New York: Wiley, 1968, 215–233.

☐ experience, law of *see* experience curve effect

■ experience curve effect

DESCRIPTION

The effect of accumulated production experience in systematically reducing per-unit product costs.

KEY INSIGHTS

The experience curve effect is a widely recognized phenomenon in production operations. Increases in cumulative production experience provide opportunities for increased labor efficiency due to learning; cost reductions due to adoption of technological innovation in the use of production inputs or processes; and increased efficiency due to economies of scale resulting from production operations size increases. Quantification of the experience curve effect is typically in the form of a percentage reduction in unit costs (e.g. 20%) each time accumulated production is doubled. Such quantifications can be portrayed numerically or graphically to show how expected cost reductions can be determined for any given future volume of production. The general relationship observed by the experience curve effect is also what the Boston Consulting Group has termed the law of experience, or BCG's law of experience, where the doubling of cumulative production is associated with costs reducing by a constant percentage.

The experience curve concept is closely related to the learning curve concept in that both emphasize the change that occurs with learning. Thus, the experience curve effect is sometimes called the learning curve effect. Unlike the learning curve effect, however, which emphasizes changes in human performance due to learning, the experience curve effect refers to a production context where the emphasis is on understanding changes in cost, which may be due in part to a learning curve effect among production workers. (See **learning curve effect**.)

KEY WORDS Production, cost reductions, experience

IMPLICATIONS

Marketers understanding the extent that unit production costs will predictably decline due to the experience curve effect can use such knowledge in establishing more appropriate pricing strategies for new products where such costs may be very high initially but much lower over planned time horizons corresponding to planned production volume and experience increases.

APPLICATION AREAS AND FURTHER READINGS

Pricing
Krishnan, Trichy V., Bass, Frank M., and Jain, Dipak C. (1999). 'Optimal Pricing Strategy for New Products,' *Management Science*, 45(12), December, 1650–1663.

Marketing Strategy
Gatignon, Hubert, Weitz, Barton, and Bansal, Pradeep (1990). 'Brand Introduction Strategies and Competitive Environments,' *Journal of Marketing Research*, 27(4), November, 390–401.
Hedley, B. (1976). 'A Fundamental Approach to Strategy Development,' *Long Range Planning*, December, 2–11.

BIBLIOGRAPHY
Day, George S., and Montgomery, David B. (1983). 'Diagnosing the Experience Curve,' *Journal of Marketing*, 47(2), Spring, 44–58.

Alberts, William W. (1989). 'The Experience Curve Doctrine Reconsidered,' *Journal of Marketing*, 53(3), July, 36–49.

Boston Consulting Group (1972). *Perspectives on Experience*. Boston: BCG Ltd.

☐ **experience goods** *see* goods

☐ **experience marketing** *see* experiential marketing

■ experiential marketing

(also called customer experience marketing or experience marketing)

DESCRIPTION

Marketing aimed at getting customers to sense, feel, think, act, and relate strongly to a brand or a company.

KEY INSIGHTS

Experiential marketing attempts to build an emotional bond between the company's brand and its customers via a sensory-rich experience. Experiential marketing approaches to marketing communication are characterized by a relatively high level of interactivity, multi-sensory communication (e.g. sight, sound, touch), and personal engagement with consumers and where such conditions are directed at eliciting favorable emotional responses on the part of the consumer. An example is an agricultural firm's use of an interactive, multi-media exhibit at a regional fair which consumers can walk through and experience, where the many elements of the exhibit demonstrate and communicate to consumers how the firm and its brands have improved the quality of life. Experiential marketing's effectiveness stems from the ability of the totality of such experiences to communicate the essence, or identity, of a brand or a firm, thereby enhancing the firm's relationship with the consumer.

KEY WORDS Senses, sensory communication, interactivity, engagement

IMPLICATIONS

Marketers can develop and implement experiential marketing approaches on a relatively large scale (e.g. a walk-through branded pavilion at a theme park) or small scale (e.g. a small traveling display for the company's brand). Further, it can be the primary marketing methodology of the firm or it can be one of its complementary methodologies. Regardless of the way in which an experiential marketing opportunity is developed and presented to consumers, the approach gives marketers an opportunity to communicate with and involve consumers in a way that may be much more holistic relative to that provided by traditional marketing media (e.g. television or print advertising).

APPLICATION AREAS AND FURTHER READINGS

Marketing Strategy

Petkus, E. (2004). 'Enhancing the Application of Experimental Marketing in the Arts,' *International Journal of Nonprofit and Voluntary Sector Marketing*, 9(1), 49–56.

Marketing Management
Berry, Leonard L., Carbone, Lewis P., and Haekel, Stephan H. (2002). 'Managing
   the Total Customer Experience,' *MIT Sloan Management Review*, 43(3), Spring, 85–
   89.
Pullman, M. E., and Gross, M. A. (2004). 'Ability of Experience Design Elements to Elicit Emotions and Loyalty Behaviors,' *Decision Sciences*, 35(3), 551–
   578.

BIBLIOGRAPHY
Schmitt, B. (1999), 'Experiential Marketing,' *Journal of Marketing Management*, 15(1/3),
   53–67.
Schmitt, Brend H. (1999). *Experiential Marketing : How to Get Customers to Sense, Feel,
   Think, Act and Relate to your Company and Brands*. New York: The Free Press.

■ experimenter effect

DESCRIPTION
Any generally unintended influence or bias of an experimenter on his or her
results.

KEY INSIGHTS
Systematically examined by Rosenthal (1966), experimenter effects are
viewed as undesirable in experimental research studies where it is
recognized that experimental results or outcomes may be a result
of systematic, inadvertent experimenter influence. Ultimately, there
are many possibilities and opportunities for unintended experimenter
influence, as where subjects interviewed by a researcher are inadvertently influenced by the researcher's manner of relating to the
subjects.

KEY WORDS Research, experiments, **bias**

IMPLICATIONS
Marketers must be aware of the possibility of experimenter effects influencing or confounding research findings. An emphasis on robust methodologies aimed at combating experimenter effects is desirable to the extent
marketers seek to eliminate or control for such effects, as when subjects
are interviewed by a researcher who has expectations regarding the
desired outcome of the research.

APPLICATION AREAS AND FURTHER READINGS
Marketing Research
Venkatesan, M. (1967). 'Laboratory Experiments in Marketing: The Experimenter
   Effect,' *Journal of Marketing Research*, 4(2), May, 142–146.
Armstrong, J. Scott (1979). 'Advocacy and Objectivity in Science,' *Management Sci-
   ence*, 25(5), May, 423–428.

BIBLIOGRAPHY
Rosenthal, Robert (1966). *Experimenter Effects In Behavioral Research*. New York:
   Appleton-Century-Crofts.

■ experimenter expectancy effect

(also called the Rosenthal effect)

DESCRIPTION

A particular type of experimenter effect whereby the experimenter's expectations act to influence or bias the findings of an experiment.

KEY INSIGHTS

Experimenter expectancy effects may be present in experimental research in many forms including unconscious experimental manipulation on the part of the experimenter as a result of knowledge of expected findings or selective interpretation or misinterpretation of data aimed at obtaining results which support an experimenter's established expectations.

KEY WORDS Research, expectations, **bias**, influence

IMPLICATIONS

When experimenters or researchers have clear expectations about the outcome of their research activities, experimenter expectancy effects may be a concern when assessing the adequacy of research designs and interpreting research findings.

APPLICATION AREAS AND FURTHER READINGS

Marketing Research

Rosenthal, R. (1985). 'From Unconscious Experimenter Bias to Teacher Expectancy Effects,' in J. B. Dusek, V. C. Hall, and W. J. Meyer (eds.), *Teacher Expectancies*. Hillsdale, NJ: Erlbaum.

Hoogstraten, Johan, and Vorst, Harrie C. M. (1978). 'Group Cohesion, Task Performance, and the Experimenter Expectancy Effect,' *Human Relations*, 31(11), 939–956.

Barone, M. J., Shimp, T. A., and Sprott, D. E. (1997). 'The Mere-Ownership Effect: "More There Than Meets their Eyes" or "Less There Than They Would Have Us Believe"?,' *Journal of Consumer Psychology*, 6(3), 299–311.

BIBLIOGRAPHY

Minor, Marshall W. (1967). 'Experimenter Expectancy Effect as a Function of Evaluation Apprehension.' Dissertation, University of Chicago.

Finkelstein, Jonathan C. (1976). 'Experimenter Expectancy Effects,' *Journal of Communication*, 26(3), September, 31.

☐ exploratory marketing research *see* marketing research

☐ extensive distribution *see* distribution strategies

☐ external validity *see* validity

F

☐ face validity *see* validity
☐ factorial validity *see* validity

■ fallacy of composition

DESCRIPTION
The mistaken assumption that, if something is true for the individual parts of a whole (e.g. members of a group), it will also hold true for the whole (e.g. group).

KEY INSIGHTS
The fallacy of composition can lead individuals or groups of individuals to mistakenly draw incorrect conclusions concerning the relationship between individual and collective behaviors. For example, the fallacy may lead an individual to believe that actions taken that are in the best interest of individuals in a group will also be in the best interest of the group—something which is inappropriately inferred. An economic illustration is the case where increased savings by an individual can clearly be beneficial to the individual but may actually be detrimental to an economy if such collective action leads to a reduction in consumer demand.

KEY WORDS Decision making, beliefs

IMPLICATIONS
Marketers concerned with the study of individual and group beliefs regarding the relationship between individual and group actions may benefit from a deeper understanding of the fallacy of composition concept. Given the broad range of phenomena where the fallacy of composition has been both observed and demonstrated (e.g. small group behaviors, economic policy), marketers should not assume that the decision-making assumptions of others will always exclude this fallacy.

APPLICATION AREAS AND FURTHER READINGS
Marketing Research
Wensley, Robin (2002). 'A Bridge over Troubled Water?' *European Journal of Marketing*, 36(3), April, 391–400.

Public Policy
Calfee, J. E. (2000). 'The Historical Significance of Joe Camel,' *Journal of Public Policy and Marketing*, 19(2), 168–182.

Marketing Modeling
Smith, Carol A. (1974). 'Economics of Marketing Systems: Models from Economic Geography,' *Annual Review of Anthropology*, 3, 167–201.

BIBLIOGRAPHY
Caballero, Ricardo J. (1992). 'A Fallacy of Composition,' *American Economic Review* (American Economic Association), 82(5), 1279–92.
Mayer, J. (2002). 'The Fallacy of Composition: A Review of the Literature,' *World Economy* (London), 25(6), 875–894.

■ fallacy of misplaced concreteness

DESCRIPTION
Fallaciously believing that an abstraction is actually something material or concrete.

KEY INSIGHTS
The fallacy of misplaced concreteness involves the concept of *reification*, or the process whereby concepts become material. As a fallacy, misplaced concreteness can lead individuals to mistakenly draw incorrect conclusions concerning the nature of ideas, concepts, and models. For example, the fallacy may lead a marketing manager to treat an ideal conceptual model of the consumer buying decision process as if it were a description of a real or actual consumer buying decision process.

KEY WORDS Abstractions, concepts

IMPLICATIONS
Marketers should be wary of the fallacy of misplaced concreteness when examining conceptual material to avoid drawing incorrect conclusions about the true nature of such material. In addition, in an effort to ensure a sense of realism in understanding and evaluating a wide range of marketing phenomena in terms of concepts and models, marketers should also be wary of the possibility that the views of others may inappropriately embody such a fallacy.

APPLICATION AREAS AND FURTHER READINGS
Marketing Strategy
Lane, P. J., Koka, B., and Pathak, S. (2006). 'The Reification of Absorptive Capacity: A Critical Review and Reconceptualization,' *Academy of Management Review*, 31(4), 833–863.
Angelmar, R., and Pinson, C. (1975). 'The meaning of "marketing",' *Philosophy of Science*, June, S. 208–214.

Marketing Research
Zinkhan, George M., and Hirschheim, Rudy (1992). 'Truth in Marketing Theory and Research: An Alternative Perspective,' *Journal of Marketing*, 56(2), April, 80–88.
Hunt, Shelby D. (1989). 'Reification and Realism in Marketing: In Defense of Reason,' *Journal of Macromarketing*, 9(2), Fall, 4–10.
Hunt, Shelby D. (1992). 'For Reason and Realism in Marketing,' *Journal of Marketing*, 56(2), April, 89–102.

BIBLIOGRAPHY
Whitehead, Alfred North (1925). *Science and the Modern World*. New York: The Free Press.

■ false consensus effect

DESCRIPTION

The tendency for individuals or groups of individuals to overestimate the extent that others are in agreement with their views.

KEY INSIGHTS

The false consensus effect is a cognitive bias among individuals or groups of individuals that leads them to believe that the collective view of others is more likely to reflect their view than is actually the case. In other words, it is the tendency to see oneself as more representative of others than one really is. While there may be multiple causes for the effect's prevalence among both individuals and groups in the general population, one explanation for the effect's prevalence among groups is the tendency for some groups to be in consensus on matters of group opinion but where the opinion is unchallenged to a large extent by others outside the group.

KEY WORDS Cognitive bias, consensus

IMPLICATIONS

In the conduct of marketing research, management, and strategy development, marketers should be aware of the general human tendency for an individual to believe their views are shared by others to a greater extent than they really are, since the existence of the false consensus effect can lead to biased perceptions and inaccurate conclusions by the marketer. For example, the effect may lead a group of marketing strategists in a firm to believe that certain views regarding consumers are also shared to a great extent by competing firms in the industry when it may not be the case at all, thereby leading the firm to fail to predict certain competitive actions.

APPLICATION AREAS AND FURTHER READINGS

Sponsorship Marketing
Bennett, Roger (1999). 'Sports Sponsorship, Spectator Recall and False Consensus,' *European Journal of Marketing*, 33(3–4), 291–312.

Marketing Research
Sherman, S. J., Presson, C. C., Chassin, L., Corty, E., and Olshavsky, P. (1983). 'The False Consensus Effect in Estimates of Smoking Prevalence: Underlying Mechanisms,' *Personality and Social Psychology Bulletin*, 9, 197–207.
Moore, M., and Urbany, J. (1994). 'Blinders, Fuzzy Lenses, and the Wrong Shoes,' *Marketing Letters*, 5(3), 247–258.

BIBLIOGRAPHY
Fields, James M., and Schuman, Howard (1976–7). 'Public Beliefs about the Beliefs of the Public,' *Public Opinion Quarterly*, 40, 427–448.
Ross, L., Greene, D., and House, P. (1977). 'The False Consensus Effect: An Egocentric Bias in Social Perception and Attribution Processes,' *Journal of Experimental Social Psychology*, 13, 279–301.
Marks, G., and Miller, N. (1987). 'Ten Years of Research on the False Consensus Effect: An Empirical and Theoretical Review,' *Psychological Bulletin*, 102, 72–81.

■ fan effect

DESCRIPTION

A tendency in individual learning and long-term memory retrieval where the greater the number of specific facts an individual links to a general mental construct, the less likely it is that any particular fact will be retrieved or recalled by the individual when the general mental construct is present later on.

KEY INSIGHTS

According to pioneering research by Anderson (1974) on the fan effect, when an increasingly large number of facts is associated with a particular category or mental construct by an individual (e.g. the category of 'currency' in contrast with the category of 'tableware'), the retrieval of any given fact by the individual becomes increasingly difficult when the mental construct is subsequently present. Retrieval difficulty, for example, may be in terms of the time it takes the individual to verify that any particular fact is, in fact, linked to the particular category or general mental construct.

KEY WORDS Learning, memory retrieval

IMPLICATIONS

Marketers concerned with how and to what extent consumers may ultimately retrieve information learned regarding a category (e.g. a product category, a service provider category, an industry, or a market) may benefit from a greater appreciation and understanding of the fan effect. In particular, the prevalence of the fan effect in memory retrieval suggests that marketers should seek to understand how and when it may work to the marketer's disadvantage or advantage as well as how and when the effect may be increased or decreased. The fan effect is decreased, for example, when an individual, through increased expertise, creates subcategories or additional mental constructs that are linked with smaller sets of facts that would otherwise be associated with larger categories or broader mental constructs.

APPLICATION AREAS AND FURTHER READINGS

Marketing Strategy
Till, B. D., and Nowak, L. I. (2000). 'Toward Effective Use of Cause-Related Marketing Alliances,' *Journal of Product & Brand Management*, 9(7), 472–484.

Consumer Behavior
Till, B. D., and Shimp, T. A. (1998). 'Endorsers in Advertising: The Case of Negative Celebrity Information,' *Journal of Advertising*, 27(1), 67–82.
Yoon, C. (1997). 'Age Differences in Consumers' Processing Strategies: An Investigation of Moderating Influences,' *Journal of Consumer Research*, 24, 329–342.
Gerard, L., Zacks, R., Hasher, L., and Radvansky, G. A. (1991). 'Age Deficits in Retrieval: The Fan Effect,' *Journals of Gerontology*, 46(4), 131–136.

BIBLIOGRAPHY
Anderson, J. R., and Reder, L. M. (1999). 'The Fan Effect: New Results and New Theories,' *Journal of Experimental Psychology: General*, 128, 186–197.
Anderson, John R. (1974). 'Retrieval of Prepositional Information from Long-Term Memory,' *Cognitive Psychology*, 6, 451–474.

☐ fast follower *see* market entry timing
☐ fast moving consumer goods *see* goods
☐ fax marketing *see* e-marketing; direct marketing

■ field marketing

DESCRIPTION
A marketing approach involving the deployment of marketing, sales, or other staff by a firm to engage in person-to-person interaction in the field, such as at locations visited by customers.

KEY INSIGHTS
A field marketing approach enables a firm's staff to use and offer their personal expertise to enhance distributor effectiveness and/or customer experiences. Field marketing encompasses a range of approaches and activities that take place at or closer to places where customers engage with the firm's offerings. Field marketing can therefore be said to encompass marketing approaches including event marketing and experiential marketing. (See **event marketing; experiential marketing**.)

KEY WORDS Customer interaction, distributor interaction

IMPLICATIONS
Marketers seeking a greater marketing presence in the field where distributors and/or customers are present can benefit from a deeper understanding of the scope and range of the field marketing concept and approaches. In particular, knowing how the approach has been used effectively by other firms in marketing efforts for a variety of other product and service categories can provide the marketer with a rich set of field marketing strategies, techniques, and tactics to subsequently evaluate for use in the marketing of the firm's own products or services.

APPLICATION AREAS AND FURTHER READINGS
Marketing Strategy
Sepe, E., Ling, P. M., and Glantz, S. A. (2002). 'Smooth Moves: Bar and Nightclub Tobacco Promotions that Target Young Adults,' *American Journal of Public Health*, 92, 414–419.
Eisenberg, M., Ringwalt, C., Driscoll, D., Vallee, M., and Gullette, G. (2004). 'Learning from Truth (SM): Youth Participation in Field Marketing Techniques to Counter Tobacco Advertising,' *Journal of Health Communication*, 9(3), 223–232.
Mistry, B. (1998). 'Field Marketing: Event Marketing is Overtaking Traditional Techniques,' *Promotions and Incentives*, November–December, 61–66.
Barrand, D. (2004). 'Field Marketing: Experiential Marketing is Having a Huge Effect on the Sector,' *Promotions and Incentives*, September, 27–30.

BIBLIOGRAPHY
Cramp, B. (1995). 'Field Marketing: There's More to Field Marketing than Sampling Cheese In-store,' *Promotions and Incentives*, 10, 46–54.
Cummings, K. M., Morley, C. P., Horan, J. K., Steger, C., and Leavell, N. R. (2002). 'Marketing to America's Youth: Evidence from Corporate Documents,' *Tobacco Control*, 11(Supplement 1), i5–i17.

■ field theory

DESCRIPTION

Theory or theories viewing behavior as being determined by the totality of an individual's situation.

KEY INSIGHTS

Field theory approaches to the study of phenomena in the social sciences involve focusing on the interactions that occur in the space between various objects of analysis as opposed to focusing on relations within the objects of analysis. In the context of individual behavior, field theory views individual behavior as being determined by an individual's entire situation or life space, including the individual's goals, needs, and perceptions of the environment.

In addition to marketing, field theory research spans disciplines in the social sciences including psychology, sociology, and anthropology. Field theory is also an area of study in both physics and mathematics, but the field theory term has different emphases in each of these other fields and is not directly relevant to marketing even though both fields can be said to have contributed to field theory application in the social sciences. One of the early pioneers of field theory development in the social sciences is Lewin (1951) and much of field theory in the social sciences is therefore referred to as *Lewin's field theory*.

KEY WORDS Behavior, goals, **need(s)**

IMPLICATIONS

Marketers recognizing the complexity of consumer behavior may benefit from a greater understanding of individual behaviors by adopting a field theory perspective in their analysis and research efforts. In particular, insights gained from a field theory perspective may enable marketers to offer products and services which are more closely aligned with consumer goals, needs, and perceptions of their purchase, service use, and consumption environments.

APPLICATION AREAS AND FURTHER READINGS

Services Marketing
Houston, M. B., Bettencourt, L. A., and Wenger, S. (1998). 'The Relationship between Waiting in a Service Queue and Evaluations of Service Quality: A Field Theory Perspective,' *Psychology and Marketing*, 15(8), 735-754.
Mittal, B., and Baker, J. (1998). 'The Services Marketing System and Consumer Psychology,' *Psychology and Marketing*, 15(8), 727-734.

Consumer Behavior
Solomon, M. R. (1983). 'The Role of Products as Social Stimuli: A Symbolic Interactionism Perspective,' *Journal of Consumer Research*, 10, 319-329.

BIBLIOGRAPHY
Lewin, K. (1951). *Field Theory in Social Science*. New York: Harper.
Wheelan, S. A., Pepitone, E. A., and Abt, V. (eds.) (1990). *Advances in Field Theory*. Newbury Park, Calif.: Sage Publications.

☐ fighter brand *see* brand positioning
☐ final goods *see* goods
☐ firm, behavioral theories of the *see* firm, theory of the
☐ firm, managerial theories of the *see* firm, theory of the

■ firm, theory of the

DESCRIPTION
Theory or theories aimed at understanding, explaining, and predicting the conduct and behavior of firms.

KEY INSIGHTS
Theories of the firm comprise multiple theoretical perspectives on the nature of the firm, with more specific emphases including firm pricing decisions, investment decisions, choice of production process, output decisions, and dividend policy. Major distinctions in various theories of the firm include that of *managerial theories of the firm*, where the emphasis is on analyses of the consequences of the firms' conduct when managers emphasize objectives other than that of profit maximization, and *behavioral theories of the firm*, where the emphasis is on consideration of the objectives and motives of multiple individuals and groups within the firm.

KEY WORDS Management objectives, organizational behavior

IMPLICATIONS
Although there are multiple theories of the firm and specific research emphases, an understanding of perspective associated with each can potentially sensitize the marketer to issues and practices that may be otherwise under-appreciated drivers, or consequences, of firm- and strategic marketing-related actions. For example, the various theories may help to gain insight into issues important to small firms (e.g. extent of ambition within the firm to actually grow) as well as large firms (e.g. the possibility that managers may engage in empire building at the expense of overall firm profitability).

APPLICATION AREAS AND FURTHER READINGS
Marketing Strategy
Anderson, Paul F. (1982). 'Marketing, Strategic Planning and the Theory of the Firm,' *Journal of Marketing*, 46(2), Spring, 15–26.
Heide, Jan B. (1994). 'Interorganizational Governance in Marketing Channels,' *Journal of Marketing*, 58(1), January, 71–85.
Hallen, Lars, Johanson, Jan, and Seyed-Mohamed, Nazeem (1991). 'Interfirm Adaptation in Business Relationships,' *Journal of Marketing*, 55(2), April, 29–37.
Jaworski, Bernard J. (1988). 'Toward a Theory of Marketing Control: Environmental Context, Control Types, and Consequences,' *Journal of Marketing*, 52(3), July, 23–39.
Noble, Charles H., and Mokwa, Michael P. (1999). 'Implementing Marketing Strategies: Developing and Testing a Managerial Theory,' *Journal of Marketing*, 63(4), October, 57–73.

International Marketing
Andersen, O. (1993). 'On the Internationalization Process of Firms: A Critical Analysis,' *Journal of International Business Studies*, 24(2), 209.

Marketing Research
Day, George S., and Montgomery, David B. (1999). 'Charting New Directions for Marketing,' *Journal of Marketing*, 63, Fundamental Issues and Directions for Marketing, 3–13.

BIBLIOGRAPHY
Bartlett, C. A., and Ghoshal, S. (1993). 'Beyond the M-form: Toward a Managerial Theory of the Firm,' *Strategic Management Journal*, 14, Winter Special Issue, 23–46.
Cyert, R., and March, J. (1963). *A Behavioral Theory of the Firm*. Englewood Cliffs, NJ: Prentice Hall.
Simon, Herbert A., and Bonini, Charles P. (1958). 'The Size Distribution of Business Firms,' *American Economic Review*, 48(4), September, 607–617.
Simon, Herbert A. (1991). 'Organizations and Markets,' *Journal of Economic Perspectives*, 5(2), Spring 25–44.

☐ first law of marketing *see* marketing, laws of
☐ first-mover advantage *see* market entry timing
☐ fixed cost *see* cost

■ floor effect

(also called basement effect)

DESCRIPTION
Any effect on measurement or response where a lower limit to the range of possible responses leads to a skewing of the distribution of responses.

KEY INSIGHTS
The floor effect becomes an issue in measurement and response when the imposition of a lower limit on possible responses impedes understanding the true nature of responses for a phenomenon as a result of its prominent effects on statistical analyses. Oftentimes, the existence of the floor effect in a set of measurements means only limited insights can be drawn about a phenomenon. For example, if consumers were surveyed to indicate the number of car brands they are able to name, where the range of choices given to them is, say, from five or fewer to ten or more, information from the survey would be lost if a relatively large proportion of respondents indicated the answer of five or fewer.

KEY WORDS Measurement, response, statistical analysis

IMPLICATIONS
Marketers should be aware of the possibility of a floor effect in conducting marketing research when the lower limit to a range of possible responses to be collected or measured is essentially arbitrary.

APPLICATION AREAS AND FURTHER READINGS

Marketing Research

Mela, Carl F., Gupta, Sunil, and Lehmann, Donald R. (1997). 'The Long-Term Impact of Promotion and Advertising on Consumer Brand Choice,' *Journal of Marketing Research*, 34(2), May, 248–261.

Smith, Robert E. (1993). 'Integrating Information from Advertising and Trial: Processes and Effects on Consumer Response to Product Information,' *Journal of Marketing Research*, 30(2), May, 204–219.

BIBLIOGRAPHY

Singh, Surendra N., Rothschild, Michael L., and Churchill, Gilbert A., Jr. (1988). 'Recognition versus Recall as Measures of Television Commercial Forgetting,' *Journal of Marketing Research*, 25(1), February, 72–80.

Joyce, William F. (1986). 'Matrix Organization: A Social Experiment,' *Academy of Management Journal*, 29(3), September, 536–561.

Cook, Thomas D., and Campbell, Donald T. (1979). *Quasiexperimental Designs for Research*. Chicago: Rand McNally.

☐ FMCGs *see* goods

☐ focus group *see* marketing research

☐ focus strategy *see* strategies, generic

☐ follow-up *see* selling process

☐ follower advantage *see* market entry timing

☐ follower firm *see* market entry timing

■ foot-in-the-door technique

DESCRIPTION

A technique for persuading an individual to accept or adopt a particular large course of action where the individual is first presented with a request to accept a much smaller course of action which has the effect of making the individual more amenable to subsequently accepting the larger course of action.

KEY INSIGHTS

Based on pioneering research by Freedman and Fraser (1966), the foot-in-the-door technique was observed to be more effective in obtaining individuals' commitments to particular causes relative to the condition where individuals were sought for the same causes without using the technique. The technique therefore involves presenting a small request that is relatively palatable to an individual and where the individual's commitment to accepting the request weakens the individual's interest in rejecting a subsequently larger request.

KEY WORDS Persuasion, compliance, negotiation, selling

IMPLICATIONS

While the technique may certainly not be appropriate for use in all or even in most instances where marketers seek to persuade as it is one technique among many, it nevertheless may be an alternative; marketers may wish to explore its viability in areas of persuasive communication including personal selling and negotiations.

APPLICATION AREAS AND FURTHER READINGS

Marketing Research

Fern, Edward F., Monroe, Kent B., and Avila, Ramon A. (1986). 'Effectiveness of Multiple Request Strategies: A Synthesis of Research Results,' *Journal of Marketing Research*, 23(2), May, 144–152.

Scott, Carol A. (1977). 'Modifying Socially-Conscious Behavior: The Foot-in-the-Door Technique,' *Journal of Consumer Research*, 4(3), December, 156–164.

Hansen, Robert A., and Robinson, Larry M. (1980). 'Testing the Effectiveness of Alternative Foot-in-the-Door Manipulations,' *Journal of Marketing Research*, 17(3), August, 359–364.

BIBLIOGRAPHY

Freedman, J. L., and Fraser, S. C. (1966). 'Compliance without Pressure: The Foot-in-the-Door Technique,' *Journal of Personality and Social Psychology*, 4(2), 195–202.

Dillard, James P., Hunter, John E., and Burgoon, Michael (1984). 'Sequential-Request Persuasive Strategies: Meta-analysis of Foot-in-the-Door and Door-in-the-Face,' *Human Communication Research*, 10(4), June, 461.

□ for-profit marketing *see* commercial marketing

■ forecasting methods

DESCRIPTION

Any of an array of methods for estimating or predicting future events or conditions.

KEY INSIGHTS

Marketers have a range of methods to draw upon in making forecasts concerning events and conditions which vary in the likelihood of their occurrence in both the short and long term. Three notable forecasting methods used in marketing are: the *market factor index method*, where market factors found to correlate with market potential are identified and then combined to form a weighted index; the *Delphi method*, where the views of individual experts forming an expert panel are obtained, summarized, and fed back to individuals for reconsideration and where successive iterations of the process are aimed at arriving at panel consensus; and the *jury method*, where the views of a certain number of customers (e.g. 50 to 100) are used to establish a collective opinion about an event's or condition's likelihood of occurrence, which may include opinions regarding the degree of consumer acceptance of a new offering by the firm. No single method is considered superior to any other as each has benefits and limitations which must be weighed in accordance with the marketer's objectives.

KEY WORDS Estimates, predictions

IMPLICATIONS

In forecasting, marketers should evaluate multiple methods for characteristics including accuracy and bias potential, resource requirements (e.g. time, money, effort), and potential for contribution to the firm's marketing objectives. To the extent that stakes are high regarding the accuracy and usefulness of an estimate or prediction, marketers may benefit from the adoption of multiple forecasting methods, which may further include a combination of both quantitative and qualitative approaches.

APPLICATION AREAS AND FURTHER READINGS

Marketing Research
Yokum, T., and Armstrong, J. S. (1995). 'Beyond Accuracy: Comparison of Criteria Used to Select Forecasting Methods,' *International Journal of Forecasting*, 11, 591-597.
Urban, Glen L., Weinberg, Bruce D., and Hauser, John R. (1996). 'Premarket Forecasting for Really New Products,' *Journal of Marketing*, 60(1), 47-60.
Armstrong, J. S., and Collopy, F. (1992). 'Error measures for Generalizing about Forecasting Methods: Empirical Comparisons,' *International Journal of Forecasting*, 8, 69-80.

Marketing Management
Fildes, R., and Hastings, R. (1994). 'The Organization and Improvement of Market Forecasting,' *Journal of the Operational Research Society*, 45, 1-16.

BIBLIOGRAPHY
Armstrong, J. S., Brodie, R. J., and McIntyre, S. H. (1987). 'Forecasting Methods for Marketing: Review of Empirical Research,' *International Journal of Forecasting*, 3, 335-376.
Armstrong, J. S. (2001). *Principles of Forecasting: A Handbook for Researchers and Practitioners*. Dordrecht: Kluwer.

☐ **Forer effect** *see* Barnum effect
☐ **forgetting, law of** *see* forgetting curve

■ forgetting curve

(also called the Ebbinghaus forgetting curve, Ebbinghaus curve of forgetting, Ebbinghaus forgetting function, Ebbinghaus effect, Ebbinghaus's law of forgetting, or, more generally, the law of forgetting)

DESCRIPTION
A curve depicting the outcome of Ebbinghaus's recall experiments relating the time since a learning session to the percentage of recall.

KEY INSIGHTS
Ebbinghaus (1913) conducted pioneering experimental research on memory. As a result of experiments which involved using sets of items to be committed to memory that had no previous associations, he produced a now-famous curve summarizing his findings. With time since learning session on the x-axis and percentage of recall on the y-axis, a plot of the following numbers can be used to show the Ebbinghaus forgetting curve:

Time since Learning Session	Percentage of Recall
28 minutes	58.2%
1 hour	44.2%
9 hours	35.8%
1 day	33.7%
2 days	27.8%
6 days	25.4%
31 days	21.1%

The forgetting curve involves recall, which is simply trying to recall each item. Ebbinghaus also examined recollection, which involves trying to recognize which items had been on the list studied, and found that recollection is a more sensitive test of memory than recall as people may be able to recognize items that they cannot recall.

Ebbinghaus further developed the concept of savings in relation to rememorization. Specifically, in trying to rememorize a list of items after some long period of time (i.e. after a time when neither recall nor recollection demonstrate much evidence of prior learning), an individual can attempt to rememorize the list through further trials. By comparing the number of trials required to rememorize the list (e.g. five trials) to the number of trials required to memorize the list the first time (e.g. ten trials), a percent savings can be calculated (e.g. 5/10 or 50%). Ebbinghaus views the concept of savings to be the most sensitive test of memory, as it characterizes a residual effect of previous learning, especially when recall and recognition show little evidence of prior learning. The savings concept of Ebbinghaus is often referred to in research as the Ebbinghaus savings function.

It is important to note that the forgetting curve should not be confused with the power law of forgetting which mathematically characterizes the forgetting function as a specific power function. (See **power law of forgetting**.)

Note also that the forgetting curve should not be confused with the *forgetting law*, also known as *Jost's law*, or Jost's law of forgetting. The forgetting law encompasses two specific, formal ideas developed by Jost (1897) concerning aspects of memory. Specifically, the forgetting law states that if two associations or memories are of the same strength but different ages, the older will (a) benefit more from a learning trial and (b) decay more slowly in a given period of time than the younger one. While of interest in the field of psychology, the forgetting law as developed by Jost has not received significant research attention in marketing.

KEY WORDS Forgetting, memory, recall

IMPLICATIONS

Much marketing practice is aimed at encouraging consumer recall and recognition of a marketer's products and brands. Recognizing that consumers have a systematic tendency to forget part of what they learn over time, knowledge of such tendencies, and its quantification can form the basis for marketing models, policies, and practices that help to make the best use of marketing resources and strategies for particular marketing objectives for short- and long-term consumer learning. Advertising policies and practices are particularly influenced by a careful understanding of consumers' forgetting tendencies.

APPLICATION AREAS AND FURTHER READINGS

Consumer Behavior

Lodish, Leonard M. (1971). 'Empirical Studies on Individual Response to Exposure Patterns,' *Journal of Marketing Research*, 8(2), May, 212–218.

Advertising

Bagozzi, Richard P., and Silk, Alvin J. (1983). 'Recall, Recognition, and the Measurement of Memory for Print Advertisements,' *Marketing Science*, 2(2), Spring, 95–134.

Mahajan, Vijay, and Muller, Eitan (1986). 'Advertising Pulsing Policies for Generating Awareness for New Products,' *Marketing Science*, 5(2), Spring, 89–106.

Krugman, Herbert E. (1965). 'The Impact of Television Advertising: Learning without Involvement,' *Public Opinion Quarterly*, 29(3), Autumn, 349–356.

BIBLIOGRAPHY

Anderson, J. R. (2000). *Learning and Memory: An Integrated Approach*, 2nd edn. New York: Wiley.

Ebbinghaus, H. (1913). *Memory: A Contribution to Experimental Psychology*, trans. H. A. Ruger and C. E. Bussenius. New York: Teachers College, Columbia University. (Original work published 1885.)

Jost, A. (1897). 'Die Assoziationsfestigkeit in ihrer Abhangigkeit von der Verteilung der Wiederholungen' (The Strength of Associations in their Dependence on the Distribution of Repetitions), *Zeitschrift für Psychologie und Physiologie der Sinnesorgane*, 16, 436–472.

☐ forgetting law *see* forgetting curve

☐ forward integration *see* integration

☐ four Ps *see* marketing mix

■ framing effect

DESCRIPTION

Any effect of how a problem is described, presented, or labeled on an individual's response to it.

KEY INSIGHTS

Based on pioneering research by Tversky and Kahneman (1981), the framing effect is observable when significantly different responses (e.g. decisions) are obtained by individuals when the same problem is merely presented in different ways, as when saying a surgical operation has a 10% chance of failure vs. a 90% chance of success. How problems are framed can therefore influence the way problems are evaluated, which may include leading individuals to pay more or less attention to their tendencies to be either risk averse or risk seeking.

KEY WORDS Problem framing, choice, decision making

IMPLICATIONS

Marketers should seek to understand how the framing of particular problems presented to individuals for their consideration may systematically influence their decision making. Whether in using persuasive communications with consumers or internal marketing communications in efforts to persuade employees within an organization, a better understanding of the relative influence and importance of framing effects may assist the marketer in proactively developing effective marketing message content for both tactical and strategic marketing communications.

APPLICATION AREAS AND FURTHER READINGS

Consumer Behavior

Levin, Irwin P., and Gaeth, Gary J. (1988). 'How Consumers are Affected by the Framing of Attribute Information before and after Consuming the Product,' *Journal of Consumer Research*, 15(3), December, 374–378.

Marketing Research

Block, Lauren G., and Keller, Punam Anand (1995).'When to Accentuate the Negative: The Effects of Perceived Efficacy and Message Framing on Intentions to Perform a Health-Related Behavior,' *Journal of Marketing Research*, 32(2), May, 192–203.

Levin, I. P., Gaeth, G. J., Schreiber, J., and Lauriola, M. (2002). 'A New Look at Framing Effects: Distribution of Effect Sizes, Individual Differences, and Independence of Types of Effects,' *Organizational Behavior and Human Decision Processes*, 88(1), 411–429.

BIBLIOGRAPHY

Tversky, Amos, and Kahneman, Daniel (1986). 'Rational Choice and the Framing of Decisions,' *Journal of Business*, 59(4), Part 2: The Behavioral Foundations of Economic Theory, October, S251–S278.

Tversky A., and Kahneman, D. (1981). 'The Framing of Decisions and the Psychology of Choice,' *Science*, 211(4481), January, 453–458.

Kahneman, Daniel, and Tversky, Amos (2000). *Choices, Values, and Frames.* New York: Russell Sage Foundation.

■ free rider effect

DESCRIPTION

A situation where an individual or organization is able to benefit from the actions of another without contributing to the cost associated with such actions.

KEY INSIGHTS

The free rider effect, where one outcome of an action is that others are able to benefit from the action without contributing to its cost, is typically viewed as a problem for those bearing the cost of the action and an opportunity for those who are able to benefit from the action. A firm choosing to be a market pioneer, for example, typically bears a higher cost to develop a new product than those that follow with a copy of the product since follower firms can frequently reverse-engineer, or at least learn from, the pioneer's product.

KEY WORDS Cost(s), benefits

IMPLICATIONS

Whether involved in new product development efforts or in the management of public goods and services, a marketer should be concerned with the extent to which free rider effects are either created by the actions of the marketer's organization or by the actions of others. In doing so, the marketer will be in a better position to assess the extent that free rider effects create problems or opportunities for the firm.

APPLICATION AREAS AND FURTHER READINGS

Marketing Strategy
Golder, Peter N., and Tellis, Gerard J. (1993). 'Pioneer Advantage: Marketing Logic or Marketing Legend?' *Journal of Marketing Research*, 30(2), May, 158–170.
Kerin, Roger A., Varadarajan, P. Rajan, and Peterson, Robert A. (1992). 'First-Mover Advantage: A Synthesis, Conceptual Framework, and Research Propositions,' *Journal of Marketing*, 56(4), October, 33–52.

Green Marketing
Wiser, R., and Pickle, S. (1997). *Green Marketing, Renewables, and Free Riders: Increasing Customer Demand for a Public Good*. Berkeley, Calif.: Lawrence Berkeley National Laboratory, LBNL-40632.

BIBLIOGRAPHY
Groves, T., and Ledyard, J. (1977). 'Optimal Allocation of Public Goods: A Solution to the Free Rider Problem,' *Econometrica*, 45, 783–809.

☐ **freight-absorption pricing** *see* pricing strategies

■ **frequency marketing**

DESCRIPTION
Marketing which involves rewarding customers for the volume or frequency of their purchases in order to enhance customer profitability.

KEY INSIGHTS
Frequency marketing emphasizes the development and implementation of marketing strategies and tactics aimed at increasing the frequency of customer purchases, visits, orders, and the like in an effort to maximize the profit contributions of customers. Frequency marketing can therefore involve a process of identifying 'best,' or most valuable customers, recognizing that the Pareto principle may apply to customer profitability (where, for example, 80% of the firm's profits may be attributed to 20% of the firm's customers). The practice of frequency marketing by many firms is typically through formal loyalty programs, which aim to encourage repeat purchase and increase customer retention.

KEY WORDS Purchase frequency, loyalty, customer retention

IMPLICATIONS
Marketers concerned with increasing repeat purchases by customers valued by the firm may benefit from a greater understanding of the benefits, costs, and limitations associated with the practice of frequency marketing. For example, marketers should recognize that, while customers may

increase their purchase frequency in response to a marketer's frequency program and ultimately become habitual or steadfast buyers, it is also possible that customer loyalty may be short-lived among other customers, particularly if the frequency marketing programs of competitors become relatively more attractive to such customers.

APPLICATION AREAS AND FURTHER READINGS

Marketing Strategy
Barlow, R. G. (1995). 'Five Mistakes of Frequency Marketing,' *Direct Marketing*, 57 (11), 16–18.
Pruden, D. (1995). 'There's a Difference between Frequency Marketing and Relationship Marketing,' *Direct Marketing*, June, 30–31.
Barlow, R. (1999). 'Frequency Marketing: The Shift from First to Second Generation Programs will Challenge our Ingenuity as Marketers,' *Brandweek* (New York), 40(7), 20–21.

Consumer Behavior
Kivetz, Ran, and Simonson, Itamar (2002). 'Earning the Right to Indulge: Effort as a Determinant of Customer Preferences towards Frequency Program Rewards,' *Journal of Marketing Research*, 39, May, 155–170.

BIBLIOGRAPHY
Barlow, Richard (1990). 'Building Customer Loyalty through Frequency Marketing,' *Bankers Magazine*, May–June, 73–76.
Mohs, Julia (1999). 'Frequency Marketing,' *Retail Report*, 12(4), 3.

☐ **functional area strategy** *see* marketing strategy
☐ **functional theory of attitudes** *see* attitudes, functional theory of

■ fundamental attribution error

DESCRIPTION
The common tendency for individuals to underestimate the influences of external circumstances in interpretations of others' behaviors as well as to overestimate the importance of others' dispositions in such interpretations.

KEY INSIGHTS
The pervasive phenomenon of the fundamental attribution error is a major area of focus in the broader area of attribution theory. The phenomenon is a form of dispositional bias which may result in significant misjudgments of others' attitudes and behaviors.

KEY WORDS Causality, circumstances, behavioral explanations

IMPLICATIONS
Particularly in service encounters, marketers must be aware of how consumers may fail to consider sufficiently how external circumstances have influenced particular individual behaviors (as in explaining the slowness of a department store cashier) as well as how the same consumers may also give excessive attention to the influence of other's personality characteristics and related dispositions. Adjusting marketing communications to draw attention to the influences of external conditions may be a means

to counter individual tendencies for making a fundamental attribution error.

APPLICATION AREAS AND FURTHER READINGS

Consumer Behavior
Cowley, Elizabeth (2005). 'Views from Consumers Next in Line: The Fundamental Attribution Error in a Service Setting,' *Journal of the Academy of Marketing Science*, 33(2), 139–152.

International Marketing
Krull, D. S., Loy, M. H.-M., Lin, J., Wang, C.-F., Chen, S., and Zhao, X. (1999). 'The Fundamental Fundamental Attribution Error: Correspondence Bias in Individualist and Collectivist Cultures,' *Personality and Social Psychology Bulletin*, 25(10), 1208–1219.

BIBLIOGRAPHY
Heider, Fritz (1958). *The Psychology of Interpersonal Relations*. New York: John Wiley & Sons.
Ross, L. (1977). 'The Intuitive Psychologist and his Shortcomings,' in L. Berkowitz (ed.), *Advances in Experimental Social Psychology*, 10. New York: Academic Press, 173–220.
Ichheiser, Gustav (1943). 'Misinterpretations of Personality in Everyday Life and the Psychologist's Frame of Reference,' *Journal of Personality*, 12(2), December, 145.

■ fusion marketing

DESCRIPTION
Marketing involving the use of multiple forms of promotion, communication, and/or interactivity.

KEY INSIGHTS
The emphasis on fusion marketing is that of combining alternate means of marketing to enhance overall marketing effectiveness. In an online marketing environment, a fusion marketing approach may therefore involve a coherent mix of e-mail advertising, banner ad presentations, and relevant web page-based content in an effort to achieve a firm's marketing objectives. The approach may also involve efforts to coordinate and profit from marketing performed across firms, as where two firms endorse or promote each other's products. As the term is used by practitioners to indicate marketing activities that vary in their emphasis (e.g. as part of online marketing, as part of guerrilla marketing), the actual scope of fusion marketing remains relatively vague and certainly overlaps with hybrid marketing and convergence marketing (see **hybrid marketing**; **convergence marketing**).

KEY WORDS Multiple marketing approaches

IMPLICATIONS
While conceptually vague, fusion marketing nevertheless provides the marketers with a perspective suggesting the possibility of increased marketing effectiveness as a result of the adoption of multiple marketing methods. In addition, given that the term is used in certain contexts (e.g. guerrilla marketing) to achieve increased cost effectiveness, the concept

also lends itself to the notion that there may be multiple low-cost methods that the marketer can employ given limited marketing resources.

APPLICATION AREAS AND FURTHER READINGS

Online Marketing
Koogle, Tim (2000). 'Building Yahoo!' *Business Strategy Review*, 11(4), April, 15–20.

Services Marketing
Crandall, Richard C. (1998). *1001 Ways To Market Your Services—Even If You Hate To Sell*. New York: McGraw-Hill.

BIBLIOGRAPHY
Levinson, Jay Conrad, and Rubin, Charles (1996). *Guerrilla Marketing Online Weapons: 100 Low-Cost, High-Impact Weapons for Online Profits and Prosperity*. Boston: Houghton Mifflin Co.

■ fuzzy set theory

DESCRIPTION
Theory relating to fuzzy sets, where elements' membership in relation to a set is viewed as gradual or continuously graded.

KEY INSIGHTS
The notion of fuzzy sets was developed in pioneering research by Zadeh (1965) as a result of the observation that many phenomena (e.g. attractiveness, newness) involve categories with indistinct boundaries. In contrast to a view that elements either are or are not members of a set, fuzzy sets enable elements to have graded degrees of set membership ranging from zero to one, where zero indicates non-membership and one indicates full membership.

KEY WORDS Sets, models, membership

IMPLICATIONS
Fuzzy set theory has potential for use in the development and application of marketing models where categories are viewed as having indistinct boundaries, as in categorizations of products or in characterizations of consumer choice behavior.

APPLICATION AREAS AND FURTHER READINGS

Marketing Modeling
Viswanathan, Madhubalan, and Childers, Terry L. (1999). 'Understanding How Product Attributes Influence Product Categorization: Development and Validation of Fuzzy Set-Based Measures of Gradedness in Product Categories,' *Journal of Marketing Research*, 36(1), February, 75–94.
Wu, Jianan, and Rangaswamy, Arvind (2003). 'A Fuzzy Set Model of Search and Consideration with an Application to an Online Market,' *Marketing Science*, 22(3), Summer, 411–434.

BIBLIOGRAPHY
Zimmermann, H.-J. (1991). *Fuzzy Set Theory and its Applications*. Boston: Kluwer Academic.
Zadeh, L. A. (1965). 'Fuzzy Set,' *Information and Control*, 8, 338–353.

G

■ gain-loss effect

DESCRIPTION
An effect characterizing situations whereby an outcome is more dependent on the degree of increase or decrease of an influencing factor than the overall level of the influencing factor.

KEY INSIGHTS
Based on pioneering experimental research by Aronson and Linder (1965), the gain–loss effect is embodied in the finding that an individual's attraction to another is commonly observed to be more dependent on the degree that the other individual's liking of them has increased or decreased rather than the overall level of the other's degree of liking. In such a context, an individual's attraction to another tends to be high when the other's liking of the individual has appeared to increase and low when the other's liking of the individual has appeared to decrease.

KEY WORDS Decision making, gains, losses

IMPLICATIONS
Marketers should consider how gains or losses associated with a customer relationship or product or service offering, whether experienced or simply perceived by a consumer or other individual, may have more influence on the individual's behaviors or decisions than the overall level of a factor of influence. As such, the gain–loss effect may embody itself in elements of marketing relationships with consumers as well as in decision-maker evaluations of problems involving gains or losses.

APPLICATION AREAS AND FURTHER READINGS
Consumer Behavior
Huston, T. L., and Levinger, G. (1978). 'Interpersonal Attraction and Relationships,' *Annual Review of Psychology*, 29, January, 115–156.
Putler, Daniel S. (1992). 'Incorporating Reference Price Effects into a Theory of Consumer Choice,' *Marketing Science*, 11(3), Summer, 287–309.

Decision Making
Fischer, Gregory W., Kamlet, Mark S., Fienberg, Stephen E., and Schkade, David (1986). 'Risk Preferences for Gains and Losses in Multiple Objective Decision Making,' *Management Science*, 32(9), September, 1065–1086.

BIBLIOGRAPHY
Aronson, E., and Linder, D. (1965). 'Gain and Loss of Esteem as Determinants of Interpersonal Attractiveness,' *Journal of Experimental Social Psychology*, 1, 156–172.

■ gambler's fallacy

DESCRIPTION

The misconception that future occurrences of a repeating random event are influenced by past occurrences.

KEY INSIGHTS

The gambler's fallacy characterizes an error in understanding probabilities where an individual believes that the frequency or recency of repeated random events of the past is influential in determining the outcome of a future random event. The fallacy is therefore present in believing that a random event is more or less likely to occur because it has not happened for a long time or because it recently happened. A common example is when believing that not winning a jackpot on a slot machine after playing it for a long period of time means that the next time the slot machine is played, the chances of winning a jackpot are greater.

KEY WORDS Probabilities, random events

IMPLICATIONS

Consumers who fail to understand the nature of random events may make an error of reasoning in the form of the gambler's fallacy. Such a misconception may influence consumer behavior in activities such as gambling. Marketers and consumers should seek to understand the nature of random events to ensure that actions are consistent with actual probabilities as opposed to misconceived probabilities.

APPLICATION AREAS AND FURTHER READINGS

Decision Making
Armstrong, J. S., Coviello, N., and Safrane, B. (1993). 'Escalation Bias: Does it Extend to Marketing?' *Journal of the Academy of Marketing Science*, 21(3), 247.

Consumer Behavior
Johnson, Joseph, Tellis, Gerard J., and Macinnis, Deborah J. (2005). 'Losers, Winners, and Biased Trades,' *Journal of Consumer Research*, 32, 324–329.
Roshwalb, Irving (1975). 'A Consideration of Probability Estimates Provided by Respondents,' *Journal of Marketing Research*, 12(1), February, 100–103.

BIBLIOGRAPHY
Jarvik, M. E. (1951). 'Probability Learning and a Negative Recency Effect in the Serial Anticipation of Alternative Symbols,' *Journal of Experimental Psychology*, 41, 291–297.

■ game theory

DESCRIPTION

Theory relating to the study of decision making, strategy, and competition in situations typically characterized by interaction and interdependence among rival players under conditions of imperfect information about other rivals' intentions.

KEY INSIGHTS
Game theory, based on pioneering research by von Neumann and Morgenstern (1944), draws upon principles and concepts in mathematics and economics and aims to understand, explain, and predict how and why interdependent rival players will choose from among different courses of action in an effort to maximize their returns under specific conditions and rules for interaction. As such, models based on game theory involve player interaction and are concerned with optimal decisions and strategies under situations where costs and benefits are not fixed but rather are dependent on other players' choices. For example, one outcome of a game-theoretic model involving several interacting players may be that of *Nash equilibrium*, where there exists a stable state in which no participant can gain by a change of strategy as long as the strategies of all the other participants remain unchanged.

Particular characterizations of game theory can be a focus of further theory in the study of games, as in the cases of cooperative and non-cooperative game theory, where *cooperative game theory* involves the study of games where cooperative behavior through coalitions of groups of players is allowed and enforceable and *non-cooperative game theory* where such behavior is not allowed. Games within game theory can be characterized in many other ways as well, including whether the game is zero sum vs. non-zero sum (where a *zero-sum game* is one where a player's gain is at the equal expense of others), sequential vs. simultaneous (where sequential indicates a player has knowledge of earlier actions as opposed to no knowledge), symmetric vs. asymmetric (where symmetric indicates that payoffs are dependent only on strategy and not on who is playing), and fixed duration vs. infinitely long.

One of the better-known games within game theory is the Prisoner's Dilemma, which in game theory terminology is a two-person, non-zero-sum, symmetric, fixed duration, simultaneous game of cooperative behavior. The game involves an intriguing tension through the incentives presented to the players. Specifically, two persons suspected of a crime are caught and interrogated, but there is not enough evidence to convict them unless one of them confesses. If both remain silent, they both will be released. But if one confesses and the other is silent, the one who confesses will be released while the other will be sentenced to prison for a long time.

A major contribution of game theory research, models, and particular games such as the Prisoner's Dilemma is in making sense of particular situations where costs and benefits for various courses of action are not fixed but rather are dependent on the choices of other competitors.

KEY WORDS Games, decision making, **strategy**, uncertainty, **competition**, cooperation

IMPLICATIONS
Research into game theory provides a rich set of principles and concepts that may be drawn upon to model areas of marketing including

competitive dynamics and strategic choices. Marketers can benefit from understanding how game theory can potentially provide useful insights through modeling to assist with decision making, strategy formulation, and understanding, explaining, and predicting competitive responses and other behaviors.

APPLICATION AREAS AND FURTHER READINGS

Marketing Modeling

Moorthy, K. Sridhar (1985). 'Using Game Theory to Model Competition,' *Journal of Marketing Research*, 22(3), August, 262–282.

McAfee, R. Preston, and McMillan, John (1996). 'Competition and Game Theory,' *Journal of Marketing Research*, 33(3), August, 263–267.

Marketing Strategy

Brandenburger, A. M., and Nalebuff, B. J. (1995). 'The Right Game: Use Game Theory to Shape Strategy,' *Harvard Business Review*, 73(4), 57.

Corfman, K. P., and Lehmann, D. R. (1994). 'The Prisoner's Dilemma and the Role of Information in Setting Advertising Budgets,' *Journal of Advertising (Utah)*, 23(2), 35.

Cable, D. M., and Shane, S. (1997). 'A Prisoner's Dilemma Approach to Entrepreneur-Venture Capitalist Relationships,' *Academy of Management Review*, 22(1), 142–176.

BIBLIOGRAPHY

Von Neumann, J., and Morgenstern, O. (1944). *Theory of Games and Economic Behavior*. Princeton: Princeton University Press.

Kreps, David M. (1990). *Game Theory and Economic Modeling*. Oxford: Clarendon Press.

Rapoport, Anatol, and Chammah, Albert M. (1965). *Prisoner's Dilemma: A Study in Conflict and Cooperation*. Ann Arbor: University of Michigan Press.

☐ gatekeepers *see* industrial buyer behavior
☐ gender segmentation *see* segmentation
☐ general systems theory *see* systems theory

■ generalizability theory

DESCRIPTION

A theoretical approach in quantitative measurement where analysis of variance is used to estimate the extent that derived results are applicable beyond the specific conditions under which they were obtained.

KEY INSIGHTS

Generalizability theory as a theory of measurement focuses on the identification and quantification of multiple sources of measurement error. As such, generalizability theory enables a researcher to examine the influences of sources of error within the context of a measurement situation and use such information to tailor the measurement conditions of subsequent studies to maximize reliability within the constraints of the measurement situation.

KEY WORDS Measurement, generalizability, analysis of variance, **reliability**

IMPLICATIONS

Generalizability theory provides a basis for the development and application of measurement analysis frameworks and methods in the area of testing (e.g. psychometric testing) and other approaches to data collection for an array of measures. In particular, marketers concerned with assessing or improving the reliability or dependability of marketing measures in data analyses may benefit from understanding the principles and elements of generalizability theory.

APPLICATION AREAS AND FURTHER READINGS

Marketing Research

Hughes, Marie Adele, and Garrett, Dennis E. (1990). 'Intercoder Reliability Estimation Approaches in Marketing: A Generalizability Theory Framework for Quantitative Data,' *Journal of Marketing Research*, 27(2), May, 185–195.

Rentz, Joseph O. (1987). 'Generalizability Theory: A Comprehensive Method for Assessing and Improving the Dependability of Marketing Measures,' *Journal of Marketing Research*, 24(1), February, 19–28.

Peter, J. Paul (1979). 'Reliability: A Review of Psychometric Basics and Recent Marketing Practices,' *Journal of Marketing Research*, 16(1), February, 6–17.

BIBLIOGRAPHY

Shavelson, Richard J., and Webb, Noreen M. (1991). *Generalizability Theory: A Primer.* Newbury Park, Calif.: Sage Publications.

Brennan, Robert L. (1983). *Elements of Generalizability Theory.* Iowa City: American College Testing Program.

Brennan, R. L. (1994). 'Variance Components in Generalizability Theory,' in C. R. Reynolds (ed.), *Cognitive Assessment: A Multidisciplinary Perspective.* New York: Plenum Press, 175–207.

Kane, M. (2002). 'Inferences about Variance Components and Reliability-Generalizability Coefficients in the Absence of Random Sampling,' *Journal of Educational Measurement*, 39(2), 165–181.

☐ generation X/Y/Z *see* generational marketing

■ generational marketing

DESCRIPTION

Marketing to a group of individuals who are born and live at the same general time.

KEY INSIGHTS

Generational marketing emphasizes the tailoring of marketing approaches to appeal to the characteristics of particular generations of individuals. Of relevance to marketers are generations given particular names, even though such generational cohorts are not always well defined. Popularly named generations include: *baby boomers*—individuals born in a period of increased birth rates (e.g. 1946-64); *generation X* (or *X-generation*)—the generation following the baby boom generation, comprising individuals born in the 1960s and 1970s (with definitions including 1965-75, 1965-76, and 1963-78); *generation Y* (or *Y-generation*)— the generation following generation X (with definitions including 1976-85, 1977-94, and 1977-97); and *generation Z* (or *Z-generation*)—the generation following generation Z (defined generally as being from the mid-2000s to a date estimated at 2017). According to various marketing researchers, each of the above generational cohorts shares certain characteristics that enable them to have identifiable influences in the societies in which they live.

KEY WORDS Age, cohorts

IMPLICATIONS
Marketers of offerings that have generational appeal may benefit from a greater understanding of the different characteristics of generational cohorts. Whether the marketer is concerned with targeting a single generation or multiple generations, a greater awareness of the many different generational differences, expectations, and influences can assist the marketer in being responsive to changes that, while occurring relatively slowly, may nevertheless be important influences to the firm's longer-term marketing strategy.

APPLICATION AREAS AND FURTHER READINGS

Marketing Research
Cleaver, M., and Muller, T. E. (2002). 'The Socially Aware Baby Boomer: Gaining a Lifestyle-Based Understanding of the New Wave of Ecotourists,' *Journal of Sustainable Tourism*, 10(3), 173–190.

Marketing Strategy
Muller, T. E., and Cleaver, M. (2000). 'Targeting the CANZUS Baby Boomer Explorer and Adventurer Segments,' *Journal of Vacation Marketing*, 6(2), 154–169.
Richie, K. (1995). 'Marketing to Generation X,' *American Demographics*, 17, April, 34–39.
Mitchell, V., and Freestone, O. (2004). 'Generation Y Attitudes towards E-ethics and Internet-Related Misbehaviours,' *Journal of Business Ethics*, 54, 121–128.
Bennett, G., and Lachowetz, T. (2004). 'Marketing to Lifestyles: Action Sports and Generation,' *Y. Sport Marketing Quarterly*, 13(4), 239–243.

BIBLIOGRAPHY
Smith, J. W., and Clurman, A. (1997). *Rocking the Ages: The Yankelovich Report on Generational Marketing*. New York: Harper.
Coupland D. (1991). *Generation X: Tales for an Accelerated Culture*. New York: St Martin's.
Bainbridge, J. (1999). 'Keeping up with Generation Y,' *Marketing*, 18, February, 37–38.
Wellner, A. S. (2000). 'Generation Z,' *American Demographics*, 22(9), September, 61–64.

☐ generic strategies *see* strategies, generic
☐ geographic segmentation *see* segmentation

■ **gestalt theory**

DESCRIPTION
Theory aimed at understanding and explaining phenomena that are perceived as possessing qualities which transcend the sum of their elements and which are unable to be described only in terms of their elements.

KEY INSIGHTS
Based on research by Wertheimer (1912) and others, gestalt theory encompasses a range of psychological and philosophical principles involving perceptions in their relation to forms, complete patterns, organized wholes in experience or other characterizations of phenomena. For example, one principle of gestalt perception is that the perception of ambiguous stimuli tends to be as good (e.g. meaningful, simple, or strong) as the sensory input allows.

KEY WORDS Systems, forms, elements, organization

IMPLICATIONS
Gestalt theory's emphasis on understanding and explaining perceptions of phenomena where perceptions of qualities transcend the sums of their respective elements suggests the potential for the theory to provide unique marketing insights into complex phenomena ranging from ethics to consumption behavior.

APPLICATION AREAS AND FURTHER READINGS
Marketing Ethics
Hunt, Eugene H., and Bullis, Ronald K. (1991). 'Applying the Principles of Gestalt Theory to Teaching Ethics,' *Journal of Business Ethics*, 10(5), May, 341–347.

Consumer Behavior
Hoyt, Elizabeth E. (1944). 'The Place of Gestalt Theory in the Dynamics of Demand,' *American Journal of Economics and Sociology*, 4(1), October, 81.
Thompson, Craig J. (1997). 'Interpreting Consumers: A Hermeneutical Framework for Deriving Marketing Insights from the Texts of Consumers' Consumption Stories,' *Journal of Marketing Research*, 34(4), November, 438–455.

Marketing Research
Hunt, Shelby D. (1993). 'Objectivity in Marketing Theory and Research,' *Journal of Marketing*, 57(2), April, 76–91.

BIBLIOGRAPHY
King, D. Brett, and Wertheimer, Michael (2004). *Max Wertheimer & Gestalt Theory*. New Brunswick: Transaction Publishers.
Wertheimer, M. (1912). 'Experimentelle studien über das sehen von Bewegung,' *Zeitschrift für Psychologie*, 61, 161–165.

☐ Giffen goods *see* goods

■ global marketing

(also called worldwide marketing)

DESCRIPTION
Marketing by a firm on a worldwide scale.

KEY INSIGHTS
Firms engaged in global marketing commit themselves to applying their assets and competencies on a broad international scale where global operations are managed and coordinated to meet global objectives. While a global marketing approach sometimes conveys the view that the firm's

marketing is performed in essentially the same way globally, a firm's global marketing strategy and practice can be far more complex and adaptations based on global differences are clearly within the broad scope of global marketing.

KEY WORDS Worldwide operations

IMPLICATIONS
Whether a firm is seeking to expand marketing operations to a worldwide scale or the firm is already operating on such a scale, a greater knowledge of the many marketing strategies and practices within the domain of global marketing can be beneficial for increasing the firm's global marketing effectiveness as well as in country and regional markets. For example, global marketing concepts and frameworks can assist the global marketer with assessing better the extent to which the firm's offerings are sensitive to different economic and sociocultural environments, thereby providing the marketer with insight into how and to what extent the interactions of the firm's offerings with such environments can and should be managed.

APPLICATION AREAS AND FURTHER READINGS
Marketing Strategy
Jeannet, J. P., and Hennessey, H. D. (1998). *Global Marketing Strategies*, 4th edn. Boston: Houghton Mifflin.
Johansson, J. K. (1997). *Global Marketing: Foreign Entry, Local Marketing, and Global Management*. Chicago: IRWIN.
Samiee, Saeed, and Roth, Kendall (1992). 'The Influence of Global Marketing Standardization on Performance,' *Journal of Marketing*, 56(2), April, 1–17.

Marketing Management
Keegan, Warren J. (2002). *Global Marketing Management*. Upper Saddle River, NJ: Prentice Hall.

Advertising
de Mooij, Marieke K. (2005). *Global Marketing and Advertising*. Thousand Oaks, Calif.: Sage Publications Inc.

BIBLIOGRAPHY
Kotabe, M., and Helsen, K. (2000). *Global Marketing Management*, 2nd edn. New York: John Wiley & Sons, Inc.

☐ **glocal** *see* glocal marketing

■ glocal marketing

DESCRIPTION
Marketing on a global scale that emphasizes customization at the level of local culture.

KEY INSIGHTS
Glocal marketing involves a combination of global marketing and local marketing. Firms adopting such an approach thus have clear global aspirations yet also recognize the benefit of understanding and working

with local culture in the development and provision of their offerings. Despite the fact that the approach has significant intuitive appeal among marketers, the term is rarely used in conveying the concept and implications that it represents.

KEY WORDS **Global marketing, local marketing,** culture

IMPLICATIONS
As global marketing presents numerous challenges and opportunities to marketers with global aspirations, a better understanding of the glocal marketing concept can help to focus the marketer's efforts in achieving an appropriate balance between global and local marketing. Whether the marketer's efforts rely on global information technologies or a global presence of the firm's personnel, the need to establish a compromise between global and local efforts should clearly be examined as a means to increase overall marketing effectiveness.

APPLICATION AREAS AND FURTHER READINGS
Business-to-Business Marketing
Karlsson, Christer (2003). 'The Development of Industrial Networks: Challenges to Operations Management in an Extraprise,' *International Journal of Operations & Production Management*, 23(1), 44–61.

Marketing Strategy
Svensson, G. (2001). ' "Glocalisation" of Business Activities: A "Glocal Strategy" Approach,' *Management Decision*, 39(1), 6–18.
Kickbush, I. (1999). 'Global + Local = Glocal Public Health,' *Journal of Epidemiology and Community Health*, 53, 451–452.
Cobley, Paul (2004). 'Marketing the "Glocal" in Narratives of National Identity,' *Semiotica*, 150(1–4), 197–225.

BIBLIOGRAPHY
Dovey, Kim (1999). *Framing Places: Mediating Power in Built Form*. London: Routledge.

☐ golden rule *see* marketing, rules of

■ **Goodhart's law**

DESCRIPTION
The general principle that, once an economic or social indicator is made a target as part of an economic or social policy, the target becomes distorted by the very act of targeting it.

KEY INSIGHTS
Developed in the context of monetary policy by Goodhart (1975), Goodhart's law has since expanded in scope to include target indicators for any policy having social or economic consequences. In essence, the law asserts that any effort to develop specific rules aimed at pursuing a particular economic or social initiative will inevitably foster rational behaviors to evade such rules. Indicators, measures, or surrogate measures considered to have valuable information content for the purpose of assessing or evaluating economic or social performance will ultimately lose their

usefulness as a result of the visibility given to them and the ensuing rational behavior of individuals or organizations to use such information in ways that run counter to the original purpose of using such measures.

KEY WORDS Economic indicators, social indicators, targets, policy, performance measures

IMPLICATIONS
Marketers involved in establishing measures and indicators for the purpose of pursuing particular economic or social agendas must be aware of the possibility for such measures to lose usefulness as a result of the very act of targeting such measures. Marketers must recognize that Goodhart's law may apply at a level influencing the actions of groups or individuals in an organization as well. For example, if a large firm were to assess the value of subsidiaries' research and development efforts by counting the number of patents each subsidiary generates per year, such a target might lead subsidiaries to diminish the quality of their research and development efforts and focus instead on increasing the quantity of patents generated, even though patent quality forms part of the firm's valuation of the research itself.

APPLICATION AREAS AND FURTHER READINGS
Marketing Strategy
Beckett, R., and Jonker, J. (2002). 'AccountAbility 1000: A New Social Standard for Building Sustainability,' *Managerial Auditing Journal*, 17(1–2), 36–42.
Kopits, George, and Craig, Jon (1998). *Transparency in Government Operations*. IMF Occasional Paper 158. Washington, DC: International Monetary Fund.

International Marketing
Jao, Y. C. (2001). *The Asian Financial Crisis and the Ordeal of Hong Kong*. Westport, Conn.: Quorum Books.
Grote, Rainer, and Marauhn, Thilo (2006). *The Regulation of International Financial Markets: Perspectives for Reform*. Cambridge: Cambridge University Press.

BIBLIOGRAPHY
Goodhart, C. A. E. (1975). 'Monetary Relationships: A View from Threadneedle Street,' in *Papers in Monetary Economics*, volume i. Reserve Bank of Australia.
Chrystal, K. Alec, and Mizen, Paul D. (2001). 'Goodhart's Law: Its Origins, Meaning and Implications for Monetary Policy,' paper prepared for the Festschrift in honour of Charles Goodhart, 15–16 November 2001, the Bank of England.

■ goods

DESCRIPTION
Tangible, physical entities that increase utility or, more generally, anything pertaining to commerce that increases utility.

KEY INSIGHTS
Goods are often associated with tangible physical products but broader use of the term includes that which is intangible, e.g. services. Key characterizations of goods include:

Brown goods—televisions, stereos, and more generally, audio, video, telecommunications, computing and printing goods (the term being derived from the historically brown finish of television and stereo cabinets).

Capital goods—fixed assets (e.g. machinery, equipment) used in the production of other goods.

Consumer goods—goods purchased for individual or household use.

Credence goods—goods for which the utility derived from its use or consumption is almost equally difficult to ascertain at all points in time (e.g. vitamin supplements).

Durable goods or *hard goods*—goods that do not wear out quickly and are used over time as opposed to being consumed all at once (e.g. automobiles, appliances).

Experience goods—goods with features and characteristics which are difficult to observe in advance of purchase but are easily observable upon use or consumption.

Fast moving consumer goods (or *FMCGs*)—frequently purchased consumer goods further characterized by low prices and low purchase risk (e.g. toiletries, detergent, batteries, light bulbs).

Final goods—goods which are ready to use or consume and require no further processing.

Giffen goods—goods for which demand decreases as their price decreases and for which demand increases and their price increases (e.g. inferior-quality staple foods where demand is driven by poverty).

Inferior goods—goods for which demand decreases as income increases.

Intermediate goods—goods used as inputs in the production of other goods (e.g. raw materials, partly finished goods).

Luxury goods—goods at the high end of the market in terms of quality and price and for which demand increases as income increases but to an extent proportionally more than income (e.g. luxury automobiles).

Non-durable goods or soft goods—goods that are used up when consumed and which generally last three years or less (e.g. food, clothing).

Normal goods—goods for which demand increases as income increases.

Private goods—goods for which one person's consumption reduces the quantity available to others and for which there can be exclusion by both producers and consumers in the sense that the producer can restrict use of the product to those willing to pay for it and where the consumer is not forced to consume the good.

Public goods—commodities or services which, if supplied to one person, can be made available to others at no extra cost.

Search goods—goods with features and characteristics easily observable before purchase.

Service goods—goods characterized by their inherent intangibility as well as their inability to be stored, and with their production occurring at the same time as consumption (see **service characteristics**).

Superior goods—goods which make up a larger proportion of consumption as income rises.

Veblen goods—goods (e.g. certain expensive wines or perfumes) where consumers' preference for buying the goods increases as their price increases and for which consumers' preference for buying them decreases as their price falls, a phenomenon also referred to as the *Veblen effect* as it indicates that such goods are sought precisely because of their expensiveness.

White goods—large electrical home appliances such as refrigerators, freezers, washing machines, diswashers, and dryers (the term being derived from their typical white enamel finish).

Yellow goods—goods associated with construction and earth-moving equipment, quarrying equipment, and forklift trucks.

KEY WORDS Products, services, **utility**

IMPLICATIONS

Clearly, goods can be viewed as varying categorically including the extent to which the utility derived from their use can be observed before purchase and upon consumption and in the change in their demand with price and consumer income. As such, it is imperative that the marketer of the firm's offerings understand such characteristics and more in order to stimulate and manage better the demand for the offerings in competitive markets. For example, when firms in an industry offer consumers a range of high- and low-value credence goods, there may clearly be instances where some firms offer low-value goods at high prices as consumers are unable to assess value easily. At the same time, marketers should seek to understand carefully how and to what extent demand for their goods is sensitive to changes in price—something that may vary dramatically between, and within, given categories of goods.

APPLICATION AREAS AND FURTHER READINGS

Marketing Strategy

Avlonitis, G. J., and Gounaris, S. P. (1997). 'Marketing Orientation and Company Performances: Industrial vs. Consumer Goods Companies,' *Industrial Marketing Management*, 26(5), September, 385–402.

Desai, Preyas, and Purohit, Devavrat (1998). 'Leasing and Selling: Optimal Marketing Strategies for a Durable Goods Firm,'*Management Science*, 44(11), Part 2 of 2, November, S19–S34.

Vickers, J. S., and Renand, F. (2003). 'The Marketing of Luxury Goods: An Exploratory Study: Three Conceptual Dimensions,' *Marketing Review*, 3(4), 459–478.

Wernerfelt, Birger (1994). 'Selling Format for Search Goods,' *Marketing Science*, 3, Summer, 298–309.

Marketing Management

Dupre, K., and Gruen, T. (2004). 'The Use of Category Management Practices to Obtain a Sustainable Competitive Advantage in the Fast-Moving-Consumer-Goods-Industry,' *Journal of Business & Industrial Marketing*, 19(7), 444–459.

Marketing Modeling

Erdem, Tulin, and Keane, Michael P. (1996). 'Decision-Making under Uncertainty: Capturing Dynamic Brand Choice Processes in Turbulent Consumer Goods Markets,' *Marketing Science*, 15(1), 1–20.

Neelamegham, R., and Jain, D. (1999). 'Consumer Choice Process for Experience Goods: An Econometric Model and Analysis,' *Journal of Marketing Research*, 36(3), 373–386.

International Marketing
Baden-Fuller, C. W. L., and Stopford, J. M. (1991). 'Globalization Frustrated: The Case of White Goods,' *Strategic Management Journal*, 12, 493–507.

Retail Marketing
Bucklin, Louis P. (1963). 'Retail Strategy and the Classification of Consumer Goods,' *Journal of Marketing*, 27(1), January, 50–55.

Services Marketing
Vargo, S. L., and Lusch, R. F. (2004). 'The Four Service Marketing Myths,' *Journal of Service Research*, 6(4), May, 324–335.

Advertising
Ekelund, R., Mixon, F., and Ressler, R. (1995). 'Advertising and Information: An Empirical Study of Search, Experience and Credence Goods,' *Journal of Economic Studies*, 22, 33–43.

BIBLIOGRAPHY
Leibenstein, H. (1950). 'Bandwagon, Snob, and Veblen Effects in the Theory of Consumers' Demand,' *Quarterly Journal of Economics*, 64, 183–207.
Hunt, Shelby D. (1976). 'The Nature and Scope of Marketing,' *Journal of Marketing*, 40(3), July, 17–28.
Kotler, Philip, and Armstrong, Gary (2006). *Principles of Marketing*, 11th edn. Upper Saddle River, NJ: Pearson Education, Inc.

☐ goods-characteristics theory *see* characteristics theory

■ government marketing

(also called public sector marketing or governmental marketing)

DESCRIPTION

Marketing efforts associated with the legislative and public administration activities of organizations and institutions.

KEY INSIGHTS

Government marketing encompasses a range of activity in organizations tasked with the provision of offerings for the good of the public. Such organizations may be in areas of the public sector and at any level, including central government (e.g. federal), regional government, and local or municipal government. For any government organization, government marketing is therefore concerned with enhancing the effectiveness and efficiency of the organization in terms of its ability to identify and meet the needs and wants of the set of individuals that it has been tasked to serve. In the provision of health services, for example, a government organization may be involved in the promotion practices supporting healthy lifestyles (e.g. eating five servings of vegetables a day) while at the same time involved in counter-marketing initiatives (e.g. in efforts to target smoking—see **counter-marketing**). Still other organizations serving the public may be involved in demarketing initiatives (e.g. to reduce road congestion in a city—see **demarketing**). In addition, while firms in the private sector are regularly engaged in marketing activities to fend off competition from other firms in their industries, government organizations may also use marketing initiatives as a means to respond to private and public competition, as when a government postal service faces increasingly stiff competition from private parcel delivery firms.

KEY WORDS Public administration, government operations

IMPLICATIONS

A greater understanding of government marketing may assist marketers engaging in such efforts to become increasingly effective and efficient in meeting public needs and wants in relation to their organizations' aims and objectives and overall charters. While the institutional nature of many government organizations may pose certain unique challenges (see **institutional marketing**), marketers in such organizations nevertheless have a wide range of marketing approaches to consider and pursue in developing effective marketing strategies and programs for the benefit of their constituents and their own organizations.

APPLICATION AREAS AND FURTHER READINGS

Marketing Strategy

Conway, A., and Whitelock, J. (2004). 'Can Relationship Marketing Enhance Strategic Thinking in the Public Sector? A Study of the Perceived Relationship between Subsidised Theatres and their Government Funders/Regulators,' *International Journal of Nonprofit and Voluntary Sector Marketing*, 9(4), 325-334.

Walsh, K. (1989). *Marketing in Local Government*. London: Longman.

Tourism Ireland (2003). *Marketing Strategy 2004-2006: Operating Plans 2004*. Dublin: Tourism Ireland.

Marketing Management

Lovelock, C. H., and Weinberg, C. B. (1984). *Marketing for Public and Nonprofit Managers*. New York: John Wiley & Sons.

Walsh, K. (1994). 'Marketing and Public Sector Management,' *European Journal of Marketing*, 28(3), 63-71.

Services Marketing

Kearsey, A., and Varey, R. J. (1998). 'Managerialist Thinking on Marketing for Public Services,' *Public Money and Management*, January-March, 51-61.

Massey, A. (ed.) (1997). *Globalization and Marketization of Government Services*. Basingstoke: Macmillan Press Ltd.

Online Marketing

Leatherman, John (2001). *Internet Commerce: Challenges for the Rural Public Sector*. Madison: Center for Community Economic Development, University of Wisconsin—Extension.

International Marketing

Lovelock, C. H. (1981). 'International Perspectives on Public Sector Marketing,' in M. P. Mokwa and S. E. Permut (eds.), *Government Marketing: Theory and Practice*. New York: Praeger Publishing.

Marketing Research
Bernhardt, K. J. (1981). 'Consumer Research in the Federal Government,' in M. P.
Mokwa and S. E. Permut (eds.), *Government Marketing: Theory and Practice*. New
York: Praeger Publishing.

BIBLIOGRAPHY
Lamb, Charles W. (1987). 'Public Sector Marketing is Different,' *Business Horizons*,
July–August, 56–60.
Chapman, D., and Cowdell, T. (1998). *New Public Sector Marketing*. London: Financial
Times/Pitman, London.
Mokwa, M. P., and Permut, S. E. (eds.) (1981). *Government Marketing: Theory and
Practice*. New York: Praeger Publishing.
Coffman, Larry L. (1986). *Public-Sector Marketing: A Guide for Practitioners*. New York:
Wiley.

☐ governmental marketing *see* government marketing
☐ grassroots marketing *see* word-of-mouth marketing

gravity theory

DESCRIPTION
In the context of trade, a view which holds that the amount of trade between
any two entities is negatively influenced by their distance apart and positively
influenced by the product of their respective outputs.

KEY INSIGHTS
According to gravity theory, distance is viewed as a deterrent to travel.
Shorter distances between trading partners will be likely to result in
more trade than that for longer distances. Such a view finds empirical
support in many urban and international trade studies and provides
a basis for much site location analysis in evaluating the relationship
between trade and travel for destination locations of the same type and
size.

KEY WORDS Location analysis, distance, trade

IMPLICATIONS
Gravity theory provides a basis for evaluating business locations in relation to customer locations or trading partner locations. As such, analytical
models drawing upon gravity theory can be used to establish the attractiveness of a location for trade, as in establishing the best location for a
new grocery store in a particular city.

APPLICATION AREAS AND FURTHER READINGS
Marketing Modeling
Curry, B., and Moutinho, L. (1994). 'Intelligent Computer Models for Marketing
Decisions,' *Management Decision* (London, Bradford), 32(4), 30.
Stanley, Thomas J., and Sewall, Murphy A. (1976). 'Image Inputs to a Proba-
bilistic Model: Predicting Retail Potential,' *Journal of Marketing*, 40(3), July, 48–
53.
Cadwallader, Martin (1975). 'A Behavioral Model of Consumer Spatial Decision
Making,' *Economic Geography*, 51(4), October, 339–349.

BIBLIOGRAPHY
Matyas, L. (1998). 'The Gravity Model: Some Econometric Considerations,' *World Economy* (London), 21(3), 397–401.

■ gray markets

(also referred to by the alternate spelling 'grey markets')

DESCRIPTION

Markets involving the flow and purchase of new goods through channels of distribution other than those intended by the supplier.

KEY INSIGHTS

Gray markets, as opposed to black markets, can potentially provide purchasers with an alternative legal means of acquiring goods from a supplier. Thus, although a producer of denim jeans varies the wholesale prices of its jeans across countries in a way that seeks to maximize its profits from retailers in each country, it may also be the case that a retailer in one country could purchase large quantities of the jeans in another country and resell them at a greater profit in its home country relative to the practice whereby most retailers purchase them at wholesale prices in supplier-intended channels.

KEY WORDS Distribution, channels of distribution

IMPLICATIONS

Marketers concerned with distribution strategy and management should examine the distribution channels for their firm's—and competitor firms'—offerings to determine to what extent there may be opportunities for purchasers to acquire the offerings through gray market. Given that gray markets vary significantly by industry (being relatively prevalent, for example, in the automobile, wine, and photographic equipment industries), marketers may benefit from a greater understanding of gray market issues (e.g. their legal status and competitive implications) to assess better the marketing and financial risks and opportunities facing the firm from their current or possible use.

APPLICATION AREAS AND FURTHER READINGS

Marketing Strategy
Lim, G. H., Lee, K. S., and Tan, S. J. (2001). 'Gray Marketing as an Alternative Market Penetration Strategy for Entrepreneurs,' *Journal of Business Venturing*, 16(4), 405–427.
Antia, D. Kersi, Bergen, Mark, and Dutta, Shantanu (2004). 'Competing with Gray Market,' *Sloan Management Review*, 46(1), 63–69.

Marketing Management
Bergen, Mark, Heide, Jan, and Dutta, Shantanu (1998). 'Managing Gray Markets through Tolerance of Violations: A Transaction Cost Perspective,' *Managerial and Decision Economics*, 19(3), May, 157–165.

International Marketing
Duhan, Dale F., and Sheffet, Mary Jane (1988). 'Gray Markets and the Legal Status of Parallel Importation,' *Journal of Marketing*, 52(3), July, 75–83.

BIBLIOGRAPHY
Cross, James, Stephan, James, and Benjamin, Robert E. (1990). 'Gray Markets: A Legal Review and Public Perspectives,' *Journal of Public Policy & Marketing*, 9, 183–194.

■ greater fool theory

DESCRIPTION

The view that investing in a fully valued or questionable asset can still be worthwhile if one can soon find a 'greater fool' in the market to whom the investment can be resold.

KEY INSIGHTS

The greater fool theory provides a basis for the investment practices of some investors in the stock market and other investment markets where, although a certain investment may appear to be high, fully priced, or overpriced by one or more measures, the investor thinks he or she can still profit from it by soon reselling it at a higher price to a 'greater fool.' Clearly, investors vary in the extent that they adopt the theory in investment practice, but the theory is often used to partially explain the existence of 'bubbles,' or large increments to asset prices that are present only because the prices are expected to be even higher in the near future. In such an instance, individuals believe they might be a fool to purchase such assets but they believe they can soon find a greater fool to sell to at a higher price. While the theory is often cited in reference to stock market investing and stock market bubbles in particular, it can also help to explain investment behaviors concerning a range of investment opportunities.

KEY WORD Investments

IMPLICATIONS

Marketers concerned with investment opportunity evaluation and participation who seek to understand better investment motives and behaviors should recognize that some investors may be adopting the greater fool theory either implicitly or explicitly. As there may not always be a 'greater fool' for any given investment, marketers must, of course, exercise caution in their advocacy of investment opportunities, particularly ones seemingly characterized by 'bubbles.'

APPLICATION AREAS AND FURTHER READINGS

Marketing Strategy
Dickson, P. R., Farris, P. W., and Verbeke, W. J. M. I. (2001). 'Dynamic Strategic Thinking,' *Journal of the Academy of Marketing Science*, 29(3), 216–237.

Online Marketing
Oliva, R., Sterman, J. D., and Giese, M. (2003). 'Limits to Growth in the New Economy: Exploring the "Get Big Fast" Strategy in E-commerce,' *System Dynamics Review*, 19(2), 83–118.

BIBLIOGRAPHY
Lynch, A. (2000). 'Thought Contagions in the Stock Market,' *Journal of Psychology and Financial Markets*, 1, 10–23.

■ green marketing

(also called eco-marketing, eco-centric marketing, environmental marketing, environmentally responsible marketing, or responsible marketing)

DESCRIPTION

Marketing strategies and activities that emphasize sensitivity to environmental impact.

KEY INSIGHTS

Green marketing strategies and activities may involve any number of means to protect, improve, or reduce damage to the natural environment as well as human health. While green marketing seeks to maintain the quality of the natural world in some way, a major benefit of its use is often in its appeal to environmentally conscious consumers.

KEY WORDS Environmental impact

IMPLICATIONS

Marketers concerned with environmental impact may benefit from a better understanding of green marketing strategies and tactics to enable the firm to appeal to a greater extent to consumers with similar concerns. At the same time, marketers will be in a better position to evaluate the extent that green marketing can potentially provide the firm with reputational, financial, and competitive advantages over firms that are less environmentally focused in their marketing efforts.

APPLICATION AREAS AND FURTHER READINGS

Marketing Strategy
Mendleson, N., and Polonsky, M. J. (1995). 'Using Strategic Alliances to Develop Credible Green Marketing,' *Journal of Consumer Marketing*, 12(2), 4.
Mcdaniel, Stephen W., and Rylander, David (1993). 'Strategic Green Marketing,' *Journal of Consumer Marketing*, 10(3), 4–10.
Menon, Ajay, and Menon, Anil (1997). 'Enviropreneurial Marketing Strategy: The Emergence of Corporate Environmentalism as Market Strategy,' *Journal of Marketing*, 61(1), January, 51–67.
Miles, M. P., and Covin, J. G. (2000). 'Environmental Marketing: A Source of Reputational, Competitive, and Financial Advantage,' *Journal of Business Ethics*, 23(3), 299–311.

Marketing Management
Wasik, J. (1996). *Green Marketing and Management: A Global Perspective*. Cambridge, Mass.: Blackwell Publishers Inc.

Marketing Research
Kalafatis, S. P., Pollard, M., East, R., and Tsogas, M. H. (1999). 'Green Marketing and Ajzen's Theory of Planned Behaviour: A Cross-Market Examination,' *Journal of Consumer Marketing*, 16(4–5), 441–460.

BIBLIOGRAPHY
Coddington, W. (1993). *Environmental Marketing*. New York: McGraw-Hill.
Ottman, J. A. (1994). *Green Marketing*. Chicago: NTC Business Books.
Charter, Martin, and Polonsky, Michael J. (1999). *Greener Marketing: A Global Perspective on Greening Marketing Practice*. Sheffield: Greenleaf.

■ Gresham's law

DESCRIPTION
The term characterizing the view that 'bad money drives out good money' and originally referencing money in circulation but further used with reference to instances where bad practices or products drive good ones out of markets.

KEY INSIGHTS
Named after English financier Sir Thomas Gresham, Gresham's law encompasses the observation that individuals spending money prefer to hand over bad money and keep the good, where bad money is money that has a commodity market value lower than its exchange value and where good money has little difference between its commodity market value and exchange value. An example is in the case of a gold coin and a gold bar or ingot having the same commodity market value but where people prefer to trade in gold coins rather than in gold bars as they attribute less intrinsic value to bullion and more intrinsic value to coins, thereby leading to situations where coining frequently becomes profitable.

KEY WORDS **Value**, exchange, market practice

IMPLICATIONS
While Gresham's law originally applied to the specific context of money in circulation, the view it encompasses can be used to characterize any of a variety of instances where bad market practices are observed to drive out good ones, as where an inferior product may drive a superior product out of a market. In this context, Gresham's law can be used to characterize and provide additional insight to a range of phenomena within domains including ethical decision making and competition in the marketing of products and services.

APPLICATION AREAS AND FURTHER READINGS
Marketing Research
Nelson, J. E., and Kiecker, P. L. (1996). 'Marketing Research Interviewers and their Perceived Necessity of Moral Compromise,' *Journal of Business Ethics*, 15(10), 107–117.

Marketing Strategy
Cook, P. Lesley (1961). 'Orderly Marketing or Competition?' *Economic Journal*, 71(283), September, 497–511.

Marketing Education
Ashworth, K. (1980). 'Gresham's Law in the Marketplace of Ideas: Are Bad Degrees Driving Out the Good?' *Chronicle of Higher Education*, 21, October, 64.
Litten, Larry H. (1980). 'Marketing Higher Education: Benefits and Risks for the American Academic System,' *Journal of Higher Education*, 51(1), January–February, 40–59.

BIBLIOGRAPHY
Rolnick, A. J., and Weber, W. E. (1986). 'Gresham's Law or Gresham's Fallacy?' *Journal of Political Economy*, 94, 185–199.

■ group polarization

DESCRIPTION

The tendency for discussion among members of a group to result in more extreme attitudes, opinions, inclinations, and decisions of group members.

KEY INSIGHTS

Based on research by Moscovici and Zavalloni (1969) and earlier researchers, the group polarization phenomenon has been experimentally observed as a significant tendency in many groups. A particular form of group polarization is the risky shift effect, also referred to as choice shift, where group decisions are found to be riskier than the average of the individual decisions of the members before the group has met. Explanations for the group polarization phenomenon tend to be based on mechanisms related to social comparison (e.g. where culturally, people tend to admire riskiness rather than caution in most circumstances) as well as informational influences (e.g. where individual choices are based on weighing remembered pro and con arguments).

KEY WORDS Groups, decision making, choice, risk

IMPLICATIONS

Marketers must be aware of how participation in groups, whether in a group of an organization's employers or in a group of consumers, can lead to views which are more extreme than those of individuals prior to group participation or where views are amplified and shift in the direction of dominant norms. The effect may present itself in the form of more extreme attitudes, opinions, or riskier decisions. Assessing individual views prior to group discussions and decision making and comparing individual views with group views is one way to identify the extent of group polarization.

APPLICATION AREAS AND FURTHER READINGS

Decision Making

Whitney, John C., and Smith, Ruth A. (1983). 'Effects of Group Cohesiveness on Attitude Polarization and the Acquisition of Knowledge in a Strategic Planning Context,' *Journal of Marketing Research*, 20(2), May, 167–176.

Consumer Behavior

Rao, Vithala R., and Steckel, Joel H. (1991). 'A Polarization Model for Describing Group Preferences,' *Journal of Consumer Research*, 18(1), June, 108–118.

Woodside, Arch G. (1974). 'Is There a Generalized Risky Shift Phenomenon in Consumer Behavior?' *Journal of Marketing Research*, 11(2), May, 225–226.

Ward, James C., and Reingen, Peter H. (1990). 'Sociocognitive Analysis of Group Decision Making among Consumers,' *Journal of Consumer Research*, 17(3), December, 245–262.

Sia, C. L., Tan, B. C. Y., and Wei, K. K. (2002). 'Group Polarization and Computer-Mediated Communication: Effects of Communication Cues, Social Presence, and Anonymity', *Information Systems Research*, 13(1), 70–90.

BIBLIOGRAPHY

Moscovici, S., and Zavalloni, M. (1969). 'The Group as a Polarizer of Attitudes,' *Journal of Personality and Social Psychology*, 12, 125–135.

■ groupthink

DESCRIPTION
A term characterizing the situation where a group's drive for consensus
overrides the drive to realistically evaluate alternative courses of action,
ultimately distorting the testing of reality, lessening critical thinking, and
generally rationalizing a shared illusion of invulnerability and infallibility. The
result of groupthink is typically poor or irrational decisions.

KEY INSIGHTS
Based on pioneering research by Janis (1972) and subsequent researchers,
groupthink is a potential risk in group decision making which may
increase in likelihood under conditions including that where the group is
acting in relation to and constrained by certain characteristics of an external threat, being generally insulated from outside sources of information,
the group is cohesive and homogeneous, and the group has a persuasive,
directive leader. In addition, symptoms indicative of groupthink include
illusions of invulnerability, unquestioned belief in the group's inherent
morality, collective rationalization of group decisions, shared stereotypes
of other groups including opponents, self-censorship where members
withhold criticisms, illusion of unanimity, pressure on dissenters to
conform to the group, and self-appointed individuals who protect the
group from negative information. Symptoms of decisions affected by
groupthink include incomplete surveys of alternatives, incomplete surveys of objectives, failures to examine risks of preferred choices, failures to reappraise rejected alternatives, poor information search, selective bias in information processing, and failures to develop contingency
plans.
   Mechanisms suggested for the prevention of groupthink include
appointing a devil's advocate within a group whose purpose is to disagree
with any suggestion presented, allowing anonymous feedback as through
a suggestion box, and placing decision-making responsibility and authority with one group member who is able to consult with other members
of the group.

KEY WORDS Groups, decision making, rationality

IMPLICATIONS
Marketers involved in group decision-making processes, as when formulating marketing strategies, must be vigilant for various symptoms
of groupthink as well as its resultant influence on decision-making
processes and decisions. Adopting means to prevent or reduce the possibility of groupthink in groups may result in higher-quality decisions
than would otherwise be achieved.

APPLICATION AREAS AND FURTHER READINGS
Marketing Managment
Peterson, R. S., Owens, P. D., Tetlock, P. E., Fan, E. T., and Martorana, P. (1998).
   'Group Dynamics in Top Management Teams: Groupthink, Vigilance, and Alter-
   native Models of Organizational Failure and Success,' *Organizational Behavior and
   Human Decision Processes*, 73(2–3), 272–305.

Ayers, Doug, Dahlstrom, Robert, and Skinner, Steven J. (1997). 'An Exploratory Investigation of Organizational Antecedents to New Product Success,' *Journal of Marketing Research*, 34(1), Special Issue on Innovation and New Products, February, 107–116.

Andrews, Jonlee, and Smith, Daniel C. (1996). 'In Search of the Marketing Imagination: Factors Affecting the Creativity of Marketing Programs for Mature Products,' *Journal of Marketing Research*, 33(2), May, 174–187.

BIBLIOGRAPHY

Janis, I. (1972). *Victims of Groupthink: A Psychological Study of Foreign-Policy Decisions and Fiascoes*. Boston: Houghton Mifflin.

Janis, I., and Mann, L. (1977). *Decision Making: A Psychological Analysis of Conflict, Choice and Commitment*. New York: The Free Press.

☐ **growth-share matrix** *see* product portfolio analysis

☐ **growth stage** *see* product life cycle

☐ **growth strategies** *see* product-market investment strategies

■ guerrilla marketing

(also referred to by the alternate spelling of guerilla marketing and sometimes incorrectly referred to as gorilla marketing)

DESCRIPTION

Guerrilla marketing involves the use of unconventional, creative marketing strategies and activities to accomplish a firm's objectives and where such approaches typically require lower marketing expenditures in comparison to more traditional means.

KEY INSIGHTS

Guerrilla marketing, with its emphasis on marketing approaches not traditionally employed by other established firms in an industry, is often associated with opportunities for use by smaller and/or 'upstart' firms in an industry to compete more effectively with larger or traditional competitors in their promotional and broader marketing efforts. In support of a firm's strategic objectives, guerrilla marketing approaches may therefore assist the firm in acquiring market share from a larger competitor by discrediting the larger competitor in the minds of consumers. An example is where a small, new airline labels a larger, established airline as a 'bully always trying to keep out new competition' in periodic public relations attacks, thereby swaying public opinion against the larger airline and also demoralizing the larger airline's staff in the process, and where the outcome of the approach is to ultimately allow the small airline to expand its flight operations and increase market share.

KEY WORDS **Unconventional marketing**, promotion

IMPLICATIONS

While the ethics associated with various guerrilla marketing strategies and tactics may be a matter of debate among marketers, it nevertheless is an approach that some firms can—and do—incorporate into their marketing and promotion efforts. To be sure, the approach carries marketing risks as well as the potential for greater cost-effectiveness. At the same time, astute marketers will recognize that, regardless of whether or not guerrilla marketing approaches are adopted to, say, discredit a competitor through the media, the firm must ultimately deliver real value to its customers if it is to remain viable in the longer term.

APPLICATION AREAS AND FURTHER READINGS

Marketing Strategy

Stasch, S. F. (1999). 'Guerilla Marketing in New Venture Marketing Strategies,' in G. Hills, W. Siu, and D. Malewicki (eds.), *Research at the Marketing/Entrepreneurship Interface—Proceedings of the UIC Symposium on Marketing and Entrepreneurship*. Chicago: University of Illinois at Chicago, 57–67.

Slack, M. (1999). *Guerilla Marketing Breaking through the Clutter with Word-of-Mouth*. Darien, Conn.: Jupiter Research.

Online Marketing

Levinson, Jay Conrad, and Rubin, Charles (1996). *Guerrilla Marketing Online Weapons: 100 Low-Cost, High-Impact Weapons for Online Profits and Prosperity*. Boston: Houghton Mifflin Co.

BIBLIOGRAPHY

Levinson, Jay Conrad (1984). *Guerilla Marketing: Secrets for Making Big Profits from your Small Business*. Boston: Houghton-Mifflin.

H

□ habitual buying behavior *see* consumer buyer behavior

■ halo effect

(also called the horns and halo effect)

DESCRIPTION

A cognitive bias where a perception of a particular characteristic or quality has an aural influence on perceptions and judgment beyond the characteristic or quality as a result of some association.

KEY INSIGHTS

Based on pioneering research by Thorndike (1920), the halo effect characterizes the situation where positive trait perceptions influence judgments of related traits, while the 'horns and halo effect' term characterizes any such influence. The effect is a form of cognitive bias which may present itself in perceptions of judgments of individuals, organizations, products, brands, service experiences, and the like. An example is where individuals perceiving a brand to be strong in an aspect such as name recognition or aesthetics in product design have subsequent positive perceptions of lesser-known qualities such as product durability and reliability. Whereas halo effect refers to positive aural influences, negative influences are sometimes referred to by the 'horns effect' term.

KEY WORDS **Bias**, perception, judgment, quality

IMPLICATIONS

Marketers must seek to be aware of halo effects in the consumer's perceptions of a marketer's offerings and should strive to leverage such effects. In the case of a brand, certain halo effects may be used strategically, as in the case where a well-received new product under the company's brand name enhances the perceived value of all of the company's same-branded products and enables the firm to introduce more easily another new product under the same brand as well.

APPLICATION AREAS AND FURTHER READINGS

Branding
Leuthesser, L., Kohli, C. S., and Harich, K. R. (1995). 'Brand Equity: The Halo Effect Measure,' *European Journal of Marketing*, 29(4), 57.

Marketing Modeling
Beckwith, Neil E., and Lehmann, Donald R. (1975). 'The Importance of Halo Effects in Multi-attribute Attitude Models,' *Journal of Marketing Research*, 12(3), August, 265–275.

Holbrook, Morris B. (1983). 'Using a Structural Model of Halo Effect to Assess Perceptual Distortion Due to Affective Overtones,' *Journal of Consumer Research*, 10(2), September, 247–252.

Marketing Management
Wu, B., and Petrshiuses, S. (1987). 'The Halo Effect in Store Image Management,' *Academy of Marketing Science Journal*, 15(3), 25–45.

BIBLIOGRAPHY
Thorndike, E. L. (1920). 'A Constant Error on Psychological Rating,' *Journal of Applied Psychology*, 4, 25–29.

☐ handling objections *see* selling process
☐ hard goods *see* goods
☐ harvest strategy *see* decline strategies

■ Hawthorne effect

DESCRIPTION
The apparent phenomenon in group-based observational research where behaviors of individuals in a group being studied change as a result of their being aware that they are participating in a study as opposed to behaviors changing as a result of any actual treatment or changes being made. More broadly, the term is used in referring to unexpected influences of non-experimental variables in experiments.

KEY INSIGHTS
Named after the plant where the effect was first observed and described in the 1920s–1930s, the Hawthorne effect leads to a confounding situation where experimental effects are observed in the direction expected but not necessarily for the reason expected, where effects may be attributed to participants' knowing they are being studied. Explanations for the effect include the view that the extra attention given to individuals as a result of their participation in a study positively motivates the individuals to change their behaviors which may include their working harder, faster, or more efficiently. Subsequent research focused on replicating the Hawthorne effect in work situations has resulted in mixed and alternatives interpretations of findings, however, as in cases where it can be argued that individuals' performance improved as a result of receiving performance feedback that they would not have otherwise received and where such feedback improved individuals' learning.

KEY WORDS Experiments, observation, behavior, confounding influences

IMPLICATIONS
Given the ambiguity and controversy surrounding the original interpretations of the Hawthorne effect and the prevalence of alternative explanations, the effect's implications for marketers extend to the development of proper research methodologies for experimental research as much as actual influences of experimental observation on the behaviors of individuals being studied. Marketing researchers must strive to eliminate

confounding influences in their research through appropriately rigorous methods.

APPLICATION AREAS AND FURTHER READINGS
Marketing Research
Hubbard, Raymond, and Armstrong, Scott (1994). 'Replications and Extensions in Marketing: Rarely Published but Quite Contrary,' *International Journal of Research in Marketing*, 11, 233–248.
Cadotte, Ernest R., and Robinson, Larry M. (1978). 'Measurement of Consumer Satisfaction: An Innovation,' *Journal of Marketing*, 42(3), July, 8–58.

BIBLIOGRAPHY
Schwartzman, H. B. (1993). 'Ethnography in Organizations,' *Qualitative Research Methods Series*, 27.
Franke, R. H., and Kaul, J. O. (1978). *Hawthorne Effect*. London: Sage Publications.
Parsons, H. M. (1974). 'What Happened at Hawthorne?' *Science*, 183, 922–932.

☐ **heavy half, law of the** *see* Pareto principle

■ Herzberg's theory of motivation

DESCRIPTION
The theory of motivation proposed by Herzberg which characterizes factors affecting people's attitudes about work.

KEY INSIGHTS
Herzberg's theory of motivation distinguishes between hygiene factors (e.g. working conditions, interpersonal relationships) and motivators which enrich a person's job. According to Herzberg, the absence of hygiene factors can create dissatisfaction but their presence does not motivate. Motivators include achievement, recognition, the work itself, responsibility, and advancements. As such, motivators are satisfiers associated with long-term effects in job performance while hygiene factors are dissatisfiers which produce only short-term changes.

KEY WORDS Work motivation, motivation, satisfaction

IMPLICATIONS
The principles and concepts found in Herzberg's theory of motivation can be applied to obtain useful insights into work motivation in marketing organizations. Distinguishing between hygiene factors and motivators provides a means to understand better how motivated and satisfied individuals may be in performing particular jobs such as those in the sales function of an organization.

APPLICATION AREAS AND FURTHER READINGS
Marketing Management
Walker, Orville C., Jr., Churchill, Gilbert A., Jr., and Ford, Neil M. (1977). 'Motivation and Performance in Industrial Selling: Present Knowledge and Needed Research,' *Journal of Marketing Research*, 14(2), May, 156–168.
Alvesson, M. (1998). 'Management of Knowledge Intensive Companies,' *Organization Studies* (Berlin—European Group for Organizational Studies), 19(6), 1053.

BIBLIOGRAPHY
Herzberg, F., Mausner, B., and Snyderman, B. B. (1959). *The Motivation to Work*, 2nd edn. New York: John Wiley & Sons.

■ Hick's law

DESCRIPTION

The general proposition that one's reaction time for making a choice increases as the logarithm of the number of alternatives.

KEY INSIGHTS

Hick's law indicates a systematic and generally predictable non-linear relationship between the time required by an individual to choose from a set of alternatives and the number of alternatives in the choice set. It is often more formally expressed by the formula $RT = a + b\log_2(n+1)$ (where RT is reaction time, a is a constant representing the intercept of the function, b is a constant representing the slope of the function, and n is the number of alternatives). Hick's law is sometimes referred to as Merkel's law as a result of Merkel's earlier research on the relationship.

KEY WORDS Choice, reaction time

IMPLICATIONS

Hick's law suggests that each additional choice available to a person makes it increasingly difficult for people to make choices. Marketers involved in the establishment of choices available to individual consumers must be aware of how individual reaction time will increase with the number of alternatives. In computer–human interaction, for example, such an issue may influence consumer participation and satisfaction.

APPLICATION AREAS AND FURTHER READINGS

Online Marketing
Travis, David (2003). *E-commerce Usability*. London: Taylor & Francis.
Raskin, Jef (2000). *The Humane Interface: New Directions for Designing Interactive Systems*. Reading, Mass.: Addison Wesley.

BIBLIOGRAPHY
Hick, W. E. (1952). 'On the Rate of Gain of Information,' *Quarterly Journal of Experimental Psychology*, 4, 11–26.
Hyman, R. (1953). 'Stimulus Information as a Determinant of Reaction Time,' *Journal of Experimental Psychology*, 45, 188–196.

■ hierarchy of effects

(also called the hierarchy of effects model)

DESCRIPTION

The view that advertising is effective to the extent that it moves individuals through a series of defined stages in consumer purchasing.

KEY INSIGHTS

Based on pioneering research by Lavidge and Steiner (1961), a hierarchy of effects modeling approach for predicting advertising effectiveness considers the effect of advertising to be that of moving consumers through purchasing stages including awareness, knowledge, liking, preference, conviction, and purchase. Similarly, Palda (1966) considers the critical stages to be attention, interest, desire, and action (AIDA). More generally, the view can be said to extend to broader models of information response including, for example, consumer response to information presented through persuasive methods of personal selling.

KEY WORDS Advertising effectiveness, persuasion, consumer purchasing, stages, models

IMPLICATIONS
The hierarchy of effects model suggests an approach for the structured development of persuasive marketing communications where the ultimate aim is to persuade consumers to take action through purchase. In essence, the approach suggests that composition and presentation of marketing messages must be carefully developed and evaluated for the extent that they encourage, persuade, and reinforce consumers to move successfully through a set of distinct stages of consumer purchasing.

APPLICATION AREAS AND FURTHER READINGS
Marketing Modeling
Smith, Robert E., and. Swinyard, William R. (1982). 'Information Response Models: An Integrated Approach,' *Journal of Marketing*, 46(1), Winter, 81–93.

Advertising
Vakratsas, Demetrios, and Ambler, Tim (1999). 'How Advertising Works: What Do We Really Know?' *Journal of Marketing*, 63(1), January, 26–43.

BIBLIOGRAPHY
Palda, Kristian S. (1966). 'The Hypothesis of a Hierarchy of Effects: A Partial Evaluation,' *Journal of Marketing Research*, 3(1), February, 13–24.
Lavidge, Robert J., and Steiner, Gary A. (1961). 'A Model for Predictive Measurements of Advertising Effectiveness,' *Journal of Marketing*, 25, October, 59–62.

☐ hierarchy of effects model *see* hierarchy of effects

■ hierarchy of needs theory

(also called Maslow's theory of motivation, need hierarchy theory, Maslow's need hierarchy, or Maslow's theory of self-actualization)

DESCRIPTION
The view that human needs are categorical and hierarchical, where it is not until certain categories of lower-level needs are met or reasonably well satisfied that other higher-level categories of needs can be attended to.

KEY INSIGHTS
The hierarchy of needs theory as developed by Maslow (1943, 1954, 1970) considers human needs as consisting of five categories in ascending order: physiological or biological needs (e.g. food, water, sleep), safety needs (e.g. physical security, financial security), belongingness and love

needs (e.g. friends, relationships, intimacy), esteem needs (respect, status), and self-actualization needs (e.g. making the most of one's unique abilities). While the theory is viewed as having merit over earlier theories, some subsequent research including that of Wahba and Bridwell (1976) has questioned elements of the view including support for the existence of a definite hierarchy and further has drawn attention to vagueness in terminology including that for the self-actualization concept.

KEY WORDS **Need(s)**, need categories, need hierarchy

IMPLICATIONS
While the hierarchy of needs theory is not without detractors, it nevertheless provides a means with which to categorize and analyze human needs in ways suggestive of priorities for needs being met. Marketers should seek to understand how consumers define and prioritize their own particular needs in relation to those that can be met through the marketer's offerings.

APPLICATION AREAS AND FURTHER READINGS
International Marketing
Malhotra, N. K., Ulgado, F. M., Agarwal, J., and Baalbaki, I. B. (1994). 'International Services Marketing: A Comparative Evaluation of the Dimensions of Service Quality between Developed and Developing Countries,' *International Marketing Review*, 11(2), 5.

Marketing Management
Salancik, Gerald R., and Pfeffer, Jeffrey (1977). 'An Examination of Need-Satisfaction Models of Job Attitudes,' *Administrative Science Quarterly*, 22(3), September, 427–456.

Marketing Research
Sirgy, M. Joseph, and Samli, A. Coskun (1995). *New Dimensions in Marketing/Quality-of-Life Research*. Westport, Conn.: Quorum Books.
Oleson, Mark (2004). 'Exploring the Relationship between Money Attitudes and Maslow's Hierarchy of Needs,' *International Journal of Consumer Studies*, 28(1), January, 83.

BIBLIOGRAPHY
Maslow, A. H. (1943). 'A Theory of Human Motivation,' *Psychological Review*, 50, 370–396.
Maslow, A. H. (1954). *Motivation and Personality*. New York: Harper & Row.
Maslow, A. H. (1970). *Motivation and Personality*, 2nd edn. New York: Harper & Row.
Wahba, M. A., and Bridwell, L. G. (1976). 'Maslow Reconsidered: A Review of Research on the Need Hierarchy Theory,' *Organizational Behavior and Human Performance*, 15, 212–240.

■ hindsight bias

(also called the I-knew-it-all-along effect)

DESCRIPTION
A tendency where an individual's knowledge of the occurrence of a past event leads them to overestimate in hindsight the likelihood that it would have been predicted in foresight.

KEY INSIGHTS

The hindsight bias phenomenon was first studied in pioneering research by Fischhoff and Beyth (1975) where it was found that individuals' recall of their predictions tended to be biased in the direction of events which have actually occurred. Mechanisms leading to a hindsight bias tendency in an individual include the view that actual events are more available to the individual in their recall when compared to that for events which did not occur. Hindsight bias has been observed to be a tendency in a variety of settings where past events are reflected upon.

Formal examinations of possible alternatives by individuals may lead to reductions in hindsight bias.

KEY WORDS **Bias**, perception, hindsight, event likelihood

IMPLICATIONS

Marketers must be aware of how individuals' assessments of past events may be affected by hindsight bias, where the result is a distorted current view of what could, or should, have been able to be predicted in foresight. Consumer and managerial perceptions alike may be subject to hindsight biases. Efforts to remove, control for, or draw attention to such biases to a greater extent may include engaging an individual in critical evaluations of possible alternatives.

APPLICATION AREAS AND FURTHER READINGS

Marketing Ethics
Sligo, F., and Stirton, N. (1998). 'Does Hindsight Bias Change Perceptions of Business Ethics?' *Journal of Business Ethics*, 17(2), 111–124.

Services Marketing
Pieters, R., Koelemeijer, K., and Roest, H. (1995). 'Assimilation Processes in Service Satisfaction Formation,' *International Journal of Service Industry Management*, 6(3), 17.

Consumer Behavior
Pieters, R., and Zwick, R. (1993). 'Hindsight Bias in the Context of a Consumption Experience,' *European Advances in Consumer Research*, 1, 307–11.

BIBLIOGRAPHY
Fischhoff, B., and Beyth, R. (1975). ' "I Knew it would Happen": Remembered Probabilities of Once-Future Things,' *Organizational Behavior and Human Performance*, 13, 1–16.

■ hockey stick effect

DESCRIPTION

A phenomenon where an organization's quarterly performance (e.g. sales) is characterized by a steep upturn in the performance measure as a fiscal period nears a close.

KEY INSIGHTS

The hockey stick effect, named after the hockey stick-shaped graph that results when daily performance is plotted over a fiscal period (e.g. one quarter), is an artificial phenomenon that is observed among some firms in different industries and markets (e.g. computing and business software). Explanations for the phenomenon vary and include the view that increases in sales at the end of each quarter may be a result of managers of firms in buying situations making purchases to avoid the loss of budget money within their firms.

KEY WORDS Buying cycle, fiscal performance

IMPLICATIONS
To the extent the phenomenon of the hockey stick effect is present in a firm's industry and market, there may be important implications for the firm's internal operations. In particular, the cyclical nature of the aggregate customer buying cycle may require the marketer's firm to adopt more flexible manufacturing practices. At the same time, the phenomenon may present an opportunity to the marketer to adopt marketing practices aimed at smoothing the customer buying cycle.

APPLICATION AREAS AND FURTHER READINGS

Marketing Strategy
Gerwin, D. (1993). 'Manufacturing Flexibility: A Strategic Perspective,' *Management Science*, 39, 395–410.
Klein, William, and Ramseyer, J. Mark (1997). *Business Associations*, 3rd edn. Westbury, Conn.: Foundation Press.

Marketing Management
Rehfeld, John E. (1994). *Alchemy of a Leader: Combining Western and Japanese Management Skills to Transform your Company*. New York: J. Wiley.

BIBLIOGRAPHY
O'Guinn, M. C. (1991). *The Complete Guide to Activity-Based Costing*. Englewood Cliffs, NJ: Prentice-Hall.

■ honeymoon effect

DESCRIPTION
A positive initial effect on performance attributed to conditions that are most favorable at the early stages of a new relationship or venture in comparison to conditions encountered as the relationship or venture continues.

KEY INSIGHTS
Any time a new relationship or ventures is established by an organization with customers, suppliers, or firms in alliance with the organization, there is a possibility that performance may be enhanced initially as the newness of the relationship or venture may be chacterized initially by harmony, euphoria, calmness, or similar qualities analogously associated with that of a marital honeymoon. As honeymoons, by definition, are temporary, however, perceptions of the relationship or venture and associated actions of the participants may change over time resulting in differences (e.g. decreases) in performance relative to that demonstrated during the honeymoon period.

KEY WORDS Performance, relationships, ventures

IMPLICATIONS

Marketers involved in developing or managing any new venture or relationship of the firm with others, whether it is in constructing a new stadium to draw sports fans or engaging in a new comarketing alliance with another organization, may benefit from anticipating the occurrence of honeymoon effects in managing and measuring new venture or relationship performance over time. Depending on the context, performance measures, and information available, the effect may be assessed (e.g. predicted or retrospectively examined) either qualitatively or through rigorous and systematic quantitative methods.

APPLICATION AREAS AND FURTHER READINGS

Sports Marketing

McEvoy, C., Nagel, M., DeSchriver, T., and Brown, M. (2005). 'Facility Age and Attendance in Major League Baseball,' *Sport Management Review*, 8(1), 19–41.

Leadley, John C., and Zygmont, Zenon X. (2005). 'When is the Honeymoon Over? National Basketball Association Attendance 1971–2000,' *Journal of Sports Economics*, 6(2), 203–221.

Consumer Behavior

Crosby, Lawrence A., and Taylor, James R. (1983). 'Psychological Commitment and its Effects on Post-Decision Evaluation and Preference Stability among Voters,' *Journal of Consumer Research*, 9(4), March, 413–431.

Heilman, C. M., Bowman, D., and Wright, G. P. (2000). 'The Evolution of Brand Preferences and Choice Behaviors of Consumers New to a Market,' *Journal of Marketing Research*, 37(2), 139–155.

Marketing Strategy

Bucklin, Louis P., and Sengupta, Sanjit (1993). 'Organizing Successful Co-marketing Alliances,' *Journal of Marketing*, 57(2), April, 32–46.

BIBLIOGRAPHY

Clapp, Christopher M., and Hakes, Jahn K. (2005). 'How Long a Honeymoon? The Effect of New Stadiums on Attendance in Major League Baseball,' *Journal of Sports Economics*, 6(3), 237–63.

☐ horizontal integration *see* integration

☐ horns and halo effect *see* halo effect

■ house of quality

DESCRIPTION

A house-shaped planning matrix that is developed during organizational decision making involving customer needs assessments and shows the relationship of customer requirements to the means of achieving those requirements.

KEY INSIGHTS

The house of quality, a graphical planning tool, helps to define the relationship between customer preferences and the way the firm is able to fulfill such preferences. The specific planning approach is considered to be most effective when it is used as part of a broader planning process involving flexible and comprehensive group decision making focused on developing products or services that are aligned closely with customer needs.

KEY WORDS Quality, customer needs, product development, service development

IMPLICATIONS
Marketers involved in new product and service development efforts may benefit from adopting a house of quality-based planning approach to help ensure the firm's offerings are well matched with customer needs. In particular, mastering the methodology provides the marketer with a means to develop and articulate critical product or service plans collaboratively with others in a range of organizational functions.

APPLICATION AREAS AND FURTHER READINGS
Marketing Strategy
Griffin, Abbie, and Hauser, John R. (1993). 'The Voice of the Customer,' *Marketing Science*, 12(1), Winter, 1–27.

Marketing Research
Bech, A., Hansen, M., and Wienberg, L. (1997). 'Application of House of Quality in Translation of Consumer Needs into Sensory Attributes Measurable by Descriptive Sensory Analysis,' *Food Quality and Preference*, 8, 329–348.
Vairaktarakis, G. L. (1999). 'Optimization Tools for Design and Marketing of New/Improved Products Using the House of Quality,' *Journal of Operations Management*, 17, 645–663.

Marketing Modeling
Ramaswamy, Rajan, and Ulrich, Karl (1993). 'Augmenting the House of Quality with Engineering Models,' *Research in Engineering Design*, 5(2), 70–79.

BIBLIOGRAPHY
Hauser, John R., and Clausing, Don (1988). 'The House of Quality,' *Harvard Business Review*, 88(3), May–June, 68–72.

■ hybrid marketing

(also called multimarketing)

DESCRIPTION
Marketing involving multiple strategies, methods, processes, and/or tactical approaches in order to achieve the firm's marketing objectives.

KEY INSIGHTS
Hybrid marketing encompasses many areas of marketing ranging from the combined use of multiple strategic planning processes to the strategic use of multiple, distinct distribution channels. *Multimarketing* may be viewed as an equivalent term to hybrid marketing as it conveys the use of more than one marketing approach, although the term is also used by Weigand (1977) to refer more specifically to the use of multiple marketing channels to distribute the same product to markets differing in some important way. When the firm's objectives involve reaching and influencing a firm's target market, hybrid marketing may be used to increase the likelihood that those within the firm's target market will be successfully reached and persuaded at some point in their purchase deliberations. On the other hand, hybrid marketing may also be beneficial when a single marketing approach is insufficient to reach multiple market segments.

KEY WORDS Multiple marketing approaches, channels, distribution

IMPLICATIONS

While it may be tempting to conclude that some distinct marketing approaches (e.g. distribution strategies) are most effective when adopted to the mutual exclusion of other approaches, hybrid marketing emphasizes the view that superior results may be achievable through the interactions of multiple marketing approaches. Convergence marketing, for example, adopts such a view, as does fusion marketing (see **convergence marketing; fusion marketing**). Toward assisting efforts evaluating alternative combinations, marketers may therefore benefit from a greater knowledge of research examining not only the relative effectiveness of hybrid approaches but the many issues associated with their development and implementation as well.

APPLICATION AREAS AND FURTHER READINGS

Marketing Strategy

Moriarty, Rowland T., and Moran, Ursula (1990). 'Marketing Hybrid Marketing Systems,' *Harvard Business Review*, 6, 146–155.

Duan, Y., and Burrel, P. (1995). 'A Hybrid System for Strategic Marketing Planning,' *Marketing Intelligence & Planning*, 13(11), 5–12.

Webb, K. L., and Hogan, J. E. (2002). 'Hybrid Channel Conflict: Causes and Effects on Channel Performance,' *Journal of Business & Industrial Marketing*, 17(5), 338–356.

Marketing Management

Littman, M. (2000). 'Hybrid Engine Cars do Better with Hybrid Marketing Tactics,' *Marketing News*, 6.

BIBLIOGRAPHY

Moriarty, R. T., and Moran, U. (1990). 'Managing Hybrid Marketing Systems,' *Harvard Business Review*, 68(6), 146–155.

Gandolfo, A., and Padelleti, F. (1999). 'From Direct to Hybrid Marketing: A New IBM Go-to-Market Model,' *European Journal of Innovation Management*, 2(3), 109–117.

Weigand, R. E. (1977). 'Fit Products and Channels to your Markets,' *Harvard Business Review*, 1, 95–105.

I

■ Icarus paradox

DESCRIPTION
The situation where an organization's great success precedes its severe decline.

KEY INSIGHTS
The Icaraus paradox phenomenon as developed and researched by Miller (1990) views an effect of organizational success as contributing to blinding it to future threats, thereby increasing the likelihood of failure in the future. Such organizations become slow in their ability to react to changing environments as a result of success contributing to an overall sense of organizational superiority.

KEY WORDS Success, failure

IMPLICATIONS
Marketers must be aware of how an organization's successes may ultimately contribute to its vulnerability to decline. Anticipating competitive moves, for example, is an activity that could increase in importance and scope as an organization becomes increasingly successful.

APPLICATION AREAS AND FURTHER READINGS
Marketing Management
Chen, Ming-Jer (2002). 'Transcending Paradox: The Chinese "Middle Way" Perspective,' *Asia Pacific Journal of Management*, 19(2–3), August.
Mumby-Croft, Roger, and Williams, Juliet (2002). 'The Concept of Workplace Marketing: A Management Development Model for Corporate and Enterprise Sectors,' *Strategic Change*, 11(4), 205–214.
Moulton, Wilbur N., Thomas, Howard, and Pruett, Mark (1996). 'Business Failure Path Ways: Environmental Stress and Organizational Response,' *Journal of Management*, 22(4), 571–595.

BIBLIOGRAPHY
Miller, D. (1990). *The Icarus Paradox: How Exceptional Companies Bring about their Downfall*. New York: HarperBusiness.
Miller, Danny (1993). 'The Architecture of Simplicity,' *Academy of Management Review*, 18(1), January, 116–138.

■ iceberg principle

DESCRIPTION
A general view that only a small part of an issue will often be visible initially. More specifically, the view that in aggregate or summary data, there can be hidden much good or important information.

KEY INSIGHTS
As where approximately 90% of an iceberg is below the surface of the water, the iceberg principle points to how initial or summary views of a phenomenon may miss drawing attention to details which may be deemed important upon further inspection or analyses.

KEY WORDS Data analysis, information, aggregate data

IMPLICATIONS
Marketers must consider how summary data and information obtained in research may potentially conceal further findings which may be important or essential. For example, while summary knowledge of average consumer responses to a marketer's offerings may be useful for marketing planning, it can also be misleading if such information hides important understandings of dramatic variation in the range of responses.

APPLICATION AREAS AND FURTHER READINGS
Marketing Analysis
Ramaprasad, M. V. (2004). 'Trends in Marketing Cost Analysis,' *Management Accountant* (Calcutta), 39(2), 145–147.

BIBLIOGRAPHY
Palia, Aspy (2005). 'Online Cumulative Simulation Team Performance Package,' *Developments in Business Simulations and Experiential Learning*, 32, 233–241.

☐ idea generation *see* new product development
☐ idea marketing *see* social marketing
☐ idea screening *see* new product development
☐ I-knew-it-all-along effect *see* hindsight bias

■ illusion of control

DESCRIPTION
The tendency for individuals to believe they have the ability to control or influence outcomes over which they have no demonstrable influence, as where outcomes are actually determined by chance.

KEY INSIGHTS
Based on pioneering research by Langer and Roth (1975), the illusion of control phenomenon characterizes the finding that people often behave as if chance events have a potential for influence through personal control. The likelihood of the phenomenon occurring may increase under situations where there is a resemblance to situations where skill is involved

and where situations appear familiar and involve free choice among other factors. Some research (e.g. Taylor and Brown 1988) argues that the illusion of control, when positive, is adaptive in that it acts to increase motivation and persistence. The illusion of control is often evident in gambling and lottery play.

KEY WORDS Control, influence, behavior, chance

IMPLICATIONS
While marketers may perceive and sometimes act in ways that reinforce the illusion of control among consumers as in certain cases of gambling and lottery play, where it may contribute to consumers' anticipation and enjoyment of participating, for example, marketers must recognize how the illusion of control may also contribute to irrational behaviors. Beyond consumers, the illusion of control may also be present in activities within a firm, as where it may influence organizational forecasts.

APPLICATION AREAS AND FURTHER READINGS
Consumer Behavior
Hoch, Stephen J., and Ha, Young-Won (1986). 'Consumer Learning: Advertising and the Ambiguity of Product Experience,' *Journal of Consumer Research*, 13(2), September, 221–233.
Clotfelter, Charles T., and Cook, Philip J. (1990). 'On the Economics of State Lotteries,' *Journal of Economic Perspectives*, 4(4), Autumn, 105–119.

Forecasting
Durand, R. (2003). 'Predicting a Firm's Forecasting Ability: The Roles of Organizational Illusion of Control and Organizational Attention,' *Strategic Management Journal*, 24(9), 821–838.

BIBLIOGRAPHY
Langer, E. J., and Roth, J. (1975). 'Heads I Win, Tails it's Chance: The Illusion of Control as a Function of the Sequence of Outcomes in a Purely Chance Task,' *Journal of Personality and Social Psychology*, 32(6), 191–198.
Langer, E. J. (1982). 'The Illusion of Control', in D. Kahneman, P. Slovic, and A. Tversky (eds.), *Judgment under Uncertainty: Heuristics and Biases*. New York: Cambridge University Press.
Taylor, S. E., and Brown, J. D. (1988). 'Illusion and Well-Being: A Social Psychological Perspective on Mental-Health,' *Psychological Bulletin*, 103(2), 193–210.

■ imitation effect

DESCRIPTION
An effect of social influence in the diffusion of innovations whereby an innovation's diffusion in the marketplace is a result of the interaction of non-adopters with adopters.

KEY INSIGHTS
The imitation effect is considered to be one of two important parameters in models of demand and diffusion of innovation, where the other key parameter is the innovation effect. The new-product growth model developed by Bass (1969) is one of the first to formally characterize its role in diffusion of innovation descriptions, explanations, and predictions. In essence, the imitation effect is due to what has also been referred

to as social contagion, where in the case of innovation diffusion, the spread of an innovation is due to non-adopters interacting with and learning about an innovation (e.g. in terms of its features and benefits) through its adopters, with some non-adopters subsequently adopting the innovation themselves, thereby leading to further innovation diffusion in the marketplace.

KEY WORDS Diffusion, imitation, social influence

IMPLICATIONS
Marketers should seek to understand how the imitation effect may assist in explaining the rate and extent of diffusion of an innovation such as a new product if the aim is to enhance an innovation's diffusion. Such an effect may be critical in some instances, as where positive word-of-mouth is a primary driver of new product or service acceptance in a marketplace. The overall popularity of a new restaurant, for example, may be highly dependent on communication dynamics characterized by the imitation effect.

APPLICATION AREAS AND FURTHER READINGS
Marketing Modeling
Mahajan, Vijay, and Muller, Eitan (1979). 'Innovation Diffusion and New Product Growth Models in Marketing,' *Journal of Marketing*, 43(4), Autumn, 55–68.
Dolan, Robert J., and Jeuland, Abel P. (1981). 'Experience Curves and Dynamic Demand Models: Implications for Optimal Pricing Strategies,' *Journal of Marketing*, 45(1), Winter, 52–62.
Dekimpe, Marnik G., and Hanssens, Dominique M. (1995). 'The Persistence of Marketing Effects on Sales,' *Marketing Science*, 14(1), 1–21.
Swami, S., and Khairnar, P. J. (2003). 'Diffusion of Products with Limited Supply and Known Expiration Date,' *Marketing Letters* (New York), 14(1), 33–46.

BIBLIOGRAPHY
Bass, Frank M. (1969). 'A New-Product Growth Model for Consumer Durables,' *Management Science*, 15, January, 215–227.

■ inbound marketing

(also referred to as in-bound marketing)

DESCRIPTION
Any marketing approach where it is the current or prospective customer that initiates contact with an organization.

KEY INSIGHTS
Inbound marketing, as where current or prospective customers can call a company call center, reach an interactive voice response system, and/or visit a company website, can be considered in some ways to be more effective than outbound marketing where the organization initiates contact with the customer. Specifically, inbound marketing approaches may

be a relatively effective way of meeting customers' personal needs and helping to build customer relationships, since individuals who contact a company are more apt to give the organization their time and attention in comparison to approaches where the organization cold-calls its customers on the telephone, for example. In addition, inbound marketing provides a means for the firm to obtain information from customers that customers wish to share with the firm (e.g. ideas, complaints, compliments).

KEY WORDS Customer contact

IMPLICATIONS
Inbound marketing provides marketers with a means to become acutely aware of current and prospective customers' particular needs and wants, where such information can be used by the marketers' firm to build stronger relationships with such individuals as well as to become more responsive to overall customer needs.

APPLICATION AREAS AND FURTHER READINGS
Marketing Strategy
Moffett, T., Stone, M., and Crick, P. (2002). 'The Use of New Customer-Facing Technology in Fast-Moving Consumer Goods,' *Journal of Brand Management*, 9(6), 437–451.
Pawsey, N. (2005). 'Ideas Factory: Planning for Success,' *Engineering Management Journal*, 15(3), June–July, 40–43.

BIBLIOGRAPHY
Thomas, G. S., and Kleiner, B. H. (1995). 'New Developments in Organizing around Markets,' *Work Study*, 44(8), 4–8.

□ incipient demand *see* demand

■ income effect

DESCRIPTION
Any effect on consumer behaviors as a result of a consumer's change in real income. In economic terms, the income effect may also be viewed as any change in a consumer's real income resulting from a change in the price of a good or service.

KEY INSIGHTS
As a consumer's real income changes, consumer purchasing and consumption behaviors may also change. For example, when a consumer faces greater increased real income, such a change may prompt him or her to eat more often at restaurants as opposed to eating at home. Beyond actual consumption behavior, consumer perceptions of products and services may also be influenced by income, as when a consumer's income influences his or her perceptions of product quality (Wheatley and Chiu 1991).

KEY WORDS Consumer behavior, consumption, perception

IMPLICATIONS

For many products and services, an understanding of the income effect may be essential for understanding how consumer purchase behaviors and consumer perceptions may change with real income. When an individual receives additional income through a new job after a university education, for example, the income effect on consumption behavior and perceptions of product quality can be quite dramatic.

APPLICATION AREAS AND FURTHER READINGS

Consumer Behavior

Chiang, Jeongwen (1991). 'A Simultaneous Approach to the Whether, What and How Much to Buy Questions,' *Marketing Science*, 10(4), Autumn, 297–315.

Wheatley, John J., and Chiu, John S. Y. (1977). 'The Effects of Price, Store Image, and Product and Respondent Characteristics on Perceptions of Quality,' *Journal of Marketing Research*, 14(2), May, 181–186.

BIBLIOGRAPHY

Kingma, Bruce Robert (1989). 'An Accurate Measurement of the Crowd-out Effect, Income Effect, and Price Effect for Charitable Contributions,' *Journal of Political Economy*, 97(5), October, 1197–1207.

☐ **income segmentation** *see* segmentation
☐ **increasing opportunity cost, law of** *see* diminishing returns, law of
☐ **incremental validity** *see* validity
☐ **in-cultural marketing** *see* multicultural marketing

■ indirect marketing

DESCRIPTION

Marketing activities that rely on any indirect means for attracting, persuading, or otherwise influencing and eliciting a desired response from a firm's customers or end-users of its offerings.

KEY INSIGHTS

Indirect marketing encompasses any of a range of marketing approaches where there is a reliance on intervening marketing approaches to reach and interact with the customer. Thus, firms using wholesalers, brokers, or other independent distributors as part of their marketing channels engage indirect marketing, where such firms rely upon motivating such intermediaries to market the firm's offerings to consumers. A benefit of the approach is that, compared to direct marketing approaches, it may take less time and marketing effort, involve a lower capital expenditure, and allow the firm to reach a larger number of customers.

Another less common meaning attached to indirect marketing relates to the marketing value of any firm activity or action that is not directly associated with the firm's main marketing activities, as where spotless offices, well-dressed staff, and courteous receptionists can indirectly create positive, lasting impressions or influences on customers, or any other instance where elements of a firm's service quality indirectly facilitate its major efforts in product marketing.

KEY WORDS Intermediaries, marketing intermediaries

IMPLICATIONS
Given that marketing exchanges are often indirect, marketers should
seek to understand how such exchanges can be enhanced by the firm's
many indirect marketing efforts. In particular, marketers may find it
beneficial to compare indirect marketing approaches with those of direct
marketing (see **direct marketing**) to determine to what extent either
or both contribute to the marketer's objectives, which may include
expanding customer reach as well as cost-effectively meeting individual
customer needs.

APPLICATION AREAS AND FURTHER READINGS
Marketing Management
Rolnicki, Kenneth (1998). *Managing Channels of Distribution: The Marketing Executive's
Complete Guide.* New York: Amacom.

International Marketing
Bello, Daniel C., and Williamson, Nicholas C. (1985). 'Contractual Arrangement
and Marketing Practices in the Indirect Export Channel,' *Journal of International
Business Studies*, 16(2), Summer, 65–82.

Online Marketing
De Koster, M. B. M. (2003). 'Distribution Strategies for Online Retailers,' *IEEE
Transactions on Engineering Management*, 50(4), 448–457.

Services Marketing
Danaher, P. J., and Rust, R. T. (1996).'Indirect Marketing Benefits from Service
Quality,' *Quality Management Journal*, 3(2), 63–88.

BIBLIOGRAPHY
Bagozzi, Richard P. (1975). 'Marketing as Exchange,' *Journal of Marketing*, 39, October, 32–39.

☐ **individual marketing** *see* one-to-one marketing

■ **industrial buyer behavior**

(also called business buyer behavior or organizational buyer behavior)

DESCRIPTION
The buying behavior of organizations involved in the purchase of goods or
services for resale or for use in the production of other goods or services by
the firm.

KEY INSIGHTS
Given that a major proportion of all marketing activity is in the area
of business-to-business marketing, industrial buyer behavior constitutes
a major area of research in marketing and involves many related concepts. The *buygrid* framework, for example, is a common way of characterizing the organizational buying process and the associated behavior
of industrial buyers, where the framework comprises two dimensions:
buyclass and *buyphase*. Buyclass categorizes or frames the nature of the

business buying situation: *new task*—situations where the buyer is a first-time buyer of a product or service; *straight rebuy*—situations where the buyer is reordering the same product or service previously purchased; and *modified rebuy*—situations where the buyer wants to make adjustments to product or service specifications relative to a previous purchase. Buyphase relates to the stages in the industrial buying process—i.e. need recognition, need definition, need description, seller identification, proposal solicitation, proposal evaluation, proposal selection, ordering procedures, and a review of performance.

Further concepts related to the *business buying process*—the business process comprising multiple stages of business-to-business buying activity—include that of *product specification* (the stage where the organization establishes the desired specifications or characteristics according to which purchased products or services are needed and to which they must conform) and *order-routine specification* (the stage where the buyer incorporates such specifications, along with further requirements for delivery, service, and warranty, into a final order with chosen supplier(s)). Finally, the concept of the *buying center* is key to much of industrial buyer behavior as it focuses on the roles that multiple individuals perform in the customer organization in industrial buying. Given that the buying center comprises the set of individuals involved in business buying in the customer organization, such roles can be further decomposed into: *deciders*—those individuals with formal or informal influence over the final selection of a supplier; *influencers*—those individuals who affect the buying decision through specification definition or alternative evaluation, for example; and *gatekeepers*—those individuals who, through their position in the buying organization, are able to restrict external access to key individuals in the organization or, similarly, impede or facilitate the flow of information to key others in the organization.

KEY WORDS Organizations, buying behavior

IMPLICATIONS
As much of industrial buying is characterized by sophisticated buyers and complex product and services, an in-depth understanding of the buyer behavior and the decision process actually followed for a firm's products or services can help to increase both the effectiveness and efficiency of the firm's business-to-business marketing efforts. Drawing upon conceptual and empirical research on industrial buyer behavior can not only assist the marketer in evaluating and refining the firm's current strategic and tactical approaches to be consistent with such buying behavior, but also help to increase buying receptivity to the firm's business-to-business marketing initiatives, given diverse customer needs and a highly competitive marketing environment (See also **buyer decision process**).

APPLICATION AREAS AND FURTHER READINGS
Marketing Strategy
Choffray, Jean-Marie, and Lilien, Gary L. (1978). 'Assessing Response to Industrial Marketing Strategy,' *Journal of Marketing*, 42(2), April, 20–31.

Sheth, Jagdish N. (1996). 'Organizational Buying Behavior: Past Performance and Future Expectations,' *Journal of Business & Industrial Marketing*, 11(3/4), June, 7–24.

McQuiston, Daniel H. (1989). 'Novelty, Complexity, and Importance as Causal Determinants of Industrial Buyer Behavior,' *Journal of Marketing*, 53(2), April, 66–79.

Lehmann, Donald R., and O'Shaughnessy, John (1974). 'Difference in Attribute Importance for Different Industrial Products,' *Journal of Marketing*, 38(2), April, 36–42.

Marketing Management

Anderson, Erin, Chu, Wujin, and Weitz, Barton (1987). 'Industrial Purchasing: An Empirical Exploration of the Buyclass Framework,' *Journal of Marketing*, 51(3), July, 71–86.

Johnston, Wesley J., and Bonoma, Thomas V. (1981). 'The Buying Center: Structure and Interaction Patterns,' *Journal of Marketing*, 45(3), Summer, 143–156.

International Marketing

Money, R. Bruce, Gilly, Mary C., and Graham, John L. (1998). 'Explorations of National Culture and Word-of-Mouth Referral Behavior in the Purchase of Industrial Services in the United States and Japan,' *Journal of Marketing*, 62(4), October, 76–87.

Online Marketing

Klein, Lisa R., and Quelch, John A. (1997). 'Business-to-Business Market Making on the Internet,' *International Marketing Review*, 14(5), 345–361.

Deeter-Schmelz, Dawn R., Bizzari, Aric, Graham, Rebecca, and Howdyshell, Catherine (2001). 'Business-to-Business Online Purchasing: Suppliers' Impact on Buyers' Adoption and Usage Intent,' *Journal of Supply Chain Management*, 37(1), December, 4–10.

Lucking-Reiley, David, and Spulber, Daniel F. (2001). 'Business-to-Business Electronic Commerce,' *Journal of Economic Perspectives*, 15(1), Winter, 55–68.

BIBLIOGRAPHY
Sheth, Jagdish N. (1973). 'A Model of Industrial Buyer Behavior,' *Journal of Marketing*, 37(4), October, 50–56.

Webster, Frederick E., Jr., and Wind, Yoram (1972). 'A General Model for Understanding Organizational Buying Behavior,' *Journal of Marketing*, 36(2), April, 12–19.

☐ industrial marketing *see* business-to-business marketing

☐ inelastic demand *see* elasticity of demand

☐ inferior goods *see* goods

☐ influencers *see* industrial buyer behavior

■ information processing theory

DESCRIPTION

Theory or theories related to describing, understanding, and explaining how individuals or organizations process, analyze, or change information, as where information is gathered, stored, retrieved, manipulated, and transformed for some purpose.

KEY INSIGHTS

Information-processing theory encompasses a broad base of research sharing a view that cognition can be characterized as computational in nature, with information being transformed and converted. Information-processing theory is often concerned with the depth with which incoming information is processed as well as its quality (e.g. processed free of distortion), and its short- and long-term influences. Such a view further suggests that the properties of information have an influence on the way information is processed.

KEY WORDS Information, communication, processing

IMPLICATIONS

Information-processing theory provides a means to model and frame a wide range of phenomena involving both consumers and organizations. For example, viewing individuals or organizations as information processors enables marketers to focus attention on the ways that the means by which information is communicated (e.g. formally or informally) may influence the nature and extent of information reception and processing and its effects on individual or organization behaviors. Consumer responses to advertising and an organization's competitive response time are specific areas that may be viewed in terms of information-processing dynamics.

APPLICATION AREAS AND FURTHER READINGS

Marketing Strategy

Tybout, Alice M., Calder, Bobby J., and Sternthal, Brian (1981). 'Using Information Processing Theory to Design Marketing Strategies,' *Journal of Marketing Research*, 18(1), February, 73–79.

Egelhoff, William G. (1991). 'Information-Processing Theory and the Multinational Enterprise,' *Journal of International Business Studies*, 22, 341–368.

Consumer Behavior

MacInnis, Deborah J., and Jaworski, Bernard J. (1989). 'Information Processing from Advertisements: Toward an Integrative Framework,' *Journal of Marketing*, 53(4), October, 1–23.

Bettman, James R. (1979). *An Information Processing Theory of Consumer Choice*. Reading, Mass.: Addison-Wesley.

BIBLIOGRAPHY

Craik, F. I. M., and Lockhart, R. S. (1972). 'Levels of Processing: A Framework for Memory Research,' *Journal of Verbal Learning and Verbal Behavior*, 11, 671–684.

Shannon, Claude E., and Weaver, Warren (1949). *The Mathematical Theory of Communication*. Urbana, Ill: University of Illinois Press.

☐ information search *see* buyer decision process

■ information systems theory

DESCRIPTION

Theory or theories of information systems where information or data are collected, transmitted, processed, or disseminated by some means.

Information systems theory, of which an earlier contributor was Shannon (1948), currently encompasses a broad base of research where a common aim is the examination of information systems in relation to their role in obtaining or developing meaningful information. Information processing is a key concept within information systems theory. Characteristics of information systems examined by theory in the area include structures or repositories for holding data, interfaces for exchanging information, channels for connecting repositories, and the subsequent meanings and value provided to its users.

KEY WORDS Systems, information, data, processing, **value**

IMPLICATIONS
The effective development of marketing information systems owes much to information systems theory. Subsequent developments of effective marketing information systems and, more broadly, effective systems for electronic commerce may also draw upon information systems theory-related research to obtain potentially useful insights for increased value to their developers and users.

APPLICATION AREAS AND FURTHER READINGS
Online Marketing
Venkatesh, Alladi, Member, Laurie, and Firat, A. Fuat (1998). 'Cyberspace as the Next Marketing Frontier (?): Questions and Issues,' in S. Brown and D. Turley (eds.), *Consumer Research: Postcards from the Edge*. London: Routledge, 301–321.
Suh, Bomil, and Han, Ingoo (2003). 'The Impact of Customer Trust and Perception of Security Control on the Acceptance of Electronic Commerce,' *International Journal of Electronic Commerce*, 7(3), Spring, 135–161.

Marketing Information Systems
Talvinen, J. M. (1995). 'Information Systems in Marketing: Identifying Opportunities for New Applications,' *European Journal of Marketing*, 29(1), 8–26.
Banker, R. D., and Kauffman, R. J. (2004). 'The Evolution of Research on Information Systems: A Fiftieth-Year Survey of the Literature in Management Science,' *Management Science*, 50(3), 281–298.

BIBLIOGRAPHY
Hirschheim, R., Klein, H. K., and Lyytinen, K. (1995). *Information Systems Development and Data Modeling: Conceptual and Philosophical Foundations*. Cambridge: Cambridge University Press.
Khazanchi, D., and Munkvold, B. E. (2000). 'Is Information Systems a Science? An Inquiry into the Nature of the Information Systems Discipline,' *DataBase for Advances in Information Systems*, 31(3), 24–42.
Shannon, Claude E. (1948). 'A Mathematical Theory of Communication,' *Bell System Technical Journal*, 27, 379–423, 623–656.

■ innovation effect

DESCRIPTION
An effect in the diffusion of innovations whereby an innovation's diffusion and adoption in the marketplace are the result of a tendency for individuals in a population to innovate, where such activity is independent of the availability of social influence.

KEY INSIGHTS

The innovation effect is considered to be one of two important parameters in models of demand and diffusion of innovation, where the other key parameter is the imitation effect. The new-product growth model developed by Bass (1969) formally characterizes its role in diffusion of innovation descriptions, explanations, and predictions. In essence, the innovation effect is due to individuals in a population acting mainly on external sources of influence (e.g. new product advertising), as opposed to social influences, in adopting innovations as a result of the innovations' differences in comparison to existing products or services. Thus, to the extent that a population is receptive to an innovation independent of social influence, the innovation's diffusion is facilitated.

KEY WORDS Diffusion, innovation, adoption

IMPLICATIONS

Marketers should seek to understand how the innovation effect may contribute to explaining or anticipating the rate and extent of diffusion of an innovation among any given target population. Whether the population of the firm's current product users or the population of an entire country, the innovation effect resulting from communicating the nature of a product's or service's innovative features and benefits may have significant influence on the innovation's diffusion and overall market acceptance.

APPLICATION AREAS AND FURTHER READINGS

Marketing Modeling

Mahajan, Vijay, and Muller, Eitan (1979). 'Innovation Diffusion and New Product Growth Models in Marketing,' *Journal of Marketing*, 43(4), Autumn, 55-68.

Dolan, Robert J., and Jeuland, Abel P. (1981). 'Experience Curves and Dynamic Demand Models: Implications for Optimal Pricing Strategies,' *Journal of Marketing*, 45(1), Winter, 52-62.

Parthasarathy, M., Jun, S., and Mittelstaedt, R. A. (1997). 'Multiple Diffusion and Multicultural Aggregate Social Systems,' *International Marketing Review*, 14(4-5), 233-247.

Gjerde, K. A. P., Slotnick, S. A., and Sobel, M. J. (2002). 'New Product Innovation with Multiple Features and Technology Constraints,' *Management Science*, 48(10), 1268-1284.

BIBLIOGRAPHY

Bass, Frank M. (1969). 'A New-Product Growth Model for Consumer Durables,' *Management Science*, 15, January, 215-227.

☐ innovative marketing *see* enlightened marketing
☐ innovators *see* adopter categories

■ inoculation theory

DESCRIPTION

A theory of resistance to persuasion where a belief or attitude is made stronger through a series of repeated mild attacks.

KEY INSIGHTS

Based on pioneering research by McGuire (1964), inoculation theory represents a view that an individual's resistance to persuasion can be increased through a pre-established process of inoculative communications. Specifically, communication steps which may lead to increased resistance to persuasion by the individual when he or she is ultimately exposed to a future persuasive argument include: providing a warning to the individual of future efforts aimed at persuading so as to lead the individual to psychologically prepare, or even over-prepare, to resist them; subjecting the individual to a weak persuasive argument aimed at overcoming the individual's defenses, yet where the argument is sufficiently strong to encourage the individual to defend it; and encouraging the individual to actively defend the argument through words or actions as opposed to merely thoughts.

KEY WORDS Persuasion, arguments, resistance

IMPLICATIONS

Marketers aiming at changing or reinforcing particular consumer behaviors can draw upon inoculation theory to design potentially more effective marketing communications. For example, providing inoculative arguments to consumers may prevent their switching to a competitor's product. When a firm knows a competitor will soon be introducing an alternative product aimed at taking away the firm's current customers, the firm can use communications aimed at warning them that a competitor will soon be trying to persuade them to switch as well as providing them with reasons why they should still prefer the firm's product over any competitor's product.

APPLICATION AREAS AND FURTHER READINGS

Marketing Communications

Lessne, Greg J., and Didow, Nicholas M., Jr. (1987). 'Inoculation Theory and Resistance to Persuasion in Marketing,' *Psychology and Marketing*, 4(2), 157–165.

Crowley, Ayn E., and Hoyer, Wayne D. (1994). 'An Integrative Framework for Understanding Two-Sided Persuasion,' *Journal of Consumer Research*, 20(4), March, 561–574.

Buttle, F. A. (1998). 'Word of Mouth: Understanding and Managing Referral Marketing,' *Journal of Strategic Marketing*, 6(3), 241–254.

Compton, J. A., and Pfau, M. (2004). 'Use of Inoculation to Foster Resistance to Credit Card Marketing Targeting College Students,' *Journal of Applied Communication Research*, 32(4), 343–364.

BIBLIOGRAPHY

Szybillo, George J., and Heslin, Richard (1973). 'Resistance to Persuasion: Inoculation Theory in a Marketing Context,' *Journal of Marketing Research*, 10(4), November, 396–403.

McGuire, W. J. (1964). 'Inducing Resistance to Persuasion: Some Contemporary Approaches', in L. Berkowitz (ed.), *Advances in Experimental Social Psychology*, vol. i. New York: Academic Press, 191–229.

☐ **inseparability** *see* service characteristics

■ institutional marketing

DESCRIPTION
Organizational marketing efforts aimed at influencing broad audiences within a common industry, function, or issue orientation, with particular emphasis on the marketing efforts of large public organizations.

KEY INSIGHTS
Institutional marketing, being concerned with the marketing efforts of organizations such as higher education institutions, hospitals, and other public organizations, emphasizes marketing to accomplish institutional aims and objectives. As such, institutional marketing can be viewed as an imperative for institutions seeking to increase institutional awareness in the marketplace, stimulate interest in the institution among prospective customers, facilitate positive evaluations among such individuals as well as diverse publics (e.g. employers, government agencies), and ultimately encourage customers to adopt the institution's offerings. Yet, the nature of some institutions, given characteristics such as large size and public status, is such that institutional marketing efforts may lead certain organizations to be slow or unresponsive in the development and implementation of their marketing efforts. Furthermore, individuals on the receiving end of such efforts may view the institution as being impersonal, necessitating a challenge for marketers at such institutions to implement approaches to encourage greater responsiveness to marketplace needs.

KEY WORDS Large organizations, public organizations

IMPLICATIONS
A greater understanding of institutional marketing enables marketers engaging in such efforts to recognize more clearly the many challenges and opportunities that are associated with large public institutions, which may include timely responsiveness to changes in market conditions. In addition, marketers within such organizations may benefit from leveraging the institution's marketing efforts in reaching and engaging with current and prospective customers on a more personal level—something that may facilitate the development of stronger (and more profitable) customer relationships.

APPLICATION AREAS AND FURTHER READINGS
Marketing Education
Brown, John Anthony (1978). 'The Role of Academic Programs in Institutional Marketing; Administrator Role; College Choice; Higher Education; Institutional Characteristics; Marketing; Presidents; Publicize; School Holding Power; Student Recruitment,' *New Directions for Higher Education*, 21 (Marketing Higher Education), 6(1), Spring, 1–6.
Krause, Robin D. (2003). 'Managing Higher ed Web Sites: Balancing the Need for Timely Updates, the Requirements of Institutional Marketing, and the Development of Content,' User Services Conference archive, Proceedings of the 31st

annual ACM SIGUCCS conference on User services, San Antonio, Tex. New York: ACM Press, 139-141.

O'Brian, Edward J. (1973). 'Marketing Higher Education: Administration; Distributive Education; Educational Administration; Educational Objectives; Extension Education; Higher Education; Institutional Role; Marketing; Planning; Tuition,' *College and University Journal*, 12(4), September, 22-23.

Marketing Ethics

Jones, J. W., McCullough, L. B., and Richman, B. W. (2003). 'Ethics of Institutional Marketing: Role of Physicians,' *Journal of Vascular Surgery*, 38(2), August, 409-410.

Marketing Strategy

Stumpf, Stephen, and Longman, Robert (2000). 'The Ultimate Consultant: Building Long-Term, Exceptional Value Client Relationships,' *Career Development International*, 5, 124-134.

BIBLIOGRAPHY

Michael, Steve, Holdaway, Ed, and Young, H. Clifton (1993). 'Administrators' Perceptions of Institutional Marketing,' *Journal of Marketing for Higher Education*, 4, 3-25.

☐ in-store marketing *see* retail marketing

☐ intangibility *see* service characteristics

☐ integrated direct marketing *see* direct marketing

☐ integrated marketing *see* concurrent marketing

■ integrated marketing communications

DESCRIPTION

Marketing emphasizing the full integration or merging of multiple, different marketing communication approaches with the aim of achieving synergistic effects and superior results relative to approaches where multiple marketing communication activities are pursued but not coordinated.

KEY INSIGHTS

An integrated marketing communications (IMC) approach is aimed at assisting the firm in communicating with customers and other stakeholders in a clear, consistent, and compelling manner. Given an understanding of customer and stakeholder profiles (e.g. demographics, psychographics), a firm adopting an IMC approach is then able to draw upon such information to develop communication strategies involving the integrated use of multiple communication methods including advertising, sales promotions, and public relations, where the net effect of the approach is a strengthening of the firm's relationships with its customers and/or stakeholders.

KEY WORDS Marketing communication, communications integration, **integration**

IMPLICATIONS

As a central part of marketing involves effective marketing communication with current or potential customers and other stakeholders, marketers may benefit from a better understanding of the both the breadth and depth of integrated marketing communications research. For example, in the development and implementation of effective advertising and sales promotions, IMC-related research can assist the marketer with understanding how and to what extent the two approaches may be used in combination to achieve a superior customer response.

APPLICATION AREAS AND FURTHER READINGS

Marketing Strategy
Percy, Larry (1997). *Strategies for Implementing Integrated Marketing Communications.* Lincolnwood, Ill.: NTC Business Books.
Keller, Kevin Lane (2001). 'Mastering the Marketing Communications Mix: Micro and Macro Perspectives on Integrated Marketing Communication Programs,' *Journal of Marketing Management,* 17(7–8), August, 819–847.

Marketing Management
McArthur, D. N., and Griffin, T. (1997). 'A Marketing Management View of Integrated Marketing Communication,' *Journal of Advertising Research,* 37(5), 19–26.

Advertising
Schultz, D., and Kitchen, P. J. (1997). 'Integrated Marketing Communications in U.S. Advertising Agencies,' *Journal of Advertising Research,* 37(5), 7–18.

BIBLIOGRAPHY
Schultz, Don, Lauterborn, Robert, and Tannenbaum, Stanley (1993). *Integrated Marketing Communications.* Lincolnwood, Ill.: NTC Business Books.
Schultz, Don E., Tannenbaum, Stanley I., and Lauterborn, Robert F. (1994). *The New Marketing Paradigm.* New York: McGraw-Hill Professional.

■ integration

DESCRIPTION
A process whereby firms combine or merge for a strategic purpose.

KEY INSIGHTS
Integration among firms can take place along several dimensions. Common characterizations of integration include *vertical integration*, where two firms at different stages in a production processs merge to form a single business entity, and *horizontal integration*, where two firms at the same stage of the production process merge to form a single business entity. In addition, firms vertically integrating can be said to engage in either *backward integration*, where a firm merges with (or acquires) an upstream supplier for its production process, or *forward integration*, where a firm merges with (or acquires) a downstream distributor or customer. Firms pursuing vertical integration often do so to control sources of supply or demand and/or as a means to increase profit potential, whereas firms pursuing horizontal integration may do so to achieve greater economies of scale.

KEY WORDS Mergers, acquisitions

IMPLICATIONS
Marketing strategists seeking to understand better the benefits as well as risks associated with different integration approaches may benefit

from greater knowledge of integration processes. Such knowledge may assist the marketer in understanding how and to what extent different approaches may provide the firm or others in the firm's industry with a possible competitive advantage. At the same time, marketers must take care to weigh such options with alternatives that may include strategic alliances, technology license agreements, and franchises, for example.

APPLICATION AREAS AND FURTHER READINGS

Marketing Strategy
Anderson, E., and Weitz, B. (1986). 'Make-or-Buy Decisions: Vertical Integration and Marketing Productivity,' *Sloan Management Review*, 27(3), 3–19.
Balakrishnan, Srinivasan, and Wernerfelt, Berger (1986). 'Technical Change, Competition and Vertical Integration,' *Strategic Management Journal*, 7, 347–355.
Varadarajan, P. Rajan, and Rajaratnam, Daniel (1986). 'Symbiotic Marketing Revisited,' *Journal of Marketing*, 50(1), January, 7–17.
Kenneth, Arrow (1975). 'Vertical Integration and Communication,' *Bell Journal of Economics*, 6, Spring, 173–183.
Morton, F. M. S. (2002). 'Horizontal Integration between Brand and Generic Firms in the Pharmaceutical Industry,' *Journal of Economics and Management Strategy*, 11(1), 135–168.

BIBLIOGRAPHY
McDaniel, Stephen W., and Kolari, James W. (1987). 'Marketing Strategy Implications of the Miles and Snow Strategic Typology,' *Journal of Marketing*, 51(4), October, 19–30.

■ intellectual property

DESCRIPTION
Products of intellectual work that have commercial value.

KEY INSIGHTS
Firms engaged in creative endeavors, whether developing innovative new products or simply a new brand name, have a potential ownership stake in intellectual property. Major forms of intellectual property include *patents*, which are legal rights to exclude others from making, using, or selling some combination of elements that are new, useful, and unobvious; *copyrights*, which are protective legal rights covering literary, musical, and artistic works; *trademarks*, which are protective legal rights covering words, symbols, phrases, names, or other devices or combinations of such devices associated with ownership of a product or service, and *trade secrets*, which are processes, patterns, formulas, devices, information, and the like that are known only to their owner (or, in the case of a firm, the owner's employees). Trade secrets are often viewed as an alternative to the legal and public registration of intellectual property, where trade secrets have strategic and commercial value to the extent that they are not known or knowable to competitors of the firm.

KEY WORDS Property rights, legal protection

IMPLICATIONS
As much of marketing involves creative initiatives within an organization, marketers should seek to understand the many options available to

the firm for protecting and exploiting the firm's intellectual property. Just as importantly, marketers should seek to understand how and to what extent different options have potential benefits, costs, risks, and limitations for the firm from marketing, competitive, and legal standpoints.

APPLICATION AREAS AND FURTHER READINGS

Marketing Strategy

Borg, E. A. (2001). 'Knowledge, Information and Intellectual Property: Implications for Marketing Relationships,' *Technovation*, 21(8), 515–524.

Cohen, Dorothy (1991). 'Trademark Strategy Revisited,' *Journal of Marketing*, 5, July, 46–59.

Peterson, R. A., Smith, K. H., and Zerillo, P. C. (1999). 'Trademark Dilution and the Practice of Marketing,' *Journal of the Academy of Marketing Science*, 27(2), 255–268.

Miaoulis, G., and D'Amato, N. (1978). 'Consumer Confusion and Trademark Infringement,' *Journal of Marketing*, 42, 48–55.

BIBLIOGRAPHY

Ostergard, R. L. (2000). 'The Measurement of Intellectual Property Rights Protection,' *Journal of International Business Studies*, 31(2), 349–360.

Maskus, Keith (2000). *Intellectual Property Rights in the Global Economy*. Washington: Institute for International Economics.

☐ **intensive distribution** *see* distribution strategies

☐ **interactive marketing** *see* online marketing

☐ **interest** *see* adoption process

☐ **intermarket segmentation** *see* segmentation

☐ **intermediate good** *see* goods

■ internal marketing

DESCRIPTION

Marketing efforts within a firm that are directed at its internal stakeholders.

KEY INSIGHTS

Just as most firms recognize that marketing principles and practices enable a firm to accomplish marketplace objectives when they are directed at current and prospective customers and other external stakeholders, internal marketing is viewed as beneficial when a firm's management seeks to gain support for some initiative from its internal stakeholders (e.g. employees, organizational volunteers). Internal marketing therefore adopts the view that it is important to understand the needs and wants of internal stakeholders and that the firm should consider how communications and other elements of marketing (e.g. compensation, working conditions, job responsibilities) may be used to encourage such stakeholders to buy into what the firm's management has to offer. Unlike external offerings, however, the firm's internal offerings may consist of a new marketing strategy that the firm's management would like to pursue or a new programme that the firm would like to implement in support of a new or different marketing strategy.

KEY WORDS Employees, organizational buy-in

IMPLICATIONS

Marketing managers and strategists should not assume that their enthusiasm and commitment for new firm initiatives will be shared to the same extent with other internal stakeholders. To overcome resistance to change, management should consider developing and implementing internal marketing strategies that encourage appropriate organizational internal stakeholder buy-in to the marketer's proposed (or in-progress) strategies, plans, and tactics.

APPLICATION AREAS AND FURTHER READINGS

Marketing Strategy
Piercy, N., and Morgan N. (1991). 'Internal Marketing: The Missing Half of the Marketing Programme,' *Long Range Planning*, 24(2), 82–93.

Marketing Management
Piercy, N. (1995). 'Customer Satisfaction and the Internal Market: Marketing our Customers to our Employees,' *Journal of Marketing Practice and Applied Marketing Science*, 1(1), 22–44.
Bak, Constance A., Vogt, Leslie H., George, William R., and Greentree, I. Richard (1994). 'Management by Team: An Innovative Tool for Running a Service Organization through Internal Marketing,' *Journal of Services Marketing*, 8(1), 37–47.
George, William R. (1990). 'Internal Marketing and Organizational Behavior: A Partnership in Developing Customer-Conscious Employees at Every Level,' *Journal of Business Research*, 20(1), 63–70.

Services Marketing
Greene, W. E., Walls, G. D., and Schrest, L. J. (1994). 'Internal Marketing: The Key to External Marketing Success,' *Journal of Services Marketing*, 8(4), 5–13.

BIBLIOGRAPHY
Grönroos, C. (1985). 'Internal Marketing: Theory and Practice,' in T. M. Bloch, G. D. Upah, and V. A. Zeithaml (eds.), *Services Marketing in a Changing Environment*. Chicago: American Marketing Association, 41–47.

☐ **internal validity** *see* validity

■ **internalization theory**

DESCRIPTION

A theory aimed at explaining and predicting the growth and structure of multinational enterprise where internalization of imperfections in external markets across national boundaries is viewed as leading to the creation of multinational enterprises.

KEY INSIGHTS

Based on pioneering research by Buckley and Casson (1976), the development of internalization theory emphasizes the role of imperfections in intermediate product markets, such as those associated with knowledge, expertise, intellectual property, and human capital, in the creation of multinational enterprises (MNEs). Such market imperfections generate benefits of internalization. Furthermore, the theory suggests that internalization occurs only to the point where benefits equal the costs. While the internalization decision for a firm may be complex, it can be viewed as influenced by factors related to the industry, region, nation, and the firm. The theory therefore can be used to support suggestions including that where MNEs choose to set up subsidiaries to exploit technological advantages abroad as a result of licensing arrangements being too difficult with indigenous firms.

KEY WORDS Multinational enterprise, international operations

IMPLICATIONS

Internalization theory provides a rich set of concepts and perspectives with which to analyze current states of multinational enterprise and anticipate future states. Marketers may therefore aim to achieve relevant knowledge of particular firms, industries, regions, and nations to enable analyses supporting strategic decisions related to MNE structure and growth.

APPLICATION AREAS AND FURTHER READINGS

International Marketing

Doherty, A. M. (1999). 'Explaining International Retailers' Market Entry Mode Strategy: Internalization Theory, Agency Theory and the Importance of Information Asymmetry,' *International Review of Retail Distribution and Consumer Research*, 9(4), 379–402.

Buckley, P. J., and Casson, M. C. (1998). 'Analyzing Foreign Market Entry Strategies: Extending the Internalization Approach,' *Journal of International Business Studies*, 29(3), 539–562.

Chen, Shih-Fen S. (2005). 'Extending Internalization Theory: A New Perspective on International Technology Transfer and its Generalization,' *Journal of International Business Studies*, 36(2), March, 231–245.

BIBLIOGRAPHY

Buckley, Peter J., and Casson, M. C. (1976). *The Future of the Multinational Enterprise*. London: Macmillan.

Buckley, P. J., and Casson, M. C. (1998). 'Models of the Multinational Enterprise,' *Journal of International Business Studies*, 29(1), 21–44.

Rugman, A. M., and Verbeke, A. (2003). 'Extending the Theory of the Multinational Enterprise: Internalization and Strategic Management Perspectives,' *Journal of International Business Studies*, 34(2), 125–137.

■ international marketing

DESCRIPTION

Marketing concerned with developing and managing trade across international boundaries.

KEY INSIGHTS

While international marketing has much in common with cross-cultural marketing (see **cross-cultural marketing**) in its emphasis on spanning and/or bridging markets that differ in important broad respects, international marketing may involve efforts that span multiple countries but where countries do not differ significantly on a cultural dimension as much as on other characteristics (e.g. legal or economic dimensions). Nevertheless, international marketing is necessarily concerned with any and all country market differences that may ultimately influence the accomplishment of the firm's marketing objectives. As most firms do not initiate operations in multiple countries all at once but rather internationalize incrementally, a considerable amount of international marketing research is focused on criteria and approaches for expanding a firm's international market presence.

KEY WORDS Trade, country markets

IMPLICATIONS
While there are many major issues facing international marketers (e.g. assessments of country market attractiveness, international market distribution strategy development) an important broad issue facing many international marketers is the extent to which the firm's offerings should be standardardized across countries versus adapted to account for country-specific conditions. Given that such decisions may be influenced by both macroenvironmental and microenvironmental criteria, a greater knowledge of international marketing issues, frameworks, and methods may clearly assist the international marketer with more effective decision making.

APPLICATION AREAS AND FURTHER READINGS
Marketing Strategy
Szymanski, David M., Bharadwaj, Sundar G., and Varadarajan, P. Rajan (1993). 'Standardization versus Adaptation of International Marketing Strategy: An Empirical Investigation,' *Journal of Marketing*, 57(4), October, 1–17.

Marketing Management
Tse, David K., Lee, Kam-hon, Vertinsky, Ilan, and Wehrung, Donald A. (1988). 'Does Culture Matter? A Cross-cultural Study of Executives' Choice, Decisiveness, and Risk Adjustment in International Marketing,' *Journal of Marketing*, 52(4), October, 81–95.
Jain, S. (1990). *International Marketing Management*. Boston: Kent-PWS Publishing.

Online Marketing
Hamill, J. (1997). 'The Internet and International Marketing,' *International Marketing Review*, 14(4/5), 300–323.

International Marketing
Kaynak, Erdener (1999). 'Cross-national and Cross-cultural Issues in Food Marketing: Past, Present and Future,' *Journal of International Food and Agribusiness Marketing*, 10(4), 1–11.

BIBLIOGRAPHY
Onkvisit, S., and Shaw, J. (2004). *International Marketing: Analysis and Strategy*. London: Routledge.
Terpstra, V., and Sarathy, R. (2000). *International Marketing*. Fort Worth: Dryden Press.
Czinkota, M. R., and Ronkainen, I. A. (1993). *International Marketing*, 3rd edn. Fort Worth: Dryden Press.
Hofstede, Geert H. (1980). *Culture's Consequences: International Differences in Work-Related Values*. Beverly Hills, Calif.: Sage Publications.

☐ internet-centric marketing *see* online marketing
☐ internet marketing *see* online marketing

■ intertemporal substitution

DESCRIPTION
The extent to which similar goods offered at different times can take the place of each other.

KEY INSIGHTS
Products or services may be characterized by varying intertemporal substitutability among consumers. In the case of air fares to a travel destination being higher on weekdays and lower on weekends, for example, intertemporal substitutability is lower for a consumer flying to a business meeting than for a leisure traveler. High intertemporal substitutability for a product or service may thus lead consumers to delay purchase or consumption of an offering to a time that is more favorable, such as where travel to the same destination can be made off-peak at a lower price.

KEY WORDS Time, substitutability

IMPLICATIONS
When a product or service is offered to consumers at an array of times, marketers should seek to understand how and to what extent such offerings are intertemporally substitutable among consumers in order to explain and predict consumer demand to a greater extent. Such knowledge can have important implications for price setting involving services that vary regularly in both supply and demand, for example, as when daily train commuters with little time flexibility are more resigned to paying higher fares on weekday mornings.

APPLICATION AREAS AND FURTHER READINGS
Consumer Behavior
Winer, Russell S. (1997). 'Discounting and its Impact on Durables Buying Decisions,' *Marketing Letters*, 8(1), 109–118.

Marketing Research
Hartmann, Wesley R. (2006). 'Intertemporal Effects of Consumption and their Implications for Demand Elasticity Estimates,' *Quantitative Marketing and Economics*, 4(4), December, 325–349.

BIBLIOGRAPHY
Hendel, I., and Nevo, A. (2004). 'Intertemporal Substitution and Storable Products,' *Journal of European Economic Association*, 2(2–3), 536–547.

☐ interval scale *see* scale
☐ introduction stage *see* product life cycle

■ intrusive marketing

DESCRIPTION

Exposing consumers to marketing without their permission or invitation.

KEY INSIGHTS

Intrusive marketing may involve any number of specific marketing approaches which are aimed at current or prospective consumers without their consent and which may be perceived by a consumer as an invasion of privacy. Outbound telemarketing is intrusive as it encroaches on an individual's privacy when it involves calling a consumer at his or her residence and where the consumer must listen at least for a moment to the caller's message. Free newspapers delivered to one's door are intrusive as the consumer must inevitably pick them up to read or toss. In out-of-home marketing, intrusive marketing may take the form of flat panel television screens running a series of advertisements that a consumer cannot help but watch while standing in line at a shop waiting for service.

KEY WORDS Uninvited marketing, unwelcome communication

IMPLICATIONS

Intrusive marketing's aim is to get in the way of the consumer so as to capture the consumer's attention. In some cases, approaches may involve forms of direct marketing (see **direct marketing**) or out-of-home marketing where marketing messages, either through sight or sound, are displayed or broadcast in places that consumers happen to be and where they cannot help but be exposed to them. In many instances, such marketing communications may be unwelcome to a consumer but the consumer may nevertheless tolerate it. Marketers seeking to reach consumers through an intrusive marketing approach must therefore give consideration to how such communications may be received by the target audience, lest they become turned off or tuned out prematurely to the marketer's message. On a larger scale, marketers must be concerned about the possibility of a consumer backlash against a particular intrusive marketing approach.

APPLICATION AREAS AND FURTHER READINGS

Marketing Strategy

Rowe, W. G., and Barnes, J. G. (1998). 'Relationship Marketing and Sustained Competitive Advantage,' *Journal of Market Focused Management*, 2(3), 281–292.

Marketing Management

Hackley, C. E., and Kitchen, P. J. (1999). 'Ethical Perspectives on the Postmodern Communications Leviathan,' *Journal of Business Ethics*, 20(1), 15–26.

Cohn, E., and Zengerle, J. (1997). 'Devil in the Details,' *American Prospect*, 35, 14–17.

Marketing Research

Day, G. S., and Montgomery, D. B. (1999). 'Charting New Directions for Marketing,' *Journal of Marketing*, 63(1), 3–13.

Mobile Marketing

Unni, R., and Harmon, R. (2003). 'Location-Based Services: Models for Strategy Development in M-Commerce,' in *Proceedings of the Portland International Conference on Management of Engineering and Technology (PICMET'03)*, 416–424.

BIBLIOGRAPHY
Brown, D. J., and Browne, B. A. (1998). 'Vulnerability and Attitudes toward Intrusive Marketing,' *Psychological Reports*, 83(33), 1348–1350.

■ isolation effect

DESCRIPTION
A tendency in individual evaluations of alternatives where an individual generally disregards components that the alternatives share and focuses on the components that distinguish them.

KEY INSIGHTS
Based on pioneering research by Tversky (1972) and Kahneman and Tversky (1979), the isolation effect is a phenomenon that stems from people's need or desire to simplify the choice between alternatives. Such an approach to choice problems may, however, result in inconsistent preferences to the extent that alternatives are able to be decomposed into common and distinctive components in more than one way, with different decompositions thereby leading to potentially different preferences.

NOTE
The isolation effect as described here should not be confused with the Restorff effect or von Restorff effect, which is also referred to as the isolation effect. (See **von Restorff effect**.)

KEY WORDS Alternative evaluation, choice

IMPLICATIONS
Whether marketer or consumer, individuals evaluating alternatives are prone to the isolation effect. As a result, there is potential for bias in evaluations of alternatives where individuals tend to overly focus on features that differentiate alternatives and under-focus on features that the alternatives share, even if the shared features have an important influence on the desirability of, or satisfaction with, the outcome associated with the evaluation. Consumers evaluating risk in financial products may, for example, not give sufficient attention to the degree of risk that is common to all alternatives examined, instead overly focusing on differentiating features. Marketers concerned with alternative evaluations should therefore be aware of potential biasing tendencies and strive to provide greater attention to important features shared by all alternatives. Similarly, marketers seeking to understand better how consumers evaluate alternatives should be aware of such tendencies in consumer behavior. Such tendencies in alternative evaluations may, for example, lead to consumers considering two similar products to view one product more favorably if it is placed next to a more expensive alternative.

APPLICATION AREAS AND FURTHER READINGS
Marketing Strategy
Tellis, Gerard J. (1986). 'Beyond the Many Faces of Price: An Integration of Pricing Strategies,' *Journal of Marketing*, 50(4), October, 146–160.

Consumer Behavior
Byrne, K. (2005). 'How do Consumers Evaluate Risk in Financial Products?' *Journal of Financial Services Marketing*, 10(1), 21–36.

BIBLIOGRAPHY
Kahneman, Daniel, and Tversky, Amos (1979). 'Prospect Theory: An Analysis of Decision under Risk,' *Econometrica*, 47, 263–292.
Tversky, Amos (1972). 'Elimination by Aspects: A Theory of Choice,' *Psychological Review*, 79, 281–299.

■ item response theory

(also called latent trait theory)

DESCRIPTION
A theoretical approach to the scaling of items and persons based on responses to items contained within assessments or other related data collection instruments.

KEY INSIGHTS
An item response theory-based approach to measurement and analysis is based on the assumption that the probabilities of responses to items are joint functions of individual characteristics as well as other items. A benefit of the approach is that it not only facilitates the development of formal data collection instruments but allows more systematic comparisons of results over successive occasions of use.

KEY WORDS Measurement, response, items

IMPLICATIONS
Item response theory provides a basis for the development and evaluation of a range of data collection instruments including surveys and tests. The theory enables marketing scales to be developed and appropriately interpreted as well.

APPLICATION AREAS AND FURTHER READINGS
Marketing Research
Singh, Jagdip, Howell, Roy D., and Rhoads, Gary K. (1990). 'Adaptive Designs for Likert-Type Data: An Approach for Implementing Marketing Surveys,' *Journal of Marketing Research*, 27(3), August, 304–321.
Salzberger, T., Sinkovics, R. R., and Schlegelmilch, B. B. (1999). 'Data Equivalence in Cross-Cultural Research: A Comparison of Classical Test Theory and Latent Trait Theory Based Approaches,' *Australasian Marketing Journal*, 7(2), 23–38.

BIBLIOGRAPHY
Sijtsma, Klaas, and Molenaar, Ivo W. (2002). *Introduction to Non-parametric Item Response Theory*. London: Sage Publications.
DeVellis, R. F. (2003). 'Scale Development Theory and Applications Second Edition,' *Applied Social Research Methods Series*, 26(2).
Lord, F. M. (1980). *Applications of Item Response Theory to Practical Testing Problems*. Hillsdale, NJ: Lawrence Erlbaum Associates, Inc.

J

☐ JND *see* Weber–Fechner law

■ job characteristics theory

DESCRIPTION
Theory relating job design to work motivation, satisfaction, and performance.

KEY INSIGHTS
Job characteristics theory as originally developed by Hackman and Old-ham (1976) views the relationship between job characteristics and their outcomes as a three-stage model where certain job characteristics ultimately lead to certain end states of motivation and satisfaction. More specifically, job characteristics such as skill variety, task significance, task identity, autonomy, and feedback are viewed as contributing to certain intermediate psychological states including experienced meaningfulness, experienced responsibility, and knowledge of results. These psychological states, in turn, act to influence outcomes including satisfaction, growth satisfaction, and motivation. Such views have subsequently stimulated a wide range of studies on job characteristics including those aimed at evaluating the relationships involved in the above factors as well as the inclusion and influences of other factors into broader job characteristics-related theory such as work pressure and its effects.

While similar in terminology, job characteristics theory is not to be confused with goods-characterstics theory. (See **characteristics theory**.)

KEY WORDS Job design, satisfaction, motivation, performance

IMPLICATIONS
Marketers involved in job design can potentially benefit from understanding the concepts and relationships suggested in job characteristics theory if the aim of a job's design is to achieve high levels of job satisfaction, motivation, and performance. Whether a job involves individual performance or team performance, the theory may potentially provide insights into more effective designs for a range of marketing functions and jobs.

APPLICATION AREAS AND FURTHER READINGS
Marketing Management
Hartline, Michael D., and Ferrell, O. C. (1996). 'The Management of Customer-Contact Service Employees: An Empirical Investigation,' *Journal of Marketing*, 60(4), October, 52–70.

Emery, Charles R., and Fredendall, Lawrence D. (2002). 'The Effect of Teams on Firm Profitability and Customer Satisfaction,' *Journal of Service Research*, 4(3), 217–229.

Simon, W., Vickie, S., and Nelson, T. (1999). 'The Impact of Demographic Factors on Hong Kong Hotel Employees' Choice of Job-Related Motivators,' *International Journal of Contemporary Hospitality Management*, 11(5), 230—241.

BIBLIOGRAPHY

Hackman, J. R., and Oldham G. R. (1976). 'Motivation through the Design of Work: Test of a Theory,' *Organizational Behavior and Human Performance*, 16, 250–279.

Hackman, J. R., and Oldham, G. R. (1980). *Work Redesign*. Reading, Mass.: Addison-Wesley.

■ John Henry effect

DESCRIPTION

A possible adverse experimental effect where the actions and outcomes of members of a control group are influenced by members' knowledge of an experiment involving an experimental group where specifically, the control group members engage in competing with the experimental group in an effort to obtain increased performance.

KEY INSIGHTS

Named after a worker who outperformed a machine because he knew his performance was being compared to the machine, the John Henry effect is a potential threat to the internal validity in experiments where control of control groups is an issue. While an experimenter may wish to simply compare the performance of one means of accomplishing a task with another to assess the extent of difference if any, individuals involved in accomplishing the task by the original means may feel threatened by the new approach and become competitive, thereby increasing their performance to levels not normally achieved. The effect is also referred to by some as a reverse-Hawthorne effect.

KEY WORDS Experiments, control

IMPLICATIONS

Marketers involved in the development and testing of new means to accomplish tasks involving individuals or teams (e.g. in comparing the efficiency of a bank teller with an automated teller for certain complex transactions) may wish to consider the possibility of the John Henry effect potentially confounding the results of a study. Carefully controlling conditions so as to eliminate or compensate the effect should be considered, as where individuals or teams have no knowledge of efforts to compare different methods for accomplishing a task.

APPLICATION AREAS AND FURTHER READINGS

Marketing Education

Phipps, Ronald, and Merisotis, Jamie (1999). 'What's the Difference? A Review of Educational Research on the Effectiveness of Distance Learning in Higher Education,' *Report Prepared for the American Federation of Teachers*. Washington: Institute for Higher Education Policy.

Zdep, S. M., and Irvine, S. H. (1970) 'A Reverse Hawthorne Effect in Educational Evaluation,' *Journal of School Psychology*, 8, 89–95.

BIBLIOGRAPHY
Saretsky, Gary (1975). 'The John Henry Effect: Potential Confounder of Experimental vs. Control Group Approaches to the Evaluation of Educational Innovations,' *The Education Resources Information Center (ERIC)*, sponsored by the Institute of Education Sciences of the US Department of Education.

☐ joint marketing *see* cooperative marketing
☐ Jost's law *see* forgetting curve
☐ junk e-mail marketing *see* mass marketing; viral marketing
☐ jury method *see* forecasting methods
☐ just noticeable difference *see* Weber-Fechner law

■ just world hypothesis

(also called the just world effect or the just world phenomenon)

DESCRIPTION
The tendency for people to falsely believe that the world is essentially fair and just, with the result being that people get what they deserve.

KEY INSIGHTS
With the just world hypothesis, people believe that the good will be rewarded and the bad will be punished. The view also leads to people who suffer misfortunes to blame themselves. Conceptually developed by Lerner (1965), the view is usually explained as a result of an illusion of control.

KEY WORDS Attributions, justice, control

IMPLICATIONS
As the view of the world being just is a relatively widespread belief among individuals, marketers must recognize that individuals may hold biased and false perspectives about the causes and consequences of events. Such a view may reinforce a belief that nothing bad should happen to a person who does nothing wrong as well as that persons who experience misfortunes must have done something wrong to deserve it. (See **blaming the victim.**) Carrying such a view over to individual and collective consumption behaviors, consumers may hold false beliefs about both causes of consumption problems as well as solutions to consumption problems. Particularly in the context of social marketing, marketers seeking to influence such beliefs and encourage rational thought and action can understand better consumer motivations and tendencies with further knowledge of the phenomenon characterized by the just world hypothesis.

APPLICATION AREAS AND FURTHER READINGS

Social Marketing

Belk, Russell, Painter, John, and Semenik, Richard (1981). 'Preferred Solutions to the Energy Crisis as a Function of Causal Attributions,' *Journal of Consumer Research*, 8(3), December, 306–312.

Devine, P. G., Plant, E. A., and Harrison, K. (1999). 'The Problem of "Us" Versus "Them" and AIDS Stigma,' *American Behavioural Scientist*, 42(7), 1212–1228.

BIBLIOGRAPHY

Lerner, M. J. (1965). 'Evaluation of Performance and Reward as a Function of Performer's Reward and Attractiveness,' *Journal of Personality and Social Psychology*, 1, 355–360.

Lerner, M. J., and Miller, Donald T. (1978). 'Just World Research and the Attribution Process: Looking Back and Ahead,' *Psychological Bulletin*, 85, 1030–1051.

K

■ key success factors

(also abbreviated as KSFs)

DESCRIPTION
Any asset or competence that is needed to compete successfully in the marketplace.

KEY INSIGHTS
Key success factors are those that any firm in a particular market should possess in order to be a viable competitor in the market. Thus, when introducing a new product into an existing market, the success of the introduction may hinge on the extent to which the firm has certain assets and competencies that enable it to compete successfully. Assets forming KSFs may include a strong brand name and financial resources. Competencies forming KSFs may include personal selling competence or online marketing competence. More specific uses of the key success factors term are also found in relation to particular aspects of marketing such as new product development.

KEY WORDS Marketplace competitiveness, firm success

IMPLICATIONS
Marketers should consider understanding key success factors to be an essential input to marketing strategy development. For example, in being able to compete successfully in the e-commerce marketplace, marketers should recognize that KSFs include abilities such as being able to monitor and track individual buying behavior and motivations and being able to tailor the firm's marketing to individual customers.

APPLICATION AREAS AND FURTHER READINGS
Marketing Strategy
Di Benedetto, C. A. (1999). 'Identifying the Key Success Factors in New Product Launch,' *Journal of Product Innovation Management*, 16, 530–544.

Retail Marketing
Dupuis, M., and Prime, N. (1996). 'Business Distance and Global Retailing: A Model for Analysis of Key Success/Failure Factors,' *International Journal of Retail and Distribution Management*, 24(11), 30–38.

Business-to-Business Marketing
De Vasconcellos, J. A. (1991). 'Key Success Factors in Marketing Mature Products,' *Industrial Marketing Management*, 20, 263–278.

Marketing Research
Grunert, K. G., and Ellegaard, C. (1992). 'The Concept of Key Success Factors: Theory and Method,' in M. J. Baker (ed.), *Perspectives on Marketing Management*. Chichester: Wiley, iii. 245–274.

Mobile Marketing
Facchetti, A., Rangone, A., Renga, F. A., and Savoldelli, A. (2005). 'Mobile Marketing: An Analysis of Key Success Factors and the European Value Chain,' *International Journal of Management and Decision Making*, 6(1), 65–80.

BIBLIOGRAPHY
Sa, Jorge Alberto Sousa de Vasconcellos E., and Hambrick, Donald C. (1989). 'Key Success Factors: Test of a General Theory in the Mature Industrial-Product Sector,' *Strategic Management Journal*, 10(4), July–August, 367–382.

☐ **knowledge** *see* buyer influence/readiness
☐ **KSFs** *see* key success factors

L

■ laddering

DESCRIPTION
A knowledge acquisition technique where the core attributes and values that drive the consumer of a product are identified through a form of in-depth interview.

KEY INSIGHTS
The laddering technique aims to establish underlying motivations for the purchase of an offering (e.g. a product) by asking a consumer why he or she buys the product and then, given the response, asking 'why' to that response and each subsequent response until the respondent can no longer provide an explanation. The approach therefore enables a marketer to understand why the consumer *really* buys the product.

KEY WORDS Interviewing, in-depth interviewing, purchase drivers

IMPLICATIONS
The laddering technique can be very useful to marketing researchers conducting in-depth interviews of product consumers or service users to understand the real drivers behind product or service purchase. Marketers must exercise caution, however, to ensure that interviewees are sufficiently comfortable with such lines of questioning.

APPLICATION AREAS AND FURTHER READINGS
Marketing Research
Reynolds, Thomas J., and Gutman, Jonathan (1988). 'Laddering Theory, Method, Analysis, and Interpretation,' *Journal of Advertising Research*, 28(1) February–March, 11–31.
Grunert, K. G., and Grunert, S. C. (1995). 'Measuring Subjective Meaning Structures by the Laddering Method: Theoretical Considerations and Methodological Problems,' *International Journal of Research in Marketing*, 12(3), October, 209–225.
Hofstede, F. T., Audenaert, A., Steenkamp, J. B. E. M., and Wedel, M. (1998). 'An Investigation into the Association Pattern Technique as a Quantitative Approach to Measuring Means-End Chains,' *International Journal of Research in Marketing*, 15(1), February, 37–50.

Marketing Strategy
Reynolds, T. J., and Whitlark, D. B. (1995). 'Applying Laddering Data to Communications Strategy and Advertising Practice,' *Journal of Advertising Research*, 35(4), 9.

BIBLIOGRAPHY
Wansink, B. (2000). 'New Techniques to Generate Key Marketing Insights,' *Marketing Research*, 12(2), 28—36.

☐ laggards *see adopter categories*

■ lagged effect

(also called lagged response or delayed response effect)

DESCRIPTION
Any delay in time between an action and its intended effect.

KEY INSIGHTS
Lagged effects represent a lack of synchronism between cause and effect. In the context of consumer purchase as the intended effect for which there is a delay in its occurrence, reasons for why the effect is not always immediate and fully realized in the period for which the change takes place include: delays in response, as when there is a delay in execution of a marketing action, a delay in the time the marketing action is observed by a consumer, a delay in a consumer's decision to purchase, or a delay in fulfillment of a customer order; customer holdover effects where marketing actions have an effect which carries over to periods beyond the period of study; and anticipatory response effects, such as consumer anticipation of a marketing action (e.g. a delay in sales due to an anticipated price reduction).

KEY WORDS Delay, lag time, effect

IMPLICATIONS
Marketers will invariably face lags in the time between marketing actions and the action's effects. Marketers should consider the various causes of lagged effects to ensure realistic planning and implementation as well to be able to proactively take action to control and reduce undesirable delays. Marketers should also consider how current marketing actions may be affected by earlier marketing actions (e.g. previous advertising campaigns) which have produced lagged effects as well.

APPLICATION AREAS AND FURTHER READINGS
Advertising
Bass, Frank M., and Clarke, Darral G. (1972). 'Testing Distributed Lag Models of Advertising Effect,' *Journal of Marketing Research*, 9(3), August, 298–308.

Marketing Modeling
Weinberg, Charles B. (1976). 'Dynamic Correction in Marketing Planning Models,' *Management Science*, 22(6), February, 677–687.
Doyle, Peter, and Saunders, John (1985). 'The Lead Effect of Marketing Decisions,' *Journal of Marketing Research*, 22(1), February, 54–65.

BIBLIOGRAPHY
Kotler, P. (1971). *Marketing Decision Making: A Model Building Approach*. New York: Holt, Rinehart & Winston.

☐ **lagged response** *see* **lagged effect**
☐ **Lancaster's characteristics theory** *see* **characteristics theory**

■ large numbers, law of

DESCRIPTION
A principle of probability and statistics which indicates that the average of a random sample of a population is increasingly likely to be close to the mean of the population as the sample size becomes increasingly large.

KEY INSIGHTS
The law of large numbers enables conclusions, such as estimates and forecasts, to be drawn about populations based on random samples. More specifically, as the number in a sample increases, the more likely it will be that the estimate obtained, i.e. the average of the sample, will reflect the actual value for the larger population, including that for what is not measured.

KEY WORDS Sampling, probabilities, statistical analysis

IMPLICATIONS
Marketers involved in making forecasts and estimates from random samples can understand better to what extent findings are likely to be representative of larger populations based on the statistical principle embodied in the law of large numbers. The law also provides insight into appropriate sample design in support of marketing research and marketing model development for new marketing initiatives including online marketing.

APPLICATION AREAS AND FURTHER READINGS
Marketing Modeling
Bakos, Yannis, and Brynjolfsson, Erik (1999). 'Bundling Information Goods: Pricing, Profits, and Efficiency,' *Management Science*, 45(12), December, 1613–1630.

Online Marketing
Bakos, Yannis (2001). 'The Emerging Landscape for Retail E-commerce,' *Journal of Economic Perspectives*, 15(1), Winter, 69–80.
Bakos, Y., and Brynjolfsson, E. (2000). 'Bundling and Competition on the Internet,' *Marketing Science*, 19(1), 63–82.

BIBLIOGRAPHY
Grimmett, G. R., and Stirzaker, D. R. (1992). *Probability and Random Processes*, 2nd edn. Oxford: Clarendon Press.

☐ late follower *see* market entry timing
☐ late majority *see* adopter categories
☐ late response bias *see* bias
☐ latent demand *see* demand
☐ latent trait theory *see* item response theory
☐ later market entrant *see* market entry timing

■ lateral marketing

DESCRIPTION

A marketing approach involving exploration and creativity in the restructuring of a good by adding needs, uses, situations, or targets that would otherwise be unreachable without the appropriate changes.

KEY INSIGHTS

Developed by Kotler and de Bes (2003) in a book by the same name, the approach emphasizes the opportunity for a firm's offerings to reach beyond its current boundaries. An example is that of organic food, which is defined based on specially labelled and regulated products. If firms in the organic food industry were to claim and build upon a 'well-being' positioning, the organic food industry could aim to develop new products, uses, and situations that might not only add to industry sales volume but might also lessen their cannibalization with existing organic food offerings.

KEY WORDS Repositioning, product repositioning, creativity

IMPLICATIONS

Marketers looking for ways to move the firm's offerings beyond their traditional boundaries may benefit from a greater understanding of the lateral marketing approach and its associated exploration-based and creativity-based methods. In using the approach to reposition and restructure their offerings, marketers may identify not only multiple new repositioning directions but also particular ones that potentially provide the firm with higher growth prospects than that constrained by the firm's current offerings.

APPLICATION AREAS AND FURTHER READINGS

Marketing Strategy
Fodness, Dale (2005). 'Rethinking Strategic Marketing: Achieving Breakthrough Results,' *Journal of Business Strategy*, 26(3), 20–34.

Marketing Research
Abubakar, Binta, and Austin, Nathan (2006). 'An Exploratory Analysis for the Modeling of Effective Marketing in Sensitive Historical Sites: The Consortium,' *Journal of Hospitality and Tourism*, 10(1), 5–19.

BIBLIOGRAPHY
Kotler, Philip, and de Bes, Fernando Trías (2003). *Lateral Marketing: New Techniques for Finding Breakthrough Ideas*. New York: John Wiley & Sons.

☐ law(s) of . . . *see specific entries, e.g.* diminishing returns, law of

☐ leadership strategy *see* decline strategies

☐ lean-over marketing *see* stealth marketing

■ leapfrogging

DESCRIPTION

Strategic action involving the skipping of a strategic move that is inferior, less efficient, or more costly than that of a subsequent strategic move adopted.

KEY INSIGHTS

Given the steady or rapid pace of technological change affecting many markets today, some firms, organizations, and even countries that have (intentionally or unintentionally) not kept up with more nimble competitors who are continually adopting the latest technology may find their organizations are in a position to bypass the adoption of certain technologies altogether and embrace instead a more advanced technology that is superior, more efficient, or less costly than that currently adopted by competitors. In this sense, the organization is said to be engaged in a process of technological leapfrogging over competitors. Leapfrogging as a strategy is not necessarily limited to that of technological influence, however.

KEY WORDS Competitive strategy, strategic moves

IMPLICATIONS

While opportunities for leapfrogging clearly vary depending on the rate and extent of change of technological and other factors, and factors internal to the organization as well, the approach as a strategy is something that marketers in organizations operating in a dynamic marketing environment need to give careful consideration to if the aim is to remain competitive over the longer term. The long-term evolution of many markets is such that leapfrogging may enable currently weak competitors to become future strong competitors in terms of their processes used, their offerings, or both.

APPLICATION AREAS AND FURTHER READINGS

Marketing Strategy

Morgan, R. E., and Hunt, S. D. (2002). 'Determining Marketing Strategy: A Cybernetic Systems Approach to Scenario Planning,' *European Journal of Marketing*, 36(4), 450–478.

Glazer, Rashi, and Weiss, Allen M. (1993). 'Marketing in Turbulent Environments: Decision Processes and the Time-Sensitivity of Information,' *Journal of Marketing Research*, 30(4), November, 509–521.

Marketing Research

Danaher, P. J., Hardie, B. G. S., and Putsis, W. P. (2001). 'Marketing-Mix Variables and the Diffusion of Successive Generations of a Technological Innovation,' *Journal of Marketing Research*, 38(4), 501–514.

John, George, Weiss, Allen M., and Dutta, Shantanu (1999). 'Marketing in Technology-Intensive Markets: Toward a Conceptual Framework,' *Journal of Marketing*, 63, Fundamental Issues and Directions for Marketing, 78–91.

Chen, Y., Narasimhan, C., and Zhang, Z. J. (2001). 'Individual Marketing with Imperfect Targetability,' *Marketing Science*, 20(1), 23–41.

BIBLIOGRAPHY

Weiss, Allen M., and John, George (1989). *Leapfrogging Behavior and the Purchase of Industrial Innovations: Theory and Evidence*. Cambridge, Mass.: Marketing Science Institute.

■ learning curve effect

DESCRIPTION

The systematic positive effect on human performance of accumulated learning through practice.

KEY INSIGHTS

Developed in pioneering research by Thurstone (1919), the learning curve effect emphasizes the view that systematic changes in human performance as a result of accumulations in learning can be mathematically examined and graphically illustrated. Depiction of the systematic effects of learning is typically through a graph of accumulated learning on the x-axis and some performance measure on the y-axis. Performance may be measured any number of ways including time it takes to complete a task or the number of errors made in performing a task, both of which would be shown to systematically decrease with cumulative learning as indicated over time or the number of tasks performed.

The learning curve effect may also be described through a percentage term for a given performance measure, as where an 80% learning curve for the time to complete a task means that the average time to complete the task falls to 80% of the previous average for every doubling in the number of tasks completed.

The learning curve concept is closely related to the experience curve concept in that both emphasize the change that occurs with learning. Unlike the experience curve effect, however, the learning curve effect refers to changes in the performance of individuals or, more broadly, organizations through learning, whereas the experience curve more often than not relates to the context of changes in production outcomes as a result of accumulated production experience, which may be due in part to a learning curve effect among production workers. (See **experience curve effect**.)

KEY WORDS Learning, performance, individuals, organizations

IMPLICATIONS

As marketers are engaged in a process of encouraging consumers to learn about their brands, products, and services, the learning curve effect has relevance for the development and design of marketing communications aimed at systematically increasing a consumer's learning about the marketer's offerings which enables the consumer to respond more effectively to the offerings. In addition, learning within the marketing manager's own organization becomes an issue when the organization seeks to be able to respond better and faster to information originating from outside the organization including that from the firm's own customers (e.g. responding to customer complaints).

APPLICATION AREAS AND FURTHER READINGS

Marketing Research

Balachander, Subramanian, and Srinivasan, Kannan (1998). 'Modifying Customer Expectations of Price Decreases for a Durable Product,' *Management Science*, 44(6), June, 776–786.

Marketing Management
Lapre, M. A., and Tsikriktsis, N. (2006). 'Organizational Learning Curves for Customer Dissatisfaction: Heterogeneity across Airlines,' *Management Science*, 52(3), 352–366.
Argote, Linda, Beckman, Sara L., and Epple, Dennis (1990). 'The Persistence and Transfer of Learning in Industrial Settings,' *Management Science*, 36(2), February, 140–154.

BIBLIOGRAPHY
Thurstone, L. L. (1919). 'The Learning Curve Equation,' *Psychological Monographs*, 26, 1–51.

■ learning theory

DESCRIPTION
Theory or theories aimed at explaining the individual learning process.

KEY INSIGHTS
There are multiple theories of learning, including those characterized by constructivism and behaviorism. Constructivism is where a learner is viewed as constructing ideas based upon past and current knowledge. Behaviorism is where a learner is viewed as being conditioned to learn as a result of environmental reinforcement or punishment. There are also more specialized theories of learning such as Hullian learning theory as developed by Hull (1943), which elaborately relates concepts including work, energy, reinforcement, and response. While the aim of all such theories is to help understand and explain the process of learning, the diversity of learning approaches and contexts makes any particular learning theory difficult to generalize.

KEY WORDS Learning processes, individuals

IMPLICATIONS
Theoretical perspectives on learning continue to attract the interest and attention of marketers as such perspectives can often provide unique insights into how marketing activities can be developed and implemented to enhance consumer learning about the marketer's offerings. While there are multiple theoretical approaches, marketers can nevertheless aim to understand better such approaches, particularly when their views are argued to be relevant to particular marketing activities such as sales promotions or advertising.

APPLICATION AREAS AND FURTHER READINGS
Learning
Kolb, David A., Boyatzis, Richard E., and Mainemelis, Charalampos (2000). 'Experiential Learning: Previous Research and New Directions,' in R. J. Sternberg and L. F. Zhang (eds.), *Perspectives on Cognitive, Learning, and Thinking Styles*. Mahwah, NJ: Lawrence Erlbaum Associates.

Marketing Communications
Rothschild, Michael L., and Gaidis, William C. (1981). 'Behavioral Learning Theory: Its Relevance to Marketing and Promotions,' *Journal of Marketing*, 45(2), Spring, 70–78.

Weiss, R. F. (1968). 'An Extension of Hullian Learning Theory to Persuasive Communication,' in A. G. Greenwald, T. C. Brock, and T. M. Ostrum (eds.), *Psychological Foundations of Attitudes*. New York: Academic Press.

BIBLIOGRAPHY
Ormrod, J. E. (2003). *Educational Psychology: Developing Learners*, 4th edn. Upper Saddle River, NJ: Merrill-Prentice Hall.
Skinner, B. F. (1938). *The Behavior of Organisms: An Experimental Analysis*. New York: Appleton-Century.
Hull, C. L. (1943). *Principles of Behavior*. New York: Appleton-Century-Crofts.

■ least effort, principle of

DESCRIPTION
The view that in an individual's efforts to achieve a goal, the individual will generally seek a method involving the minimum expenditure of effort or energy.

KEY INSIGHTS
The principle of least effort has been put forth in contexts including human ecology (Zipf 1949), cognitive processes (Allport 1954), and, most recently, information search (Mann 1987). While each of these contexts shares the same general view of individuals minimizing their effort when striving to achieve their goals, the differing contexts suggest different methods of goal achievement. Mann (1987), for example, considers the principle in the context of search approaches, and therefore emphasizes that individuals will tend to use the most convenient search method and in the least exacting mode available.

KEY WORDS Behavior, effort, individuals

IMPLICATIONS
The principle of least effort is of considerable importance to marketers since it suggests consumers will tend to follow the path of least resistance in their search and purchase behaviors, all else being equal. Minimizing consumer search effort and maximizing convenience and ease of use (e.g. in terms of physical distance traveled or time required to find sought-after information) can therefore be strategic aims of marketers who seek to take advantage of consumers' systematic tendencies to minimize effort and energy in their goals to be satisfied.

APPLICATION AREAS AND FURTHER READINGS
Consumer Behavior
Woods, Walter A. (1960). 'Psychological Dimensions of Consumer Decision,' *Journal of Marketing*, 24(3), January, 15–19.
Hubbard, Raymond (1978). 'A Review of Selected Factors Conditioning Consumer Travel Behavior,' *Journal of Consumer Research*, 5(1), June, 1–21.
Larsen, Otto N., and De Fleur, Melvin L. (1987). *The Flow of Information*. New Brunwick, NJ: Transaction Publishers.

BIBLIOGRAPHY
Zipf, G. K. (1949). *Human Behaviour and the Principle of Least Effort: An Introduction to Human Ecology*, 1st edn. Hafner reprint, New York: Addison-Wesley.

Allport, G. W. (1954). *The Nature of Prejudice*. Cambridge, Mass.: Addison-Wesley.
Mann, Thomas (1987). *A Guide to Library Research Methods*. Oxford: Oxford University Press.

■ least interest, principle of

DESCRIPTION

A principle stating that the person who is the least interested in the continuation of a relationship is able to dictate the conditions of association.

KEY INSIGHTS

Put forth and developed by Waller (1938), the principle of least interest suggests that power in any relationship lies with the least interested individual. The principle also suggests that such an individual is in a position to exploit those most interested in the relationship's continuation. As such, the principle can be considered to be a generalized view of what Ross (1921) termed the 'law of personal exploitation,' namely, that 'in any sentimental relation, the one who cares less can exploit the one who cares more.' While such views originated in a sociological context, they have since been extended to contexts beyond marital relationships to provide insights into areas including effective working relationships and bargaining.

KEY WORDS Exchange relationships, power

IMPLICATIONS

Marketers concerned with understanding or evaluating the nature of power in any exchange relationship may benefit from a greater knowledge of the principle of least interest. In particular, the principle suggests that power depends on the relative interests of parties to an exchange relationship. As such, the principle can be viewed as applicable in explaining power in exchange relationships occurring not only at the level of the individual but also the level of the organization as well as the level of broader economic or political entities such as nations where exchange relationships are present.

APPLICATION AREAS AND FURTHER READINGS

Marketing Management

Anderson, James C., and Narus, James A. (1984). 'A Model of the Distributor's Perspective of Distributor–Manufacturer Working Relationships,' *Journal of Marketing*, 48(4), Autumn, 62–74.

Cook, Karen S., and Emerson, Richard M. (1978). 'Power, Equity and Commitment in Exchange Networks,' *American Sociological Review*, 43(5), October, 721–739.

Marketing Research

Beniger, James R. (1980). 'Using the Principle of Least Interest to Derive a Dominance Hierarchy from Interaction or Exchange Data,' *American Statistical Association*, Proceedings of the Survey Research Methods Section (SRMS).

Consumer Behavior

Webster, C., and Reiss, M. C. (2001). 'Do Established Antecedents of Purchase Decision-Making Power Apply to Contemporary Couples?,' *Psychology and Marketing*, 18(9), 951–972.

BIBLIOGRAPHY
Waller, W. (1938). *The Family: A Dynamic Interpretation*. New York: Gordon.
Ross, Edward A. (1921). *Principles of Sociology*. New York: Century.

☐ **leisure class, theory of the** *see* conspicuous consumption
☐ **Lewin's field theory** *see* field theory
☐ **life cycle** *see* product life cycle
☐ **life-cycle segmentation** *see* segmentation

■ lifestyle marketing

DESCRIPTION
Marketing based on knowledge of individuals' actual or desired patterns of living, in areas including their activities and interests.

KEY INSIGHTS
Lifestyle marketing is concerned with understanding the lifestyles of consumers, as demonstrated by consumers' preferences and behaviors in their social relations, consumption, entertainment, dress, and the like, and using such an understanding as a central element in an organization's marketing efforts. Given that consumers' lifestyles are determined in part by their values and attitudes, lifestyle marketing necessarily involves understanding not only particular lifestyle patterns but an understanding of the drivers of such patterns as well. Lifestyle marketing can emphasize how a firm's offerings can assist consumers with leading lifestyles they would like to have or it can be based on reinforcing a lifestyle a consumer is already leading. Lifestyle marketing may be the primary focus of a firm's efforts or it may be a part, as when lifestyle market segmentation is combined with other segmentation approaches. (See **segmentation**.)

KEY WORDS Consumer interests, consumer activities, consumer values

IMPLICATIONS
Marketers may benefit from assessing how and to what extent a marketing approach based on lifestyle marketing may assist the marketer's firm in reaching existing markets and developing new markets for the firm's offerings.

APPLICATION AREAS AND FURTHER READINGS
Marketing Strategy
Cahill, Dennis J. (2006). *Lifestyle Market Segmentation*. New York: Haworth Press.

Consumer Behavior
Englis, Basil G., and Solomon, Michael R. (1995). 'To Be and Not to Be: Lifestyle Imagery, Reference Groups and the Clustering of America,' *Journal of Advertising*, 24, Spring, 13–28.
Swenson, C. A. (1990). *Selling to a Segmented Market: The Lifestyle Approach*. New York: Quorum Books.

Marketing Ethics
Niebuhr, J. (1998). 'Target Group: Poor Neighbourhood. The Ethical Implications of Lifestyle Marketing in Low Income Residential Neighborhoods,' *Business Ethics* (Oxford), 7(3), 182–185.

BIBLIOGRAPHY
Michman, Ronald D., Mazze, Edward M., and Greco, Alan James (2003). *Lifestyle Marketing: Reaching the New American Consumer.* Westport, Conn.: Praeger.
Michman, R. D. (1991). *Lifestyle Market Segmentation.* New York: Greenwood Publishing Group.

☐ lifestyle segmentation *see* segmentation
☐ Likert scale *see* scale
☐ liking *see* buyer influence/readiness
☐ limit pricing *see* pricing strategies

■ Little's law

(also called Little's result or Little's theorem)

DESCRIPTION
A queuing formula for a stable system stating that the average number of customers in a system (over some interval) is equal to their average arrival rate multiplied by their average time in the system.

KEY INSIGHTS
Based on pioneering research by John D. C. Little, the relationship presented in Little's law is demonstrated through his proof of the queuing formula $L = \lambda W$ (Little 1961). While Little's law may appear to be somewhat intuitive, a key contribution is that it is proven to hold independent of assumptions about customers' arrival schedules, service schedules, or service order. One constraint for the relationship is that the system must be stable (e.g. not in a transition state of starting up or shutting down).

Applied more broadly to any production system, as opposed to that for a customer queuing system context, Little's law can also be used to support the view that average throughput time through a production system is directly proportional to average work-in-progress (WIP) inventory. Hence, in the context of a production system for manufacturing, as capacity utilization increases, WIP inventory increases, throughput time increases, and delivery performance declines.

Little's law also has corollary. Again referring to the context of a customer queuing system, the corollary statement added to the law is: the average time in the system is equal to the average time in queue plus the average time it takes to receive service.

To illustrate Little's law with an example, assume that customers arrive at a set of supermarket checkout counters at an average rate of one customer every 15 seconds. Assume also that each customer ends up spending an average of 8 minutes in the queue and 4 minutes actually checking out or receiving service. Little's law can be used to calculate the average number of customers that will be in the system:

Avg. arrival rate = 1 customer every 15 seconds = 4 customers per minute

Avg. time in the system = avg. time in queue + avg. time to receive service
= 8 minute + 4 minutes = 12 minutes

Avg. no. of customers in queue = avg. arrival rate × avg. time in the system
= 4 customers per minute × 12 minutes
= 48 customers

KEY WORDS Queuing, systems, performance, production, service

IMPLICATIONS
The principle embodied by Little's law has clear implications for customer queuing systems as well as most systems of production and manufacturing. When capacity utilization and system performance are of strategic importance, Little's law provides valuable insights into how these systems will function when stable.

APPLICATION AREAS AND FURTHER READINGS
Marketing Management
Hua, Stella Y., and Wemmerlöv, Urban (2006). 'Product Change Intensity, Product Advantage, and Market Performance: An Empirical Investigation of the PC Industry,' *Journal of Product Innovation Management*, 23(4), July, 316.
Bitran, G. R., and Mondschein, S. V. (1996). 'Mailing Decisions in the Catalog Sales Industry,' *Management Science*, 42(9), 1364–1381.
Hopp, W. J., and Sturgis, M. L. R. (2000). 'Quoting Manufacturing Due Dates Subject to a Service Level Constraint,' *IIE Transactions*, 32(9), 771–784.
Berman, O., and Kim, E. (2001). 'Dynamic Order Replenishment Policy in Internet-Based Supply Chains,' *Mathematical Methods of Operations Research* (Heidelberg), 53(3), 371–390.

BIBLIOGRAPHY
Little, J. D. C. (1961). 'A Proof of the Queueing Formula L = λ W,' *Operations Research*, 9, 383–387.

■ local marketing

DESCRIPTION
Marketing tailored to the wants and needs of local markets such as cities, neighborhoods, or stores.

KEY INSIGHTS
Local marketing emphasizes a perceived net marketing benefit to tailoring certain aspects of a firm's offerings (e.g. promotions, product prices, brands) to reflect the wants and needs of local organizations or communities of consumers. Local marketing may vary in the extent of such tailoring in terms of the firm's offerings as well as a local area's size and other characteristics (e.g. city vs. neighborhood marketing).

KEY WORDS Tailored offerings, local needs, neighborhoods, cities

IMPLICATIONS

Firms with offerings that may vary in their appeal among local markets may benefit from a greater understanding of local marketing-based approaches. In the case of firms providing local markets with multiple offerings, for example, such as where a food and snack foods firm supplies many neighborhood stores, local marketing practices may include the careful tailoring of the mix of offerings provided to each local retailer.

APPLICATION AREAS AND FURTHER READINGS

Retail Marketing

Byrom J. (2001). 'The Role of Loyalty Card Data Within Local Marketing Initiatives,' *International Journal of Retail and Distribution Management*, 29(7), 333–341.

Fish, K. R. (2001). 'Fresh Choice Restaurants, Inc.: Good Practices in Neighborhood Marketing,' *Journal of Restaurant and Foodservicing Marketing*, 4(2), 95–98.

International Marketing

Solberg, C. A. (2002). 'The Perennial Issue of Adaptation or Standardization of International Marketing Communication: Organizational Contingencies and Performance,' *Journal of International Marketing*, 10(3), 1–21.

BIBLIOGRAPHY

Johansson, J. K. (1997). *Global Marketing: Foreign Entry, Local Marketing and Global Management*. New York: McGraw-Hill.

■ locality, principle of

DESCRIPTION

A general principle stating that, when reasoning, an individual does not use all he or she knows about the world, but only a subset of it.

KEY INSIGHTS

Not to be confused with the physics-based principle of locality (i.e. 'no action at a distance'), the sociological-based principle of locality (i.e. the empowerment of localities to make decisions of local concern and the acknowledgment and respect of such rights), or the computing-based principle of locality for local computational resource usage, the principle of locality emphasizes the role and influence of context in determining how and to what extent individuals reason in accomplishing tasks or for achieving goals. Whether acting for themselves or acting as agents on behalf of others (e.g. managers employed to pursue the goals of the firm's owners), the principle of locality indicates that individuals will draw upon only part of their total knowledge when reasoning, where such knowledge drawn is heavily influenced by the context in which the need for reasoning occurs.

KEY WORDS Individual reasoning, decision making

IMPLICATIONS

While the principle of locality is a very general principle of reasoning, it nevertheless emphasizes the importance of local context in determining how and to what extent individuals will draw upon their base of knowledge. Marketing models of consumer behavior can therefore draw upon the principle of locality in establishing assumptions about decision-making behavior and implications for consumer action.

APPLICATION AREAS AND FURTHER READINGS
Marketing Modeling

Bouquet, Paolo, and Warglien, Massimo (1999). 'Mental Models and Local Models Semantics: The Problem of Information Integration,' *European Conference in Cognitive Science*, University of Siena.
Gregory, Aaron L. (2004). 'Prediction of Commuter Choice Behavior Using Neural Networks,' Master's Thesis, University of South Florida.
Nelson, Bardin H. (1962). 'Seven Principles in Image Formation,' *Journal of Marketing*, 26(1), January, 67–71.

BIBLIOGRAPHY
Giunchiglia, F., and Ghidini, C. (1998). 'Local Models Semantics, or Contextual Reasoning = Locality + Compatibility,' *Proceedings of the Sixth International Conference on Principles of Knowledge Representation and Reasoning (KR'98)*, Trento: Morgan Kaufmann, 282–289.

☐ location marketing *see* place marketing

■ location theory

DESCRIPTION
Theory aimed at understanding, explaining, and predicting the locational and spatial choices of economic entitities.

KEY INSIGHTS
Location theory encompasses a broad base of research aimed at understanding, explaining, and/or predicting firms' geographic location choices in relation to such factors as sources of supply and demand. Taking into account the nature of the firm's production processes, for example, location theory as developed by Weber (1929) supports the view that (1) firms will locate near raw material sources when the goods produced are not as heavy, bulky, or perishable as the raw materials from which they are manufactured, (2) firms will locate near markets for their goods when the goods produced are heavier, bulkier, or more perishable than the raw materials from which they are produced, and (3) firms will not locate at intermediate points as such locations incur additional costs. Theories of location with more specific emphases include *retail location theory*, which is concerned with understanding, explaining, and predicting the locational and spatial choices of retailers. More broadly, central place theory is an area of study with theoretical perspectives which are related to location theory. (See **central place theory.**)

KEY WORDS Physical locations, spatial locations

IMPLICATIONS
Marketers in firms evaluating choice of firm location may benefit from a greater knowledge of location theory-based research. In addition, the theory may also provide marketers with insights into the possible and likely locational choices of industry and market competitors as a result of

a greater understanding of the different factors influencing firm location choice.

APPLICATION AREAS AND FURTHER READINGS

Retail Marketing

Brown, S. (1989). 'Retail Location Theory: The Legacy of Harold Hotelling,' *Journal of Retailing*, 65(4), Winter, 450–470.
Brown, S. (1993). 'Retail Location Theory: Evolution and Evaluation,' *International Review of Retail, Distribution, and Consumer Research*, 3(2), 185–229.
Grether, E. T. (1983). 'Regional-Spatial Analysis in Marketing,' *Journal of Marketing*, 47, 36–43.

Business-to-Business Marketing

Olson, F. L. (1959). 'Location Theory as Applied to Milk Processing Plants,' *Journal of Farm Economics*, 1546–1559.

BIBLIOGRAPHY

Weber, Alfred (1929). *Theory of the Location of Industries*. Chicago: Chicago University Press.
Francis, R. L., and Goldstein, J. M. (1974). 'Location Theory: A Selective Bibliography,' *Operations Research*, 22, 400–409.

☐ loss leader pricing *see* pricing strategies

■ low-ball technique

(also called the low-ball procedure)

DESCRIPTION

A technique for persuading an individual to accept or adopt a particular course of action, where the individual is first induced to agree to the action through presentation of a favorable proposition which, soon after but before final commitment, is then disclosed less favorably.

KEY INSIGHTS

Based on pioneering research by Cialdini, Cacioppo, Bassett, and Miller (1978), the low-ball technique (or procedure) was observed to be more effective in obtaining individuals' commitments to volunteer under conditions disclosed subsequently as less desirable than initially disclosed relative to instances where individuals were sought as volunteers for the immediately disclosed less desirable condition. The technique therefore involves obtaining a commitment to an action prior to disclosing the full and true cost, where the initial commitment acts to increase the likelihood of sustained agreement, and likewise reduce the likelihood that the individual will subsequently reverse his or her initial decision, even under conditions of greater cost or other less favorable conditions.

KEY WORDS Persuasion, compliance, negotiation, selling

IMPLICATIONS

While the technique clearly has ethical implications which should be examined by marketers in considering its use, its effectiveness nevertheless suggests it may be an alternative that marketers may wish to explore in personal selling, negotiation, and other forms of persuasion.

APPLICATION AREAS AND FURTHER READINGS
Negotiation
Evans, Kenneth R., and Beltramini, Richard F. (1987). 'A Theoretical Model of
    Consumer Negotiated Pricing: An Orientation Perspective,' *Journal of Marketing*,
    51(2), April, 58–73.

Non-profit Marketing
Lindahl, W. E., and Conley, A. T. (2002). 'Literature Review: Philanthropic Fundrais-
    ing,' *Nonprofit Management and Leadership*, 13(1), 91–112.

Marketing Research
Hornik, J., Zaig, T., Shadmon, D., and Barbash, G. I. (1990). 'Comparison of Three
    Inducement Techniques to Improve Compliance in a Health Survey Conducted
    by Telephone,' *Public Health Reports*, 105(5), September–October, 524–9.

Consumer Behavior
Joule, R. V. (1987). 'Tobacco Deprivation: The Foot-in-the-Door Technique versus the
    Lowball Technique,' *European Journal of Social Psychology*, 17(3), 361–365.

BIBLIOGRAPHY
Cialdini, R. B., Cacioppo, J. T., Bassett, R., and Miller, J. A. (1978). 'Low-Ball Procedure
    for Eliciting Compliance: Commitment then Cost,' *Journal of Personality and Social
    Psychology*, 34, 366–375.
Burger, J. M., and Petty, R. E. (1981). 'The Low-Ball Compliance Technique: Task or
    Person Commitment?' *Journal of Personality and Social Psychology*, 40, 492–500.

■ loyalty effect

DESCRIPTION
Beneficial effects to a firm and its marketing efforts that are attributed to brand
loyalty by customers.

KEY INSIGHTS
Research by Reichheld (1996) argues that marketing costs for serving
loyal customers are lower than those for attracting new customers
because loyal customers are familiar with the firm's products or services
and are less dependent on the firm and its employees for assistance and
information. As a result, loyal customers contribute much to the bottom
line of a firm. In quantifying the contribution of loyalty, Reichheld's
(1996) research suggests that in certain industries such as automobile and
life insurance and credit cards, attracting new customers can cost up to
five times the cost associated with retaining current customers.

More broadly, effects of increases in customer loyalty to a firm include:
increases in the long-term and continuous profit accumulation from
individual customers, reduced marketing costs as a result of less marketing effort to attract new customers, increases in per-customer revenue
growth as loyal customers tend to increase their spending over time,
lower operating costs as a result of less employee time spent on answering the queries of loyal customers, increases in referrals by loyal customers to friends and others, a greater willingness to pay and a reduced
sensitivity to price increases as a result of loyal customers' perceptions of
unique value in the brand.

While there are many benefits associated with customer loyalty, the two major dimensions of the loyalty effect according to Reichheld (1996) are the 'customer volume effect' (also called the 'volume effect') and the 'profit-per-customer effect.' The *customer volume effect* is the effect on the growth rate of a firm resulting from adding new customers each year while also reducing the rate at which it is losing customers. Thus, while two firms may have identical customer acquisition rates, the firm with the lower customer attrition rate has the advantage in terms of increasing its installed base is of customers more quickly over time. The *profit-per-customer effect* is the effect of increasing profits the longer a customer stays with a company, where such increasing profits are due to greater customer spending and lower operating costs in serving loyal customers.

KEY WORDS Loyalty, growth, profit, **value**

IMPLICATIONS
Marketers should not underestimate the beneficial effects of customer loyalty to a firm and its marketing efforts. Marketing aimed at maintaining and increasing customer loyalty is likely to produce far greater rewards than marketing of a similar financial expenditure that is aimed at attracting new customers.

APPLICATION AREAS AND FURTHER READINGS
Marketing Strategy
Oliver, R. L. (1999). 'Whence Consumer Loyalty,' *Journal of Marketing*, 63(SPI/1), 33–44.
Reichheld, F. F., Markey, R. G., and Hopton, C. (2000). 'The Loyalty Effect,' *European Business Journal*, 12(3), 134–139.
Sheth, J. N., and Sisodia, R. N. (2002). 'Marketing Productivity, Issues and Analysis,' *Journal of Business Research*, 55, 349–362.

Online Marketing
Reichheld, F. F., and Schefter, P. (2000). 'E-Loyalty: Your Secret Weapon on the Web,' *Harvard Business Review*, 78(4), 105–113.

BIBLIOGRAPHY
Reichheld, Frederick F. (1996), *The Loyalty Effect: The Hidden Force behind Lasting Growth, Profits, and Lasting Value*. Boston: Harvard Business School Press.

■ loyalty marketing

DESCRIPTION
Marketing that is aimed at encouraging or increasing customer loyalty to a firm and its branded offerings.

KEY INSIGHTS
Loyalty marketing seeks to create and take strategic advantage of the loyalty effect (see **loyalty effect**) and/or the loyalty ripple effect (see **loyalty ripple effect**). As such, a firm may make loyalty marketing central to the firm's marketing efforts, such as when a new airline opts to compete by offering highly favorable terms to its frequent flyers, or in combination with other marketing approaches, such as a supermarket

offering shoppers a loyalty program to encourage repeat shopping but also to learn about ongoing customer purchase behavior.

KEY WORDS Loyalty, competitive advantage

IMPLICATIONS
Given that customer loyalty can have strategic value to a firm operating in a highly competitive industry, marketers may benefit from a greater understanding of loyalty marketing approaches. While in some markets, loyalty marketing may simply provide a firm with a means to achieve and maintain competitive parity, in other industries the approach may provide the firm with a competitive advantage that is not easily eroded over the longer term.

APPLICATION AREAS AND FURTHER READINGS

Marketing Strategy
Duffy, D. L. (1998). 'Customer Loyalty Strategies,' *Journal of Consumer Marketing*, 15(5), 435–448.

Online Marketing
Sindell, Kathleen (2000). *Loyalty Marketing for the Internet Age: How to Identify, Attract, Serve and Retain Customers in an E-commerce Environment.* Chicago: Dearborn Financial Publishing.

Marketing Research
Dick, A. S., and Basu, K. (1994). 'Customer Loyalty: Toward an Integrated Conceptual Framework,' *Journal—Academy of Marketing Science*, 22(2), 99.
Shoemaker, S., and Lewis, R. C. (1999). 'Customer Loyalty: The Future of Hospitality Marketing—Determining and Measuring Customer Value,' *International Journal of Hospitality Management*, 18(4), 345–370.
Dowling, G. R., and Uncles, M. (1997). 'Do Customer Loyalty Programs Really Work?' *Sloan Management Review*, 38(4), 71–82.

BIBLIOGRAPHY
Woolf, Brian (2002). *Loyalty Marketing: the Second Act.* Greenville, SC: Teal Books.

■ loyalty ripple effect

DESCRIPTION
Direct and indirect influences that customers have on a firm as a result of their generating interest in the firm by encouraging patronage from new customers as well as any other of their actions or behaviors that create value for the organization.

KEY INSIGHTS
Conceptually developed by Gremler and Brown (1999), the loyalty ripple effect conveys the notion that there is a gradually spreading effect or influence of customer loyalty to an organization. Beyond loyal customers' influence on a company's ongoing revenues, actions including positive word-of-mouth communication add further value to a firm and reduce the firm's costs.

KEY WORDS Loyalty, **value, word-of-mouth communication**

IMPLICATIONS

Marketers concerned with developing customer loyalty should not under-estimate its ripple effect, which can include not only generating more customers but also more customers that are also loyal. Appreciating and understanding better the loyalty ripple effect may therefore help firms to exploit more of the true value of loyalty.

APPLICATION AREAS AND FURTHER READINGS

Online Marketing

Ribbink, Dina, van Riel, Allard C. R., Liljander, Veronica, and Streukens, Sandra (2004). 'Comfort your Online Customer: Quality, Trust and Loyalty on the Internet,' *Managing Service Quality*, 14(6), 446–456.

Marketing Strategy

Uncles, M. D., Dowling, G. R., and Hammond, K. (2003). 'Customer Loyalty and Customer Loyalty Programs,' *Journal of Consumer Marketing*, 20(4/5), 294–316.

BIBLIOGRAPHY

Gremler, D. D., and Brown, S. W. (1999). 'The Loyalty Ripple Effect: Appreciating the Full Value of Customers,' *International Journal of Service Industry Management*, 10(3), 271–291.

☐ **luxury goods** *see* **goods**

M

☐ m-marketing *see* mobile marketing
☐ macro marketing environment *see* macroenvironment

■ macroenvironment

DESCRIPTION
The set of societal forces that have a major influence on industries and markets. (also called macro marketing environment)

KEY INSIGHTS
The macroenvironment can be considered to consist of multiple forces of influence to industries and markets. Examples of such forces, or pressures on the firm, include political, economic, social, cultural, demographic, technological, legal, regulatory, environmental, and natural forces. To ensure that a firm's marketing efforts are compatible with these and other broad societal forces, an analysis of the macroenvironment is recommended, where the implications for the firm's marketing efforts receive critical attention. Aside from the general term environmental analysis, there are a number of generally equivalent terms used for such an analysis, including *PEST analysis* (also called *STEP analysis*), which involves an analysis of political (including legal and regulatory), economic, social, and technological forces of the macroenvironment, and *PESTLE analysis*, which also involves analysis of the same set of forces as for PEST but makes legal forces distinct from political forces and further includes environmental forces. What is most important in the environmental analysis is not so much the precise categorizations used but the identification of important forces of influence, both current and potential, to the firm's marketing efforts. For example, a firm involved in developing new teleworking products may find that there are numerous important influences in the area of technological forces, which may further include influences associated with technological advances in both communications hardware and software. At the same time, the firm would not want to neglect analyses of cultural forces and economic forces, both of which may be important in the firm's plans to offer the product in multiple countries.

KEY WORDS Societal forces

IMPLICATIONS
While the marketing strategies supporting a firm's offerings must clearly take into account the firm's immediate operating environment (e.g. competitor and customer environment), astute marketers recognize the importance of understanding the firm's macroenvironment to ensure the firm's marketing strategy fits with broader forces of influence. Such forces cannot be influenced but trends and events associated with such forces may have a profound impact on firm success, as when a food products firm anticipates a cultural trend toward healthier eating and incorporates knowledge of the trend into new food offerings and their supporting marketing communications.

APPLICATION AREAS AND FURTHER READINGS

Marketing Management
Andrews, Jonlee, and Smith, Daniel C. (1996). 'In Search of the Marketing Imagination: Factors Affecting the Creativity of Marketing Programs for Mature Products,' *Journal of Marketing Research*, 33(2), May, 174–187.

Marketing Strategy
Mavondo, F. T. (1999). 'Environment and Strategy as Antecedents for Marketing Effectiveness and Organizational Performance,' *Developments in Marketing Science*, 22, 363–370.

BIBLIOGRAPHY
Sheth, J. N. (1992). 'Emerging Marketing Strategies in a Changing Macroeconomic Environment: A Commentary,' *International Marketing Review*, 9(1), 57–63.

■ macromarketing

DESCRIPTION
Marketing focused on issues relating to the broader environmental influences on societies and economies.

KEY INSIGHTS
Macromarketing is concerned with the interplay between marketing actions and the broad needs of societies and economies. As such, issues such as quality of life, societal well-being, and sustainable consumption receive primary (as opposed to secondary) focus in terms of how marketing-led actions positively or negatively influence their current and future levels and vice versa.

KEY WORDS Societal needs, economies

IMPLICATIONS
As marketing is performed in a broader societal context, it behooves marketers to understand a broad range of issues having a possible influence on marketing as well as the broad societal and economic issues that are influenced, directly or indirectly, by marketing practice. A greater understanding of macromarketing-based research provides the marketer with such a perspective and may further assist the marketer with considering the longer-term consequences of the firm's marketing actions.

APPLICATION AREAS AND FURTHER READINGS

Marketing Strategy
Kilbourne, W., McDonagh, P., and Prothero, A. (1997). 'Sustainable Consumption and the Quality of Life: A Macromarketing Challenge to the Dominant Social Paradigm,' *Journal of Macromarketing*, 17(1), 4-24.

Marketing Management
Priddle, J. (1994). 'Marketing Ethics, Macromarketing, and the Managerial Perspective Reconsidered,' *Journal of Macromarketing*, 14(2), 3, 47.

Marketing Research
Ahuvia, A. C., and Friedman, D. C. (1998). 'Income, Consumption, and Subjective Well-Being: Toward a Composite Macromarketing Model,' *Journal of Macromarketing*, 18(2), 153-168.

BIBLIOGRAPHY
Bartels, Robert, and Jenkins, Roger L. (1977). 'Macromarketing,' *Journal of Marketing*, 41(4), October, 17-20.
Hunt, S. D., and Burnett, J. J. (1982). 'The Macromarketing–Micromarketing Dichotomy: A Taxonomical Model,' *Journal of Marketing*, 46(3), Summer, 11-26.

■ magical number seven

DESCRIPTION
A term capturing the notion that individuals are limited in their capacity for processing information, where the limitation consists of spans involving of about seven distinct categories or items of information.

KEY INSIGHTS
Based on pioneering research by Miller (1956), evidence suggests that an individual's ability to process information is strictly limited. More specifically, individual attention spans tend to encompass about six items of information at any given time, while spans of short-term memory tend to encompass about seven items, and spans of judgment tend to distinguish about seven categories. One recognized approach for helping to overcome such limitations involves grouping together items of information into chunks, an approach referred to as chunking, where the individual items of information can be more easily perceived, interpreted, and remembered. An example is the telephone number 118 TAXI, which is more easily remembered than the seven-digit telephone number 118 8294.

KEY WORDS Information processing capacity, individuals

IMPLICATIONS
Marketers should be critically sensitive to how individual's information processing capacities are limited and how such limitations may influence memory, attention, and judgments of a marketer's offerings. Specifically, marketers should be wary of overloading consumer's processing capability and emphasize marketing communications and other actions that are easily remembered, attended to, and judged as a result of being within individual limits of information processing capacity.

APPLICATION AREAS AND FURTHER READINGS

Consumer Behavior

Jacoby, Jacob, Speller, Donald E., and Kohn, Carol A. (1974). 'Brand Choice Behavior as a Function of Information Load,' *Journal of Marketing Research*, 11(1), February, 63–69.

Jacoby, Jacob (1984). 'Perspectives on Information Overload,' *Journal of Consumer Research*, 10(4), March, 432–435.

Marketing Research

Cox, Eli P., III (1980). 'The Optimal Number of Response Alternatives for a Scale: A Review,' *Journal of Marketing Research*, 17(4), November, 407–422.

Green, Paul E., and Rao, Vithala R. (1970). 'Rating Scales and Information Recovery: How Many Scales and Response Categories to Use?' *Journal of Marketing*, 34(3), July, 33–39.

BIBLIOGRAPHY

Miller, George A. (1956). 'The Magical Number Seven, Plus or Minus Two: Some Limits on our Capacity for Processing Information,' *Psychological Review*, 63, 81–97.

☐ **mail marketing** *see* direct marketing

■ majority fallacy

DESCRIPTION

Generally, an error in logical reasoning stemming from inappropriate consideration of a popular or majority view. In a more specific marketing context, the view that larger markets or market segments will be more profitable than smaller ones simply due to their size.

KEY INSIGHTS

The majority fallacy encompasses the notion that one's actions, attitudes, or beliefs can be inappropriately influenced by perceptions of behaviors, attitudes, and beliefs held by a majority or sufficiently large-sized population. Examples are when an individual views an action as more acceptable as a result of its practice by the majority, or when an individual views an action to be more commonly practiced by a majority in comparison to the individual. Similarly, an individual deliberating an action may view it as increasingly acceptable to the extent that the action is increasingly practiced by a large enough number of others.

KEY WORDS Judgment, errors

IMPLICATIONS

Marketers can fall prey to the majority fallacy when erroneously adopting the view that large markets and market segments are always better than small ones (e.g. in terms of attractiveness, profitability, etc.), or in believing that the majority position adopted by competitors in terms of product attributes is likely to be best and should therefore be adopted as well. In the former example, large markets may be less attractive due to a greater number of competitors, while in the latter example, adopting such a position results in a lack of product differentiation. At the same time, consumers can fall prey to the fallacy in persuasive arguments, as when told that, since the majority of consumers have purchased a particular brand, the brand is clearly the right one for them (e.g. '50 million consumers can't be wrong'). Marketers should therefore understand how the majority fallacy can intentionally or inadvertently influence marketing or consumer judgments, where knowledge or beliefs about majority views or actions have an influence on personal views, decisions, and actions.

APPLICATION AREAS AND FURTHER READINGS

Marketing Strategy
Holbrook, Morris B., and Holloway, Douglas V. (1984). 'Marketing Strategy and the Structure of Aggregate, Segment-Specific, and Differential Preferences,' *Journal of Marketing*, 48(1), Winter, 62–67.

Marketing Education
Smead, Raymond J., and Finn, David W. (1979). 'Discovering the Majority Fallacy,' *Insights into Experiential Pedagogy*, 6, 178–181.

BIBLIOGRAPHY
Kuehn, Alfred A., and Day, Ralph. L. (1962). 'Strategy of Product Quality,' *Harvard Business Review*, 40(6), 100–110.
Moore, W. L. (1980). 'Levels of Aggregation in Conjoint Analysis: An Empirical Comparison,' *Journal of Marketing Research*, 17, 516–523.

■ management theory

DESCRIPTION
Theory or theories of effective and efficient management.

KEY INSIGHTS
While management theory encompasses a broad base of research and continues to receive considerable research attention, many theories of management often refer to, and are based upon, the scientific view of management theory as put forth by Taylor (1911). Principles embodied in the classic view of management theory include: assuming full responsibility for work planning, applying scientific methods to work design to achieve maximum efficiency, staffing jobs with the most appropriate individuals, adequately training such individuals, and providing such individuals with feedback to ensure desired performance. Management theory continues to advance beyond the classic view and now encapsulates many complementary as well as competing views.

KEY WORDS Management, effectiveness, efficiency

IMPLICATIONS
Management theories, whether explicit or implicit, form a basis for much marketing management practice. Issues such as determining the most effective means to motivate a sales force (e.g. salary, commission, or a combination), are the subject of debate and discussion in organizations that are ultimately dependent on managerial views on what constitutes effective and efficient management. The topic of management theory therefore provides marketers with an ongoing source of concepts

for consideration in establishing effective and efficient marketing management practices.

APPLICATION AREAS AND FURTHER READINGS

Marketing Management
Dean, James W., Jr., and Bowen, David E. (1994). 'Management Theory and Total Quality: Improving Research and Practice through Theory Development,' *Academy of Management Review*, 19(3), Special Issue: 'Total Quality', July, 392–418.
Gummesson, E. (2002). 'Practical Value of Adequate Marketing Management Theory,' *European Journal of Marketing*, 36(3), 325–349.
Locke, Edwin A. (1982). 'The Ideas of Frederick W. Taylor: An Evaluation,' *Academy of Management Review*, 7(1), January, 14–24.

BIBLIOGRAPHY
Cole, Kris (2005). *Management: Theory and Practice*. Frenchs Forest, NSW: Pearson-Prentice Hall.
Nelson, Daniel (1980). *Frederick W. Taylor and the Rise of Scientific Management*. Madison: University of Wisconsin Press.
Taylor, Frederick W. (1911/1967). *The Principles of Scientific Management*. New York: Norton (originally published 1911).

☐ **managerial theories of the firm** *see* firm, theory of the

☐ **many-to-many marketing** *see* affiliate marketing

☐ **marginal cost pricing** *see* pricing strategies

☐ **market development** *see* product-market investment strategies

■ market entry timing

DESCRIPTION
The time at which a firm enters a market, either chronologically or in relation to competitors or other market conditions.

KEY INSIGHTS
Market entry timing is an important element in a firm's marketing strategy when the firm seeks to make the most of its limited resources in relation to perceived market opportunities. Being 'too early' to market can waste a firm's resources, whereas being 'too late' to market can reduce the opportunity available to a firm. In relation to other firms entering a market, a firm may be a *pioneer*—the very first to enter a market, or one of the first firms collectively entering a market in close temporal proximity, or a *follower firm*—a firm which enters a market after the market pioneer(s). A follower firm may be further characterized as being an *early follower*—a firm that enters a market sooner after the market pioneer(s) or a *late follower* or *later market entrant*—a firm that enters a market some time after both the market pioneer(s) and after early follower firms. Firms may therefore pursue a *pioneering*, or *market pioneering* strategy—where the aim is to be first among competitors to enter a market, or a *market follower* strategy—where the aim is to let other firms pioneer markets before entering them. In deliberating pursuing a particular market entry timing strategy a firm is either implicitly or explicitly concerned with

achieving particular advantages associated with time of market entry in relation to competitors. Specifically, pioneers seek an opportunity to pursue and exploit some form of *first mover advantage*, where the firm's entry timing enables it to reap greater economic or behaviorally based benefits in relation to those achieveable by follower firms, such as more favorable distribution terms with retailers or increased ability to shape consumer preferences. On the other hand, a firm either implicitly or explicitly pursuing a market follower strategy seeks opportunities to pursue and exploit some form of follower advantage, where the firm's entry strategy enables it to obtain greater economic or behavior benefits in comparison to those achievable by pioneering firms, such as lower-cost product development (as a result of evaluations of the pioneer's new product) or more effective product positioning (as a result of learning from the pioneer's marketing mistakes).

As it is usually the case that multiple firms enter a given market with their new products once the markets are pioneered, it is almost always the case that there will be many more followers in the market than pioneers. In such a case, *order-of-entry effects*, or those effects on marketing performance that are directly attributable to the precise sequence of entry of a firm into a market relative to that of competitors, can also be an important consideration having both strategic and tactical implications. For example, research on frequently purchased consumer goods has found that, as a firm's order-of-entry increases (e.g. the later it enters in relation to competitors), market share, probability of consumer trial and probability of repeat purchase by the consumer are all observed to decrease, but at different relative rates (Kalyanaram and Urban 1992).

KEY WORDS Timing, order of entry

IMPLICATIONS
In order to make the most of a firm's limited resources in accomplishing the firm's objectives, marketers should take care to consider market entry timing strategy in their overall marketing strategy. As there are benefits, costs, and risks associated with each of the different approaches, marketers should analyze factors including the firm's objectives, characteristics of the firm, its current products, competitors, competitors' products, and characteristics of the market to enable the firm to identify, evaluate, and pursue market entry timing strategies that may be more beneficial to the firm than others.

APPLICATION AREAS AND FURTHER READINGS
Marketing Strategy
Lilien, G., and Yoon, E. (1990). 'The Timing of Competitive Market Entry: An Exploratory Study of New Industrial Products,' *Management Science*, 36(5), 568–585.
Kalish, Shlomo, and Lilien, Gary L. (1986). 'A Market Entry Timing Model for New Technologies,' *Management Science*, 32, February, 194–205.
Wilson, L., and Norton, J. (1989). 'Optimal Entry Timing for a Product Line Extension,' *Marketing Science*, 8(1), Winter, 1–17.

Shankar, Venkatesh, Carpenter, Gregory S., and Lakshman, Krishnamurthi (1998). 'Late Mover Advantage: How Innovate Late Entrants Outsell Pioneers,' *Journal of Marketing Research*, 35, February, 54–70.

Dacko, Scott G. (2002). 'Understanding Market Entry Timing Decisions: The Practitioner–Academic Gap,' *Marketing Intelligence and Planning*, 20, 70–81.

Marketing Management

Dacko, Scott G. (2000). 'Benchmarking Competitive Responses to Pioneering New Product Introductions,' *Benchmarking: An International Journal*, 7(5), 324–342.

International Marketing

Mitra, D., and Golder, P. N. (2002). 'Whose Culture Matters? Near-Market Knowledge and its Impact on Foreign Market Entry Timing,' *Journal of Marketing Research*, 39(3), 350–365.

BIBLIOGRAPHY

Kerin, Roger A., Varadarajan, Rajan, and Peterson, Robert A. (1992). 'First-Mover Advantage: A Synthesis, Conceptual Framework, and Research Propositions,' *Journal of Marketing*, 56(4), 33–52.

Lambkin, Mary (1988). 'Order of Entry and Performance in New Markets,' *Strategic Management Journal*, 9, Summer, 127–140.

Kalyanaram, G., and Urban, G. L. (1992). 'Dynamic Effects of the Order of Entry on Market Share, Trial Penetration and Repeat Purchases for Frequently Purchased Consumer Goods,' *Marketing Science*, 11, 235–250.

☐ market expansion *see* product-market investment strategies
☐ market factor index method *see* forecasting methods
☐ market follower *see* market entry timing
☐ market penetration *see* product-market investment strategies
☐ market pioneering *see* market entry timing
☐ market segmentation *see* segmentation

■ market share

DESCRIPTION

Expressed in percentage terms, a firm's or brand's sales (or unit) volume divided by the total category sales (or unit) volume for the market or market segment within which the firm or brand competes.

KEY INSIGHTS

Market share-based objectives (such as capturing a certain market share or maintaining a particular market share) are among the most common marketing objectives as such objectives enable relative performance comparisons with other firms or brands. Additionally market share measures of firm performance, as opposed to total sales or total unit volume measures may be generally less dependent on, or sensitive to, fluctuations in macroeconomic conditions to the extent that other firms or brands competing in the same market or market segment and similarly affected by the same fluctuating conditions.

KEY WORDS Markets, share, competitive position

IMPLICATIONS

Marketers often use market share-based measures as part of firm objectives. Market share calculations, however, depend on the marketer's definition of the market in which the firm or brand competes, which may broadly include substitute products or narrowly be restricted to a group of well-defined competitors within a particular industry who are competing in a specific market segment. As such, the ultimate choices of market definitions should be those which provide the marketer with the most strategic insight into a firm's or brand's competitive position.

APPLICATION AREAS AND FURTHER READINGS

Marketing Strategy

Urban, Glen L., Carter, Theresa, Gaskin, Steven, and Mucha, Zofia (1986). 'Market Share Rewards to Pioneering Brands: An Empirical Analysis and Strategic Implications,' *Management Science*, 32(6), June, 645–659.

Anderson, Eugene W., Fornell, Claes, and Lehmann, Donald R. (1994). 'Customer Satisfaction, Market Share, and Profitability: Findings from Sweden,' *Journal of Marketing*, 58(3), July, 53–66.

BIBLIOGRAPHY

Cooper, Lee G., and Nakanishi, Masa (1988). *Market-Share Analysis: Evaluating Competitive Marketing Effectiveness*. Boston: Kluwer Academic Publishers.

■ market share effect

DESCRIPTION

The enhancing effect of a high market share on firm performance.

KEY INSIGHTS

Some research on the effect of market share on firm performance has suggested that firm performance is enhanced to the extent a firm achieves a high market share. While results of studies suggesting evidence of such a linkage are a subject of debate among marketing researchers, theories have nevertheless been put forth to explain possible mechanisms for such an effect. Specifically, there is the quality explanation, where high market share can act as a signal of superior quality to consumers; there is the market power explanation, where high market share creates the ability to command higher prices, more favorable vendor terms, better shelf space, etc.; and there is the efficiency explanation, where the scale and experience associated with high market share can lead to lower costs and higher profits. Ultimately, multiple explanations may apply in explaining such a relationship, where unobservable factors such as luck may also be a contributor.

KEY WORDS Firm performance, **market share**

IMPLICATIONS

While strategic efforts to increase market share by a firm may be a goal in and of itself, it is also possible that a firm's increased market share may positively influence other firms' performance measures. Yet, what is most important for marketing managers to understand is the mechanism or mechanisms by which market share may have a possible facilitating effect. Understanding the state of research on the market share effect and exploring competing theories on the topic may provide marketers with insights into likely mechanisms given the context of their firm's product offerings, market, and competitors.

APPLICATION AREAS AND FURTHER READINGS

Marketing Strategy

Hellofs, Linda L., and Jacobson, Robert (1999). 'Market Share and Customers' Perceptions of Quality: When Can Firms Grow their Way to Higher versus Lower Quality?' *Journal of Marketing*, 63(1), January, 16–25.

Szymanski, David M., Bharadwaj, Sundar G., and Varadarajan, P. Rajan (1993). 'An Analysis of the Market Share–Profitability Relationship,' *Journal of Marketing*, 57(3), July, 1–18.

Jacobson, Robert, and Aaker, David A. (1985). 'Is Market Share All That It's Cracked up to Be?' *Journal of Marketing*, 49(4), Autumn, 11–22.

Jacobson, Robert (1990). 'Unobservable Effects and Business Performance,' *Marketing Science*, 9(1), Winter, 74–85.

Wensley, R. (1997). 'Explaining Success: The Rule of Ten Percent and the Example of Market Share,' *Business Strategy Review*, 8(1), 63–70.

BIBLIOGRAPHY

Jacobson, Robert (1988). 'Distinguishing among Competing Theories of the Market Share Effect,' *Journal of Marketing*, 52(4), October, 68–80.

☐ market-skimming pricing *see* pricing strategies

■ **marketing**

DESCRIPTION

An organizational function and a set of processes for creating, communicating, and delivering value to customers and for managing customer relationships in ways that benefit the organization and its stakeholders.

KEY INSIGHTS

The definition of marketing has changed over the years. Defined by the Board of Directors of the American Marketing Association (AMA) in July 2004, the current definition of marketing reflects the changes in the nature of marketing which have occurred in the last two decades. Prior to the current definition, marketing was defined by the AMA in 1985 as the process of planning and executing the conception, pricing, promotion, and distribution of ideas, goods, and services to create exchanges that satisfy individual and organizational objectives. In 1935, the AMA originally defined marketing as the performance of business activities that direct the flow of goods and services from producers to consumers. Unlike previous definitions, the current definition reflects a paradigm that accounts for the continuous nature of relationships among marketing actors.

KEY WORDS Organizational function, processes, **value**, customer relationships, stakeholders

IMPLICATIONS
While some marketers may have a different personal definition of marketing, the current view of marketing emphasizes a need to deliver value to customers and managing customer relationships, where the ultimate aim of such activity is to benefit the organization and its many stakeholders. In this regard, marketing can be viewed as having a broad charter within an organization. As such, regardless of the nature of an organization's marketing function and offerings, it is imperative that marketers strive to actively manage the organization's many value delivery processes as well as its ongoing relationships with its customers to ensure maximum organizational and stakeholder benefits.

APPLICATION AREAS AND FURTHER READINGS
Marketing's Definition
Lichtenthal, J. D., and Beik, L. L. (1984). 'A History of the Definition of Marketing,' in J. N. Sheth (ed.), *Research in Marketing*, 7, Greenwich, Conn.: JAI Press, 133–163.
Gronroos, C. (1990). 'Marketing defined,' *Management Decision*, 28, 5–9.

Marketing Management
Webster, Frederick E., Jr. (1992). 'The Changing Role of Marketing in the Corporation,' *Journal of Marketing*, 56(4), October, 1–17.

BIBLIOGRAPHY
Keefe, Lisa M. (2004). 'What is the Meaning of "Marketing"?' *Marketing News*, 15, September, 17–18.

■ marketing, laws of

DESCRIPTION
Broad generalizations concerning the nature or practice of effective marketing.

KEY INSIGHTS
Unlike disciplines and practices governed by one or more physical laws or laws of nature which are widely accepted as a result of extensive empirical observation and scientific investigation, marketing has at most laws consisting of broad generations which appear to have considerable merit based on empirical observation and scientific investigation into the domain and practice of marketing.

One of the earliest statements in a marketing-related journal referring to a law of marketing is the *First Law of Marketing*, given by Dik Warren Twedt, Director of Marketing Research, Oscar Mayer & Company, which reads:

'The consumer psychologist helps the manufacturer to observe the First Law of Marketing, "Make what people want to buy, don't try to sell what you happen to make" ' (Twedt 1965).

In a subsequent publication in the *Journal of Marketing* by the same author (Twedt 1966), the law is again referenced:

'The First Law of Marketing has been suggested as, "Make what people want to buy; don't try to sell what you happen to make." '

Another indication of a marketing law is given in a journal article discussing distance education which states:

'understanding the nature of products and services that one is attempting to sell constitutes the first law of marketing' (Michael 1997).

Beyond laws of marketing which are explicitly presented in marketing and marketing-related journals, there are also a number of 'laws of marketing' that have been put forth in books on marketing and other publications about marketing. These include a reference to a law of marketing in a book on internal marketing, which is referred to as:

'Cahill's First Law of Marketing: Take care of the Customer and Profits Will Take Care of Themselves' (Cahill 1996).

and another in a book on strategic marketing planning, which, in a chapter entitled 'The Formulation of Strategy 3: Strategies for Leaders, Followers, Challengers, and Nichers', has a section entitled

'The inevitability of strategic wearout (or, the law of marketing gravity and why dead cats only bounce once)' (Gilligan and Wilson 2003);

and, finally, receiving much popular attention, a book on twenty-two "immutable' marketing laws by Ries and Trout (1993).

Still other laws of marketing have been put forth by individuals in less-formal publications including one on website design which states:

'It's the first law of marketing: if they can't find you, then they won't buy your products' (Dysart 2003).

Beyond laws referring specifically to marketing, there are also laws related to particular aspects and elements of marketing such as the 'Laws of Service' (see **service, laws of**) and the 'Law of Exchange' (see **exchange, law of**).

KEY WORDS Marketing generalizations, effective marketing

IMPLICATIONS

Laws of marketing, or broad generalizations about effective marketing, provide marketers with perspectives worthy of reflection. While the merits of any generalization may vary depending on the context in which it is considered (e.g. online marketing versus internal marketing), marketers may wish to give particular attention to Twedt's reference to the First Law of Marketing, as it reflects a dominant view of that which constitutes effective marketing.

APPLICATION AREAS AND FURTHER READINGS

Marketing Management
Little, John D. C. (1979). 'Decision Support Systems for Marketing Managers,' *Journal of Marketing*, 43(3), 9–26.
Harris, Phil, Lock, Andrew, and Rees, Patricia (2000). *Machiavelli, Marketing, and Management*. London: Routledge.
Teare, R. E. (1998). 'Interpreting and Responding to Customer Needs,' *Journal of Workplace Learning*, 10(2), 76–94.

Marketing Strategy
Bell, Gordon H. (2001). 'Physics and the Laws of Marketing,' *Direct Marketing*, 64(1), 46–47.

Marketing Theory
Rossiter J. R. (2001). 'What is Marketing Knowledge,' *Marketing Theory*, 1, 9–26.
Wierenga, B. (2002). 'On Academic Marketing Knowledge and Marketing Knowledge that Managers Use for Decision-Making,' *Marketing Theory*, 2(4), 355–362.
Ehrenberg, A. S. C. (1966). 'Laws in Marketing: A Tail-Piece,' *Applied Statistics*, 15(3), 257–267.
Ehrenberg, A. S. C. (1969). 'The Discovery and Use of Laws of Marketing,' *Journal of Advertising Research*, 9.
Skipper, R. B., and Hyman, M. R. (1995). 'On Foundations Research in the Social Sciences,' *International Journal of Applied Philosophy*, 10, Summer/Fall, 23–38.

BIBLIOGRAPHY
Dysart, Joe (2003). 'A Primer for Website Design,' www.nature.com/bioent /building/pr/042003/box/bioent728_BX1.html Accessed: 8 October 2007.
Cahill D. J. (1996). *Internal Marketing: Your Companys's Next Stage of Growth*. The Haworth Press: New York.
Michael, Steve O. (1997). 'Distance Education in the New Russia: The Relevance of Strategic Marketing Planning,' *Educational Technology Research and Development*, 45(4), 106–117.
Twedt, Dik Warren (1966). 'Is an "Audit Bureau of Interviews" Needed Now?' *Journal of Marketing*, 30(2), April, 59–60.
Twedt, Dik Warren (1965). 'Consumer Psychology,' *Annual Review of Psychology*, 16, January, 265–294.
Gilligan, Colin, and Wilson, Richard M. S. (2003). *Strategic Marketing Planning*. Oxford: Butterworth Heinemann.
Ries, A., and Trout, J. (1993). *The 22 Immutable Laws of Marketing: Violate Them at your Own Risk*. New York: HarperCollins Publishers.

■ marketing, principles of

DESCRIPTION
Basic marketing generalizations that are frequently accepted as true and which can be used as a basis for reasoning and/or marketing conduct.

KEY INSIGHTS
A more-specific view on the definition and scope of 'principles of marketing' is that given by Armstrong and Schultz (1993), namely, 'principles of marketing are normative statements about marketing that specify a condition followed by a suggested action.' However, there are a great many academic and practitioner-generated texts, journal articles, and written works that espouse principles of marketing in the sense that they each provide bases for marketing reasoning and action. What varies within each, however, are indications of the extent that such principles generalize across different areas of marketing. Clearly, it would be a challenge for any single written work to present, address, evaluate, and critique the many principles of marketing as developed and advocated by multiple authors. As such, those interested in understanding the different principles of marketing will find benefit in reading influential and popular texts and articles concerning marketing, either generally, or any of marketing's topical areas (e.g. services marketing, social marketing).

Examples of principles of marketing put forth in the academic marketing-related literature include:

'... a basic principle of marketing [is] that business performance is enhanced by satisfying customers.' (Yeung and Ennew 2001)

'... the underpinning principle of marketing is that the buyers... know what is best for themselves.' (Nims 1999)

'... the guiding principle of marketing practice is "market segmentation."' (Nagle 1984)

'A centrally important principle of marketing is that all marketing activities should be geared towards what the customers want.' (Binsardi and Ekwulugo 2003)

'... the fundamental principle of marketing—namely orientation towards the customer in particular and society in general—...' (Bauer, Huber, and Herrmann 1996)

'The first principle of marketing, and the foundation and basis for all success in marketing, is concentration or focus.' (Keegan 1984)

KEY WORDS Basic marketing generalizations, effective marketing

IMPLICATIONS

Principles of marketing, as advocated by academicians and practitioners alike, provide individuals serious about the study of marketing with 'food for thought' about the nature and practice of marketing. Developing a greater understanding of the many principles of marketing may ultimately assist marketers with the identification, evaluation, selection, and implementation of effective marketing practice.

APPLICATION AREAS AND FURTHER READINGS

Marketing Strategy
Henry, Aasael (1993). *Marketing Principles & Strategy*, 2nd edn. Orlando, Fla.: The Dryden Press.

Online Marketing
Hughes, T. J. (2002). 'Marketing Principles in the Application of E-commerce,' *Qualitative Market Research*, 5(4), 252–260.

Services Marketing
Palmer, A., and Cole, C. (1995). *Services Marketing: Principles and Practices*. Englewood Cliffs, NJ: Prentice-Hall.

Marketing Research
Armstrong, J. Scott, and Schultz, Randall L. (1993). 'Principles Involving Marketing Policies: An Empirical Assessment,' *Marketing Letters*, 4, July, 253–65.

Social Marketing
Donovan, R., and Henley, N. (2003). *Social Marketing: Principles and Practice*. Melbourne: IP Communications.

BIBLIOGRAPHY
Bartels, Robert (1944). 'Marketing Principles,' *Journal of Marketing*, 9 (October), 151–157.
Kotler, Philip, and Armstrong, Gary (2006). *Principles of Marketing*, 11th edn. Upper Saddle River, NJ: Pearson Education, Inc.

Keegan, Warren J. (1984). 'International Competition: The Japanese Challenge,' *Journal of International Business Studies*, 3, Winter, 188–193.

Bauer, H. H., Huber, F., and Herrman A. (1996). 'Political Marketing: An Information-Economic Analysis,' *European Journal of Marketing*, 30(10/11), 159–172.

Binsardi, A., and Ekwulugo, F. (2003). 'International Marketing of British Education: Research on the Students' Perceptions and the UK Market Penetration,' *Marketing Intelligence and Planning*, 21(5), 318–327.

Nagle, T. (1984). 'Economic Foundations for Pricing,' *Journal of Business*, 57(1), January, s3–s26.

Yeung, M. C. H., and Ennew, C. T. (2001). 'Measuring the Impact of Customer Satisfaction on Profitability: A Sectoral Analysis,' *Journal of Targeting, Measurement and Analysis for Marketing*, 10(2), 106–116.

Nims, J. (1999). 'Marketing Library Instruction Services: Changes and Trends,' *Reference Services Review*, 27(3), 249–253.

■ marketing, rules of

DESCRIPTION

Authoritative statements concerning the conduct of effective marketing.

KEY INSIGHTS

While much academic and practitioner marketing research has focused on the search for laws and principles of marketing, there are also advocates of effective marketing practice who offer guidance in the form of rules governing effective marketing practice. One example from the business literature is:

'... the golden rule of marketing, i.e., that marketing activities should always take place in the language of the customer.' (Guillen 2002)

Examples of rules of marketing put forth in the broader academic literature include:

'The first rule of marketing is to understand the target audience.' (Brown, Long, Gould, Weitz, and Milliken 2000)

'A general rule of marketing, borne out by years of practical experience and research, is that if you want to sell more of something, target the people (or type of people) who are already buying it.' (Buford 2000)

Beyond references to rules of marketing in academic journals, there are also a number of rules of marketing that are presented in books on marketing topics. Examples include:

'What's the first rule of marketing? Understand your market. The second rule? Understand your consumer.' (Barletta 2003).

and a book on the practice of marketing by Lewis Kornfeld of Radio Shack, where he provides 129 rules of marketing including:

'The First Rule of Marketing: Without a product, you don't have a business; the formula is $0 \times 1 = 0$' (Kornfeld 1992)

Finally, beyond rules 'of' marketing, there are also a number of rules 'for' marketing, in that they are viewed as facilitating effective marketing and are linked with the success of the organization. Notable examples of such rules include:

> *The Ten Foot Rule*—a rule of customer service strongly advocated by Wal-Mart founder Sam Walton, which stated that, whenever an associate is within ten feet of a customer, the associate should look the customer in the eye, greet the customer, and ask if they can help the customer. Today, Wal-Mart considers the Ten Foot Rule to be one of its 'secrets' to customer service.

> *The Sundown Rule*—a rule supporting an organizational culture promoting a respect for other's time, a sense of urgency, and a desire to exceed customer expectations, also advocated by Wal-Mart founder Sam Walton, which states that the organization should try to answer requests (from, quite simply, anyone) by the close of business on the day which they are received.

KEY WORDS Authoritative marketing statements, effective marketing

IMPLICATIONS

The experiences and views of other marketers provide yet another means for marketers to obtain perspectives on effective marketing for further reflection. While some espoused rules of marketing overlap to some extent with 'laws of marketing' and 'principles of marketing,' and where others are not as formal or rigorous, such statements can nevertheless assist the marketer further by providing points of reference for marketers engaged in processes of developing and evaluating marketing alternatives for their potential effectiveness. Finally, while not a law, principle, or rule, marketers may also want to take heed of what is referred to in the marketing literature as both an 'adage' and 'venerable phrase': 'Know thy customer.'

APPLICATION AREAS AND FURTHER READINGS

Marketing Strategy

Ryan, C. (2000). 'How Disintermediation is Changing the Rules of Marketing, Sales and Distribution,' *Interactive Marketing* (London), 1(4), 368–374.

Newell, F. (1997). *The New Rules of Marketing: How to Use One-to-One Relationship Marketing to be the Leader in your Industry.* New York: McGraw-Hill.

Nunes, Paul, and Johnson, Brian (2004). *Mass Affluence: Seven New Rules of Marketing to Today's Consumer.* Cambridge, Mass.: Harvard Business School Press.

Kotler, P. (2004). *Ten Deadly Marketing Sins: Signs and Solutions.* Hoboken, NJ: John Wiley & Sons.

BIBLIOGRAPHY

Buford, H. (2000). 'Understanding Gay Consumers: What Matters is not Affluence but Discretionary Income and Time,' *Gay and Lesbian Review*, 7(2), Spring, 26–27.

Barletta, Martha (2003). *Marketing to Women: How to Understand, Reach and Increase your Share of the World's Largest Market Segment.* Chicago: Dearborn Trade Publishing.

Brown, B. A., Long, H. L., Gould, H., Weitz, T., and Milliken, N. (2000). 'A Conceptual Model for the Recruitment of Diverse Women into Research Studies,' *Journal of Women's Health and Gender-Based Medicine*, 9(6), 625–632.

Guillén, M. F. (2002). 'What is the Best Global Strategy for the Internet?' *Business Horizons*, May–June, 39–46.

Kornfeld, Lewis (1992). *To Catch a Mouse, Make a Noise Like a Cheese.* Denton, Tex.: University of North Texas Press.

Wal-Mart (2007). 'The Sundown Rule,' www.walmartstores.com, following links to People, The Wal-Mart Culture, Sundown Rule. Accessed: 7 March 2007.

Wal-Mart (2007). 'The Ten Foot Rule,' www.walmartstores.com, following links to People, The Wal-Mart Culture, The Ten Foot Rule. Accessed: 7 March 2007.

■ marketing, theories of

DESCRIPTION
Theory or theories aimed at understanding, explaining, and/or predicting the nature of marketing and/or its conduct.

KEY INSIGHTS
According to Hunt (1991), a theory is a 'systematically related set of statements, including some law-like generalizations, that is empirically testable.' Given that the scope of marketing is unquestionably broad, it should come as no surprise that agreement upon a general theory of marketing remains elusive. There are, however, theories of marketing that have been suggested for areas within marketing, such as marketing ethics (Hunt and Vitell 1986) and marketing control (Jaworski 1988). Marketing theory therefore comprises a collection of theoretical perspectives, with each varying in the extent that they fit the rigorous definition of theory as given by Hunt (1991).

KEY WORDS Nature of marketing, marketing conduct, effective marketing

IMPLICATIONS
Marketers seeking a greater understanding of broad marketing theory may benefit from a deeper understanding of the many issues associated with its development as discussed and developed in marketing theory research. In support of a better understanding of effective marketing practice, marketers may also wish to obtain greater knowledge of particular theoretical perspectives in marketing, such as those focusing on relationship marketing or internal marketing. While theories continue to develop in many areas of marketing, recognizing that a major source of inspiration of theory development is found in the practice of marketing can assist the marketer in appreciating how the marketer's own actions ultimately contribute to marketing theory development and theoretical knowledge dissemination.

APPLICATION AREAS AND FURTHER READINGS
Marketing Strategy
Day, G. S., and Wensley, R. (1983). 'Marketing Theory with a Strategic Orientation,' *Journal of Marketing*, 47, 79–89.

Marketing Management
Jaworski, B. J. (1988). 'Toward a Theory of Marketing Control: Environmental Context, Control Types and Consequences,' *Journal of Marketing*, 52, July, 23–39.
Hunt, S. D., and Vitell, S. (1986). 'A General Theory of Marketing Ethics,' *Journal of Macromarketing*, 6(1), 5–16.
Buttle, Francis (1996). *Relationship Marketing: Theory and Practice*. London: Chapman.

Services Marketing
Murray, Keith B. (1991). 'A Test of Services Marketing Theory: Consumer Information Acquisition Activities,' *Journal of Marketing*, 55, January, 10–25.

Gronroos, C. (1985). 'Internal Marketing—Theory and Practice,' in T. Block, G. Upah, and V. Zeithlman (eds.), *Services Marketing in a Changing Environment*. Chicago: American Marketing Association, 41–47.

BIBLIOGRAPHY
Hunt, Shelby D. (1991). *Modern Marketing Theory: Critical Issues in the Philosophy of Marketing Science*. Cincinnati: South-Western Publishing Co.
Cornelissen, J. (2002). 'Academic and Practitioner Theories of Marketing,' *Marketing Theory*, 2(1), 133–143.
Hunt, Shelby D. (2002). *Foundations of Marketing Theory: Toward a General Theory of Marketing*. Armonk, NY: M. E. Sharpe
Hunt, Shelby D. (2003). *Controversy in Marketing Theory: For Reason, Realism, Truth, and Objectivity*. Armonk, NY: M. E. Sharpe.
Sheth, Jagdish N., Gardner, David M., and Garrett, Dennis E. (1988). *Marketing Theory: Evolution and Evaluation*. New York: John Wiley & Sons.
Zaltman, Gerald, LeMasters, Karen, and Heffring, Michael (1982). *Theory Construction in Marketing: Some Thoughts on Thinking*. New York: John Wiley & Sons.
Alderson, Wroe (1965). *Dynamic Marketing Behavior, A Functionalist Theory of Marketing*. Homewood, Ill.: R. D. Irwin.
Hunt, S. D. (1993). 'Objectivity in Marketing Theory and Research,' *Journal of Marketing*, 57, April, 76–91.

■ marketing approaches

DESCRIPTION
Marketing characterized by emphases on different purposes, methodologies, strategies, tactics, or techniques which may further involve an emphasis on a particular type or form of offering characteristic, organizational arrangement, information technology, communication approach, communication technique, marketing channel, market emphasis, or market relationship.

KEY INSIGHTS
The increasingly advanced nature of marketing has led to numerous, specific characterizations of marketing. Each, in turn, has resulted in research emphases and practical developments aimed at understanding and explaining better their usefulness and scope for more effective and efficient marketing management and strategy. The following alphabetized list identifies the many different approaches, types, or forms of marketing which are elaborated upon in this dictionary:

above-the-line marketing
affiliate marketing
affinity marketing
ambient marketing *see*
out-of-home marketing
ambush marketing
antimarketing
B2B marketing *see*
business-to-business marketing

B2C marketing *see* **consumer marketing**
below-the-line marketing
bespoke marketing
blog marketing
bottom-up marketing
brick(s)-and-click(s) marketing *see* *entry at* **online marketing**
brick(s)-and-mortar marketing *see* *entry at* **online marketing**

business marketing *see*
**business-to-business
marketing**
business-to-business marketing
business-to-consumer
marketing *see* **consumer
marketing**
buzz marketing *see*
word-of-mouth marketing
by-the-book marketing *see*
traditional marketing
cause marketing *see* **cause-related
marketing**
cause-related marketing
celebrity marketing
cell phone marketing *see* **mobile
marketing**
click(s)-and-brick(s) marketing *see*
entry at **online marketing**
click(s)-and-mortar marketing
see entry at **online
marketing**
collaborative marketing
comarketing *see* **cooperative
marketing**
commercial marketing
comparative marketing
concentrated marketing *see* **niche
marketing**
concurrent marketing
confusion marketing
consumer marketing
contrarian marketing *see*
unconventional marketing
convergence marketing
cooperative marketing
copycat marketing *see* **me-too
marketing**
corporate marketing
counter-marketing
cross-cultural marketing
cross-marketing *see* **cooperative
marketing**
cultural marketing *see*
multicultural marketing
custom marketing *see* **one-to-one
marketing**

customer-centric marketing *see*
customer-oriented marketing
customer experience marketing
see **experiential marketing**
customer-oriented marketing
customer relationship marketing
see **relationship marketing**
customer value marketing *see*
value-based marketing
customized marketing *see*
one-to-one marketing
cybermarketing *see* **online
marketing; Web marketing**
cyberspace marketing *see* **online
marketing; Web marketing**
database marketing
defensive marketing
demarketing
destination marketing *see* **place
marketing**
differentiated marketing
digital marketing *see* **e-marketing**
direct mail marketing *see* **direct
marketing**
direct marketing
direct response marketing *see*
direct marketing
direct-to-consumer marketing
diversity marketing *see*
multicultural marketing
door-to-door marketing *see* **direct
marketing**
eco-centric marketing *see* **green
marketing**
eco-marketing *see* **green
marketing**
electronic marketing *see*
e-marketing
electronic word-of-mouth
marketing *see* **viral marketing**
e-mail marketing *see* **e-marketing;
direct marketing**
e-marketing
enlightened marketing
entrepreneurial marketing
environmental marketing *see*
green marketing

environmentally responsible marketing *see* **green marketing**
ethical marketing
ethnic marketing *see* **multicultural marketing**
ethnomarketing *see* **multicultural marketing**
evangelism marketing *see* **word-of-mouth marketing**
event marketing
experience marketing *see* **experiential marketing**
experiential marketing
fax marketing *see* **e-marketing**
field marketing
for-profit marketing *see* **commercial marketing**
frequency marketing
fusion marketing
generational marketing
global marketing
glocal marketing
government marketing
governmental marketing *see* **government marketing**
grassroots marketing *see* **word-of-mouth marketing**
green marketing
guerrilla marketing
hybrid marketing
idea marketing *see* **social marketing**
inbound marketing
in-cultural marketing *see* **multicultural marketing**
indirect marketing
individual marketing *see* **one-to-one marketing**
industrial marketing *see* **business-to-business marketing**
innovative marketing *see* **enlightened marketing**
institutional marketing
in-store marketing *see* **retail marketing**

integrated direct marketing *see* **direct marketing**
integrated marketing *see* **concurrent marketing**
interactive marketing *see* **e-marketing; online marketing; Web marketing**
internal marketing
international marketing
internet marketing *see* **online marketing; Web marketing**
internet-centric marketing *see* **online marketing; Web marketing**
intrusive marketing
joint marketing *see* **cooperative marketing**
junk e-mail marketing *see* **mass marketing; viral marketing**
lateral marketing
lean-over marketing *see* **stealth marketing**
lifestyle marketing
local marketing
location marketing *see* **place marketing**
loyalty marketing
macromarketing
mail marketing *see* **direct marketing**
many-to-many marketing *see* **affiliate marketing**
markets-of-one marketing *see* **one-to-one marketing**
mass marketing
mass media marketing *see* **mass marketing**
matrix marketing *see* **network marketing**
megamarketing
me-too marketing
micromarketing
minority marketing *see* **multicultural marketing**
mission-based marketing *see* **non-profit marketing**

m-marketing *see* **mobile marketing**

mobile marketing

mobile phone marketing *see* **mobile marketing**

multicultural marketing

multi-level marketing *see* **network marketing**

multimarketing *see* **hybrid marketing**

network marketing

new economy marketing *see* **online marketing; Web marketing**

niche marketing

non-profit marketing

non-profit sector marketing *see* **non-profit marketing**

not-for-profit marketing *see* **non-profit marketing**

offensive marketing

offline marketing *see entry at* **online marketing**

one-to-many marketing *see* **traditional marketing**

one-to-one marketing

online marketing

on-the-edge marketing *see* **unconventional marketing**

OOH marketing *see* **out-of-home marketing**

opt-in marketing *see* **permission marketing**

opt-out marketing *see* **permission marketing**

organizational marketing *see* **business-to-business marketing**

out-of-home marketing

outbound marketing

outdoor marketing *see* **out-of-home marketing**

parity marketing *see* **me-too marketing**

partner marketing *see* **affiliate marketing**

partnership marketing *see* **cooperative marketing**

pay-for-performance marketing *see* **affiliate marketing**

pay-per-click marketing *see* **affiliate marketing**

peer-to-peer marketing *see* **word-of-mouth marketing**

performance-based marketing *see* **affiliate marketing**

permission marketing

person marketing *see* **celebrity marketing**

personal marketing *see* **one-to-one marketing**

personalized marketing *see* **one-to-one marketing**

person-to-person marketing *see* **word-of-mouth marketing**

place-based marketing *see* **out-of-home marketing**

place marketing

point-of-purchase marketing

point-of-sale marketing

postal marketing *see* **direct marketing**

precision marketing

private sector marketing *see* **commercial marketing**

product marketing

public sector marketing *see* **government marketing**

pull marketing

push marketing

radical marketing *see* **unconventional marketing**

reciprocal marketing *see* **cooperative marketing**

referral marketing *see* **affiliate marketing; word-of-mouth marketing**

relationship marketing

remarketing

responsible marketing *see* **ethical marketing; social marketing; green marketing**

retail marketing
retro-marketing
revenue-sharing marketing *see* **affiliate marketing**
right-time marketing *see* **outbound marketing**
search engine marketing *see entry at* **Web marketing**
segment-of-one marketing
segmented marketing *see* **differentiated marketing**
selective marketing *see* **differentiated marketing**
sense of mission marketing *see* **enlightened marketing**
services marketing
short message service marketing/short messaging service marketing *see entry at* **mobile marketing**
SMS marketing *see entry at* **mobile marketing**
social cause marketing *see* **cause-related marketing; social marketing**
social idea marketing *see* **social marketing**
social marketing
socially responsible marketing *see* **social marketing**
societal marketing *see* **enlightened marketing**
spam marketing *see* **mass marketing; viral marketing**
sponsorship marketing
sports marketing
status quo marketing *see* **defensive marketing**
stealth marketing
STP marketing
strategic marketing
supermarketing *see* **retail marketing**
symbiotic marketing *see* **cooperative marketing**
tactical marketing

tailored marketing *see* **one-to-one marketing**
target marketing
telemarketing
telephone marketing *see* **telemarketing**
test marketing
text marketing *see entry at* **mobile marketing**
third sector marketing *see* **non-profit marketing**
through-the-line marketing *see entry at* **above-the-line marketing; below-the-line marketing**
top-down marketing
total integrated marketing
trade marketing *see* **business-to-business marketing**
traditional marketing
transactional marketing
tribal marketing
text marketing *see entry at* **mobile marketing**
unconventional marketing
undercover marketing *see* **stealth marketing**
under-the-radar marketing *see* **stealth marketing**
undifferentiated marketing
value-based marketing
value marketing *see* **enlightened marketing**
viral marketing
virtual marketing *see* **online marketing**
voice mail marketing *see* **direct marketing**
voluntary sector marketing *see* **non-profit marketing**
Web marketing
Web-based marketing *see* **Web marketing; online marketing**
Web-centric marketing *see* **Web marketing; online marketing**
wholesale marketing

wikimarketing *see entry at* **online marketing**
wireless marketing *see* **mobile marketing**
word-of-mouse marketing *see* **viral marketing**
word-of-mouth marketing

World Wide Web marketing *see* **Web marketing; online marketing**
worldwide marketing *see* **global marketing**
WWW marketing *see* **Web marketing; online marketing**

There are also further marketing approaches that are primarily practitioner-generated and, as such, are termed and characterized by businesspersons and business writers through popular books. While not included in this dictionary, they nevertheless provide additional perspectives on marketing. Examples of marketing approaches for which such books exist include:

Accountable Marketing, by Peter Rosenwald
Ageless Marketing, by David B. Wolfe and Robert Snyder
Connected Marketing, by Justin Kir and Paul Marsden
Credibility Marketing, by Larry Chambers
Duct Tape Marketing, by John Jantsch
Gonzo Marketing, by Christopher Locke
Hot Button Marketing, by Barry Feig
Method Marketing, by Denny Hatch
Outrageous Marketing, by Joe Vitale
Power Marketing, by Peter Urs Bender and George Torok
Predatory Marketing, by C. Britt Beemer and Robert L. Shook
Red Zone Marketing, by Maribeth Kuzmeski
Robin Hood Marketing, by Katya Andresen
Seven Second Marketing, by Ivan Misner
Simplicity Marketing, by Steven M. Cristol and Peter Sealey
Testosterone-Free Marketing, by Denise Michaels

Finally, there are still other marketing approaches which are characterized by the marketing of a *highly specific* product, service, or other characteristic. While such terms are also not elaborated upon in this dictionary, due to either their specialized nature or more obvious meaning, individuals interested in their marketing may refer to any number of books on the topics. Examples of highly specific marketing topics for which various books have been written include:

aquaculture marketing
arts marketing
catalog marketing
church marketing
destination marketing
e-mail marketing
ethical marketing
exhibit marketing

fashion marketing
food marketing
furniture marketing
government marketing
guest-based marketing
healthcare marketing
hospitality marketing
leisure marketing
location marketing
membership marketing
multicultural marketing
pharmaceutical marketing
political marketing
search engine marketing
small business marketing
tourism marketing
venue marketing
white paper marketing
youth marketing

KEY WORDS Marketing characteristics, marketing forms, marketing types, marketing purposes, marketing methodologies, marketing techniques

IMPLICATIONS

Marketers have a wide array of marketing approaches, methods, techniques, and tools at their disposal in their efforts to fulfill intended purposes and accomplish specific organizational and marketing objectives. Understanding the benefits and costs associated with the many marketing approaches, as well as assessing the extent of strategic marketing opportunity or threat associated with each, may ultimately benefit organizations and individuals seeking to make the most of their marketing efforts through effective and efficient marketing management and strategies.

APPLICATION AREAS AND FURTHER READINGS

Marketing Strategy
Coviello, N. E., Brodie, R. J., and Munro, H. J. (2000). 'An Investigation of Marketing Practice by Firm Size,' *Journal of Business Venturing*, 15(5–6), 523–545.
Watson, R. T., Pitt, L. F., Berthon, P., and Zinkhan, G. M. (2002). 'U-Commerce: Expanding the Universe of Marketing,' *Journal of the Academy of Marketing Science*, 30(4), 333–347.
Traynor, K., and Traynor, S. C. (1989). 'Marketing Approaches Used by High-Tech Firms,' *Industrial Marketing Management*, 18, 281–287.

Marketing Management
Levitt, Theodore (1983). *The Marketing Imagination*. New York: Free Press.

BIBLIOGRAPHY
Baker, Michael (2003). *The Marketing Book*. Oxford: Butterworth-Heinemann.
Dibb, Sally, Simkin, Lyndon, Pride, William M., and Ferrell, O. C. (2006). *Marketing: Concepts and Strategies*, 5th edn. New York: Houghton Mifflin.

Doyle, Peter, and Stern, Philip (2006). *Marketing Management and Strategy*, 4th edn. Harlow: Pearson Education Limited.

Hunt, Shelby D. (1976). 'The Nature and Scope of Marketing,' *Journal of Marketing*, 40(3), July, 17–28.

Kotler, Philip, and Armstrong, Gary (2004). *Principles of Marketing*, 10th international edn. Upper Saddle River, NJ: Pearson Education International.

Kotler, Philip, and Armstrong, Gary (2006). *Principles of Marketing*, 11th edn. Upper Saddle River, NJ: Pearson Education, Inc.

☐ marketing concept *see* marketing management orientation

■ marketing management orientation

DESCRIPTION

An organization's conceptualization of the way that marketing should be managed to achieve its organizational goals.

KEY INSIGHTS

There are four distinct philosophies concerning how an organization conceives of and manages marketing in the pursuit of organizational goals: the *product concept*—the view that consumers are mainly concerned with purchasing products having the highest levels of performance, quality, or features, thereby prompting the organization to develop such products; the *production concept*—the view that consumers are mainly concerned with purchasing affordable products which are readily available, thereby prompting the organization to develop and implement production and distribution approaches that accommodate such needs; the *selling concept*—the view that consumers will only be motivated to purchase the organization's products in sufficient quantities if the organization engages in extensive sales and promotion efforts; the *marketing concept*—the view that determining the wants and needs of a firm's target market and satisfying customers more effectively and efficiently than competitors is central to the achievement of the organization's goals; and the *societal marketing concept*—the view that the organization should determine the wants and needs of a firm's target market and satisfy customers more effectively and efficiently than competitors in a way that considers company, consumer, and societal interests and ultimately seeks to maintain or improve the well-being of consumers and society. Although each of the concepts has certain merits depending on the nature of the organization and its marketplace, it can also be argued that, by embracing the marketing concept and societal marketing concepts to a greater extent, a firm may be able to enhance its organizational and marketing effectiveness in ways that are more sustainable over the longer term.

KEY WORDS Organizational philosophies, firm orientations

IMPLICATIONS
In support of achieving greater organizational and marketing effectiveness, marketers should seek to understand carefully the conceptual orientations of their organizations toward marketing management. For example, in organizations with diverse functional areas, marketers may find that multiple strong orientations exist within the firm, thereby necessitating initiatives by the marketer to consolidate the firm's orientations to achieve greater focus, as when the firm primarily adopts either the marketing concept or societal marketing concept.

APPLICATION AREAS AND FURTHER READINGS
Marketing Strategy
Avlonitis, G. J., and Gounaris, S. P. (1999). 'Marketing Orientation and its Determinants: An Empirical Analysis,' *European Journal of Marketing*, 33(11/12), 1003–1037.

Marketing Management
Gummesson, Evert (1991). 'Marketing-Orientation Revisited: The Crucial Role of the Part-Time Marketer,' *European Journal of Marketing*, 25(22), 60–75.

Services Marketing
Knights, D., Sturdy, A., and Morgan, G. (1994). 'The Consumer Rules? An Examination of the Rhetoric and "Reality" of Marketing in Financial Services,' *European Journal of Marketing*, 28(3), 42.

BIBLIOGRAPHY
Howard, John A. (1983). 'Marketing Theory of the Firm,' *Journal of Marketing*, 47(4), Autumn, 90–100.
Houston, Franklin S. (1986). 'The Marketing Concept: What It Is and What It Is Not,' *Journal of Marketing*, 50(2), April, 81–87.
Hirschman, Elizabeth C. (1983). 'Aesthetics, Ideologies and the Limits of the Marketing Concept,' *Journal of Marketing*, 47(3), Summer, 45–55.
Kotler, Philip, and Armstrong, Gary (2006). *Principles of Marketing*, 11th edn. Upper Saddle River, NJ: Pearson Education, Inc.

■ marketing mix

(also called the Four Ps or the Seven Ps)

DESCRIPTION
The set of controllable marketing elements that marketers are able to blend either tactically or in support of broader marketing strategies.

KEY INSIGHTS
The marketing mix is traditionally known as consisting of the *Four Ps* (4Ps) of marketing—price, product, promotion, and place (or distribution)—a classification suggested by McCarthy (1960). Yet the marketing mix may certainly have elements beyond the 4Ps when one considers that the marketing of an offering may be influenced by other vitally important elements. Some marketers, therefore, refer to the marketing mix by the Five Ps, where 'people' is added as another key element. Further extensions of the marketing mix found in the academic literature include a reference to a sixth P—'point in time,' i.e. the marketing effort must involve the right point in time (Seiss 2003).

The service marketing mix, also called the extended marketing mix, is traditionally recognized as comprising the *Seven Ps*, namely, the Four Ps plus people, process, and physical evidence. The Ps of marketing have many variations, however. Sets of Ps put forth by marketers include the '9Ps of the consultant's marketing mix'— planning, price, place, packaging, positioning, people, product, promotion, and professionalism (Greenbaum 1990) and variously suggested new Ps for e-marketing, including penetration, permission, personalization, and profitability.

Alternatives to the consideration of marketing mix Ps also are raised by various marketers. Adopting a relationship marketing perspective, Gummesson (1999) advocates the use of '30Rs' instead of the 4Ps. Adopting a customer perspective to the original four Ps of the marketing mix, 'four Cs' have also been put forth—customer solution, customer cost, convenience, and communication, where they are customer equivalents to product, price, place, and promotion, respectively (Lauterborn 1990).

KEY WORDS Ps, controllable marketing elements

IMPLICATIONS

The Four Ps classification of the marketing mix may certainly assist marketers with the identification and evaluation of combinations of marketing elements in support of a firm's tactical and strategic marketing approaches. At the same time, marketers should not be constrained by its use, or even led to believe that the focus of a successful marketing effort resides in the Four Ps alone. Understanding alternative marketing mix classifications to a greater extent can provide the knowledge with additional perspectives that may lead to the development of marketing plans and strategies of greater effectiveness.

APPLICATION AREAS AND FURTHER READINGS

Marketing Strategy
Yoo, B., Donthu, N., and Lee, S. (2000). 'An Examination of Selected Marketing Mix Elements and Brand Equity,'*Academy of Marketing Science*, 28(2), 195–211.
Robinson, William T. (1988). 'Marketing mix reactions to entry,' *Marketing Science* 7, 368–385.
Bowman, D., and Gatignon, H. (1996). 'Order of Entry as a Moderator of the Effect of the Marketing Mix on Market Share,' *Marketing Science*, 15(3), 222–242.

Marketing Management
Gronroos, C. (1997). 'From Marketing Mix to Relationship Marketing—Towards a Paradigm Shift in Marketing,' *Management Decision*, 35(4), 322–339.

Global Marketing
Kreutzer, R. T. (1988) 'Marketing-Mix Standardization: An Integrated Approach in Global Marketing', *European Journal of Marketing*, 22(10): 19–30.

BIBLIOGRAPHY
Van Waterschoot, W., and Van Bulte, C. (1992). 'The 4P Classification of the Marketing Mix Revisited,' *Journal of Marketing*, 56(4), 83–93.
Lauterborn, Robert (1990). 'New Marketing Litany: 4Ps Passé; C-Words Take Over,' *Advertising Age*, October, 26.

Gummesson, E. (1999). *Total Relationship Marketing. Rethinking Marketing Management: From 4Ps to 30Rs*. Oxford: Butterworth-Heinemann.

McCarthy, E. Jerome (1960). *Basic Marketing: A Managerial Approach*. Homewood, Ill.: Richard D. Irwin.

Greenbaum, Thomas L. (1990). *The Consultant's Manual: A Complete Guide to Building a Successful Consulting Practice*. New York: Wiley.

Siess, Judith A. (2003). *The Visible Librarian: Asserting your Value with Marketing and Advocacy*. Chicago: American Library Association.

Dibb, Sally, Simkin, Lyndon, Pride, William M., and Ferrell, O. C. (2006). *Marketing: Concepts and Strategies*, 5th edn. New York: Houghton Mifflin.

Kotler, Philip, and Armstrong, Gary (2004). *Principles of Marketing*, 10th international edn. Upper Saddle River, NJ: Pearson Education International.

Kotler, Philip, and Armstrong, Gary (2006). *Principles of Marketing*, 11th edn. Upper Saddle River, NJ: Pearson Education, Inc.

■ marketing myopia

DESCRIPTION

Short-sightedness in marketing planning and strategy development and, more specifically, a failure to define adequately the scope of the firm's business.

KEY INSIGHTS

Coined and characterized by Levitt (1960), marketing myopia encompasses the view that firms can be short-sighted in their planning and strategy efforts, where short-sightedness involves overly narrow definitions of a firm's markets and excessive attention to present circumstances as opposed to future considerations. Ultimately, a narrow view of a firm's mission leads it to focus excessively on products as opposed to customer wants or needs, thereby posing a threat to the firm's existence as customer wants and needs change over the longer term.

KEY WORDS Marketing planning, **marketing strategy**, short-sightedness

IMPLICATIONS

In an effort to ensure the long-term viability of their firm, marketers should be wary of overly narrow definitions of their business shaping marketing planning and strategy development. In addition, rather than discounting the impact of possible future events and trends due to their unpredictability, marketers should strive to adopt methods that enable them to systematically incorporate knowledge of future possibilities into their ongoing marketing planning and strategy development efforts.

APPLICATION AREAS AND FURTHER READINGS

Marketing Strategy

Webster, Frederick E., Jr. (1992). 'The Changing Role of Marketing in the Corporation,' *Journal of Marketing*, 56(4), October, 1–17.

Services Marketing

Wright, Lauren K. (1995). 'Avoiding Services Marketing Myopia', in William J. Glynn and James G. Barnes (eds.), *Understanding Services Management*. Chichester. John Wiley & Sons.

March, R. (1994). 'Tourism Marketing Myopia,' *Tourism Management*, 15(6), 411.

International Marketing

Douglas, Susan P., and Craig, C. Samuel (1986). 'Global Marketing Myopia,' *Journal of Marketing Management*, 2, Winter.

BIBLIOGRAPHY
Levitt, T. (1960). 'Marketing Myopia', *Harvard Business Review*, 38(4), July–August, 45–56.

■ marketing research

DESCRIPTION

The process of systematically gathering and analyzing data in support of more effective marketing decision making.

KEY INSIGHTS

Marketing reseach, involving the collection and interpretation of data from sources including customers, competitors, and the broader market of the firm, can be characterized several ways. For example, the marketing research that an organization conducts may be causal, exploratory, or descriptive. Firms engage in *causal marketing research* when they seek to understand the cause-and-effect nature of a phenomenon; e.g. the phenomenon is either influenced by the firm's marketing efforts or influences the firm's marketing efforts and the aim is to understand to what extent and why such relationships occur. Firms pursue *descriptive marketing research* when they wish to merely understand more about the nature of a phenomenon on its own (e.g. what habits consumers follow when they get up in the morning). Firms pursuing *exploratory research* seek to understand little-known or emerging phenonomena, where there is no real indication or expectation of what understanding will be obtained (e.g. exploring consumer's game-playing experiences as a means to gain insight into possible trends in game playing).

In addition, firms conducting marketing research often have multiple methods from which to choose. For example, firms may conduct *observational marketing research*, where the research methods involve first-hand observations of consumer's interactions with products and services (e.g. watching how female consumers go about shopping for casual shoes); firms may use *syndicated research*, where data is obtained from an independent research organization whose efforts are financed by member firms in a particular industry (e.g. sales trends in retail shopping by teenagers); firms may use a *focus group*, where a small group of, say, six to ten individuals is personally interviewed by the marketer and, as a result of focusing the group's attention on particular topics, the marketer can listen to the group's views on the topics (e.g. consumer evaluations of a new hybrid automobile); and firms may use *panel data*, where data is collected over an extended period of time from the same sample of respondents (e.g. where multiple consumers comprising a panel keep track of their individual beverage purchase habits over several months).

KEY WORDS Research characteristics, research methods, data collection methods

IMPLICATIONS

Sound marketing research is essential for effective marketing decision making. Marketers involved in the planning, implementation, or use of marketing research initiatives will find considerable benefit in developing a deeper understanding of general marketing research approaches as well as specific data collection methods. Such knowledge will enable the marketer to target efforts which are likely to be both meaningful and relatively cost effective.

APPLICATION AREAS AND FURTHER READINGS

Marketing Strategy
Aaker, D. A., Kumar, V., and Day, G. S. (1998). *Marketing Research*, 6th edn. New York: Wiley.

Marketing Management
Kinnear, T., and Taylor, J. (1991). *Marketing Research: An Applied Approach*, 4th edn. London: McGraw-Hill.

International Marketing
Douglas, Susan P., and Craig, Samuel C. (1983). *International Marketing Research*. Englewood Cliffs, NJ: Prentice-Hall.

Marketing Research
Calder, Bobby J. (1977). 'Focus Groups and the Nature of Qualitative Marketing Research,' *Journal of Marketing Research*, 14(3), Special Issue: Recent Developments in Survey Research, August, 353–364.
Haire, Mason (1950). 'Projective Techniques in Marketing Research,' *Journal of Marketing*, 14(5), April, 649–656.
Hoffman, Elizabeth, Menkhaus, Dale J., Chakravarti, Dipankar, Field, Ray A., and Whipple, Glen D. (1993). 'Using Laboratory Experimental Auctions in Marketing Research: A Case Study of New Packaging for Fresh Beef,' *Marketing Science*, 12(3), Summer, 318–338.
Kozinets, R. V. (2002). 'The Field behind the Screen: Using Netnography for Marketing Research in Online Communities,' *Journal of Marketing Research*, 39(1), 61–72.

BIBLIOGRAPHY
Churchill, Gilbert A. (1983). *Marketing Research: Methodological Foundations*. Chicago: Dryden Press.

■ marketing strategy

DESCRIPTION
The set of marketing decisions made by a firm determining its choice of product markets in which to invest and compete and how the firm decides to compete in terms of its customer value proposition, assets and competencies, and functional area strategies and programs.

KEY INSIGHTS
Marketing strategy comprises decisions that have a major impact on an organization over a long-term time horizon. Firms with a strategic marketing focus (see **strategic marketing**) are concerned with marketing strategy development and implementation to enable the firm to achieve and sustain a competitive advantage. A comprehensive marketing strategy provides the basis for sound marketing planning, as opposed to being mere aspirations for a firm. As such, marketing strategy development necessarily involves external analyses including that for customers, competitors, markets/submarkets, and the environment as well as analyses of

the internal organization. Outputs of strategic analyses include identification of opportunities, threats, trends, and strategic uncertainties as well as strategic strengths, weaknesses, problems, constraints, and uncertainties. In the identification, selection, and implementation of a firm's marketing strategy, the choice of where and how a firm decides to compete includes decisions about the nature of product-market investment by the firm, its value proposition, its assets, competencies, and synergies, and its functional area strategies and programs. Examples of *functional area strategies*, where a functional area strategy can be viewed as any strategy within an organization concerned with a particular function or related activity that is part of a process, are those for individual elements of the firm's marketing mix (e.g. product strategy, pricing strategy, promotion strategy, and distribution strategy) as well as areas often highly influential to marketing strategy development and implementation such as manufacturing strategy and information technology strategy.

KEY WORDS **Strategy**, product markets, **value**, assets, competencies, functional strategies

IMPLICATIONS
Marketing strategy is an area of marketing that receives considerable attention as a result of its importance in enabling a firm to achieve major long-term objectives. As such, marketers should strive to understand the different strategic options available to a firm as well as the processes by which the firm's marketing strategy is developed and implemented.

APPLICATION AREAS AND FURTHER READINGS
Marketing Strategy
Schnaars, Steven P. (1998). *Marketing Strategy*. New York: The Free Press.
Ferrell, O. C., and Hartline, Michael (2004). *Marketing Strategy*, 3rd edn. Mason, Oh.: Thomson Learning/South-Western College Publishing.
Walker, Orville C., Mullins, Jr., John, Boyd, Harper, W., and Larreche, Jean-Claude (2005). *Marketing Strategy: A Decision-Focused Approach*. New York: McGraw-Hill.

Consumer Behavior
Peter, J. Paul, Grunert, Klaus G., and Olson, Jerry C. (1999). *Consumer Behaviour and Marketing Strategy*. London: McGraw-Hill.

BIBLIOGRAPHY
Aaker, David A. (2004). *Strategic Market Management*, 7th edn. New York: John Wiley & Sons.

☐ markets-of-one marketing *see* one-to-one marketing
☐ Maslow's theory of motivation *see* hierarchy of needs theory

■ mass marketing

DESCRIPTION
A marketing approach involving an offering intended for wide appeal among a large market of consumers.

KEY INSIGHTS

Mass marketing involves marketing to a very large group of individuals. Such an approach frequently involves standardization in one or more elements of the firm's offering (see **undifferentiated marketing**). In the area of marketing communications, for example, mass marketing involves the use of *mass media marketing*, an approach where marketing efforts emphasize the use of one or more mass media including television, radio, magazines, books, newspapers, and movie theaters for purposes including advertising and sales promotion. Mass marketing involving the use of the internet can also take many forms, including *spam marketing*, or *junk e-mail marketing*, which involves indiscriminately sending unsolicited and unwanted e-mails in mass quantities in the hope that at least some recipients will respond favorably to the e-mail messages. A mass marketing approach can be contrasted with a niche marketing approach (see **niche marketing**) in that the aim is to profit from standardized marketing efforts conducted on a large scale as opposed to profiting from uniquely serving the needs of one or a few segments.

KEY WORDS Large markets, broad appeal

IMPLICATIONS

The offerings of many firms are intended for mass market appeal where the aim is to benefit from economies of scale associated with serving a large market. Yet, astute marketers also recognize that the effective mass marketing of offerings with broad appeal also involves market segmentation and targeting to at least some or even a great extent. Such a view distinguishes mass marketing practices in the early-to-mid twentieth century from those in much of marketing today.

APPLICATION AREAS AND FURTHER READINGS

Marketing Strategy

Tedlow, Richard S., and Jones, Geoffrey (1993). *The Rise and Fall of Mass Marketing*. London: Routledge.

Kubacki, K., and Croft, R. (2004). 'Mass Marketing, Music, and Morality,' *Journal of Marketing Management* (Helensburgh), 20(5/6), 577–590.

Kotler, P. (1989). 'From Mass Marketing to Mass Customization,' *Planning Review*, September–October, 10–12.

Retail Marketing

Upah, G. D. (1980). 'Mass Marketing in Service Retailing: A Review and Synthesis of Major Methods,' *Journal of Retailing*, 56 (Fall), 59–76.

Public Sector Marketing

Newman, B. I. (ed.) (1999). *The Mass Marketing of Politics*. Thousand Oaks, Calif.: Sage.

BIBLIOGRAPHY

Tedlow, Richard S. (1990). *New and Improved: The Story of Mass Marketing in America*. New York: Basic Books.

Petty, Ross (1995). 'Peddling the Bicycle in the 1890s: Mass Marketing Shifts into High Gear,' *Journal of Macromarketing*, 15(1), 32.

☐ **mass media marketing** *see* mass marketing

☐ matrix marketing *see* network marketing
☐ maturity stage *see* product life cycle

☐ meaningless differentiation *see* positioning
☐ measurability *see* segmentation viability

■ megamarketing

DESCRIPTION
The strategically coordinated application of economic, psychological, political, and public relations skills to gain the cooperation of a number of parties in order to enter and/or operate in a given market.

KEY INSIGHTS
Coined and developed by Kotler (1986), megamarketing takes an enlarged view of marketing where activities, resources, and skills beyond those ordinarily used in marketing are needed to enter and operate in certain markets. An example is when there is a need to use inducements or sanctions to gain the desired response of a market's gatekeepers. As such, public relations and power need to be added to marketing's four Ps of price, promotion, product, and place. Power refers to the art of managing power in relation to the power structures involved and, along with public relations, enables a firm to manage better certain elements of its external environment such as governments, media, or pressure groups. Megamarketing therefore helps a firm in its efforts to enter as well as stay in difficult markets such as those characterized by various forms of protectionism.

KEY WORDS Broadened marketing concept, market entry, market operations

IMPLICATIONS
Marketers seeking to expand a firm's efforts to enter or operate in difficult markets may benefit from understanding and applying concepts found in megamarketing. More broadly, the concept may be a vehicle to help broaden the thinking of marketers about the nature and scope of marketing itself.

APPLICATION AREAS AND FURTHER READINGS

Marketing Concept
Kotler, P. (1987). *Broadening the Concept of Marketing Still Further: The Megamarketing Concept. Contemporary Views on Marketing Practice.* Lexington, Mass.: Lexington Books, 3–18.

Services Marketing
Mobley, M. F., and Elkins, R. L. (1990). 'Megamarketing Strategies for Health Care Services,' *Health Marketing Quarterly*, 7(1–2), 13–19.

Relationship Marketing
Gummesson, Evert (1994). 'Making Relationship Marketing Operational,' *International Journal of Service Industry Management*, 5(5), December, 5–20.

BIBLIOGRAPHY
Kotler, P. (1986). 'Megamarketing,' *Harvard Business Review*, March–April, 117-24.

■ mere exposure effect

DESCRIPTION
An effect where the familiarity obtained simply by being exposed to something results in its increased liking.

KEY INSIGHTS
First quantitatively examined by Zajonc (1968), the mere exposure effect characterizes the phenomenon where individuals demonstrate an increased liking for something simply as a result of their being familiar with it. The effect has been further demonstrated even under conditions where individuals are not able to consciously remember the exposure. One explanation given for the phenomenon is that a greater feeling of safety results from the recognition of a familiar environment.

KEY WORDS Exposure, liking, attitudes

IMPLICATIONS
The phenomenon where an increased liking of something results merely by being exposed to it forms the basis for much of advertising and other forms of promotion and marketing communication. While measurement of the effect in marketing practice is much more difficult than that which could be achieved experimentally, marketers should nevertheless seek to understand the extent to which increased liking of their offerings results from consumers' exposure to various forms of marketing, which may even include a consumer's seeing a product in use by another consumer.

APPLICATION AREAS AND FURTHER READINGS
Consumer Behavior
Janiszewski, Chris (1993). 'Preattentive Mere Exposure Effects,' *Journal of Consumer Research*, 20(3), December, 376-392.
Lee, A. Y. (2001). 'The Mere Exposure Effect: An Uncertainty Reduction Explanation Revisited,' *Personality and Social Psychology Bulletin*, 27(10), 1255-1266.
Miller, Richard L. (1976). 'Mere Exposure, Psychological Reactance and Attitude Change,' *Public Opinion Quarterly*, 40(2), Summer, 229-233.
Holden, S. J. S., and Vanhuele, M. (1999). 'Know the Name, Forget the Exposure: Brand Familiarity versus Memory of Exposure Context,' *Psychology and Marketing*, 16(6), 479-496.

BIBLIOGRAPHY
Zajonc, R. B. (1968). 'Attitudinal Effects of Mere Exposure', *Journal of Personality and Social Psychology*, 9(2), 1-27.
Bornstein, R. F. (1989) 'Exposure and Affect: Overview and Meta-Analysis of Research, 1968-1987,' *Psychological Bulletin*, 106(2), 265-289.
Kunst-Wilson, W. R., and Zajonc, R. B. (1980). 'Affective Discrimination of Stimuli that Cannot be Recognized,' *Science*, 207, 557-558.

□ Merkel's law *see* Hick's law

■ Metcalfe's law

DESCRIPTION
The assertion that the value, utility, or usefulness of a network is proportional to the square of the network size.

KEY INSIGHTS
Named after Robert Metcalfe, inventor of the Ethernet, who originated the idea in 1970, the law's emphasis has been that of telecommunications networks, with the internet, World Wide Web, and fax machines being a few prominent examples of such networks. With a fax machine example, the law conveys the notion that the value of every fax machine increases to the extent there are more fax machines in a given network as a result of there being more total people who are able to receive and send documents. While Metcalfe's law has received widespread acceptance among telecommunications network researchers, the mathematical relationship contained within Metcalfe's law is not without relatively recent critics, some of whom have proposed different mathematical relationships that, in some instances, reflect the view that a network's value may be overstated when equated with the square of the network size. Nevertheless, few argue with the fundamental basis of Metcalfe's law.

KEY WORDS Networks, size, **value**

IMPLICATIONS
Marketers seeking to take advantage of new or existing telecommunication technologies or systems (e.g. e-commerce use by a service industry) can understand better the notion of network value, and hence, value to the network's users, by assessing value in relation to Metcalfe's law.

APPLICATION AREAS AND FURTHER READINGS
Online Marketing
Wymbs, C. (2000). 'How E-commerce is Transforming and Internationalizing Service Industries,' *Journal of Services Marketing*, 14(6-7), 463–478.
Wind, Jerry, and Mahajan, Vijay (2001). *Digital Marketing: Global Strategies from the World's Leading Experts*. New York: John Wiley & Sons, Inc.

Pricing
Bakos, Yannis, and Brynjolfsson, Erik (1999). 'Bundling Information Goods: Pricing, Profits, and Efficiency,' *Management Science*, 45(12), December, 1613–1630.

BIBLIOGRAPHY
Gilder, George (1993). 'Metcalf's Law and Legacy,' *Forbes ASAP*, September.

■ me-too marketing

(also called copycat marketing or parity marketing)

DESCRIPTION
Marketing involving approaches, programs, and techniques that are essentially identical to those of others in a particular industry.

KEY INSIGHTS

Firms with me-too marketing approaches demonstrate little inventiveness and instead rely on practices adopted by many other firms, even though such practices may ultimately reduce differentiation from competitors from a customer perspective. An example is where the marketing efforts of most firms involved in wine tourism have relied on minor changes in branding and packaging along with wine tastings and cellar tours. Such an approach does very little to accommodate variety-seeking behavior among wine consumers. While there are many reasons why firms may pursue me-too marketing, one possible contributor is the existence of the *me-too syndrome* among marketing managers—that if so many others are following a certain practice (e.g. using a particular marketing strategy), they should as well. One suggested alternative to me-too marketing practices in service-related markets is the pursuit of marketing initiatives aimed at creating memorable or 'extraordinary' experiences (Arnould and Price 1993).

KEY WORDS Conventional marketing strategy

IMPLICATIONS

Marketers should recognize that me-too marketing strategies may enable a firm to remain on-par with competitors but that such a strategic approach can have clear limitations for the firm in that it may lead to being blandly associated with competitors. Thus, marketers should assess carefully their marketing strategies for adverse effects when such strategies become common among competitors.

APPLICATION AREAS AND FURTHER READINGS

Marketing Strategy
Mitchell, A. (1996). 'With Copycat Goods and Me-Too Marketing Strategies Abounding, it is Real Difference that will Gain the Edge,' *Marketing Week*, 19(25), 26–29.

Marketing Management
Andrew, J., and Smith, D. (1994). 'Getting beyond Me-Too Marketing: Determinants of the Creativity of Marketing Programs for Mature Products,' *Working Paper: Case Western Reserve*.
Boster, K. (2002). 'Avoiding the "Me Too" Syndrome,' *Textile Rental*, 86(2), 84–89.

Services Marketing
'An Exploration of the use of 'Extraordinary' Experiences in Wine Tourism,' www.unisa.edu.au/winemarketing/conferences/docs/File019.pdf Accessed: 8 October 2007.

BIBLIOGRAPHY

Arnould, E. J., and Price, L. (1993). 'River Magic: Extraordinary Experience and the Extended Service Encounter,' *Journal of Consumer Research*, 20(1), June, 24–47.
Chiagouris, Larry, and Perrell, Leslie (1989). 'Asking the Right Questions,' *Review of Business*, 11(1), 5–8.

☐ me-too syndrome *see* me-too marketing
☐ micro marketing environment *see* microenvironment

■ microenvironment

(also called micro marketing environment)

DESCRIPTION

The set of actors close to the organization that influence its ability to meet the wants and needs of its customers.

KEY INSIGHTS

An organization's microenvironment consists of multiple influential actors which, including the organization itself and its customers, may also include suppliers, competitors, distributors, and other marketing intermediaries, and various publics (e.g. media organizations, citizen groups, etc.). Such influences will be unique to each organization operating in a particular market.

KEY WORDS Actors, organizational relationships

IMPLICATIONS

Astute marketers recognize that there are multiple influences in the firm's macroenvironment that can have a major impact on the firm's marketing effectiveness. In support of accomplishing the firm's marketing objectives, the marketer may find a benefit in identifying more clearly the many different influential macroenvironmental actors and then striving to proactively manage the firm's relationships with such actors as needed.

APPLICATION AREAS AND FURTHER READINGS

Marketing Strategy
Mavondo, F. T. (1999). 'Environment and Strategy as Antecedents for Marketing Effectiveness and Organizational Performance,' *Developments in Marketing Science*, 22, 363–370.
Varey, R. J. (1998). 'Locating Marketing within the Corporate Communication Managing System,' *Journal of Marketing Communications*, 4(3), 177–190.

Marketing Management
Zineldin, Mosad Amin (1998). 'Towards an Ecological Collaborative Relationship Management: A "Co-operative" Perspective,' *European Journal of Marketing*, 32(11–12), December, 1138–1164.
Weitz, Barton A. (1981). 'Effectiveness in Sales Interactions: A Contingency Framework,' *Journal of Marketing*, 45(1), Winter, 85–103.

BIBLIOGRAPHY
Sandhusen, R. L. (2000). *Marketing*. New York: Barron's Educational Services.

■ micromarketing

DESCRIPTION

Marketing emphasizing the tailoring of an organization's offerings to meet the wants and needs of local customers and specific individuals.

KEY INSIGHTS

Micromarketing's emphasis on tailoring to local and individual wants and needs means that its scope clearly includes both local marketing and one-to-one (or individual) marketing. (See **local marketing; one-to-one**

marketing.) Drivers of its use, which is generally on the rise, include the fragmentation of customer markets, increasing competition, and the proliferation of technologies which make it more cost effective for firms to tailor its offerings to the local and individual level. Firms providing offerings to multiple local retailers, for example, often customize their marketing mixes to the level of individual stores.

KEY WORDS Customization, marketing mix tailoring

IMPLICATIONS
Given such factors as increasing market fragmentation and advances in information technologies, marketers should assess regularly their macroenvironment and microenvironment for opportunities to adopt micromarketing approaches in their marketing efforts. While the level at which such approaches may vary from the individual to that of groups of customers, marketers may find that its use, either selectively or as a major focus of the firm, may provide a means of achieving greater customer satisfaction and increased profitability.

APPLICATION AREAS AND FURTHER READINGS
Marketing Strategy
Montgomery, Alan L. (1997). 'Creating Micro-Marketing Pricing Strategies Using Supermarket Scanner Data,' *Marketing Science*, 16(4), 315–337.

Business-to-Business Marketing
Wotruba, T. R. (1996). 'The Transformation of Industrial Selling: Causes and Consequences,' *Industrial Marketing Management*, 25(5), 327–338.

Retail Marketing
Hoch, Stephen J., Kim, Byung-Do, Montgomery, Alan L., and Rossi, Peter E. (1995). 'Determinants of Store-Level Price Elasticity,' *Journal of Marketing Research*, 32(1), February, 17–29.

Marketing Management
Brooksbank, R. (1995). 'The New Model of Personal Selling: Micro-Marketing,' *Journal of Personal Selling and Sales Management*, 15, 61–66.

BIBLIOGRAPHY
Hunt, Shelby D., and Burnett, John J. (1982). 'The Macromarketing/Micromarketing Dichotomy: A Taxonomical Model,' *Journal of Marketing*, 46(3), Summer, 11–26.
Pearce, M. R. (1997). 'Succeeding with Micromarketing,' *Ivey Business Quarterly*, 62(1), 69–72.

☐ milking strategy *see* decline strategies
☐ minority marketing *see* multicultural marketing
☐ mission-based marketing *see* non-profit marketing

■ mobile marketing

(also called mobile phone marketing, m-marketing, wireless marketing, or cell phone marketing)

DESCRIPTION

Marketing aimed at consumers who move readily from place to place or, similarly, any form of marketing by the firm that moves readily to different consumer locations.

KEY INSIGHTS

Mobile marketing is widely viewed as marketing that makes use of mobile communications technologies to reach consumers on the go. Yet, mobile marketing may also involve marketers on the go, as when a firm uses traveling promotional tours to communicate its offerings to consumers at places where consumers are congregated or when a company car carrying an oversized replica of one of the firm's products is driven regularly around a city. Nevertheless, the ability of firms to communicate with consumers on the go, particularly through consumers' mobile telephones and other wirelessly connected communications devices (e.g. notebook computers), is the area that is receiving by far the most attention from firms interested in mobile marketing. For example, *SMS marketing* (or *short message service marketing*, *short messaging service marketing*, *text message marketing*, or *txt marketing*) involves the sending and receiving of short alphanumeric text messages (i.e. up to 160 characters) over a wireless network, where such messages may be initiated or responded to by either the marketer or current or potential customers of the marketer's offerings. While many factors may ultimately influence the successful use of mobile marketing approaches, an area that mobile marketers tend to give considerable attention is the extent that consumers implicitly and/or explicitly agree to be willing recipients of mobile marketing communications.

KEY WORDS Mobile consumers

IMPLICATIONS

Firms offering both products and services aimed at meeting the current or unmet needs and wants of consumers on the go may benefit from a greater understanding of the considerable body of research in the area of mobile marketing. Furthermore, as mobile communications technologies continue their rapid pace of advancement, marketers should strive to remain up to date in their knowledge of a growing array of tactical mobile marketing approaches in addition to those approaches of a more strategic nature, recognizing that consumer receptivity to mobile marketing is evolving simultaneously with its use.

APPLICATION AREAS AND FURTHER READINGS

Marketing Strategy

Facchetti, A., Rangone, A., Renga, F. A., and Savoldelli, A. (2005). 'Mobile Marketing: An Analysis of Key Success Factors and the European Value Chain,' *International Journal of Management and Decision Making*, 6(1), 65–80.

Scharl, A., Dickinger, A., and Murphy, J. (2004). 'Diffusion and Success Factors of Mobile Marketing,' *Electronic Commerce Research and Applications*, 4, 159–173.

Barnes, S. J., and Scornavacca, E. (2004). 'Mobile Marketing: The Role of Permission and Acceptance,' *International Journal of Mobile Communication*, 2(2), 128–139.

Consumer Behavior
Heinonen, K., and Strandvik, T. (2003). *Consumer Responsiveness to Mobile Marketing.* Stockholm: The Stockholm Mobility Roundtable.

BIBLIOGRAPHY
Haig, H. (2002). *Mobile Marketing: The Message Revolution.* London: Kogan Page.
Keen, Peter G. W., and Mackintosh, Ron (2001). *The Freedom Economy: Gaining the M-commerce Edge in the Era of the Wireless Internet.* Berkeley, Calif.: McGraw-Hill.

□ mobile phone marketing *see* mobile marketing
□ modified rebuy *see* industrial buyer behavior
□ monopolistic competition *see* competition
□ monopoly *see* competition
□ monopoly power *see* competition
□ monopsony *see* competition

■ mood effect

DESCRIPTION
Any influence on an individual's behavior, attitudes, or recall characteristics that is attributed to the individual's affective state or disposition.

KEY INSIGHTS
Moods, as affective states, can have influences on an individual's cognitive processes which lead to observable influences on behaviors, attitudes, and the nature of recall. Positive moods, for example, can lead to less cognitive elaboration and observable biases in evaluations of argument quality. More generally, extensive research on consumer moods suggests that consumers' mood states have direct and indirect effects on a range of consumer behaviors, evaluations, and recall characteristics. In particular, mood effects are most evident in areas involving service encounters, point-of-purchase situations, and marketing communications. Negative moods involving anger and uncertainty which result from service delays, for example, are found to clearly influence evaluations of service quality.

KEY WORDS Affective state, behavior, attitudes

IMPLICATIONS
Understanding, explaining, and predicting the influence of consumer mood states on individual actions and attitudes constitutes a significant area of consumer behavior research which marketers may draw upon to increase the effectiveness of various marketing strategies and tactics. From enhancing evaluations of new brand extensions to service quality, the pervasiveness and importance of consumers' mood state influences should not be underestimated.

APPLICATION AREAS AND FURTHER READINGS

Consumer Behavior

Batra, Rajeev, and Stayman, Douglas M. (1990). 'The Role of Mood in Advertising Effectiveness,' *Journal of Consumer Research*, 17(2), September, 203–214.

Barone, Michael J., Miniard, Paul W., and Romeo, Jean B. (2000). 'The Influence of Positive Mood on Brand Extension Evaluations,' *Journal of Consumer Research*, 26(4), March, 386–400.

Miniard, P. W., Bhatla, S., and Sirdeshmukh, D. (1992). 'Mood as a Determinant of Postconsumption Product Evaluations: Mood Effects and their Dependency on the Affective Intensity of the Consumption Experience,' *Journal of Consumer Psychology*, 1, 171–195.

BIBLIOGRAPHY

Gardner, Meryl Paula (1985). 'Mood States and Consumer Behavior: A Critical Review,' *Journal of Consumer Research*, 12(3), December, 281–300.

■ Moore's law

DESCRIPTION

The observation that the number of transistors occupying a square inch of integrated circuit material doubles approximately every eighteen months.

KEY INSIGHTS

Attributable to Gordon E. Moore, co-founder of Intel, based on his earlier observations and predictions (Moore 1965), Moore's law reflects the view that the power of microprocessor technology doubles about every eighteen months. While early observations saw the complexity of integrated circuits doubling about every year since its invention—an observation which held into the late 1970s—the current rate of doubling is expected to hold for at least another decade.

For technology-intensive industries and markets, and especially for semiconductor and other computer component suppliers, Moore's law is as much an important observation as it is a benchmark in technological and competitive goal setting which is influencing the rate of development of next-generation components. Organizations directly or indirectly dependent on such technologies for their success therefore face enormous pressure to develop and launch new products according to windows of time where lateness—and uncompetitiveness—may occur in as little as two to three months.

KEY WORDS Technology, rate of change

IMPLICATIONS

As many new products and services are becoming increasingly influenced by technological developments, Moore's law provides a clear indication of the current and expected rate of change of integrated circuit-related technologies. Marketers must seek to understand the cost and value implications of the rapid yet predictable rate of such change for their products and services to ensure timely provisions of value to customers and industry competitiveness. Moore's law also suggests the imperative of careful planning of next-generation product and service development to ensure future competitiveness and to avoid technological obsolescence.

APPLICATION AREAS AND FURTHER READINGS

Marketing Strategy
Schaller, R. R. (1997). 'Moore's Law: Past, Present and Future,' *IEEE Spectrum*, 34(6), June, 52–59.

Online Marketing
Meijer, J. W. (2003). 'Internet Traffic Growth: A Combination of Moore's Law and Smart Marketing,' *Journal—Communications Network*, 2(3), 83–88.

Marketing Research
Lambert, D. R., Joyce, M. L., and Krentler, K. A. (2004). 'The Multiplying Literature: Moore's Law at Work in Marketing,' *Developments in Marketing Science*, 27, 114–120.

BIBLIOGRAPHY
Moore, Gordon E. (1965). 'Cramming More Components onto Integrated Circuits,' *Electronics*, April 19, 114–117.

■ moral hazard

DESCRIPTION
The risk associated with the presence of an incentive for a party to an agreement or understanding to act in a way that may lead to the party's gain but would not result in its incurring the action's full costs.

KEY INSIGHTS
Moral hazards represent incentives for individuals to breach agreements out of self-interest where there is an absence of sufficient penalties for such behavior and where it is unrealistic for all parties involved to establish conditions which would prevent fully any possibility of such behavior. The concept of the moral hazard is a particularly important one to individuals and organizations operating under contracts, agreements, or other understandings where the nature of the transactions and relationships involved includes a risk of problematic behavior by others which must be carefully managed to avoid a financial loss. Examples of moral hazards include cases where consumers have little incentive to disclose certain pre-existing health conditions prior to their obtaining insurance that would cover them as well as cases where insured automobile drivers may act more recklessly as a result of their having a high level of automobile insurance coverage.

KEY WORDS Risk, self-interest behavior, agreements, contracts

IMPLICATIONS
Marketers should seek to identify and manage moral hazard situations in their business transactions and relationships with customers as well as suppliers, distributors, and other business stakeholders as such problems often cannot be eliminated but can be sought to be minimized. Providing incentives and imposing conditions which help to minimize moral hazards cost-effectively should be the aim of marketers affected by their presence outside and/or within the organization.

APPLICATION AREAS AND FURTHER READINGS

Consumer Behavior

Zweifel, P., and Manning, W. G. (2000). 'Moral Hazard and Consumer Incentives in Health Care,' *Handbooks in Economics*, 17(1A), 409–460.

Hess, J. D., Chu, W., and Gerstner, E. (1996). 'Controlling Product Returns in Direct Marketing,' *Marketing Letters* (New York), 7(4), 307–318.

Marketing Management

Romano, Richard E. (1994). 'Double Moral Hazard and Resale Price Maintenance,' *RAND Journal of Economics*, 25(3), Autumn, 455–466.

Mann, Duncan P., and Wissink, Jennifer P. (1988). 'Money-Back Contracts with Double Moral Hazard,' *RAND Journal of Economics*, 19(2), Summer, 285–292.

BIBLIOGRAPHY

Pauly, Mark V. (1968). 'The Economics of Moral Hazard: Comment,' *American Economic Review*, 58, June, 531–537.

Holmstrom, Bengt (1979). 'Moral Hazard and Observability,' *Bell Journal of Economics*, 10(1), Spring, 74–91.

☐ **motivation, Herzberg's theory of** *see* Herzberg's theory of motivation

☐ **multi-level marketing** *see* network marketing

■ multicultural marketing

(also called cultural marketing, diversity marketing, ethnic marketing, ethnomarketing, in-culture marketing, or minority marketing)

DESCRIPTION

Marketing aimed at consumers of one or more ethnicities and/or cultural backgrounds.

KEY INSIGHTS

Multicultural marketing's emphasis is on efforts to concurrently market to individuals situated within and among multiple cultures. As culture relates to sets of learned behaviors of groups of people, which may therefore include associated values, attitudes, beliefs, traditions, and habits, multicultural marketing emphasizes understanding, whereas ethnicity relates to an individual's identification or affiliation with certain others as a result of one or more factors that may include cultural or racial ties, language, religion, and national origin, multicultural marketing recognizes the benefit of developing and implementing customized marketing initiatives for communicating with and meeting the needs of culturally or ethnically diverse consumers. Growing cultural and ethnic diversity in many cities, regions, and countries is often cited for an increasing interest in multicultural and ethnic marketing by marketers.

While there is much similarity between multicultural marketing and cross-cultural marketing in terms of the marketing emphasis on understanding cultural differences, cross-cultural marketing places greater emphasis on comparisons of differences that exist across cultures which are typically more geographically diverse or dispersed and which are more prevalent across national boundaries. (See **cross-cultural marketing**.)

KEY WORDS Cultural diversity, ethnic diversity

IMPLICATIONS

To the extent that a marketer recognizes diversity among current and prospective customers, which may include differences in beliefs, values, expectations, or preferences for particular products and services, the marketer has an opportunity to develop and implement multicultural or ethnic marketing approaches in the firm's strategies and tactics. While a firm may choose to maintain standardized offerings in response to growing ethnic diversity, for example, such an approach can still involve marketing communications which are customized along some aspect of cultural diversity, such as when a firm develops several outdoor ads for a single product but where the individuals shown in each of the ads differ in ethnicity according to where the ad is displayed.

APPLICATION AREAS AND FURTHER READINGS

Marketing Strategy

Cui, Geng, and Choudhury, Pravat (2002). 'Marketplace Diversity and Cost-Effective Marketing Strategies,' *Journal of Consumer Marketing*, 19(1), 54–73.

Gore, J. P. (1998). 'Ethnic Marketing May Become the Norm,' *Bank Marketing*, 30(9), 12–15.

Nwankwo, S., and Lindridge, A. (1998). 'Marketing to Ethnic Minorities in Britain,' *Journal of Marketing Practice*, 4(7), 200–216.

Schreiber, Alfred (2001). *Multicultural Marketing*. Chicago: NTC Business Books.

DePalma, D. (2000). 'Meet your Customers' Needs through Cultural Marketing,' *E-business Advisor*, 18(8), 18–21.

BIBLIOGRAPHY

Rossman, Marlene L. (1994). *Multicultural Marketing: Selling to a Diverse America*. New York: AMACOM, American Management Association.

Pires, G., and Stanton, J. (2005). *Ethnic Marketing: Accepting the Challenge of Cultural Diversity*. London: Thomson Learning.

Cui, Geng (2001). 'Marketing to Ethnic Minority Consumers: A Historical Journey (1932–1997),' *Journal of Macromarketing*, 21(1), 23–31.

Dahl, Stephan (2002). *Diversity Marketing*. London: Thomson.

Valdes, M. Isabel (2000). *Marketing to American Latinos: A Guide to the In-Culture Approach*. Ithaca, NY: Paramount Market Publishing.

■ Murphy's law

DESCRIPTION

The popular adage often stated as, 'whatever can go wrong, will go wrong.'

KEY INSIGHTS

Although it is not clear who originated the phrase, with its origins possibly being 1948 at Edwards Air Force Base, Murphy's law remains a topic of ongoing attention, particularly in Western cultures, as a result of its proverbial nature made memorable through long and repeated use by both individuals and organizations. Originally relating to a product development context, Murphy's law has since been adopted by individuals and organizations to characterize the prediction that, if something is given a chance to go wrong, it will go wrong.

KEY WORDS Planning, problems

IMPLICATIONS

Marketers involved in any marketing initiative, whether product development or promotion implementation, must strive to anticipate possible problems and, if such problems are critical to the effort's success, make room for their occurrence in marketing plans. In particular, marketers should recognize that the likelihood of marketing problem occurrence increases as the complexity of marketing plans increase.

APPLICATION AREAS AND FURTHER READINGS

International Marketing
Harvey, Michael G. (1983). 'The Multinational Corporation's Expatriate Problem: An Application of Murphy's Law,' *Business Horizons*, 26(1), 71–78.

Marketing Management
Fearn-Banks, Kathleen (2006). *Crisis Communications: A Casebook Approach*. Mahwah, NJ: Lawrence Erlbaum Associates, Inc.

New Product Development
Anderson, David M. (2003). *Design for Manufacturability & Concurrent Engineering: How to Design for Low Cost, Design in High Quality, Design for Lean Manufacture, and Design Quickly for Fast Production*. Cambria, Calif.: CIM Press.

BIBLIOGRAPHY
Dimson, E., and Marsh, P. (1999). 'Murphy's Law and Market Anomalies,' *Journal of Portfolio Management*, 25(2), 53–69.
Bloch, A. (1977). *Murphy's Law and Other Reasons Why Things Go Wrong*. London: Methuen.

☐ **myopia** *see* marketing myopia

N

☐ Nash equilibrium *see* game theory
☐ natural selection theory *see* Darwinian evolution theory

■ need

DESCRIPTION

An innate feeling of deprivation in a person.

KEY INSIGHTS

Humans have a variety of needs, which may be described, categorized, and related in any number of ways. Examples are needs for safety, love/belonging, and esteem which have been proposed as hierarchically related by Maslow (1943). (See **hierarchy of needs theory**.) It is clearly within the scope of marketing to aim to satisfy human needs as well as wants, yet it is also recognized within the marketing discipline that consumption needs are just one of several types of human needs. Beyond recognized needs, astute marketers further strive to be sensitive to consumes' unmet needs in efforts to achieve competitive advantages through their offerings.

KEY WORDS Consumer deprivation

IMPLICATIONS

Within marketing is an implicit concern with sensitively serving and satisfying human needs. In terms of the process by which consumers may seek to satisfy their needs through a marketer's offerings, need recognition is a considered a key phase in the buyer decision process. In addition, marketers should also focus on the identification of unmet needs in the development of marketing strategies to assist in achieving competitive advantages.

APPLICATION AREAS AND FURTHER READINGS

Consumer Behavior

Wilk, R. (2002). 'Consumption, Human Needs, and Global Environmental Change,' *Global Environmental Change* (Guildford), 12(1), 5–13.

Gallup, George H. (1976–77). 'Human Needs and Satisfactions: A Global Survey,' *Public Opinion Quarterly*, 40(4), Winter, 459–467.

Marketing Strategy

Siderman, Ben (2003). *Leonardo's Laptop: Human Needs and the New Computing Technologies*. Cambridge, Mass.: MIT Press.

Social Responsibility
Abratt, Russell, and Sacks, Diane (1988). 'The Marketing Challenge: Towards Being
   Profitable and Socially Responsible,' *Journal of Business Ethics*, 7(7), July, 497–
   507.

BIBLIOGRAPHY
Maslow, A. H. (1943). 'A Theory of Human Motivation,' *Psychological Review*, 50, 370–
   396.

☐ need hierarchy theory *see* hierarchy of needs theory
☐ need recognition *see* buyer decision process
☐ negative demand *see* demand

■ network effect

(also called network externality)

DESCRIPTION
The change in value or utility that is derived from a product or service as a
result of it also being used or consumed by others.

KEY INSIGHTS
When a good is influenced by network effects, new users or consumers of
it indirectly influence the value of the good to other users or consumers.
Typically, the value to those using such offerings (whether individuals or
organizations) increases to the extent others also use such offerings as a
result of certain benefits associated with a large number of users. Physical
connectedness of products, compatibility of a product's use among others
in a diverse network, standardization of components, and the availability
of post-purchase service for a durable good are just a few examples
of where a product or service functions better when large numbers of
others are also involved in its consumption or use. Yet, not all network
effects are positive. Network effects can be negative when problems
associated with networks influence its member users, as when too high
a call volume on a mobile telephone network leads to delays for all
users.

KEY WORDS Networks, **utility**, **value**, users

IMPLICATIONS
Marketers should seek to understand how and to what extent consumers'
use of their offerings is influenced by network effects in order to assess
better such effects on customer purchase motivations, adoption likeli-
hoods, and post-purchase evaluations. Managing network effects to leverage positive influences and reduce adverse influences over the life cycle
of a product or service should be the aim of the marketer involved in
managing the offerings' perceived and actual value among customers in
the firm's market. Understanding positive and negative network effects
associated with competitive offerings, irrespective of the offerings' actual

superiority/inferiority, may also be beneficial to a firm in developing appropriate marketing strategies.

APPLICATION AREAS AND FURTHER READINGS

Marketing Strategy

Basu, A., Mazumdar, T., and Raj, S. P. (2003). 'Indirect Network Externality Effects on Product Attributes,' *Marketing Science*, 22(2), 209–221.
Liebowitz, Stan J., and Margolis, Stephen E. (1999). *Winners, Losers & Microsoft*. Oakland, Calif.: The Independent Institute.
Shankar, V., and Bayus, B. L. (2003). 'Network Effects and Competition: An Empirical Analysis of the Home Video Game Industry,' *Strategic Management Journal*, 24(4), 375–384.

Marketing Management

Katz, Michael L., and Shapiro, Carl (1986). 'Technology Adoption in the Presence of Network Externalities,' *Journal of Political Economy*, 94(4), September, 822–841.

Marketing Research

Park, Sangin (2004). 'Quantitative Analysis of Network Externalities in Competing Technologies: The VCR Case,' *Review of Economics and Statistics*, 86(4), November, 937–945.

BIBLIOGRAPHY

Katz, Michael L., and Shapiro, Carl (1985). 'Network Externalities, Competition, and Compatibility,' *American Economic Review*, 75(3), June, 424–440.

☐ **network externality** *see* network effect

■ network marketing

(also called matrix marketing or multi-level marketing)

DESCRIPTION

Marketing involving the use of an interconnected system of distributors as the primary means to accomplish an organization's marketing objectives.

KEY INSIGHTS

While network marketing may take many forms, the common element in any network marketing approach is the use of an interconnected system of firms or other individuals outside the organization who essentially act as agents of the firm in facilitating the distribution of the firm's offerings and in securing sales from end-customers. (The scope of network marketing can thus be said to overlap with many aspects of affiliate marketing—see **affiliate marketing**.) Organizations or individuals in the firm's marketing network may be franchisees of the firm or independent contractors who are compensated by the firm based on their sales of the firm's offerings. 'Multi-level,' as a concept, simply refers to the use of multiple levels of distribution by the firm in providing its offerings to current and potential customers and in achieving revenue. Contrary to what some have been led to believe, multi-level marketing is not illegal strictly by definition. It becomes illegal, however, when most of the firm's revenue comes from the recruitment of network members as opposed to revenue which comes from end-customers. In such a case, the firm can be said to be engaging in an illegal 'pyramid scheme' or 'Ponzi scheme.' Firms engaged in network marketing frequently assist with the management of the firm's marketing network by providing support to network members including product storage and distribution as well as information systems to manage network member compensation. In addition, given the trend of increased use of online marketing, network marketing arrangements have the opportunity to become increasingly sophisticated in terms of how online and offline network interactions are facilitated and integrated.

KEY WORDS Marketing networks, distribution systems

IMPLICATIONS

Firms in any number of markets may use a network marketing approach as their primary means of marketing. (Avon and Tupperware are two of many notable firms using the approach.) Marketers therefore have an opportunity to evaluate the network marketing approach for its benefits and costs as part of a major focus of the firm or a supplemental emphasis. Assuming the approach is implemented, marketers must take care to ensure they conform to laws regarding its use, which may include proper disclosures to new or potential network members of the likelihood that network members may actually profit from being part of the firm's marketing network as well as how profitability is to be calculated.

APPLICATION AREAS AND FURTHER READINGS

Marketing Strategy
Grayson, K. (1996). 'Examining the Embedded Markets of Network Marketing Organizations,' in D. Iacobucci (ed.), *Networks in Marketing*. Thousand Oaks, Calif.: Sage, 325–341.

Marketing Management
Coughlan, A. T., and Grayson, K. (1998). 'Network Marketing Organizations: Compensation Plans, Retail Network Growth, and Profitability,' *International Journal of Research in Marketing*, 15, 401–426.
Berry, R. (1998). *Direct Selling: From Door to Door to Network Marketing*. Oxford: Butterworth-Heinemann.

International Marketing
Croft, R., and Woodruffe, H. (1996). 'Network Marketing: The Ultimate in International Distribution?' *Journal of Marketing Management*, 12, 201–214.

BIBLIOGRAPHY
Poe, R. (1995). *Wave 3: The New Era in Network Marketing*. Taipei: Shy-Mau Publications Co.
Poe, R. (1999). *Wave 4: Network Marketing in the 21st Century*. Rockland, Calif.: Prima Publishing.
Hawkins, L. S. (1991). *How to Succeed in Network Marketing*. London: Piatkus.
Woods, T. (1998). 'Let's Just Call it Matrix Marketing,' *Mc Technology Marketing Intelligence*, 18(5), May, 52–53.

■ network theory

DESCRIPTION
Theory aimed at understanding and explaining how, why, and to what extent networks of organizations or individuals in various forms are, or are likely to be, effective and/or efficient means to achieve the particular goals and aims of one or more organizations or individuals associated with a network.

KEY INSIGHTS
From the perspective of the ongoing performance and capabilities of a particular actor, whether organization or individual, network theory recognizes that the actor's relationships with other organizations or individuals is an important dimension that is interrelated to the dimension characterized by the actor's own activities and resources. Given this view, numerous strategic issues can be explored and understood better within various theoretical frameworks, such as in understanding and explaining better the relevance of network connectivity in combining common and complementary skills, resources, assets, and/or competencies found within inter-firm relationships to enhance a particular firm's production levels and capabilities. The scope of network theory is therefore broad and encompasses a range of theoretical frameworks on which to base examinations of issues in more specific contexts.

KEY WORDS Networks, interorganizational relationships, connectivity

IMPLICATIONS
Frameworks and concepts grounded in network theory can be potentially useful to marketers seeking to understand, explain, or predict the effectiveness and/or efficiency of strategic actions and initiatives ranging from firm-level marketing activities to the development of international markets. Of particular growing interest to many marketers is the view that the broader market economy can be increasingly viewed as being networked and therefore able to analyzed and evaluated from network theory-based perspectives.

APPLICATION AREAS AND FURTHER READINGS
Marketing Strategy
Achrol, Ravi S., and Kotler, Philip (1999). 'Marketing in the Network Economy,' *Journal of Marketing*, 63, Fundamental Issues and Directions for Marketing, 146–163.
Rowley, T. J. (1997). 'Moving beyond Dyadic Ties: A Network Theory of Stakeholder Influences,' *Academy of Management Review*, 22(4), 887–910.

Marketing Research
Webster, C. M., and Morrison, P. D. (2004). 'Network Analysis in Marketing,' *Australasian Marketing Journal*, 12(2), 8–18.

BIBLIOGRAPHY
Achrol, R. S. (1997). 'Changes in the Theory of Interorganizational Relationships in Marketing: Toward a Network Paradigm,' *Journal of the Academy of Marketing Science*, 25(1), 56–71.
Johanson, J., and Mattson, L.-G. (1992). 'Network Positions and Strategic Action: An Analytical Framework', in B. Axelsson and G. Easton (eds.), *Industrial Networks: A New View of Reality*. London: Routledge, 205–217.

☐ **new economy marketing** *see* online marketing

■ new product

DESCRIPTION

A good, either a product or service or product and service combination, that is perceived as new by some potential customers in the marketplace.

KEY INSIGHTS

New products, in being viewed as new by potential consumers along at least one dimension or attribute, may range from products incrementally different from the firm's current products to the radically different. At one end of the spectrum, a new product may involve a simple change in aesthetics, as when it has a more appealing package. At the other end of the spectrum, the new product may be a new-to-the-world product, where there is nothing quite like it anwhere, thereby making it very difficult for potential customers to evaluate. Such products are rare, however. In between are new products that typically involve a change in value, such as when a new product has twice the performance of an existing product but where it is also offered at less than twice the existing product's price. In addition to decisions about the type and degree of product newness, marketers also face many other decisions regarding the development and effective use of such products (see **product levels**; **new product development**), for example) in support of achieving the firm's broader objectives. Clearly, the pursuit and adoption of practices and approaches associated with effective marketing will likely provide the marketer with considerable assistance in making the most of all of the firm's new products.

KEY WORDS Original products, recent products

IMPLICATIONS

Given the dynamic of most markets, new products are the life blood of most organizations. Marketers may therefore benefit tremendously from a greater understanding of the many options and issues associated with the use of new products as part of the firm's marketing and business strategies and broader organizational aims.

APPLICATION AREAS AND FURTHER READINGS

Marketing Strategy
Cooper, Robert G., and Kleinschmidt, E. J. (1999). *New Products: The Key Factors in Success*. Chicago: American Marketing Association.

Marketing Management
Crawford, C. Merle (1994). *New Product Management*, 4th edn. Burr Ridge, Ill.: Irwin.

Services Marketing
Berry, Leonard L., and Parasuraman, A. (1991). *Marketing Services: Competing through Quality*. New York: Free Press.

BIBLIOGRAPHY
Urban, G. L., and Hauser, J. R. (1993). *Design and Marketing of New Products*, 2nd edn. Englewood Cliffs, NJ: Prentice Hall.

■ new product development

DESCRIPTION

The set of actions of an organization aimed at developing a new product intended for introduction into the market.

KEY INSIGHTS

While every organization differs in its specific approach to new product development (NPD), the process of developing new products is often viewed as consisting of a number of interrelated and overlapping activities. These activities may include: *idea generation*, where the firm systematically searches for new ideas and seeks to generate a large number of ideas from which to draw upon for further development; *idea screening*, where the firm performs an initial cut to filter out the many bad ideas and keep the smaller number of good ones; *business analysis*, where the firm conducts reviews of sales, cost, and profit projections for the envisioned new product to determine if it is likely to contribute sufficiently to meeting the firm's overall objectives; *concept testing*, where the firm tests new product concepts with small numbers of consumers to assess better the appeal associated with each concept; *product development*, where the product concept is transformed into a physical product; *test marketing*, where the product is marketed realistically on a small scale and in a controlled manner so as to be able to learn about the new product's receptivity and fine-tune the overall marketing approach; and *commercialization*, where the firm enters the new product into the market on a larger scale than the test marketing and where the firm commits to competing with the new product for some substantial period of time. Depending on the nature of the good to be developed and the preferences of the firm's management, a firm may choose to pursue such NPD activities either sequentially, where a next step in the process is only begun when the previous step is completely finished, or simultaneously, where the firm performs multiple activities in parallel. One advantage of a simultaneous approach is that it may help the firm to reduce the overall time of NPD.

Aside from the many possible benefits accruing from new product development, there are, of course, many challenges and risks associated with NPD. One general challenge that may be encountered across one or more areas of NPD within the organization is the *not-invented-here syndrome* (or *NIH syndrome*), where there is resistance to the acceptance or adoption of others' new ideas or actions as a result of such ideas or actions not having been developed within the organization already (e.g. 'if we didn't think of it or do it already, it must not be worth doing'). In addition, there are clear risks associated with individual NPD activities that must also be managed. In idea generation, too few ideas may be generated and/or such ideas may be of insufficient quality. In idea screening, there is the risk of rejecting a good idea as well as the risk of accepting a bad idea. In business analysis, there are risks of bias or inadequate analysis. In concept testing, there is the risk that the concepts developed are sub-optimal in some way. In product development, there is the risk that quality problems are missed that only surface when larger quantities are produced later on. In test marketing, there is a risk that competitors may learn from the presence of the offering in the market and gain from the knowledge to develop a more effective competitive response. In commercialization, there is the risk that the product will fail to meet either the expectations of customers or the firm's management or both.

KEY WORDS Product development, market introduction process

IMPLICATIONS
In order to increasing the likelihood of success of a firm's NPD efforts, marketers may benefit from developing a greater knowledge of the different considerations and risks associated with NPD. For example, astute marketers will recognize that not only are time and money required for effective NPD, commitment from the organization is essential, and gaining commitment is a responsibility of management that can be facilitated by many different managerial actions (e.g. showing how the effort is aligned with the firm's strategy, encouraging risk-taking behavior, providing managerial guidance).

APPLICATION AREAS AND FURTHER READINGS

Marketing Strategy
Cohen, M. A., Eliashberg, J., and Ho, T. H. (1996). 'New Product Development: The Performance and Time-to-Market Tradeoff,' *Management Science*, 42(12), 1753–1755.
Leonard-Barton, D. (1992). 'Core Capabilities and Core Rigidities: A Paradox in Managing New Product Development,' *Strategic Management Journal*, 13, 111–125.

Marketing Management
Schilling, M. A., and Hill, C. W. L. (1998). 'Managing the New Product Development Process,' *Academy of Management Executive*, 12(3), 67–81.

Services Marketing
de Brentani, U. (1991). 'Success Factors in Developing New Business Services,' *European Journal of Marketing*, 25(2), 33–59.

Marketing Education
Dacko, Scott G. (2001). 'Narrowing Skill Development Gaps in Marketing and MBA Programs: The Role of Innovative Technologies for Distance Learning,' *Journal of Marketing Education*, 23, 228–239.

BIBLIOGRAPHY
Cooper, R. G., and Kleinschmidt, E. J. (1995). 'Benchmarking the Firm's Critical Success Factors in New Product Development,' *Journal of Product Innovation Management*, 12(5), 374–391.

☐ new task *see* industrial buyer behavior

■ niche marketing

(also called concentrated marketing)

DESCRIPTION
The approach of making a particular small group or segment of buyers the focus of a firm's marketing efforts.

KEY INSIGHTS

Marketers often engage in niche marketing with the aim of uniquely serving the needs of one or a few segments and achieving niche dominance. When firms serve the needs of particular niches, they also have the opportunity to develop specialized knowledge of the needs and wants of customers in the niches, which may provide them with a competitive advantage relative to firms focusing their marketing efforts more broadly. In addition, the small size of some niches can also mean there is relatively little competition as a result of the niches being either ignored or overlooked by competitors. Finally, niche marketing may be beneficial to firms having relatively limited resources since the approach enables the firm to concentrate their resources on a niche with greater effectiveness.

KEY WORDS Focused marketing, market segments

IMPLICATIONS

Increasing market fragmentation in some markets may provide the marketer with an opportunity to identify and ultimately serve certain emerging market niches more profitably than competitors. Given the attractiveness of niche marketing to firms with limited resources, marketers should also recognize that new competitors may enter a market using a niche marketing approach but eventually expand to become competitors in the broader market for a firm's offerings.

APPLICATION AREAS AND FURTHER READINGS

Marketing Strategy

Raynor, M. E. (1992). 'The Pitfalls of Niche Marketing,' *Journal of Business Strategy*, 13(2), 19–24.

Dalgic, T., and Leeuw, M. (1994). 'Niche Marketing Revisited: Concept, Applications and Some European Cases,' *European Journal of Marketing*, 28(4), 39.

Shani, D., and Chalasani, S. (1993). 'Exploiting Niches Using Relationship Marketing,' *Journal of Business and Industrial Marketing*, 8(4), 58.

Marketing Research

Weinstein, Art (1994). *Market Segmentation: Using Demographics, Psychographics, and Other Niche Marketing Techniques to Predict and Model Customer Behavior.* Chicago: Probus Pub. Co.

Leeming, E. Janice, and Tripp, Cynthia F. (1994). *Segmenting the Women's Market: Using Niche Marketing to Understand and Meet the Diverse Needs of Today's Most Dynamic Consumer Market.* Chicago: Probus.

BIBLIOGRAPHY

Linneman, R. E., and Stanton, J. L. (1991). *Making Niche Marketing Work: How to Grow Big by Acting Smaller.* New York: McGraw Hill.

☐ **niche strategy** *see* decline strategies

☐ **NIH syndrome** *see* new product development

☐ **nine effect** *see* odd price effect

☐ **nominal scale** *see* scale

☐ **nomological validity** *see* validity

☐ non-cooperative game theory *see* game theory
☐ non-durable goods *see* goods
☐ non-price competition *see* competition

■ non-profit marketing

(also referred to as nonprofit marketing; also called non-profit sector marketing, non-profit marketing, not-for-profit marketing, mission-based marketing, third sector marketing, or voluntary sector marketing)

DESCRIPTION
Marketing with an emphasis on achieving organizational objectives that are not commercially motivated, where income generated is for its operations and stated purpose rather than for the private gain of any individual having an interest in the organization.

KEY INSIGHTS
Given that a non-profit organization's goals are not focused directly on profitability, the organization's purpose or mission clearly becomes prominent in guiding and shaping the non-profit firm's marketing efforts. At the same time, there are also markets where multiple non-profit firms vie for the same customers, thereby creating a need within the firm to increase its competitiveness. Adopting this perspective of non-profit marketing, Brinckerhoff (1997) uses the term *mission-based marketing* to denote the set of mission-directed marketing actions that help a non-profit organization pursue its organizational goals more effectively in relation to the marketing actions of competitors. Non-profit marketing may therefore involve marketing activities directed at individuals whom it seeks to serve or other individuals or organizations which may, for example, serve as sources of funding for the non-profit organization's activities. Numerous marketing approaches are therefore potentially relevant to the non-profit organization, with affinity marketing, event marketing, internal marketing, counter-marketing, and demarketing being just some examples. (See **affinity marketing; event marketing; internal marketing; counter-marketing; demarketing**.)

KEY WORDS Mission, organizational mission

IMPLICATIONS
The increasingly competitive environment facing many non-profit organizations is leading some to adopt marketing practices that have been traditionally associated with commercial or for-profit marketing. Marketers within non-profit organizations thus have an opportunity to become more familiar with a wide array of marketing approaches as a means to evaluate better their appropriateness in supporting their organization's mission.

APPLICATION AREAS AND FURTHER READINGS

Marketing Strategy

Kotler, P., and Andreasan, A. (1991). *Strategic Marketing for Nonprofit Organizations*, 4th edn. Upper Saddle River, NJ: Prentice-Hall.

Hatten, M. L. (1982). 'Strategic Management in Not-for-Profit Organisations,' *Strategic Management Journal*, 3, 89–104.

Marketing Management

Lovelock, Christopher H., and Weinberg, Charles B. (1984). *Marketing for Public and Nonprofit Managers*. New York: John Wiley & Sons.

Arnett, D. B., German, S. D., and Hunt, S. D. (2003). 'The Identity Salience Model of Relationship Marketing Success: The Case of Nonprofit Marketing,' *Journal of Marketing*, 67(2), 89–105.

Brinckerhoff, Peter C. (2003). *Mission-Based Marketing: An Organizational Development Workbook: A Companion to Mission-Based Marketing*, 2nd edn. Hoboken, NJ: Wiley.

BIBLIOGRAPHY

Rados, D. L. (1996). *Marketing for Nonprofit Organizations*, 2nd edn. London: Auburn House.

Brinckerhoff, P. (1997). *Mission-Based Marketing: How your Not-for-Profit Organization can Succeed in a More Competitive World*. Dillon, Colo.: Alpine Guild, Inc.

☐ **non-profit sector marketing** *see* non-profit marketing

☐ **non-response bias** *see* bias

☐ **normal goods** *see* goods

☐ **not-for-profit marketings** *see* non-profit marketing

☐ **not-invented-here syndrome** *see* new product development

☐ **NPD** *see* new product development

O

□ O, theory *see* E and O theories of change
□ objective-and-task method *see* promotion budget setting methods
□ observation bias *see* bias
□ observational marketing research *see* marketing research
□ Occam's razor *see* parsimony, law of
□ occasion segmentation *see* segmentation

■ odd price effect

DESCRIPTION
Any effect on product purchase amounts or purchase frequencies resulting from a product's price ending in odd-numbered digits.

KEY INSIGHTS
Pricing decisions where odd numbered prices are used (or avoided) indicates that the pricing approach is a form of psychological pricing, where the aim is to manipulate consumers' perceptions of price desirability through the selection of a price's ending digits. Research on the topic for a wide array of products clearly suggests that most managers believe that price endings are important in influencing product sales as a result of believing that most customers are more receptive to some price endings over others. While many managers are found to advocate the use of odd pricing to generate additional demand and increase sales at the level of an individual brand, particularly where endings of five or nine are used as means to make the product appear significantly cheaper in comparison to pricing to the next round number or even number, other managers are also observed to advocate the use of even-numbered pricing. Actual influences of price endings are observed to vary among product categories and price amounts. Beyond operational considerations, explanations for managerial use of price endings to achieve desired effects include the acknowledgment of consumer behaviors such as tendencies for consumers to round prices down, limited consumer memories, and consumers using price endings to draw conclusions about whether or not a product is on sale.

KEY WORDS Pricing, perception

IMPLICATIONS

Marketers involved in price setting should seek to understand both through prior research and experience how price endings can be used as a means to influence subtly a consumer's perceptions of a product's or brand's price or its attributes such as value or quality.

APPLICATION AREAS AND FURTHER READINGS

Pricing

Estelami, H. (1999). 'The Computational Effect of Price Endings in Multi-Dimensional Price Advertising,' *Journal of Product and Brand Management*, 8(2-3), 244-256.

Gendall, P., Holdershaw, J., and Garland, R. (1997). 'The Effect of Odd Pricing on Demand,' *European Journal of Marketing*, 31(11-12), 799-813.

Naipaul, S., and Parsa, H. G. (2001). 'Menu Price Endings that Communicate Value and Quality,' *Cornell Hotel and Restaurant Administration Quarterly*, 42(1), 26-37.

BIBLIOGRAPHY

Stiving, Mark, and Winer, Russell S. (1997). 'An Empirical Analysis of Price Endings with Scanner Data,' *Journal of Consumer Research*, 24(1), June, 57-67.

Gendall, Philip (1998). 'Title: Estimating the Effect of Odd Pricing,' *Journal of Product & Brand Management*, 7(5), October, 421-432.

■ offensive marketing

DESCRIPTION

Marketing focused on attacking, directly or indirectly, the strategic positions of any number of a firm's competitors.

KEY INSIGHTS

In adopting an offensive marketing approach, a firm may use any number of 'attack' or 'assault' strategies to strengthen its own position and weaken the positions of its current or future competitors in the marketplace. In some situations, offensive marketing may be used to challenge a firm which is either dominant or which has greater dominance in the marketplace. In this context, examples of offensive marketing approaches—where each is based on a military analogy—include: a 'frontal attack,' where the firm matches the dominant firm's marketing in some area (e.g. pricing, product features, or promotions); a 'flanking assault,' where the firm pits its strengths against a competitor's identified weaknesses (e.g. entering a geographic market where the competitor's presence is very limited); an 'encirclement attack,' where the firm pursues a multi-pronged onslaught against the competitor to dilute its resources (e.g. introducing numerous new product lines to overwhelm the competitor's ability to respond in any one area); a 'bypass attack,' where the firm pursues markets where the competitor is absent (e.g. diversifying into an unrelated product market), and 'guerrilla warfare,' where the firm engages in a series of small intermittent attacks on the competitor's position in an effort to disorient the competitor and ultimately obtain some kind of concession from the competitor (e.g. using public relationships campaigns to put a market-monopolizing competitor in a bad light in the eyes of the public, prompting the competitor to loosen its stranglehold on the market; see **guerrilla marketing**).

In other situations, offensive marketing may be used by a market leader to defend its position, such as when a firm initiates a 'pre-emptive strike' against one or more firms who are encroaching on its position. An example of a pre-emptive strike in this context is when a firm engages in a strategy of saturating the market with multiple product offerings, thereby leaving less space for current and future competitors to gain a foothold. Such an approach may be viewed as an 'offensive defense' marketing strategy.

KEY WORDS Attack strategies, proactive marketing strategy

IMPLICATIONS
There are a number of proactive strategies available to the marketer seeking to strengthen its firm's position in the marketplace through offensive means. Ultimately, marketers must evaluate such approaches for their benefits and costs—not only in relation to other offensive strategies but perhaps in relation to different defensive strategies as well. In addition, as there are many marketing strategies that correspond to different military strategies, marketers may benefit from a greater understanding of military analogies for marketing and business strategy. One marketing lesson to be reinforced from military strategy, for example, is that frontal attacks have a number of disadvantages when compared to other strategies, including that of an increased likelihood that they will provoke strong competitor retaliation.

APPLICATION AREAS AND FURTHER READINGS
Marketing Strategy
Keegan, W. J., and Davidson, H. (2004). 'Offensive Marketing: An Action Guide to Gaining Competitive Advantage,' *Elsevier* (Amsterdam), 1–36.
Trout, J., and Ries, A. (1985). *Marketing Warfare*. New York: McGraw Hill,
Paley, N. (1989). *The Manager's Guide to Competitive Marketing Strategies*. New York: AMACOM.

BIBLIOGRAPHY
Ho, S. K., and Choi, A. S. F. (1997). 'Achieving Marketing Success Through Sun Tzu's Art of Warfare,' *Marketing Intelligence & Planning*, 15(1), 38–47.
Davidson, J. H. (1997). *Even More Offensive Marketing: An Exhilarating Action Guide to Winning in Business*. London: Penguin Books.
Sun, Tzu (1963). *The Art of War*, trans. S. B. Griffith. Oxford: Oxford University Press.

☐ offline marketing *see entry at* online marketing
☐ OLI paradigm *see* eclectic paradigm
☐ oligopolistic competition *see* competition
☐ oligopoly *see* competition
☐ oligopsony *see* competition
☐ omnibus survey *see* survey research

■ one price, law of

DESCRIPTION

The economic view that in an efficient market, all identical goods will have only one price at any given time.

KEY INSIGHTS

The law of one price encapsulates the view that the forces of competition operating in an efficient market act to ensure that any given good will be sold for the same price everywhere after adjusting for exchange rates and allowing for transport and transaction costs. While the law is observed to hold most strongly for commodities that are standardized and heavily traded internationally, the law is also observed to be violated in many empirical research studies. Factors that may explain observed deviations from the law include those related to the costs of firms ascertaining rivals asking prices, buyers' search costs, and the occurrence of new and inexperienced buyers and sellers entering a market. Other studies finding deviations from the law suggest that price differences between locations are attributable to the markets not being fully integrated.

KEY WORDS Pricing, efficient markets, international markets, **goods**, commodities

IMPLICATIONS

Marketers involved in pricing decisions, particularly ones involving international markets, should seek to understand through careful market analysis the extent that market characteristics support adherence to, or deviations from, the law of one price for the firm's good. At the same time, to the extent that a firm's goods are commodity-like, marketers may wish to explore opportunities for de-commoditizing or differentiating such goods if an important aim is to enable further pricing flexibility by the firm.

APPLICATION AREAS AND FURTHER READINGS

Pricing
Hviid, M., and Shaffer, G. (1999). 'Hassle Costs: The Achilles' Heel of Price-Matching Guarantees,' *Journal of Economics and Management Strategy*, 8(4), 489–522.

Consumer Behavior
Frank, R. G. (2001). 'Prescription Drug Prices: Why Do Some Pay More Than Others Do?' *Health Affairs*, 20(2), 115–128.

Online Marketing
Schmitz, S. W., and Latzer, M. (2002). 'Competition in B2C E-commerce: Analytical Issues and Empirical Evidence,' *Electronic Markets*, 12(3), 163–174.

BIBLIOGRAPHY
Engel, Charles, and Rogers, John H. (1996). 'How Wide is the Border?' *American Economic Review*, 86(5), 1112–1125.
Isard, Peter (1977). 'How Far Can We Push the Law of One Price?' *American Economic Review*, 67(5), 942–948.

☐ one-to-many marketing *see* traditional marketing

■ one-to-one marketing

(also called custom marketing, customized marketing, individual marketing, markets-of-one marketing, personal marketing, personalized marketing, or tailored marketing)

DESCRIPTION
Tailoring a firm's offerings to meet the specific needs of individual customers.

KEY INSIGHTS
In contrast to a mass marketing or even differentiated marketing approach where the wants or needs of all or some customers are provided with the same marketing approach, one-to-one marketing involves an approach that tailors the marketing effort according to the wants or needs of individual customers. Customization of marketing frequently occurs in business-to-business marketing, for example, when customers express unique wants or needs and the magnitude of customer purchases (e.g. order size) is relatively high, thereby providing a greater incentive for a firm to supply business customers with tailored offerings. At the same time, one-to-one marketing is clearly not just business-to-business marketing's domain; it can be a viable option in business-to-consumer marketing where, even though customer purchase quantitites may be low, the expense of tailored marketing offerings can also be held low such as through the use of advanced information technologies, for example.

KEY WORDS Tailored offerings, unique offerings

IMPLICATIONS
Firms pursuing one-to-one marketing approaches may be involved in the tailoring or customization of any number of elements of the firm's offerings to meet the unique needs and wants of its individual customers in both industrial and consumer markets. Given the increasing ease with which customer knowledge can be understood and managed as a result of advances in information technologies, marketers may find that one-to-one marketing will only grow in importance.

APPLICATION AREAS AND FURTHER READINGS
Marketing Strategy
Shapiro, C., and Varian, H. R. (1998). *Information Rules*. Cambridge, Mass.: Harvard University Press.
Wind, Jerry, and Rangaswamy, Arvind (2001). 'Customerization: The Next Revolution in Mass Customization,' *Journal of Interactive Marketing*, 15(1), 13–32.

Marketing Management
Peppers, D., and Rogers, M. (1999). *The One to One Manager: Real-World Lessons in Customer Relationship Management*. New York: Doubleday.

Marketing Research
Pitta, D. A. (1998). 'Marketing One-to-One and its Dependence on Knowledge Discovery in Databases,' *Journal of Consumer Marketing*, 15(5), 468–480.
Kahan, R. (1998). 'Using Database Marketing Techniques to Enhance your One-to-One Marketing Initiatives,' *Journal of Consumer Marketing*, 15(5), 491–493.

Online Marketing
Weiber, R., and Kollmann, T. (1998). 'Competitive Advantages in Virtual Markets: Perspectives of "Information-Based Marketing" in Cyberspace,' *European Journal of Marketing*, 32(7–8), 603–615.
Mitchell, A. (2000). 'In One-to-One Marketing, which "One" Comes First?' *Interactive Marketing*, 1(4), 354–367.

BIBLIOGRAPHY
Peppers, D., Rogers, M., and Dorf, R. (1999). 'Is your Company Ready for One-to-One Marketing,' *Harvard Business Review*, January–February, 151–160.

■ online marketing

(also called cybermarketing, cyberspace marketing, interactive marketing, internet marketing, internet-centric marketing, new economy marketing, Web marketing, Web-based marketing, Web-centric marketing, World Wide Web marketing, or WWW marketing)

DESCRIPTION
Marketing making use of a connection to a computer network and the internet in particular.

KEY INSIGHTS
The scope of online marketing is markedly broad. In its simplest form, online marketing may involve the active diplay of user-accessible marketing material on a computer screen that results from a computer connection. In actuality, online marketing has become synonymous with internet marketing, which involves any number of marketing uses of the internet, the vast network of globally connected computers, where such connections are established by copper wire, fiber-optic cable, and wireless connectivity, and for which there is a common set of communications protocols. Thus, a key benefit of online marketing to firms is the ability to reach and interactively communicate with large numbers of network-connected individuals in ways that would be relatively more involved or resource intensive (in terms of time, effort, resources) if conducted via offline marketing methods. While simple text may be used in internet marketing communication, the World Wide Web also provides a rich set of more advanced graphics-based approaches from which to choose (see **Web marketing**). In accomplishing online marketing, firms may therefore adopt and pursue multiple marketing strategies, ranging from e-mail marketing as a form of direct marketing to viral marketing to blog marketing (see **direct marketing; viral marketing; blog marketing**).

Many marketing concepts and approaches are continuing to emerge in the area of online marketing. For example, *wikimarketing* is a term that is starting to be used in practice but with several different meanings including: (1) using wikipedia.com as a starting point in online searches to gain a basic understanding of unfamiliar topics that may have marketing relevance, while also recognizing its potential for inaccuracies, (2) using a 'wiki' approach in conjunction with marketing, where an online collaboration model or specific Web application is used that allows multiple individuals to add content to a website as well as freely edit such content, and (3) in the writing and editing of an entry contained within **wikipedia.com**, deleting all material that is negative and further including material that has the purpose of advertising or promoting something.

Online marketing can also, of course, be compared and contrasted with *offline marketing*, also called *brick(s)-and-mortar marketing*, which consists of marketing activities that do not involve the use of, or connection to, a computer or computer network. Given that the use of either approach does not necessarily exclude the use of the other, *click(s)-and-mortar marketing*, or *click(s)-and-brick(s) marketing*, refers to marketing that combines online marketing and offline marketing approaches. While there is an enormous amount of research into online marketing, most references to 'offline marketing' as a marketing approach are found in discussions of comparisons and contrasts between online and offline marketing.

KEY WORDS Internet, interactivity, computer network, web

IMPLICATIONS

Online marketing provides marketers with a rich and growing set of marketing opportunities. In using an affiliate marketing approach, *pay-per-click marketing* is just one example (see **affiliate marketing**). While its use may be a cost-effective means of achieving many of the firm's marketing objectives, it is also widely viewed as an approach that affords considerable flexibility and speed. It is, however, not suited to many areas of marketing where in-person, face-to-face interaction is highly benefi-cial, or when consumers prefer to see, touch, and feel products they are considering for purchase. For some products such as many luxury goods, for example, part of the experience consumers seek when shopping is that of also being seen by other shoppers.

APPLICATION AREAS AND FURTHER READINGS

Marketing Strategy
Hanson, Ward A. (2000). *Principles of Internet Marketing*. Cincinnati: South-Western College Publishing.
Allen, E., and Fjermestad, J. (2001). 'E-commerce Marketing Strategies: Integrated Framework and Case Analysis,' *Logistics Information Management*, 14(1–2), 14–23.

Marketing Management
Newell, F. (2000). *Loyalty.com: Customer Relationship Management in the New Era of Internet Marketing*. New York: McGraw Hill Professional Books.
Turban, Ephraim (2006). *Electronic Commerce: A Managerial Perspective*. Upper Saddle River, NJ: Pearson Prentice Hall.

Consumer Behavior
Wang, H., Lee, M. K. O., and Wang, C. (1998). 'Consumer Privacy Concerns about Internet Marketing,' *Communications—ACM*, 41(3), 63–70.

Marketing Research
Kozinets, R. V. (2002). 'The Field behind the Screen: Using Netnography for Market-ing Research in Online Communities,' *Journal of Marketing Research*, 39(1), 61–72.
Grossnickle, Joshua, and Raskin, Oliver (2000). *The Handbook of Online Marketing Research: Knowing your Customer Using the Net*. New York: McGraw-Hill.

International Marketing
White, G. K. (1997). 'International Online Marketing of Focus to US Consumers,' *International Marketing Review*, 14, 376–384.

Marketing Education
Kaynama, S. A., and Keesling, G. (2000). 'Development of a Web-Based Internet Marketing Course,' *Journal of Marketing Education*, 22(2), 84–89.

BIBLIOGRAPHY
Janal, D. (1998). *Online Marketing Handbook: How to Promote, Advertise, and Sell your Products and Services on the Internet*. New York: John Wiley & Sons.
Leuf, Bo, and Cunningham, Ward (2001). *The Wiki Way: Quick Collaboration on the Web*. Boston: Addison-Wesley.
Shapiro, Carl, and Varian, Hal R. (1999). *Information Rules*. Boston: Harvard Business School Press.

☐ **on-the-edge marketing** *see* unconventional marketing
☐ **OOH marketing** *see* out-of-home marketing

■ opinion leader

DESCRIPTION
Individuals that wield a disproportionately large influence over the attitudes, opinions, and behaviors of others and where such individuals are ones to whom others turn for advice or information.

KEY INSIGHTS
In the context of purchase intentions and purchase decisions, opinion leaders are those that have influence over others as a result of their personal characteristics, which may include their product or service experience, expertise, or knowledge, their interest in seeking out and communicating information on new products or services, their interest and vocal ability in persuading others to adopt their personal views, and their status in a particular group or community.

KEY WORDS Consumer influence, advice, information, attitudes, opinions, behavior

IMPLICATIONS
Whether through their abilities to influence large-scale public opinion through communication channels such as the internet, or key groups of individuals through face-to-face communication, marketers may benefit from identifying individuals who are likely to be opinion leaders for the firm's offerings and targeting them with effective marketing communications. 'Winning over' such individuals may facilitate the firm's efforts to accelerate the diffusion of positive information about the firm's offerings in the marketplace.

APPLICATION AREAS AND FURTHER READINGS
Consumer Behavior
King, Charles W., and Summers, John O. (1970). 'Overlap of Opinion Leadership across Consumer Product Categories,' *Journal of Marketing Research*, 7(1), February, 43–50.

Marketing Management
Feick, Lawrence F., and Price, Linda L. (1987). 'The Market Maven: A Diffuser of Marketplace Information,' *Journal of Marketing*, 51(1), January, 83–97.
Leonard-Barton, Dorothy (1985). 'Experts as Negative Opinion Leaders in the Diffusion of a Technological Innovation,' *Journal of Consumer Research*, 11(4), March, 914–926.
Chan, Kenny K., and Shekhar, Misra (1990). 'Characteristics of the Opinion Leader: A New Dimension,' *Journal of Advertising*, 19, Summer, 53.

BIBLIOGRAPHY
Myers, James H., and Robertson, Thomas S. (1972). 'Dimensions of Opinion Leadership,' *Journal of Marketing Research*, 9(1), February, 41–46.

□ **opportunity cost** *see* cost
□ **opt-in marketing** *see* permission marketing
□ **opt-out marketing** *see* permission marketing

■ options theory

DESCRIPTION
Theory or theories aimed at understanding, explaining, and predicting phenomena where an individual or organization has the freedom or right, but not the obligation, to pursue one or more courses of action.

KEY INSIGHTS
Options theory comprises an area of study concerned with phenomena involving choice. The theory has a grounding in finance when one considers the scope of financial options involving contracts or agreements between buyers and sellers where a buyer has a right, but not an obligation, to a purchase or sale of a financial asset. When one considers options as not being limited to those that are purely financial or restricted to trade, the scope of the theory becomes that of *real options theory*, where the emphasis is on a phenomenon where an individual, or more commonly a business entity, has the freedom, but not the obligation, to undertake one or more courses of action, such as the freedom to either double or quadruple production capacity in response to market demand, for example.

KEY WORDS Choice, freedom of choice

IMPLICATIONS
While phenomena involving real options are not new, there have been many recent advances in analytical methodologies concerning their study. Marketers desiring to be more rigorous in the identification and analysis of real options as a means to increasing both marketing and organizational effectiveness may benefit from a deeper understanding of real options theory-related research.

APPLICATION AREAS AND FURTHER READINGS
Marketing Strategy
Adner, R., and Levinthal, D. (2004). 'What is not a Real Option: Considering Boundaries for the Application of Real Options to Business Strategy,' *Academy of Management Review*, 29, 74–85.

Achrol, R. S., and Kotler, P. (1999). 'Marketing in the Network Economy,' *Journal of Marketing*, 63, 146–63.

McGrath, R. G. (1999). 'Falling Forward: Real Options Reasoning and Entrepreneurial Failure,' *Academy of Management Review*, 24(1), 13–30.

Marketing Management

Foote, D. A., and Folta, T. B. (2002). 'Temporary Workers as Real Options,' *Human Resource Management Review*, 12(4), 579–597.

Marketing Research

Dias, S., and Ryals, L. (2002). 'Options Theory and Options Thinking in Valuing Returns on Brand Investments and Brand Extensions,' *Journal of Product & Brand Management*, 11, 115–128.

New Product Development

Paxson, D. A. (2003). *Real R & D Options: Theory, Practice and Implementation*. Oxford: Butterworth-Heinemann.

BIBLIOGRAPHY

Leslie, K. J., and Michaels, M. P. (1997). 'The Real Power of Real Options,' *McKinsey Quarterly*, 3, 5–23.

■ order effect

(also called placement effect)

DESCRIPTION

Any effect of the serial order or placement of stimuli on the response of an individual.

KEY INSIGHTS

Order effects are of particular concern in research designs where the influence of the order of questions in questionnaires and other data collection instruments must be considered if results are to be interpreted accurately. Over the course of completing a long questionnaire, for example, individuals may express less accurate views later in the questionnaire as a result of their experiencing fatigue, or individuals' responses to later questions may change as a result of their learning in certain ways from earlier questions.

KEY WORDS Individual responses, data collection

IMPLICATIONS

Marketers must be sensitive to order effects possibly confounding the interpretation of results of particular research approaches and should consider methods to control for such effects, such as by presenting different randomizations of question orders to different respondents of a survey.

APPLICATION AREAS AND FURTHER READINGS

Consumer Behavior

Haugtvedt, Curtis P., and Wegener, Duane T. (1994). 'Message Order Effects in Persuasion: An Attitude Strength Perspective,' *Journal of Consumer Research*, 21(1), June, 205–218.

Buda, R., and Zhang, Y. (2000). 'Consumer Product Evaluation: The Interactive Effect of Message Framing, Presentation Order, and Source Credibility,' *Journal of Product and Brand Management*, 9(4–5), 229–242.

Forecasting
Urban, Glen L., Weinberg, Bruce D., and Hauser, John R. (1996). 'Premarket Forecasting of Really-New Products,' *Journal of Marketing*, 60(1), January, 47–60.

BIBLIOGRAPHY
Jain, Arun K., and Pinson, Christian (1976). 'The Effect of Order of Presentation of
  Similarity Judgments on Multidimensional Scaling Results: An Empirical Exami-
  nation,' *Journal of Marketing Research*, 13(4), November, 435–439.

☐ **order of entry effect** *see* market entry timing
☐ **order-routine specification** *see* industrial buyer behavior

■ organization theory

DESCRIPTION
Theory or theories aimed at understanding, explaining, and predicting how,
why, and to what extent various organizational designs, structures, and
decision-making processes are, or are likely to be, effective for achieving
particular aims.

KEY INSIGHTS
Organization theory views organizations as social systems and is therefore concerned with understanding and explaining relationships within
such systems. The role and influence of organizational politics on individual and group decision making is one of many topics examined within the
domain of organization theory.

KEY WORDS Organization, design, structure, decision making

IMPLICATIONS
While the scope of organization theory is very broad, it encompasses
numerous frameworks and concepts on which marketers can draw
to help understand, explain, or predict the usefulness of particular
approaches for organizing marketing or the broader organization. Marketers may also draw upon organization theory-based concepts in seeking to understand how organizational politics may influence marketing
decision making.

APPLICATION AREAS AND FURTHER READINGS
Marketing Management
Ruekert, Robert W., Walker, Orville C., Jr., and Roering, Kenneth J. (1985). 'The
  Organization of Marketing Activities: A Contingency Theory of Structure and
  Performance,' *Journal of Marketing*, 49(1), Winter, 13–25.
Ruekert, Robert W., and Walker, Orville C., Jr. (1987). 'Marketing's Interaction
  with Other Functional Units: A Conceptual Framework and Empirical Evidence,'
  Journal of Marketing, 51(1), January, 1–19.

BIBLIOGRAPHY
Workman, John P., Jr., Homburg, Christian, and Gruner, Kjell (1998). 'Marketing
  Organization: An Integrative Framework of Dimensions and Determinants,' *Jour-
  nal of Marketing*, 62(3), July, 21–41.

□ organizational buyer behavior *see* industrial buyer behavior
□ organizational marketing *see* business-to-business marketing

■ out-of-home marketing

(also called OOH marketing, outdoor marketing, ambient marketing, or place-based marketing)

DESCRIPTION

Any and all marketing activity directed at consumers where they happen to be, in places other than their places of residence.

KEY INSIGHTS

Out-of-home marketing (OOH marketing) encompasses a broad range of more specific marketing activities, with many of such activities being in the areas of advertising and sales promotion. As such, a more common term for OOH marketing is out-of-home advertising or OOH advertising. Such efforts may involve, for example, advertising via billboards, street furniture, or transit (e.g. buses). Out-of-home advertising need not necessarily take place outdoors, as practices including advertising in shopping malls and in shops via flat screen television displays are also within the scope of out-of-home advertising. Such displays may be used alone or in conjunction with other displays, where a closed-circuit television network is used for broadcasting or displaying marketing-related information to be seen and/or heard by current and prospective customers.

Ambient marketing refers to marketing in a consumer's surrounding environment. Ambient marketing may therefore involve advertising anywhere a consumer might be including bus shelters, toilets, or on the sidewalk along a city street. It may involve the use of small posters or flyers on lamp-posts or something more dramatic such as branded hot air balloons. While the term is often used synonymously with outdoor marketing and OOH marketing, it also has more specific meanings including that of marketing activities that blend in closely with the consumer's surrounding environment (e.g. writing the marketer's message in the sand at a public beach), marketing activities in the natural environment that also convey a sense of being special (e.g. a salesperson handing out leaflets in a public place to selected individuals, as opposed to all, as a means to suggest such activities are special to those encountering them), and marketing activities where consumers are located which are implemented in ways that try to catch consumers when they will be highly receptive to the marketer's message.

KEY WORDS Marketing communication, advertising, outdoors

IMPLICATIONS

Marketers seeking to reach consumers outside their homes have a wide range of more specific marketing approaches from which to choose. Even though many forms of mass media, such as newspapers and magazines, are available outside the home, they are differentiated from out-of-home approaches in that they are usually for home or office viewing. To the extent that out-of-home approaches involve reaching and communicating with consumers at places and times when they are likely to be receptive to the marketer's message, such approaches may be a beneficial component of the firm's marketing strategy.

APPLICATION AREAS AND FURTHER READINGS

Marketing Strategy

Thode, Stephen F., and Maskulka, James M. (1998). 'Place-Based Marketing Strategies, Brand Equity and Vineyard Valuation,' *Journal of Product & Brand Management*, 7(5), 379–399.

Sepe, Edward, Ling, Pamela M., and Glantz, Stanton A. (2002). 'Smooth Moves: Bar and Nightclub Tobacco Promotions that Target Young Adults,' *American Journal of Public Health*, 92(3), 414–419.

Ling, P. M., and Glantz, S. A. (2002). 'Why and How the Tobacco Industry Sells Cigarettes to Young Adults: Evidence from Industry Documents,' *American Journal of Public Health*, 92(6), 908–916.

Schooler, C., Basil, M. D., and Altman, D. G. (1996). 'Alcohol and Cigarette Advertising on Billboards: Targeting with Social Cues,' *Health Communication*, 8(2), 109–130.

Mankins, M. (2002). 'The Digital Sign in the Wired City,' *IEEE Wireless Applications*, February, 54–58.

Marketing Research

Corbin, H. L. (1995). 'Tracking the New Thinkers,' *Public Relations Quarterly*, 39(4), 38.

BIBLIOGRAPHY

Tucker, E. M., Alvey, P. A., Mulligan, J., and Edwards, S. (1997). 'A Report on Outdoor: Current Research into the Factors of Effective Out-of-Home Advertising Campaigns,' *Proceedings of the Conference of the American Academy of Advertising*, 176.

■ outbound marketing

(also referred to as out-bound marketing)

DESCRIPTION

Any marketing approach where it is the marketer or the marketer's organization that initiates contact with current or potential customers.

KEY INSIGHTS

Outbound marketing, as where a company has a dedicated call center engaged in cold-calling potential customers, emphasizes marketing where it is the firm that takes the initiative to reach out to customers rather than the other way around (see **inbound marketing**). What varies in outbound marketing approaches and techniques among firms is the extent to which the firm uses technologies or processes that help to increase the effectiveness of its targeting of potential customers and/or increase the receptivity of targeted customers to the firm's offerings. A significant fraction of firms using outbound marketing calls in their marketing efforts, for example, rely on predictive dialing technologies, whereas many other firms do not use such technologies. A major aim of much outbound marketing is therefore increasing its effectiveness by reducing its intrusiveness and privacy-insensitivity as perceived by its recipients. Goldstein and Lee (2005), for example, refer to this as *right-time marketing*, where firms adopt approaches that accommodate customer demands for when and how marketers should communicate with them.

KEY WORDS Proactive marketing, firm-initiated marketing

IMPLICATIONS
Outbound marketing provides marketers with a means to proactively contact and engage with current and potential customers. Rather than 'blanketing' or sporadically targeting markets with such efforts, however, astute marketers recognize the value of adopting approaches that increase the receptivity of targeted customers, such as when database marketing approaches are used in combination with telemarketing approaches (see **database marketing**; **telemarketing**).

APPLICATION AREAS AND FURTHER READINGS
Marketing Strategy
Hirschowitz, A. (2001). 'Closing the CRM Loop: The 21st Century Marketer's Challenge: Transforming Customer Insight into Customer Value,' *Journal of Targeting Measurement and Analysis for Marketing*, 10(2), 168–178.
Goldstein, Dan, and Lee, Yuchun (2005). 'The Rise of Right-Time Marketing,' *Journal of Database Marketing & Customer Strategy Management*, 12(3), April, 212–225.
Haden, Belinda (2005). 'Silent Calls Briefing,' *Interactive Marketing*, 6(3), January, 268–273.

Services Marketing
Santomero, A., and Eckles, D. L. (2000). 'The Determinants of Success in the New Financial Services Environment,' *FRBNY Economic Policy Review*, October, 11–23.

BIBLIOGRAPHY
Day, C. E. (1994). 'New Technologies that Facilitate Integrated Inbound/Outbound Marketing,' *Telemarketing*, 12(11), 75.

☐ outdoor marketing *see* out-of-home marketing

■ **outlier effect**

DESCRIPTION
Any biasing or otherwise adverse effect on the conclusions drawn regarding the relationships between variables that is directly attributable to the presence within numerical data of data that are markedly smaller or larger than other values.

KEY INSIGHTS
Outlier effects are a possible concern in marketing research that seeks to draw useful conclusions from analyses of numerical data. Inattention to outliers can lead to misleading conclusions, either by the researcher or by individuals interpreting and using the research findings. To ensure that marketing research findings are representative of the phenomenon being studied, care needs to be taken to determine to what extent outlier data should be included or excluded in the numerical analyses and, at

the very least, the methods employed in their treatment should be made explicit when communicating the findings.

KEY WORDS Numerical data, data analysis

IMPLICATIONS
Marketing researchers should always examine numerical data for the presences of outliers to ensure that appropriate methods are used for their treatment. As marketing researchers vary in the way they treat and report outliers in their research studies, care should be taken in their interpretation and use, whether such studies are used individually or in broader comparisons.

APPLICATION AREAS AND FURTHER READINGS
Marketing Research
Peterson, R. A. (2001). 'On the Use of College Students in Social Science Research: Insights from a Second-Order Meta-analysis,' *Journal of Consumer Research*, 28, December, 450–461.
Teng, C. J., Abbott, F. V., Franses, P. H., Kloek, T., and Lucas, A. (1998). 'Outlier Robust Analysis of Long-Run Marketing Effects for Weekly Scanning Data,' *Journal of Econometrics*, 89(1), November, 293–315.
Dekimpe, M. G., and Hanssens, D. M. (1999). 'Sustained Spending and Persistent Response: A New Look at Long-Term Marketing Profitability,' *Journal of Marketing Research*, 36, 397–412.
Semon, T. (1999). 'Outlier Problem has no Practical Solution,' *Marketing News*, 31(16), June, 2–7.

BIBLIOGRAPHY
Chen, C., and Liu, L. M. (1993). 'Joint Estimation of Model Parameters and Outlier Effects in Time Series,' *Journal of the American Statistical Association*, 88, 284–297.

■ overconfidence effect

DESCRIPTION
Any effect resulting from an individual having greater certainty in the correctness of his or her beliefs or judgments than circumstances warrant.

KEY INSIGHTS
Empirical research on individual probability judgments finds overconfidence to be a relatively pervasive phenomenon. While the nature and extent of overconfidence varies considerably among individuals, the cognitive process of anchoring and adjustment, where individuals make initial judgments and then adjust the judgments to arrive at a final judgment but where final judgments tend to be biased by the value of the initial judgments, is believed by some to account for much of the phenomenon.

KEY WORDS Confidence, certainty, beliefs, judgment

IMPLICATIONS
Since overconfidence is a relatively pervasive tendency among individuals, marketers, too, must be wary of being overconfident in their beliefs and judgments. Making efforts to perform 'reality checks,' for example,

by confirming or verifying the consistency of one's views with those of a number of objective others, is one way of seeking to minimize the overconfidence effect in individual and organizational decision making.

APPLICATION AREAS AND FURTHER READINGS

Marketing Strategy
Camerer, Colin, and Lovallo, Dan (1999). 'Overconfidence and Excess Entry: An Experimental Approach,' *American Economic Review*, 89(1), March, 306–318.

Marketing Research
Van Bruggen, G. H., Lilien, G. L., and Kacker, M. (2002).'Informants in Organizational Marketing Research: Why Use Multiple Informants and How to Aggregate Responses,' *Journal of Marketing Research*, 39(4), 469–478.

Marketing Education
Kennedy, E. J., Lawton, L., and Plumlee, E. L. (2002). 'Blissful Ignorance: The Problem of Unrecognized Incompetence and Academic Performance,' *Journal of Marketing Education*, 24(3), 243–252.

BIBLIOGRAPHY
Mahajan, Jayashree (1992). 'The Overconfidence Effect in Marketing Management Predictions,' *Journal of Marketing Research*, 29(3), August, 329–342.
Lichtenstein, S., and Fischhoff, B. (1977). 'Do Those Who Know More Also Know More About How Much They Know? The Calibration of Probability Judgments,' *Organizational Behavior and Human Performance*, 20, 159–183.

■ overlearning

DESCRIPTION
The additional learning achieved after something has already been learned to a high standard.

KEY INSIGHTS
While research studying the influence of overlearning, as in learning a particular concept, association, or skill, has found that it is not generally associated with improvements in individual performance in the short term, it is found to be associated with improvements in long-term retention. In addition, research on overlearning has found it can help increase one's resistance to distractive influences.

KEY WORDS Learning, performance, retention

IMPLICATIONS
Marketers concerned with the extent of consumer learning about a firm's offerings should seek to understand how, why, and to what extent consumer overlearning through marketing communications, and advertising in particular, may be beneficial in consumers' responding favorably to a firm's offerings over the longer term. At a minimum, the concept of overlearning and evidence of its demonstrated effects suggests a reason for extending marketing communications beyond the point in time where a high degree of consumer learning has already occurred.

APPLICATION AREAS AND FURTHER READINGS

Advertising

Craig, C. Samuel, Sternthal, Brian, and Leavitt, Clark (1976). 'Advertising Wearout: An Experimental Analysis,' *Journal of Marketing Research*, 13(4), November, 365–372.

Consumer Behavior

Craig, C. S., Sternthal, B., and Olshan, K. (1972). "Effect of Overlearning on Retention,' *Journal of General Psychology*, 87, 85–94.

Alba, Joseph W., and Hutchinson, J. Wesley (1987). 'Dimensions of Consumer Expertise,' *Journal of Consumer Research*, 13(4), March, 411–454.

BIBLIOGRAPHY

Carrick, Paul M., Jr. (1959). 'Why Continued Advertising Is Necessary: A New Explanation,' *Journal of Marketing*, 23(4), April, 386–398.

Krueger, W. C. F. (1929). 'The Effects of Overlearning on Retention,' *Journal of Experimental Psychology*, 12, 71–78.

☐ **own label** *see* private label

P

■ Pareto principle

(also called Pareto rule, Pareto effect, Pareto's law, eighty-twenty principle, eighty-twenty rule, or the law of the heavy half)

DESCRIPTION
The Pareto principle characterizes the situation where a disproportionately large percentage (e.g. 80%) of a particular phenomenon is caused by a disproportionately small percentage (e.g. 20%) of another phenomenon. (For example, 80% of company profit is derived from 20% of the company's customers.)

KEY INSIGHTS
The Pareto principle was originally developed by economist Vilfredo Pareto to understand and explain the relationship between national income and the benefit of such income to the population. The principle is now more broadly understood and interpreted to suggest there are often many instances where it is a relatively small fraction of some phenomenon, rather than the larger fraction, that has the most significant effect on some other phenomenon, such as where it may be found that 80% of a firm's sales volume is a result of the purchases of 20% of a firm's customers.

KEY WORDS Cause, effect, disproportional influence

IMPLICATIONS
The Pareto principle can be used as a guide to managers in deciding how to allocate limited resources. In particular, the principle suggests that priority should be given to identifying and acting upon the most significant 20% of a cause as it may have a large (e.g. 80%) influence over the desired effect. Quantitative analyses (e.g. cost analyses and profitability analyses) may be useful to identify cause and effect relationships that are found to generally follow the Pareto principle, where the exact proportion of an observed or desired effect stemming from a proportion of a particular cause may, of course, vary from 80% to 20%. The Pareto principle can be widely extended to apply to numerous areas of marketing and management ranging from advertising to marketing strategy development where the aim is to accomplish particular objectives with limited resources.

APPLICATION AREAS AND FURTHER READINGS

Advertising
Anschuetz, N. (1997). 'Profiting from the 80–20 Rule of Thumb,' *Journal of Advertising Research*, 37(6), 51–56.

Marketing Modeling
Rungie, C. M., Laurent, G., and Habel, C. A. (2002). 'A New Model for the Pareto Effect (80:20) at Brand Level,' in *Proceedings of the ANZMAC*. Melbourne: ANZMAC.

Marketing Strategy
Chen, J. C.-H., Chong, P. P., and Chen, Y.-S. (2001). 'Decision Criteria Consolidation: A Theoretical Foundation of Pareto Principle to Porter's Competitive Forces,' *Journal of Organizational Computing and Electronic Commerce*, 11(1), 1–14.

Services Marketing
Sanders, R. (1987). 'The Pareto Principle: Its Use and Abuse,' *Journal of Services Marketing*, 1(2), 37–40.

BIBLIOGRAPHY
Schmittlein, David C., Cooper, Lee G., and Morrison, Donald G. (1993). 'Truth in Concentration in the Land of (80/20) Laws,' *Marketing Science*, 12(2), Spring, 167–183.

☐ **Pareto's law** *see* Pareto principle
☐ **parity marketing** *see* me-too marketing

■ Parkinson's law

DESCRIPTION
Most commonly, the proposition that, in the context of office organization, work expands so as to fill the time available for its completion, along with other propositions of Parkinson including the proposition that the number of subordinates increase at a fixed rate regardless of the amount of work produced.

KEY INSIGHTS
Put forth and developed by C. Northcote Parkinson (1957) in his book *Parkinson's Law*, the laws of Parkinson are viewed by many to be facetious-but-true aphorisms that are most applicable to office organization and to that of large organizations in particular. The view that work expands to fill the time available is also referred to more generally as the 'excess time effect' in the field of social psychology (Aronson and Gerard 1966; Aronson and Landy 1967).

KEY WORDS Organization, management, time, work, staffing

IMPLICATIONS
Marketers involved in the management of marketing, particularly in large organizations, must strive to take steps to ensure that organizational tendencies raised in the laws of Parkinson are minimized if the aim is an effective and efficient organization. In particular, issues related to service quality within large organizations, as with public administration, may be particularly prone to the tendencies suggested by Parkinson's laws.

APPLICATION AREAS AND FURTHER READINGS

Marketing Management
Taylor, Ronald N. (1975). 'Perception of Problem Constraints,' *Management Science*, 22(1), September, 22–29.

Services Marketing
O'Toole, L. J., and Meier, K. J. (2004). 'Parkinson's Law and the New Public Management? Contracting Determinants and Service-Quality Consequences in Public Education,' *Public Administration Review*, 64(3), 342–352.

BIBLIOGRAPHY
Aronson, E., and Gerard, E. (1966). 'Beyond Parkinson's Law: The Effect of Excess Time on Subsequent Performance,' *Journal of Personality and Social Psychology*, 3, 366–399.
Aronson, E., and Landy, D. (1967). 'Further Steps beyond Parkinson's Law: A Replication and Extension of the Excess Time Effect,' *Journal of Experimental Social Psychology*, 4, 274–285.
Parkinson, C. Northcote (1957). *Parkinson's Law*. Boston: Houghton Mifflin.

■ parsimony, law of

(also called the principle of parsimony, Occam's razor, or Ockham's razor)

DESCRIPTION
The view that the simplest explanation for a phenomenon is preferable, unless it is known to be wrong.

KEY INSIGHTS
The law of parsimony, in its earliest form referred to as Occam's razor, based on the fourteenth century philosophical tenet of logician William of Ockham that advocates the 'shaving off' of assumptions that make no difference to a theoretical explanation, is mainly viewed today as a heuristic maxim that advises simplicity in explanation. The law of parsimony is often cited to further prescribe that, given two equally valid competing explanations, the simplest one should be embraced.

While the law of parsimony is considered to be of significant value in the development of theories, in arriving at explanations, and in advocating empirical generalizations (where precision and scope are also valued), it is also recognized that there may be a fine line between parsimony and oversimplification. In addition, in achieving parsimony, there may also be a tradeoff with richness of explanation. As such, any judgments about parsimony in explanation should depend on the explicit goals of a researcher.

KEY WORDS Explanation, simplicity, theories

IMPLICATIONS
The law of parsimony provides guidance to marketing researchers to strive for explanations in research that are not overly complicated. As a result, many marketing models in use today are parsimonious. At the same time, however, marketers must be wary of explanations that are overly simplistic and neglect the value of richness. Marketers should

strive to resolve such issues by making the implications of their research goals explicit in terms of the value placed on parsimony.

APPLICATION AREAS AND FURTHER READINGS

Marketing Research
Rieck, D. (1997). 'Occam's Razor and Cutting your Own Throat,' *Direct Marketing* (Garden City), 60(7), 52–53.
Starr, Martin Kenneth (1964). 'Management Science and Marketing Science,' *Management Science*, 10(3), April, 557–573.
Deshpande, Rohit (1983). '"Paradigms Lost": On Theory and Method in Research in Marketing,' *Journal of Marketing*, 47(4), Autumn, 101–110.
Cohen, Joel B., and Reed II, Americus (2006). 'Perspectives on Parsimony: How Long Is the Coast of England? A Reply to Park and MacInnis; Schwarz; Petty; and Lynch,' *Journal of Consumer Research*, 33, 28–30.
Chaiken, S., Duckworth, K. L., and Darke, P. T. (1999). 'When Parsimony Fails...,' *Psychological Inquiry*, 10(2), 118–123.
Epstein, R. (1984). 'The Principle of Parsimony and Some Applications in Psychology,' *Journal of Mind & Behavior*, 5(2), 119–130.

Marketing Modeling
Plouffe, C. R., Hulland, J. S., and Vandenbosch, M. (2001). 'Research Report: Richness Versus Parsimony in Modeling Technology Adoption Decisions: Understanding Merchant Adoption of a Smart Card-Based Payment System,' *Information Systems Research*, 12(2), 208–222.
Cheung, Gordon W., and Rensvold, Roger B. (2001). 'The Effects of Model Parsimony and Sampling Error on the Fit of Structural Equation Models,' *Organizational Research Methods*, 4(3), 236–264.

BIBLIOGRAPHY
Ariew, Roger (1976). *Ockham's Razor: A Historical and Philosophical Analysis of Ockham's Principle of Parsimony*. Champaign-Urbana, Ill: University of Illinois Press.

☐ **partner marketing** *see* affiliate marketing

☐ **partnership marketing** *see* cooperative marketing

☐ **passing stranger effect** *see* ancient mariner effect

☐ **patent** *see* intellectual property

☐ **pay-for-performance marketing** *see* affiliate marketing

☐ **pay-per-click marketing** *see* affiliate marketing

☐ **peak-load pricing** *see* pricing strategies

☐ **peer-to-peer marketing** *see* word-of-mouth marketing

☐ **penetration pricing** *see* pricing strategies

☐ **percent-of-sales method** *see* promotion budget setting methods

☐ **perfect competition** *see* competition

☐ **performance-based marketing** *see* affiliate marketing

☐ **perishability** *see* service characteristics

■ permission marketing

DESCRIPTION

Marketing where there is an emphasis on securing customers' consent or approval prior to engaging in further marketing activity with, or involving, the customer and/or customer information.

KEY INSIGHTS

Permission marketing essentially involves one of two approaches. Opt-in marketing is where the firm will only engage in further marketing activity with a customer, or use customer information, if the customer has given clear permission to do so by signing up to the arrangement. Opt-out marketing is where the firm will automatically engage in such activity unless the customer has given a clear indication that they do not wish to participate. As either approach involves a voluntary choice on the part of the customer to participate or not, much of permission marketing is concerned with marketing approaches aimed at increasing the likelihood that a customer will decide to participate initially and will want to continue doing so.

KEY WORDS Customer consent, customer approval

IMPLICATIONS

A greater knowledge of permission marketing approaches can be beneficial to marketers in industries or markets facing legal or regulatory constraints regarding the marketing use of customer information, as when there are restrictions in giving customer information to third party firms. In other instances, a greater knowledge and use of permission marketing approaches may provide the marketer with means to increase the effectiveness of the firm's marketing, as when the firm is able to avoid focusing its efforts on those customers who are clearly unreceptive to the firm's offer. Finally, permission marketing has potential benefits in terms of increasing consumer receptivity to subsequent marketing offers as a result of the marketer having the 'courtesy' to ask for the customer's permission to begin with.

APPLICATION AREAS AND FURTHER READINGS

Marketing Strategy
Bellman, S., Johnson, E. J., and Lohse, G. L. (2001). 'To Opt-in or Opt-out? It Depends on the Question,' *Communications of the ACM*, 44, February, 25–27.

Marketing Research
Krishnamurthy, S. (2001). 'A Comprehensive Analysis of Permission Marketing,' *Journal of Computer Mediated Communication*, 6(2): **http://jcmc.indiana.edu/vol6/ issue2/krishnamurthy.html.** Date accessed: 19 July 2007.
Tezinde, T., Smith, B., and Murphy, J. (2002). 'Getting Permission: Exploring Factors Affecting Permission Marketing,' *Journal of Interactive Marketing*, 16(4), 28–36.

Mobile Marketing
Kavassalis, P., Spyropoulou, N., Drossos, D., Mitrokostas, E., Gikas, G., and Hatzistamatiou, A. (2003). 'Mobile Permission Marketing: Framing the Market Inquiry,' *International Journal of Electronic Commerce*, 8(1), 55–79.

Online Marketing
Marinova, A., Murphy, J., and Massey, B. (2002). 'Permission E-mail Marketing as a
    Means of Targeted Promotion,' *Cornell Hotel and Restaurant Administration Quarterly*,
    43(1), 61–69.

BIBLIOGRAPHY
Godin, Seth (1999). *Permission Marketing: Turning Strangers into Friends and Friends into
    Customers*. New York: Simon & Schuster.

☐ person marketing *see* celebrity marketing
☐ person-to-person marketing *see* word-of-mouth marketing

■ personal construct theory

DESCRIPTION
A social psychological theory of personality concerned with the way that
individuals construct meanings and more specifically positing that an individual's personal constructs, or categories used by an individual in ordering
relationships and roles, stem from the individual's anticipation of events.

KEY INSIGHTS
Put forth in pioneering research by Kelly (1955), personal construct
theory was initially concerned with mental disorder detection but has
since been expanded in scope to examine a range of marketing phenomena. A particular approach advocated in personal construct theory is
that of repertory grid analysis, which involves evaluating an individual's
responses given a researcher's task concerning the ordering of individual
relationships and roles. A topic in marketing for which the theoretical
approach has been put to considerable use is in the evaluation of consumer perceptions of travel destinations.

KEY WORDS Personality, interpersonal relationships

IMPLICATIONS
Greater knowledge of personal construct theory can potentially provide
the marketer with both a theoretical lens and research methodology to
understand better the nature of individuals' meanings and perceptions
of a marketer's offerings, including that of travel destinations. Beyond
additional consumer insight, the theory potentially enables marketers to
obtain insights into how an individual's personal constructs are related to
the effectiveness of marketing processes managed within the marketer's
organization.

APPLICATION AREAS AND FURTHER READINGS
Marketing Management
Plank, R. E., and Greene, J. N. (1996). 'Personal Construct Psychology and Personal
    Selling Performance,' *European Journal of Marketing*, 30(7), 25–48.
Thomas, R. E. (1969). 'Marketing Processes and Personal Construct Theory,' *Adver-
    tising Quarterly*, 20, 9–21.

Marketing Research
Hankinson, G. (2004). 'Repertory Grid Analysis: An Application to the Measurement for Destination Images,' *Journal of Nonprofit & Voluntary Sector Marketing*, 9(2), 145–153.

Destination Marketing
Embacher, J., and Buttle, F. (1989). 'A Repertory Grid Analysis of Austria's Image as a Summer Vacation Destination,' *Journal of Travel Research*, 28, 3–7.
Pike, Steven (2003). 'The Use of Repertory Grid Analysis to Elicit Salient Short-Break Holiday Destination Attributes in New Zealand,' *Journal of Travel Research*, 41(3), 315–319.

Consumer Behavior
Preston, Valerie, and Taylor, S. Martin (1981). 'Personal Construct Theory and Residential Choice,' *Annals of the Association of American Geographers*, 71(3), September, 437–451.

BIBLIOGRAPHY
Kelly, G. A. (1955). *The Psychology of Personal Constructs*. New York: Norton.
Kelly, G. A. (1970). 'A Brief Introduction to Personal Construct Theory,' in D. Bannister (ed.), *Perspectives in Personal Construct Theory*. London: Academic Press, 1–8.
Adams-Webber, J. R. (1979). *Personal Construct Theory: Concepts and Applications*. Chichester: John Wiley & Sons, Inc.

☐ personal exploitation, law of *see* least interest, principle of
☐ personal marketing *see* one-to-one marketing
☐ personalized marketing *see* one-to-one marketing
☐ PEST analysis *see* macroenvironment
☐ PESTLE analysis *see* macroenvironment

■ Peter principle

DESCRIPTION
A colloquial principle of competence of human resources in a hierarchical organization that states that, in a hierarchy, every employee tends to rise to his or her level of incompetence.

KEY INSIGHTS
The Peter principle, as developed by Laurence J. Peter (Peter and Hull 1969), suggests that individuals in organizational hierarchies tend to advance based on competence to a point where they achieve positions where they lack competence for such positions, and in such positions they tend to remain, lacking the necessary competencies or skills as a result of the positions being either more difficult or simply different than previous positions. To the extent that the principle reflects promotion practices in an organization, those responsible for promotion decisions should strive to assess the extent that a promotion candidate already possesses the needed competencies and skills for a higher-level position.

KEY WORDS Organization, hierarchies, promotion, competence

IMPLICATIONS
Marketing managers involved in staffing and promotion decisions should take heed of the competence issue identified in the Peter principle to ensure the marketing organization remains viable. By seeking to ensure in promotion decisions that individuals filling higher-level roles possess the needed skills, the Peter principle may be potentially mitigated.

APPLICATION AREAS AND FURTHER READINGS
Marketing Management
Anderson, R. E., Dubinsky, A. J., and Mehta, R.(1999). 'Sales Managers: Marketing's Best Example of the Peter Principle?' *Business Horizons* (Bloomington), 42(1), 19–26.
Choy, R. M., and Savery, L. K. (1998). 'Employee Plateauing: Some Workplace Attitudes,' *Journal of Management Development*, 17(5–6), 392–401.

BIBLIOGRAPHY
Peter, Laurence J., and Hull, Raymond (1969). *The Peter Principle: Why Things Always Go Wrong*. New York: William Morrow & Company, Inc.

☐ **pioneer** *see* market entry timing
☐ **pioneering, market** *see* market entry timing
☐ **place-based marketing** *see* out-of-home marketing

■ place marketing

(also called destination marketing or location marketing)

DESCRIPTION
Marketing activity directed at creating a favorable attitude or impression of a particular area, region, or location and attracting individuals or organizations to such places.

KEY INSIGHTS
Whether a 'place' in question is for purposes of tourism, travel, investment, eating, working, learning, recreating, socializing, or living, either permanently or temporarily, place marketing emphasizes marketing approaches where the dominant element of the marketer's offering is a definable place, topographically, geographically, or otherwise. As such, places may be countries, regions, cities, towns, private properties, attractions, shopping malls, shopping mall food courts, shopping centers, office complexes, recreational complexes, parks, or any other area, region, or location. Places may be viewed as destinations that a marketer wishes to market to individuals or organizations located elsewhere, or they may be places that a marketer wishes to market to individuals or organizations already in residence.

KEY WORDS Areas, regions, physical locations

IMPLICATIONS
Marketers involved in place marketing may or may not have control over the actual physical elements or other features that are an integral

part of a particular place. To be sure, much of place marketing involves modifications to, or management of, infrastructure that makes a place more amenable to its target markets. While any given place will vary in what it has to offer and in what it can possibly offer, many well-established marketing principles and practices are applicable to the marketing of any place, particularly when the marketer adopts the view that a place is a good (product or service), albeit fixed in location, to be purchased, consumed, and/or used. At the same time, in place marketing, there is clearly a strong experiential element to the offering. Thus, effective place marketing necessarily entails developing marketing strategies based on appropriate positioning strategies and the communication of its experiential value, recognizing that any place will have both an actual value and a perceived value in the minds of current and potential customers.

APPLICATION AREAS AND FURTHER READINGS

Marketing Strategy
Buhalis, D. (2000). 'Marketing the Competitive Destination in the Future,' *Tourism Management*, 21(1), 97–116.

Marketing Management
Ritchie, R. J. B., and Ritchie, J. R. B. (2002). 'A Framework for an Industry Supported Destination Marketing System,' *Tourism Management*, 23, 439–454.

Marketing Research
Woodside, A. G. (1990). 'Measuring Advertising Effectiveness in Destination Marketing Strategies,' *Journal of Travel Research*, 29(2), 3–8.

International Marketing
Kotler, P., and Gertner, D. (2002). 'Country as Brand, Product, and Beyond: A Place Marketing and Brand Management Perspective,' *Journal of Brand Management*, 9(4–5), April, 249–261.

Public Sector Marketing
Fretter, A. D. (1993). 'Place Marketing: A Local Authority Perspective,' in G. Kearns and C. Philo (eds.), *Selling Places: The City as Cultural Capital, Past and Present*. Oxford: Pergamon.
Gartrell, R. B. (1988). *Destination Marketing for Convention and Visitor Bureaus*. Des Moines, Ia.: Kendall/Hunt Publishing Company.
Ulagaa, W., Sharmab, A., and Krishnanc, R. (2002). 'Plant Location and Place Marketing: Understanding the Process from the Business Customer's Perspective,' *Industrial Marketing Management*, 31, 393–401.

BIBLIOGRAPHY
Murray, C. (2001). *Making Sense of Place: New Approaches to Place Marketing*. Leicester: Comedia.

■ placebo effect

DESCRIPTION
A positive effect that results from administering an action or treatment that is inert or inactive but is believed by the recipient to have a benefit.

KEY INSIGHTS
While the placebo effect was initially identified and observed in the context of medical treatments by Beecher (1955), the concept and

phenomenon has since been extended beyond medicine into marketing as well as other related individual and organizational areas. Explanations for why placebo actions or treatments are observed to work (as when 30–40% of a range of symptoms from medical ailments are shown to improve as a result of administering placebos) are generally based on recipient expectancies, e.g. that it is because its recipients believe and expect the actions or treatments will work. Although the phenomenon is not fully understood, it is nevertheless recognized as a valuable concept that is shown to be present in a range of situations. Marketing research by Shiv, Carmon, and Ariely (2005) finds, for example, that consumers who paid a discounted price for an energy drink thought to increase mental acuity actually derived less benefit from it (e.g. they solved fewer puzzles) than those paying its full price.

KEY WORDS Cause, effect, expectancy

IMPLICATIONS

Like physicians, marketers, too, have tools, techniques, and methods at their disposal that include the use of placebo-like elements in offerings to their target audience. In the case of marketers, placebo effects may arise, for example, as a result of a price alteration that changes the actual customer-perceived usefulness of products or services to which they are applied.

APPLICATION AREAS AND FURTHER READINGS

Marketing Research

Shiv, B., Carmon, Z., and Ariely, D. (2005). 'Placebo Effects of Marketing Actions: Consumers May Get What They Pay For,' *Journal of Marketing Research*, 42(4), 383–393.
Lauren, Caglar Irmak, Gavan, G. Block, and Fitzsimons, J. (2005). 'The Placebo Effect in Marketing: Sometimes You Just Have to Want It to Work,' *Journal of Marketing Research*, 42(4), November, 406–409.
Borsook, D., and Becerra, L. (2005). 'Placebo: From Pain and Analgesia to Preferences and Products,' *Journal of Marketing Research*, 42(4), 394–398.
Berns, Gregory S. (2005). 'Price, Placebo, and the Brain,' *Journal of Marketing Research*, 42(4), November, 399–400.

BIBLIOGRAPHY

Beecher, H. K. (1955). 'The Powerful Placebo,' *Journal of the American Medical Association*, 159, 1602–1606.
Shiv, B., Carmon, Z., and Ariely, D. (2005). 'Ruminating about Placebo Effects of Marketing Actions,' *Journal of Marketing Research*, 42(4), 410–414.

☐ placement effect *see* order effect

■ **planned behavior, theory of**

DESCRIPTION

A theory linking attitudes and behavior that builds upon the theory of reasoned action by further incorporating the notion of an individual's perceived behavioral control.

KEY INSIGHTS

Based on pioneering research by Ajzen (1988, 1991; Ajzen and Madden 1986), the theory of planned behavior holds that individual actions are guided by beliefs about the likely outcomes of behaviors, beliefs about the expectations of others, and beliefs about the nature of control that the individual has over conditions that may facilitate or impede performing the behaviors. In relating these areas, the theory suggests, for example, that individuals' behavioral intentions will be stronger to the extent they are supported by favorable beliefs about the outcome and other's expectations. Such individuals may then carry out their intentions to perform certain behaviors when appropriate opportunities arise as a result of their beliefs that they have a sufficient actual degree of control over the behavior.

KEY WORDS Behavior, attitudes, control

IMPLICATIONS

For marketers seeking to understand and relate consumer behavior to a firm's product and service offerings, the theory of planned behavior and its associated concepts can provide a basis for analyzing how individuals' beliefs about actions, expectations of others, and personal control influence their preferences for consumption behavior as well as their actual consumption behaviors. Whether in making choices about leisure decisions or online shopping, the theory highlights the potentially important area of perceived individual control for a range of consumer actions that marketers can seek to influence and facilitate with their product and service offerings.

APPLICATION AREAS AND FURTHER READINGS

Marketing Research
Ajzen, I., and Driver, B. L. (1992) 'Application of the Theory of Planned Behavior to Leisure Choice,' *Journal of Leisure Research*, 24(3), 207–224.
Taylor, S., and Todd, P. (1995). 'Decomposition and Crossover Effects in the Theory of Planned Behavior: A Study of Consumer Adoption Intentions,' *International Journal of Research in Marketing*, 12(2), July, 137–155.
Notani, Arti Sahni (1998). 'Moderators of Perceived Behavioral Control's Predictiveness in the Theory of Planned Behavior: A Meta-analysis,' *Journal of Consumer Psychology*, 7(3), 247–271.

Online Marketing
Hoffman, Donna L., and Novak, Thomas P. (1996). 'Marketing in Hypermedia Computer-Mediated Environments: Conceptual Foundations,' *Journal of Marketing*, 60(3), July, 50–68.

BIBLIOGRAPHY

Ajzen, I. (1988). *Attitudes, Personality, and Behavior*. Milton Keynes: Open University Press.
Ajzen, I. (1991). 'The Theory of Planned Behavior,' *Organizational Behavior and Human Decision Processes*, 50, 179–211.
Ajzen, I., and Madden, T. J. (1986). 'Prediction of Goal-Directed Behavior: Attitudes, Intentions, and Perceived Behavioral Control,' *Journal of Experimental Social Psychology*, 22, 453–474.

☐ **pleasing products** *see* societal classification of products

■ point-of-purchase marketing

DESCRIPTION
Marketing where there is an emphasis on strategies and tactics involving the precise locations of purchase activity.

KEY INSIGHTS
Point-of-purchase marketing is concerned with increasing a firm's marketing effectiveness by focusing marketing efforts on the precise spots where products or services are able to be acquired by current and/or prospective customers. In retail stores, for example, point-of-purchase marketing activity involves attention to shelf space considerations (e.g. positioning a large quantity of the firm's products at eye level) and displays (e.g. colorful, eye-catching signs and other promotional materials). In some industries, such as tobacco, the majority of a firm's marketing efforts may be in point-of-purchase marketing.

KEY WORDS Purchase locations

IMPLICATIONS
Particularly in retail environments, point-of-purchase marketing can be an important strategic as well as tactical consideration in the marketing of a firm's offerings. In addition, when product purchases are sometimes the result of spontaneous or impulse purchase decisions of consumers, a strong emphasis on point-of-purchase marketing may lead to higher overall marketing effectiveness by the firm.

APPLICATION AREAS AND FURTHER READINGS
Marketing Strategy
Kapoor, T., Wildey, M. B., Pelletier, R. L., Elder, J. P., and Sallis, J. F. (1999). 'Point-of-Purchase Marketing Strategies to Increase Low Fat Chip Sales in a School Cafeteria,' *Society of Behavioral Medicine*, March, San Diego.
Wakefield, M., Terry, Y. M., Chaloupka, F., Barker, D. C., Slater, S., Clark, P. I., and Giovino, G. A. (2002). 'Tobacco Industry Marketing at Point of Purchase after the 1998 MSA Billboard Advertising Ban,' *American Journal of Public Health*, 92(6), June, 937–940.

Marketing Research
Chandon, P., Hutchinson, J. W., and Young, S. (2001). 'Measuring the Value of Point-of-Purchase Marketing with Commercial Eye-Tracking Data,' *INSEAD Working Paper*, 19/MKT.
Wertenbroch, Klaus, and Bernd, Skiera (2002). 'Measuring Consumers' Willingness to Pay at the Point of Purchase,' *Journal of Marketing Research*, 39, May, 228–241.

BIBLIOGRAPHY
Phillips, H., and Cox, J. (1998). 'Point of Purchase Marketing,' *Journal of Brand Management*, 5(3), 186–93.

■ point-of-sale marketing

DESCRIPTION

Marketing where there is an emphasis on strategies and tactics involving the precise locations of selling activity for the firm's offerings.

KEY INSIGHTS

Point-of-sale marketing overlaps strongly with point-of-purchase marketing, although the former is far more inclusive of marketing to retailers and other organizations that offer the firm's products or services for sale to current and prospective customers. As such, point-of-sale marketing may include incentives to a specific retailer to market the firm's offerings in a certain way. In addition, point-of-sale marketing may also involve approaches that systematically translate knowledge of consumer buying behavior (e.g. customer purchase histories) into the marketing plans and actions of retailers—something that is the subject of claims of a number of patents, for example.

KEY WORDS Sales locations

IMPLICATIONS

In implementing point-of-purchase marketing, particularly in retail environments, marketers must also engage in point-of-sale marketing. At the same time, marketers may engage in point-of-sale marketing but also leave the seller of the firm's offerings with a relative amount of freedom to determine appropriate point-of-sale marketing activity. In either case, a greater knowledge of point-of-sale marketing approaches provides the marketer with an opportunity to increase the firm's marketing effectiveness by focusing its efforts on key factors of influence in sales location success.

APPLICATION AREAS AND FURTHER READINGS

Marketing Strategy

Laws, M. B., Whitman, J., Bowser, D. M., and Krech, L. (2002). 'Tobacco Availability and Point of Sale Marketing in Demographically Contrasting Districts of Massachusetts,' *Tobacco Control*, 11 (Suppl. 2), ii71–ii73.

Harper, T. (2006). 'Why the Tobacco Industry Fears Point of Sale Display Bans,' *Tobacco Control*, 15(3), June, 270–271.

Donovan, R. J., Jancey, J., and Jones, S. (2002). 'Tobacco Point of Sale Advertising Increases Positive Brand User Imagery,' *Tobacco Control*, 11(3), 191–194.

BIBLIOGRAPHY

Feighery, E. C., Ribisl, K. M., Schleicher, N., Lee, R. E., and Halvorson, S. (2001). 'Cigarette Advertising and Promotional Strategies in Retail Outlets: Results of a Statewide Survey in California,' *Tobacco Control*, 10, 184–188.

Deaton, David W., and Gabriel, Rodney G. (1997). *Method and System for Selective Incentive Point-of-Sale Marketing in Response to Customer Shopping Histories.* United States Patent 5644723, US Patent Issued on July 1, 1997.

☐ political environment *see* macroenvironment

■ Pollyanna effect

(also called the Pollyanna hypothesis)

DESCRIPTION
The phenomenon where pleasant information is processed more easily and recalled better than unpleasant information, as well as the tendency for individuals to give more attention to pleasant information relative to unpleasant information in their thought and speech.

KEY INSIGHTS
The Pollyanna effect, as researched by C. E. Osgood (Boucher and Osgood 1969), where it was named after a fictional female character in a novel series, involves the tendency to process and recall positive information more easily than negative information and, more generally, the pervasive human tendency to define the experience of reality as more good than bad. At the extreme, an individual exhibiting the Pollyanna effect may recall only positive information about a past event, for example. While there are individual differences as to what is termed Pollyannism, the generally pervasive tendency associated with the phenomenon has led to a much higher frequency of certain common positive words in written language in comparison to that for certain common negative words.

KEY WORDS Information processing, recall, positive information

IMPLICATIONS
Marketers seeking to enhance consumer recall of a firm's offerings may find that consumers are much more likely to process and recall such information more easily when the information is positive or pleasant as opposed to negative or unpleasant. At the same time, marketers conducting consumer research must consider its possible effects in obtaining and evaluating positive and negative consumer views regarding their past experiences.

APPLICATION AREAS AND FURTHER READINGS
Marketing Management
Resnick, Paul, Zeckhauser, Richard, Swanson, John, and Lockwood, Kate (2006). 'The Value of Reputation on eBay: A Controlled Experiment,' *Experimental Economics*, 9(2), June, 79–101.
Olander, Folke (1977) 'Can consumer dissatisfaction and complaints guide public consumer policy?' *Journal of Consumer Policy*, 1(2), March, 124–137.

BIBLIOGRAPHY
Boucher, J., and Osgood, C. E. (1969). 'The Pollyanna Hypothesis,' *Journal of Verbal Learning and Verbal Behavior*, 8, 1–8.
Matlin, M. W., and Gawron, V. J. (1979). 'Individual Differences in Pollyannism,' *Journal of Personality Assessment*, 43, 411–412.

■ population ecology theory

DESCRIPTION

A theory holding that most of the variability in organizational structures comes about through the creation of new organizations and organizational forms and the replacement of old ones.

KEY INSIGHTS

Put forth in research by Hannan and Freeman (1977), Freeman and Hannan (1983), and McKelvey (1982), population ecology theory provides an ecologically based perspective for understanding, explaining, and predicting organizational change in terms of organizational changes occurring in a firm's industry and markets. More broadly, the theory is based on the study of the dynamics of species populations and how such populations interact with their environment.

KEY WORDS Organizational structure, organizational change

IMPLICATIONS

Marketers looking for additional perspectives for understanding how and why organizational forms and structures develop and contribute to sustaining the organization may benefit from a greater knowledge of population ecology-related research. While acceptance of the theory among marketing researchers remains variable, it nevertheless provides marketers with a broader perspective, and one which draws upon ecological analogy, that is often lacking in mainstream marketing.

APPLICATION AREAS AND FURTHER READINGS

Marketing Strategy
Achrol, Ravi S. (1991). 'Evolution of the Marketing Organization: New Forms for Turbulent Environments,' *Journal of Marketing*, 55(4), October, 77–93.
Stearns, T. M., Carter, N. M., Reynolds, P. D., and Williams, M. (1995). 'New Firm Survival: Industry, Strategy and Location,' *Journal of Business Venturing*, 10(1), 23–42.

Marketing Management
Getz, D. (2002). 'Why Festivals Fail,' *Event Management*, 7, 209–219.
Jaworski, Bernard J. (1988). 'Toward a Theory of Marketing Control: Environmental Context, Control Types, and Consequences,' *Journal of Marketing*, 52(3), July, 23–39.
Shoham, A., and Fiegenbaum, A. (2002). 'Competitive Determinants of Organizational Risk-Taking Attitude: The Role of Strategic Reference Points,' *Management Decision*, 40(2), 127–141.

BIBLIOGRAPHY
Hannan, Michael T., and Freeman, John (1977). 'The Population Ecology of Organizations,' *American Journal of Sociology*, 82, 929–964.
Freeman, John, and Hannan, Michael T. (1983). 'Niche Widths and the Dynamics of Organizational Populations,' *American Journal of Sociology*, 88, 116–145.
Hannan, M. T., and Freeman, J. (1984), 'Structural Inertia and Organizational Change,' *American Sociological. Review*, 49, 149–164.
McKelvey, Bill (1982). *Organizational Systematics*. Berkeley and Los Angeles: University of California Press.

□ population validity *see* validity

☐ portfolio analysis *see* product portfolio analysis

■ portfolio theory

DESCRIPTION
Theory and mathematical frameworks that are concerned with the use of investment portfolios of holdings to manage risks and financial returns.

KEY INSIGHTS
Portfolio theory, as developed by Markovitz (1959), is based on the views that diversifying holdings can reduce risks, that financial returns are dependent on expected risks, and that risk-averse investors will only take increased risks if compensated by adequately higher expected returns. The theory and mathematical frameworks facilitate investors' minimizing risks and maximizing returns and establishing an efficient set of portfolios from which to choose based on an investor's risk preferences.

KEY WORDS Portfolios, investments, risk, financial return

IMPLICATIONS
Marketers may benefit from understanding the theoretical frameworks and concepts of portfolio theory in assisting with a firm's efforts to minimize risks and maximize returns in its various investments, whether at the firm level or strategic marketing level. Marketers may also use the theory to gain insights into appropriate practices for managing portfolios of customers as well.

APPLICATION AREAS AND FURTHER READINGS
Marketing Strategy
Ryals, L. (2003). 'Making Customers Pay: Measuring and Managing Customer Risk and Returns,' *Journal of Strategic Marketing*, 11(3), 165–176.
Yorke, D. A., and Droussiotis, G. (1994). 'The Use of Customer Portfolio Theory: An Empirical Survey,' *Journal of Business and Industrial Marketing*, 9(3), 6–18.
Lubatkin, Michael, and Chatterjee, Sayan (1994). 'Extending Modern Portfolio Theory into the Domain of Corporate Diversification: Does It Apply?' *Academy of Management Journal*, 37(10), February, 109–136.
Lubatkin, Michael (1983). 'Mergers and the Performance of the Acquiring Firm,' *Academy of Management Review*, 8(2), April, 218–225.

BIBLIOGRAPHY
Markovitz, H. (1959). *Portfolio Selection: Efficient Diversification of Investments*. New York: John Wiley & Sons.

■ positioning

DESCRIPTION
The way a firm's offering is perceived by its target market in relation to that of competitor offerings.

KEY INSIGHTS
Whether a firm's offering is a product, service, or brand, the firm frequently has a choice regarding how the offering should be positioned in

the market. Offerings may be positioned along a few or many dimensions, where the specific dimensions considered and used are ones that are meaningful to consumers and strategically important to the firm. When there are many competitors in the marketplace, the firm must consider carefully how current and potential consumers will perceive the offering in relation to competing offerings. A key aim of positioning is to differentiate the firm's offerings from those of competitors, as there is often little to be gained by positioning in a completely identical way to a competitor. Just two examples of positioning dimensions are attribute positioning (or functional benefit positioning), where the firm seeks to position itself in a superior way relative to competitors on a product attribute valued by customers (e.g. cavity-fighting ability for a toothpaste) and product line breadth positioning, where the firm seeks to position itself in a desirable way relative to competitors on the sheer number of products that the firm offers (as a means to signal convenience and market leadership, for example). There are, of course, any number of ways a firm can position its offerings, including the important dimensions of price and quality. Additionally, firms may adopt a position that the firm is able to make meaningful in the minds of consumers, even though such a position may have no real substance. Thus, *meaningless differentiation* involves positioning an offering on an attribute that may be unique to offering but in actuality is not related to its performance (e.g. the unique but ultimately meaningless attribute of 'coffee crystals' in a firm's instant coffee offering).

KEY WORDS Attributes, **benefits**, product perceptions, competitive positioning, strategic positioning

IMPLICATIONS
While it is certainly easy to focus on major positioning dimensions such as price and quality, marketers have a wide array of positioning approaches from which to choose. As many product and service offerings involve the use of three to five important positioning dimensions, marketers must be sure to give sufficient attention to the broader set of positioning dimensions that the firm and its competitors are currently using and may use at some future point for strategic advantage.

APPLICATION AREAS AND FURTHER READINGS
Marketing Strategy
Hooley, G., Saunders, J. A., and Piercy, N. F. (1998). *Marketing Strategy and Competitive Positioning*, 2nd edn. Harlow: Prentice-Hall.
Brooksbank, R. (1994). 'The Anatomy of Marketing Positioning Strategy,' *Marketing Intelligence and Planning*, 12(4), 10–14.

Marketing Management
Hooley, Graham, and Saunders, J. (1993). *Competitive Positioning: The Key to Market Success*. Hemel Hempstead: Prentice-Hall.

Marketing Research
Kaul, A., and Rao, V. R. (1995). 'Research for Product Positioning and Design Decisions: An Integrative Review,' *International Journal of Research in Marketing*, 12, 293–320.

Services Marketing
Shostack, G. L. (1987). 'Service Positioning through Structural Change,' *Journal of Marketing*, 51, Winter, 33–43.

Business-to-Business Marketing
Doyle, P., and Saunders, J. (1985). 'Market Segmentation and Positioning in Specialized Industrial Markets,' *Journal of Marketing*, 49, Spring, 24–32.

BIBLIOGRAPHY
Myers, J. H. (1996). *Segmentation and Positioning for Strategic Marketing Decisions.* Chicago: American Marketing Association.
Carpenter, Gregory S., Glazer, Rashi, and Nakamoto, Kent (1994). 'Meaningful Brands from Meaningless Differentiation: The Dependence on Irrelevant Attributes,' *Journal of Marketing Research*, 31(3), August, 339–350.
Broniarczyk, S., and Gershoff, A. (1997). 'Meaningless Differentiation Revisited,' in Merrie Brucks and D. J. McInnis (eds.), *Advances in Consumer Research*, 24. Provo, Ut.: Association for Consumer Research, 223–228.
Ries, Al, and Trout, Jack (2001). *Positioning: The Battle for Your Mind.* New York: McGraw-Hill.
Trout, Jack, and Ries, Al (1972). 'The Positioning Era Cometh', *Advertising Age*, 17, April 24, 35–38.

☐ **postal marketing** *see* direct marketing
☐ **post-purchase behavior** *see* buyer decision process

■ power law of forgetting

DESCRIPTION
Specific characterization of the decline in memory performance with time by a mathematical power function.

KEY INSIGHTS
Studies by several memory researchers view the decline in memory performance with time or intervening events as being well fit by a mathematical power function (Wickelgren 1974, 1977; Wixsted 1990; Wixsted and Ebbesen 1997). A power function is a function with a variable base and a constant exponent (e.g. $f(x) = ax^b$). As different researchers have different views on the form and parameters of forgetting functions, the power law of forgetting is sometimes referred to more specifically as the Wickelgren power law or Wixsted's power law, for example. In studies of forgetting behavior, the power law of forgetting is typically applied to situations where forgetting is from long-term memory.

It is important to note that the power law of forgetting should not be confused with the forgetting curve, sometimes called the law of forgetting, as developed by Ebbinghaus (1885). The forgetting curve of Ebbinghaus is an empirical result based upon specific experimental conditions for learning and recall.

KEY WORDS Memory, forgetting, mathematical modeling

IMPLICATIONS
Marketers seeking to understand, explain, and predict forgetting behaviors and tendencies of consumers may potentially obtain useful insights

in the modeling of consumer behaviors through applications of the power law of forgetting. As consumer choice is often dependent on what consumers have remembered as well as forgotten, knowledge of consumer forgetting over time may be critical in establishing policies for appropriate marketing communications.

APPLICATION AREAS AND FURTHER READINGS

Consumer Behavior

McGuire, William J. (1976). 'Some Internal Psychological Factors Influencing Consumer Choice,' *Journal of Consumer Research*, 2(4), March, 302–319.

Lodish, Leonard M. (1971). 'Empirical Studies on Individual Response to Exposure Patterns,' *Journal of Marketing Research*, 8(2), May, 212–218.

Rubin, D. C., and Wenzel, A. E. (1996). 'One Hundred Years of Forgetting: A Quantitative Description of Retention,' *Psychological Review*, 103(4), 743–760.

BIBLIOGRAPHY

Anderson, J. R. (1995). *Cognitive Psychology and its Implications*, 4th edn. New York: W. H. Freeman and Company.

Wickelgren, W. A. (1974). 'Single Trace Fragility Theory of Memory Dynamics,' *Memory and Cognition*, 2, 775–780.

Wickelgren, W. A. (1977). *Learning and Memory*. Englewood Cliffs, NJ: Prentice Hall.

Wixted, J. T. (1990). 'Analyzing the Empirical Course of Forgetting,' *Journal of Experimental Psychology: Learning, Memory, and Cogition*, 16, 927–935.

Wixted, J. T., and Ebbesen, E. (1997). 'Genuine Power Curves in Forgetting,' *Memory and Cognition*, 25, 731–739.

Ebbinghaus, H. (1913). *Memory: A Contribution to Experimental Psychology*, trans. H. A. Ruger and C. E. Bussenius. New York: Teachers College, Columbia University. (Original work published 1885.)

☐ **preapproach** *see* selling process

■ **precision marketing**

DESCRIPTION

Marketing concerned with increasing the degree to which marketing outcomes are able to be sharply defined and distinguished by their exactness.

KEY INSIGHTS

Precision marketing has much in common with target marketing when the concern is targeting prospective customers with precision (see **target marketing**). Yet, the scope of precision marketing is broader when one considers that marketers may be concerned about the extent to which their efforts can lead to sharply definable outcomes in other areas of marketing, such as in selecting marketing research approaches that help the firm to fine-tune its marketing mix in an effort to increase the retention of existing customers. Nevertheless, there remains considerable opportunity in marketing to adopt approaches that enable the firm to identify, attract, and retain its most profitable customers.

KEY WORDS Marketing refinements, marketing enhancements

IMPLICATIONS

Marketers facing limited firm resources may find that the adopting of precision marketing approaches will enable them to market their offerings more cost-effectively. In firms engaged in direct mail marketing, for example, there can be considerable waste involved when the firm's brochures are sent year after year to individuals who will never have an interest in the firm's products. In such a case, a greater knowledge of precision marketing approaches may enable the firm to refine or enhance its approach to achieve greater overall effectiveness.

APPLICATION AREAS AND FURTHER READINGS

Marketing Strategy
De Reyck, Bert, and Degraeve, Zeger (2006). 'MABS: Spreadsheet-Based Decision support for Precision Marketing,' *European Journal of Operational Resesearch*, 171(3), 935–950.

Marketing Management
Brooks, David (2003). 'People Like Us,' *Atlantic Monthly*, 292, September, 29–32.

Business-to-Business Marketing
Larsson, R., and Passby, M. (1997). 'High-Precision Marketing through Customer Style Accommodation: Utility Industry Applications,' *DA/DSM Proceedings*, Amsterdam.

Retail Marketing
Hart, C., Doherty, N., and Ellis-Chadwick, F. (2000). 'Retailer Adoption of the Internet: Implications for Retail Marketing,' *European Journal of Marketing*, 34(8), 954–974.

BIBLIOGRAPHY
Zabin, Jeff, and Brebach, Gresh (2003). *Precision Marketing: The New Rules for Attracting, Retaining, and Leveraging Profitable Customers*. New York: John Wiley & Sons, Inc.

☐ predatory pricing *see* pricing strategies
☐ predictive validity *see* validity
☐ preference *see* buyer influence/readiness

■ preference reversal

DESCRIPTION
The tendency, in facing a choice between particular types of risky ventures involving nearly equal expected payoffs, to have a non-monetary preference for one approach but to prefer to place a higher monetary stake on the other.

KEY INSIGHTS
Based on pioneering research by Slovic and Lichtenstein (1968, 1983), reversals of preference occur when there is one venture, or gamble, involving a high probability of receiving a small payoff and another venture involving a low probability of receiving a high payoff. In other words, individuals have tendencies to rate risky ventures as attractive based on a stronger association with winning than with payoff size, but

ultimately individuals tend to place higher monetary values on risky ventures involving stronger associations with payoff size than with winning. Explanations offered for preference reversals include that of individual anchoring and adjustment on monetary scales leading to overpricing of low-probability gambles relative to the individual's choice preference.

KEY WORDS Risk, preference, probabilities, outcomes, payoffs

IMPLICATIONS

To the extent that marketers evaluating the attractiveness of risky ventures desire to understand fully the rationales and implications for their choices, recognizing the tendency for, and occurrence of, preference reversals may be an important consideration. In understanding consumer behavior regarding particular forms of gambles, understanding the preference reversal phenomenon may also provide the marketer with useful insights into general tendencies in consumer choice.

APPLICATION AREAS AND FURTHER READINGS

Consumer Behavior

Nowlis, Stephen M., and Simonson, Itamar (1997). 'Attribute–Task Compatibility as a Determinant of Consumer Preference Reversals,' *Journal of Marketing Research*, 34(2), May, 205–218.

Coupey, Eloise, Irwin, Julie R., and Payne, John W. (1998). 'Product Category Familiarity and Preference Construction,' *Journal of Consumer Research*, 24(4), March, 459–468.

Seidl, C. (2002). 'Preference Reversal,' *Journal of Economic Surveys*, 16(5), 621–656.

Slovic, Paul, and Lichtenstein, Sarah (1983). 'Preference Reversals: A Broader Perspective,' *American Economic Review*, 73(4), September, 596–605.

BIBLIOGRAPHY

Reilly, Robert J. (1982). 'Preference Reversal: Further Evidence and Some Suggested Modifications in Experimental Design,' *American Economic Review*, 72(3), June, 576–584.

Tversky, Amos, Slovic, Paul, and Kahneman, Daniel (1990). 'The Causes of Preference Reversal,' *American Economic Review*, 80(1), March, 204–217.

Slovic, Paul, and Lichtenstein, Sarah (1968). 'Relative Importance of Probabilities and Payoffs in Risk Taking,' *Journal of Experimental Psychology Monograph*, 78(3 Pt. 2), 1–18.

☐ premium pricing *see* pricing strategies
☐ presentation *see* selling process
☐ prestige pricing *see* pricing strategies
☐ price, law of one *see* one price, law of

■ price discrimination

DESCRIPTION

A marketing approach where a firm charges different customers different prices for identical offerings.

KEY INSIGHTS
Price discrimination is a valid marketing practice in marketplaces characterized by imperfect information and where firms consider current and
potential customers to vary in their willingness and ability to pay certain
prices for certain offerings. By charging different customers different
prices for the same offering, as when an airline charges one price for
a seat on its own website and a lower price for the exact same seat
on another website, the firm aims to pursue its marketing objectives
(e.g. profitability, sales) by taking advantage of marketplace conditions
that involve variation in search costs while also taking into account the
variability in the firm's costs to supply its offering to different areas of
the market.

KEY WORDS Discriminatory pricing

IMPLICATIONS
As a means to increase overall marketing effectiveness, marketers should
recognize how, when, and to what extent price discrimination strategies and tactics can be used beneficially by the marketer's firm. Given
the complex nature of pricing decisions, a greater knowledge of price
discrimination-related research can help to simplify and guide effective
marketing practice.

APPLICATION AREAS AND FURTHER READINGS
Marketing Strategy
Nagle, T. T., and Holden, R. K. (1995). *The Strategy and Tactics of Pricing*. Upper Saddle
    River, NJ: Prentice Hall.
Stokey, N. (1979). 'Intertemporal Price Discrimination,' *Quarterly Journal of Economics*,
    93, 355–371.
Armstrong, M., and Vickers, J. (2001). 'Competitive Price Discrimination,' *Rand
    Journal of Economics*, 32(4), 579–605.
Lederer, P. J., and Hurter, A. P., Jr. (1986). 'Competition of Firms: Discriminatory
    Pricing and Location,' *Econometrica*, 54, 623–640.

Retail Marketing
Shepard, A. (1991). 'Price Discrimination and Retail Configuration,' *Journal of Politi-
    cal Economy*, 99, 30–53.

International Marketing
Knetter, Michael M. (1989). 'Price Discrimination by U.S. and German Exporters,'
    American Economic Review, 79(1), 198–210.

BIBLIOGRAPHY
Varian, Hal (1989). 'Price Discrimination,' in R. Schmalensee and R. D. Willig (eds.),
    The Handbook of Industrial Organization. Amsterdam: North Holland Publishing.

■ price effect

DESCRIPTION
A change in consumption or any other marketing-related variable of interest
that is directly attributable to a change in the price of an offering.

KEY INSIGHTS

Price may not only be influential to the demand for an offering but to other marketing-related variables as well, such as consumer perceptions of a product's quality. Considerable marketing research is therefore directed at establishing the extent of price effects on other factors that are either directly or indirectly controllable by the marketer. Aside from price effects involving price increases or decreases, there are also price-related effects related to odd versus even pricing. (See **even price effect**; **odd price effect**.)

KEY WORDS Pricing, price changes

IMPLICATIONS

For a great many goods, price is a prime consideration in consumers' product purchase evaluations. Yet, price acts in many different ways to facilitate or hinder effective marketing. Price, for example, can be a means to communicate product quality to consumers who are unable to assess reliably a product's quality. A greater understanding of the many different types of price effects as well as the nature and scope of their influence can be beneficial to marketers who are involved directly in pricing decisions.

APPLICATION AREAS AND FURTHER READINGS

Marketing Strategy

Dekimpe, Marnik G., and Hanssens, Dominique M. (1995). 'The Persistence of Marketing Effects on Sales,' *Marketing Science*, 14(1), 1–21.

Marketing Management

Nijs, V. R., Dekimpe, M. G., Steenkamp, J. B. E. M., and Hanssens, D. M. (2001). 'The Category-Demand Effects of Price Promotions,' *Marketing Science*, 20(1), 1–22.

Rao, Akshay R., and Monroe, Kent B. (1989). 'The Effect of Price, Brand Name, and Store Name on Buyers' Perceptions of Product Quality: An Integrative Review,' *Journal of Marketing Research*, 26(3), August, 351–357.

Consumer Behavior

Lattin, James M., and Bucklin, Randolph E. (1989). 'Reference Effects of Price and Promotion on Brand Choice Behavior,' *Journal of Marketing Research*, 26(3), August, 299–310.

Marketing Research

Kingma, Bruce Robert (1989). 'An Accurate Measurement of the Crowd-out Effect, Income Effect, and Price Effect for Charitable Contributions,' *Journal of Political Economy*, 97, 1197–1207.

BIBLIOGRAPHY

Dodds, William B., Monroe, Kent B., and Grewal, Dhruv (1991). 'Effects of Price, Brand, and Store Information on Buyers' Product Evaluations,' *Journal of Marketing Research*, 28(3), August, 307–319.

☐ price elasticity of demand *see* elasticity of demand
☐ price skimming *see* pricing strategies

■ price theory

DESCRIPTION
Theory or theories that seek to understand, explain, and predict prices and pricing decisions relative to customer demand, firm supply, and market characteristics.

KEY INSIGHTS
Price theory is central in much research grounded in economics, as where market prices are often viewed as reflecting the interaction between demand considerations based on marginal utility and supply considerations based on marginal cost. Given the diversity of conditions under which products and services are supplied and demanded in the marketplace, price theory has become a rich area of study in marketing research as well, where the emphasis is typically on how managers should set prices as opposed to how markets behave. Numerous models and frameworks for pricing have subsequently been developed based on theories of pricing.

KEY WORDS Prices, pricing

IMPLICATIONS
Since price is an essential element in the marketing mix for a product or service, the area of price theory provides a marketer with a rich set of concepts and frameworks on which to draw to facilitate pricing strategy and management in marketing. Price theory-based frameworks and concepts may enable a marketer to understand better the complex interactions of firms, customers, and markets in product or service pricing.

APPLICATION AREAS AND FURTHER READINGS
Pricing
Oxenfeldt, Alfred R. (1973). 'A Decision-Making Structure for Price Decisions,' *Journal of Marketing*, 37(1), January, 48–53.
Kamen, Joseph M., and Toman, Robert J. (1970). 'Psychophysics of Prices,' *Journal of Marketing Research*, 7(1), February, 27–35.
Gabor, Andre, Granger, Clive W. J., and Sowter, Anthony P. (1971). 'Comments on "Psychophysics of Prices,"' *Journal of Marketing Research*, 8(2), May, 251–252.
Noble, Peter M., and Gruca, Thomas S. (1999). 'Industrial Pricing: Theory and Managerial Practice,' *Marketing Science*, 18(3), Special Issue on Managerial Decision Making, 435–454.
Smith, Vernon L., and Williams, Arlington W. (2000). *The Boundaries of Competitive Price Theory: Convergence, Expectations, and Transaction Costs. Bargaining and Market Behavior: Essays in Experimental Economics.* New York: Cambridge University Press, 286–319.

BIBLIOGRAPHY
Hall, R. L., and Hitch, C. J. (1939). 'Price Theory and Business Behaviour,' *Oxford Economic Papers*, 2, May, 12–45.
Hauser, John R. (1984). 'Pricing Theory and the Role of Marketing Science,' *Journal of Business*, 57(1), Part 2: Pricing Strategy, January, S65–S71.

■ pricing strategies

DESCRIPTION

Approaches to pricing offerings which are driven by strategic considerations and which have strategic implications for a firm.

KEY INSIGHTS

There are numerous strategic pricing approaches. Notable approaches include:

Basing-point pricing—a pricing approach that involves designating a particular geographic location as a basing point and then charging customers the freight cost from that location to the location of the customer.

Break-even pricing—the practice of setting a price to break even on the marketing of the product given its costs of manufacture and marketing.

By-Product Pricing—the practice of setting a price on products produced as a result of producing a main product that allows the main product to be marketed at a more competitive price.

Captive-product pricing—price setting for those products that must be used in conjunction with a main product, such as ink cartridges for a digital photo printer.

Competition-based pricing—the practice of setting prices based on the prices that competitors are charging for their (similar) products.

Cost-plus pricing—a pricing approach that involves adding a set mark-up to the cost of a product.

Dynamic pricing—the practice of charging difference prices to different customers depending on their characteristics and situations.

Freight-absorption pricing—a geographic pricing practice where the seller chooses to absorb part or all of the freight costs, typically as part of a pricing strategy to secure a particular sale or contract.

Loss leader pricing—adopting the practice of pricing particular product(s) below cost, below their normal mark-up price, or, more generally, at a very low price with the aim of drawing a greater number of customers to the seller's location than would otherwise be achieved without loss leader products.

Market skimming pricing—also called *price skimming*, the practice of setting a high initial price for a new product to enable high revenues and margins to be obtained from those in the market that are willing to pay the high initial price.

Peak-load pricing—the practice of charging a higher price for the peak period of demand for an offering relative to periods of lesser demand given a situation where the offering cannot be stored and where production capacity for the offering is not able to vary appreciably over time.

Penetration pricing—the strategy of deliberating assigning a low price to an offering, which is often new to the market, as a means to accomplish objectives including rapidly gaining market share (which may further lead to scale economies for the firm) and discouraging other firms from entering the market with competing products.

Predatory pricing—a pricing practice, typically by a leading firm in the market, that involves offering products at such low prices that other firms are discouraged from competing in the market and ultimately exit, after which prices may be raised again.

Prestige pricing—also called *premium pricing*, pricing a product sufficiently high (as when setting the price for an offering so that it is at or near the high end of a price range for a particular range of offerings) in order to associate its purchase and ownership with prestige as well as to give an impression of a high level of quality in the product and further avoid conveying a low level of quality that could arise when a product is priced much lower.

Product line pricing—a pricing approach that involves setting the steps in price between products in a product line by taking into account such factors as differences in product cost, features, customer preferences, and competing product prices.

Profit maximization pricing—efforts by a firm to price an offering, or vary the price of an offering, for particular levels of output in such a way that the firm would ultimately maximize its profitability for the offering.

Promotional pricing—temporarily lowering the price of a product relative to that which it is typically offered in an effort to increase short-term sales.

Psychological pricing—pricing that reflects the psychological influence of buyer beliefs and perceptions, including irrationalities, in the evaluations of prices, as when consumers tend to perceive that prices ending in odd numbers are significantly less expensive than those ending in even numbers or when consumers tend to associate high prices with high quality.

Target costing—an approach that assists the marketer in offering a product at an ideal or desired selling price as a result of setting targets for product costs to ensure that the desired selling price is met.

Target profit pricing—the practice of setting a price to make a target profit on a product given its costs of manufacture and marketing.

Uniform-delivered pricing—a pricing strategy that involves charging all customers the same price plus freight for a product, regardless of a customer's location.

Value pricing—a pricing approach that involves offering a product or service at a fair price relative to its quality and associated benefits.

Value-based pricing—the practice of setting the price of an offering based on buyers' perception of its value as opposed to that which is based on the seller's costs.

Zone pricing—a pricing practice that involves establishing multiple geographic zones and charging all customers in a particular zone the same total price.

KEY WORDS Price setting, pricing approaches

IMPLICATIONS

Marketers have a wide array of pricing approaches from which to choose in determining the appropriate prices for their offerings. Central to the choice and use of one or more particular strategies is, of course, the set of objectives to be accomplished through the use of price. While certain levels of profitability and/or market share are common objectives for many firms, it is also important for marketers to understand how and why particular pricing approaches can facilitate or hinder accomplishing such objectives given an understanding of consumer buying behavior as well as competitive dynamics. Finally, it is essential that marketers strive to anticipate and plan for competitive responses to particular pricing strategies adopted.

APPLICATION AREAS AND FURTHER READINGS

Pricing

Tellis, Gerard J. (1986). 'Beyond the Many Faces of Price: An Integration of Pricing Strategies,' *Journal of Marketing*, 50(4), October, 146–160.

Morris, M. H., and Morris, G. (1990). *Market-Oriented Pricing: Strategies for Management.* New York: Quorum Books.

Montgomery, Alan L. (1997). 'Creating Micro-Marketing Pricing Strategies Using Supermarket Scanner Data,' *Marketing Science*, 16(4), 315–337.

Online Marketing

Dewan, R., Jing, B., and Seidmann, A. (2000). 'Adoption of Internet-Based Product Customization and Pricing Strategies,' *Journal of Management Information Systems* 17(2), 9–28.

Marketing Modeling

Dolan, Robert J., and Jeuland, Abel P. (1981). 'Experience Curves and Dynamic Demand Models: Implications for Optimal Pricing Strategies,' *Journal of Marketing*, 45(1), Winter, 52–62.

BIBLIOGRAPHY

Kotler, Philip, and Armstrong, Gary (2004). *Principles of Marketing*, 10th international edn. Upper Saddle River, NJ: Pearson Education International.

Kotler, Philip, and Armstrong, Gary (2006). *Principles of Marketing*, 11th edn. Upper Saddle River, NJ: Pearson Education, Inc.

■ primacy, law of

DESCRIPTION

The view that, in presenting two sides of an issue involving persuasive arguments, the side presenting first will have greater effectiveness than the side presenting second.

KEY INSIGHTS

Named by Lund (1925) in his research on persuasion, the law of primacy was put forth based on the finding that communications presented first (whether pro or con to the issue) influenced an audience more than communications presented second. Subsequent research, however, has only shown limited support for the law of primacy under similar and varying conditions, suggesting that considerations of variables related to primacy in persuasion are more appropriate than a general law of primacy. For example, the findings of various research studies suggest that in persuasion efforts involving two-sided communications, non-salient, controversial topics, topics with an interesting subject matter, and highly familiar issues appear to meet with more success when presented first, where the mechanism for their effectiveness is distinctly different than that for the primacy effect involving serial learning.

KEY WORDS Persuasion, communication, arguments, primacy

IMPLICATIONS

In considering the effectiveness of persuasive communications, marketers should seek to understand through prior research and experience to what extent the characteristics of the persuasive message enable such communications to be presented first, as opposed to second in efforts to persuade receiving audiences. For example, persuasive communications involving controversial topics or interesting subject matter may benefit from being presented first to audiences, as opposed to second, in a marketer's efforts to influence and persuade its target audience through the use of persuasive arguments under conditions where both sides of the argument are presented.

APPLICATION AREAS AND FURTHER READINGS

Marketing Communications
Haugtvedt, Curtis P., and Wegener, Duane T. (1994). 'Message Order Effects in Persuasion: An Attitude Strength Perspective,' *Journal of Consumer Research*, 21(1), June, 205–218.

BIBLIOGRAPHY

Rosnow, R. L. (1966). 'Whatever Happened to the "Law of Primacy"?' *Journal of Communication*, 16(1), March, 10–31.
Lund, F. (1925). 'The Psychology of Belief: IV. The Law of Primacy in Persuasion,' *Journal of Abnormal and Social Psychology*, 20, 183–191.
Luchins, A. (1957). 'Primacy-Recency in Impression Formation,' in C. I. Hovland et al. (eds.), *The Order of Presentation in Persuasion*, New Haven: Yale University, 33–61.

■ primacy effect

DESCRIPTION

A cognitive bias in individual learning where, in a series of observations or other stimuli, initial observations or stimuli become disproportionately salient to the individual relative to those in the middle of the series.

KEY INSIGHTS

The primacy effect is considered to be a common phenomenon in individual learning, where information presented first in a series is more easily remembered than that in the middle of the series. Similarly, in forming impressions of individuals, the primacy effect is present when initial observations have a larger effect on the overall impression of an individual relative to later observations. One explanation given for the primacy effect is that short-term memory is 'less crowded' when pondering the initial observations, enabling them to be transferred more easily into long-term memory.

KEY WORDS Information, stimuli, learning, memory, primacy

IMPLICATIONS
Marketers can take advantage of the primacy effect in individual learning and impression formation by ensuring that the most important information or other stimuli is at the beginning of any series of information or stimuli that marketers wish consumers to remember. Alternatively, marketing researchers should recognize the primacy effect as a bias among consumers when they are asked to recall serial information that they have previously encountered.

APPLICATION AREAS AND FURTHER READINGS
Consumer Behavior

Buda, R., and Zhang, Y. (2000). 'Consumer Product Evaluation: The Interactive Effect of Message Framing, Presentation Order, and Source Credibility,' *Journal of Product and Brand Management*, 9(4/5), 229–242.
Haugtvedt, Curtis P., and Wegener, Duane T. (1994). 'Message Order Effects in Persuasion: An Attitude Strength Perspective,' *Journal of Consumer Research*, 21(1), June, 205–218.

Online Marketing

Murphy, J., Hofacker, C., and Mizerski, R. (2006). 'Primacy and Recency Effects on Clicking Behavior,' *Journal of Computer-Mediated Communication*, 11(2), article 7, http://jcmc.indiana.edu/vol11/issue2/murphy.html Accessed: 8 October 2007.

BIBLIOGRAPHY
Asch, S. E. (1946). 'Forming Impressions of Personality,' *Journal of Abnormal and Social Psychology*, 41, 258–290.

☐ **primary data** *see* data types
☐ **primary demand** *see* demand
☐ **principle(s) of** *see specific entries, e.g.* least effort, principle of
☐ **prisoner's dilemma** *see* game theory
☐ **private brand** *see* private label
☐ **private goods** *see* goods

■ private label

(also called own label, private brand, or store brand)
DESCRIPTION
The offering of a good under the brand of a retailer.
KEY INSIGHTS
While almost all retailers carry goods offered under any number of regional, national, or international brands (also called 'name brands' and with some of these called 'leading brands'), it is increasingly common for retailers to also carry goods under their own brand name. Today, some retailers are even pursuing marketing strategies where they offer almost all of their goods under their own label. Many of such brands are positioned as lower-priced alternatives to major brands within a product category, although some privately branded products are also positioned as higher in quality and are also offered at a higher price.

In addition to offering goods under a private label, firms may also offer goods under a *generic brand*, which is where there is only an indication of a product's category (e.g. cola, potato chips, milk) and a complete absence of any brand or brand name on its packaging. Such offerings can provide retailers with yet another way of providing customers with alternatives to well-known brands in terms of price, quality, or value.

KEY WORDS Retail, branding

IMPLICATIONS
Private label goods may be used by a retailer for any number of reasons including obtaining higher overall sales volumes and higher profit margins in relation to those for name brands. At the same time, many manufacturing firms find profitable niches in manufacturing private label goods for retailers. Some manufacturing firms even produce goods offered under both their own international brand and private labels as a means to increase their production volumes and achieve scale economies that can lower their costs. Thus, whether a marketer's firm produces and offers a product under a leading brand or one to be offered under one or more private labels, a greater knowledge of the strategies and tactics associated with the use of private label goods may assist the marketer with identifying feasible strategic options and developing competitive marketing strategies.

APPLICATION AREAS AND FURTHER READINGS
Marketing Strategy
Mills, D. E. (1999). 'Private Labels and Manufacturer Counterstrategies,' *European Review of Agricultural Economics*, 26(2), June, 125-146.
Harris, Brian F., and Strang, Roger A. (1985). 'Marketing Strategies in the Age of Generics,' *Journal of Marketing*, 49(4), Autumn, 70-81.

Marketing Management
Batra, Rajeev, and Sinha, Indrajit (2000). 'Consumer-Level Factors Moderating the Success of Private Label Brands,' *Journal of Retailing*, 76, Summer, 175-191.

Retail Marketing
Burt, S. (2000). 'The Strategic Role of Retail Brands in British Grocery Retailing,' *European Journal of Marketing*, 34(8), 875-890.

Marketing Research
Burton, S., Lichtenstein, D. R., Netemeyer, R. G., and Garretson, J. A. (1998). 'A Scale for Measuring Attitude toward Private Label Products and an Examination of its Psychological and Behavioral Correlates,' *Journal of the Academy of Marketing Science*, 26(4), 293-306.
Halstead, D., and Ward, C. (1995). 'Assessing the Vulnerability of Private Label Brands,' *Journal of Product and Brand Management*, 4(3), 38-48.

BIBLIOGRAPHY
Mills, David E. (1995). 'Why Retailers Sell Private Labels,' *Journal of Economics & Management Strategy*, 4(3), Fall, 509-528.

☐ **private sector marketing** *see* commercial marketing
☐ **problem child** *see* product portfolio analysis

☐ problem recognition *see* buyer decision process
☐ product characteristics theory *see* characteristics theory

■ product classifications, consumer

DESCRIPTION

Products purchased for individual or household use arranged into meaningful categories according to specific marketing-related criteria.

KEY INSIGHTS

Consumer product classifications arrange consumer offerings into categories that are meaningful to marketers. Common product classifications of consumer products include: *convenience products*—items that customers typically buy often, quickly, and with very little effort (including effort to make brand comparisons); *shopping products*—items for which consumers typically make product and/or brand comparisons using criteria such as price and quality; *specialty products*—items which consumers perceive to be unique in one or more characteristics, including brand identification and thereby leading a sizeable number of such consumers to make a special effort to purchase; and *unsought products*—items that are unknown to consumers or ones that the consumers do not typically think of purchasing. While such products are characterized according to criteria relating to consumer buying behavior, there are still other means of classifying consumer products including those that consider product qualities from a societal perspective (see **societal classification of products**) as well as by characteristics that may or may not be restricted to consumer products (see **goods**).

KEY WORDS Product categories

IMPLICATIONS

A better understanding of the nature of consumer products can provide marketers of such products with insights that may lead to more effective marketing strategies and tactics. For example, most makers of inkjet printers market their ink cartridges and photopaper for such printers in such a way that emphasizes their uniqueness as a means to dissuade consumers from making brand comparisons involving price, even though other such brands may be perfect equivalents.

APPLICATION AREAS AND FURTHER READINGS

Marketing Strategy
Murphy, P. E., and Enis, B. M. (1986). 'Classifying Products Strategically,' *Journal of Marketing*, 50(3), 24–42.

Marketing Management
Brown, L. G. (1989). 'The Strategic and Tactical Implications of Convenience in Consumer Product Marketing,' *Journal of Consumer Marketing*, 6(3), Summer, 13–19.

Retail Marketing
Bucklin, Louis P. (1963). 'Retail Strategy and the Classification of Consumer Goods,' *Journal of Marketing*, 27, January, 50–55.

Marketing Research
Ratneshwar, S., and Shocker, A. D. (1991). 'Substitution in Use and the Role of Usage Context in Product Category Structures,' *Journal of Marketing Research*, 28, 281–295.

Consumer Behavior
Sudman, Seymour (1971). 'Overlap of Opinion Leadership across Consumer Product Categories,' *Journal of Marketing Research*, 8(2), May, 258–259.

BIBLIOGRAPHY
Kotler, Philip, and Armstrong, Gary (2006). *Principles of Marketing*, 11th edn. Upper Saddle River, NJ: Pearson Education, Inc.

☐ **product concept** *see* marketing management orientation

☐ **product development** *see* new product development; product-market investment strategies

☐ **product development stage** *see* product life cycle

☐ **product expansion** *see* product-market investment strategies

■ product levels

DESCRIPTION
Characteristically different ways that a firm's offering is able to add customer value.

KEY INSIGHTS
The offerings of a firm are able to add customer value in three basic ways. First, any product offering ultimately has a *core benefit*, or essence, that a customer wishes to obtain. A buyer of a treadmill, for example, may ultimately be purchasing it for the core benefit of increased cardiovascular fitness, or even more generally, a greater sense of well-being. Second, any offering involves an *actual product*, which is a product in some real form (e.g. features, packaging, brand name, design, level of quality). All electric treadmills, for example, have a speed adjustment control, with some also having an elevation adjustment control. Third, an offering also involves an augmented product, which is the set of additional services and benefits that accompany the offering's purchase (e.g. warranty, installation, after-sales service, delivery, financing). Two treadmills may be identical in terms of both their core benefit and actual product, for example, but may differ in terms of the length of the warranty as well as what particular parts are covered by the warranty. Starting with the core benefit, each of the two successive levels provides a means for marketers to add more customer value

KEY WORDS **Benefits**, features, value-added characteristics

IMPLICATIONS
While some marketers focus on how a product's features provide value to a customer and others focus on what the product's core benefit is, marketers should recognize that a product can add customer value in

several interrelated ways—ways which include augmented product offerings. Thus, by giving greater attention to the many different ways that an offering can create customer value, marketers have an opportunity to develop and provide offerings in ways that not only increase their value but also in the ability of the firm to increase the profitability that corresponds with the added value.

APPLICATION AREAS AND FURTHER READINGS

Marketing Strategy

Crane, Andrew (2001). 'Unpacking the Ethical Product,' *Journal of Business Ethics*, 30(4), 361–373.

Ravald, A., and Groenroos, C. (1996). 'The Value Concept and Relationship Marketing,' *European Journal of Marketing*, 30(2), 19–30.

Services Marketing

Berry, Leonard L., and Parasuraman, A. (1991). *Marketing Services: Competing through Quality*. New York: Free Press; Toronto: Maxwell Macmillan Canada; New York: Maxwell Macmillan International.

Storey, C., and Easingwood, C. J. (1998). 'The Augmented Service Offering: A Conceptualization and Study of its Impact on New Service Success,' *Journal of Product Innovation Management*, 15, 335–351.

Marketing Research

Green, Paul E., and Srinivasan, V. (1990). 'Conjoint Analysis in Marketing: New Developments with Implications for Research and Practice,' *Journal of Marketing*, 54(4), October, 3–19.

Mittal, Vikas, Kumar, Pankaj, and Tsiros, Michael (1999). 'Attribute-Level Performance, Satisfaction, and Behavioral Intentions over Time: A Consumption-System Approach,' *Journal of Marketing*, 63(2), April, 88–101.

BIBLIOGRAPHY

Kotler, Philip, and Armstrong, Gary (2006). *Principles of Marketing*, 11th edn. Upper Saddle River, NJ: Pearson Education, Inc.

■ product life cycle

DESCRIPTION

A series of states in a product's existence described in terms of its sales and profitability.

KEY INSIGHTS

The life cycle of a product is often viewed as being characterized by a number of states, or stages, including the *product development stage*, where there are development costs and no sales as yet; the *introduction stage*, where sales growth is slow and profitability is negative due to high product introduction costs; the *growth stage*, where sales dramatically increase due to rapid market acceptance and where profits increase as well; the *maturity stage*, where sales growth slows, plateaus, and may begin to decline as a result of product saturation in the market and where profits plateau and may begin to decline as a result of increased marketing costs to defend the product against competing offerings; and the *decline stage*, where both sales and profits are falling. It is often acknowledged that there are different marketing strategies that are appropriate for different stages. However, as appealing as the product life cycle concept is to many marketers, there remains the difficulty of determining just what stage a product is actually in (e.g. one may not be able to tell whether sales have plateaued permanently or temporarily). Additionally, it is also recognized that marketers have means to lengthen or shorten a product life cycle, adding further complexity to decisions about when to develop and introduce new products to take the place of others in decline.

KEY WORDS Life cycle, sales, profitability

IMPLICATIONS

The product life cycle provides a useful means of conceptualizing the life stages of a product that a marketer might expect to observe from the time of a product's inception to its demise. In addition, the conceptualization may provide a useful means of making sense of past events associated with product sales and profitability performance. Its ability to assist with the proactive development of appropriate marketing strategies is far more limited, however, as a result of the inability to understand a product's precise location within its own in-process life cycle.

APPLICATION AREAS AND FURTHER READINGS

Marketing Strategy
Klepper, S. (1996). 'Entry, Exit, Growth and Innovation over the Product Life-Cycle,' *American Economic Review*, 86, 562–583.
Anderson, C. R., and Zeithaml, C. P. (1984). 'Stage of the Product Life Cycle, Business Strategy, and Business Performance,' *Academy of Management Journal*, 27, 5–24.
Lambkin, Mary, and Day, George S.(1989). 'Evolutionary Processes in Competitive Markets: Beyond the Product Life Cycle,' *Journal of Marketing*, 53(3), July, 4–20.

Marketing Management
Parker, Philip M. (1992). 'Price Elasticity Dynamics over the Adoption Life Cycle,' *Journal of Marketing Research*, 29(3), August, 358–367.

Business-to-Business Marketing
Thorelli, Hans B., and Burnett, Stephen C. (1981). 'The Nature of Product Life Cycles for Industrial Goods Businesses,' *Journal of Marketing*, 45(4), Autumn, 97–108.
Golder, P. N., and Tellis, G. J. (2004). 'Growing, Growing, Gone: Cascades, Diffusion, and Turning Points in the Product Life Cycle,' *Marketing Science*, 23(2), 207–218.

International Marketing
Samiee, Saeed, and Roth, Kendall (1992). 'The Influence of Global Marketing Standardization on Performance,' *Journal of Marketing*, 56(2), April, 1–17.
Niss, H. (1996). 'Country of Origin Marketing over the Product Life Cycle: A Danish Case Study,' *European Journal of Marketing*, 30(3), 6–22.

Marketing Research
Asiedu, Y., and Gu, P. (1998). 'Product Life Cycle Cost Analysis: State of the Art Review,' *International Journal of Production Research*, 36(4), 883–908.

Marketing Modeling
Cox, William E., Jr. (1967). 'Product Life Cycles as Marketing Models,' *Journal of Business*, 40(4), October, 375–384.

BIBLIOGRAPHY
Day, George S. (1981). 'The Product Life Cycle: Analysis and Applications Issues,' *Journal of Marketing*, 45(4), Autumn, 60–67.
Polli, R., and Cook, V. (1969). 'Validity of the Product Life Cycle,' *Journal of Business*, 42(4), 385–400.

Ryan, C., and Riggs, W. E. (1996). 'Redefining the Product Life Cycle: The Five-Element Product Wave,' *Business Horizons*, 39(5), 33–41.

■ product line

DESCRIPTION

Among a firm's offerings, a group of individual offerings that share one or more meaningful characateristics.

KEY INSIGHTS

A product line comprises offerings with something meaningful in common. At the same time, that which is meaningful can be described any number of ways. It is common to characterize a product line by several key dimensions. *Product line length* refers to the number of items in the product line (e.g. the number of distinctly different styles of running shoes). *Product line depth* refers to the number of versions offered for each product in the product line (e.g. the number of sizes and colors for each distinctly different style of running shoe). Additionally, when firms have multiple product lines, such lines can be characterized by *product line mix width*, which refers to the number of different product lines carried by the firm (e.g. running shoes and walking shoes).

KEY WORDS Product group, line

IMPLICATIONS

Marketers have many strategic decisions to make regarding a product line's length and depth as well as the width associated with product line mixes. While such decisions are clearly dependent on both consumer demand and the firm's assets and competencies, a greater understanding of product line-related research, and modeling approaches in particular, can potentially assist the marketer in making product line decisions that may also lead to sustainable competitive advantages.

APPLICATION AREAS AND FURTHER READINGS

Marketing Strategy
Wind, Y., and Claycamp, M. (1976). 'Planning Product Line Strategy: Matrix Approach,' *Journal of Marketing*, 40, 2–9.
Moorthy, K. Sridhar (1984). 'Market Segmentation, Self-Selection, and Product Line Design,' *Marketing Science*, 3(4), Autumn, 288–307.
Kekre, S., and Srinivasan, K. (1990). 'Broader Product Line: A Necessity to Achieve Success?' *Management Science*, 36(10), 1216–1231.

Marketing Management
Dobson, Gregory, and Kalish, Shlomo (1988). 'Positioning and Pricing a Product Line,' *Marketing Science*, 7(2), Summer, 107–125.

Marketing Research
Tang, Christopher S., and Ho, Teck-Hua (1998). *Product Variety Management: Research Advances*. Boston: Kluwer Academic.

Marketing Modeling
Green, Paul E., and Krieger, Abba M. (1985). 'Models and Heuristics for Product Line Selection,' *Marketing Science*, 4(1), Winter, 1–19.

McBride, Richard D., and Zufryden, Fred S. (1988). 'An Integer Programming Approach to the Optimal Product Line Selection Problem,' *Marketing Science*, 7(2), Summer, 126–140.

BIBLIOGRAPHY
Morein, J. (1975). 'Shift from Brand to Product Line Marketing,' *Harvard Business Review*, 53, 56–64.

☐ **product line pricing** *see* pricing strategies
☐ **product-market expansion grid** *see* product-market investment strategies

■ product-market investment strategies

(also called growth strategies)

DESCRIPTION
Generic strategies of the firm in the pursuit of growth.

KEY INSIGHTS
Firms seeking to grow for any reason (management directive, shareholder pressure, etc.) typically need to make strategic investments in one or more areas of their operations. To understand where to invest, firms must, either explicitly or implicitly, establish a strategic direction for growth. One explicit means for analyzing a firm's growth options involves the use of a *product-market expansion grid*, or *Ansoff matrix* more specifically, which characterizes options for growth and investment along 'market' and 'product' dimensions, where each is distinguished further by either being 'existing' or 'new.' The four common categories for product-market investment are therefore: *market penetration*, where the firm's growth is directed at existing markets and the use of present or existing products; *market development* (or *market expansion*), where the firm's growth is directed at new markets and the use of present or existing products; product development (or *product expansion*), where the firm's growth is directed at new product development for present or existing markets; and *diversification*, where the firm's growth is directed at new product development for new markets. In the latter category, while diversification can be considered to be a matter of degree, it is also not uncommon to distinguish conceptually between related and unrelated diversification, where *related diversification* is where there are certain assets and competencies within the firm that can be leveraged in its pursuit of synergy with its other products and/or market operations and where *unrelated diversification* is where the area of investment involves no real synergistic relationship with the firm's other products and/or market operations. An extension of the Ansoff matrix's four-quadrant approach to product-market investment analysis is to consider as well the possibility of integration as yet another avenue of firm growth, such as where a firm engages in vertical integration to acquire both suppliers and customer organizations. (See **integration.**)

KEY WORDS Investment, generic growth strategies

IMPLICATIONS
A challenging question faced by many marketers is in what direction
the firm should grow. Addressing such a question requires marketers to
identify feasible options for growth and engage in analyses to understand
better their possible benefits and costs in relation to the firm's marketing
and business objectives. As such, a greater understanding of the many
different product-market investment strategies and the many issues associated with each can assist the marketer with making growth-related
decisions that ultimately meet a set of important criteria including being
feasible, generating an attractive return on investment, and supporting a
sustainable competitive advantage.

APPLICATION AREAS AND FURTHER READINGS
Marketing Strategy
Slater, S. F., and Narver, J. C. (1993). 'Product-Market Strategy and Performance:
   An Analysis of the Miles and Snow Strategy Types,' *European Journal of Marketing*,
   27(10), 33.
Rosa, Jose Antonio, Porac, Joseph F., Runser-Spanjol, Jelena, and Saxon, Michael S.
   (1999). 'Sociocognitive Dynamics in a Product Market,' *Journal of Marketing*, 63,
   Fundamental Issues and Directions for Marketing, 64–77.
Cool, K., Dierickx, I., and Jemison, D. (1989). 'Business Strategy, Market Structure
   and Risk-Return Relationships: A Structural Approach,' *Strategic Management Journal*, 10(6), 507–522.
Gatignon, Hubert, and Xuereb, Jean-Marc (1997). 'Strategic Orientation of the Firm
   and New Product Performance,' *Journal of Marketing Research*, 34(1), Special Issue
   on Innovation and New Products, February, 77–90.

BIBLIOGRAPHY
Aaker, David A. (2005). *Strategic Market Management*. New York: John Wiley & Sons,
   Inc.

■ product marketing

DESCRIPTION
Marketing efforts involving tangible, physical offerings.

KEY INSIGHTS
While the term 'product' conveys that which is tangible, its broader usage
also includes any item of commerce more generally (e.g. services). Nevertheless, product marketing is most often used to refer to the marketing of
tangible objects or items which are created through processes of production. As such, the term is often used in comparisons and contrasts with
services marketing (see **services marketing**). Unlike service offerings, for
example, tangible offerings are able to be described precisely as they
can be subject to quantitative measure. Because physical offerings are
able to be perceived by the senses, their marketing necessarily involves
giving considerable attention to their observable elements (e.g. how such
products look to the eye, feel to the touch, taste to the tongue, sound
to the ear, and/or smell to the nose). Thus, for some products, aesthetics becomes a critically important marketing consideration in addition

to product functionality and performance. In addition to attention to physical characteristics, however, effective product marketing may also involve approaches that seek to enhance such characteristics through abstract associations, as where a relatively good-tasting carbonated drink consisting of flavored sugar water is associated with youthfulness and authenticity.

KEY WORDS Tangible goods, physical objects, items of commerce

IMPLICATIONS
Clearly, products take many shapes and forms and can be described in numerous ways (see **product classifications, consumer; goods; societal classification of products**). Understanding such characteristics is often critical to product marketing success since the actual product is a major focus of marketing attention. Yet, effective product marketing recognizes that there are other aspects of the product that also add customer value (see **product levels**). While, in comparison to service offerings, there is often less attention to people in the firm's marketing mix (see **marketing mix**) as perceived by current and potential customers, astute product marketers also recognize that effective product marketing often requires careful attention to the firm's related intangible offerings (e.g. after-sales service) as well as product positioning that involves associations with abstract concepts as a means to enhance perceived product value.

APPLICATION AREAS AND FURTHER READINGS
Marketing Strategy
Kotler, P. (1965). 'Competitive Strategies for New Product Marketing over the Life Cycle,' *Management Science*, 9, B104–119.

Marketing Management
Collier, Richard A. (1995). *Profitable Product Management*. Oxford: Butterworth-Heinemann.

Online Marketing
Shaw, M., Subramaniam, C., and Gardner, D. (1999). 'Product Marketing on the Internet,' in *Handbook of Electronic Commerce*. Berlin: Springer-Verlag.

Business-to-Business Marketing
Gordon, G. L., Calantone, R. J., and di Benedetto, C. A. (1993). 'Business-to-Business Service Marketing: How does it Differ from Business-to-Business Product Marketing?' *Journal of Business and Industrial Marketing*, 8(1), 45–57.

BIBLIOGRAPHY
Shostack, G. L. (1977). 'Breaking free from Product Marketing,' *Journal of Marketing*, 41(2), 73–80.

■ product portfolio analysis

(also called portfolio analysis)

DESCRIPTION
The systematic analysis and evaluation of a firm's set of offerings.

KEY INSIGHTS

A product portfolio analysis examines the firm's portfolio of product offerings to understand what, if anything, the firm should do to strengthen its portfolio. For example, many firms try to create and maintain a balanced portfolio in terms of their perceived product life-cycle stages, thereby working toward establishing a portfolio where, while some products are being developed, the firm's existing products are spread across the introduction, growth, maturity, and/or decline stages.

Another strategically important way of assessing the strength of the overall product portfolio, as well as the relative strengths and weaknesses of individual offerings within the portfolio, involves the use of market attractiveness and business position criteria to assess where the firm's offerings are in relation to one or more measures of market attractiveness and one or more measures of the firm's standing among competitors. A notable framework for product portfolio analyses (and, more broadly, for the analyses of the firm's strategic business units or divisions) is the *growth-share matrix* (also called the *Boston Consulting Group matrix*, the *Boston matrix*, and the *BCG growth-share matrix*) more specifically, which relies upon dimensions of market growth rate and relative market share to determine to what extent each of the firm's offerings is a star, cash cow, question mark, or dog. Adopting the terminology of the BCG growth-share matrix approach, an offering is a *star* when it has a high relative market share and the market growth rate is also high; an offering is a *cash cow* when it has a high relative market share and the market growth rate is low; an offering is a *question mark* (or *problem child*) when it has a low relative market share and the market growth rate is high; and an offering is a *dog* when it has a low relative market share and the market growth rate is low. Despite the framework's widespread recognition, however, a key issue to be addressed in its use is where the lines should be drawn along each dimension (a decision that some argue is rather arbitrary) to distinguish between market growth rates that are high vs. low and relative market shares that are high vs. low. Depending on where the line is drawn for market growth rate, for example, an offering may be a star or it may be a cash cow. An alternative to describing and evaluating the firm's offerings in terms of such categories is therefore an analysis that relies upon the major dimensions to assess the relative standings of the firm's offerings in relation to other offerings of the firm as well as those of competitors in the marketplace but avoids the step of partitioning or categorization.

KEY WORDS Balanced offerings

IMPLICATIONS

Astute marketers involved in strategy development recognize the ongoing need to analyze systematically the firm's portfolio offerings to identify relative strengths and weaknesses as well as opportunities or problems. A greater understanding of the many different approaches to product portfolio analysis put forth in the marketing literature can therefore provide the marketer with an opportunity to engage in such analyses with increased rigor and potentially greater effectiveness. For example, many different techniques have been developed for portfolio analyses involving products of different characteristics and where many of these techniques have been incorporated into commercially available decision support software packages.

APPLICATION AREAS AND FURTHER READINGS

Marketing Strategy
Anderson, Paul F. (1982). 'Marketing, Strategic Planning and the Theory of the Firm,' *Journal of Marketing*, 46, Spring, 15–26.

Marketing Management
Dickson, Peter R. (1983). 'Distributor Portfolio Analysis and the Channel Dependence Matrix: New Techniques for Understanding and Managing the Channel,' *Journal of Marketing*, 47, Summer, 35–55.
Palia, A. P. (1991). 'Strategic Market Planning with the COMPETE Product Portfolio Analysis Package: A Marketing Decision Support System,' *Developments in Business Simulations and Experiential Learning*, 18, 80–83.

Business-to-Business Marketing
Fiocca, R. (1982). 'Account Portfolio Analysis for Strategy Development,' *Industrial Marketing Management*, 11, 53–62.

BIBLIOGRAPHY
Day, George S. (1977). 'Diagnosing the Product Portfolio,' *Journal of Marketing*, 41(2), April, 29–38.

☐ product specification *see* industrial buyer behavior
☐ production concept *see* marketing management orientation
☐ profit-per-customer effect *see* loyalty effect

■ promotion budget setting methods

DESCRIPTION
Approaches for establishing the amount of a firm's expenditure on marketing activities aimed at communicating the merits of the firm's offerings and persuading target customers to purchase or use the firm's offerings.

KEY INSIGHTS
Firms can determine the amount to be allocated to its promotional activities using any number of methods. Recognized methods for promotion budget setting include: the *affordable method*, which is where the firm sets a budget based on what the firm's management believes the firm can bear without serious detriment; the *competitive-parity method*, which is where the firm's budget matches the promotional spending of competing firms; the *objective-and-task method*, which is where the firm defines its promotion objectives, identifies tasks required for their accomplishment, estimates the costs associated with the tasks, and then sums all such costs; and the *percentage-of-sales method*, which is where the firm bases the budget amount on a specified percentage of current or expected firm sales or unit selling price.

KEY WORDS Marketing expenditures, budget setting

IMPLICATIONS
Marketers involved in setting promotion budgets have a range of methods from which to consider. While the nature of the firm's marketing objectives is often key in determining which approach or approaches may be beneficial to adopt, a greater understanding of the advantages and disadvantages associated with each, along with an appreciation of the many different pitfalls in planning and implementation more generally (e.g. stubbornly adhering to a budgeting setting method in the face of strategically important changes in the marketplace) may do much to assist the marketer with making more effective promotion budget decisions.

APPLICATION AREAS AND FURTHER READINGS
Marketing Strategy
Hutt, M. D., Reingen, P., and Ronchetto, J. R., Jr. (1988). 'Tracing Emergent Processes in Marketing Strategy Formation,' *Journal of Marketing*, 52, January, 4–19.

Marketing Management
Piercy, Nigel F. (1987). 'The Marketing Budgeting Process: Marketing Management Implications,' *Journal of Marketing*, 51(4), October, 45–59.
Piercy, Nigel F. (1986). *Marketing Budgeting*. London: Croom Helm.
Little, John D. C. (1966). 'A Model of Adaptive Control of Promotional Spending,' *Operations Research*, 14(6), November–December, 1075–1097.
Gupta, Sunil (1988). 'Impact of Sales Promotions on When, What, and How Much to Buy,' *Journal of Marketing Research*, 25(4), November, 342–355.

Business-to-Business Marketing
Blasko, Vincent J., and Patti, Charles H. (1984). 'The Advertising Budgeting Practices of Industrial Marketers,' *Journal of Marketing*, 48(4), Autumn, 104–110.

BIBLIOGRAPHY
Low, G. S., and Mohr, J. J. (1999). 'Setting Advertising and Promotion Budgets in Multi-Brand Companies,' *Journal of Advertising Research*, 39(1), 67–80.

☐ promotional pricing *see* pricing strategies

■ prospect theory

DESCRIPTION
A theory relating individual risk-aversion and risk-seeking tendencies to gain and loss situations, where it is theorized and experimentally demonstrated that individuals are significantly more risk averse when facing gains and significantly more risk seeking when facing losses.

KEY INSIGHTS
According to prospect theory as developed and researched by Kahneman and Tversky (1979), individuals facing favorable conditions tend to be more risk averse, as opposed to risk seeking, because they feel they have more to lose than to gain. Conversely, individuals facing unfavorable circumstances tend to be more risk seeking, as opposed to risk averse, because they feel they have little to lose. The theory has received support

as a result of experiments conducted by the founders and subsequent academic researchers on individuals confronted with gain and loss situations under a wide variety of controlled conditions.

KEY WORDS gains, losses, risk taking, risk seeking, risk, return, decision making, framing

IMPLICATIONS

The theory has implications for explaining and predicting the tendencies of people in evaluating information. Specifically, the theory provides an explanation for why individuals and organizations may make decisions that vary from what might be considered purely rational based on maximizing expected utilities.

In the context of organizational decision making, executives facing external threats might be expected to be risk seeking, and executives facing external opportunities might be expected to be risk averse (Fiegenbaum and Thomas 1988; Wiseman and Gomez-Mejia 1998; Chattopadhyay, Glick, and Huber 2001). Executives and managers should, therefore, attempt to compensate for the possibility of inadvertent biases in their decision making as a result of the way a decision is framed in terms of gains and losses.

In the context of influencing consumer decision making, marketers should consider the fact that consumers are likely to make product and service purchase decisions based on personal valuations of gains and losses that differ significantly from a purely rational perspective. Specifically, whereas losing a dollar should be just as painful as the pleasure of gaining a dollar, experiments based on prospect theory suggest that losing a dollar is about twice as painful as the pleasure of gaining a dollar (Kahneman and Tversky 1991). Thus, according to the theory, consumers buying and holding financial market instruments will tend to hold on to losing positions in the hope of a recovery while also tending to move too quickly to sell to secure any financial gains.

Astute marketers of a wide range of products and services (e.g. financial instruments, disability insurance, electric utility services, equipment warranties) should therefore recognize consumer biases in psychologically valuing gains and losses and make adjustments to their marketing strategies and tactics in order to provide stronger psychological and actual tangible appeals. In advertising and promotions, for example, marketers may potentially increase consumer receptivity to a product or service by emphasizing the risk of significant losses without the product or service as opposed to the opportunity for significant gains with the same product or service.

APPLICATION AREAS AND FURTHER READINGS
Marketing Strategy
Qualls, William J., and Puto, Christopher P. (1989). 'Organizational Climate and Decision Framing: An Integrated Model,' *Journal of Marketing Research*, 26(2), 179–193.

Marketing Management

Shefrin, Hersh (1993). 'Behavioral Aspects of the Design and Marketing of Financial Products,' *Financial Management*, 22(2), Summer, 123–131.

Chattopadhyay, Rithviraj, Glick, William H., and Huber, George P. (2001). 'Organizational Actions in Response to Threats and Opportunities,' *Academy of Management Journal*, 44(5), October, 937–955.

Fiegenbaum, A., and Thomas, H. (1988). 'Attitudes toward Risk and the Risk-Return Paradox: Prospect Theory Explanations,' *Academy of Management Journal*, 31, 85–106.

Mowen, John C., and Mowen, Maryanne M. (1991). 'Time and Outcome Valuation: Implications for Marketing Decision Making,' *Journal of Marketing*, 55(4), October, 54–63.

Wiseman, R., and Gomez-Mejia, L. (1998). 'A Behavioral Agency Model of Managerial Risk Taking,' *Academy of Management Review*, 23, 133–153.

Services Marketing

Smith, Amy K., Bolton, Ruth N., and Wagner, Janet (1999). 'A Model of Customer Satisfaction with Service Encounters Involving Failure and Recovery,' *Journal of Marketing Research*, 36(3), August, 356–372.

Advertising

West, Douglas (1997). 'Antecedents of Risk-Taking Behavior by Advertisers: Empirical Evidence and Management Implications,' *Journal of Advertising Research*, 37(5), September/October, 27–42.

Sales

Burton, S. (1989). 'Decision-Framing Helps Make the Sale,' *Journal of Consumer Marketing*, 6(2), Spring, 15–24.

Marketing Modeling

Hardie, Bruce G. S. (1993). 'Modeling Loss Aversion and Reference Dependence Effects on Brand Choice,' *Marketing Science*, 12(4), Fall, 378–395.

BIBLIOGRAPHY

Chattopadhyay, Rithviraj, Glick, William H., and Huber, George P. (2001). 'Organizational Actions in Response to Threats and Opportunities,' *Academy of Management Journal*, 44(5), October, 937–955.

Fiegenbaum, A., and Thomas, H. (1988). 'Attitudes toward Risk and the Risk-Return Paradox: Prospect Theory Explanations,' *Academy of Management Journal*, 31, 85–106.

Kahneman, Daniel, and Tversky, Amos (1979). 'Prospect Theory: An Analysis of Decision under Risk,' *Econometrica*, 47, 263–292.

Kahneman, Daniel, and Tversky, Amos (1991). 'Loss Aversion in Riskless Choice: A Reference-Dependent Model,' *Quarterly Journal of Economics*, 106(4), November, 1039–1063.

Wiseman, R., and Gomez-Mejia, L. (1998). 'A Behavioral Agency Model of Managerial Risk Taking,' *Academy of Management Review*, 23, 133–153.

☐ prospecting *see* selling process

■ psychic distance

DESCRIPTION

In the internationalization of a business, the perceived and understood degree of closeness between a home market and a foreign market in terms of cultural and business differences.

KEY INSIGHTS

In terms of a business contemplating internationalization, psychic distance is considered to be an important factor in determining its sequence of foreign market entry, where psychically close foreign markets tend to be entered before psychically distance foreign markets. According to this view, closeness in psychic distance reduces uncertainties associated with foreign markets and makes it easier for a firm to learn from its gradual experiences in foreign markets as well. While research tends to support such a view, it may also be the case, however, that firm choices of foreign markets based on psychic distance criteria, which include both perceived cultural closeness and business closeness (e.g. closeness in business practices, industry structure, and economic legal and political climate) may not necessarily result in desired high levels of performance if such firms paradoxically underestimate cultural and business differences and fail to adapt sufficiently (O'Grady and Lane 1996).

KEY WORDS Internationalization, foreign market entry, culture

IMPLICATIONS

Marketing managers in firms contemplating internationalization, as well as those seeking to understand and explain or predict the internationalization of other firms, may benefit from understanding better the pivotal role of psychic distance in firms' decision-making processes for internationalization. Closeness in terms of psychic distance between a firm's home market and a foreign market may make learning about the foreign market much easier, yet management must also exercise caution in adopting standardized marketing practices across markets.

APPLICATION AREAS AND FURTHER READINGS

International Marketing

Evans, J., Treadgold, A., and Mavondo, F. T. (2000). 'Psychic Distance and the Performance of International Retailers: A Suggested Theoretical Framework,' *International Marketing Review*, 17(4/5), 373–391.

Evans, J., and Mavondo, F. T. (2000). 'Psychic Distance and Organizational Performance: An Empirical Examination of International Retailing Operations,' *Journal of International Business Studies*, 33(3), 515–532.

Stoettinger, B., and Schlegelmilch, B. B. (1998). 'Explaining Export Development through Psychic Distance: Enlightening or Elusive?' *International Marketing Review*, 15(5), 357–372.

BIBLIOGRAPHY

Johanson, J., and Vahlne, J.-E. (1977). 'The Internationalization Process of the Firm: A Model of Knowledge Development and Increasing Foreign Commitments,' *Journal of International Business Studies*, 8(1), 23–32.

Kogut, B., and Singh, H. (1988). 'The Effect of National Culture on Choice of Entry Mode,' *Journal of International Business Studies*, 19(3), 411–432.

O'Grady, S., and Lane, H. W. (1996). 'The Psychic Distance Paradox,' *Journal of International Business Studies*, 27(2), 309–334.

■ psychoanalytic theory

DESCRIPTION

A view of individual drives and motivations that emphasizes the role of the unconscious, or beyond awareness, and heavily influenced by emotion.

KEY INSIGHTS

Psychoanalytic theory, as developed by Freud (1955) as a psychological theory, ascribes a significant role to the unconscious in establishing individual drives and motivations. As such, certain motivational influences are viewed as being beyond awareness and may be in the form of unconscious desires, instinctual urges, and conflicts. While not initially developed as a personality theory per se, its basis and development nevertheless provide a coherent approach for explaining better individual characteristics or actions that are difficult to understand.

KEY WORDS Individual motivation, personality, unconscious drives

IMPLICATIONS

Marketers seeking to understand and explain consumer personalities and/or complex, difficult-to-understand behaviors may potentially obtain key insights through the lens of psychoanalytic theory and its associated concepts. Understanding better the early experiences of individuals, for example, may be one way to achieve insight into certain complex consumer behaviors.

APPLICATION AREAS AND FURTHER READINGS

Consumer Behavior

Kassarjian, Harold H. (1971). 'Personality and Consumer Behavior: A Review,' *Journal of Marketing Research*, 8(4), November, 409–418.

Hirschman, Elizabeth C., and Holbrook, Morris B. (1982). 'Hedonic Consumption: Emerging Concepts, Methods and Propositions,' *Journal of Marketing*, 46(3), Summer, 92–101.

BIBLIOGRAPHY

Freud, Sigmund (1955). 'The "Uncanny",' *The Standard Edition of the Complete Psychological Works of Sigmund Freud*, vol. xvii (1917–1919). London: Hogarth Press, 219–256.

☐ psychographic segmentation *see* segmentation
☐ psychological pricing *see* pricing strategies
☐ public good *see* goods
☐ public sector marketing *see* government marketing

■ pull marketing

DESCRIPTION

A strategic approach where a firm emphasizes marketing activities aimed at building up consumer demand, thereby prompting consumers to demand the offerings from intermediaries (e.g. retailers who, in turn, demand the offerings from wholesalers) who, in turn, demand the offerings from the firm.

Pull marketing emphasizes a *demand pull* (or pull strategy) approach to marketing, which is where marketing activities such as advertising and consumer promotion are directed strategically at consumers as a way to encourage them to buy the firm's offerings, thereby prompting demand for the firm's offerings from channel intermediaries such as retailers and wholesalers—a demand which is then ultimately met by the firm. Pull marketing is in contrast to push marketing which is where the firm's marketing is directed at intermediaries who, in turn, promote the offerings to consumers. (See **push marketing**.) While pull marketing strategies may be used by any firm that relies upon intermediaries, such strategies are common in consumer marketing, where advertising and sales promotions are dominant as a result of such goods typically being inexpensive or low risk and where there are often many buyers and sellers in the marketplace. Ultimately, however, many large companies use both pull marketing and push marketing approaches.

KEY WORDS Consumer demand, demand creation, advertising, sales promotion

IMPLICATIONS
Marketers in any firm should seek to understand how and to what extent pull marketing may be used to the firm's strategic advantage given the characteristics of the firm's offerings and the firm's customers. In many consumer product markets in particular, pull marketing becomes a prominent strategic approach, but one that is also supplemented by push marketing. When a consumer products firm engages in push marketing, however, the astute marketer in such a firm will recognize that it may also involve certain marketing disadvantages, including diminishing the firm's efforts to build long-term brand equity that result from more intensive pull marketing efforts.

APPLICATION AREAS AND FURTHER READINGS
Marketing Strategy
Farhoomand, A. F., and Drury, D. H. (1999). 'Information Technology Push/Pull Reactions,' *Journal of Systems and Software*, 47, 3–10.
Morris-Lee, J. (1993). 'Push-Pull Marketing with Magalogs,' *Direct Marketing*, 56(2), June, 23–26.
Liu, H. W., and Huan, H. C. (2005). 'Tradeoff between Push and Pull Strategy: The Moderating Role of Brand Awareness,' *Developments in Marketing Science*, 28, 260–265.

Marketing Management
Hultink, E. J., and Schoormans, Jan P. L. (1995). 'How to Launch a High-Tech Product Successfully: An Analysis of Marketing Managers' Strategy Choices,' *Journal of High Technology Management Research*, 6, 229–242.

Online Marketing
Sands, M. (2003). 'Integrating the Web and E-Mail into a Push-Pull Strategy,' *Qualitative Market Research*, 6(1), 27–37.

Government Marketing
Piper, W. S., and Naghshpour, S. (1996). 'Government Technology Transfer: The Effective Use of Both Push and Pull Marketing Strategies,' *International Journal of Technology Management,* 12(1), 85–94.

BIBLIOGRAPHY
Seddon, John (2000). 'From "push" to "pull": Changing the Paradigm for Customer Relationship Management,' *Journal of Interactive Marketing,* 2(1), July, 19–28.
Varadarajan, P. R. (1985). 'A Two-Factor Classification of Competitive Strategy Variables,' *Strategic Management Journal,* 6, 357–375.

☐ purchase *see* buyer influence/readiness; buyer decision process
☐ pure competition *see* competition
☐ pure monopoly *see* competition

■ push marketing

DESCRIPTION
A strategic approach where the firm's marketing is directed at intermediaries who, in turn, promote the firm's offering to consumers.

KEY INSIGHTS
Push marketing emphasizes a *supply push* (or push strategy) approach to marketing, which is where marketing activities such as personal selling and trade promotion are directed strategically at intermediaries as a way to encourage them to buy the firm's offerings and subsequently promote them to consumers via advertising, sales promotion, and other means. Push marketing is in contrast to pull marketing, which is where the firm's marketing activities are directed at consumers, thereby prompting demand for the firm's offerings from channel intermediaries such as retailers and wholesalers—a demand which is then ultimately met by the firm. (See **pull marketing**.) While push marketing strategies may be used by any firm that relies upon intermediaries, such strategies are common in business-to-business marketing involving industrial goods, where personal selling practices dominate as a result of such goods being expensive and/or risky and where there may also be relatively few buyers and sellers. Ultimately, however, many large companies use both pull marketing and push marketing approaches.

KEY WORDS Personal selling, trade promotion

IMPLICATIONS
As with pull marketing, marketers in any firm should seek to understand how and to what extent push marketing may be used to the firm's strategic advantage given the characteristics of the firm's offerings and the firm's customers. In many business-to-business markets in particular, push marketing becomes a prominent strategic approach, but one that is also supplemented by pull marketing. In some cases, push marketing may be relatively more effective than pull marketing for stimulating

short-term sales, but the astute marketer will recognize the need to consider the long-term implications of either approach as well.

APPLICATION AREAS AND FURTHER READINGS

Marketing Strategy
Levy, M., Webster, J., and Kerin, R. (1983). 'Formulating Push Marketing Strategies: A Method and Application,' *Journal of Marketing*, 1083, Winter, 25–34.
Levy, M., and Jones, G. W. (1984). 'The Effect on Sales of Changes in a "Push" Marketing Strategy in a Marketing Channel Context,' *Journal of the Academy of Marketing Science*, 12(1), 85–105.

Business-to-Business Marketing
Masuchun, W., Davis, S., and Patterson, J. W. (2004). 'Comparison of Push and Pull Control Strategies for Supply Network Management in a Make-to-Stock Environment,' *International Journal of Production Research*, 42(20), 4401–4420.

BIBLIOGRAPHY
Achenbaum, A., and Mitchel, F. K. (1987). 'Pulling away from Push Marketing,' *Harvard Business Review*, May–June, 38–40.

■ Pygmalion effect

(also called the Rosenthal effect)

DESCRIPTION
The phenomenon where an individual's performance and achievements are enhanced as a result of what is expected of them, independent of their abilities.

KEY INSIGHTS
Based on pioneering research by Rosenthal and Jacobson (1968) on the Pygmalion effect in the classroom, where enhanced teacher expectations for students led the students to achieve higher levels of intellectual development independent of their actual ability, the Pygmalion effect demonstrates the power of expectations and beliefs in shaping outcomes as a result of their subtle influences on behaviors that help lead to those outcomes. In this context, the Pygmalion effect can be viewed as similar to that of a self-fulfilling prophecy. While the extent of the effect is observed to vary based on context, subsequent research has confirmed the presence of the Pygmalion effect in settings including the classroom, industry, and the military.

KEY WORDS Expectations, beliefs, performance, outcomes

IMPLICATIONS
As the Pygmalion effect has been observed in many diverse settings, astute marketing managers, too, will recognize the potential for enhanced expectations of others leading to others' enhanced performance. Whether in sales or new product development, marketers may therefore seek to leverage the power of expectations, in conjunction with other facilitating actions, in shaping desired outcomes.

APPLICATION AREAS AND FURTHER READINGS

Marketing Management

Tierney, Pamela, and Farmer, Steven M. (2004). 'The Pygmalion Process and Employee Creativity,' *Journal of Management*, 30(3), 413–432.

Chowdhury, M. (2006). 'Pygmalion in Sales: The Influence of Supervisor Expectancies on Salespersons' Self-Expectations and Work Evaluations,' *Journal of Business and Public Affairs*, 1, 1.

BIBLIOGRAPHY

Rosenthal, R., and Jacobson, L. (1968). *Pygmalion in the Classroom: Teacher Expectations and the Pupil's Intellectual Development*. New York: Holt, Rinehart & Winston.

Q

□ **question mark** *see* product portfolio analysis

■ queuing theory

(also called waiting line theory)

DESCRIPTION
Theory or theories of queuing involving a system or systems having multiple inputs waiting to be processed.

KEY INSIGHTS
Queuing theory involves the use of mathematical modeling approaches to obtain insights into the efficiency and effectiveness of various queuing methods, processes, and systems. The theory enables types of queuing systems such as first-in/first-served, last-in/first-served, random order service, and service sharing systems to be examined in terms of their performance in relation to characteristics including arrival rates, arrival probabilities, server numbers, and system capacity.

KEY WORDS Queues, waiting lines, efficiency, effectiveness

IMPLICATIONS
Services marketing remains the major area of marketing where mathematical models based on queuing theory are able to provide insights into various queuing system behaviors. Marketers seeking to establish appropriate queuing systems in any area of services involving the queuing of customers can therefore potentially benefit from applying queuing theory principles and methods to both queuing system design and evaluation. (See also **Little's Law.**)

APPLICATION AREAS AND FURTHER READINGS
Services Marketing
Klassen, K. J., and Rohleder, T. R. (2001). 'Combining Operations and Marketing to Manage Capacity and Demand in Services,' *Service Industries Journal*, 21(2), 1–30.
Haynes, Paul J. (1990). 'Hating to Wait: Managing the Final Service Encounter,' *Journal of Services Marketing*, 4, Fall, 20–26.

BIBLIOGRAPHY
Gross, Donald, and Harris, Carl M. (1998). *Fundamentals of Queueing Theory*. New York: Wiley.
Kotler, Philip (1963). 'The Use of Mathematical Models in Marketing,' *Journal of Marketing*, 27(4), October, 31–41.

R

☐ radical marketing *see* unconventional marketing

■ random-walk theory

DESCRIPTION

A theory that share price movements in the financial markets over the short term are random in that they do not follow any predictable pattern.

KEY INSIGHTS

Random-walk theory is based on the view that the market is efficient, where any strategies that are found to work will be soon discovered and rendered unprofitable. As such, movements of share prices in the short term are considered to be unrelated to their previous movements.

KEY WORDS Firm share price, short-term performance

IMPLICATIONS

Random-walk theory provides a perspective on changes in short-term financial indicators that suggests a limitation on being able to make forecasts or predictions. Marketers seeking to relate marketing actions to short-term financial indicators of a firm may therefore benefit from understanding more fully the methods associated with short-term performance analyses as well as the potential limitations in such analyses which are suggested by the theory and its supporting assumptions.

APPLICATION AREAS AND FURTHER READINGS

Marketing Strategy
Wisner, Robert N., Blue, E. Neal, and Baldwin, E. Dean (1998). 'Preharvest Marketing Strategies Increase Net Returns for Corn and Soybean Growers,' *Review of Agricultural Economics*, 20(2), Autumn–Winter, 288–307.

New Product Development
Pauwels, K., Srinivasan, S., Silva-Risso, J., and Hanssens, D. M. (2004). 'New Products, Sales Promotions and Firm Value: The Case of the Automobile Industry,' *Journal of Marketing*, 68, 142–156.

Black, Fischer, and Scholes, Myron (1974). 'From Theory to a New Financial Product,' *Journal of Finance*, 29(2), Papers and Proceedings of the Thirty-Second Annual Meeting of the American Finance Association, New York (December 28–30, 1973), May, 399–412.

BIBLIOGRAPHY

Malkiel, Burton Gordon (1973). *A Random Walk down Wall Street*. New York: Norton.
Cohen, Jacob Willem (1992). *Analysis of Random Walks*. Amsterdam: IOS Press.

■ ratchet effect

DESCRIPTION

An outcome of an action that results in a change in state to some higher level that is resistant to returning to a previous lower level.

KEY INSIGHTS

One of the most notable ratchet effects in marketing is that where the use of a series of advertising campaigns in tandem with a series of sales promotions is commonly observed to result in higher levels of sustained sales in comparison to sales levels sustained by a series of sales promotions alone. In the former case, the advertising may reach other brand users or non-brand users, for example, whereas in the latter case, sales promotions may merely bring forward the buying of current brand users, leading to drops in sales to even lower levels than prior to the sales promotion. Moran (1978) suggests that ratchet effects are observable in a range of consumer and services markets.

Beyond the use of the term in marketing to describe the resulting pattern of sales achieved through the combination of advertising and sales promotions, the term is used in other contexts to describe ratchet-like response functions. For example, in economics, the term is used to describe the phenomenon where many households find it easier to adjust to rising incomes than to falling incomes.

KEY WORDS Cause, effect, asymmetric response functions, advertising, sales promotions

IMPLICATIONS

Given the enhancing effect on sales resulting from a combination of advertising and sales promotions as a prime example, marketers should seek to understand how marketing actions—and combinations of such actions in particular—may predictably produce desirable ratchet-like effects in the marketplace. Establishing the magnitude of such effects as well as determining their strategic and tactical importance should also be an important consideration in the development of marketing models aimed at explaining and predicting the corresponding cause-and-effect relationships.

APPLICATION AREAS AND FURTHER READINGS

Marketing Strategy

Sanne, C. (2005). 'The Consumption of our Discontent,' *Business Strategy and the Environment*, 14(5), 315–323.

Roland, Gerard, and Szafarz, Ariane (1990). 'The Ratchet Effect and the Planner's Expectations,' *European Economic Review*, 34(5), July, 1079–1098.

BIBLIOGRAPHY

Moran, William T. (1978). 'Insights from Pricing Research,' in E. B. Bailey (ed.), *Pricing Practices and Strategies*. New York: The Conference Board.

☐ **ratio scale** *see* scale

■ rational choice theory

DESCRIPTION

A theoretical view of decision making that is based on the rational evaluation of options or alternatives to arrive at the best possible choice from the perspective of the decision maker.

KEY INSIGHTS

Rational choice theory assumes that decision makers are rational in that their aims are to maximize the expected utilities that result from their decision. Further assumptions about rationality typically include time consistency in decision making over time, and a decision-maker ability to consistently compare all alternatives. Other simplifying assumptions may also be employed in the use of the theory in decision-making models such as decision-maker awareness of all possible choices and having reliable or precise information about the consequences of any given choice. While such latter assumptions may be considered unrealistic for many types of decisions, the theory nevertheless provides a significant and influential basis for describing, explaining, and predicting a range of decision-making approaches, outcomes, and behaviors from perspectives spanning economics to psychology.

KEY WORDS Decision making, rationality, alternative evaluation

IMPLICATIONS

In explaining and predicting various consumer (or organizational) behaviors, marketers must seek to understand better what assumptions of rationality are being made of the target market. To the extent that the decision making of current and potential customers demonstrates elements of rationality (e.g. in choosing where one will obtain a university education), marketers may benefit from a greater knowledge of rational choice theory-based perspectives for decision making by being able to facilitate decision making toward desired ends.

APPLICATION AREAS AND FURTHER READINGS

Consumer Behavior

Redmond, W. H. (2000). 'Consumer Rationality and Consumer Sovereignty,' *Review of Social Economy*, 58(2), 177–196.

Tremblay, P., Cusson, M., and Morselli, C. (1998). 'Market Offenses and Limits to Growth,' *Crime Law and Social Change*, 29(4), 311–330.

Jacoby, Jacob (2000). 'Is it Rational to Assume Consumer Rationality? Some Consumer Psychological Perspectives on Rational Choice Theory,' *Working Paper CLB-00-009*, NYU Pollack Center for Law & Business, August.

BIBLIOGRAPHY

Anand, Paul (1993). *Foundations of Rational Choice under Risk.* Oxford: Clarendon Press; New York: Oxford University Press.

Coleman, James Samuel, and Fararo, Thomas J. (1992). *Rational Choice Theory: Advocacy and Critique.* Newbury Park, Calif.: Sage Publications.

■ reader-response theory

DESCRIPTION

A theoretical view in the study of the reading of literature that emphasizes the role of the reader in actively creating and completing the meaning of a literary work through his or her interpretations.

KEY INSIGHTS

A reader-response theory-based view of literature and written work including that of written advertising suggests that their involvement with the reader is not unlike a 'performing art' in that a reader is able to create his or her own unique performance. In the context of understanding better consumer response to an ad, for example, the theory allows greater attention to be drawn to possible rich and complex interplays between elements of an ad and consumers' responses.

KEY WORDS Literature, written advertisements, interpretation, meaning, consumer response

IMPLICATIONS

Marketers may benefit from understanding the basis for and concepts of reader response theory in developing more-effective marketing communications. For example, the theory suggests that marketers may elicit stronger consumer responses to written advertisements that are aimed at drawing the consumer into the ad as opposed to ads that are relatively easy for a consumer to understand.

APPLICATION AREAS AND FURTHER READINGS

Consumer Behavior

McQuarrie, Edward F., and Mick, David Glen (1999). 'Visual Rhetoric in Advertising: Text-Interpretive, Experimental, and Reader-Response Analyses,' *Journal of Consumer Research*, 26(1), June, 37–54.

Scott, Linda M. (1994). 'The Bridge from Text to Mind: Adapting Reader-Response Theory to Consumer Research,' *Journal of Consumer Research*, 21(3), December, 461–480.

BIBLIOGRAPHY

Mick, David Glen, and Buhl, Claus (1992). 'A Meaning-Based Model of Advertising Experiences,' *Journal of Consumer Research*, 19, December, 317–338.

Mick, David Glen, and Politi, Laura G. (1989). 'Consumers' Interpretations of Advertising Imagery: A Visit to the Hell of Connotation,' in Elizabeth C. Hirschmann (ed.), *Interpretive Consumer Research*. Provo, Ut.: Association for Consumer Research, 85–96.

☐ real options theory *see* options theory

■ reasoned action, theory of

DESCRIPTION

A theory relating attitudes to behavior where behaviors are viewed as being determined by behavioral intentions which, in turn, are determined by attitudes to the behaviors and subjective norms.

KEY INSIGHTS
Developed in pioneering research by Fishbein and Ajzen (1975) and Ajzen and Fishbein (1977, 1980), the theory of reasoned action is based on the assumption that the most important cause of a person's behavior is his or her behavioral intent. Intentions to perform a behavior are viewed as being driven by both an individual's attitudes toward the behavior and subjective norms, or influences and motivations of the individual to comply with normative beliefs. Models based on the theory provide a basis for systematically describing, explaining, and predicting behaviors or behavioral intentions given appropriately specific characterizations of behavioral attitudes and subjective norms.

The theory is well supported in research and has considerable scope in both implications and applications. At the same time, it is generally recognized as being most applicable to completely voluntary behaviors (e.g. where individuals perceive themselves as having complete control over their choices). In an effort to address this latter limitation, the theory of planned behavior was subsequently developed which builds upon the theory of reasoned action and further includes the concept of perceived behavioral control. (See **planned behavior, theory of**.)

KEY WORDS Behavior, behavioral intentions, attitudes, subjective norms

IMPLICATIONS
Marketers seeking to understand, explain, or predict voluntary consumer behaviors may potentially obtain rich insights into behavioral intentions through application of concepts, modeling, and research approaches which are based upon the theory of reasoned action. For example, marketers may gain insights into consumer attitudes and subjective norms through consumer surveys where consumers respond to questions scaled with terms such as good/bad, like/unlike, or agree/disagree. Given the appropriate information, indications of positive intentions by consumers to perform certain behaviors can be identified when measures of both attitudes and subjective norms are positive.

APPLICATION AREAS AND FURTHER READINGS

Marketing Research
Sheppard, Blair H., Hartwick, Jon, and Warshaw, Paul R. (1988). 'The Theory of Reasoned Action: A Meta-analysis of Past Research with Recommendations for Modifications and Future Research,' *Journal of Consumer Research*, 15(3), December, 325–343.

Consumer Behavior
Shimp, Terence A., and Kavas, Alican (1984). 'The Theory of Reasoned Action Applied to Coupon Usage,' *Journal of Consumer Research*, 11(3), December, 795–809.
Bagozzi, Richard P., Baumgartner, Hans, and Yi, Youjae (1992). 'State versus Action Orientation and the Theory of Reasoned Action: An Application to Coupon Usage,' *Journal of Consumer Research*, 18(4), March, 505–518.
Randall, Donna M. (1989). 'Taking Stock: Can the Theory of Reasoned Action Explain Unethical Conduct?' *Journal of Business Ethics*, 8(11), November, 873–882.

Marketing Communications
Marin, Barbara Vanoss, Marin, Gerardo, Perez-Stable, Eliseo J., Otero-Sabogal, Regina and Sabogal, Fabio (1990). 'Cultural Differences in Attitudes toward

Smoking: Developing Messages Using the Theory of Reasoned Action,' *Journal of Applied Social Psychology*, 20(6), April, 478.

BIBLIOGRAPHY
Fishbein, Martin, and Ajzen, Icek (1975). *Belief, Attitude, Intention, and Behavior: An Introduction to Theory and Research*. Reading, Mass.: Addison-Wesley.
Ajzen, Icek, and Fishbein, Martin (1977). 'Attitude-Behavior Relations: A Theoretical Analysis and Review of Empirical Research,' *Psychological Bulletin*, 84, September, 888–918.
Fishbein, Martin (1980). 'A Theory of Reasoned Action: Some Applications and Implications,' in H. Howe and M. Page (eds.), *Nebraska Symposium on Motivation*. Lincoln, Neb.: University of Nebraska Press, 65–116.
Ajzen, I., and Fishbein, M. (1980). *Understanding Attitudes and Predicting Social Behavior*. Englewood Cliffs, NJ: Prentice Hall.

■ rebound effect

DESCRIPTION
A less-than-desired outcome of an action intended to create a change in state in a particular direction where the action also has the partial effect of creating a change in state in the opposite direction as well.

KEY INSIGHTS
Some actions aimed at particular changes in state also include effects opposite to the direction intended, as where laws to increase fuel efficiency in cars are intended to reduce a country's overall fuel consumption but where the greater fuel efficiency also leads people to drive more than they otherwise would. In this context, a rebound effect can be either qualitatively acknowledged or quantitatively evaluated. A rebound effect is typically quantified as the extent of deviation from the proportional change in an outcome expected by an action. Rebound effects are most often an issue in technology developments regulatory changes and their influence on consumption behaviors.

KEY WORDS Consumption behavior, technology

IMPLICATIONS
Marketers involved in estimating the effects of particular technology developments, regulations, or laws on the consumption behaviors of individuals, households, or broader geographic regions should consider how the rebound effect may be present as a result of changes in consumer behavior, thereby reducing the gains sought or behavioral changes desired. Whether for energy-intensive products such as those for home cooling or transportation or for energy-saving products such as home insulation, the rebound effect can present itself in ways that should be anticipated in the marketing of new products and services.

APPLICATION AREAS AND FURTHER READINGS
Marketing Strategy
Sanne, C. (2005). 'The Consumption of our Discontent,' *Business Strategy and the Environment*, 14(5), 315–323.

Technology
Birol, F., and Keppler, J. H. (2000). 'Prices, Technology Development and the Rebound Effect,' *Energy Policy*, 28(6–7), 457–469.

Marketing Research
Hofstetter P., Madjar, M., and Ozawa, T. (2005). 'The Fallacy of Ceteris Paribus and Real Consumers: An Attempt to Quantify Rebound Effects,' in E. Hertwich, T. Briceno, P. Hofstetter, and A. Inaba (eds.). *Sustainable Consumption: The Contribution of Research.* Proceedings of an International Workshop, 10–12 February 2005, Gabels Hus, Oslo, NTNU, Program for Industriell Okologi, Report No. 1/2005.

BIBLIOGRAPHY
Greene, D. L., Kahn, J., and Gibson, R. (1999). 'Fuel Economy Rebound Effect for U.S. Household Vehicles,' *Energy Journal* (Cambridge, Mass.; Cleveland, Oh.), 20(3), 1–31.

■ recency effect

DESCRIPTION

A cognitive bias in individual learning where, in a series of observations or other stimuli, the last or final observations or stimuli become disproportionately salient to the individual relative to those in the middle of the series.

KEY INSIGHTS

The recency effect is considered to be a common phenomenon in individual learning, where information presented last in a series is more easily remembered than that in the middle of the series. One explanation for the recency effect is that earlier information (e.g. that in the middle of a series) encounters associative interference from subsequent, competing information in individuals' efforts to remember such information, something that is reduced in the process of individuals' remembering the most recent information.

While the recency effect as described above generally refers to a specific effect in individual learning given a series of information to learn over a relatively short period of time, the phenomenon is sometimes referred to more generally as the 'recency rule' in the context of learning occurring over a relatively longer period of time or other less constrained learning conditions. The use of the term 'recency rule' generally refers to the view that information that is learned last is that which is best remembered. Note also the recency effect term as described above should not be viewed as having the same meaning or implications as that for the related term recency principle. (See **recency principle**.)

KEY WORDS Information, stimuli, learning, memory, recency

IMPLICATIONS

Marketers can take advantage of the primacy effect in individual learning by ensuring that the most important information or other stimuli is at the end of any series of information or stimuli that marketers wish consumers to remember. Alternatively, marketing researchers should recognize the recency effect as a potential bias among consumers when they are asked to recall serial information that they have previously encountered or when they are evaluating service experiences. Finally, marketing managers should also be aware of the potential for recency effects influencing and potentially biasing their evaluations of the performance of others.

APPLICATION AREAS AND FURTHER READINGS

Marketing Research
Lynch, John G., Jr., and Srull, Thomas K. (1982). 'Memory and Attentional Factors in Consumer Choice: Concepts and Research Methods,' *Journal of Consumer Research*, 9, June, 18-37.

Consumer Behavior
Pieters, Rik G. M., and Bijmolt, Tammo H. A. (1997). 'Consumer Memory for Television Advertising: A Field Study of Duration, Serial Position, and Competition Effects,' *Journal of Consumer Research*, 23(4), March, 362-372.

Marketing Management
Steiner, D. D., and Rain, J. S. (1989). 'Immediate and Delayed Primacy and Recency Effects in Performance Evaluation,' *Journal of Applied Psychology*, 74, 136-142.

BIBLIOGRAPHY
Crano, William D. (1977). 'Primacy and Recency in Retention of Information and Opinion Change,' *Journal of Social Psychology*, 101, February, 87-96.

■ recency principle

DESCRIPTION
The view that consumer exposure to advertising that is positioned close in time to a purchase occasion will be more beneficial to purchase than exposure to advertising positioned further away in time.

KEY INSIGHTS
Research on exposure to advertising among consumers suggests that recency of advertising exposure relative to a purchase occasion may be more beneficial in eliciting a desired consumer response than the same advertising exposure occurring with less recency. Recognizing the potential for recent ad exposure to be more effective than less recent exposures, the recency principle has been used to argue that it is not necessarily more beneficial to expose consumers to multiple (e.g. three) advertisements over time in comparison to a single recent exposure.

Note: The recency principle as described above should not be confused with the term of the same name established in research by psychologist John Broadus Watson (1930) which states that 'the most recent response is strengthened more by its frequent occurrence than is an earlier response.' While of interest to psychology researchers, the recency principle as defined by Watson (1930) is found to be lacking in interest among marketing researchers. Note also the recency principle term as described above should not be viewed as having the same meaning or implications as that for the related term recency effect. (See **recency effect**.)

KEY WORDS Advertising, exposure, recency, effectiveness

IMPLICATIONS

Marketers should clearly consider the possible enhancing effect of advertising exposures occurring close in time to a consumer's purchase occasion. Marketers may therefore benefit from marketing research aimed
at relating the degree of recency to effects on purchase for a particular
product or service offering.

APPLICATION AREAS AND FURTHER READINGS

Advertising

Sommer, Robert, and Aitkens, Susan (1982). 'Mental Mapping of Two Supermarkets,' *Journal of Consumer Research*, 9(2), September, 211–215.

BIBLIOGRAPHY

Reichel, W., and Wood, L. (1997). 'Recency in Media Planning—Re-Defined,' *Journal
of Advertising Research*, 37(4), 66–74.

Watson, John Broadus (1930). *Behaviorism*, 2nd edn., Chicago: University of Chicago
Press.

☐ **recency rule** *see* recency effect
☐ **reciprocal marketing** *see* cooperative marketing

■ red queen effect

(also called the red queen hypothesis, the red queen theory, the red
queen principle, the red queen metaphor, the red queen trap, the red
queen syndrome, the red queen game, the red queen's race, red queen
evolution, or simply the red queen)

DESCRIPTION

The effect of certain dynamics associated with a highly competitive environment on an organizational entity or strategic approach where, increasingly,
there is a need to expend high levels of exhausting effort or resources in order
for the organization or strategy to remain viable.

KEY INSIGHTS

The red queen effect originally received attention as an evolutionary
hypothesis in biology based on research by Van Valen (1973) but has
subsequently been examined in the context of a range of areas including
marketing. The term 'red queen' refers to the situation in the children's
story *Through the Looking Glass, and What Alice Found There* by Lewis Carroll
(1871) in which the Red Queen, a life-size chess piece, had prompted
Alice to run faster and faster, saying, 'Now, *here* you see, it takes all
the running you can do to keep in the same place. If you want to get
somewhere else, you must run at least twice as fast as that!' In a biological
context—which may be aptly extended to numerous organizational and
marketing contexts—the term refers to the view that enemies of an
organism continuously track its defences and evolve to bypass them,
eventually leading to a situation where the organism must run all-out
merely to maintain a successful defense. More broadly, the term refers to
competitive dynamics where there is intense pressure or a deleterious

effect on the subsequent development or evolution of an entity (e.g. organization), strategy, or marketing strategy resulting from competitive actions.

KEY WORDS **Strategy**, organization, evolution, competitive dynamics, resources

IMPLICATIONS

Marketers in firms encountering the red queen effect as a result of fierce or shrewd competition may find that levels of marketing resources required to simply cope with the competition will be at near-hemorrhaging levels or beyond. In such situations, it is imperative for the viability of the firm or strategy involved to devise and employ a break-through approach or response. At the same time, marketers involved in the development of competitive strategies should strive to recognize and anticipate possible red queen dynamics in an effort to avoid such situations altogether.

APPLICATION AREAS AND FURTHER READINGS

Marketing Strategy

Cooper, L. G. (2000). 'Strategic Marketing Planning for Radically New Products,' *Journal of Marketing*, 64(1), 1–16.

Voelpel, Sven C., Liebold, Marius, Tekie, Eden B., and Kroeg, Georg von (2005). 'Escaping the Red Queen Effect in Competitive Strategy: Sense-Testing Business Models,' *European Management Journal*, 23(1), 37–49.

Lewin, A. Y., and Volberda, H. W. (1999). 'Prolegomena on Coevolution: A Framework for Research on Strategy and New Organizational Forms,' *Organization Science*, 10(5), 519–534.

Baye, Michael R., and Morgan, John (2003). 'Red Queen Pricing Effects in E-Retail Markets,' *Social Science Research Network*, October, Available at SSRN: **http://ssrn.com/abstract=655448**.

Kauffman, S. (1995). 'Escaping the Red Queen Effect,' *McKinsey Quarterly*, 1, 118–129.

Arnott, D. C. (2004). 'The Red Queen: On Positioning in Dynamic Markets,' in K. Sausen and S. Dibb (eds.), *Proceedings of the Academy of Marketing SIG on Market Segmentation*. St Gallen: Thexis, 35–39.

BIBLIOGRAPHY

Van Valen, L. (1973). 'A New Evolutionary Law,' *Evolutionary Theory*, 1, 1–30.

Ridley, Matt (2003). *The Red Queen*. New York: HarperCollins.

Carroll, Lewis (1871) (reprinted 1960). 'The Annotated Alice: Alice's Adventures in Wonderland and Through the Looking-Glass,' illustrated by J. Tenniel, *Through the Looking-Glass and What Alice Found There*, with an Introduction and Notes by M. Gardner, The New American Library, New York, 345.

■ reference group

DESCRIPTION

The people that an individual uses as a point of reference in determining his or her own judgments, beliefs, preferences, and behaviors.

KEY INSIGHTS

Considerable research based in the social sciences suggests that reference groups both large and small can have significant influences on a range of individual judgments, beliefs, attitudes, preferences, and behaviors. In the context of many product or brand purchase decisions where individuals look to one or more others for guidance on such purchase decisions, identifying the nature and extent of reference group influences is often a vital consideration among marketers. Depending on the purchase situation, a sports group, volunteer group, church group, political group, a group of student peers, or one or more of many other groups may ultimately play a significant role in influencing an individual's attitudes and preferences, regardless of whether or not one is a member of such groups and whether or not one even aspires to become a member.

KEY WORDS Groups, influence, behavior, judgment, attitudes, beliefs, preference

IMPLICATIONS
While individuals may vary on the extent that they are susceptible to reference group influences, marketers must actively seek to understand consumer behaviors in relation to their offerings in order to leverage possible reference group influences. Tailoring marketing messages and media to either reach such groups or to acknowledge such positive or negative influences by others may enhance the effectiveness of marketing communications aimed at influencing consumer purchase decision making.

APPLICATION AREAS AND FURTHER READINGS
Consumer Behavior
Bearden, William, and Etzel, O. Michael J. (1982). 'Reference Group Influence on Product and Brand Purchase Decisions,' *Journal of Consumer Research*, 9(2), September, 183–194.
Park, C. Whan, and Lessig, V. Parker (1977). 'Students and Housewives: Differences in Susceptibility to Reference Group Influence,' *Journal of Consumer Research*, 4(2), September, 102–110.
Childers, Terry L., and Rao, Akshay R. (1992). 'The Influence of Familial and Peer-Based Reference Groups on Consumer Decisions,' *Journal of Consumer Research*, 19(2), September, 198–211.

BIBLIOGRAPHY
Merton, Robert K., and Rossi, Alice Kitt (1949). 'Contributions to the Theory of Reference Group Behavior,' in Robert K. Merton (ed.), *Social Theory and Social Structure*. New York: The Free Press, 225–275.

■ reference price

DESCRIPTION
An internal standard against which observed prices are compared.

KEY INSIGHTS
Reference prices are psychological points of reference used by consumers that have been empirically demonstrated to be influential in brand choice. The reference price formation process typically involves reliance on past prices and, as such, may vary in accuracy as a result of limitations in consumers' ability to recall prices paid, but is nevertheless an influential process in its effect on consumer judgments of price acceptability.

KEY WORDS Psychological reference point, price comparison

IMPLICATIONS

Marketers should be concerned about reference prices held by consumers for particular offerings out of consideration for reference price effects on consumer evaluations of the acceptability and desirability of future prices. For example, consistent price promotions are found to lower consumers' reference prices and, as a result, consumers tend to see non-promotion prices much more as price increases than prices which are returning to normal.

APPLICATION AREAS AND FURTHER READINGS

Marketing Management

Winer, Russell S. (1986). 'A Reference Price Model of Brand Choice for Frequently Purchased Products,' *Journal of Consumer Research*, 13(2), September, 250–256.

Rajendran, K. N., and Tellis, Gerard J. (1994).'Contextual and Temporal Components of Reference Price,' *Journal of Marketing*, 58(1), January, 22–34.

Lattin, James M., and Bucklin, Randolph E. (1989). 'Reference Effects of Price and Promotion on Brand Choice Behavior,' *Journal of Marketing Research*, 26(3), August, 299–310.

Greenleaf, Eric A. (1995). 'The Impact of Reference Price Effects on the Profitability of Price Promotions,' *Marketing Science*, 14(1), 82–104.

BIBLIOGRAPHY

Kalyanaram, Gurumurthy, and Winer, Russell S. (1995). 'Empirical Generalizations from Reference Price Research,' *Marketing Science*, 14(3), Part 2 of 2: Special Issue on Empirical Generalizations in Marketing, G161–G169.

☐ referral-based marketing *see* affiliate marketing

■ **regression towards the mean**

DESCRIPTION

A statistical phenomenon or artifact where there is a tendency for values of variables probabilistically predicted and with random error to be closer to their means than predicted.

KEY INSIGHTS

The regression towards the mean phenomenon, where there is a tendency in related measurements for the expected value of a subsequent measurement to be closer to the mean than the observed value of an initial measurement, occurs when there is asymmetric or non-random sampling from a population and measures that are imperfectly correlated. Often considered counter-intuitive, the regression towards the mean phenomenon is important in that a researcher may mistakenly interpret a measurement as occurring as a result of a treatment or stimulus when, in fact, it is due to chance.

KEY WORDS Measurement, response, prediction

IMPLICATIONS

The regression towards the mean phenomenon has important implications for marketing researchers in establishing expectations about future measures in relation to initial measures. For example, relative to a recognized average response rate for a mail survey, an extremely high response rate for a subsequent survey will not necessarily be followed by another high response rate for yet another survey but rather a response rate that is closer to the mean.

APPLICATION AREAS AND FURTHER READINGS

Marketing Strategy

Day, George S., and Wensley, Robin (1988). 'Assessing Advantage: A Framework for Diagnosing Competitive Superiority,' *Journal of Marketing*, 52(2), April, 1–20.

Marketing Research

Lee, Eunkyu, Hu, Michael Y., and Toh, Rex S. (2000). 'Are Consumer Survey Results Distorted? Systematic Impact of Behavioral Frequency and Duration on Survey Response Errors,' *Journal of Marketing Research*, 37(1), February, 125–133.

Consumer Behavior

Raj, S. P. (1982). 'The Effects of Advertising on High and Low Loyalty Consumer Segments,' *Journal of Consumer Research*, 9(1), June, 77–89.

BIBLIOGRAPHY

Reynolds, William H. (1966). 'Statistical Regression in Before-and-After Paired Comparison Studies,' *Journal of Advertising Research*, 6(1), 18–20.

☐ reification *see* fallacy of misplaced concreteness
☐ Reilly's law *see* retail gravitation, law of

■ reinforcement

DESCRIPTION

Anything accompanying a behavior that leads to an increase in the likelihood that the behavior will occur again or with increased frequency.

KEY INSIGHTS

Pioneering research by Thorndike (1911) demonstrated that a stimulus, either in the form of a reward or the removal of something unpleasant, presented to a subject immediately following a desired response increased the probability that the response will occur again. Subsequent research on reinforcement recognizes the value and role of a general reinforcement approach for systematically encouraging and obtaining the desired behaviors of individuals under a range of conditions.

KEY WORDS Behavior, stimulus, rewards

IMPLICATIONS

A greater understanding and appreciation of the concepts and principles associated with a reinforcement approach to learning may benefit marketers who are concerned with developing effective and efficient approaches that reinforce particular consumer behaviors. Encouraging

regular purchase or frequent service usage through formal reward programs that give financial incentives to consumers who demonstrate
desired purchase behaviors is but one way that reinforcement may potentially be put to effective use by marketers. Product and service usage experiences that provide customers with an immediate sense of satisfaction
may reinforce repeat purchase or service use as well.

APPLICATION AREAS AND FURTHER READINGS
Marketing Research
Kahn, Barbara E., Kalwani, Manohar U., and Morrison, Donald G. (1986). 'Measur-
    ing Variety-Seeking and Reinforcement Behaviors Using Panel Data,' *Journal of
    Marketing Research*, 23(2), May, 89–100.
Kahn, Barbara E., and Raju, Jagmohan S. (1991). 'Effects of Price Promotions on
    Variety-Seeking and Reinforcement Behavior,' *Marketing Science*, 10(4), Autumn,
    316–337.
Carey, J. Ronald, Clicque, Steven H., Leighton, Barbara A., and Milton, Frank
    (1976). 'A Test of Positive Reinforcement of Customers,' *Journal of Marketing*, 40(4),
    October, 98–100.

BIBLIOGRAPHY
Thorndike, Edward L. (1911). *Animal Intelligence*. New York: Macmillan.

☐ **rejection-then-retreat technique** *see* door-in-the-face technique
☐ **related diversification** *see* product-market investment strategies

■ relationship marketing

(also called customer relationship marketing)

DESCRIPTION
Marketing characterized by an emphasis on building long-term customer
relationships with selected customers.

KEY INSIGHTS
Relationship marketing adopts the view that it can be in the best interest
of a firm and selected customers of the firm to maintain long-term
mutual relationships as opposed to the firm and such customers simply
engaging in a series of individual commercial transactions. While not
appropriate for all product markets, the relationship marketing's emphasis on customer retention may have cost advantages to a firm when compared to the potentially higher costs associated with attracting new customers to the firm. When customer acquisition costs are high relative to
costs associated with their retention, customer relationship management
becomes increasingly important (see **customer relationship management**). Nevertheless, characteristics of the firm's offerings, the market,
and the customer may ultimately determine how beneficial it may be. For
example, when the value of products purchased is relatively high, when
there are relatively high switching costs associated with a product, and
when customers' level of involvement with the firm's products and their
production is relatively high, a relationship marketing approach may be

more beneficial than transactional marketing than when the converse is true. As an example, a specialty car manufacturer in the UK would clearly benefit from relationship marketing with current and potential customers when one considers that customers must wait patiently for up to five years to have their cars made from the time they place their order. At the same time, relationship marketing recognizes that a firm need not seek to establish long-term relationships with all of its customers, as not only do some customers prefer to avoid such relationships, but other customers, depending on their wants, needs, purchase histories, and expected future purchases, may not provide the firm with sufficient value as to warrant the effort.

KEY WORDS Customer retention, long-term relationships

IMPLICATIONS

A better understanding of the relationship marketing approach, as expressed in the considerable amount of marketing research devoted to the study of its effective use, can do much to assist a marketer with identifying, developing, and implementing strategies, methods, techniques, and tactics that help the marketer's firm to identify, create, and retain profitable customers. Given that the offerings of many firms are the subject of ongoing, periodic desire by their customers, it behooves marketers to look regularly for ways that relationship marketing approaches can be put to effective use.

APPLICATION AREAS AND FURTHER READINGS

Marketing Strategy

Foss, B., and Stone, M. (2001). *Successful Customer Relationship Marketing: New Thinking, New Strategies, New Tools for Getting Closer to your Customers.* London: Kogan Page.

Gronroos, C. (1996). 'Relationship Marketing: Strategic and Tactical Implications,' *Management Decision*, 34/3, 5–14.

Zineldin, M. (2000). 'Beyond Relationship Marketing: Technologicalship Marketing,' *Marketing Intelligence and Planning*, 18(1), 9–23.

Marketing Management

Gummesson, E. (1994). 'Making Relationship Marketing Operational,' *International Journal of Service Industry Management*, 5, 5–20.

Services Marketing

Berry, L. (1995). 'Relationship Marketing of Services: Growing Interest, Emerging Perspectives,' *Journal of the Academy of Marketing Science*, 23, 236–245.

Tax, S. S., Brown, S. W., and Chandrashekaran, M. (1998). 'Customer Evaluations of Service Complaint Experiences: Implication for Relationship Marketing,' *Journal of Marketing*, 62(2), 60–76.

Business-to-Business Marketing

Nevin, J. R. (1995). 'Relationship Marketing and Distribution Channels: Exploring Fundamental Issues,' *Journal of the Academy of Marketing Science*, 23, Fall, 327–334.

Shani, D., and Chalasani, S. (1993). 'Exploiting Niches Using Relationship Marketing,' *Journal of Business and Industrial Marketing*, 8(4), 58.

Online Marketing

Gilbert, David C., Powell-Perry, Jan, and Widijoso, Sianandar (1999). 'Approaches by Hotels to the Use of the Internet as a Relationship Marketing Tool,' *Journal of Marketing Practice: Applied Marketing Science*, 5(1), February, 21–38.

BIBLIOGRAPHY
Stone, M., Woodcock, N., and Machtynger, L. (2000). *Customer Relationship Marketing*. London: Kogan Page.
Parvatiyar, A., and Sheth, J. N. (2000). 'The Domain and Conceptual Foundations of Relationship Marketing,' in J. N. Sheth and A. Parvatiyar (eds.), *Handbook of Relationship Marketing*. Beverly Hills, Calif.: Sage Publications.
Morris, M. H., Brunyee J., and Page, M. (1998). 'Relationship Marketing in Practice—When is it Appropriate?' *Industrial Marketing Management*, 27(4), July, 359-371.

■ reliability

DESCRIPTION
The extent to which a measurement approach is able to obtain consistent, stable, and uniform measurements on repeated occasions under the same measurement conditions.

KEY INSIGHTS
Research in marketing is often concerned with reliable measurement. If, for example, a survey is developed to measure consumers' interest in using the internet for luxury goods purchases, then each time the survey is administered, the results should be approximately the same. While it is impossible to calculate reliability exactly, however, it can be estimated in different ways.

KEY WORDS Accuracy, consistency, repeatability

IMPLICATIONS
Marketers involved in marketing research should take great care to develop measurement methods that are sufficiently reliable to ensure that results are useful and that the research is able to provide sufficient insight given its cost, time, and effort. A better understanding of the different ways that reliability can be estimated may do much to assist the marketer with effective research designs. In addition, marketers making use of marketing research should be sure to understand to what extent the measurement methods employed are reliable if such findings are to be used as inputs to strategically important marketing decisions.

APPLICATION AREAS AND FURTHER READINGS
Marketing Research
Perreault, William D., Jr., and Leigh, Laurence E. (1989). 'Reliability of Nominal Data Based on Qualitative Judgments,' *Journal of Marketing Research*, 26(2), May, 135-148.
Churchill, Gilbert A., Jr., and Peter, J. Paul (1984). 'Research Design Effects on the Reliability of Rating Scales: A Meta-analysis,' *Journal of Marketing Research*, 21(4), November, 360-375.
Kolbe, Richard H., and Burnett, Melissa S. (1991). 'Content-Analysis Research: An Examination of Applications with Directives for Improving Research Reliability and Objectivity,' *Journal of Consumer Research*, 18(2), September, 243-250.
Ruekert, Robert W., and Churchill, Gilbert A., Jr. (1984). 'Reliability and Validity of Alternative Measures of Channel Member Satisfaction,' *Journal of Marketing Research*, 21(2), May, 226-233.

BIBLIOGRAPHY
Peter, J. Paul (1979). 'Reliability: A Review of Psychometric Basics and Recent Marketing Practices,' *Journal of Marketing Research*, 16(1), February, 6–17.
Churchill, Gilbert A., Jr. (1979). 'A Paradigm for Developing Better Measures of Marketing Constructs,' *Journal of Marketing Research*, 16(1), February, 64–73.

■ remarketing

DESCRIPTION

Marketing efforts by an organization to market an offering again after it has been marketed, unsuccessfully or successfully, on an earlier occasion.

KEY INSIGHTS

The nature of some firm's offerings is such that the firm may have a need to remarket them after an earlier marketing effort which may or may not have been successful. In the case of firms offering tangible leased property, for example, the firm would have a need to remarket the property when a lessee turns in the property at the end of the lease or if the lessor defaulted on the lease. Yet, the remarketing efforts of a firm may not necessarily be concerned with tangible goods, as it may involve a service or even an idea. In the instance where earlier marketing efforts were successful, it is, of course, easier to remarket an offering as there is a success story to draw upon. On the other hand, when an earlier marketing effort is unsuccessful, the firm must often find a new, alternative way of marketing its offering.

KEY WORDS Subsequent marketing strategies

IMPLICATIONS

In the case of offerings that are remarketed as a result of having seen previous use, remarketing may, of course, use any number of marketing approaches (e.g. using auctions for automobile remarketing) to reach new customer markets. However, in the case of offerings that are remarketed out of a lack of success on an earlier occasion, marketers must usually adopt new marketing strategies that emphasize different strategic positions and value propositions. For example, when the Coca-Cola Company introduced new Coke and simultaneously withdrew its original Coke in 1985, many customers were extremely dissatisfied with the new Coke and stopped buying it. In response to the crisis, the company reintroduced the original Coke, remarketing it, very successfully, as 'Coke Classic.'

APPLICATION AREAS AND FURTHER READINGS

Marketing Strategy

Beeton, S., and Pinge, I. (2003). 'Casting the Holiday Dice: Demarketing Gambling to Encourage Local Tourism,' *Current Issues in Tourism*, 6(4), 309–322.

Place Marketing

Chan, W. F. (2005). 'Planning Birmingham as a Cosmopolitan City: Recovering the Depths of its Diversity?' In *Cosmopolitan Urbanism*. London: Routledge.

Services Marketing
MacStravic, S. (1995). 'Remarketing, Yes, Remarketing Health Care,' *Journal of Health Care Marketing*, 15(4), 57–59.

Business-to-Business Marketing
Chesler, L. (1991). 'Contractual Issues in the Remarketing of Systems,' *Computer/Law Journal*, 11, 247–264.
McConocha, Diane M., and Speh, Thomas W. (1991). 'Remarketing: Commercialization of Remanufacturing Technology,' *Journal of Business and Industrial Marketing*, 6(1–2), 23–36.

BIBLIOGRAPHY
Blackwell, R. D. (1994). 'Remarketing of Autos: The Role of Auctions in the Auto Distribution Revolution,' *Journal of Consumer Marketing*, 11(2), 4–17.

■ repetition effect

DESCRIPTION
Any effect or response resulting from repetition in exposure to a stimulus.

KEY INSIGHTS
Repetition in communication, particularly advertising, is a recognized approach by marketers seeking the effect of increased recall or recognition of a stimulus (e.g. product name, brand name, or message). While any effect of repetition will vary with the amount and timing associated with the process of exposing consumers to a message on multiple occasions, the way that consumers process information from the message can also be influential in establishing the degree of a repetition effect.

KEY WORDS Message repetition, stimulus, response

IMPLICATIONS
Marketers seeking to influence consumer behavior through message repetition may benefit from understanding not only how such an approach may encourage desired behaviors but also how factors related to message repetition such as ease of message processing may have important moderating influences on repetition effects as well.

APPLICATION AREAS AND FURTHER READINGS
Advertising
Malaviya, P., Meyers-Levy, J., and Sternthal, B. (1999). 'Ad Repetition in a Cluttered Environment: The Influence of Type of Processing,' *Psychology and Marketing*, 16(2), 99–118.
Rethans, Arno J., Swasy, John L., and Marks, Lawrence J. (1986). 'Effects of Television Commercial Repetition, Receiver Knowledge, and Commercial Length: A Test of the Two-Factor Model,' *Journal of Marketing Research*, 23(1), February, 50–61.
Malaviya, Prashant (2000). 'Ad Repetition Effects: The Influence of Amount and Type of Elaboration,' *INSEAD Working Paper* No. 2000/17/MKT.

BIBLIOGRAPHY
Anand, Punam, and Sternthal, Brian (1990). 'Ease of Message Processing as a Moderator of Repetition Effects in Advertising,' *Journal of Marketing Research*, 27(3), August, 345–353.

■ reputation effect

DESCRIPTION

Any effect or response resulting from a perceived reputation of an organization, individual, product, service, or brand.

KEY INSIGHTS

Perceptions of the quality, character, or standing of an organization, individual, or marketing offering can have influences on the attitudes, judgments, and behaviors of a stakeholder (e.g. customer, shareholder) that extend beyond the stakeholder's immediate relationship with the organization, individual, or offering. Positive reputation effects stemming from favorable particular firm or brand evaluations, for example, may lead consumers to be more receptive to evaluating or adopting new, yet unfamiliar offerings of a firm relative to situations where existing firm or brand reputation effects are either neutral or negative.

KEY WORDS Perception, firm performance, brand quality

IMPLICATIONS

While the nature and extent of a reputation effect is clearly context-specific, firm and brand reputation effects in particular are considered by marketing researchers to be important areas to manage in efforts to achieve strong financial performance and customer satisfaction.

APPLICATION AREAS AND FURTHER READINGS

Marketing Strategy

Roberts, P. W., and Dowling, G. R. (2002). 'Corporate Reputation and Sustained Superior Financial Performance,' *Strategic Management Journal*, 23(12), 1077–1094.

Wirtz, J., Kum, D., and Lee, K. S. (2000). 'Should a Firm with a Reputation for Outstanding Service Quality Offer a Service Guarantee?' *Journal of Services Marketing*, 14(6–7), 502–512.

Anderson, Eugene W., and Sullivan, Mary W. (1993). 'The Antecedents and Consequences of Customer Satisfaction for Firms,' *Marketing Science*, 12(2), Spring, 125–143.

Consumer Behavior

Lee, Kyoungmi, and Shavitt, Sharon (2006). 'The Use of Cues Depends on Goals: Store Reputation Affects Product Judgments When Social Identity Goals Are Salient,' *Journal of Consumer Psychology*, 16(3), 260–271.

BIBLIOGRAPHY

Cabral, L. M. B. (2000). 'Stretching Firm and Brand Reputation,' *Rand Journal of Economics*, 31(4), 658–673.

■ resource-based view

DESCRIPTION

The view that the competitive advantage of a firm is grounded in the way it uses the collection of valuable resources that is available to the firm.

KEY INSIGHTS

Developed in research by Wernerfelt (1984), the resource-based view (or RBV) argues that attention to a firm's resources, which may include assets, capabilities, processes of the firm, and knowledge within the firm, is critically important in determining how and to what extent a firm can potentially achieve a competitive advantage. Further, given that any competitive advantage can vary in the time horizon over which it is more or less sustainable, the theory puts forward the view that understanding what key resources the firm should possess and how such resources should be configured are vitally important steps in a firm's pursuit of competitive advantage that are increasingly sustainable. More specifically, the theory suggests that, to the extent that key resources are valuable (e.g. able to create value, strengthen the firm's weaknesses, and/or neutralize competitor's strengths), rare (e.g. uncommon or not widely available among competitors), imperfectly imitable (e.g. not being able to be duplicated by competitors in the same way, as a result of being based on knowledge exclusively available within the firm, for example), and imperfectly substitutable (e.g. where other resources which are available cannot be used easily to replace the key resources).

KEY WORDS Assets, competencies, competitive advantage

IMPLICATIONS

In a firm's efforts to pursue and achieve sustainable competitive advantage, the resource-based view highlights the need for marketers to manage strategically the firm's scarce resources. A greater knowledge of the considerable body of marketing research based on the resource-based view may therefore be very useful to the marketer seeking to identify potential key resources, evaluate them for strategic importance, and ensure that the most important ones are adequately protected by the firm to prevent their loss in value.

APPLICATION AREAS AND FURTHER READINGS

Marketing Strategy

Ghosh, Mrinal, and John, George (1999). 'Governance Value Analysis and Marketing Strategy,' *Journal of Marketing*, 63, Fundamental Issues and Directions for Marketing, 131–145.

Day, George S., and Wensley, Robin (1988). 'Assessing Advantage: A Framework for Diagnosing Competitive Superiority,' *Journal of Marketing*, 52(2), April, 1–20.

Lieberman, M. B., and Montgomery, D. B. (1998). 'First-Mover (Dis)Advantages: Retrospective and Link with the Resource-Based View,' *Strategic Management Journal*, 19(12), 1111–1125.

Srivastava, Rajendra K., Shervani, Tasadduq A., and Fahey, Liam (1999). 'Marketing, Business Processes, and Shareholder Value: An Organizationally Embedded View of Marketing Activities and the Discipline of Marketing,' *Journal of Marketing*, 63, Fundamental Issues and Directions for Marketing, 168–179.

Marketing Management

Day, G. S. (2000). 'Managing Market Relationships,' *Journal of the Academy of Marketing Science*, 28(1), 24–30.

Capron, Laurence, and Hulland, John (1999). 'Redeployment of Brands, Sales Forces, and General Marketing Management Expertise Following Horizontal Acquisitions: A Resource-Based View,' *Journal of Marketing*, 63(2), April, 41–54.

Verona, G. (1999). 'A Resource-Based View of New Product Development,' *Academy of Management Review*, 24, 132–142.

Services Marketing
Fahy, J. (1996). 'Competitive Advantage in International Services: A Resource-Based View,' *International Studies of Management and Organization*, 26(2), 24–37.

International Marketing
Fahy, J. (2002). 'A Resource-Based Analysis of Sustainable Competitive Advantage in a Global Environment,' *International Business Review*, 11(1), 57–78.

Global Marketing
Zou, S., and Cavusgil, S. T. (2002). 'The GMS: A Broad Conceptualization of Global Marketing Strategy and its Effect on Firm Performance,' *Journal of Marketing*, 66(4), 40–56.

Online Marketing
Fahy, J., and Hooley, G. (2002). 'Sustainable Competitive Advantage in Electronic Business: Towards a Contingency Perspective on the Resource-Based View,' *Journal of Strategic Marketing*, 10, 241–253.

Business-to-Business Marketing
Matthyssems, P., and Koen, V. (1998). 'Creating Competitive Advantage in Industrial Services,' *Journal of Business & Industrial Marketing* (Santa Barbara), 13(4–5), 339–355.

Marketing Research
Day, George S., and Montgomery, David B. (1999). 'Charting New Directions for Marketing,' *Journal of Marketing*, 63, Fundamental Issues and Directions for Marketing, 3–13.

BIBLIOGRAPHY
Wernerfelt, B. (1984). 'A Resource-Based View of the Firm,' *Strategic Management Journal*, 5, 171–180.
Peteraf, M. A. (1993). 'The Cornerstones of Competitive Advantage: A Resource-Based View,' *Strategic Management Journal*, 14(3), 179–191.

∎ resource dependency theory

DESCRIPTION
The view that organizations lacking in needed resources will be prompted to establish relationships with other organizations in order to strengthen their resource positions while at the same time striving to minimize their dependencies.

KEY INSIGHTS
Put forth in pioneering research by Aldrich (1976) and Aldrich and Pfeffer (1976), resource dependency theory adopts the view that increasing a firm's dependence on other firms for their resources decreases the firm's chances for survival in the long run. Given that many firms must rely on others for their resources to some extent, the theory further indicates that such firms will seek ways to keep control of such relationships in an effort to lessen their dependencies.

KEY WORDS Interorganizational relationships, business relationships

IMPLICATIONS

Marketers may find that a greater knowledge of resource dependency theory and resource dependency theory-based research may help the marketer to understand and evaluate better the firm's many different interorganizational relationships and assist with the development of relationships involving greater control. As a means to establish greater control over a firm's suppliers, for example, the firm may opt to perform some of the work in-house. Terms with suppliers may be able to be renegotiated as well, further enabling the firm to obtain more power over suppliers. In addition, being in a position to switch to alternate suppliers may yet be another means to minimize the firm's resource dependencies.

APPLICATION AREAS AND FURTHER READINGS

Marketing Strategy
Anderson, Paul F. (1982). 'Marketing, Strategic Planning and the Theory of the Firm,' *Journal of Marketing*, 46(2), Spring, 15–26.

Marketing Management
Ruekert, Robert W., and Walker, Orville C., Jr. (1987). 'Marketing's Interaction with Other Functional Units: A Conceptual Framework and Empirical Evidence,' *Journal of Marketing*, 51(1), January, 1–19.

Business-to-Business Marketing
Hallen, Lars, Johanson, Jan, and Mohamed, Nazeem Seyed (1991). 'Interfirm Adaptation in Business Relationships,' *Journal of Marketing*, 55(2), April, 29–37.
Anderson, James C., Hakansson, Hakan, and Johanson, Jan (1994). 'Dyadic Business Relationships within a Business Network Context,' *Journal of Marketing*, 58(4), October, 1–15.
Heide, Jan B., and John, George (1988). 'The Role of Dependence Balancing in Safeguarding Transaction-Specific Assets in Conventional Channels,' *Journal of Marketing*, 52(1), January, 20–35.

Government Marketing
Meznar, Martin B., and Nigh, Douglas (1995). 'Buffer or Bridge? Environmental and Organizational Determinants of Public Affairs Activities in American Firms,' *Academy of Management Journal*, 38(4), August, 975–996.

Marketing Research
Oliver, Christine (1990). 'Determinants of Interorganizational Relationships: Integration and Future Directions,' *Academy of Management Review*, 15(2), April, 241–265.

BIBLIOGRAPHY
Aldrich, H. (1976). 'Resource Dependence and Inter-organizational Relations: Relations between Local Employment Service Offices and Social Service Sector Organizations,' *Administration and Society*, 7, 419–454.
Aldrich, Howard E., and Pfeffer, Jeffrey (1976). 'Environments of Organizations,' *Annual Review of Sociology*, 2, 79–105.
Aldrich, H., and Herker, D. (1976). 'Boundary Spanning Roles and Organizational Structure,' *Academy of Management Journal*, 2, 217–230.

☐ **responsible marketing** *see* ethical marketing; social marketing; green marketing

☐ **Restorff effect** *see* von Restorff effect

■ retail accordion theory

(also called accordion theory)

DESCRIPTION

The view that retail institutions change systematically over time, moving from outlets with wide assortments to outlets with narrow, more specialized assortments, but then over time moving back again to outlets with wide assortments.

KEY INSIGHTS

Based on pioneering research by Hollander (1966), the accordion theory was put forward to explain observed and expected changes in retail institution behavior over time. While not all retailers may change their assortments in ways that are completely consistent with retail accordion theory, the theory nevertheless highlights the importance of assortment width in the long-term marketing strategy of a retailer.

KEY WORDS Retailing, organizational change, product assortments, width

IMPLICATIONS

Marketers concerned with retail strategy development may potentially benefit from a better understanding of the role of product assortment in the context of retail accordion theory in terms of its relationship to possible retail organization change. In particular, a retailer's viability and competitiveness may be influenced by how the relative width of its product assortment changes over time and, as such, must be appropriately managed for optimization or maximum effectiveness.

APPLICATION AREAS AND FURTHER READINGS

Retail Marketing

Hart, C. (1999). 'The Retail Accordion and Assortment Strategies: An Exploratory Study,' *International Review of Retail Distribution and Consumer Research*, 9(2), 111–126.

Pioch, E. A., and Schmidt, R. A. (2000). 'Consumption and the Retail Change Process: A Comparative Analysis of Toy Retailing in Italy and France,' *International Review of Retail Distribution and Consumer Research*, 10(2), 183–204.

BIBLIOGRAPHY

Hollander, Stanley C. (1966). 'Notes on the Retail Accordion,' *Journal of Retailing*, 42, Summer, 29–40, 54.

■ retail gravitation, law of

(also called Reilly's law or Reilly's law of retail gravitation)

DESCRIPTION

The view that larger cities will have larger trade areas than smaller ones, thereby leading people to travel further to reach larger cities for trade relative to smaller ones.

KEY INSIGHTS

Put forth by Reilly (1931), the view summarizes research findings aimed at explaining variations in retail sales between cities and related phenomena. Reilly's law considers population and distance to be key elements related to retail trade. Key assumptions of the relationship put forward include the same ease of travel conditions between cities and consumer indifference between cities.

KEY WORDS Retail, travel, distance, trade, cities

IMPLICATIONS
While the law does not hold in all cases and is also limited by its geographical assumptions for city-to-city travel, the law of retail gravitation nevertheless highlights the importance of city size in attracting consumers for retail shopping. Marketers seeking to model expected consumer travel and retail shopping patterns may therefore benefit from the research findings that have established the relationships posed in Reilly's law.

APPLICATION AREAS AND FURTHER READINGS
Retail Marketing
Kelley, Eugene J. (1958). 'The Importance of Convenience in Consumer Purchasing,' *Journal of Marketing*, 23(1), July, 32–38.
Jung, Allen F. (1959). 'Is Reilly's Law of Retail Gravitation Always True?' *Journal of Marketing*, 24(2), October, 62–63.
Ferber, Robert (1958). 'Variations in Retail Sales between Cities,' *Journal of Marketing*, 22(3), January, 295–303.

BIBLIOGRAPHY
Reilly, William J. (1931). *The Law of Retail Gravitation*. New York: Knickerbocker Press.

☐ **retail location theory** *see* location theory

■ **retail marketing**

DESCRIPTION
Marketing involving the direct sale of offerings to customers, with such offerings not intended for resale.

KEY INSIGHTS
Retail marketing encompasses a broad set of marketing activities as it may, for example, involve the offering of goods and services online, in stores, malls, and/or markets. In addition, regardless of location, retailers may also position themselves in any number of ways including specialty retailers, discounters, and superstores. The term *supermarketing* is sometimes used to refer to retail marketing involving large, primarily self-service retail stores offering wide varieties of regularly consumed food products and other selected products and services. Purchasers of retail offerings may be individual consumers or businesses. By obtaining sets of offerings in larger quantities from upstream distributors (e.g. wholesalers) and manufacturers, retailing firms are then able to offer them in smaller quantities to customers in ways that add value (e.g. making the offerings more easily obtainable). Retailers have a range of marketing approaches at their disposal in an effort to achieve marketing

effectiveness. When a retailer has a physical presence, *in-store marketing* is essential, which is where the retailer engages in marketing practices that aim to increase the appeal of their offerings to current and potential customers who have entered a retailer's store or shop. Such practices may include attention to store ambience (e.g. appealing music, colorful wall displays), making strategic and tactical use of product signage, end-of-aisle product displays, and adopting attractive pricing practices. Still other marketing approaches, used independently or in conjunction with wholesalers and manufacturers, involve making strategic use of point-of-purchase and point-of-sale marketing approaches. (See **point-of-purchase marketing; point-of-sale marketing.**)

When a retailer has an online presence (see **online marketing**), the marketer is similarly concerned with the retail outlet's virtual appearance (e.g. visual appeal, ease of navigability). In contrast to bricks-and-mortar retail marketing, however, a key issue to many online retailers is identifying causes and solutions to the relatively pervasive problem of *shopping cart abandonment*, which is where site visitors take time to evaluate the firm's offerings and pick out some by placing them in their virtual shopping carts only to leave the website at the stage where such offerings are to be paid for by website visitors' credit cards or other means.

KEY WORDS Retailing, direct sales

IMPLICATIONS

Retail marketing enables retailers to engage more effectively with current and prospective customers in retail settings. Yet, retail marketing is not limited to the marketing activities of retailers, since manufacturers and wholesalers may also engage in retail marketing to some degree, where such activity may be either through actual physical locations or an online presence. As such, a greater understanding of retail marketing approaches may potentially provide retailers and non-retailers alike with strategic and tactical knowledge that enables their firms to achieve their marketing objectives more effectively and efficiently, either alone or in conjunction with retail organizations.

APPLICATION AREAS AND FURTHER READINGS

Marketing Strategy
Mulhern, F. (1997). 'Retail Marketing: From Distribution to Integration,' *International Journal of Research in Marketing*, 17(2), 103–124.
Balasubramanian, Sridhar (1998). 'Mail versus Mall: A Strategic Analysis of Competition between Direct Marketers and Conventional Retailers,' *Marketing Science*, 17(3), 181–195.
Dhar, Sanjay K., and Hoch, Stephen J. (1997). 'Why Store Brand Penetration Varies by Retailer,' *Marketing Science*, 16(3), 208–227.

Marketing Management
Padmanabhan, V., and Png, I. P. L. (1997). 'Manufacturer's Returns Policies and Retail Competition,' *Marketing Science*, 16(1), 81–94.
Gilbert, D. (2003). *Retail Marketing Management*, 2nd edn. London: Pearson Education.

Services Marketing
Zeithaml, Valarie A., Parasuraman, A., and Berry, Leonard L. (1985). 'Problems and Strategies in Services Marketing,' *Journal of Marketing*, 49(2), Spring, 33–46.

Online Marketing
Alba, Joseph, Lynch, John, Weitz, Barton, Janiszewski, Chris, Lutz, Richard, Sawyer, Alan, and Wood, Stacy (1997). 'Interactive Home Shopping: Consumer, Retailer, and Manufacturer Incentives to Participate in Electronic Marketplaces,' *Journal of Marketing*, 61(3), July, 38–53.

Retail Marketing
Hart, C., Doherty, N., and Chadwick, F. Ellis (2000). 'Retailer Adoption of the Internet: Implications for Retail Marketing,' *European Journal of Marketing*, 34(8), 954–974.

Consumer Behavior
Dawar, Niraj, and Parker, Philip (1994). 'Marketing Universals: Consumers' Use of Brand Name, Price, Physical Appearance, and Retailer Reputation as Signals of Product Quality,' *Journal of Marketing*, 58(2), April, 81–95.

BIBLIOGRAPHY
O'Brien, Larry, and Harris, Frank (1991). *Retailing: Shopping, Society, Space*. London: David Fulton Publishers.
Krafft, Manfred, and Mantrala, Murali K. (eds.) (2006). *Retailing in the 21st Century: Current and Future Trends*. New York: Springer Verlag.
Global Millennia Marketing (2002). 'Recent Survey Gives Online Merchants Fifteen Reasons for Shopping Cart Abandonment,' *Global Millennia Marketing Press Release*, March.
McGoldrick, P. J. (1990). *Retail Marketing*. New York: McGraw-Hill.

■ retro-marketing

DESCRIPTION
Marketing approaches involving re-representations of the past in one or more areas of marketing activity.

KEY INSIGHTS
Retro-marketing involves taking one or more aspect of marketing associated with any bygone era and reviving it for use in a firm's current marketing practice. A retro-marketing approach may, for example, involve a revived and reconfigured product (e.g. a new automobile but with styling from the 1960s) or an advertising approach adopting elements from an earlier time (e.g. a television advertisement with 1950s music and visual effects). In essence, retro-marketing adopts the view that that which is old can come back again to become the new 'new.' Going beyond mere adoptions of tangible elements of the past, however, retro-marketing suggests further that marketers have an opportunity to adopt marketing practices that may even be antithetical to modern marketing principles including that of customer centricity. Brown (2001a) argues, for example, that some consumers are tired of being 'pandered to,' and actually 'yearn to be teased, tantalized, and tortured by marketers and their wares... just like in the good old days.'

KEY WORDS Bygone marketing practices, nostalgic offerings

IMPLICATIONS

A retro-marketing approach involves looking to the past for marketing inspiration. Clearly, the approach suggests there are numerous opportunities to offer revived products and services incorporating elements of past eras that ultimately went out of fashion or which were superseded by other offerings in the marketplace but nevertheless are associated with nostalgia. Despite the relative pervasiveness in many product markets of resurrected products and services, however, marketers should be wary of only looking at the past for all future inspiration. Finally, taking knowledge of bygone marketing a step further, retro-marketing also suggests an opportunity for marketers to adopt (long-past) marketing approaches that may actually appear to run counter to the customer-centric principle associated with modern marketing.

APPLICATION AREAS AND FURTHER READINGS

Marketing Strategy

Brown, S., Kozinets, R. V., and Sherry, J. F. (2003). 'Teaching Old Brands New Tricks: Retro Branding and the Revival of Brand Meaning,' *Journal of Marketing*, 67(3), 19–33.

McCole, P. (2004). 'Refocusing Marketing to Reflect Practice: The Changing Role of Marketing for Business,' *Marketing Intelligence and Planning*, 22(5), 531–539.

Marketing Management

Brown, S. (2001). 'The Retromarketing Revolution: L'imagination au pouvoir,' *International Journal of Management Reviews*, 3(4), 303–320.

Consumer Behavior

Goedhart, D. (2005). *Capitalizing on Consumer Nostalgia: Exploring Retro Marketing and the Role of Nostalgia in Consumer Behaviour.* Rotterdam: Erasmus Universiteit.

Marketing Education

Burton, D. (2003). 'Rethinking the UK System of Doctoral Training in Marketing,' *Journal of Marketing Management* (Helensburgh), 19(7/8), 883–904.

BIBLIOGRAPHY

Brown S. (1999). 'Retro-marketing: Yesterday's Tomorrows, Today!' *Marketing Intelligence & Planning*, 17(7), 363–376.

Brown, S. (2001a), 'Torment your Customers (they'll Love it),' *Harvard Business Review*, 79(9), 82–8.

Brown, S. (2001b). *Marketing: The Retro Revolution*. London: Sage.

☐ revenue-sharing marketing *see* affiliate marketing
☐ right-time marketing *see* outbound marketing
☐ Ringelmann effect *see* social loafing effect

■ ripple effect

DESCRIPTION

Any effect gradually spreading beyond that which is primarily intended.

KEY INSIGHTS

While any possible ripple effect is clearly context specific, a recognized ripple effect of advertising is a general increase in word-of-mouth communication resulting from advertising. Such an effect can enhance the immediate effectiveness of advertising by creating awareness among individuals who are not reached directly by advertising. As ripple effects may be unintentional or intentional, such effects are important to identify in determining the broader impact of any given marketing action. Another specific type of ripple effect is that attributed to loyalty. (See **loyalty ripple effect**.)

KEY WORDS Influence, spreading effect, advertising

IMPLICATIONS
Marketers concerned with assessing the full impact of marketing actions need to anticipate possible ripple effects in marketing planning and strategy development. Ripple effects of marketing actions such as that from advertising can have significant behavioral as well as economic consequences and can vary across cultures as well.

APPLICATION AREAS AND FURTHER READINGS
Advertising
Hogan, John E., Lemon, Katherine N., and Libai, Barak (2004). 'Quantifying the Ripple: Word-of-Mouth and Advertising Effectiveness,' *Journal of Advertising Research*, 44, 271–280.

Consumer Behavior
Maddux, W. W., and Yuki, M. (2006). 'The "Ripple Effect": Cultural Differences in Perceptions of the Consequences of Events,' *Personality and Social Psychology Bulletin*, 32(5), 669–683.

BIBLIOGRAPHY
Barsade, S. G. (2002). 'The Ripple Effect: Emotional Contagion and its Influence on Group Behavior,' *Administrative Science Quarterly*, 47(4), 644–675.

☐ **risky shift phenomenon** *see* group polarization
☐ **Rosencrantz and Guildenstern effect** *see* approach–avoidance conflict
☐ **Rosenthal effect** *see* experimenter expectancy effect
☐ **rule(s) of . . .** *see specific entries, e.g.* ten percent, rule of

S

- □ sagacity segmentation *see* segmentation
- □ salutory products *see* societal classification of products
- □ sampling bias or error *see* bias
- □ satisfaction *see* customer satisfaction

■ satisficing

DESCRIPTION

A cognitive heuristic for simplifying decision making that involves making decisions that are considered likely to lead to satisfactory or sufficiently acceptable results as opposed to optimal results.

KEY INSIGHTS

Based on research by Simon (1955, 1956), the concept of satisfying reflects the view that individual cognitive capacities and decision processes are not strictly rational and, as such, are not guaranteed to arrive at optimal results. Deviations from rationality arise due to limitations in individual information-processing ability and the costs involved in comparing all available options. Individual decision making, as well as group and organizational decision making, may therefore involve satisficing as a means to cope or work more easily within limitations on information-processing capabilities and lessen the cost of comparing available options. With satisficing, the aim of decision making may therefore be to achieve some minimal level of performance rather than optimal performance. As an example, individuals and organizations engaged in satisficing behaviors may choose to regularly adopt plans for future action in much the same way they have always done in the past if past performance has always been minimally satisfactory.

KEY WORDS Decision making, satisfactory outcomes

IMPLICATIONS

Marketers involved in making strategic as well as tactical decisions should consider the extent to which objectives of the decisions involve satisficing as opposed to optimization. Drawing explicit attention to satisficing in marketing decision making and decision-making processes can potentially assist decision makers interested in achieving results further in the direction of optimality to evaluate more critically the decision-making processes involved and its associated costs and benefits.

APPLICATION AREAS AND FURTHER READINGS

Marketing Strategy
Winter, S. G. (2000). 'The Satisficing Principle in Capability Learning,' *Strategic Management Journal*, 21(10–11), 981–996.
Kahn, K. B., and Myers, M. B. (2005). 'Framing Marketing Effectiveness as a Process and Outcome,' *Marketing Theory*, 5(4), 457–469.

Marketing Research
Holbrook, A. L., Green, M. C., and Krosnick, J. A. (2003). 'Telephone versus Face-to-Face Interviewing of National Probability Samples with Long Questionnaires: Comparisons of Respondent Satisficing and Social Desirability Response Bias,' *Public Opinion Quarterly*, 67(1), 79–125.

BIBLIOGRAPHY
Simon, H. A. (1955). 'A Behavioral Model of Rational Choice,' *Quarterly Journal of Economics*, 59, 99–118.
Simon, H. A. (1956). 'Rational Choice and the Structure of the Environment,' *Psychological Review*, 63, 129–138.

☐ **SCA** *see* sustainable competitive advantage

■ scale

DESCRIPTION
A scheme of rank or order for purposes of measurement and analysis.

KEY INSIGHTS
There are a number of scales that can be used in marketing research to assist with a data collection effort: a *nominal scale*, where data are categorized (e.g. for gender, being either female or male, for industry sector, being either public or private); an *ordinal scale*, where data can be ordered or ranked (e.g. for firm size, being small, medium, or large); an *interval scale*, where the distance or interval between numbers on a scale is constant to allow precise comparisons of responses (e.g. consumer satisfaction on a scale of 1 to 10, where 1 is extremely dissatisfied and 10 is extremely satisfied); and a *ratio scale*, where values can be compared in terms of ratios (e.g. the prices consumers are willing to pay for several different memory sticks differing in storage capacity). In addition, a *Likert scale* is a scale of consecutive numbers that is used to enable a respondent to specify their level of agreement to a statement. An example is when respondents are asked to indicate their level of agreement with the following statement: cars should be taxed according to their fuel efficiency, where 1 = strongly disagree, 2 = disagree, 3 = neither agree nor disagree, 4 = agree, 5 = strongly agree.

KEY WORDS Measurement, analysis

IMPLICATIONS

Marketers engaged in marketing research must choose carefully the scales used in data collection since each scale varies in its power for statistical analysis. While data collection using nominal scales contains the least information and that using ratio scales contains the most, the choice of scale ultimately depends on the marketer's objectives, where, for example, interval scales may be all that are needed to gain important marketing insights.

APPLICATION AREAS AND FURTHER READINGS

Marketing Research

Bearden, William O., Netemeyer, Richard G., and Mobley, Mary F. (1993). *Handbook of Marketing Scales: Multi-item Measures for Marketing and Consumer Behavior Research.* Newbury Park, Calif.: Sage Publications.

Anderson, David Ray, Sweeney, Dennis J., and Williams, Thomas Arthur (1984). *Statistics for Business and Economics.* St Paul, Minn.: West Publishing Company.

BIBLIOGRAPHY

Aaker, David A. (2003). *Marketing Research.* Chichester: John Wiley & Sons, Inc.
Velleman, P., and Wilkinson, L. (1993). 'Nominal, Ordinal, Interval, and Ratio Typologies are Misleading,' *American Statistician*, 47(1), 65–72.

☐ search engine marketing *see* entry at Web marketing
☐ search goods *see* goods
☐ secondary data *see* data types
☐ secondary demand *see* demand

■ segment-of-one marketing

DESCRIPTION

A marketing approach involving segmentation which starts with an individual customer and builds on that profile.

KEY INSIGHTS

Segment-of-one marketing involves a 'bottom-up' segmentation approach. In the context of micromarketing (see **micromarketing**), segment-of-one marketing is an approach where solutions are tailored for individual customers through unique and individualized products or services.

KEY WORDS Individualized offerings, mass customization

IMPLICATIONS

Segment-of-one marketing entails understanding the specific needs of an individual customer representing a target segment, one where a one-to-one relationship is established (Pitta 1998). In the context of a service, effective communication and efficient customer service can be very important in its use. As part of a broader marketing strategy, segment-of-one marketing can help track, understand, and respond to behaviors of individual customers.

APPLICATION AREAS AND FURTHER READINGS

Marketing Strategy
Dibb, S. (2001). 'New Millennium, New Segments: Moving towards the Segment of One?' *Journal of Strategic Marketing*, 9(3), 193–214.

Marketing Management
Christopher, Martin, and Peck, Helen (1997). *Marketing Logistics*. Oxford: Butterworth-Heinemann on behalf of the Chartered Institute of Marketing.
Forsyth, J., Gupta, S., Haldar, S., Kaul, A., and Kettle, K. (1999). 'A Segmentation You Can Act on,' *McKinsey Quarterly*, 3, 6–15.

Marketing Research
Green, Paul E., and Krieger, Abba M. (1991). 'Segmenting Markets with Conjoint Analysis,' *Journal of Marketing*, 55(4), October, 20–31.

Services Marketing
Dibb, S. (2001). 'Banks, Customer Relationship Management and Barriers to the Segment of One,' *Journal of Financial Services Marketing*, 6(1), 10–23.

Marketing Modeling
Rao, C. P., and Ali, J. (2002). 'Neural Network Model for Database Marketing in the New Global Economy,' *Marketing Intelligence and Planning*, 20(1), 35–43.

BIBLIOGRAPHY
Pitta, D. A. (1998). 'Marketing One-to-One and its Dependence on Knowledge Discovery in Databases,' *Journal of Consumer Marketing*, 15(5), 468–480.
Pine, J. B. (1993). *Mass Customization*. Cambridge, Mass.: Harvard Business School Press.

■ segmentation

(also called market segmentation)

DESCRIPTION
Dividing a market into distinct groups of buyers who have relatively distinct behaviors, needs, or other characteristics.

KEY INSIGHTS
Segmentation refers to the process of aggregating customers into groups based on common characteristics and needs, where they are expected to respond similarly to marketing actions. Segmentation can be beneficial to the extent the approach provides the marketer with insights and opportunities to offer one or more distinct market segments a particular market offering. Offerings corresponding to particular segments may vary in any number of ways including distinct products or services, or other elements of the marketing mix such as price, promotion, or distribution. There are many different ways that segmentation may be performed including:

Age segmentation—a type of demographic segmentation, dividing a market into groups based on consumers' ages (e.g. under 18, 18–25, 25–45, 46 and over).

Behavioral segmentation—dividing a market into groups based on consumers' knowledge, attitudes, or product or service usage behaviors (e.g. heavy product users, light product users).

Benefit segmentation—dividing a market into groups based on the different gains to be derived from purchase and consumption (e.g. using a bicycle for fitness versus transportation to and from work).

Demographic segmentation—dividing a market into groups based on demographic variables (e.g. age, gender, income, family size, education, occupation).

Gender segmentation—a type of demographic segmentation, dividing a market into males and females.

Geographic segmentation—dividing a market into different geographic units (e.g. states, cities, neighborhoods).

Income segmentation—a type of demographic segmentation, dividing a market into groups based on consumers' annual incomes (e.g. under $100,000, over $100,000).

Intermarket segmentation—segmentation involving the identification of particular groups of consumers who have similar needs or characteristics even though consumers in such groups are located in different country markets (e.g. babies, teenagers).

Life-cycle segmentation—a type of demographic segmentation, dividing a market into groups based on life-cycle stages (e.g. babies, toddlers, children, young adults, adults).

Lifestyle segmentation—a type of psychographic segmentation, dividing a market into groups based on preferences for the way one wishes to live one's life (e.g. active, passive, outdoor, indoor).

Occasion segmentation—dividing a market into groups based on situational factors or contingencies driving purchase and consumption (e.g. buying chocolate for a Valentine's Day gift vs. everyday consumption).

Psychographic segmentation—dividing a market into different groups based on psychological traits or characteristics (e.g. personality, values).

Sagacity segmentation—dividing a market into groups based on how discerning and discriminating consumers are in their judgments in relation to some activity (e.g. in drinking a fine wine, those that are highly discerning and those that are relatively undiscerning).

KEY WORDS Consumer groups, consumer characteristics

IMPLICATIONS

Segmentation forms a basis for much of marketing strategy. Studying markets to identify their segments before choosing target groups is a process that can be vital to the success of subsequent marketing actions. Choosing the right product or service, price, promotional programs, and distribution channels, for example, are all areas that can be dictated by the needs of consumer groups identified through market segmentation.

APPLICATION AREAS AND FURTHER READINGS

Marketing Strategy

Dickson, Peter R., and Ginter, James L. (1987). 'Market Segmentation, Product Differentiation, and Marketing Strategy,' *Journal of Marketing*, 51(2), April, 1-10.

Firat, A. F., and Shultz, C. J. (1997). 'From Segmentation to Fragmentation: Markets and Marketing Strategy in the Postmodern Era II,' *European Journal of Marketing*, 31(3/4), 183–207.

Marketing Management
Dibb, Sally, and Simkin, Lyndon (1997). 'A Program for Implementing Market Segmentation,' *Journal of Business and Industrial Marketing*, 12(1), 51–65.
Haley, Russell I. (1968). 'Benefit Segmentation: A Decision-Oriented Research Tool,' *Journal of Marketing*, 32(3), July, 30–35.
Plummer, Joseph T. (1974). 'The Concept and Application of Life Style Segmentation,' *Journal of Marketing*, 38(1), January, 33–37.
Moorthy, K. Sridhar (1984). 'Market Segmentation, Self-Selection, and Product Line Design,' *Marketing Science*, 3(4), Autumn, 288–307.
Bucklin, Randolph E., Gupta, Sunil, and Siddarth, S. (1998). 'Determining Segmentation in Sales Response across Consumer Purchase Behaviors,' *Journal of Marketing Research*, 35(2), May, 189–197.

Marketing Research
Wind, Yoram (1978). 'Issues and Advances in Segmentation Research,' *Journal of Marketing Research*, 15(3), August, 317–337.

Marketing Modeling
Kamakura, Wagner A., and Russell, Gary J. (1989). 'A Probabilistic Choice Model for Market Segmentation and Elasticity Structure,' *Journal of Marketing Research*, 26(4), November, 379–390.
Dawar, Niraj, and Parker, Philip (1994). 'Marketing Universals: Consumers' Use of Brand Name, Price, Physical Appearance, and Retailer Reputation as Signals of Product Quality,' *Journal of Marketing*, 58(2), April, 81–95.

Business-to-Business Marketing
Doyle, Peter, and Saunders, John (1985). 'Market Segmentation and Positioning in Specialized Industrial Markets,' *Journal of Marketing*, 49(2), Spring, 24–32.

BIBLIOGRAPHY
Dibb, Sally (1998). 'Market Segmentation: Strategies for Success,' *Marketing Intelligence and Planning*, 16(7), 394–406.
Kotler, Philip, and Armstrong, Gary (2006). *Principles of Marketing*, 11th edn. Upper Saddle River, NJ: Pearson Education, Inc.

■ segmentation viability

DESCRIPTION
The extent to which a particular form of segmentation is useful or workable from multiple perspectives including having characteristics of sufficient accessibility, substantiality, measurability, and actionability.

KEY INSIGHTS
The four major characteristics of *accessibility*, *substantiality*, *measurability*, and *actionability* are often used to define and establish segmentation viability. The notion of accessibility suggests that the targeted segment must be sufficiently reachable and servable via the firm's various marketing efforts. Substantiality, or significance, relates to the notion that the targeted segment must be sufficiently large or significant to enable profitability. Measurability, or identifiability, relates to the extent to which the targeted segment's buying power and overall size can be adequately assessed. Actionability relates to the notion that the firm must have

necessary and sufficient marketing resources to be able to manage the targeted segment given its characteristics including its size.

KEY WORDS Segmentation implementation, segmentation feasibility

IMPLICATIONS
Segmentation viability necessarily involves assessing accessibility, substantiality, measurability, and actionability to determine appropriateness for inclusion as part of a firm's marketing strategy. Tradeoffs are likely to be necessary as well, as different segmentation approaches will inevitably possess different levels of attractiveness relative to these four characteristics.

APPLICATION AREAS AND FURTHER READINGS

Marketing Strategy
Dibb, Sally (1999). 'Criteria Guiding Segmentation Implementation: Reviewing the Evidence,' *Journal of Strategic Marketing*, 7, 107–129.
Dibb, Sally (1998), 'Market Segmentation: Strategies for Success,' *Marketing Intelligence & Planning*, 16(7), 394–406.

Marketing Management
Dibb, Sally, and Simkin, Lyndon (1997). 'A Program for Implementing Market Segmentation,' *Journal of Business and Industrial Marketing*, 12(1), 51–65.

Retail Marketing
Segal, M. N., and Giacobbe, R. W. (1994). 'Market Segmentation and Competitive Analysis for Supermarket Retailing,' *International Journal of Retail & Distribution Management*, 22(1), 38–48.

BIBLIOGRAPHY
Wedel, M., and Kamakura, W. A. (2000). *Market Segmentation: Conceptual and Methodological Foundations*, 2nd edn. Boston: Kluwer Academic Publishers.

☐ segmented marketing *see* differentiated marketing
☐ selective distribution *see* distribution strategies

■ selective exposure

DESCRIPTION
The tendency for individuals to expose themselves to information that reinforces their current beliefs or attitudes.

KEY INSIGHTS
Individuals tend to seek out and pay more attention to information that supports their current beliefs and attitudes relative to information that is not supportive or to that which runs counter to current beliefs and attitudes. As individuals are typically exposed to a considerable amount of information in the course of a day, selective attention allows individuals to give relatively more time to information and messages that reinforce their pre-existing views relative to that which does not. As a result, selective exposure among individuals may lead to individuals selectively watching television programs, reading newspaper editorials,

and attending to advertisements that tend to reinforce, as opposed to not reinforce or contradict, their beliefs and attitudes.

KEY WORDS Information, beliefs, attitudes, reinforcement

IMPLICATIONS
Marketers developing advertising and marketing communications as well as those involved in evaluating the effectiveness of such communication may benefit from a greater understanding of the extent to which consumers are selectively exposing themselves to certain communications as a result of the communication's ability to reinforce their beliefs and attitudes. Such an understanding may help marketers gauge to a better degree the actual and anticipated composition of consumer audiences for marketing messages.

APPLICATION AREAS AND FURTHER READINGS
Advertising
Norris, C. E., Colman, A. M., and Aleixo, P. A. (2003). 'Selective Exposure to Television Programmes and Advertising Effectiveness,' *Applied Cognitive Psychology*, 17(5), 593–606.
Silk, Alvin J., and Geiger, Frank P. (1972). 'Advertisement Size and the Relationship between Product Usage and Advertising Exposure,' *Journal of Marketing Research*, 9(1), February, 22–26.

Consumer Behavior
Fischer, P., Jonas, E., Frey, D., and Schulz-Hardt, S. (2005). 'Selective Exposure to Information: The Impact of Information Limits,' *European Journal of Social Psychology*, 35(4), 469–492.

BIBLIOGRAPHY
Zillmann, Dolf, and Jennings, Bryant (1985). *Selective Exposure to Communication*. Hillsdale, NJ: L. Erlbaum Associates.

☐ **selective marketing** *see* differentiated marketing
☐ **self-actualization, Maslow's theory of** *see* hierarchy of needs theory

■ self-fulfilling prophecy

DESCRIPTION
A prediction that becomes true as a result of the prediction having been made.

KEY INSIGHTS
Self-fulfilling prophecies involve predictions that in and of themselves are not necessarily true but become true as a result of the prediction evoking behaviors that lead to the prediction becoming true. For example, an industry expert predicting a shortage of a popular new children's toy just before Christmas may result in such a shortage if it encourages parents to rush out and buy the product in anticipation of a possible shortage.

KEY WORDS Prediction, forecast, self-fulfillment

IMPLICATIONS
Marketers involved in forecasting, planning, and marketing strategy development should be cognizant of potential self-fulfilling prophecies as a result of actions evoked from predictions. To the extent that such actions are unintended, anticipating possible self-fulfilling prophecies may result in more effective planning efforts.

APPLICATION AREAS AND FURTHER READINGS

Marketing Strategy
Hoch, Stephen J., and Deighton, John (1989). 'Managing What Consumers Learn from Experience,' *Journal of Marketing*, 53(2), April, 1–20.
Spangenberg, E. R. (1997). 'Increasing Health Club Attendance through Self-Prophecy,' *Marketing Letters*, 8(1), 23–32.

Consumer Behavior
Spangenberg, E. R., and Greenwald, A. G. (1999). 'Social Influence by Requesting Self-Prophecy,' *Journal of Consumer Psychology*, 8(1), 61–90.

BIBLIOGRAPHY
Merton, R. K. (1948). 'The Self-Fulfilling Prophecy,' *Antioch Review*, 8, 193–210.
Darley, J. M., and Fazio, R. H. (1980). 'Expectancy Confirmation Processes Arising in the Social Interaction Sequence,' *American Psychologist*, 35, 867–881.

■ self-perception theory

DESCRIPTION
A theory that views an individual's attitudes and opinions as being inferred partly as a result of the individual's observations of their own behaviors and the circumstances surrounding the behaviors.

KEY INSIGHTS
Based on pioneering research by Bem (1965, 1967), self-perception theory considers an individual's attitude development to be a result of self-observed behaviors, where such observations are used by the individual to draw conclusions about what attitudes must have caused them. An example is where a consumer is asked if she likes cappuccino and she responds, 'I must like it; I'm always drinking it.' Self-perception theory further asserts that the use of behavioral observation for interpreting internal states has inherent strengths over introspection for the same purpose in that internal cues are often weak or ambiguous.

KEY WORDS Behavior, self-observation, attitude formation

IMPLICATIONS
Self-perception theory provides an explanatory perspective that may be beneficial in understanding better consumer attitudes and opinions as well as consumer changes in attitudes and opinions. Specifically, since the theory asserts that attitudes and opinions are inferred by consumers from their own behaviors, marketing research on a particular topic that draws a consumer's attention to his or her current or past behaviors

may assist the consumer in expressing his or her attitudes and opinions toward the topic.

APPLICATION AREAS AND FURTHER READINGS

Marketing Research
Hansen, Robert A. (1980). 'A Self-Perception Interpretation of the Effect of Monetary and Nonmonetary Incentives on Mail Survey Respondent Behavior,' *Journal of Marketing Research*, 17(1), February, 77–83.

Marketing Strategy
Allen, Chris T. (1982). 'Self-Perception Based Strategies for Stimulating Energy Conservation,' *Journal of Consumer Research*, 8(4), March, 381–390.

BIBLIOGRAPHY
Bem, D. J. (1965). 'An Experimental Analysis of Self-Persuasion,' *Journal of Experimental Social Psychology*, 1, 199–218.
Bem, D. J. (1967). 'Self-Perception: An Alternative Interpretation of Cognitive Dissonance Phenomena,' *Psychological Review*, 74, 183–200.
Bem, D. J. (1972). 'Self-Perception Theory,' in L. Berkowitz (ed.), *Advances in Experimental Social Psychology*, 6. New York: Academic Press, 1–62.

☐ **selling concept** *see* marketing management orientation

■ **selling process**

DESCRIPTION
A series of steps undertaken by a salesperson to sell a firm's product or service to a potential customer.

KEY INSIGHTS
The selling process as implemented by a salesperson is composed of multiple steps. Common characterizations of the steps in a selling process include: *prospecting*—the step of identifying qualified potential customers; *preapproach*—the step of preparing for a sales call by researching the potential customer's need and background; *approach*—the step of meeting with a potential customer at a particular time and place; *presentation*—the step of making a sales pitch to a potential customer, where the benefits of the offering to the potential customer are raised; *handling objections*—the step of identifying, clarifying, and overcoming a potential customer's objections or obstacles to the purchase of the offering; *closing*—the step of asking for a potential customer's order for the offering and getting him or her to say 'yes'; and *follow-up*—after the sale of the firm's offering to a customer, the step of checking with the customer about the customer's satisfaction with the offering as a means to building a long-term relationship with the customer and encouraging repeat business. The selling process is not always a straightforward and linear process, however, as the implementation involves iterating back and forth between the different steps.

KEY WORDS Sales, sales force

IMPLICATIONS

The success of a firm's personal selling efforts often relies on effective salespeople. As such, the development and training of salespeople can be a vital part of the firm's marketing planning. Issues that should be given consideration by marketers involved in the selling process include salespersons' knowledge of the product or service they are selling, understanding the firm's potential customers prior to approaching them, and identifying various strategies to change potential customers' attitudes favorably towards the product or service. Managing salespeople also requires their motivation, which has clear implications for sales managers in terms of selecting, training, and compensating sales personnel.

APPLICATION AREAS AND FURTHER READINGS

Marketing Strategy
Crosby, Lawrence A., and Stephens, Nancy (1987). 'Effects of Relationship Marketing on Satisfaction, Retention, and Prices in the Life Insurance Industry,' *Journal of Marketing Research*, 24(4), November, 404–411.

Marketing Management
Piercy, N. F., Cravens, D. W., and Morgan, N. A. (1999). 'Relationships between Sales Management Control, Territory Design, Salesforce Performance and Sales Organization Effectiveness,' *British Journal of Management*, 10(2), 95–112.
Weitz, Barton A., Sujan, Harish, and Sujan, Mita (1986). 'Knowledge, Motivation, and Adaptive Behavior: A Framework for Improving Selling Effectiveness,' *Journal of Marketing*, 50(4), October, 174–191.
Netemeyer, Richard G., Boles, James S., McKee, Daryl O., and McMurrian, Robert (1997). 'An Investigation into the Antecedents of Organizational Citizenship Behaviors in a Personal Selling Context,' *Journal of Marketing*, 61(3), 85–98.

Business-to-Business Marketing
Wotruba, T. R. (1996). 'The Transformation of Industrial Selling: Causes and Consequences,' *Industrial Marketing Management*, 25(5), 327–338.
Leigh, Thomas W., and Rethans, Arno J. (1984). 'A Script-Theoretic Analysis of Industrial Purchasing Behavior,' *Journal of Marketing*, 48(4), Autumn, 22–32.

Marketing Research
Spiro, Rosann L., and Weitz, Barton A. (1990). 'Adaptive Selling: Conceptualization, Measurement, and Nomological Validity,' *Journal of Marketing Research*, 27(1), February, 61–69.

International Marketing
Hart, Susan J., Webb, John R., and Jones, Marian V. (1994). 'Export Marketing Research and the Effect of Export Experience in Industrial SMEs,' *International Marketing Review*, 11(6), December, 4–22.

BIBLIOGRAPHY
Weitz B. A., and Bradford, K. D. (1999). 'Personal Selling and Sales Management: A Relationship Marketing Perspective,' *Journal of the Academy of Marketing Science*, 27(2), 241–254.
Kotler, Philip, and Armstrong, Gary (2006). *Principles of Marketing*, 11th edn. Upper Saddle River, NJ: Pearson Education, Inc.

☐ **sense-of-mission marketing** *see* enlightened marketing
☐ **sequence bias** *see* bias

■ serial position effect

(also called edge effect or end effect)

DESCRIPTION

A tendency in serial learning for individuals to recall better items at the beginning and end of the series than items in the middle of the series.

KEY INSIGHTS

The serial position effect is characterized by a U-shaped curve in a plot of item recall versus serial position, where item recall is highest for beginning and end items and lowest for middle items. In essence, the effect can be considered to be a combination of the primacy effect and recency effect (see **primacy effect**; **recency effect**) and potentially the von Restorff effect (see **von Restorff effect**). A possible explanation for the effect is that items at the beginning of a series are more easily taken into long-term memory relative to other items and items at the end of the series are more easily kept in short-term memory relative to other items, and items in the middle of the series, as a result of their intermediate serial position, are not kept or taken into either short- or long-term memory as effectively.

KEY WORDS Recall, serial position

IMPLICATIONS

Marketers concerned with maximizing the likelihood that information will be remembered by consumers exposed to serial information, as when a series of commercials are presented to consumers, can benefit from awareness of the serial position effect phenomenon by placing information to be remembered either at the beginning or end of a series and avoiding the middle of a series.

APPLICATION AREAS AND FURTHER READINGS

Advertising
Terry, W. S. (2005). 'Serial Position Effects in Recall of Television Commercials,' *Journal of General Psychology*, 132(2), 151–163.
Zhao, X. (1997). 'Clutter and Serial Order Redefined and Retested,' *Journal of Advertising Research*, 37(5), 57–74.

Online Marketing
Murphy, J., Hofacker, C., and Mizerski, R. (2006). 'Primacy and Recency Effects on Clicking Behavior,' *Journal of Computer-Mediated Communication*, 11(2), article 7. http://jcmc.indiana.edu/vol11/issue2/murphy.html. Accessed: 1 March 2007.

BIBLIOGRAPHY

Frensch, P. A. (1994). 'Composition during Serial Learning: A Serial Position Effect,' *Journal of Experimental Psychology: Learning, Memory, and Cognition*, 20(2), 423–443.
Murdock, B. B., Jr. (1962). 'The Serial Position Effect in Free Recall,' *Journal of Experimental Psychology*, 64, 482–488.
Glanzer, M., and Cunitz, A. R. (1966). 'Two Storage Mechanisms in Free Recall,' *Journal of Verbal Learning and Verbal Behaviour*, 5, 351–360.

■ service, laws of

DESCRIPTION
A set of three assertions relating to services marketing comprising (1) satisfaction equals perception minus expectation, (2) first impressions are the most important, and (3) a service-oriented attitude alone will not achieve good service.

KEY INSIGHTS
Developed and asserted by Davidoff (1994), the three laws of service are intended to summarize key marketing considerations in the provision of services. The three laws are considered to be most applicable in the context of hospitality and tourism in particular.

KEY WORDS Service offerings

IMPLICATIONS
According to Davidoff (1994), implications of the three laws of service are that, in a firm's provision of service, basic customer expectations will include service accessibility, courtesy, personal attention, empathy, job knowledge, consistency, and teamwork. In addition, marketers should recognize that first impressions in service can make lasting impressions and that service staff attitudes must be backed up with knowledge and training.

APPLICATION AREAS AND FURTHER READINGS
Services Marketing
Lepiller, Marlyse (2003). 'Language Skills of Tourist Professionals in Normandy.' Dissertation, MA in European Tourism Management, Bournemouth University.
O'Neill, M. A., Williams, P., MacCarthy, M., and Groves, R. (2000). 'Diving into Service Quality: The Dive Tour Operator Perspective,' *Managing Service Quality*, 10(3), 131–140.

BIBLIOGRAPHY
Davidoff, D. M. (1994). *Contact: Customer Service in the Hospitality and Tourism Industry.* Englewood Cliffs, NJ: Prentice Hall.

■ service characteristics

DESCRIPTION
Factors associated with service offerings which are influential to their effective marketing.

KEY INSIGHTS
Service offerings can be characterized in any number of ways, yet it is also recognized that there are several characteristics that make services relatively unique in comparison to non-service offerings. Specifically, services can be said to involve: *inseparability*—where services are usually produced and consumed at the same time and place (e.g. in the presence of the customer); *intangibility*—where services do not have physical substance in that they cannot be touched; *perishability*—where unused service capacity cannot be stored for future use or sale; and *variability*—where the quality of a service can vary by many factors, including who provides it, where it is provided, when it is provided, and how it is provided. This latter

factor arises because service businesses rely on people for delivering services.

KEY WORDS Service factors

IMPLICATIONS
The characteristics of services should be carefully understood in developing competitive service strategies and marketing plans. Customer service and continuous assessment of customer satisfaction are important aspects in the provision of services. Unlike products, services do not have tangible qualities that enable physical observation and evaluation by prospective customers, so service firms have to provide marketing communications about the firm's services through an array of sources. Researching demand and supply and timing of shifting service demand levels is important to develop pricing and promotional strategies to stimulate demand. To deal with variability of services, firms need to establish standard procedures and implement training practices among personnel in order to ensure consistent service delivery.

APPLICATION AREAS AND FURTHER READINGS
Marketing Strategy
Lovelock, Christopher H. (1983). 'Classifying Services to Gain Strategic Marketing Insights,' *Journal of Marketing*, (47)3, Summer, 9–20.
Lievens, A., and Moenaert, R. K. (2000). 'Communication Flows during Financial Service Innovation,' *European Journal of Marketing*, 34(9–10), October, 1078–1110.

Marketing Management
Webster, Cynthia (1995). 'Marketing Culture and Marketing Effectiveness in Service Firms,' *Journal of Services Marketing*, 9(2), May, 6–21.

Services Marketing
Blankson, Charles, and Kalafatis, Stavros P. (1999). 'Issues and Challenges in the Positioning of Service Brands: A Review,' *Journal of Product & Brand Management*, 8(2), April, 106–118.
Pires, Guilherme, and Stanton, John (2000). 'Marketing Services to Ethnic Consumers in Culturally Diverse Markets: Issues and Implications,' *Journal of Services Marketing*, 14(7), December, 607–618.

BIBLIOGRAPHY
de Chernatony, Leslie, and Segal-Horn, Susan (2001). 'Building on Services' Characteristics to Develop Successful Services Brands,' *Journal of Marketing Management*, 17, 645–669.
Clemes, Michael, Mollenkopf, Diane, and Burn, Darryl (2000). 'An Investigation of Marketing Problems across Service Typologies,' *Journal of Services Marketing*, 14(7), 573–594.

■ services marketing

DESCRIPTION
Marketing involving the provision of intangible offerings to consumers.

KEY INSIGHTS
A services marketing approach relies on the notion that differences among services are as important as differences between products and services. Marketing a service-base business differs from marketing a product-base service in that what the customer buys is intangible and

cannot be returned, it is harder to compare the quality of similar services, production and consumption are inseparable, and the consumer purchase is perishable. In addition, that which is offered by a firm may also be characterized by more variability. As such, the marketing of services often involves finding means to make a service more tangible and providing evidence and indicators of service quality to consumers.

KEY WORDS Intangible offerings

IMPLICATIONS

In comparison to product marketing (see **product marketing**), services marketing typically requires far more marketing attention to the marketing mix elements of people, process, and physical evidence (see **marketing mix**). As such, the personnel providing the services, the physical environment in which a service is offered, and the service process itself must all be strategically as well as tactically managed by the service marketer.

APPLICATION AREAS AND FURTHER READINGS

Marketing Strategy
Zeithaml, Valarie A., Parasuraman, A., and Berry, Leonard L. (1985). 'Problems and Strategies in Services Marketing,' *Journal of Marketing*, 49(2), Spring, 33–46.
Bharadwaj, Sundar G. P., Varadarajan, Rajan, and Fahy, John (1993). 'Sustainable Competitive Advantage in Service Industries: A Conceptual Model and Research Propositions,' *Journal of Marketing*, 57(4), October, 83–99.
Berry, Leonard L. (1995). 'Relationship Marketing of Services: Growing Interest, Emerging Perspectives,' *Journal of the Academy of Marketing Science*, 23(4), 236–245.

Marketing Management
Lovelock, Christopher H. (1992). *Managing Services: Marketing, Operations, and Human Resources.* Englewood Cliffs, NJ: Prentice Hall.

Online Marketing
Peterson, Robert A., Balasubramanian, Sridhar, and Bronnenberg, Bart J. (1997). 'Exploring the Implications of the Internet for Consumer Marketing,' *Journal of the Academy of Marketing Science*, 25(4), 329–346.

Consumer Behavior
Murray, Keith B. (1991). 'A Test of Services Marketing Theory: Consumer Information Acquisition Activities,' *Journal of Marketing*, 55(1), January, 10–25.

BIBLIOGRAPHY
Zeithaml, Valarie A., and Bitner, Mary Jo (1996). *Services Marketing.* New York: McGraw Hill.
Berry, L. L. (1980). 'Services Marketing is Different,' *Business Week*, 30, May–June, 24–29.

■ set theory

DESCRIPTION
Mathematical theory or theories for characterizing and examining sets or collections of abstract objects.

KEY INSIGHTS
In broad terms, set theory constitutes a major branch of mathematics involving the study of sets or collections of abstract objects. Key concepts

of set theory include sets (collections of objects) and membership (elements contained within a set), with the theory providing a rich language for analyzing and evaluating both. While there are numerous mathematical approaches within the domain of set theory—so many that their descriptions and insights are best covered in textbooks—it should be noted that there are also alternatives to standard set theory approaches, such as fuzzy set theory. (See **fuzzy set theory.**)

KEY WORDS Sets, objects

IMPLICATIONS
Set theory provides a means to mathematically describe and characterize sets in marketing models in numerous areas of marketing. Complex marketing research studies in particular may draw upon set theory in order to facilitate effective examinations of data associated with specific marketing phenomena.

APPLICATION AREAS AND FURTHER READINGS
Marketing Research
Brown, Robert G. (1973). 'A Model for Measuring the Influence of Promotion on Inventory and Consumer Demand,' *Journal of Marketing Research*, 10(4), November, 380–389.

Dupin, D. (2000). 'Direct Response Multi-list Market Testing,' *Interactive Marketing*, 2(2), 120–128.

Salzberger, Thomas, and Sinkovics, Rudolf R. (2006). 'Reconsidering the Problem of Data Equivalence in International Marketing Research: Contrasting Approaches Based on CFA and the Rasch Model for Measurement,' *International Marketing Review*, 23(4), 390–417.

BIBLIOGRAPHY
Hrbacek, K., and Jech, T. J. (1999). *Introduction to Set Theory*. New York: Marcel Dekker, Inc.

☐ **seven Ps** *see* marketing mix

■ **share of voice**

DESCRIPTION
The percentage of a brand's advertising relative to the overall advertising weight of the associated product category in a market over a given period.

KEY INSIGHTS
Also known as SOV, share of voice reflects the advertising expenditure of a firm's brand expressed as a weight in the total competitive spending in the market for the category. It is usually calculated as a ratio of the brand's annual advertising expenditures to those of the entire industry (including all other brands).

KEY WORD Advertising

IMPLICATIONS
SOV can be a potentially important indicator to a firm as it may be influential to market share, in addition to brand differentiation (Jones

1990). As it results from advertising expenditures, it may also influence the relative price of the product or service.

APPLICATION AREAS AND FURTHER READINGS

Marketing Strategy

Chaudhuri, Arjun, and Holbrook, Morris B. (2001). 'The Chain of Effects from Brand Trust and Brand Affect to Brand Performance: The Role of Brand Loyalty,' *Journal of Marketing*, 65(2), April, 81-93.

Kent, Robert J., and Allen, Chris T. (1994). 'Competitive Interference Effects in Consumer Memory for Advertising: The Role of Brand Familiarity,' *Journal of Marketing*, 58(3), July, 97-105.

Marketing Management

Pedrick, James H., and Zufryden, Fred S. (1991). 'Evaluating the Impact of Advertising Media Plans: A Model of Consumer Purchase Dynamics Using Single-Source Data,' *Marketing Science*, 10(2), Spring, 111-130.

Marketing Research

Nevett, Terence (1991). 'Historical Investigation and the Practice of Marketing,' *Journal of Marketing*, 55(3), July, 13-23.

Advertising

Pollay, Richard W., Siddarth, S., Siegel, Michael, Haddix, Anne, Merritt, Robert K., Giovino, Gary A., and Eriksen, Michael P. (1990). 'The Last Straw? Cigarette Advertising and Realized Market Shares among Youths and Adults, 1979-1993,' *Journal of Marketing*, 60(2), April, 1-16.

BIBLIOGRAPHY

Jones, John P. (1990), 'Ad Spending: Maintaining Market Share,' *Harvard Business Review*, 68, January-February, 38-48.

■ shared-cost effect

DESCRIPTION

In market situations where the customer is not the payer but rather some other party is the payer, the resultant effect where price sensitivity is reduced.

KEY INSIGHTS

The observation of the shared-cost effect in a range of market conditions suggests that, in determining price sensitivity, it is important to know who the payer of a product or service is. When the individual choosing a product or service is not the payer, price sensitivity is lower than when the individual is both the chooser and the payer. In instances where the individual is not the payer, the payer may be another individual, or it may be an organization that may or may not be employing the individual.

KEY WORDS Price sensitivity

IMPLICATIONS

Marketers seeking to understand price sensitivity among consumers or buyers should clearly understand whether or not such individuals are also the actual payers. Such knowledge can be vital for the development and implementation of optimal pricing strategies and tactics.

APPLICATION AREAS AND FURTHER READINGS
Marketing Research
Gonul, F. F., Carter, F., Petrova, E., and Srinivasan, K. (2001). 'Promotion of Prescription Drugs and its Impact on Physicians' Choice Behavior,' *Journal of Marketing*, 65(3), 79–90.
Kashyap, Rajiv, and Bojanic, David C. (2000). 'A Structural Analysis of Value, Quality, and Price Perceptions of Business and Leisure Travelers,' *Journal of Travel Research*, 39(1), 45–51.

BIBLIOGRAPHY
Nagle, T. T., and Holden, R. K. (1995). *The Strategy and Tactics of Pricing: A Guide to Profitable Decision Making*, 2nd edn. Englewood Cliffs, NJ: Prentice Hall.

■ shareholder value analysis

DESCRIPTION
An analysis method used in marketing-related value-based management to assess the firm's value to investors, taking into account the sources of value creation and the time horizon over which the firm enjoys competitive advantages over its rivals.

KEY INSIGHTS
Also known as SVA, shareholder value analysis values the company and its strategies based on cash generated and not on accounting conventions. Marketing managers can use it to identify the value of their strategies relative to future cash flow as this reflects the value to investors.

KEY WORDS Shareholders, analysis, **value**

IMPLICATIONS
Shareholder value analysis can be a potentially valuable method in developing and justifying marketing strategies. It can provide a highly effective way of demonstrating the contribution of marketing to the firm's overall financial performance. SVA shows that value creation relies heavily on how effective the firm is in developing its marketing assets (Doyle 2000). This is because marketing assets drive the four determinants of shareholders' value, which are future cash flow, its timing, the risk attached to the business, and its continuing value.

APPLICATION AREAS AND FURTHER READINGS
Marketing Strategy
Srivastava, Rajendra K., Shervani, Tasadduq A., and Fahey, Liam (1998). 'Market-Based Assets and Shareholder Value: A Framework for Analysis,' *Journal of Marketing*, 62(1), January, 2–18.
Srivastava, Rajendra K., Shervani, Tasadduq A., and Fahey, Liam (1990). 'Marketing, Business Processes, and Shareholder Value: An Organizationally Embedded View of Marketing Activities and the Discipline of Marketing,' *Journal of Marketing*, 63, Fundamental Issues and Directions for Marketing, 168–179.
Doyle, Peter, and Wong, Veronica (1998). 'Marketing and Competitive Performance: An Empirical Study,' *European Journal of Marketing*, 32(5/6), June, 514–535.

Marketing Management
Duncan, Tom, and Moriarty, Sandra E. (1998). 'A Communication-Based Marketing Model for Managing Relationships,' *Journal of Marketing*, 62(2), April, 1–13.

Marketing Research
Agrawal, Jagdish, and Kamakura, Wagner A. (1995). 'The Economic Worth of Celebrity Endorsers: An Event Study Analysis,' *Journal of Marketing*, 59(3), July, 56–62.

BIBLIOGRAPHY
Doyle, Peter (2000). 'Value-Based Marketing,' *Journal of Strategic Marketing*, 8(4), 299–310.

☐ shopping cart abandonment *see* retail marketing

☐ shopping product *see* product classifications, consumer

☐ short message service marketing/short messaging service marketing *see* mobile marketing

☐ skimming *see* pricing strategies

■ skunkworks

DESCRIPTION
An approach to product development and innovation that utilizes firm resources, design activities, and team relationships in a more timely and effective manner by breaking away from organizational bureaucracy and standard frameworks.

KEY INSIGHTS
Skunkworks involve organizing a subset of the firm's product development initiatives in a way that insulates the product developers engaged in such initiatives from many of the mainstream demands and constraints imposed on the rest of the organization. Skunkworks are often associated with relatively secretive new product development projects and are viewed as a way of fostering successful innovations (Quinn 1996).

KEY WORDS **New product development**, innovation, bureaucracy

IMPLICATIONS
Marketers involved in new product development may potentially benefit from initiating a skunkworks structure within their organization as it is an approach to structuring new product development that provides a means to eliminate bureaucracy, permit creative communication, create high motivation, emphasize group identity, and enable a loose operating structure (Tushman and O'Reilly 1999). It involves breaking the rules, where the structure, planning of resources and budgets, and decisions lie within the product development team.

APPLICATION AREAS AND FURTHER READINGS

Marketing Strategy
Bower, J., and Christensen, C. (1995). 'Disruptive Technologies: Catching the Wave,' *Harvard Business Review*, 73(1), 43–53.

Marketing Management
Gordon, Geoffrey L., Ayers, Douglas J., Hanna, Nessim, and Ridnour, Rick E. (1995). 'The Product Development Process: Three Misconceptions Which Can Derail

Even the "Best-Laid" Plans,' *Journal of Product & Brand Management*, 4(1), March, 7–17.
Rosenau, Milton D. Jr. (1988). 'Faster New Product Development,' *Journal of Product Innovation Management*, 5(2), 150–153.
Cordero, Rene (1991). 'Managing for Speed to Avoid Product Obsolescence: A Survey of Techniques,' *Journal of Product Innovation Management*, 8(4), 283–294.

BIBLIOGRAPHY
Quinn, J. B. (1996). 'Team Innovation,' *Executive Excellence*, 13(7), 13–17.
Tushman, M. L., and O'Reilly, C. A., III (1999). 'Building Ambidextrous Organizations: Forming your Own "Skunk Works," ' *Health Forum Journal*, 42(2), March–April, 20–23.

■ sleeper effect

DESCRIPTION
An effect where the persuasiveness of a message increases with time.

KEY INSIGHTS
While there may be many explanations for the occurrence of a sleeper effect in persuasive communication, some predictions of the occurrence of a sleeper effect in persuasion are based on the view that low source credibility or some other discounting factor inhibits the immediate persuasiveness of an otherwise compelling message but, with the passage of time, the source becomes dissociated from the message, thereby leading to increased message influence. Research on the effect has been somewhat mixed in both findings and interpretation, however, resulting in a degree of controversy over its existence and the conditions under which it may occur, if at all.

KEY WORDS Persuasion, communication, time

IMPLICATIONS
While research on the sleeper effect may be controversial and somewhat inconclusive, the concept of the sleeper effect and the possible mechanisms in support of it nevertheless provide marketers involved in researching persuasive communication methods with additional perspectives that may potentially assist in understanding and explaining the many factors that influence their effectiveness.

APPLICATION AREAS AND FURTHER READINGS
Consumer Behavior
Mazursky, David, and Schul, Yaacov (1988). 'The Effects of Advertisement Encoding on the Failure to Discount Information: Implications for the Sleeper Effect,' *Journal of Consumer Research*, 15(1), June, 24–36.
Hannah, Darlene B., and Sternthal, Brian (1984). 'Detecting and Explaining the Sleeper Effect,' *Journal of Consumer Research*, 11(2), September, 632–642.

BIBLIOGRAPHY
Kumkale, G. T., and Albarracin, D. (2004). 'The Sleeper Effect in Persuasion: A Meta-analytic Review,' *Psychological Bulletin*, 130(1), 143–172.
Hovland, C. I., Lumsdaine, A., and Sheffield, F. (1949). *Experiments on Mass Communication*. Princeton: Princeton University Press.

■ small group theory

DESCRIPTION

Theory or theories aimed at understanding, explaining, and/or predicting small group behavior.

KEY INSIGHTS

Small group theory is concerned with the study of small groups of psychologically interrelated individuals. Such groups are considered to consist of interdependent relationships among individuals in terms of beliefs, attitudes, and behaviors. The many conceptualizations and hypotheses comprising the theory provide a basis for small group evaluations.

KEY WORDS Small groups, behavior

IMPLICATIONS

Marketers seeking to understand better the small group behavior of consumers may potentially obtain insights into such behaviors through greater knowledge of small group theory. Whether in exploratory marketing research or the development of marketing models aimed at explaining and predicting small group consumer behavior, the concepts contained within small group theory can assist the marketing researcher in systematically examining a range of small group phenomena associated with the evaluation, purchase, and repeat purchase of a marketer's offerings.

APPLICATION AREAS AND FURTHER READINGS

Consumer Behavior

Rudd, Joel, and Kohout, Frank J. (1983). 'Individual and Group Consumer Information Acquisition in Brand Choice Situations,' *Journal of Consumer Research*, 10(3), December, 303–309.

Marketing Modeling

Lilien, Gary L., Rao, Ambar G., and Kalish, Shlomo (1981). 'Bayesian Estimation and Control of Detailing Effort in a Repeat Purchase Diffusion Environment,' *Management Science*, 27(5), May, 493–506.

BIBLIOGRAPHY

Davis, Harry L., and Silk, Alvin J. (1971). *Small Group Theory and Marketing Research*. Cambridge, Mass.: MIT Press.

□ SMS marketing *see* mobile marketing

■ snob effect

DESCRIPTION

Buying behavior characterized by the desire to own goods which are uncommon, where consumers' preference for buying such goods increases as their exclusivity increases and for which consumers' preference for buying them decreases as their exclusivity diminishes.

KEY INSIGHTS

The snob effect is a phenomenon observable with certain products and services among certain groups of consumers. For example, when a new night club strictly limits who can get in, its exclusivity will have a strong appeal to certain individuals, but if the same night club were to suddenly throw its doors open to the general public, the night club would be completely unappealing to the same individuals.

KEY WORDS Exclusive offerings, prestige, luxury goods

IMPLICATIONS

Marketers should seek to understand carefully consumer buying behavior for their offerings, which may include the snob effect phenomenon. For some offerings, the prevalence of the snob effect may mean that limiting an offering's availability may increase its desirability among certain consumers and vice versa.

APPLICATION AREAS AND FURTHER READINGS

Marketing Strategy
Mason, R.(1998). *The Economics of Conspicuous Consumption.* Northampton, Mass.: Edward Elgar.

Consumer Behavior
Vigneron, F., and Johnson, L. W. (1999). 'A Review and a Conceptual Framework of Prestige-Seeking Consumer Behavior,' *Academy of Marketing Science Review*, 1999(1), 1–15.
Mason, R. (1981). *Conspicuous Consumption: A Study of Exceptional Consumer Behavior.* Farnborough: Gower.

BIBLIOGRAPHY
Leibenstein, Harvey (1950). 'Bandwagon, Snob, and Veblen Effects in the Theory of Conspicuous Demand,' *Quarterly Journal of Economics*, 64, 183–207.

■ snowball effect

DESCRIPTION
Any accumulating effect originating from an action of smaller relative significance.

KEY INSIGHTS
While the snowball effect term is figurative and based on the analogy of a rolling snowball picking up more snow and thereby increasing in size, mass, and momentum, the term nevertheless captures the notion that some processes starting from small states of significance can build upon themselves to ultimately produce highly significant outcomes, where such outcomes may be either beneficial or detrimental.

KEY WORDS Effect, significance

IMPLICATIONS
Marketers considering particular marketing strategies to achieve a set of objectives, such as awareness of a new product in the market, should consider to what extent particular strategies exhibit properties characteristic of snowball effects. Word-of-mouth communication, for example,

has significant potential to build upon itself in establishing further word-of-mouth communication.

APPLICATION AREAS AND FURTHER READINGS

Marketing Strategy

Helm, S. (2000). 'Viral Marketing: Establishing Customer Relationships by "Word-of-mouse,"' *Electronic Markets*, 10(3), 158–161.

Hellofs, L. L., and Jacobson, R. (1999). 'Market Share and Customers' Perceptions of Quality: When Can Firms Grow their Way to Higher Versus Lower Quality,' *Journal of Marketing*, 63(1), 16–25.

BIBLIOGRAPHY

Krishna, K. (1999). 'Auctions with Endogenous Valuations: The Snowball Effect Revisited,' *Economic Theory*, 13(2), 377–392.

■ snowballing

DESCRIPTION

A technique for sample identification in research which involves identifying subjects through a referral system whereby existing subjects suggest others for interviewing or responding to surveys.

KEY INSIGHTS

The snowballing technique is one way of conducting convenience sampling, where the sample selected is not random. After administering the research on a set of subjects, the subjects are then asked to refer others who would be willing and interested to also take part in the research.

KEY WORDS Research sampling, referrals

IMPLICATIONS

Snowballing has the advantage of convenience and low cost as a sampling technique. However, the risk that the selected convenience sample is not representative of the population of concern is high. Researchers using this technique have to be careful about the limitations it poses on their findings.

APPLICATION AREAS AND FURTHER READINGS

Marketing Strategy

Menon, Ajay, and Menon, Anil (1997). 'Enviropreneurial Marketing Strategy: The Emergence of Corporate Environmentalism as Market Strategy,' *Journal of Marketing*, 61(1), January, 51–67.

Marketing Management

Phillips, Lynn W. (1982). 'Explaining Control Losses in Corporate Marketing Channels: An Organizational Analysis,' *Journal of Marketing Research*, 19(4), Special Issue on Causal Modeling, November, 525–549.

Online Marketing

Bradley, N. (1999). 'Sampling for Internet Surveys: An Examination of Respondent Selection for Internet Research,' *Journal of the Market Research Society*, 41(4), 387–395.

Marketing Research

Helsen, Kristiaan, and Schmittlein, David C. (1993). 'Analyzing Duration Times in Marketing: Evidence for the Effectiveness of Hazard Rate Models,' *Marketing Science*, 12(4), Autumn, 395–414.

Gummesson, Evert (2001). 'Are Current Research Approaches in Marketing Leading Us Astray?' *Marketing Theory*, 1(1), 27–48.

BIBLIOGRAPHY
Moriarty, Rowland T., and Bateson, John E. G. (1982). 'Exploring Complex Decision Making Units: A New Approach,' *Journal of Marketing Research*, 19(2), May, 182–191.

☐ social cause marketing *see* cause-related marketing; social marketing

■ social cognitive theory

DESCRIPTION
A psychological theory of social learning that views individual behavior in terms of dynamic and reciprocal interactions between environment, behavior, and personal factors including cognitive, affective, and biological events.

KEY INSIGHTS
Social cognitive theory, developed by Bandura (1986), views individual behavior as something that is learned, regulated, and changing with time. In addition, vicarious learning is considered to be a key means of learning a behavior. In the theory, behaviors are understood and explained through interactions of person–behavior, person–environment, and behavior–environment. As such, the theory provides a means for understanding and predicting individual as well as group behavior. Its theoretical and conceptual basis further provides a means for identifying methods for changing or modifying behaviors. The theory is considered to be an advancement to social learning theory (see **social learning theory**).

KEY WORDS Behavior, social learning, cognition

IMPLICATIONS
Marketers seeking to understand, explain, predict, or influence consumer behavior to a greater extent may obtain potentially valuable insights as a result of examining behavioral, environmental, and personal interactions from the perspective of social cognitive theory. In particular, the theory has been found to be of significant benefit in health promotion development and in explaining health-related consumer behaviors.

APPLICATION AREAS AND FURTHER READINGS
Marketing Communications
Bandura, A. (2001). 'Social Cognitive Theory of Mass Communication,' *Media Psychology*, 3(3), 265–298.
Bandura, A. (1998). 'Health Promotion from the Perspective of Social Cognitive Theory,' *Psychology and Health*, 13(4), 623–650.

Consumer Behavior
Sheeshka, J. D., Woolcott, D. M., and MacKinnon, N. J. (1993). 'Social Cognitive Theory as a Framework to Explain Intentions to Practice Healthy Eating Behaviors,' *Journal of Applied Social Psychology*, 23(19), 1547–1573.

BIBLIOGRAPHY
Bandura, Albert (1986). *Social Foundations of Thought and Action: A Social Cognitive Theory*. Englewood Cliffs, NJ: Prentice-Hall.

☐ social environment *see* macro environment

■ social exchange theory
(also called exchange theory)

DESCRIPTION
A theory of human relationships and social interaction based on the view that individuals expect equity in the costs and benefits associated with social exchanges.

KEY INSIGHTS
Pioneered by Homans (1950, 1961) and developed further by subsequent researchers, social exchange theory considers the notion of equity to be central in human relationships and social interactions. Equity in costs and benefits leads to stability in such relationships, whereas mismatches lead to instabilities. The theory therefore predicts that an individual would choose to discontinue a social relationship where subjective costs exceed subjective benefits or rewards.

KEY WORDS Social interaction, relationships, equity, **cost(s)**, **benefits**

IMPLICATIONS
As social exchange theory is concerned with explaining and predicting stability in social relationships, marketers seeking to establish and maintain strong relationships should consider carefully the nature and full extent of relationship costs and benefits from the other party's perspective. Whether the relationship is a buyer–seller relationship or a relationship among firms jointly seeking to meet customer needs, satisfaction with the relationship and its stability may ultimately hinge upon the balance of costs and benefits.

APPLICATION AREAS AND FURTHER READINGS
Marketing Strategy
Luo, Xueming (2002). 'Trust Production and Privacy Concerns on the Internet: A Framework Based on Relationship Marketing and Social Exchange Theory,' *Industrial Marketing Management*, 31, 111–118.
Young-Ybarra, Candace, and Wiersema, Margarethe (1999). 'Strategic Flexibility in Information Technology Alliances: The Influence of Transaction Cost Economics and Social Exchange Theory,' *Organization Science*, 10(4), July–August, 439–459.

BIBLIOGRAPHY
Homans, George (1950). *The Human Group*. London: Routledge & Kegan Paul Ltd.
Homans, George (1961). *Social Behavior: Its Elementary Forms*. London: Routledge & Kegan Paul Ltd.

☐ social idea marketing *see* social marketing

■ social identity theory

DESCRIPTION

A psychological theory of social categorization, identification, and comparison based on individual self-concept derived from group membership.

KEY INSIGHTS

Developed by Tajfel (1978) and Tajfel and Turner (1986), social identity theory is concerned with understanding and explaining the cognitive and motivational bases for intergroup differentiation. Originally developed to understand the psychological bases for intergroup discrimination, the theory has since developed to encompass broader issues related to social identity. The major elements of the theory consist of social categorizations or labels, social identification and its relationship to self-esteem, and social comparisons including favorability biases to one's own group. The theory suggests, for example, that social categories provide individuals with a sense of identity, that social identities involve prescriptions of appropriate behaviors, and that group memberships provide bases for behavioral evaluations.

KEY WORDS Social categorizations, social identification, social comparison

IMPLICATIONS

Marketers seeking to understand better how consumers' social identities are related to their identifications with group memberships, categorizations of group memberships, and comparisons of groups may benefit from understanding the principles and concepts of social identity theory. Such understandings may enable marketers to develop offerings of a social nature which resonate more strongly with consumers. Similarly, marketing managers concerned with developing effective organizations may benefit from an understanding of the theory's concepts in terms of the social identities of their employees.

APPLICATION AREAS AND FURTHER READINGS

Marketing Strategy

Ashforth, Blake E., and Mael, Fred (1989). 'Social Identity Theory and the Organization,' *Academy of Management Review*, 14(1), January, 20–39.

Hatch, M. J., and Schultz, M. (1997). 'Relations between Organizational Culture, Identity and Image,' *European Journal of Marketing*, 31(5–6), 356–365.

Madrigal, R. (2001). 'Social Identity Effects in a Belief–Attitude–Intentions Hierarchy: Implications for Corporate Sponsorship,' *Psychology and Marketing*, 18(2), 145–166.

Consumer Behavior

Kleine, Robert E., III, Kleine, Susan Schultz, and Kernan, Jerome B. (1993). 'Mundane Consumption and the Self: A Social-Identity Perspective,' *Journal of Consumer Psychology*, 2(3), 209–235.

BIBLIOGRAPHY

Tajfel, H. (1978). 'Social Categorization, Social Identity, and Social Comparison,' in H. Tajfel (ed.), *Differentiation between Social Groups: Studies in the Social Psychology of Intergroup Relations*. London: Academic Press.

Tajfel, H., and Turner, J. C. (1986). 'The Social Identity Theory of Inter-group Behavior,' in S. Worchel and L. W. Austin (eds.), *Psychology of Intergroup Relations*. Chicago: Nelson-Hall.

■ social learning theory

DESCRIPTION

A psychological theory concerned with the study of individual learning in a social context, where behaviors are learned by individuals through observation, imitation, and/or modeling of others' behaviors.

KEY INSIGHTS

Social learning theory recognizes that individuals can learn from one another and views learning as something that can occur without a change in an individual's behavior. The social learning perspective as developed by Bandura (1977) focuses on how and why individuals can learn from others through means including observation of other people's behaviors, imitation of others' behaviors, and modeling their own behavior after the behavior of others. Concepts within the theory such as attention, retention, and motivation further explain the conditions under which effective social learning occurs.

KEY WORDS Individual learning, social context, observation, imitation, behavioral modeling

IMPLICATIONS

Marketers concerned with understanding and explaining how individuals—whether consumers or employees in one's organization—can learn either desirable or undesirable behaviors in a social context may benefit from a greater knowledge of social learning theory. Such knowledge may ultimately enable marketers to increase both the effectiveness and efficiency associated with individual learning in support of accomplishing organizational and marketing objectives which may include social marketing objectives. To the extent a marketer's actions are aimed at influencing individual learning through social settings, marketers should therefore strive to create and responsibly manage the conditions supporting the learning of desirable behaviors and discouraging undesirable behaviors, such as by making more evident the consequences of both types of behaviors.

APPLICATION AREAS AND FURTHER READINGS

Marketing Strategy
Ginter, Peter M., and White, Donald D. (1982). 'A Social Learning Approach to Strategic Management: Toward a Theoretical Foundation,' *Academy of Management Review*, 7(2), April, 253–261.

Marketing Management
McKee, Daryl O., Conant, Jeffery S., Varadarajan, R. Rajan, and Mokwa, Michael R. (1992). 'Success-Producer and Failure-Preventer Marketing Skills: A Social Learning Theory Interpretation,' *Journal of the Academy of Marketing Science*, 20(1), 17–26.

Social Marketing
Andreasen, A. R. (2002). 'Marketing Social Marketing in the Social Change Marketplace,' *Journal of Public Policy and Marketing*, 21(1), 3–13.

BIBLIOGRAPHY
Bandura, Albert (1977). *Social Learning Theory*. Englewood Cliffs, NJ: Prentice Hall.

Ormrod, J. E. (1999). *Human Learning*, 3rd edn. Upper Saddle River, NJ: Prentice-Hall.

■ social loafing

(also called the Ringelmann effect)

DESCRIPTION
The phenomenon where individuals are observed to exert less effort when working cooperatively within a group than when working individually.

KEY INSIGHTS
Based on pioneering research by Ringelmann (1913) and by subsequent researchers including Latane (Latane, Williams, and Harkins 1979), social loafing is an observable phenomenon under a range of tasks. Experiments examining the phenomenon have found that individuals engaged in group tasks tend to exert less effort (e.g. physically, mentally) on average in contributing to group outcomes than when the same individuals are sole contributors to task outcomes. Social loafing tends to occur under conditions where individuals contribute in a group setting to produce a group product, as opposed to conditions where individuals contribute in a group setting to produce individual products. Social loafing as a phenomenon can be reduced when individual contributions in a group setting are made easily identifiable.

KEY WORDS Cooperative work, cooperative effort, individual behavior

IMPLICATIONS
Marketing managers and educators concerned with the possibility of social loafing in group settings should seek to implement means where individual contributions are more easily identifiable. Explicit discussions of the phenomenon may also contribute to its reduction to the extent it encourages individuals to reflect on its individual and collective implications. Understanding the extent to which the phenomenon varies across cultures may also be of benefit to marketers involved in effective international marketing management.

APPLICATION AREAS AND FURTHER READINGS
Marketing Management
Harkins, Stephen G., and Jackson, Jeffrey M. (1985). 'The Role of Evaluation in Eliminating Social Loafing,' *Personality and Social Psychology Bulletin*, 11(4), 457–465.

Marketing Education
McCorkle, D. E., Reardon, J., Alexander, J. F., Kling, N. D., Harris, R. C., and Vishwanathan Iyer, R. (1999). 'Undergraduate Marketing Students, Group Projects, and Teamwork: The Good, the Bad, and the Ugly?' *Journal of Marketing Education*, 21(2), 106–117.
Pfaff, E., and Huddleston, P. (2003). 'Does It Matter if I Hate Teamwork? What Impacts Student Attitudes toward Teamwork,' *Journal of Marketing Education*, 25(1), 37–45.

International Marketing
Gabrenya, William K., Jr., Latane, Bibb, and Wang, Yue-Eng (1983). 'Social Loafing in Cross-cultural Perspective: Chinese on Taiwan,' *Journal of Cross-cultural Psychology*, 14(3), 368–384.

BIBLIOGRAPHY
Ringelmann, M. (1913). 'Recherches sur les moteurs animés: travail de l'homme,' *Annales de l'Institut National Argonomique*, 2nd ser., 12, 1–40.
Latane, B., Williams, K., and Harkins, S. (1979). 'Many Hands Make Light the Work: The Causes and Consequences of Social Loafing,' *Journal of Personality and Social Psychology*, 37, 822–832.
Karau, S. J., and Williams, K. D. (1993). 'Social Loafing: A Meta-analytic Review and Theoretical Integration,' *Journal of Personality and Social Psychology*, 65, 681–706.

■ social marketing

(also called idea marketing, responsible marketing, social idea marketing, social cause marketing, or socially responsible marketing)

DESCRIPTION
Marketing concerned with influence on the voluntary behavior of individuals and the promotion of personal and societal welfare.

KEY INSIGHTS
Social marketing is characterized by having a customer orientation where the marketing principles are drawn upon to design behavior change interventions. Critical to the success of social marketing efforts is research into the desires and needs of the target market segment. At the same time, social marketing also involves recognizing competitive influences and ensuring continuous monitoring and revision of marketing programs and tactics in order to achieve desired outcomes.

KEY WORDS Voluntary behaviour, societal welfare, personal welfare

IMPLICATIONS
Social marketing places consumers in the centre of the exchange process, where consumers act primarily out of self-interest. In commercial programs, firms design marketing messages to promote a social concern or idea as well as the 'product,' where the focus is on the behavior associated with such a product.

In pursuing a social marketing approach, marketers must therefore take an active interest in people's aspirations and desires in addition to their social and commercial needs.

APPLICATION AREAS AND FURTHER READINGS
Marketing Strategy

Kotler, Philip, and Zaltman, Gerald (1971). 'Social Marketing: An Approach to Planned Social Change,' *Journal of Marketing*, 35(3), July, 3–12.
Robin, Donald P., and Reidenbach, R. Eric (1987). 'Social Responsibility, Ethics, and Marketing Strategy: Closing the Gap between Concept and Application,' *Journal of Marketing*, 51(1), January, 44–58.
Abratt, Russell, and Sacks, Diane (1988). 'The Marketing Challenge: Towards Being Profitable and Socially Responsible,' *Journal of Business Ethics*, 7(7), July, 497–507.

Menon, Ajay, and Menon, Anil (1997). 'Enviropreneurial Marketing Strategy: The Emergence of Corporate Environmentalism as Market Strategy,' *Journal of Marketing*, 61(1), January, 51–67.

Goolsby, Jerry R., and Hunt, Shelby D. (1992). 'Cognitive Moral Development and Marketing,' *Journal of Marketing*, 56(1), January, 55–68.

Marketing Management

Bloom, Paul N., and Novelli, William D. (1981). 'Problems and Challenges in Social Marketing,' *Journal of Marketing*, 45(2), Spring, 79–88.

McKenzie-Mohr, Doug (2000). 'New Ways to Promote Proenvironmental Behavior: Promoting Sustainable Behavior: An Introduction to Community-Based Social Marketing,' *Journal of Social Issues*, 56(3), 543–554.

BIBLIOGRAPHY

Kotler, P., Roberto, N., and Lee, N. (2002). *Social Marketing: Improving the Quality of Life*, 2nd edn. Thousand Oaks, Calif.: Sage.

Kotler, P. (1972). 'What Consumerism Means for Marketers,' *Harvard Business Review*, 50, 48–57.

Bagozzi, Richard P. (1975). 'Marketing as Exchange,' *Journal of Marketing*, 39(4), October, 32–39.

☐ **socially responsible marketing** *see* social marketing

■ **societal classification of products**

DESCRIPTION

The grouping of products according to the extent that they provide consumers with certain short-term and long-term benefits.

KEY INSIGHTS

The societal classification of products is based on two dimensions, one of which addresses immediate satisfaction and the other long-run consumer benefit (Kotler 1972). *Deficient products* offer neither short nor long-term benefits; *desirable products* combine immediate satisfaction with long-run benefit; *salutary products* have low immediate appeal but offer long-term consumer benefits; and *pleasing products* have a high immediate appeal but can cause long-term harm to consumers.

KEY WORDS Short-term benefits, long-term benefits

IMPLICATIONS

The societal marketing concept suggests that firms should identify the current classification of their products and examine how to modify their products, if any, if they are to apply the societal marketing concept to their businesses. For example, in applying the societal marketing concept, deficient products should be deleted from product ranges and salutary and pleasing products should have to undergo modifications to upgrade them to the desirable products level, which should be the ultimate goal of the marketer.

APPLICATION AREAS AND FURTHER READINGS

Marketing Strategy

Crane, Andrew, and Desmond, John (2002). 'Societal Marketing and Morality,' *European Journal of Marketing*, 36(5–6), June, 548–569.

Kotler, Philip (1972). 'A Generic Concept of Marketing,' *Journal of Marketing*, 36(2), April, 46–54.

Marketing Management

Krapfel, Robert E., Jr. (1982). 'Marketing by Mandate,' *Journal of Marketing*, 46(3), Summer, 79–85.

Consumer Behavior

Grubb, Edward L., and Grathwohl, Harrison L. (1967). 'Consumer Self-Concept, Symbolism and Market Behavior: A Theoretical Approach,' *Journal of Marketing*, 31(4), Part 1, October, 22–27.

Marketing Research

Punj, Girish, and Stewart, David W. (1983). 'Cluster Analysis in Marketing Research: Review and Suggestions for Application,' *Journal of Marketing Research*, 20(2), May, 134–148.

BIBLIOGRAPHY

Kotler, P. (1972). 'What Consumerism Means for Marketers,' *Harvard Business Review*, 50, 48–57.

☐ societal marketing *see* enlightened marketing
☐ societal marketing concept *see* marketing management orientation
☐ soft goods *see* goods
☐ spam marketing *see* mass marketing; viral marketing
☐ specialty product *see* product classifications, consumer

■ spillover effect

DESCRIPTION

Any effect of an action that has an effect on a different area than the area where the action, especially when it is performed in excess, is clearly expected, intended, and desired to have a significant effect.

KEY INSIGHTS

Spillover effects, in essence, are those effects that 'spill over' to areas other than the areas where effects are widely anticipated, particularly when such actions are performed in excess. Such effects may be beneficial or detrimental to another area. In marketing, for example, a firm engaged in a strategic alliance with another firm may experience negative spillover effects in the form of increased consumer mistrust from certain negative (e.g. unethical) behaviors of the other firm. Spillover effects may also occur in the area of consumer buying behavior. According to research on spillover effects by Janakiraman, Meyer, and Morales (2006), for example, both unexpected price increases and decreases in quality cause people to buy fewer discretionary items, and to pass up other goods offered at attractive, discounted prices.

KEY WORDS Marketing planning, unexpected consequences

IMPLICATIONS

While the planning of marketing activity necessarily involves developing an understanding and expectation about the intended effects of such activity, it may also be the case that such activity extends to areas beyond that which is given primary consideration. At the same time, certain unplanned actions (e.g. unethical behavior of a strategic alliance partner) may have effects on areas other than those where the effect is clearly expected. While spillover effects may occur in virtually any area of marketing, marketers must strive to consider how and to what extent marketing-related actions, whether planned or unplanned, may positively or negatively influence strategic outcomes desired by the marketer. In some strategic planning efforts, for example, consideration of spillover effects may lead firms to develop contingency plans to address their possible occurrence.

APPLICATION AREAS AND FURTHER READINGS

Marketing Strategy

Balachander, S., and Ghose, S. (2003). 'Reciprocal Spillover Effects: A Strategic Benefit of Brand Extensions,' *Journal of Marketing*, 67, January, 4–12.
Simonin, Bernard, and Ruth, Julie A. (1998). 'Is a Company Known by the Company it Keeps? Assessing the Spillover Effects of Brand Alliances on Consumer Brand Attitudes,' *Journal of Marketing Research*, 35(1), 30–42.
Erdem, T., and Sun, B. (2002). 'An Empirical Investigation of the Spillover Effects of Advertising and Sales Promotions in Umbrella Branding,' *Journal of Marketing Research*, 39, November, 408–420.

Marketing Management

Ahluwalia, R., Unnava, H. R., and Burnkrant, R. E. (2001). 'The Moderating Role of Commitment on the Spillover Effect of Marketing Communications,' *Journal of Marketing Research*, 38, 458–470.
Roehm, Michelle L., and Tybout, Alice M. (2006). 'When Will a Brand Scandal Spill Over, and How Should Competitors Respond?' *Journal of Marketing Research*, 43(3), August, 366–373.

BIBLIOGRAPHY

Votolato, N. L., and Unnava, H. R. (2006). 'Spillover of Negative Information on Brand Alliances,' *Journal of Consumer Psychology*, 16(2), 196–202.
Janakiraman, Narayan, Meyer, Robert J., and Morales, Andrea C. (2006). 'Spillover Effects: How Consumers Respond to Unexpected Changes in Price and Quality,' *Journal of Consumer Research*, 33, 361–369.

■ sponsorship marketing

DESCRIPTION

A marketing approach involving a firm's support of an event, activity, or unrelated organization.

KEY INSIGHTS

Unlike other marketing approaches which involve a clearly explicit message communicated to consumers (e.g. direct marketing—see **direct marketing**), sponsorship marketing is a marketing approach involving communication via indirect argument and emotional appeal. Thus, by sponsoring sports, competitions, performing arts, or charities, for example, consumers associate characteristics of such events, activities, or organizations with those of the sponsoring organization. A benefit of sponsorship marketing to some organizations that use it is that it can be less expensive than advertising. In addition, it may act as a morale booster to the organization's employees.

KEY WORDS Activities, events, unrelated organizations, organizational support

IMPLICATIONS

Sponsorship marketing's effectiveness stems from the recognition and acceptance of an event, activity, or organization by the target market of interest to a firm. To the extent the sponsored event, activity, or organization sponsored has a quality reputation, sponsorship marketing's effectiveness is enhanced.

APPLICATION AREAS AND FURTHER READINGS

Marketing Strategy
Meenaghan, Tony (1991). 'Sponsorship: Legitimising the Medium,' *European Journal of Marketing*, 25(11), 5–10.
Gwinner, Kevin (1997). 'A Model of Image Creation and Image Transfer in Event Sponsorship,' *International Marketing Review*, June, 14(3), 145–158.

Marketing Management
Crimmins, James, and Horn, Martin (1996). 'Sponsorship: From Management Ego Trip to Marketing Success,' *Journal of Advertising Research*, 36(4), 11–21.
Meenaghan, John A. (1983). 'Commercial Sponsorship,' *European Journal of Marketing*, 17(7).

International Marketing
Farrelly, Francis John, Quester, Pascale G., and Burton, Richard (1997). 'Integrating Sports Sponsorship into the Corporate Marketing Function: An International Comparative Study,' *International Marketing Review*, June, 14(3), 170–182.
Cornwell, T. B. (1997). 'The Use of Sponsorship-Linked Marketing Programs by Tobacco Firms: International Public Policy Issues,' *Journal of Consumer Affairs*, 31(2), 238–254.

Marketing Research
Cornwell, T. B., Weeks, C. S., and Roy, D. P. (2005). 'Sponsorship-Linked Marketing: Opening the Black Box,' *Journal of Advertising* (Utah), 34(2), 21–42.

BIBLIOGRAPHY
McDonald, Colin (1991). 'Sponsorship and the Image of the Sponsor,' *European Journal of Marketing*, 25(11), 31–38.

■ sports marketing

(also called sport marketing)

DESCRIPTION

Marketing involving associations with, or promotion of, sports-related events, activities, and organizations.

KEY INSIGHTS
While sports marketing clearly involve the use of any number of marketing approaches for the benefit of a sports organization, activity, event, or cause, and their stakeholders, sports marketing may also involve organizational associations with sports entities and phenomena for the marketing benefit of an organization not directly involved in such activities or initiatives. An organization's association with sports in any form may be through sponsorship, for example (see **sponsorship marketing**), or by affinity, where the firm aims to make use of fans' affinities with particular sports organizations or activities to present such individuals with products or services associated with those areas (see **affinity marketing**).

KEY WORDS Sponsorship, events, activities, sports organizations, athletics

IMPLICATIONS
Given that sports marketing encompasses a broad range of marketing approaches, it can potentially provide the marketer with multiple means of effectively reaching and interacting with the firm's target market in support of the firm's marketing objectives. As the appeal of many sports-related events, activities, and organizations is related to sport's characteristic elements of structured competition, teamwork, physical dexterity, physical exertion, and the pursuit of superior physical performance, the area provides marketers with numerous opportunities to create and attach rich meanings to their product and service offerings.

APPLICATION AREAS AND FURTHER READINGS
Marketing Strategy
Bridgewater, Susan (2007). 'Alternative Paradigms and Sport Marketing,' in John Beech and Simon Chadwick (eds.), *The Marketing of Sport*. Harlow: FT Prentice Hall.
Shank, Matthew D. (1999). *Sports Marketing: A Strategic Perspective*. Upper Saddle River, NJ: Prentice Hall.

Marketing Management
Speed, R., and Thompson, P. (2000). 'Determinants of Sports Sponsorship Response,' *Academy of Marketing Science*, 28(2), 226–238.

Services Marketing
Tomlinson, M., Buttle, F., and Moores, B. (1995). 'The Fan as Customer: Customer Service in Sports Marketing,' *Journal of Hospitality and Leisure Marketing*, 3(1), 19–36.

Marketing Research
Shani, D., Sandler, D. M., and Long, M. M. (1992). 'Courting Women Using Sports Marketing: A Content Analysis of the US Open,' *International Journal of Advertising*, 11(4), 377–392.

BIBLIOGRAPHY
Beech, John, and Chadwick, Simon (eds.) (2007). *The Marketing of Sport*. Harlow: FT Prentice Hall.
Mullin, Bernard James, Hardy, Stephen, and Sutton, William Anthony (2000). *Sport Marketing*. Champaign, Ill.: Human Kinetics.
Graham, S., Goldblatt, J. J., and Neirotti, L. D. (2001). *The Ultimate Guide to Sports Marketing*, 2nd edn. New York: McGraw-Hill.
Shilbury, David, Quick, Shayne, and Westerbeek, Hans (1998). *Strategic Sport Marketing*. St Leonards, NSW: Allen & Unwin.

■ spurious correlation

DESCRIPTION

A misleading conclusion that a correlation exists between data when in fact there is no such relationship.

KEY INSIGHTS

A spurious correlation between two variables may be a result of a statistical aberration, as opposed to a true causal relationship, or it may be due to a situation where a third variable influences each of the variables in the same way, thereby making it appear that the two variables are related. Efforts to reduce the possibility of spurious correlations include research designs that hold relevant variables constant in order to more readily observe causal effects on given variables of interest.

KEY WORDS Statistical analysis, correlations, misleading conclusions

IMPLICATIONS

Marketing researchers must be concerned about research conclusions that may involve spurious correlations. Robust research designs with suitable controls must be developed and implemented to minimize their possible occurrence.

APPLICATION AREAS AND FURTHER READINGS

Marketing Research

Bradburd, Ralph M. (1980). 'Advertising and Market Concentration: A Reexamination of Ornstein's Spurious Correlation Hypothesis,' *Southern Economic Journal*, 47(2), October, 531–539.

Wensley, R. (1997). 'Explaining Success: The Rule of Ten Percent and the Example of Market Share,' *Business Strategy Review*, 8(1), 63–70.

BIBLIOGRAPHY

Simon, H. A. (1954). 'Spurious Correlation: A Causal Interpretation,' *Journal of the American Statistical Association*, 49, 467–479.

■ stakeholder theory

DESCRIPTION

Theory concerned with the identification and evaluation of groups of stakeholders of a firm for subsequent managerial attention and action.

KEY INSIGHTS

Stakeholder theory as advocated by researchers including Freeman (1984) recognizes the potential importance of stakeholder groups beyond the traditionally acknowledged groups comprising employees, suppliers, customers, and investors. Communities, political groups, government bodies, and trade associations are examples of such stakeholders. Conceptual elements of stakeholder theory enable the identification of such groups as well as assisting in firm decisions to treat such groups as important stakeholders to which the firm should be responsible and accountable. Issues such as stakeholder power, legitimacy, and urgency

of stakeholder claims are developed and integrated in stakeholder theory. While it can be argued that it may not be possible to balance the
needs of all stakeholders against each other, the theory nevertheless
provides a basis for understanding and negotiating possible stakeholder
conflicts.

KEY WORDS Organizational stakeholders, marketing stakeholders, groups

IMPLICATIONS
Beyond meeting customer needs and balancing such needs with those
of the firm, its employees, and its investors, marketing has become
increasingly concerned with meeting the needs of its many and varied
stakeholders. Stakeholder theory provides a means for marketers to identify and evaluate better groups and parties that should be considered key
stakeholders relative to the firm as a whole as well as any marketing
strategy approach initiative.

APPLICATION AREAS AND FURTHER READINGS
Marketing Strategy
Polonsky, M. J. (1995). 'A Stakeholder Theory Approach to Designing Environ-
    mental Marketing Strategy,' *Journal of Business and Industrial Marketing*, 10(3), 29–
    42.
Polonsky, M. J. (1996). 'Stakeholder Management and the Stakeholder Matrix:
    Potential Strategic Marketing,' *Journal of Market Focused Management*, 1(3), 209–
    230.
Payne, A., Ballantyne, D., and Christopher, M. (2005). 'A Stakeholder Approach
    to Relationship Marketing Strategy,' *European Journal of Marketing*, 39(7–8), 855–
    871.
Donaldson, T., and Preston, L. 1995. 'The Stakeholder Theory of the Corporation:
    Concepts, Evidence, and Implications,' *Academy of Management Review*, 20(1), 65–
    91.

BIBLIOGRAPHY
Freeman, R. E. (1984). *Strategic Management: A Stakeholder Approach*. Boston: Pitman.
Friedman, A. L., and Miles, S. (2002). 'Developing Stakeholder Theory,' *Journal of
    Management Studies*, 39(1), 1–21.
Mitchell, R. K., Agle, B. R., and Wood, D. J. (1997). 'Toward a Theory of Stakeholder
    Identification and Salience: Defining the Principle of Who and What Really
    Counts,' *Academy of Management Review*, 22(4), 853–886.

■ standardization

DESCRIPTION
The process or strategy of developing standardized goods or services to meet
the needs and preferences of a particular market or set of consumers, where
such markets and consumers are typically examined and managed within an
international marketing context.

KEY INSIGHTS
As an element of a firm's international marketing strategy, standardization relies on a uniform marketing effort over similar worldwide
segments. As opposed to adaptation or customization in the firm's
marketing strategies, standardization aims to benefit from 'marketing

universals,' which are consumer behaviors within a segment and consumer preferences within a particular product category that are invariant across cultures (Dawar and Parker 1994).

KEY WORDS Uniform marketing, marketing universals

IMPLICATIONS

The choice between standardization and adaptation across markets must explicitly consider the similarities and differences in consumer attitudes and behavior in a particular market (Dawar and Parker 1994). Pursuing the international marketing approach of standardization entails the identification of a segment of consumers who do not differ across cultures in their preferences for a particular good or service offering, allowing for a standardized marketing program across countries and cultures. In considering standardization, marketers must be careful in drawing conclusions about the similarities between markets, where too much standardization, for example, may leave room for competitors to meet local needs to a greater extent.

APPLICATION AREAS AND FURTHER READINGS

Marketing Strategy
Jain, Subhash C. (1989). 'Standardization of International Marketing Strategy: Some Research Hypotheses,' *Journal of Marketing*, 53(1), January, 70–79.
Anderson, Eugene W., Fornell, Claes, and Rust, Roland T. (1997). 'Customer Satisfaction, Productivity, and Profitability: Differences between Goods and Services,' *Marketing Science*, 16(2), 129–145.

Marketing Management
Ferrell, O. C., and Skinner, Steven J. (1988). 'Ethical Behavior and Bureaucratic Structure in Marketing Research Organizations,' *Journal of Marketing Research*, 25(1), February, 103–109.
Cavusgil, S. Tamer, and Zou, Shaoming (1994). 'Marketing Strategy–Performance Relationship: An Investigation of the Empirical Link in Export Market Ventures,' *Journal of Marketing*, 58(1), January, 1–21.

International Marketing
Szymanski, David M., Bharadwaj, Sundar G., and Varadarajan, P. Rajan (1993). 'Standardization versus Adaptation of International Marketing Strategy: An Empirical Investigation,' *Journal of Marketing*, 57(4), October, 1–17.

Global Marketing
Samiee, Saeed, and Roth, Kendall (1992). 'The Influence of Global Marketing Standardization on Performance,' *Journal of Marketing*, 56(2), April, 1–17.

BIBLIOGRAPHY
Dawar, Niraj, and Parker, Philip (1994). 'Marketing Universals: Consumers' Use of Brand Name, Price, Physical Appearance, and Retailer Reputation as Signals of Product Quality,' *Journal of Marketing*, 58(2), April, 81–95.

☐ star *see* product portfolio analysis
☐ statistical validity *see* validity
☐ status quo bias *see* endowment effect
☐ status quo marketing *see* defensive marketing

■ stealth marketing

(also called undercover marketing or under-the-radar marketing)

DESCRIPTION
Marketing that is not immediately perceived as marketing.

KEY INSIGHTS
Stealth marketing is a relatively unconventional marketing approach where customers are targeted without realizing they are being marketed to. It has similarities with guerrilla marketing in that promotional activities may be unobvious to the marketer's target market and of relatively low cost, but where the effects of the effort can be widespread (see **guerrilla marketing**). Stealth marketing is often performed on a face-to-face basis in ways where customers are usually unaware of such activities as being marketing attempts, since the approach involves interaction with customers at places or times when their defences are most likely to be down (Kaikati and Kaikati 2004). An example is when a celebrity drinks a certain branded beverage in public but where consumers are unaware that the celebrity is being paid to do so. The goal of an undercover stealth marketing campaign is to generate a buzz in the market that can reach consumers and spread among them spontaneously. It may actually rely more on consumer trust than more conventional marketing approaches if, for example, it involves a trusted celebrity who endorses the product in public and the behavior passes unconsciously to consumers. A variant of under-the-radar marketing is *lean-over marketing*, where individuals are paid by a firm to intentionally situate themselves within earshot of the firm's target market and then begin talking about the merits of the firm's particular product or service offering, where the aim is to catch attention and interest and generate a subsequent market buzz.

KEY WORDS Hidden marketing, unobvious marketing, questionable marketing practice

IMPLICATIONS
Stealth marketing may involve less financial risk and can be cost effective if it generates the sought-after buzz in the market. Its problems reside in its ethical implications. If consumers conclude that they are being manipulated into liking the product, the company runs the risk of a backlash. Thus, the ethics of a stealth marketing approach is a topic worthy of debate in a marketer's firm. Nevertheless, the appeal of its use revolves around the possibility that its effects, while very hard to predict, may ultimately be a high level of buzz or word-of-mouth communication that spreads very quickly.

APPLICATION AREAS AND FURTHER READINGS
Marketing Strategy
Biener, L., Nyman, A. L., Kline, R. L., and Albers, A. B. (2004). 'Adults Only: The Prevalence of Tobacco Promotions in Bars and Clubs in the Boston Area,' *Tobacco Control*, 13(4), 403–408.
Rushkoff, Douglas, Dretzin, Rachel, and Goodman, Barak (2001). 'Merchants of Cool,' *Frontline*. Boston: PBS, WGBH.

Online Marketing
Dubas, K. M., and Brennan, I. (2002). 'Marketing Implications of Webcasting and Extranets,' *Marketing Intelligence and Planning*, 20(4–5), 223–228.

BIBLIOGRAPHY
Kaikati, A. M., and Kaikati, J. G. (2004). 'Stealth Marketing: How to Reach Consumers Surreptitiously,' *California Management Review*, 46(4), 6–22.

☐ **STEP analysis** *see* macroenvironment
☐ **store brand** *see* private label

■ STP marketing

DESCRIPTION
A methodical approach in marketing planning whereby a marketer follows a three-step process involving segmentation, targeting, and positioning.

KEY INSIGHTS
STP marketing adopts the view that segmentation is a key part of the competitive strategy of many organizations. As such, it can be argued that the tasks of identifying, characterizing, and targeting appropriate marketing segments form the basis for much of strategic marketing and an organization's strategic thinking more generally. In the process of STP marketing, the marketer gives critical consideration to segmentation, which is the identification of groups of customers that have similarities in characteristics or needs who are likely to exhibit similar purchase behavior (Smith 1956); targeting, or selecting particular segments to target; and positioning, which necessarily involves selecting a desirable positioning strategy (see **positioning**) and subsequently developing marketing programs that convey the desired brand position.

KEY WORDS Marketing planning, planning process, **segmentation**, **targeting**, **positioning**

IMPLICATIONS
As part of the overall strategic marketing planning process, a marketer may conduct an internal analysis of the firm, a competitive analysis, and a market analysis. All such marketing research efforts may support the firm's efforts to engage in STP marketing, where, after establishing market segments and targeting appropriate segments, positioning plays a centrally important role after segmenting and targeting the appropriate market segments. As a follow-on to the STP marketing process, marketers must then ensure the development of effective marketing programs and mixes, implement such efforts, and then ensure their adequate control.

APPLICATION AREAS AND FURTHER READINGS
Marketing Strategy
Weinstein, Art (1998). *Defining your Market: Winning Strategies for High-Tech, Industrial, and Service Firms*. New York: Haworth Press.

Marketing Management
Dibb, Sally, and Simkin, Lyndon (1996). *The Market Segmentation Workbook: Target Marketing for Marketing Managers*. New York: Routledge.

Online Marketing
Geissler, Gary L. (2001). 'Building Customer Relationships Online: The Web Site Designers' Perspective,' *Journal of Consumer Marketing*, 18(6), November, 488–502.

Services Marketing
Michalska-Dudek, I. (2003). 'STP Marketing Concept in Tourism Enterprises,' *Prace Naukowe: Akademii Ekonomicznej Imienia Oskara Langego We Wroclawiu*, 964, 212–223.

Marketing Research
Wind, Yoram (1978). 'Issues and Advances in Segmentation Research,' *Journal of Marketing Research*, 15, August, 317–337.

BIBLIOGRAPHY
Weinstein, Art (1997). 'Strategic Segmentation: A Planning Approach for Marketers,' *Journal of Segmentation in Marketing*, 1(2), 7–16.
Smith, Wendell (1956). 'Product Differentiation and Market Segmentation as Alternative Marketing Strategies,' *Journal of Marketing*, 21, July, 3–8.
Kotler, Philip (1999). *Kotler on Marketing: How to Create, Win, and Dominate Markets*. New York: Free Press.

☐ **straight rebuy** *see* industrial buyer behavior

■ strategic approaches

DESCRIPTION
Substantially different ways of focusing the firm's strategic marketing management efforts.

KEY INSIGHTS
In strategic marketing management, firms are faced with varying strategic approaches to pursue. Two notable approaches include strategic vision and strategic opportunism. Strategic vision defines a company's direction with respect to the scope of the product/service markets in which it will compete, orientation in terms of product or service positioning, and scale of operation. A strategic vision is focused on the future, where it involves an insightful analysis of the current and anticipated market environment to determine where the greatest opportunities and threats are at present and where they will be in the future. Strategic opportunism, on the other hand, focuses mainly on identifying and exploiting the immediate market opportunities at hand. This strategy seeks to leverage the company's existing strategic assets and competencies and avoid commitment, as the future is viewed as uncertain due to the dynamic nature of the changing business environment.

KEY WORDS Vision, opportunism

IMPLICATIONS
While each strategic approach clearly has certain benefits attached to it, each also carries certain strategic risks. Strategic vision faces a danger of strategic stubbornness whereas strategic opportunism faces a danger of strategic drift. For either approach, marketers must therefore be vigilant

of problems arising as a result of the firm ultimately reacting too slowly or too quickly to environmental change.

APPLICATION AREAS AND FURTHER READINGS

Marketing Strategy

McDaniel, Stephen W., and Kolari, James W. (1987). 'Marketing Strategy Implications of the Miles and Snow Strategic Typology,' *Journal of Marketing*, 51(4), October, 19–30.

Menon, Ajay, and Menon, Anil (1997). 'Enviropreneurial Marketing Strategy: The Emergence of Corporate Environmentalism as Market Strategy,' *Journal of Marketing*, 61(1), January, 51–67.

Boeker, Warren (1989). 'Strategic Change: The Effects of Founding and History,' *Academy of Management Journal*, 32(3), September, 489–515.

Marketing Management

Deshpande, Rohit, and Webster, Frederick E., Jr. (1989). 'Organizational Culture and Marketing: Defining the Research Agenda,' *Journal of Marketing*, 53(1), January, 3–15.

Moorman, Christine, and Rust, Roland T. (1999). 'The Role of Marketing,' *Journal of Marketing*, 63, Fundamental Issues and Directions for Marketing, 180–197.

Marketing Research

Day, George S., and Montgomery, David B. (1999). 'Charting New Directions for Marketing,' *Journal of Marketing*, 63, Fundamental Issues and Directions for Marketing, 3–13.

BIBLIOGRAPHY

Aaker, David A. (2005). *Strategic Market Management*. New York: John Wiley & Sons, Inc.

■ strategic asset

DESCRIPTION

A resource of the firm that is strong relative to competitors.

KEY INSIGHTS

In a marketing strategy context, strategic assets, such as a firm's brand or its installed customer base, provide the firm with resources with which to pursue a sustainable competitive advantage.

KEY WORDS Firm resource

IMPLICATIONS

In formulating marketing strategies, marketers should consider the cost and feasibility of the firm creating or maintaining strategic assets, in addition to any strategic competencies, to achieve sustainable competitive advantages. When a firm chooses to not use its well-known and highly regarded brand in support of a new product introduction, for example, it is losing a resource on which to draw in pursuing and achieving a sustainable competitive advantage.

APPLICATION AREAS AND FURTHER READINGS

Marketing Strategy

Glazer, Rashi (1991). 'Marketing in an Information-Intensive Environment: Strategic Implications of Knowledge as an Asset,' *Journal of Marketing*, 55(4), October, 1–19.

Piercy, N. (1986a). 'Marketing Asset Accounting: Scope and Rationale,' *European Journal of Marketing*, 20(1), 5–15.
Piercy, N. (1986b). 'Marketing Asset Accounting: The Way Forward?' *European Journal of Marketing*, 20(1), 104–106.

BIBLIOGRAPHY
Srivastava, Rajendra K., Shervani, Tasadduq A., and Fahey, Liam (1998). 'Market-Based Assets and Shareholder Value: A Framework for Analysis,' *Journal of Marketing*, 62(1), January, 2–18.

■ strategic competency

DESCRIPTION
A combination of distinctive capabilities that assists the firm in obtaining a sustainable competitive advantage.

KEY INSIGHTS
Strategic competencies involve combined intellectual abilities in skills, processes, and knowledge bases, in addition to the provision of significant customer value. It is not just about a unique product, current market strength, or asset but rather a sustained ability that differentiates it from the competition. Examples include a production process that allows the development of creative products or partnerships with other firms that allow for a capability gap that endures over time.

KEY WORDS Distinctive capabilities, **sustainable competitive advantage**

IMPLICATIONS
An in-depth identification of the key strategic competencies of a firm is essential, ensuring that these are not mixed with basic competencies or strengths. Effectively formulating a company's overall marketing strategy relies on determining those strategic competencies as well as those of competitors.

APPLICATION AREAS AND FURTHER READINGS
Marketing Strategy
Black, J. A., and Boal, K. B. (1994). 'Strategic Resources: Traits, Configurations and Paths to Sustainable Competitive Advantage,' *Strategic Management Journal*, 15, 131–148.

Marketing Management
Thompson, J., and Cole, M. (1997). 'Strategic Competency: The Learning Challenge,' *Journal of Workplace Learning*, 9(4–5), 153–162.

BIBLIOGRAPHY
Zingheim, P. K., Ledford G. E., Jr., and Schuster, J. R. (1996). 'Competencies and Competency Models: Does One Size Fit All,' *ACA Journal*, 5(1), 56–65.
Aaker, David A. (2005). *Strategic Market Management*. New York: John Wiley & Sons, Inc.

■ strategic group

DESCRIPTION

A set of firms within an industry that follow the same basic strategy or business model and have similar reactions to environmental changes.

KEY INSIGHTS

The number of groups within an industry and their composition depend on what dimensions are used to define the groups. Strategic groups are influenced by market entry barriers that deter a firm's mobility in shifting its strategic position to diversification in new products, segments, or distribution channels. Mobility barriers define the strategic groups in that they reinforce patterns of rivalry among group members (Day and Wensley 1983). Strategic groups are influenced by the stability of mobility barriers and the ability of the firms in the group to resist the pressure on profits from direct competitors.

KEY WORDS Competitive analysis, industry structure

IMPLICATIONS

The membership and classification of strategic groups are not stable over time (Hatten and Hatten 1985). As such, in using the strategic group concept in evaluations of a firm's strategic options, it is important to be clear about the theoretical and methodological grounds for the common strategies and mobility barriers in one's industry.

APPLICATION AREAS AND FURTHER READINGS

Marketing Strategy

Dess, G. D., and Davis, P. S. (1984). 'Porter's (1980) Generic Strategies as Determinants of Strategic Group Membership and Organizational Performance,' *Academy of Management Studies*, 27(3), 467–488.

Cool, K., and Schendel, D. (1988). 'Performance Differences among Strategic Group Members,' *Strategic Management Journal*, 9(3), 207–223.

Conant, Jeffrey S., Mokwa, Michael P., and Varadarajan, P. Rajan (1990). 'Strategic Types, Distinctive Marketing Competencies and Organizational Performance: A Multiple Measures-Based Study,' *Strategic Management Journal*, 11(5), September, 365–383.

Marketing Research

Harrigan, K. R. (1985). 'An Application of Clustering for Strategic Group Analysis,' *Strategic Management Journal*, 6(1), 55–73.

Fiegenbaum, A., Sudharsan, D., and Thomas, H. (1987). 'The Concept of Strategic Time Periods in Strategic Group Research,' *Managerial and Decision Economics*, 8, 139–148.

Fiegenbaum, A., and Thomas, H. (1995). 'Strategic Groups as Reference Groups: Theory, Modeling and Empirical Examination of Industry and Competitive Strategy,' *Strategic Management Journal*, 13, 461–476.

BIBLIOGRAPHY

Day, George S., and Wensley, Robin (1983). 'Marketing Theory with a Strategic Orientation,' *Journal of Marketing*, 47(4), Autumn, 79–89.

Hatten, K. J., and Hatten, M. L. (1985). 'Some Empirical Insights for Strategic Marketers: The Case of Beer,' in H. Thomas and D. M. Gardner (eds.), *Strategic Marketing and Management*. New York: John Wiley & Sons, Inc.

■ strategic marketing

DESCRIPTION
Marketing with an emphasis on achieving important long-term marketing aims and objectives that further provide a basis for competitive advantage.

KEY INSIGHTS
Strategic marketing emphasizes decisions and actions that have a major impact on an organization over a long-term time horizon. More specifically, it is a marketing approach that involves setting the strategic direction for the firm with a long-term vision to guide investments in marketing assets and competencies, which can be leveraged within business processes towards providing sustainable competitive advantages. Actual time horizons associated with strategic marketing initiatives are broad, however, and might range anywhere from six months to one year in the future, to three to five years or beyond. Firms engaged in strategic marketing are concerned with the development and implementation of marketing strategies (see **marketing strategy**) that are focused on particular future timeframes having important competitive advantage implications. Models, frameworks, concepts, and analytical tools used in strategic marketing help the analysis of marketing decisions from an organizational perspective. Along with competencies of the firm, strategic marketing deals with long-term assets such as brand equity and customer equity (Rust et al. 2004), out of which marketing actions are derived. Firms can make decisions about which strategic marketing orientations to take based on developing competitive benchmarking and investigating the business environment. An integrative strategic marketing-planning framework enables the company to formulate effective marketing policies. For example, such a framework enables the firm to take into account total quality management issues using feedback from the major forces that impact the company such as customers, employees, and competitors (Lu et al. 1994).

KEY WORDS Competitive advantage, long-term horizon, planning

IMPLICATIONS
While the scope of marketing is sufficiently broad as to encompass day-to-day marketing initiatives as well as the very long term, marketers should recognize the importance of planning and implementing marketing initiatives concerning any timeframe in such a way that they provide the marketer's organization with a possible source of competitive advantage. Such a focus can assist the marketer with efforts aimed at not only achieving appropriate short-term objectives (e.g. reducing inventory) but also ensuring such efforts give sufficient consideration to the evolutionary dynamics of competition and customer wants and needs.

APPLICATION AREAS AND FURTHER READINGS
Marketing Strategy
Cravens, David W. (1982). *Strategic Marketing*. Homewood, Ill.: R. D. Irwin.

Marketing Management
Wilson, R. M. S., Gilligan, Colin, and Pearson, David J. (1992). *Strategic Marketing Management: Planning, Implementation, and Control*. Boston: Butterworth-Heinemann.

Business-to-Business Marketing
Bowersox, Donald J., and Cooper, M. Bixby (1992). *Strategic Marketing Channel Management*. New York: McGraw-Hill.

Services Marketing
Lovelock, C. H. (1983). 'Classifying Services to Gain Strategic Marketing Insights,' *Journal of Marketing*, 47, Summer, 9–20.

Non-profit Marketing
Kotler, Philip, and Andreasen, Alan R. (1987). *Strategic Marketing for Nonprofit Organizations*. Englewood Cliffs, NJ: Prentice-Hall.

Online Marketing
Bishop, Bill (1997). *Strategic Marketing for the Digital Age*. New York: HarperBusiness.

International Marketing
Naumann, Earl, and Lincoln, Douglas J. (1991). 'Non-Tariff Barriers and Entry Strategy Alternatives: Strategic Marketing Implications,' *Journal of Small Business Management*, 29(2), 60–70.

BIBLIOGRAPHY
Aaker, David A. (2004). *Strategic Market Management*, 7th edn. New York: John Wiley & Sons.
Rust, R. T., Ambler, T., Carpenter, G. S., Kumar, V., and Srivastava, R. K. (2004). 'Measuring Marketing Productivity: Current Knowledge and Future Directions,' *Journal of Marketing*, 68(4), 76–89.
Lu, Min Hua, Madu, Christian N., Kuei, Chu-hua, and Winokur, Dena (1994). 'Integrating QFD, AHP and Benchmarking in Strategic Marketing,' *Journal of Business & Industrial Marketing*, 9(1), 41–50.

■ strategic options

DESCRIPTION

The options available to a firm at any level that assist it with achieving important long-term marketing aims and objectives that further provide a basis for competitive advantage.

KEY INSIGHTS

In support of a firm's business and marketing strategies, strategic options are any of a set of particular value propositions for a specific product market along with supporting assets, competencies, and functional area strategies and programs. Firms may pursue any number of strategic options as part of their broader business and marketing strategies. Examples of strategic options include an emphasis on: quality, value, innovation, a particular product attribute (e.g. safety), product design (e.g. aesthetics), product line breadth (e.g. an array of home entertainment products), corporate social responsibility, brand familiarity, customer intimacy. Ultimately, the strategies of most firms involve a combination of strategic options.

KEY WORDS Value propositions, competitive advantage, product markets

IMPLICATIONS
In identifying and characterizing its strategic options, a firm is able to more clearly evaluate them as part of marketing strategy formulation. When they become part of the firm's strategy, the particular strategic options pursued can then be articulated more clearly to all of the firm's key stakeholders (e.g. employees, investors, customers).

APPLICATION AREAS AND FURTHER READINGS
Marketing Strategy
Doyle, P. (1989). 'Building Successful Brands: The Strategic Options,' *Journal of Marketing Management*, 5(1), 77–95.
Anderson, Paul F. (1982). 'Marketing, Strategic Planning and the Theory of the Firm,' *Journal of Marketing*, 46, Spring, 15–26.
Schoemaker, P. (1997). 'Disciplined Imagination: From Scenarios to Strategic Options,' *International Studies of Management and Organization*, 27(2), 43–70.
Abell, Derek F. (1978). 'Strategic Windows,' *Journal of Marketing*, 42(3), July, 21–26.
Glazer, Rashi (1991). 'Marketing in an Information-Intensive Environment: Strategic Implications of Knowledge as an Asset,' *Journal of Marketing*, 55(4), October, 1–19.

Marketing Management
Day, George S. (1984). *Strategic Market Planning: The Pursuit of Competitive Advantage.* St Paul, Minn.: West Publishing Company.
Wheelen, Thomas L., and Hunger, J. David (1983). Strategic Management and Business Policy. Reading, Mass.: Addison-Wesley Publishing Company.

Online Marketing
Stroud, D. (1998). *Internet Strategies: A Corporate Guide to Exploiting the Internet.* Basingstoke: Macmillan.

Retail Marketing
Nicholls, Alexander J. (2002). 'Strategic Options in Fair Trade Retailing,' *International Journal of Retail and Distribution Management*, 30(1), 6–17.

International Marketing
Ayal, Igal, and Zif, Jehiel (1979). 'Market Expansion Strategies in Multinational Marketing,' *Journal of Marketing*, Spring, 84–94.
Cavusgil, S. Tamer, and Zou, Shaoming (1994). 'Marketing Strategy Performance Relationship: An Investigation of the Empirical Link in Export Market Ventures,' *Journal of Marketing*, 58(1), January, 1–21.
Coviello, Nicole E., and Munro, Hugh J. (1995). 'Growing the Entrepreneurial Firm: Networking for International Market Development,' *European Journal of Marketing*, 29(7), 49–61.

Marketing Modeling
Menon, Anil, Bharadwaj, Sundar G., Adidam, Phani Tej, and Edison, Steven W. (1999). 'Antecedents and Consequences of Marketing Strategy Making: A Model and a Test,' *Journal of Marketing*, 63(2), April, 18–40.

Business-to-Business Marketing
Webster, Frederick E. (1979). *Industrial Marketing Strategy.* New York: Wiley.

BIBLIOGRAPHY
Aaker, David A. (2005). *Strategic Market Management.* New York: John Wiley & Sons, Inc.

■ strategic window

DESCRIPTION
Also called a window of opportunity, the period of time where propitious or desirable conditions exist for a firm to implement a strategic action aimed at taking advantage of a particular marketing opportunity.

KEY INSIGHTS
The strategic window concept provides a basis for anticipating and responding to changes in the marketplace. The classic journal article on the subject by Abell (1978), for example, advocates that firms should time their investments in products or markets when such strategic windows are open. In this sense, the concept captures the notion that there are only limited periods of time when there is a good fit between market conditions and a firm's capabilities and competencies relative to a particular strategic marketing objective.

KEY WORDS Window of opportunity, timing, strategic action

IMPLICATIONS
Marketers engaged in planning processes aimed at anticipating and responding to changes in the marketing environment may benefit from a greater appreciation and understanding of the strategic windows concept. For example, the timing and size of commitments of marketing funds to new marketing initiatives and the phasing out of funding to current initiatives are just some of the issues that marketing strategists must address. Identifying and evaluating strategic windows in such contexts can be of major importance to the long-term viability of a firm.

APPLICATION AREAS AND FURTHER READINGS
Marketing Strategy
Lilien, Gary L., and Yoon, Eunsang (1990). 'The Timing of Competitive Market Entry: An Exploratory Study of New Industrial Products,' *Management Science*, 36(5), May, 568–585.
Dickson, Peter R., and Giglierano, Joseph J. (1986). 'Missing the Boat and Sinking the Boat: A Conceptual Model of Entrepreneurial Risk,' *Journal of Marketing*, 50(3), July, 58–70.

BIBLIOGRAPHY
Abell, Derek F. (1978). 'Strategic Windows,' *Journal of Marketing*, 42(3), July, 21–26.

■ strategies, generic

DESCRIPTION
Logical frameworks endorsed by firms which are definable according to dimensions of strategic scope and strategic strength.

KEY INSIGHTS
Put forth by Porter (1980), strategic scope looks at the size and composition of the market the firm intends to target from a demand-side perspective, whereas strategic strength looks at the strengths or core competencies of the firm from a supply-side perspective. Types of generic

strategies in marketing can be said to include a product differentiation strategy, a cost leadership strategy, and a focus/market segmentation strategy, where the first two are broad in market scope and where the focus strategy has a narrow target market focus. Each strategy has its own direction, conditions, and implications for an organization's objectives. For example, a product differentiation strategy would focus on producing a product that is unique and providing superior value to customers. As customers perceive its uniqueness and value, it is unrivaled by competitors and creates brand loyalty, unaffected by the price. A cost leadership strategy would focus on large-volume production of a standardized product, relying on economies of scale to achieve efficiency. The product is usually basic, addressing a large customer base, and the firm's reduced cost results in a lower price that differentiates it in the market. It requires heavy investments to produce large volume and good relationships with suppliers. A market segmentation strategy, also called a focus or niche strategy, would require the firm to focus on only a few selected target markets. It seeks to identify and meet the specific needs of one or two market segments, tailoring appropriate marketing mix plans for each, focusing on effectiveness rather than efficiency.

KEY WORDS Strategic frameworks, cost leadership, focus, product differentiation

IMPLICATIONS
Each of the generic strategies entails different costs, skills, and resources. Differentiation strategy may dictate a premium pricing approach due to the high R&D costs involved, and it requires skills, creativity and a strong R&D department in the firm. To maintain cost leadership strategy, the firm has to seek all possible cost reductions in all business aspects, with a considerable market share advantage and preferential access to resources, such as material, labour, and other process inputs. Losing on such advantages can subject it to being copied by competitors. Market segmentation strategy entails finding target segments least approached by competitors and, as such, is often suitable for smaller firms, although it can be used by any firm. Generic strategies have received criticism on the basis of their lack of specificity, flexibility, and having a limiting approach. Some firms move between strategies along their growth and development.

APPLICATION AREAS AND FURTHER READINGS
Marketing Strategy
Zajac, E., and Shortell, S. M. (1989). 'Changing Generic Strategies: Likelihood, Direction, and Performance,' *Strategic Management Journal*, 10, 413–430.
Murray, A. (1988). 'A Contingency View of Porter's "Generic strategies,"' *Academy of Management Review*, 13(3), 390–400.
Karnani, A. (1984). 'Generic Competitive Strategies: An Analytical Approach,' *Strategic Management Journal*, 5, 367–380.
Dess, Gregory G., and Davis, Peter S. (1980). 'Porter's (1980) Generic Strategies as Determinants of Strategic Group Membership and Organizational Performance,' *Academy of Management Journal*, 27(3), September, 467–488.

Glazer, Rashi (1991). 'Marketing in an Information-Intensive Environment: Strategic Implications of Knowledge as an Asset,' *Journal of Marketing*, 55(4), October, 1–19.

International Marketing
Kim, Linsu, and Lim, Y. (1988). 'Environment, Generic Strategies, and Performance in a Rapidly Developing Country,' *Academy of Management Journal*, 31, 802–827.
Szymanski, David M., Bharadwaj, Sundar G., and Varadarajan, P. Rajan (1993). 'Standardization versus Adaptation of International Marketing Strategy: An Empirical Investigation,' *Journal of Marketing*, 57(4), October, 1–17.

Marketing Research
Wind, Yoram, and Robertson, Thomas S. (1983). 'Marketing Strategy: New Directions for Theory and Research,' *Journal of Marketing*, 47(2), Spring, 12–25.

Small Businesses
Lee, K. S., Lim, G. H., and Tan, S. J. (1999). 'Dealing with Resource Disadvantage: Generic Strategies for SMEs,' *Small Business Economics*, 12(4), 299–311.

BIBLIOGRAPHY
Porter, M. E. (1980). *Competitive Strategy*. New York: Free Press.

■ strategy

DESCRIPTION
A long-term approach or logical framework advancing a plan of action designed to achieve a particular goal.

KEY INSIGHTS
Strategies, as reflected in marketing strategies, are the foundations set before any marketing plans or actions are undertaken. They provide long-term direction in achieving marketing goals and objectives. The viability of any strategy is enhanced to the extent that it is aligned with the overall business strategy of the organization.

KEY WORDS Plans, long-term plans

IMPLICATIONS
Among other elements, developing strategies requires careful consideration of the main players in a market environment (sometimes referred to as the 'three Cs')—the company, customers, and competitors. Marketing strategies are usually consciously adapted to improve performance through constant monitoring of the market in terms of market trends, competitive reactions, and buying behavior. Ideally, every individual in an organization, and not just within the marketing function, should understand the overall marketing strategy driving any tactical marketing programs undertaken. This is also the essence of a total integrated marketing approach (see **total integrated marketing**).

APPLICATION AREAS AND FURTHER READINGS
Marketing Strategy
Cavusgil, S. Tamer, and Zou, Shaoming (1994). 'Marketing Strategy–Performance Relationship: An Investigation of the Empirical Link in Export Market Ventures,' *Journal of Marketing*, 58(1), January, 1–21.

Arnould, Eric J., and Wallendorf, Melanie (1994). 'Market-Oriented Ethnography: Interpretation Building and Marketing Strategy Formulation,' *Journal of Marketing Research*, 31(4), November, 484–504.

Smith, Wendell R. (1956). 'Product Differentiation and Market Segmentation as Alternative Marketing Strategies,' *Journal of Marketing*, 21(1), July, 3–8.

Services Marketing
Zeithaml, Valarie A., Parasuraman, A., and Berry, Leonard L. (1985). 'Problems and Strategies in Services Marketing,' *Journal of Marketing*, 49(2), Spring, 33–46.

Buisness-to-Business Marketing
Boyle, Brett, Dwyer, F. Robert, Robicheaux, Robert A., and Simpson, James T. (1992). 'Influence Strategies in Marketing Channels: Measures and Use in Different Relationship Structures,' *Journal of Marketing Research*, 29(4), November, 462–473.

Marketing Research
Gupta, Ashok K., Raj, S. P., and Wilemon, David (1986). 'A Model for Studying R&D. Marketing Interface in the Product Innovation Process,' *Journal of Marketing*, 50(2), April, 7–17.

BIBLIOGRAPHY
Aaker, David A. (2005). *Strategic Market Management*. New York: John Wiley & Sons, Inc.

Walker, Orville C., Jr., and Ruekert, Robert W. (1987). 'Marketing's Role in the Implementation of Business Strategies: A Critical Review and Conceptual Framework,' *Journal of Marketing*, 51(3), July, 15–33.

■ subcultural theory

DESCRIPTION

A theory that certain groups or subcultures in society share values and attitudes that influence them in assimilating dominant cultural consumption patterns.

KEY INSIGHTS

While subcultural theory receives considerable attention in anthropology and psychology, it also provides a basis for marketing research. For example, groups of people forming subcultures may share demographic and social characteristics and values, but they may also share common motivations, consumption attitudes, and consumption behaviors.

KEY WORDS Values, attitudes, culture

IMPLICATIONS

Consumer typologies which are based on subcultural theory can help enhance an understanding of subcultures' common needs and motives and assist in predicting consumption behavior. This can help target communication strategies and marketing mix plans towards specific subcultures more effectively.

APPLICATION AREAS AND FURTHER READINGS

Marketing Strategy
Cova, Bernard, and Cova, Véronique (2002). 'Tribal Marketing: The Tribalisation of Society and its Impact on the Conduct of Marketing,' *European Journal of Marketing*, 36(5–6), June, 595–620.

Marketing Management
Deshpande, Rohit, and Webster, Frederick E., Jr. (1989). 'Organizational Culture and Marketing: Defining the Research Agenda,' *Journal of Marketing*, 53(1), January, 3–15.

Consumer Behavior
Schouten, John W., and McAlexander, James H. (1995). 'Subcultures of Consumption: An Ethnography of the New Bikers,' *Journal of Consumer Research*, 22(1), June, 43–61.
Harris, Lloyd C. (1998). 'Cultural Domination: The Key to Market-Oriented Culture?' *European Journal of Marketing*, 32(3–4), April, 354–373.
Mathur, Anil, and Moschis, George P. (2005). 'Antecedents of Cognitive Age: A Replication and Extension,' *Psychology and Marketing*, 22(12), October, 969–994.

Marketing Research
Thompson, Craig J. (1997). 'Interpreting Consumers: A Hermeneutical Framework for Deriving Marketing Insights from the Texts of Consumers' Consumption Stories,' *Journal of Marketing Research*, 34(4), November, 438–455.

International Marketing
Steenkamp, Jan-Benedict E. M. (2001). 'The Role of National Culture in International Marketing Research,' *International Marketing Review*, 18(1), February, 30–44.

BIBLIOGRAPHY
Blackman, Shane (2005). 'Youth Subcultural Theory: A Critical Engagement with the Concept, its Origins and Politics, from the Chicago School to Postmodernism,' *Journal of Youth Studies*, 8(1), March, 1–20.
Calluri, R. (1985). 'The Kids are All Right: New Wave Subcultural Theory,' *Social Text*, 12, 43–53.

■ subjective expected utility theory

DESCRIPTION

A theory of decision making under risk involving making choices among alternatives in order to maximize a decision maker's subjective expected utility.

KEY INSIGHTS

Developed in pioneering research by Savage (1954), subjective expected utility theory views decision making under uncertainty in terms of two major subjectivities of an individual decision maker: the individual's personal utility function and the individual's personal probability analysis. In contrast to decision-making where objective probabilities can be established based on the relative frequencies of observable events, subjective probabilities are used in the decision-making process. The theory enables decision making to be characterized by the determination and use of such probabilities in combination with the decision maker's subjective utility function to maximize the decision maker's overall subjective expected utility.

KEY WORDS Decision making, uncertainty, subjective probability, subjective utility

IMPLICATIONS

Marketers concerned with the modeling of decision making under risk where probabilities are based on a decision maker's beliefs, as opposed to being purely objective, may benefit from a greater understanding of subjective expected utility theory. In particular, where there is significant ambiguity involved in the decision-making process, as in strategic marketing decisions involving uncertain future events, the theoretical approach to modeling the decision may be beneficial to provide structure and rigor for greater clarity and consistency in the decision-making process.

APPLICATION AREAS AND FURTHER READINGS

Marketing Modeling

Kahn, Barbara E., and Sarin, Rakesh K. (1988). 'Modeling Ambiguity in Decision Making under Uncertainty,' *Journal of Consumer Research*, 15, September, 265–272.

Lynch, J. J., and Cohen, J. L. (1982). 'The Use of Subjective Expected Utility Theory as an Aid to Understanding Variables that Influence Helping Behavior,' *Journal of Personality and Social Psychology*, 36(10), 1138–1151.

Eliashberg, Jehoshua (1980). 'Consumer Preference Judgments: An Exposition with Empirical Applications,' *Management Science*, 26(1), January, 60–77.

BIBLIOGRAPHY

Savage, Leonard J. (1954). *The Foundations of Statistics*. New York: John Wiley & Sons.

■ subliminal advertising

DESCRIPTION

The incorporation of persuasive messages in advertising which are presented at a level that is below the threshold of a viewer's consciousness.

KEY INSIGHTS

While early uses of subliminal advertising with consumer audiences considered the approach to be effective in influencing consumer behavior, subsequent research on subliminal advertising suggests a lack of robust results on which to draw any such conclusion. Nevertheless, claims of its use in advertising periodically arise resulting in public controversy over the ethical nature of its use as well as its actual effect.

KEY WORDS Advertising, persuasive messages, unconscious processing

IMPLICATIONS

Marketers involved in the development of advertising campaigns should avoid practices that either use such a method or give the appearance of using such a method in order to ensure the advertising is evaluated fairly on the basis of accepted practices by individuals or organizations that represent consumer interests.

APPLICATION AREAS AND FURTHER READINGS

Advertising

Trappey, C. (1996). 'A Meta-analysis of Consumer Choice and Subliminal Advertising,' *Psychology and Marketing*, 13(5), 517–530.

Theus, K. T. (1994). 'Subliminal Advertising and the Psychology of Processing Unconscious Stimuli: A Review of Research,' *Psychology and Marketing*, 11(3), 271–290.

BIBLIOGRAPHY

Moore, Timothy E. (1982). 'Subliminal Advertising: What You See Is What You Get,' *Journal of Marketing*, 46(2), Spring, 38–47.

☐ **substantiality** *see* segmentation viability

■ substitute awareness effect

DESCRIPTION

An effect on consumer price sensitivity resulting from a consumer's awareness of one or more substitutes for a particular product or service offering.

KEY INSIGHTS

Consumer awareness of alternatives to a given product or service offering has the potential to significantly influence the consumer's price sensitivity to the offering. In particular, increased awareness of substitutes is associated with a reduction in the price the consumer is willing to pay for the offering.

KEY WORDS **Substitute product(s)**, consumer awareness, price sensitivity

IMPLICATIONS

Marketers involved in price setting should strive to understand consumer price sensitivity for any given offering in order to set and manage prices effectively. Recognizing how and to what extent price sensitivity is due to consumer awareness of substitutes can be beneficial in dynamically setting prices as consumer knowledge of substitute offerings also changes with time.

APPLICATION AREAS AND FURTHER READINGS

Online Marketing

Dou, Wenyu (2004). 'Will Internet Users Pay for Online Content?' *Journal of Advertising Research*, 44, 349–359.

Marketing Strategy

White, Gerald B., and Uva, Wen-fei L. (2000). *Developing a Strategic Marketing Plan for Horticultural Firms*. Ithaca, NY: New York State College of Agriculture and Life Sciences, Cornell University.

BIBLIOGRAPHY

Erdem, T., Keane, M., and Sun, B. (2004). *The Impact of Advertising on Consumer Price Sensitivity in Experience Goods Markets*. New Haven: Yale University Mimeograph.

■ substitute product

DESCRIPTION
A product perceived by the consumer as an alternative to another product.

KEY INSIGHTS
A substitute product, as an alternative to a product that it is able to replace, may vary from the original product in price or availability, but it usually meets the required utility. An understanding of brand-switching behavior relies on studies related to motivations behind seeking substitutes, which can relate to variety-seeking behaviour, complementarity among brands, brand unavailability, changing prices, or shifting consumer needs.

KEY WORD   Alternative products

IMPLICATIONS
Identifying competitive substitutes and studying them is essential for marketers. Substitute products pose threats such as competitive pricing that can impose a ceiling on prices companies charge for their products. The presence of close substitutes also gives consumers a chance to make quality, performance, and price comparisons, having the luxury of another alternative to shift to. Lower switching costs also entice consumers to move to substitutes.

APPLICATION AREAS AND FURTHER READINGS
Marketing Strategy
Moorthy, K. Sridhar (1984). 'Market Segmentation, Self-Selection, and Product Line Design,' *Marketing Science*, 3(4), Autumn, 288–307.

Marketing Management
Dobson, Gregory, and Kalish, Shlomo (1993). 'Heuristics for Pricing and Positioning a Product-Line Using Conjoint and Cost Data,' *Management Science*, 39(2), February, 160–175.
Miller, Danny (1988). 'Relating Porter's Business Strategies to Environment and Structure: Analysis and Performance Implications,' *Academy of Management Journal*, 31(2), June, 280–308.

Retail Marketing
Walters, Rockney G. (1991). 'Assessing the Impact of Retail Price Promotions on Product Substitution, Complementary Purchase, and Interstore Sales Displacement,' *Journal of Marketing*, 55(2), April, 17–28.

Marketing Research
Hoffman, Elizabeth, Menkhaus, Dale J., Chakravarti, Dipankar, Field, Ray A., and Whipple, Glen D. (1993). 'Using Laboratory Experimental Auctions in Marketing Research: A Case Study of New Packaging for Fresh Beef,' *Marketing Science*, 12(3), Summer, 318–338.
Sullivan, Mary (1990). 'Measuring Image Spillovers in Umbrella-Branded Products,' *Journal of Business*, 63(3), July, 309–329.

BIBLIOGRAPHY
Lattin, James M., and McAlister, Leigh (1985). 'Using a Variety-Seeking Model to Identify Substitute and Complementary Relationships among Competing Products,' *Journal of Marketing Research*, 22(3), August, 330–339.

■ substitution effect

DESCRIPTION

An effect of a price change that causes a consumer to purchase another good of similar utility as a substitute for a good that becomes comparatively more expensive. More generally, any effect on buyer behavior resulting from the availability of substitutes for a good.

KEY INSIGHTS

The substitution effect suggests that, as the price of a product or service rises, a consumer will tend to shift purchases to substitute products or services of similar utility to the consumer in its place. While the availability of substitute products or services enables the consumer to switch, the costs associated with switching are also a factor that must be taken into consideration. When switching costs are low and when there are multiple substitutes available that provide consumers with similar utility to the original product or service, substitution effects may be most pronounced.

KEY WORDS **Substitute product(s)**, price changes

IMPLICATIONS

Marketers involved in setting prices and managing price changes should seek to understand how and to what extent price changes may lead consumers to shift to substitute products. As many products or services do not have perfect substitutes, understanding in what way other products or services are substitutes (e.g. in form and function) may also be beneficial to marketers considering price changes.

APPLICATION AREAS AND FURTHER READINGS

Consumer Behavior

Allenby, Greg M., and Rossi, Peter E. (1991). 'Quality Perceptions and Asymmetric Switching between Brands,' *Marketing Science*, 10(3), Summer, 185–204.

Huber, Joel, and Puto, Christopher (1983). 'Market Boundaries and Product Choice: Illustrating Attraction and Substitution Effects,' *Journal of Consumer Research*, 10(1), June, 31–44.

Johnson, W. C., and Bhatia, K. (1997). 'Technological Substitution in Mobile Communications,' *Journal of Business and Industrial Marketing*, 12(5-6), 383–399.

BIBLIOGRAPHY

Walters, Rockney G. (1991). 'Assessing the Impact of Retail Price Promotions on Product Substitution, Complementary Purchase, and Interstore Sales Displacement,' *Journal of Marketing*, 55(2), April, 17–28.

☐ sundown rule *see* marketing, rules of
☐ sunk cost *see* cost

■ sunk cost fallacy

(also called the Concorde fallacy)

DESCRIPTION
The mistaken belief that a continued investment in a project or similar initiative is warranted based on past investment in it.

KEY INSIGHTS
As sunk costs, by definition, have already occurred and cannot be recovered to any significant degree, the fallacy involves inappropriately considering what investment has already occurred as opposed to assessing the current rationality for any additional investment.

KEY WORDS Decision making, judgment, **bias**, error

IMPLICATIONS
Marketers making investments in marketing strategies and programs must be aware of committing the sunk cost fallacy in making judgments lest further investment becomes at risk of becoming sunk costs as well. For example, the term is referred to as the Concorde fallacy due to the observed behaviors of investors supporting the development of the Concorde supersonic jet: after a point was reached where the high development costs made continued investment clearly uneconomical, the British and French governments ultimately supported the project to justify the past investments.

APPLICATION AREAS AND FURTHER READINGS
Decision Making
Armstrong, J. Scott, Coviello, Nicole, and Safranek, Barbara (1993). 'Escalation Bias: Does it Extend to Marketing?' *Journal of the Academy of Marketing Science*, 21(3), 247–253.
Soman, Dilip (2001). 'The Mental Accounting of Sunk Time Costs: Why Time is Not Like Money,' *Journal of Behavioral Decision Making*, 14(3), 169–185.
Hsee, Christopher K., Zhang, Jiao, Yu, Fang, and Xi, Yiheng (2003). 'Lay Rationalism and Inconsistency between Predicted Experience and Decision,' *Journal of Behavioral Decision Making*, 16(4), 257–272.

BIBLIOGRAPHY
Arkes, Hal R., and Ayton, Peter (1999). 'The Sunk Cost and Concorde Effects: Are Humans Less Rational Than Animals?' *Psychological Bulletin*, 125(5), 591–600.

☐ **superior goods** *see* goods
☐ **supermarketing** *see* retail marketing

■ supply, law of

DESCRIPTION
An economic principle that holds that, all else equal, the quantity of a good supplied rises as the price of the good rises and falls as the price of the good falls.

KEY INSIGHTS

Developed by economist Alfred Marshall, the law of supply asserts that the supply and price of a good are directly proportional. That is, the amount of a good that a producer or supplier will be willing to bring to market to sell at a given price at a given time will be in proportion to the price of the good. Higher prices will lead a supplier to offer more of the product in the market, whereas lower prices will lead a supplier to offer less of the product.

KEY WORDS Supply, price, modeling

IMPLICATIONS

In order to manage effectively both the price and supply of an offering, marketing strategists should seek to understand the nature and extent of the price–supply relationship. While there may be deviations from the law of supply based on market and/or product characteristics that the marketer should also seek to appreciate and understand fully, the law of supply nevertheless emphasizes an important economic principle of influence to marketing strategy development and management over time.

APPLICATION AREAS AND FURTHER READINGS

Marketing Modeling
Engl, G., and Scotchmer, S. (1997). 'The Law of Supply in Games, Markets and Matching Models,' *Economic Theory*, 9(3), 539–550.

Marketing Strategy
Low, Linda (2000). *The Economics of Information Technology and the Media.* Singapore: Singapore University Press.

BIBLIOGRAPHY
Buchholz, Todd G. (1990). *New Ideas from Dead Economists.* New York: Penguin Books.

■ supply and demand, law of

DESCRIPTION

An economic principle of free markets in equilibrium that holds that prices are determined such that demand equals supply, and where changes in prices are a result of a shift in demand and/or supply.

KEY INSIGHTS

In free markets, the law of supply and demand asserts that the prices and quantities of goods produced are determined by the relationship between supply and demand. When either the demand or supply for goods changes, the result will be either changes in prices or in the quantities of goods produced, or both, in order to achieve equilibrium in the market.

KEY WORDS Demand, supply, prices, market equilibrium

IMPLICATIONS

Marketers involved in marketing strategy development and implementation should strive to understand how and to what extent the relative

balance or imbalance between demand and supply may potentially influence the prices of the marketer's offerings. As marketers are constantly
engaged in managing demand relative to supply for products and additionally frequently concerned with setting prices, an appreciation of
the law of supply and demand and its implications for the marketing
strategies of the firms' offerings is essential.

APPLICATION AREAS AND FURTHER READINGS
Marketing Strategy
Einav, Liran, Orbach, Barak Y., and Olin, John M. (2001). *Uniform Prices for Differen-
tiated Goods: The Case of the Movie-Theater Industry*. Cambridge, Mass.: Harvard Law
School.
Brewer, P. J., Huang, M., Nelson, B., and Plott, C. R. (2002). 'On the Behavioral
Foundations of the Law of Supply and Demand Human Convergence and Robot
Randomness,' *Experimental Economics*, 5(3), 179–208.

BIBLIOGRAPHY
Gale, D. (1955). 'The Law of Supply and Demand,' *Mathematica Scandinavica*, 3,
155–169.

☐ **supply push** *see* push marketing

■ **survey research**

DESCRIPTION
In marketing research, a method of collecting data about a certain population
using a systematic approach for measurement.

KEY INSIGHTS
Research involving surveys, also called questionnaires, can be conducted
with varying levels of interaction with the subjects of interest. Examples
are *omnibus surveys*, which are surveys covering a number of topics that
can be answered by a national and general sample of the population;
telephone surveys, which are typically calls to respondent's residences
and involve questioning the respondents over the phone; mail surveys,
which are sent by mail to selected respondents to be filled out and
sent back (or similarly, e-mail surveys sent via the internet); in-person or
face-to-face surveys, which involve direct questioning by an interviewer.
Questions asked can be very structured, especially in mail surveys, or
less structured, which is often the case in face-to-face surveys. The data
generated varies along a continuum of highly quantitative data for purposes of statistical analysis to highly qualitative data for sense making
and exploratory interpretation.

KEY WORDS Data gathering, information, measurement, research

IMPLICATIONS
The use of surveys in marketing research has been a long-held method of
conducting field studies. The choice of the specific method depends on
the research question, the population of interest, and its accessibility. As
all types of surveys involve a cost in collecting the information required,

in terms of time, effort, and money, the detailed planning of survey questions and layout must be based not only on the research objectives but also on its means of administration (e.g. e-mail, mail, or face to face).

APPLICATION AREAS AND FURTHER READINGS

Marketing Research

Deshpande, Rohit (1983). ' "Paradigms Lost": On Theory and Method in Research in Marketing,' *Journal of Marketing*, 47(4), Autumn, 101–110.

Hunt, Shelby D., Sparkman, Richard D., Jr., and Wilcox, James B. (1982). 'The Pretest in Survey Research: Issues and Preliminary Findings,' *Journal of Marketing Research*, 19(2), May, 269–273.

Schwarz, N., and Sudman, S. (eds.) (1996). *Answering Questions: Methodology for Determining Cognitive and Communicative Processes in Survey Research*. San Francisco: Jossey-Bass.

Sudman, S., and Bradburn, N. M. (1982). *Asking Questions: A Practical Guide to Questionnaire Design*. San Francisco: Jossey-Bass.

BIBLIOGRAPHY

Babbie, E. (1990). *Survey Research Methods*, 2nd edn. Belmont, Calif.: Wadsworth.

Krosnick, Jon A. (1999). 'Survey Research,' *Annual Review of Psychology*, 50, 537–567.

Bagozzi, R. P. (1994). 'Measurement in Marketing Research: Basic Principles of Questionnaire Design,' in R. P. Bagozzi (ed.), *Principles of Marketing Research*. Malden, Mass.: Blackwell Publishers, 1–49.

☐ **sustainability** *see* segmentation viability

■ **sustainable competitive advantage**

(also abbreviated as SCA)

DESCRIPTION

An element of a business or marketing strategy that provides a meaningful advantage over both existing and future competitors.

KEY INSIGHTS

While there are many possible strategic options that provide routes to a sustainable competitive advantage or SCA (e.g. quality, product design, value through low production costs, etc.) obtaining a highly effective SCA is often difficult to achieve as it means the SCA is both substantial and difficult to imitate or replicate by competitors. An SCA provides a firm with an advantage relative to competing firms that is able to be sustained by the firm and not easily eroded by competitors over time. As such, a firm may have a *competitive advantage* in that they are able to offer consumers greater value (e.g. through low prices or more benefits at a higher price) relative to that of competing firms, but such competitive advantages may not be sustainable, as when the rate and benefits of technological change outpace the firm's abilities to take advantage of such changes. Whatever strategic options are chosen by a firm, managers should recognize that the strategy should exploit organizational assets and competencies and neutralize weaknesses. Much of marketing strategy development and implementation is concerned with the pursuit of SCAs by a firm.

KEY WORDS Competitive advantage, sustainability, **marketing strategy**

IMPLICATIONS

Marketers should recognize that a major aim of a firm's marketing strategy should be to achieve and maintain a sustainable competitive advantage. While almost all SCAs may be only temporarily achieved in the long run, their pursuit should nevertheless be the foremost consideration in strategic decisions including the way the firm decides to compete (e.g. its product strategy, manufacturing strategy), its basis of competition in terms of assets and competencies, what is offered in terms of its value proposition, and its choice of where to compete in terms of product-market and competitor selection.

APPLICATION AREAS AND FURTHER READINGS

Marketing Strategy

Bharadwaj, Sundar G., Varadarajan, P. Rajan, and Fahy, John (1993). 'Sustainable Competitive Advantage in Service Industries: A Conceptual Model and Research Propositions,' *Journal of Marketing*, 57(4), October, 83–99.

Mata, Francisco J., Fuerst, William L., and Barney, Jay B. (1995). 'Information Technology and Sustained Competitive Advantage: A Resource-Based Analysis,' *MIS Quarterly*, 19(4), December, 487–505.

Fahy, J. (2002). 'A Resource-Based Analysis of Sustainable Competitive Advantage in a Global Environment,' *International Business Review*, 11(1), February, 57–77.

Williams, Jeffrey R. (1992). How Sustainable is your Competitive Advantage? Berkeley and Los Angeles: University of California Press.

Vorhies, Douglas W., and Morgan, Neil A. (2005). 'Benchmarking Marketing Capabilities for Sustainable Competitive Advantage,' *Journal of Marketing*, 69(1), January, 80–94.

BIBLIOGRAPHY

Ghemawat, Pankaj (1986). 'Sustainable Advantage,' *Harvard Business Review*, 64, September–October, 53–58.

Aaker, David A. (2005). *Strategic Market Management*. New York: John Wiley & Sons, Inc.

☐ switching cost *see* cost

■ SWOT analysis

DESCRIPTION

An internal and external assessment of a firm in terms of its strengths, weaknesses, opportunities, and threats of its operations in a market.

KEY INSIGHTS

As a situational scanning of a firm's internal and external environment, SWOT analysis helps match a firm's internal capabilities with its external prospects. It is a framework used extensively in marketing management as it entails an in-depth view of a firm. This involves looking at the political and legislative environment, socioeconomic variables, industry trends, technological advances, competitive advantages, competitors, and all organizational factors that may impact its strategy and plans. Strengths and weaknesses are related to factors in the firm's internal environment, whereas opportunities and threats are linked to its external environment.

KEY WORDS Strengths, weaknesses, opportunities, threats

IMPLICATIONS
A SWOT analysis can potentially provide some important insights into the factors that are encouraging or hampering the achievement of a firm's objectives. It can help answer questions related to where the firm is currently and where it is planning to move and it can be of value in helping direct a firm's strategy development.

APPLICATION AREAS AND FURTHER READINGS
Marketing Strategy
Brooksbank, Roger (1994). 'The Anatomy of Marketing Positioning Strategy,' *Marketing Intelligence & Planning*, 12(4), May, 10–14.
Li, Shuliang, Davies, Barry, Edwards, John, Kinman, Russell, and Duan, Yanqing (2002). 'Integrating Group Delphi, Fuzzy Logic and Expert Systems for Marketing Strategy Development: The Hybridisation and its Effectiveness,' *Marketing Intelligence & Planning*, 20(5), September, 273–284.

Marketing Research
Anwar, S. F., and Siddique, S. R. (2000). 'SWOT with a Quantitative Outlook: Revisiting the Analysis,' *Proceedings of the 2000 IEEE International Conference on Management of Innovation and Technology*, Institute of Business Administration, Dhaka University, 1, 128–133.

BIBLIOGRAPHY
Piercy, Nigel, and Giles, William (1989). 'Making SWOT Analysis Work,' *Marketing Intelligence & Planning*, 7(5), June, 5–7.

☐ symbiotic marketing *see* cooperative marketing
☐ symbolic adoption *see* adoption process

■ symbolic interaction theory

DESCRIPTION
Sociological theory or theories aimed at describing and explaining human action and interaction through the exchange of symbols or meaningful communication.

KEY INSIGHTS
Symbolic interaction theory, or more broadly symbolic interactionism as developed and advocated by Blumer (1969) and other researchers, adopts the view that individual action is based on the meanings that the action has for the individual, where such meanings arise out of social interactions, and where social actions are a result of the combination of individual actions. The emphasis of the theory is thus not on characterizing the objective reality of individuals and society but rather on the meanings individuals associate with subjectively defined objects.

KEY WORDS Symbolic interactionism, individual action, social interaction

IMPLICATIONS
In adopting a symbolic interaction perspective to product consumption and use, marketers can obtain potentially useful insights into complex areas of consumer behavior. In particular, the theoretical perspective suggests that there are psychological and social meanings that individual consumers attach to products, where such meanings are a result of the interactions between the individual and others and their associated actions with the products. Such knowledge, in turn, can inform the development of appropriate marketing strategies aimed at increasing a product's perceived value among consumers.

APPLICATION AREAS AND FURTHER READINGS
Marketing Strategy
Leigh, J. H., and Gabel, T. G. (1992). 'Symbolic Interactionism: Its Effects on Consumer Behavior and Implications for Marketing Strategy,' *Journal of Consumer Marketing*, 9(1), 27–38.

Consumer Behavior
Solomon, Michael R. (1983). 'The Role of Products as Social Stimuli: A Symbolic Interactionism Perspective,' *Journal of Consumer Research*, 10(3), December, 319–329.

BIBLIOGRAPHY
Blumer, H. (1969). *Symbolic Interactionism: Perspective and Method*. Englewood Cliffs, NJ: Prentice-Hall.

☐ syndicated research *see* marketing research

■ synergy
DESCRIPTION
A harmonious combination of parts that achieves coordination and which results in enhanced joint outcomes.

KEY INSIGHTS
Within many firms with marketing functions, improving cooperation between the firm's marketing department and other functions is viewed as important in achieving combined goals. An example is how many leading firms recognize that marketing and R&D functions need to work together in harmony in order for the firm to continue to be successful (Rein 2004).

KEY WORDS Enhanced performance

IMPLICATIONS
Synergy leads to increased customer value, lower operating costs, and reduced investment. A lack of synergy within a firm can result in tensions and struggles within functional areas of the firm. As marketing involves identifying and serving customers, the requirements of marketing often have implications for many other business functions, such as R&D, production, and finance. Harmoniously integrating the work of business

functions operating at the front and the back ends of the firm's business processes through improved organizational interactions can therefore provide a basis for greater marketing success.

APPLICATION AREAS AND FURTHER READINGS

Marketing Strategy

Wind, Yoram, and Robertson, Thomas S. (1983). 'Marketing Strategy: New Directions for Theory and Research,' *Journal of Marketing*, 47(2), Spring, 12–25.

Shani, David, and Chalasani, Sujana (1993). 'Exploiting Niches Using Relationship Marketing,' *Journal of Business & Industrial Marketing*, 8(4), December.

New Product Development

Griffin, Abbie, and Hauser, John R. (1996). 'Integrating R&D and Marketing: A Review and Analysis of the Literature,' *Journal of Product Innovation Management*, 13(3), May, 191.

Cooper, R. G., and Kleinschmidt, E. J. (1987). 'New Products: What Separates Winners from Losers?' *Journal of Product Innovation Management*, 4(3), September, 169.

Song, X. Michael, and Parry, Mark E. (1997). 'The Determinants of Japanese New Product Successes,' *Journal of Marketing Research*, 34(1), Special Issue on Innovation and New Products, February, 64–76.

BIBLIOGRAPHY

Rein, G. L. (2004). 'From Experience: Creating Synergy between Marketing and Research and Development,' *Journal of Product Innovation Management*, 21(1), 33–43.

■ systems theory

(also called general systems theory)

DESCRIPTION

A theory aimed at understanding, explaining, and predicting the behaviors of complex systems where the emphasis is on studying systems as a whole.

KEY INSIGHTS

Based on pioneering research by von Bertalanffy (1968) on general systems theory, the theory adopts a holistic view of systems behavior, where systems are more than the sums of their parts. In the theory, the term systems is viewed broadly and as such, encompasses the study of organizations, management, and marketing from perspectives including that of economics, psychology, and sociology. Systems theory views a system as being composed of interacting and interdependent parts where relationships emerge to form the whole.

KEY WORDS Systems, holistic perspective, complexity

IMPLICATIONS

Principles and concepts from systems theory can be potentially applied to obtain insights into many areas of marketing where systems are present. Such systems may be relatively focused and defined (e.g. departments within organizations) or quite broad (e.g. all of marketing practice). Recognizing principles including that where every system is an interaction of elements manifesting as a whole allows the potential to study relationships among elements and interactions among elements that may be otherwise overlooked without such a holistic view. Some services within marketing, for example, are sufficiently complex as to warrant consideration of a systems approach for measuring service quality.

APPLICATION AREAS AND FURTHER READINGS

Marketing Research
Sirgy, M. Joseph (1984). *Marketing as Social Behavior: A General Systems Theory*. New York: Praeger, 1984.
Johnson, R. L., Tsiros, M., and Lancioni, R. A. (1995). 'Measuring Service Quality: A Systems Approach,' *Journal of Services Marketing*, 9(5), 6–21.

BIBLIOGRAPHY
Bertalanffy, Ludwig von (1968). *General System Theory: Foundations, Development, Applications*. New York: George Braziller.
Bertalanffy, Ludwig von (1972). 'The History and Status of General Systems Theory,' *Academy of Management Journal*, 15(4), December, 407–426.

T

■ tactic

DESCRIPTION

Tools or actions designed to operationalize a higher-level strategy.

KEY INSIGHTS

Marketing plans which are established to meet strategic goals are, in essence, tactics. They can be viewed as short-term measures for addressing or solving a specific problem, such as increasing sales or enhancing the market share of a product.

KEY WORDS Tools, plans, operationalization, resource deployment

IMPLICATIONS

Tactics have direct implications on the firm and its consumers as they represent detailed plans of action for accomplishing higher-level objectives. While some marketing tactics may be perceived by consumers as acceptable marketing practice (e.g. see **price discrimination**), other tactics may be seen as unethical and manipulative (e.g. see **low-ball technique**).

APPLICATION AREAS AND FURTHER READINGS

Marketing Strategy

McKee, Daryl O., Varadarajan, P. Rajan, and Pride, William M. (1989). 'Strategic Adaptability and Firm Performance: A Market-Contingent Perspective,' *Journal of Marketing*, 53(3), July, 21–35.

Marketing Management

Hunt, Shelby D., and Chonko, Lawrence B. (1984). 'Marketing and Machiavellianism,' *Journal of Marketing*, 48(3), Summer, 30–42.

Robin, Donald P., and Reidenbach, R. Eric (1987).'Social Responsibility, Ethics, and Marketing Strategy: Closing the Gap between Concept and Application,' *Journal of Marketing*, 51(1), January, 44–58.

Services Marketing

Dibb, S., and Simkin, L. (1993). 'Strategy and Tactics: Marketing Leisure Facilities,' *Service Industries Journal*, 13(3), 110–124.

Consumer Behavior

Hoyer, Wayne D. (1984). 'An Examination of Consumer Decision Making for a Common Repeat Purchase Product,' *Journal of Consumer Research*, 11(3), December, 822–829.

Marketing Research

Thomas, J. S. (2001). 'A Methodology for Linking Customer Acquisition to Customer Retention,' *Journal of Marketing Research*, 38(2), 262–268.

Marcus, C. (1998). 'A Practical Yet Meaningful Approach to Customer Segmentation,' *Journal of Consumer Marketing*, 15(5), 494–504.

BIBLIOGRAPHY
Nagle, T. T., and Holden, R. K. (1995). *The Strategy and Tactics of Pricing*. Upper Saddle River, NJ: Prentice Hall.

■ tactical marketing

DESCRIPTION

An approach that moves marketing from the strategic to the operational level, designing and implementing plans for the short term.

KEY INSIGHTS

Marketing strategies are usually the driver of tactical marketing actions that influence the consumer directly, such as advertising programs and other operational actions that require marketing expenditure (Rust, Ambler, Carpenter, Kumar, and Srivastava 2004). In some firms, however, marketing strategy initiatives may take a back seat to that which is urgent, resulting in fire-fighting activity which resembles tactical marketing but where such activity may or may not be as effective as when it is based on a sound marketing strategy.

KEY WORDS Operationalization, short-term plans

IMPLICATIONS

Setting tactical marketing plans directly affects the firm's financial resources as it relates to marketing mix programs to be implemented. As such, marketers should seek to develop a sound understanding of tactical marketing approaches as it is clearly the implementation of the firm's marketing in the marketplace.

APPLICATION AREAS AND FURTHER READINGS

Marketing Strategy
McDonald, Malcolm (1989). *Ten Barriers to Marketing Planning*. Cranfield: Cranfield School of Management.

Marketing Management
McDonald, Malcolm, and Morris, Peter (2000). *The Marketing Plan in Colour: A Pictorial Guide for Managers*. Oxford: Butterworth-Heinemann.

Services Marketing
Zeithaml, Valarie A., Parasuraman, A., and Berry, Leonard L. (1985). 'Problems and Strategies in Services Marketing,' *Journal of Marketing*, 49(2), Spring, 33–46.

International Marketing
Samiee, Saeed, and Roth, Kendall (1992). 'The Influence of Global Marketing Standardization on Performance,' *Journal of Marketing*, 56(2), April, 1–17.
Rust, R. T., Ambler, T., Carpenter, G. S., Kumar, V., and Srivastava, R. K. (2004). 'Measuring Marketing Productivity: Current Knowledge and Future Directions,' *Journal of Marketing*, 68(4), 76–89.

BIBLIOGRAPHY
Rust, R. T., Ambler, T., Carpenter, G. S., Kumar, V., and Srivastava, R. K. (2004). 'Measuring Marketing Productivity: Current Knowledge and Future Directions,' *Journal of Marketing*, 68(4), 76–89.

☐ tailored marketing *see* one-to-one marketing

■ takeoff

DESCRIPTION

The transitional point in the life cycle of a new product or service where it moves from introduction to growth to achieve its viability.

KEY INSIGHTS

Takeoff is a concept in diffusion models of new products or services that represents an important stage in the product's market development. It is usually represented by a dramatic increase in sales. It requires an increase in support of the offering, through investing more resources where marketers make decisions on issues including investing in research on the product/process, spending more on promotion, and enhancing distribution (Golder and Tellis 1997).

KEY WORDS   New product introductions, growth, product viability

IMPLICATIONS

The concept of takeoff is in opposition to the assumption of constant and linear growth pattern of new products. Hence, takeoff and its implications have to be foreseen and accounted for from early planning stages. A better understanding of its nature, drivers, systematic patterns, and when it takes place can provide the marketer with highly beneficial insights for marketing planning and strategy development.

APPLICATION AREAS AND FURTHER READINGS

Marketing Strategy
Agarwal, Rajshree, and Bayus, Barry L. (2002). 'The Market Evolution and Sales Take-off of Product Innovations,' *Management Science*, 48, August, 1024-1041.

International Marketing
Tellis, G. J., Stremersch, S., and Yin, E. (2002). 'The International Takeoff of New Products: The Role of Economics, Culture, and Country Innovativeness,' *Report of the Marketing Science Institute Cambridge Massachusetts*, ISSU 121.

Marketing Research
Tellis, Gerard J., Golder, Peter N., and Foster, Joseph A. (2004). 'Predicting Sales Takeoff for Whirlpool's New Personal Valet,' *Marketing Science*, 23(2), 180-191.

BIBLIOGRAPHY
Golder, Peter N., and Tellis, Gerard J. (1997). 'Will It Ever Fly? Modeling the Takeoff of Really New Consumer Durables,' *Marketing Science*, 16(3), 256-270.

□ target costing *see* pricing strategies

■ target marketing

DESCRIPTION

A marketing approach involving evaluations of different market segments' attractiveness and selecting one or more segments to enter.

KEY INSIGHTS

Target marketing involves the use of market segmentation for subsequently directing marketing efforts at one or more specific groups of customers considered beneficial or desirable by the marketer. The aim of target marketing is to identify the most viable segments—ones where a firm can profitably generate the most customer value and sustain such value over time. Through such focus, marketers are able to develop and provide offerings that may be positioned as attractive or appealing to the target market.

KEY WORDS Segment attractiveness

IMPLICATIONS
Target marketing necessarily involves effective targeting, one of the most important concepts in marketing. As such, marketers should strive to develop a strong working knowledge of targeting strategies along with a solid understanding of targeting's conceptual and practical relationship with segmentation and positioning as a means to ensure the development and pursuit of viable marketing strategies.

APPLICATION AREAS AND FURTHER READINGS
Marketing Strategy
Freeman, K. M. (1992). 'Target Marketing: The Logic of It All,' *Journal of Consumer Marketing*, 9(3), 15–18.

Marketing Management
Smith, N. Craig, and Martin, Elizabeth Cooper (1997). 'Ethics and Target Marketing: The Role of Product Harm and Consumer Vulnerability,' *Journal of Marketing*, 61(3), July, 1–20.

Marketing Research
Rossi, Peter E., McCulloch, Robert E., and Allenby, Greg M. (1996). 'The Value of Purchase History Data in Target Marketing,' *Marketing Science*, 15(4), 321–340.
Zahavi, J., and Levin, N. (1997). 'Applying Neural Computing to Target Marketing,' *Journal of Direct Marketing*, 11(1), 5–22.

Consumer Behavior
Aaker, J. L., Brumbaugh, A. M., and Grier, S. A. (2000). 'Nontarget Markets and Viewer Distinctiveness: The Impact of Target Marketing on Advertising Attitudes,' *Journal of Consumer Psychology*, 9(3), 127–140.
Ringold, Debra Jones (1995). 'Social Criticisms of Target Marketing,' *American Behavioral Scientist*, 38(4), 578–592.

BIBLIOGRAPHY
Dibb, Sally, and Simkin, Lyndon (1996). *The Market Segmentation Workbook: Target Marketing for Marketing Managers*. London: Routledge.

☐ **target profit pricing** *see* pricing strategies

■ **targeting**

DESCRIPTION
The process of selecting one or more market segments that the firm decides to serve with its offerings.

KEY INSIGHTS
Targeting involves the process of defining the specific needs and profiles of customer market segments and selecting from those segments

the ones to target with appropriate offerings, strategies, and marketing programs. The process of targeting involves a number of strategies from which marketers may select, including concentrated targeting (e.g. focusing on a particular niche), undifferentiated targeting (e.g. adopting a mass marketing strategy), and differentiated targeting (e.g. adopting a selective marketing strategy). Advertising, along with many other forms of marketing communication, for example, may involve targeting particular groups of consumers with particular messages which are specifically aimed at audiences possessing the characteristics of such consumer groups.

KEY WORDS Segment selection

IMPLICATIONS
At a strategic level, making choices about targeting strategies to use in relation to chosen customer segments is something that can have a major influence on a firm's overall operations in the selected markets. At an operational level, appropriate targeting in, say, advertising has the potential to improve the advertiser's return on investment and make an advertising campaign efficient in accomplishing its objectives.

APPLICATION AREAS AND FURTHER READINGS
Marketing Strategy
McLauglin, R. (2000). 'Targeting Teens,' *Target Marketing*, 23(1), 84–87.
Moschis, G. P., Lee, E., and Mathur, A. (1997). 'Targeting the Mature Market: Opportunities and Challenges,' *Journal of Consumer Marketing*, 14(4), 282–293.
Mahajan, Vijay, and Muller, Eitan (1998). 'When is it Worthwhile Targeting the Majority instead of the Innovators in a New Product Launch?' *Journal of Marketing Research*, 35, November, 488–495.

Marketing Research
Sivadas, E., Grewal, R., and Kellaris, J. (1998). 'The Internet as a Micro Marketing Tool: Targeting Consumers through Preferences Revealed in Music Newsgroup Usage,' *Journal of Consumer Research*, 41, 179–186.

BIBLIOGRAPHY
Kotler, Philip, and Armstrong, Gary (2006). *Principles of Marketing*, 11th edn. Upper Saddle River, NJ: Pearson Education, Inc.

☐ **technological environment** *see* macroenvironment

■ **telemarketing**
(also called telephone marketing)

DESCRIPTION
A direct marketing approach that involves using the telephone as a medium to market products or services to consumers.

KEY INSIGHTS
Telemarketing is a form of direct marketing (see **direct marketing**). There are two forms of telemarketing: inbound and outbound. In inbound telemarketing, prospective customers call the company to seek

assistance to get a product or ask for information in response to an advertisement or offer (see **inbound marketing**). In outbound telemarketing, the company proactively calls potential customers, which can be businesses or consumers, to offer its product or service to them (see **outbound marketing**). Some companies use their own telemarketing built-in capabilities whereas others use other telemarketing firms when it is more cost effective.

KEY WORD Telephone

IMPLICATIONS
The telemarketing approach is an 'invisible medium' that has grown to be largely and successfully used as a direct marketing technique. Its advantage to a firm is that its high cost can be offset by the maximum consumer selectivity and interactivity it offers. The power to capture the attention of the prospect and hold them in place represents both its strengths and weaknesses, the latter being because if the message is poorly timed, perceived, or executed, it can end long-term customer relationships (Nash 2000).

APPLICATION AREAS AND FURTHER READINGS
Marketing Strategy
Webster, Frederick E., Jr. (1992). 'The Changing Role of Marketing in the Corporation,' *Journal of Marketing*, 56(4), October, 1–17.
Boyd, D. E. (1996). 'Defensive Marketing's Use of Post-Purchase Telecommunications to Create Competitive Advantages: A Strategic Analysis,' *Journal of Consumer Marketing*, 13(1), 26–34.

Marketing Research
Talvinen, J. M. (1995). 'Information Systems in Marketing: Identifying Opportunities for New Applications,' *European Journal of Marketing*, 29(1), 8.

Public Policy
Petty, R. D. (2000). 'Marketing without Consent: Consumer Choice and Costs, Privacy, and Public Policy,' *Journal of Public Policy and Marketing*, 19(1), 42–53.

BIBLIOGRAPHY
Nash, Edward L. (1982). *Direct Marketing: Strategy, Planning, Execution*. New York: McGraw-Hill.

☐ **telephone marketing** *see* telemarketing

■ telescoping

DESCRIPTION
Among individuals asked to place the time of a past event, the systematic tendency for individuals to recall that recent events occurred farther back in time and distant events occurred more recently than is actually the case.

KEY INSIGHTS
Telescoping, where individuals systematically err in their recall and reporting of the timing of events, is a generally pervasive phenomenological tendency among individuals. Backward telescoping is where

individuals recall that recent events occurred farther back in time than is actually the case. Forward telescoping is where individuals recall that distant events occurred more recently in time than is actually the case. An example of forward telescoping is when a respondent who is asked if she had purchased an expensive pair of shoes in the past year recalls and reports on an expensive shoe purchase that actually occurred eighteen months prior.

KEY WORDS Event recall, reporting, time

IMPLICATIONS
Telescoping has important implications for marketing researchers concerned with accurately understanding and predicting consumer behavior. For example, research by Morwitz (1997) suggests that on average, consumers underestimate the time since purchasing a durable good. Further, findings by Morwitz (1997) suggest that the magnitude of forward telescoping errors increases and the propensity to make backward telescoping errors decreases with the time since the purchase of a good. Marketing researchers should be cognizant of telescoping errors in recall and reporting since telescoping can have a significant effect on future purchase intentions. At the same time, marketing researchers should also consider that telescoping biases are observed to vary across different demographic segments.

APPLICATION AREAS AND FURTHER READINGS
Marketing Research
Cook, W. A. (1987). 'Telescoping and Memory's Other Tricks,' *Journal of Advertising Research*, 27, February–March, RC5–RC8.
Morwitz, V. G. (1997). 'Why Consumers Don't Always Accurately Predict their own Future Behavior,' *Marketing Letters* (New York), 8(1), 57–70.

BIBLIOGRAPHY
Morwitz, Vicki G. (1997). 'It Seems like Only Yesterday: The Nature and Consequences of Telescoping Errors in Marketing Research,' *Journal of Consumer Psychology*, 6(1), 1–29.

■ temperament theory

DESCRIPTION
A theory that models human behavior into personality types, where it predisposes individuals to think, act, relate, learn, and be motivated in systematically varying ways.

KEY INSIGHTS
Temperament theory falls within the realms of behavioral studies and psychological influences on personalities. The different dimensions of temperament, such as emotionality and sociability, are tested in research for their influence on receptivity to marketing communication activities, such as advertising responses, consumer preferences and lifestyles (Moore and Homer 2000).

KEY WORDS Personality, behavior

IMPLICATIONS

As marketing involves a study of consumer psychology in understanding behavior, attitudes, and forecasted actions, a greater knowledge of temperament theory-based research on personality types may potentially provide the marketer with fresh insights which are ultimately useful for developing segmentation and positioning strategies.

APPLICATION AREAS AND FURTHER READINGS

Marketing Strategy
Penrose, Edith Tilton (1995). *The Theory of the Growth of the Firm.* Oxford: Oxford University Press.

Marketing Management
Volkema, R. J., and Gorman, R. H. (1998). 'The Influence of Cognitive-Based Group Composition on Decision-Making Process and Outcome,' *Journal of Management Studies* (Oxford), 35(1), 105–121.

International Marketing
Samli, A. Coskun (1995). *International Consumer Behavior: Its Impact on Marketing Strategy Development.* Westport, Conn.: Quorum Books.

Marketing Research
Walle, A. H. (2001). 'Machiavelli, Humanistic Empiricism and Marketing Research,' *Management Decision*, 39(5/6), 403–406.

Consumer Behavior
Grubb, Edward L., and Grathwohl, Harrison L. (1967). 'Consumer Self-Concept, Symbolism and Market Behavior: A Theoretical Approach,' *Journal of Marketing*, 31(4), 1, October, 22–27.

BIBLIOGRAPHY
Moore, D. J., and Homer, P. M. (2000). 'Dimensions of Temperament: Affect Intensity and Consumer Lifestyles,' *Journal of Consumer Psychology*, 9(4), 231–232.

☐ **ten foot rule** *see* marketing, rules of

■ **ten percent, rule of**

DESCRIPTION
The generalization that it is almost impossible for any single research study to come up with a variable which accounts for more than ten percent of the variation in any particular measure of business performance.

KEY INSIGHTS
Put forth by Wensley (1997), the rule of ten percent (or rule of 10%) is a generalization that draws upon decades of research on factors that seek to explain business performance. In particular, reviews of such studies lead to the generally accepted conclusion among marketing researchers that the number of factors which account for business performance is so many that it is extremely unlikely that any single research study will ever be able to explain more than 10% of the variability in any business performance measure (e.g. return on investment). While the inclusion of additional measures has been shown to explain a considerably greater

amount of variation in performance between different businesses—in some cases between 25% and 33%—the disadvantage of the complexity introduced by such studies is that they present a far greater challenge to providing managerially useful guidance.

KEY WORDS **Marketing research**, firm performance, management guidance

IMPLICATIONS
Based upon the rule of 10%, marketers should be wary of pursuing strategies based on the assumption that there exists a simple relationship between a particular business approach and the achievement of strong business performance. Instead, marketers should recognize that there are, more often than not, multiple and interacting factors that influence business performance and any strategy based on the pursuit of a single approach to achieve success is likely to be poorly guided and ultimately insufficient.

APPLICATION AREAS AND FURTHER READINGS
Marketing Strategy
Vining, A., and Meredith, L. (2000). 'Metachoice for Strategic Analysis,' *European Management Journal*, 18(6), 605–618.

BIBLIOGRAPHY
Wensley, Robin (1997). 'Explaining Success: The Rule of Ten Percent and the Example of Market Share,' *Business Strategy Review*, 8(1), 63–70.

■ test marketing

DESCRIPTION
A pilot trial of a firm's offering on a small scale in actual or simulated market conditions at a time before its full-scale introduction and commercialization.

KEY INSIGHTS
The aim of test marketing is to understand better the market's acceptance of the offering and how well the marketing will perform if fully commercialized. Test marketing further allows the opportunity for fine-tuning the marketing strategy and marketing mix elements developed in support of a new product development effort. (See also **new product development.**) Test marketing can be done in certain representative geographic areas in the market or otherwise done through the use of product development simulation models.

KEY WORDS Market testing, new product introduction

IMPLICATIONS
The aim of market testing before introducing the new offering to the market on a much larger scale is to reconcile the difference between what marketers think consumers want and what consumers actually want. Test marketing can help define the difference or similarity in order to improve any of the marketing mix elements before commercial market introduction. Problems in using simulated test marketing techniques may

arise, however, out of the inability of some models and techniques to capture realistic market dynamics. On the other hand, when an offering is test marketed in the actual market, there is the risk that competing firms may become aware of the firm's plans and learn from the effort in a way that gives the competitor a head start in developing a competitive response.

APPLICATION AREAS AND FURTHER READINGS

Marketing Strategy
Mohammed, Salleh A., and Easingwood, C. (1993). 'Why European Financial Institutions do not Test-Market New Consumer Products,' *International Journal of Bank Marketing*, 11(3), 23.

Marketing Research
Silk, Alvin J., and Urban, Glen L. (1978). 'Pre-Test-Market Evaluation of New Packaged Goods: A Model and Measurement Methodology,' *Journal of Marketing Research*, 15(2), May, 171–191.
Urban, Glen L., and Katz, Gerald M. (1983). 'Pre-Test-Market Models: Validation and Managerial Implications,' *Journal of Marketing Research*, 20(3), August, 221–234.
Clancy, Kevin J., Shulman, Robert S., and Wolf, Marianne (1994). *Simulated Test Marketing: Technology for Launching Successful New Products*. New York: Lexington Books.
Cameron, Trudy A., and James, Michelle D. (1987). 'Estimating Willingness to Pay from Survey Data: An Alternative Pre-Test-Market Evaluation Procedure,' *Journal of Marketing Research*, 24(4), November, 389–395.

BIBLIOGRAPHY
Klompmaker, J. E., Hughes, G., and Haley, R. (1976). 'Test Marketing in New Product Development,' *Harvard Business Review*, 54, 128–138.

■ testing effect

DESCRIPTION
Any effect of testing or test taking on the responses of an individual.

KEY INSIGHTS
In the measurement of responses of individuals exposed to some stimuli or experimental treatment, respondent views are often obtained through comparisons of pre-treatment and post-treatment tests. Yet, such an approach is vulnerable to a testing effect where the pre-treatment test may sensitize and distort consumer reactions to the treatment itself.

Another type of testing effect is where, relative to information that is to be remembered by an individual, the likelihood of retrieving such information from memory is enhanced when an individual engages in periodic self-testing activity.

KEY WORDS Testing, measurement, **bias**

IMPLICATIONS
Marketers engaged in marketing research should be aware of possible testing effects adversely influencing or biasing the findings and interpretations of research studies. Designing research studies that control for such effects, such as through studies that include the use of control groups, may be beneficial in obtaining more meaningful research results.

APPLICATION AREAS AND FURTHER READINGS

Marketing Research
Banks, Seymour (1964). 'Designing Marketing Research to Increase Validity,' *Journal of Marketing*, 28(4), October, 32–40.
Lohse, G. L., Bellman, S., and Johnson, E. J. (2000). 'Consumer Buying Behavior on the Internet: Findings from Panel Data,' *Journal of Interactive Marketing*, 14 (1), 15–29.

Marketing Education
Deck, D. William, Jr. (1998). 'The Effects of Frequency of Testing on College Students in a Principles of Marketing Course', Ph.D. Dissertation, Virginia Tech.

BIBLIOGRAPHY
Churchill, Gilbert A., and Iacobucci, Dawn (2005). *Marketing Research: Methodological Foundations*, 9th edn. Mason, Oh.: Thomson-South-Western.
Glover, J. A. (1989). 'The "Testing" Phenomenon: Not Gone But Nearly Forgotten,' *Journal of Educational Psychology*, 81, 392–399.

☐ text message marketing *see* mobile marketing

☐ theory . . . *see specific entries, e.g.* X, theory

☐ theory of/theories of . . . *see specific entries, e.g.* marketing, theory of

☐ third sector marketing *see* non-profit marketing

☐ through-the-line marketing *see* above-the-line marketing; below-the-line marketing

■ top-down marketing

DESCRIPTION
An approach to market analysis, market definition, and marketing strategy development that tends to specify markets in terms of competitive capabilities and resource transferability.

KEY INSIGHTS
The top-down marketing approach reflects the need of corporate and business level management to understand the capacity of a business unit to compete and apply resources to secure a sustainable competitive advantage (Day 1981). The other approach to market analysis is a bottom-up approach emphasizing customer requirements or usage patterns when defining markets (see **bottom-up marketing**). While the latter is employed by marketing planners and programme managers within the framework of a chosen product market, the top-down approach is more at a corporate strategic planning level.

KEY WORDS Capabilities, resources

IMPLICATIONS
The top-down approach involves viewing markets as arenas of profitable competition where corporate resources can be utilized to achieve differential advantage (Day 1981). Using this approach involves defining the scope of the business, the broad strategic thrust of each strategic business

unit, its opportunities in new markets as well as current and forecasted performance within served markets. Achieving a clearer, deeper, and more comprehensive market definition and understanding, however, often calls for integrating the top-down and the bottom-up approaches to market analysis and marketing strategy development.

APPLICATION AREAS AND FURTHER READINGS

Marketing Strategy

Jaworski, B. J., and Kohli, A. K. (1996). 'Market Orientation: Review, Refinement, and Roadmap,' *Journal of Market Focused Management*, 1(2), 119–136.

Hutt, Michael D., Reingen, Peter H., and Ronchetto, John R., Jr. (1988). 'Tracing Emergent Processes in Marketing Strategy Formation,' *Journal of Marketing*, 52(1), January, 4–19.

Marketing Management

McDonald, Malcolm, and Morris, Peter (2000). *The Marketing Plan in Colour: A Pictorial Guide for Managers*. Oxford: Butterworth-Heinemann.

Mantrala, Murali K., Sinha, Prabhakant, and Zoltners, Andris A. (1992). 'Impact of Resource Allocation Rules on Marketing Investment-Level Decisions and Profitability,' *Journal of Marketing Research*, 29(2), May, 162–175.

Ambler, T. (2000). 'Marketing Metrics,' *Business Strategy Review*, 11(2), 59–66.

BIBLIOGRAPHY

Day, George S. (1981). 'The Product Life Cycle: Analysis and Applications Issues,' *Journal of Marketing*, 45(4), Autumn, 60–67.

Park, C. Whan, and Smith, Daniel C. (1989). 'Product-Level Choice: A Top-Down or Bottom-Up Process?' *Journal of Consumer Research*, 16, December, 289–299.

■ total integrated marketing

DESCRIPTION

An integrated approach for firms to manage change in the marketplace and maintain competitiveness by integrating marketing imperatives into all functions in the firm creating an integrated system.

KEY INSIGHTS

Rather than viewing marketing as the domain of the marketing department of a firm, the total integrated marketing approach establishes the primacy of marketing by requiring that every single person in the firm work toward winning and keeping customers. The lack of integration of all the firms' capabilities towards this goal is considered to be the main reason why firms fail (Hulbert, Capon, and Piercy 2003).

KEY WORDS Integration, functional integration

IMPLICATIONS

The total integrated marketing approach implies dropping long-held marketing assumptions and moving towards accepting an integrated change process aimed at improving profits and increasing sales. In adopting the total integrated marketing approach, the firm puts the focus of marketing within the implicit functions of each of the firm's departments. Attracting and keeping customers becomes the overriding goal emanating from a customer-centric organization, with integrated planning towards that starting at the firm's top level.

APPLICATION AREAS AND FURTHER READINGS

Marketing Strategy
Moenart, R. K., Souder, W. E., De Meyer, A., and Deschoolmester, D. (1994). 'R&D–Marketing Integration Mechanisms, Communication Flows, and Innovation Success,' *Journal of Product Innovation Management*, 11, 31–45.

Marketing Management
Parry, M. E., and Song, X. M. (1993). 'Determinants of R&D: Marketing Integration in High Tech Japanese Firms,' *Journal of Product Innovation Management*, 10(1), 4–22.

Services Marketing
Ho, K., Jacobs, L., and Cox, J. (2003). 'Go away! Don't Bother me! I Don't Want your Money!' *Journal of Services Marketing*, 17(4/5), 379–392.

Sales
Piercy, N. F., and Lane, N. (2005). 'Strategic Imperatives for Transformation in the Conventional Sales Organization,' *Journal of Change Management*, 5(3), 249–266.
Piercy, N. F., and Lane, N. (2003). 'Transformation of the Traditional Salesforce: Imperatives for Intelligence, Interface and Integration,' *Journal of Marketing Management* (Helensburgh), 19(5/6), 563–582.

BIBLIOGRAPHY
Hulbert, James M., Capon, Noel, and Piercy, Nigel (2003). *Total Integrated Marketing: Breaking the Bounds of the Function*. New York: Free Press.

☐ **trade marketing** *see* business-to-business marketing

☐ **trade secret** *see* intellectual property

☐ **trademark** *see* intellectual property

■ traditional marketing

(also called by-the-book marketing or one-to-many marketing)

DESCRIPTION
The use of marketing approaches that rely on conventional wisdom and where such practices have typically proven to be sufficiently effective in the past.

KEY INSIGHTS
Such a marketing approach, which may include the use of traditional mass promotion (a one-to-many marketing approach), may be adopted by organizations that are interested in relying on traditional practices for their marketing but they may miss out on opportunities in pioneering new approaches and can be vulnerable to competitors who do so.

KEY WORDS Conventional wisdom, tradition

IMPLICATIONS
While an organization may embrace tradition in selecting its marketing approaches, the current rate of change in marketing practice suggests that marketers should not discount adopting pioneering new approaches—even when pursuing the firm's traditional strategic marketing objectives. In particular, marketers should continually seek to

identify and understand new approaches to marketing in order to be able to evaluate their costs and benefits relative to approaches traditionally adopted and pursued by the organization.

APPLICATION AREAS AND FURTHER READINGS

Online Marketing
Scullin, S. S., Fjermestad, J., Jr, and Romano, N. C. (2004). 'E-relationship Marketing: Changes in Traditional Marketing as an Outcome of Electronic Customer Relationship Management,' *Journal of Enterprise Information Management*, 17(6), 410–415.

Social Marketing
Shrum, L. J., Lowrey, Tina M., and McCarty, John A. (1995). 'Applying Social and Traditional Marketing Principles to the Reduction of Household Waste,' *American Behavioral Scientist*, 38(4), 646–657.
Sleich, K. (1986). 'Traditional Marketing of Livestock and Meat in West Africa: Experiences from the Ivory Coast,' *Quarterly Journal of International Agriculture*, 25, 6–21.

BIBLIOGRAPHY
Rowsom, M. (1998). 'Bridging the Gap from Traditional Marketing to Electronic Commerce,' *Direct Marketing*, 60(9), 23–25.

☐ **trait centrality** *see* warm/cold effect
☐ **trait validity** *see* validity
☐ **transaction cost** *see* cost

■ transaction cost theory

DESCRIPTION
A theory that departs from the view of the firm as a complex structure of marketing exchanges to one that is based on governance mechanisms that improve efficiency of operations and internal resource allocations, reducing transaction costs.

KEY INSIGHTS
The theory as applied to marketing addresses mechanisms for interorganizational governance in marketing channels. It accounts for the efficiency implications of organizing relationships in marketing channels through means for reducing potential costs related to carrying out safeguarding, adaptation, and evaluation processes of marketing relationships (Heide 1994).

KEY WORDS Governance, channels, interorganizational relationships

IMPLICATIONS
A greater knowledge of transaction cost theory-based research can potentially assist the marketer with the more effective structuring of inter-firm relationships. Decisions about where decision-making should lie, for example, are focal issues which are directly assessed with the transaction cost theory perspective.

APPLICATION AREAS AND FURTHER READINGS

Marketing Strategy

Chiles, Todd H., and McMackin, John F. (1996). 'Integrating Variable Risk Preferences, Trust, and Transaction Cost Economics,' *Academy of Management Review*, 21(1), January, 73–99.

Rangan, V. K., Corey, E. R., and Cespedes, F. (1993). 'Transaction Cost Theory: Inferences from Clinical Field Research on Down Stream Vertical Integration,' *Organization Science*, 4, 454–477.

Marketing Management

Heide, Jan B., and John, George (1992). 'Do Norms Matter in Marketing Relationships?' *Journal of Marketing*, 56(2), April, 32–44.

Rugman, A. M., and Verbeke, A. (1992). 'A Note on the Transnational Solution and the Transaction Cost Theory of Multinational Strategic Management,' *Journal of International Business Studies*, 23(4), 761–771.

International Marketing

Hennart, Jean-François (1991). 'The Transaction Costs Theory of Joint Ventures: An Empirical Study of Japanese Subsidiaries in the United States,' *Management Science*, 37(4), April, 483–497.

Business-to-Business Marketing

Dahlstrom, Robert, and Nygaard, Arne (1999). 'An Empirical Investigation of Ex Post Transaction Costs in Franchised Distribution Channels,' *Journal of Marketing Research*, 36(2), May, 160–170.

BIBLIOGRAPHY

Heide, J. B. (1994). 'Interorganizational Governance in Marketing Channels,' *Journal of Marketing*, 58(1), 71–91.

Williamson, O. E. (1998). 'Transaction Cost Economics: How it Works; Where it is Headed,' *De Economist*, 146(1), 23–58.

Williamson, O. E. (1979). 'Transaction-Cost Economics: The Governance of Contractual Relations,' *Journal of Law and Economics*, 22, October, 233–261.

■ transactional marketing

DESCRIPTION

Marketing focused on transactions with customers as opposed to ongoing relationships with customers.

KEY INSIGHTS

The emphasis of transactional marketing is on single transactions or individual exchange events. By being only concerned with each individual transaction independent of other transactions with a customer, the marketing approach is not concerned with the firm's relationship with the customer. In business-to-business marketing, it is an approach to marketing that relies on selling to intermediaries in one-off transactions, where competition between those intermediaries creates higher value for the transaction marketer and improved choice for the end buyer. Compared to relationship marketing that relies on maintaining interdependence and partnering between value chain players, transaction marketing focuses on the independence of marketing actors. This allows freedom of choice to those marketing actors to choose transaction partners on the basis of self-interest when making their decisions (Sheth and Parvatiyar 1994).

KEY WORDS Individual transactions

IMPLICATIONS
In business-to-business marketing, the transactional marketing approach allows for bargaining and bidding and resultant efficiencies in support of lower-cost purchases. The rationale behind using it is that competition and self-interest are the drivers of creating value. Relationships between marketing actors are kept at a distance. It is challenged by the emergence of relationship marketing, where it is based on creating higher quality and reducing transactional costs by sharing resources, hence improving marketing productivity (Sheth and Sisodia 1995). In consumer marketing, transaction marketing is also challenged by relationship marketing, where the view is that, in certain product markets, it can be more expensive to attract new customers than to keep existing customers.

APPLICATION AREAS AND FURTHER READINGS
Marketing Strategy
Webster, F. E., Jr. (1992). 'The Changing Role of Marketing in the Corporation,' *Journal of Marketing*, 56, October, 1–17.

Business-to-Business Marketing
Cornette, Guy, and Pontier, Suzanne (2002). 'Transactional Marketing versus Relationship Marketing: The US Automobile Market Evolution,' *International Journal of Automotive Technology and Management*, 2(2), 177–189.

BIBLIOGRAPHY
Sheth, Jagdish N., and Parvatiyar, Atul (1994). *Relationship Marketing: Theory, Methods and Applications*, Atlanta: Center for Relationship Marketing.
Sheth, Jagdish N., and Sisodia, Rajendra S. (1995). 'Feeling the Heat,' *Marketing Management*, 4, Fall, 8–23.

☐ **trial** *see* adoption process

■ tribal marketing

DESCRIPTION
A marketing approach which presents consumers with offerings that not only satisfy their specific needs for it, but also allows them to connect to others.

KEY INSIGHTS
The tribal marketing approach focuses on the importance for consumers to link in to their surroundings and to a communal co-presence through the offerings they consume. It is represented through a micro-social group of individuals who share similar experiences and emotions and form links together in loosely interconnected communities (Cova and Cova 2002).

KEY WORDS Connecting, community

IMPLICATIONS
The tribal marketing approach is most suitable for specific products and services that can hold people together, strengthening community links

and fostering a sense of tribal integration and belongingness (Muniz and O'Guinn 2001). (See **brand community**.) In adopting the approach, the marketer should then focus on the creation of a linking value rather than a use value particular only to such products and services. In a sense, the tribal marketing approach abandons certain traditional notions of marketing, as it emphasizes the importance of identifying shared experience of consumers in their tribal groupings and puts such knowledge at the center of the firm's business model and marketing.

APPLICATION AREAS AND FURTHER READINGS

Marketing Strategy
Cova, B. (1997). 'Community and Consumption: Towards a Definition of the "Linking Value" of Product or Services,' *European Journal of Marketing*, 31, 297–316.

Marketing Research
Cova, B., and Cova, V. (2001). 'Tribal Aspects of Postmodern Consumption Research: The Case of French In-line Roller Skaters,' *Journal of Consumer Behavior*, 1(1), 67–76.

BIBLIOGRAPHY
Cova, B., and Cova, V. (2002). 'Tribal Marketing: The Tribalisation of Society and Its Impact on the Conduct of Marketing,' *European Journal of Marketing*, 36(5/6), 595–620.
Muniz, A. M., and O'Guinn, T. C. (2001), 'Brand Community,' *Journal of Consumer Research*, 27(4), March, 412–32.

■ trickle down theory

DESCRIPTION

A theory of fashion propagation or diffusion positing a social pattern of influence in which each social class is influenced by a higher social class.

KEY INSIGHTS

Proposed and developed by Simmel (1904), trickle down theory posits a social class influence on fashion propagation and change, where new styles are first adopted by upper class elites and then spread gradually to lower classes. In this context, fashion is viewed as a social institution that allows individuals to emulate others (e.g. others of higher social status) as well as differentiate themselves from others as a member of a particular social class or group. While the theory has received considerable attention in fashion research, it is now generally accepted among fashion researchers that fashions propagate more across social classes rather than down (or up). Nevertheless, the trickle down theory remains important in fashion research due to its pioneering nature, its conceptual development, and its use in supporting subsequent and related explanations of fashion diffusion and change.

KEY WORDS Fashion, diffusion, social class

IMPLICATIONS

Marketers seeking to understand better the process of diffusion for particular fashion goods can potentially benefit from a greater knowledge of trickle down theory as it provides a basis for developing similar or complementary explanations and an approach for comparing with alternative or competing explanations.

APPLICATION AREAS AND FURTHER READINGS

Consumer Behavior

King, C. W. (1963). 'Fashion Adoption: A Rebuttal to the "Trickle Down Theory,"' in G. B. Sproles (ed.), *Perspectives of Fashion*, Minneapolis: Burgess Publishing Company, 31–39.

Sproles, George B. (1981). 'Analyzing Fashion Life Cycles: Principles and Perspectives,' *Journal of Marketing*, 45(4), Autumn, 116–124.

Law, K. M., Zhang, Z. M., and Leung, C. S. (2004). 'Fashion Change and Fashion Consumption: The Chaotic Perspective,' *Journal of Fashion Marketing and Management*, 8(4), 362–374.

BIBLIOGRAPHY

Simmel, Georg (1904). 'Fashion,' *International Quarterly*, 10, 130–155.

☐ **txt marketing** *see* mobile marketing

U

■ unconventional marketing

(also called on-the-edge marketing, contrarian marketing, or radical marketing)

DESCRIPTION

Marketing approaches that depart from accepted standard practice in marketing.

KEY INSIGHTS

A firm's marketing approach is clearly unconventional when it is contrary to the practices of other firms in the same industry or market. Durgee (1992) calls this *contrarian marketing*, where a firm adopts a marketing approach that is diametrically opposed to contemporary marketing strategies. Firms adopting unconventional marketing approaches may find that going 'against the grain' of standard practice or commonly defined attributes relative to a product or service category, for example, enables the firm to position its offering in a nonconformist way. According to Hill and Rifkin (1999), any marketing approach or strategy that challenges existing long-held conventional marketing approaches can be considered to be 'radical marketing,' with guerrilla marketing being a notable example (see **guerrilla marketing**).

KEY WORDS Counter-intuitive marketing, non-traditional marketing

IMPLICATIONS

The changing face and role of marketing in a global environment characterized by relative instability has made it inevitable that new marketing approaches, strategies, and tactics will evolve. While the benefits of any unconventional marketing approach ultimately depend on the nature of the offering and the target audience, the adoption of such approaches may ultimately depend on how conservative the firm is in trying and accepting new means of reaching and engaging customers.

APPLICATION AREAS AND FURTHER READINGS

Marketing Strategy

Sutton, R. (2002). 'Ready for Radical Marketing,' *Credit Union Magazine*, 34, September.

Clancy, Kevin, and Krieg, Peter (2000). *Counter-Intuitive Marketing*. New York: The Free Press.

BIBLIOGRAPHY

Durgee, Jeffrey F. (1992). 'Contrarian Marketing,' *Journal of Consumer Marketing*, 9, Winter, 51–59.

Hill, Sam, and Rifkin, Glenn (1999). *Radical Marketing: From Harvard to Harley, Lessons from Ten that Broke the Rules and Made it Big.* New York: HarperBusiness.

☐ **undercover marketing** *see* stealth marketing
☐ **under-the-radar marketing** *see* stealth marketing

■ undifferentiated marketing

DESCRIPTION

A marketing approach that forgoes segmentation and product tailoring, targeting an audience with a single offering and a single marketing mix.

KEY INSIGHTS

Undifferentiated marketing was a prevailing approach of the product-oriented era of marketing, where businesses viewed the marketplace as an aggregate market and, hence, focused on the common needs of customers rather than their differences. Today, such an approach is often associated with serving commodity markets where firms strive to be a low-cost producer (Jain 1985).

KEY WORDS Single offering

IMPLICATIONS

As a marketing approach, undifferentiated marketing can provide the advantage of cost leadership through producing a comparatively standard and low-cost product and offering it to customers at the lowest prevailing market price (Dalgic and Leeuw 1994). As such, the marketer's firm can pursue higher sales volumes in comparison to firms using a niche marketing strategy which are in the pursuit of higher profit margins (see also **niche marketing**).

APPLICATION AREAS AND FURTHER READINGS

Marketing Strategy
Holbrook, Morris B., and Holloway, Douglas V. (1984). 'Marketing Strategy and the Structure of Aggregate, Segment-Specific, and Differential Preferences,' *Journal of Marketing*, 48(1), Winter, 62–67.
Biggadike, E. Ralph (1981). 'The Contributions of Marketing to Strategic Management,' *Academy of Management Review*, 6(4), October, 621–632.
Kara, A., and Kaynak, E. (1997). 'Markets of a Single Customer: Exploiting Conceptual Developments in Market Segmentation,' *European Journal of Marketing*, 31(11/12), 873–895.

Marketing Management
Dawes, J., and Worthington, S. (1996). 'Customer Information Systems and Competitive Advantage: A Case Study of a Top Ten Building Society,' *International Journal of Bank Marketing*, 14(4), 36–44.

Consumer Behavior
Addis, M., and Holbrook, M. B. (2001). 'On the Conceptual Link between Mass Customisation and Experiential Consumption: An Explosion of Subjectivity,' *Journal of Consumer Behavior*, 1(1), 50–66.

BIBLIOGRAPHY
Jain, Subhash C. (1985). *Marketing Planning and Strategy*. Cincinnati: South-Western Publishing Co.
Dalgic, T., and Leeuw, M. (1994). 'Niche Marketing Revisited: Concept, Applications and Some European Cases,' *European Journal of Marketing*, 28(4), 39–56.

☐ uniform-delivered pricing *see* pricing strategies

■ unintended consequences

DESCRIPTION

Situations where marketing activities result in organizational or consumer outcomes which are unexpected or unanticipated, which can be positive or negative.

KEY INSIGHTS

It is not always possible to foresee the full consequences of many marketing actions. At the firm level, in responding to economic uncertainties with pricing decisions, some marketing managers follow risk-averse policies which can result in unanticipated consequences that entail a good deal of risk (Guiltinan 1976). Among consumers, unintended exposure to media and promotional messages can bring unexpected benefits of better information and learning gains to the consumers, even though such media and message exposures may be seen as intrusive at times (Redmond 2005). In other situations, successful marketing activities by firms can result in negative impact on consumers, society, or other stakeholders in an unanticipated way as they have not taken into consideration the wider exchange process (Fry and Polonsky 2004). Environmental impact of production processes can be an example, which involves a wider responsibility on the part of a business.

KEY WORDS Unexpected consequences, unanticipated consequences

IMPLICATIONS

Outcomes that are not expected can be seen in some situations as side effects of marketing approaches or strategies. They imply that marketing approaches and tactics have to be analyzed in depth to avoid negative unanticipated consequences. In a marketplace, dyadic relationships only encompassing the firm and its customers may result in unintended consequences for other parties. This implies that it is imperative for firms to make effective decisions based on a trade off between the positive and the negative outcomes that may result from their operations. Allowing for a wider process of exchange through taking all possible stakeholders into consideration can reduce the probability of unanticipated negative outcomes.

APPLICATION AREAS AND FURTHER READINGS

Marketing Strategy

Menon, Ajay, and Menon, Anil (1997). 'Enviropreneurial Marketing Strategy: The Emergence of Corporate Environmentalism as Market Strategy,' *Journal of Marketing*, 61(1), January, 51–67.

Kitchen, P. J. (1994). 'The Marketing Communications Revolution: A Leviathan Unveiled?' *Marketing Intelligence and Planning*, 12(2), 19–25.

Marketing Management
Fisher, Robert J., Maltz, Elliot, and Jaworski, Bernard J. (1997). 'Enhancing Communication between Marketing and Engineering: The Moderating Role of Relative Functional Identification,' *Journal of Marketing*, 61(3), July, 54–70.

Social Marketing
Brenkert, G. G. (2002). 'Ethical Challenges of Social Marketing,' *Journal of Public Policy and Marketing*, 21(1), 14–25.
Ringold, D. J. (2002). 'Boomerang Effect: In Response to Public Health Interventions. Some Unintended Consequences in the Alcoholic Beverage Market,' *Journal of Consumer Policy*, 25(1), 27–63.

Marketing Research
Tybout, Alice M., and Zaltman, Gerald (1974). 'Ethics in Marketing Research: Their Practical Relevance,' *Journal of Marketing Research*, 11(4), November, 357–368.

Advertising
Goldberg, Marvin E., and Gorn, Gerald J. (1978). 'Some Unintended Consequences of TV Advertising to Children,' *Journal of Consumer Research*, 5(1), June, 22–29.
Holbrook, Morris B. (1987). 'Mirror, Mirror, on the Wall, What's Unfair in the Reflections on Advertising?' *Journal of Marketing*, 51(3), July, 95–103.

BIBLIOGRAPHY
Fry, Marie-Louise, and Polonsky, Michael Jay (2004). 'Examining the Unintended Consequences of Marketing,' *Journal of Business Research*, 57(11), November, 1303–1306.
Guiltinan, J. P. (1976), 'Risk-Aversive Pricing Policies: Problems and Alternatives,' *Journal of Marketing*, 40(1), 10–15.
Redmond, William H. (2005). 'Intrusive Promotion as Market Failure: How Should Society Impact Marketing?' *Journal of Macromarketing*, 25, 12–21.

■ unique value effect

DESCRIPTION
An effect on consumer price sensitivity resulting from a product or service offering's unique features and benefits.

KEY INSIGHTS
When a product or service offers unique value to potential customers as a result of having one or more desirable features or benefits that are not available or replicated in competing products in the market, the unique value of the product or service has the potential to significantly influence the consumer's price sensitivity toward the offering. In particular, uniqueness in the value of an offering is associated with a lowering of consumer price sensitivity to the offering as well as an increase in the price the consumer is willing to pay for it.

KEY WORDS **Value**, uniqueness, price sensitivity, willingness-to-pay

IMPLICATIONS
Marketers involved in developing new product or service offerings as well as in setting their prices should strive to understand consumer price sensitivity to the offering in order to manage its price effectively.

Recognizing how and to what extent lower price sensitivity and higher willingness-to-pay may be achievable as a result of developing and providing an offering of unique value can be beneficial in setting prices and in managing price changes when a product's unique value varies as competing product characteristics change.

APPLICATION AREAS AND FURTHER READINGS

Pricing

Kupiec, B., and Revell, B. (2001). 'Measuring Consumer Quality Judgments,' *British Food Journal*, 103(1), 7–22.

Sullivan, P. (2003). 'Comparing Price Sensitivity Research Models for New Products,' *Product Innovation and Management*, August, School of Business Administration, Portland State University.

BIBLIOGRAPHY

Rao, Vithala R. (1984). 'Pricing Research in Marketing: The State of the Art,' *Journal of Business*, 57(1), Part 2, S39–S60.

■ unmet need

DESCRIPTION

An unsatisfied utility that can initiate firms to strategically develop products or services that can fill that gap for customers.

KEY INSIGHTS

A firm searching for a distinctive competitive advantage can find marketing opportunities in pursuing unmet needs for existing target segments or other previously untargeted segments in the market. This can be done by studying consumers' unmet needs and finding ways to meet them through new or modified product or service offerings. Consumers are sometimes unaware of such needs, and marketing efforts and communication tactics can help bring these to the conscious level, stressing their importance and converting them into effective demand.

KEY WORDS **Needs**, gaps

IMPLICATIONS

Using unmet needs as a base for developing marketing strategies may involve a need-based segmentation analysis (Peltier and Schribrowsky 1997) that studies specific target segments for the benefits they seek and the motives underlying their purchases. To the extent that such knowledge is translated expediently into a commercialized offering by the marketer's firm, the firm has the opportunity to have a distinctive first-mover advantage among competitors in the marketplace.

APPLICATION AREAS AND FURTHER READINGS

Marketing Strategy

Hoekstra, J. C., Leeflang, P. S., and Wittink, D. R. (1999). 'The Customer Concept: The Basis for a New Marketing Paradigm,' *Journal of Market Focused Management*, 4(1), 43–76.

Jaworski, B., Kohli, A. K., and Sahay, A. (2000). 'Market-Driven Versus Driving Markets,' *Journal of the Academy of Marketing Science*, 28(1), 45–54.

Plummer, Joseph T. (1974). 'The Concept and Application of Life Style Segmentation,' *Journal of Marketing*, 38(1), January, 33–37.

Marketing Management
Bearden, William O., and Teel, Jesse E. (1983). 'Selected Determinants of Consumer Satisfaction and Complaint Reports,' *Journal of Marketing Research*, 20(1), February, 21–28.

Services Marketing
Kennett, P. A., Moschis, G. P., and Bellenger, D. N. (1995). 'Marketing Financial Services to Mature Consumers,' *Journal of Services Marketing*, 9(2), 62–72.

Marketing Research
Deshpande, Rohit, Farley, John U., and Webster, Jr., Frederick E. (1993). 'Corporate Culture, Customer Orientation, and Innovativeness in Japanese Firms: A Quadrad Analysis,' *Journal of Marketing*, 57(1), January, 23–37.

BIBLIOGRAPHY
Peltier, J. W., and Schribrowsky, J. A. (1997). 'The Use of Need-Based Segmentation for Developing Segment-Specific Direct Marketing Strategies,' *Journal of Direct Marketing*, 11(4), 53–62.

■ unrealistic optimism

DESCRIPTION

A judgmental bias in an individual's estimation of the likelihood of future events or outcomes where the likelihood of positive events occurring is overestimated and the likelihood of negative events occurring is underestimated.

KEY INSIGHTS

Based on pioneering research by Lund (1925) and Cantril (1928) and subsequent research by Weinstein (1980), unrealistic optimism is considered to be a pervasive phenomenon, where individuals tend to believe that desirable events or outcomes are more likely to happen to them than others and undesirable events or outcomes are less likely to happen to them than others. Such a bias leads individuals to have a distorted, overly optimistic view of the future that, while serving to enhance an individual's sense of well-being, may nevertheless be potentially detrimental to others to the extent others perceive such assessments as providing them with unbiased, albeit subjective, guidance on the likelihood of occurrence of future events.

KEY WORDS **Bias**, optimism

IMPLICATIONS

As experts are prone to the judgmental bias of unrealistic optimism, marketing strategists should be concerned about the possibility of an expert providing overly optimistic forecasts of future events. Obtaining a mix of views by outsiders—i.e. individuals not having close, personal stakes attached to the occurrence of particular future events or outcomes—may help to reduce unrealistic optimism. Marketers should also recognize that consumers may have this judgmental bias which may, in turn, influence consumers' beliefs, attitudes, or consumption behaviors associated with beneficial personal activities (e.g. need for healthy eating) and harmful personal activities (e.g. smoking). Understanding and overcoming such a judgmental bias among consumers enables the phenomenon to be recognized as an explicit challenge for marketers to address through effective marketing communications.

APPLICATION AREAS AND FURTHER READINGS

International Marketing
Heine, S. J., and Lehman, D. R. (1995). 'Cultural Variation in Unrealistic Optimism: Does the West Feel More Invulnerable than the East?' *Journal of Personality and Social Psychology*, 68(4), 595–607.

Marketing Communications
Weinstein, Neil D. (1983). 'Reducing Unrealistic Optimism about Illness Suscepti-bility,' *Health Psychology*, 2, 11–20.
Davidson, K., and Prkachin, K. (1997). 'Optimism and Unrealistic Optimism Have an Interacting Impact on Health-Promoting Behavior and Knowledge Changes,' *Personality and Social Psychology Bulletin*, 23(6), 617–625.
Henriksen, L., and Flora, J. A. (1999). 'Third-Person Perception and Children: Per-ceived Impact of Pro- and Anti-Smoking Ads,' *Communication Research*, 26(6), 643–665.

Marketing Strategy
Tichy, G. (2004). 'The Over-Optimism among Experts in Assessment and Foresight,' *Technological Forecasting and Social Change*, 71(4), 341–63.

Consumer Behavior
Taylor, S. E., and Brown, J. D. (1988). 'Illusion and Well Being: A Social Psychological Perspective on Mental Health,' *Psychological Bulletin*, 103, 193–210.

BIBLIOGRAPHY
Lund, F. H. (1925). 'The Psychology of Belief: A Study of its Emotional and Volitional Determinants,' *Journal of Abnormal and Social Psychology*, 20, 63–81.
Cantril, H. (1928). 'The Prediction of Social Events,' *Journal of Abnormal and Social Psychology*, 33, 364–389.
Weinstein, Neil D. (1980). 'Unrealistic Optimism about Future Life Events,' *Journal of Personality and Social Psychology*, 39(5), November, 806–820.
McKenna, F. P. (1993). 'It Won't Happen to Me: Unrealistic Optimism or Illusion of Control?' *British Journal of Psychology*, 84(1), 39–50.

☐ **unrelated diversification** *see* product-market investment strategies
☐ **unsought product** *see* product classifications, consumer

■ upper echelons theory

DESCRIPTION
A theory that considers organizational outcomes to be partially predicted by top managements' background characteristics.

KEY INSIGHTS
Based on research by Hambrick and Mason (1984) and subsequent researchers, upper echelons theory posits that, as upper level managers are selectively perceptive and boundedly rational, a behavioral element derived from managements' idiosyncratic characteristics should be evi-dent in the outcomes of the organization. In this context, the theory pro-vides a rationale for examining the nature and extent of the relationship between various managerial backgrounds and organizational outcomes.

While the strength of research findings for the theory may ultimately be dependent on the specific management background characteristics examined (e.g. career experience, gender) as well as specific organizational outcomes examined (e.g. profitability, diversification posture), there is general support for the view that certain organizational outcomes can be at least partially predicted by certain top management characteristics.

KEY WORDS Top management, background characteristics, organizational performance

IMPLICATIONS

Marketing strategists should recognize the possibility that organizational outcomes may be influenced to a significant degree by the background characteristics of the organization's top management. To the extent that marketing strategy development is also influenced by top management backgrounds, marketing strategy outcomes may be affected as well. While it is difficult to generalize how and to what extent there may be such influences, knowledge of upper echelons theory-based research may provide marketers with insights that may influence top management selection and/or more effective marketing management and strategy development and implementation.

APPLICATION AREAS AND FURTHER READINGS

Marketing Strategy

Herrmann, Pol, and Datta, Deepak K. (2005). 'Relationships between Top Management Team Characteristics and International Diversification: An Empirical Investigation,' *British Journal of Management*, 16(1), March, 69.

Michel, J., and Hambrick, D. C. (1992). 'Diversification Posture and Top Management Team Characteristics,' *Academy of Management Journal*, 35, 9-37.

Wiersema, M. F., and Bantel, K. A. (1992). 'Top Management Team Demography and Corporate Strategic Change,' *Academy of Management Journal*, 35, 91-121.

Marketing Management

Waldman, D. A., Ramirez, G. G., House, R. J., and Puranam, P. (2001). 'Does Leadership Matter? CEO Leadership Attributes and Profitability under Conditions of Perceived Environmental Uncertainty,' *Academy of Management Journal*, 44(1), 134-143.

Burke, L. A., and Steensma, H. K. (1998). 'Toward a Model for Relating Executive Career Experiences and Firm Performance,' *Journal of Managerial Issues*, 10(1), 86-102.

BIBLIOGRAPHY

Hambrick, Donald C., and Mason, Phyllis A. (1984). 'Upper Echelons: The Organization as a Reflection of Its Top Managers,' *Academy of Management Review*, 9(2), April, 193-206.

Hambrick, D. C. (2005). 'Upper Echelons Theory: Origins, Twists and Turns, and Lessons Learned,' in K. G. Smith and M. A. Hitt (eds.), *Great Minds in Management: The Process of Theory Development*. Oxford: Oxford University Press, 109-127.

■ utility

DESCRIPTION

A satisfaction derived from acquisition and consumption of an offering.

KEY INSIGHTS

In making choice decisions, consumers seek to achieve maximum utility. However, as this may involve higher sacrifices which they may not be able to afford, they may seek alternatives that are optimizing (choices that achieve the most out of available resources) or satisficing (choices that provide at least a satisfactory outcome—see **satisficing**). Different utility models, such as the Stochastic Utility model (Chapman and Staelin 1982), the Reference Price model (Winer 1986), and the Random Utility (RU) model (Baltas and Doyle 2001), have been proposed in the marketing literature to explain choice behavior based on utility.

KEY WORDS Satisfaction, acquisition, consumption

IMPLICATIONS

Increasing perceived utility for consumers is an important challenge for marketers. In evaluating alternatives and making choices among brands, consumers use a number of different heuristics to arrive at optimal, if not maximum, utility. A greater understanding of the utility concept and its link with offering complexity, price, and value may therefore be very beneficial in assisting the marketer's efforts to provide attractive offerings (e.g. offerings providing possession utility as well as place and time utility) that fit the consumer's choice criteria.

APPLICATION AREAS AND FURTHER READINGS

Marketing Strategy
Vargo, S. L., and Lusch, R. F. (2004). 'Evolving to a New Dominant Logic for Marketing,' *Journal of Marketing*, 68(1), 1-17.
Dellaert, B. G. C., and Stremersch, S. (2005). 'Marketing Mass Customized Products: Striking the Balance between Utility and Complexity,' *Journal of Marketing Research*, 42(2), May, 219-227.
Wilkie, William L., and Moore, Elizabeth S. (1999). 'Marketing's Contributions to Society,' *Journal of Marketing*, 63, Fundamental Issues and Directions for Marketing, 198-218.

Services Marketing
Pullman, M., and Moore, W. (1999). 'Optimal Service Design: Integrating Marketing and Operations Perspectives,' *International Journal of Service Industry Management*, 10(2), 239-260.

Online Marketing
Breitenbach, Craig S., and Van Doren, Doris C. (1998). 'Value-Added Marketing in the Digital Domain: Enhancing the Utility of the Internet,' *Journal of Consumer Marketing*, 15(6), 558-575.

BIBLIOGRAPHY
Chapman, Randall G., and Staelin, Richard (1982). 'Exploiting Rank Ordered Choice Set Data within the Stochastic Utility Model,' *Journal of Marketing Research*, 19(3), August, 288-301.
Winer, Russell S. (1986). 'A Reference Price Model of Brand Choice for Frequently Purchased Products,' *Journal of Consumer Research*, 13(2), September, 250-256.
Baltas, George, and Doyle, Peter, 2001. 'Random Utility Models in Marketing Research: A Survey,' *Journal of Business Research*, 51(2), February, 115-125.

■ utility theory

DESCRIPTION

Theory or theories concerned with understanding, explaining and predicting an individual's choices and decisions in relation to the individual's preferences, values, and judgments of preferability, worth, or value.

KEY INSIGHTS

Utility theory emphasizes the numerical or quantitative representation of an individual's preferences, values, and judgments to provide insights into choice and decision making. The theory provides a basis for the development and evaluation of numerical models of an individual's preferences, preference–indifference relationships, decision alternatives, and associated assumptions. In particular, the theory enables risk analyses to be performed where such analyses involve the subjective views of individuals about the benefits or personal utility associated with taking certain risks.

KEY WORDS Choice, decision making, preference, values, judgment, **utility**

IMPLICATIONS

Strategic marketers seeking to develop numerical models of decision making and choice involving risk may benefit from an understanding of the concepts associated with utility theory. In addition, while there are many variants of utility theory, a working knowledge of the rigorous and commonly accepted modeling methods can enable marketers to more clearly specify and articulate preferences, values, and judgments leading to choices and decisions.

APPLICATION AREAS AND FURTHER READINGS

Marketing Modeling

Inman, J. Jeffrey, Dyer, James S., and Jia, Jianmin (1997). 'A Generalized Utility Model of Disappointment and Regret Effects on Post-Choice Valuation,' *Marketing Science*, 16(2), 97–111.

Eliashberg, Jehoshua, LaTour, Stephen A., Rangaswamy, Arvind, and Stern, Louis W. (1986). 'Assessing the Predictive Accuracy of Two Utility-Based Theories in a Marketing Channel Negotiation Context,' *Journal of Marketing Research*, 23(2), May, 101–110.

Turban, Efraim, and Metersky, Morton L. (1971). 'Utility Theory Applied to Multi-variable System Effectiveness Evaluation,' *Management Science*, 17(12), August, Application Series, B817–B828.

BIBLIOGRAPHY

Fishburn, Peter C. (1968). 'Utility Theory,' *Management Science*, 14(5), Theory Series, January, 335–378.

V

■ validity

DESCRIPTION
A criterion in measurement research referring to the degree to which an instrument measures what it is intending to measure.

KEY INSIGHTS
Validity measurement is one of the three standard measurement criteria (in addition to reliability and sensitivity) that are drawn upon in facilitating the conduct of high-quality research (Churchill 1979). There are a number of different validity measures used in marketing research, including those referred to by the following terms:

A priori validity—see *face validity* (below).

Concurrent validity—a type of *criterion validity* in that it is validity based on the degree to which a measurement approach predicts an outside criterion, or established standard against which other things can be compared and evaluated, where such criterion measures are obtained at the same time as the measurement.

Consensual validity—the degree to which there is agreement of validity among a knowledgeable community or group of individuals.

Construct validity—the degree to which a measurement approach actually measures the underlying theoretical construct it is supposed to be measuring.

Content validity—based on expert judgment, the degree to which a measurement scale contains items which experts consider to be representative of that which is to be measured.

Convergent validity—validity that is based on hypotheses and examinations of the overlap between different measurement approaches which are presumed to measure the same construct.

Criterion validity—validity based on the degree to which a measurement approach predicts an outside criterion, or established standard against which other things can be compared and evaluated.

Discriminant validity—also known as *divergent validity*, discriminant validity is the opposite of *convergent validity* as it is validity based on the degree to which the construct fails to correlate with other theoretically distinct constructs.

Divergent validity—see *discriminant validity* (above).

Ecological validity—the degree to which the settings, methods, and materials used in a study approximate the larger, real-life situation that is being studied.

External validity—the degree to which the results of the findings of a study are generalizable in that they are relevant to subjects and settings beyond those used in the study.

Face validity—also called *a priori validity*, the degree to which, by the face of it, a measure seems to make sense in that it looks like it is going to measure what it is intended to measure on the basis of reason as opposed to experience.

Factorial validity—a form of *construct validity* (see above) established through factor analysis where multiple measurement approaches purported to be measuring the same constructs are factor analyzed to determine the degree to which they share common variance and thus can be said to be tapping into the same underlying construct.

Incremental validity—the degree to which a measure is able to explain or predict a phenomenon of interest, relative to other measures having the same purpose.

Internal validity—the degree to which an experiment is able to demonstrate a causal relationship between two variables, i.e. that 'cause' precedes 'effect' in time, 'cause' and 'effect' are shown to be related, and there is a lack of alternative explanations (e.g. problems in the research design) for the relationship observed between the two variables.

Nomological validity—the degree to which the correlation between a measure and another related construct behaves as expected in theory, in that a construct predicts measures of other constructs from the perspective of a formal theoretical network of relationships.

Population validity—the degree to which the findings of a study are generalized from the sample to the larger population.

Predictive validity—a type of *criterion validity* in that it is validity based on the degree to which a measurement approach predicts an outside criterion, or established standard against which other things can be compared and evaluated, where such criterion measures are obtained at a time after the measurement.

Statistical validity—the degree to which appropriate choices are made concerning the statistical methods and tests used in relation to the measurement approach and the nature of the data collection process.

Trait validity—the degree to which a construct and its measures are in accordance with theory only at the level of a single trait or distinguishing characteristic (i.e. theory that does not consider the interrelationships of constructs within a nomological network).

KEY WORDS Measurement, intended measurement, **marketing research**

IMPLICATIONS

A greater knowledge of all measures of validity can clearly be beneficial in assisting the marketing researcher with designing, implementing, and evaluating marketing research—whether one's own or those of others—for appropriate usability by the marketer. While some measures of validity may be potentially more of an issue in quantitative research and others more of an issue in qualitative research, understanding better the many different perspectives on measurement validity further allows the marketing researcher to conduct tradeoffs in the selection and use of a wide range of marketing research approaches.

APPLICATION AREAS AND FURTHER READINGS

Marketing Research

Peter, J. P. (1981). 'Construct Validity: A Review of Basic Issues and Marketing Practices,' *Journal of Marketing Research* 18, 133–145.

Loyd, B. H., and Gressard, C. (1984). 'Reliability and Factorial Validity of Computer Attitude Scales,' *Educational and Psychological Measurement*, 44, 501–505.

John, George, and Reve, Torger (1982). 'The Reliability and Validity of Key Informant Data from Dyadic Relationships in Marketing Channels,' *Journal of Marketing Research*, 19(4), Special Issue on Causal Modeling, November, 517–524.

Ruekert, Robert W., and Churchill, Gilbert A. (1982). *The Reliability and Validity of Alternative Measures of Channel Member Satisfaction.* Madison: Graduate School of Business, University of Wisconsin-Madison.

Spiro, Rosann L., and Weitz, Barton A. (1990). 'Adaptive Selling: Conceptualization, Measurement, and Nomological Validity,' *Journal of Marketing Research*, 27(1), February, 61–69.

Netemeyer, Richard G., Durvasula, Srinivas, and Lichtenstein, Donald R. (1991). 'A Cross-National Assessment of the Reliability and Validity of the CETSCALE,' *Journal of Marketing Research*, 28(3), August, 320–327.

Perreault, William D., Jr., and Leigh, Laurence E. (1989). 'Reliability of Nominal Data Based on Qualitative Judgments,' *Journal of Marketing Research*, 26(2), May, 135–148.

Green, Paul E., and Srinivasan, V. (1990). 'Conjoint Analysis in Marketing: New Developments with Implications for Research and Practice,' *Journal of Marketing*, 54(4), October, 3–19.

Malhotra, Naresh K. (1981). 'A Scale to Measure Self-Concepts, Person Concepts, and Product Concepts,' *Journal of Marketing Research*, 18(4), November, 456–464.

Peter, J. Paul, and Churchill, Gilbert A., Jr. (1986). 'Relationships among Research Design Choices and Psychometric Properties of Rating Scales: A Meta-analysis,' *Journal of Marketing Research*, 23(1), February, 1–10.

Winer, R. S. (1999). 'Experimentation in the 21st Century: The Importance of External Validity,' *Academy of Marketing Science*, 27(3), 349–358.

BIBLIOGRAPHY

Gilbert A. Churchill, Jr. (1979). 'A Paradigm for Developing Better Measures of Marketing Constructs,' *Journal of Marketing Research*, 16(1), February, 64–73.

Heeler, Roger M., and Ray, Michael L. (1972). 'Measure Validation in Marketing,' *Journal of Marketing Research*, 9, November, 361–370.

Brewer, M. (2000). 'Research Design and Issues of Validity,' in H. Reis and C. Judd (eds.), *Handbook of Research Methods in Social and Personality Psychology.* Cambridge: Cambridge University Press.

■ value

DESCRIPTION
What something is perceived to be worth.

KEY INSIGHTS
The value of an offering, as perceived by a consumer, is the estimation of the merit of the offering in terms of money, quality, or any other measure of worth. For example, value can be assessed in terms of the offering's perceived benefits in relation to its price or perceptions of actual quality in relation to expected quality. The notion of value provides a basis for most marketing approaches. For example, it strongly links to relationship marketing, where providing superior value to the customer is the way to establish and maintain long-term relationships. If the ultimate aim is to enhance customer loyalty, value-adding attempts have to be customer oriented, rather than focused only on investing more on product development (Ravald and Groenroos 1996). Shareholder value is also an important outcome achievable through value chain analysis, for example (see **value chain analysis**).

KEY WORDS Worth, perceived value, added value

IMPLICATIONS
Adding value to products and services entails not only improving customers' perceived value through increasing benefits, but also working to reduce costs or customer-perceived sacrifices (Monroe 1991). Such a view suggests that marketers' firms may benefit in pursuing cost leadership in combination with differentiation strategies aimed at providing value to the firm's customers.

APPLICATION AREAS AND FURTHER READINGS
Marketing Strategy
Ravald, A., and Groenroos, C. (1996). 'The Value Concept and Relationship Marketing,' *European Journal of Marketing*, 30(2), 19–30.

Retail Marketing
Dawar, Niraj, and Parker, Philip (1994). 'Marketing Universals: Consumers' Use of Brand Name, Price, Physical Appearance, and Retailer Reputation as Signals of Product Quality,' *Journal of Marketing*, 58(2), April, 81–95.

Services Marketing
Devlin, J. F. (2000). 'Adding Value to Retail Financial Services,' *International Journal of Bank Marketing*, 18(4–5), 222–232.

Business-to-Business Marketing
Anderson, J. C., and Narus, J. A. (1998). 'Business Marketing: Understand What Customers Value,' *Harvard Business Review*, 76(6), 53–67.
Eggert, A., and Ulaga, W. (2002). 'Customer Perceived Value: A Substitute for Satisfaction in Business Markets?' *Journal of Business and Industrial Marketing*, 17(2–3), 107–118.

Online Marketing
Breitenbach, C. S., and Van Doren, D. C. (1998). 'Value-Added Marketing in the Digital Domain: Enhancing the Utility of the Internet,' *Journal of Consumer Marketing*, 15(6), 558–575.

Consumer Behavior
Zeithaml, Valerie A. (1988). 'Consumer Perceptions of Price, Quality, and Value: A Means–End Model and Synthesis of Evidence,' *Journal of Marketing*, 52 (July), 2–22.

BIBLIOGRAPHY
Wood, L. M. (1996). 'Added Value: Marketing Basics?' *Journal of Marketing Management*, 12(8), 735–755.
Monroe, Kent B. (1991). *Pricing: Making Profitable Decisions.* New York: McGraw Hill.

☐ **value, characteristics theory of** *see* characteristics theory

■ value-based marketing

(also called customer value marketing)

DESCRIPTION

A marketing approach that involves the pursuit of marketing strategies and tactics that provide a high degree of meaningful value and satisfaction to customers as well as achieving improved business leverage.

KEY INSIGHTS

Value-based marketing entails a strategy that focuses on ongoing analysis of the company, the competition, and the customer, observing opportunities to deliver superior value to customers based on the company's niche competencies. The approach recognizes that the firm must also be responsive to changes in the competitive environment, where the firm strives to remain competitive with sustainable advantages, while providing consumers with credible offerings that are value based. As such, the company's value proposition becomes a primary organizing force for doing business and creating shareholder value.

KEY WORDS **Value**, ongoing analysis

IMPLICATIONS

Value-based marketing emphasizes the need for marketers to consistently develop and implement marketing approaches that are of high value in multiple stakeholders—to the organization and its employees, to the organization's shareholders, and to customers. A greater understanding of value-based marketing approaches may therefore be potentially beneficial to marketers involved in any area of marketing, including strategy development, brand management, pricing, and marketing communications, as it may assist with the identification and pursuit of high-value marketing initiatives from multiple perspectives.

APPLICATION AREAS AND FURTHER READINGS

Marketing Strategy
Walters, D., and Lancaster, G. (1999). 'Value-Based Marketing and its Usefulness to Customers,' *Management Decision*, 37(9), 697–708.
Doyle, P. (2001). 'Shareholder Value-Based Brand Strategies,' *Journal of Brand Management*, 9(1), 20–31.

Marketing Management
Webster, F. E. (1994). *Market Driven Management.* New York: John Wiley & Sons, Inc.

BIBLIOGRAPHY
Doyle, P. (2000a). 'Value-Based Marketing,' *Journal of Strategic Marketing*, 8(4), 299–310.
Doyle, Peter (2000b). *Value-Based Marketing: Marketing Strategies for Corporate Growth and Shareholder Value*. New York: Wiley.
Davidow, W. H., and Malone, M. S. (1992). *The Virtual Corporation*. New York: Harper-Collins.

■ value chain analysis

DESCRIPTION

An in-depth scan of a firm's value chain activities and functions aimed at a better understanding of areas of improvement towards higher levels of efficiency and effectiveness.

KEY INSIGHTS

A value chain analysis is a method for decomposing the firm into strategically important activities and understanding their impact on cost behavior and differentiation (Hergert and Morris 1989, Porter 1985). Activities analyzed may include primary activities associated with inbound and outbound logistics, operations, marketing and sales, and service, as well as support activities associated with firm infrastructure, human resource management, technology development, and procurement.

KEY WORDS **Value**, organizational activities, strategic analysis

IMPLICATIONS

A marketer's examination of the firm's value chain allows it to optimize its activities economically, efficiently, and effectively, where the interdependencies between activities in the chain, buyers and sellers, as well as between the different strategic business units are analyzed and coordinated. As this entails better management of market-based assets, incorporation of value chain analyses into the firm's marketing strategy development and evaluation processes may ultimately act to increase shareholder value.

APPLICATION AREAS AND FURTHER READINGS

Marketing Strategy
Day, G. S., and Wensley, R. (1988). 'Assessing Advantage: A Framework for Diagnosing Competitive Superiority,' *Journal of Marketing*, 52, 1–20.

International Marketing
Fitter, R., and Kaplinsky, R. (2001). 'Who Gains from Product Rents as the Coffee Market Becomes More Differentiated? A Value-Chain Analysis,' *IDS Bulletin*, 32(3), 69–82.

Business-to-Business Marketing
Kothandaraman, P., and Wilson, D. T. (2001). 'The Future of Competition: Value-Creating Networks,' *Industrial Marketing Management*, 30, 379–389.

Online Marketing
Amit, R., and Zott, C. (2001). 'Value Creation in E-business,' *Strategic Management Journal*, 22(6–7), 493–520.

Marketing Education
Elloumi, F. (2004). 'Value Chain Analysis: A Strategic Approach to Online Learning,' in *Theory and Practice of Online Learning*, Athabasca: Athabasca University Press, 61–92.

BIBLIOGRAPHY
Hergert, M., and Morris, D. (1989). 'Accounting Data for Value Chain Analysis,' *Strategic Management Journal*, 10(2), 175–188.
Porter, Michael E. (1985). *Competitive Advantage*. New York: The Free Press.

□ value marketing *see* enlightened marketing
□ value pricing *see* pricing strategies

■ value proposition

DESCRIPTION
An element of a firm's marketing strategy that is a definable statement which spells out what value a firm's offering provides a buyer and user of the offering.

KEY INSIGHTS
The value proposition of a firm's offering is ultimately that which it provides to its customers. As such, the value proposition is not limited to an offering's functional benefits but can include benefits which are social, emotional, or self-expressive, for example.

KEY WORDS Proposed value, value provision, **benefits**

IMPLICATIONS
As part of the firm's marketing strategy, the value proposition of an offering should also strive to be consistent with the overall business strategy (Lawler 2005) and the firm's overall value proposition. Marketers should seek to develop value propositions that not only highlight important consumer needs and wants but also take into consideration the firm's distinctive competencies, resources, capabilities, and limitations and assist with the firm's efforts to achieve a competitive advantage that is sustainable. In support of its effective delivery in the marketplace, marketers should ensure that the firm's value propositions are also communicated effectively throughout the organization.

APPLICATION AREAS AND FURTHER READINGS
Marketing Strategy
Kaplan, R. S., and Norton, D. P. (2000). 'Having Trouble with your Strategy? Then Map it,' *Harvard Business Review*, 78(5), 167–176.

Marketing Management
Srivastava, R. K., Shervani, T. A., and Fahey, L. (1999). 'Marketing, Business Processes, and Shareholder Value: An Organizationally Embedded View of Marketing Activities and the Discipline of Marketing,' *Journal of Marketing*, 63(SPI/1), 168–179.

Online Marketing
Porter, M. E. (2001). 'Strategy and the Internet,' *Harvard Business Review*, 9(3), 62–79.

Services Marketing
Lovelock, Christopher H. (1991). *Services Marketing*. Englewood Cliffs, NJ: Prentice Hall.
Webster, Frederick E. (1979). *Business-to-Business Marketing: Industrial Marketing Strategy*. New York: Wiley.
Levina, N., and Ross, J. (2003). 'From the Vendor's Perspective: Exploring the Value Proposition in IT Outsourcing,' *MIS Quarterly*, 27(3), 331–364.

BIBLIOGRAPHY
Aaker, David A. (2005). *Strategic Market Management*. New York: John Wiley & Sons, Inc.
Lawler, Edward E., III (2005). 'Creating High Performance Organizations,' *Asia Pacific Journal of Human Resources*, 43(1), 10–17.

☐ **variability** *see* service characteristics

☐ **variable costs** *see* cost

☐ **variable proportions, law of** *see* diminishing returns, law of

■ variety effect

DESCRIPTION
Any effect where the existence and availability of product or brand variety results in an increased benefit to consumers.

KEY INSIGHTS
Consumers of a particular product or brand may benefit from another firm's new product or brand introduction when such an introduction provides the consumer with consumption variety. Given the availability of variety, a consumer may periodically choose the new alternative to experience diversity in consumption where, previously, all consumption experiences were the same. At the same time, the availability of variety may also act to enhance consumer perceptions of current products or brands as well as potentially give consumers greater satisfaction with the overall set of products or brands for which there is increased variety.

KEY WORDS Product variety, brand variety, consumer benefit

IMPLICATIONS
Marketers should strive to understand through research how and to what extent expanded product or brand variety, whether offered by competitors or within a firm, may lead to an increase in particular consumer benefits. For example, increased variety may lead to expanded consumption from a product category while in other instances the effect may be greater consumer satisfaction with one or more of the alternatives within a particular category.

APPLICATION AREAS AND FURTHER READINGS
Marketing Strategy
Hausman, J. A., and Leonard, G. K. (2002). 'The Competitive Effects of a New Product Introduction: A Case Study,' *Journal of Industrial Economics*, 50(3), 237–264.
Chernev, A. (2003). 'When More Is Less and Less Is More: The Role of Ideal Point Availability and Assortment in Consumer Choice,' *Journal of Consumer Research*, 30(2), 170–183.

Brynjolfsson, E., Hu, Y., and Smith, M. D. (2003). 'Consumer Surplus in the Digital
    Economy: Estimating the Value of Increased Product Variety at Online Book-
    sellers,' *Management Science*, 49(11), 1580–1596.

BIBLIOGRAPHY
Dhar, T., and Foltz, J. D. (2005). 'Milk by Any Other Name…Consumer Benefits
    from Labeled Milk,' *American Journal of Agricultural Economics*, 87(1), 214–228.

☐ variety-seeking buying behavior *see* consumer buyer behavior

☐ Veblen effect *see* goods

☐ Veblen goods *see* goods

☐ vertical integration *see* product-market investment strategies; integration

☐ vertical marketing system *see* channel arrangement

■ viral marketing

(also called electronic word-of-mouth marketing, or word-of-mouse marketing)

DESCRIPTION
An approach involving the dissemination of marketing messages or brand
information via online channels that develop through social networks.

KEY INSIGHTS
Viral marketing relies on a strategy that encourages individuals to pass
on marketing messages in a form that multiplies with a virus-spreading
effect. Its use can involve any number of internet marketing or stealth
marketing approaches (see **online marketing**; **stealth marketing**) to
have a network effect that reaches a large base of consumers. Off
the internet, it can have a buzz effect that is more closely associated
with word-of-mouth marketing (see **word-of-mouth marketing**). Because
recipients of the message are the ones who take action to pass on the
message to friends, family, and/or colleagues, viral marketing tends to
avoid problems associated with *spam marketing*, or *junk e-mail marketing*,
which involves indiscriminately sending unsolicited and unwanted e-
mails in mass quantities in the hope that at least some recipients will
respond favorably to the e-mail messages.

KEY WORDS Social networks

IMPLICATIONS
Viral marketing has several possible benefits including relative ease of
implementation, potential for broad reach, and low cost. To the extent
that marketers using viral marketing target the proper audience with a
salient message, the marketer's message can potentially 'explode' with
exponential growth to reach thousands of interested people.

APPLICATION AREAS AND FURTHER READINGS

Marketing Strategy
Wilson, R. F. (2000) 'The Six Principles of Viral Marketing,' *Web Marketing Today*, 70(2), 16–20.

Online Marketing
Helm, S. (2000). 'Viral Marketing: Establishing Customer Relationships by "Word-of-mouse,"' *Electronic Markets*, 10(3), 158–161.

Consumer Behavior
Phelps, Joseph E., Lewis, Regina, Mobilio, Lynne, Perry, David, and Raman, Niranjan (2004). 'Viral Marketing or Electronic Word-of-Mouth Advertising: Examining Consumer Responses and Motivations to Pass along Email,' *Journal of Advertising Research*, 44, 333–348.

BIBLIOGRAPHY
Goldenberg, J., Libai, B., and Muller, E. (2001). 'Talk of the Network: A Complex Systems Look at the Underlying Process of Word-of-Mouth,' *Marketing Letters* (New York), 12(3), 211–224.

☐ **virtual marketing** *see* online marketing

☐ **VMS** *see* channel arrangement

☐ **voice mail marketing** *see* direct marketing

☐ **volume effect** *see* loyalty effect

☐ **voluntary sector marketing** *see* non-profit marketing

■ **von Restorff effect**

(also called distinctiveness effect, Restorff effect, isolation effect)

DESCRIPTION
The tendency for individuals to have superior recall for items having a high degree of salience.

KEY INSIGHTS
Named after Hedwig von Restorff, a pioneer of research on the phenomenon (von Restorff 1933), the von Restorff effect finds that items such as words to be learned are more likely to be remembered when such items are salient in some way. The salience may be a result of the words being in a different color ink or any other way in which the items are distinctive in relation to other items to be learned.

Note: While the von Restorff effect is also called the isolation effect, the description and discussion of the effect present here should not be confused with that for another, more common meaning of the isolation effect term. See **isolation effect**.

KEY WORDS Memory, recall, salience, distinctiveness

IMPLICATIONS
Marketers concerned with facilitating superior recall of a message or information associated with a marketer's offerings may benefit from

making such information distinctive or salient in some way from the perspective of the consumer. Marketers can employ a variety of means to make such information stand out, which may include placement of an item where it is unexpected or making such information unique to surrounding or previously encountered messages through the use of distinctive language or graphic design.

APPLICATION AREAS AND FURTHER READINGS

Consumer Behavior

Lynch, John G., Jr., and Srull, Thomas K. (1982). 'Memory and Attentional Factors in Consumer Choice: Concepts and Research Methods,' *Journal of Consumer Research*, 9(1), June, 18–37.

Janiszewski, C., Noel, H., and Sawyer, A. G. (2003). 'A Meta-analysis of the Spacing Effect in Verbal Learning: Implications for Research on Advertising Repetition and Consumer Memory,' *Journal of Consumer Research*, 30(1), 138–149.

BIBLIOGRAPHY

von Restorff, H. (1933). 'Über die Wirkung von Bereichsbildungen im Spurenfeld' (The Effects of Field Formation in the Trace Field), *Psychologie Forschung*, 18, 299–342.

Hunt, R. R. (1995). 'The Subtlety of Distinctiveness: What von Restorff Really Did,' *Psychonomic Bulletin and Review*, 2, 105–112.

W

☐ waiting line theory *see* queuing theory

■ Wal-Mart effect

DESCRIPTION
Any of a range of effects stemming from Wal-Mart's way of doing business and its large market share.

KEY INSIGHTS
Wal-Mart, a large US and international retailer with annual sales that consistently put it in the top rankings of retailers in the USA and the world, is credited with having an influence on business as well as local and national economies. Wage rates, prices, pricing practices, and supplier relations are just some of the areas influenced. The Wal-Mart effect also includes an economy-wide effect of lower inflation and increased productivity that have resulted from the operating practices of Wal-Mart that have been replicated by the retailer on a large scale. On a local level, the Wal-Mart effect includes a tendency for communities with Wal-Marts to have faster per-capita retail sales and tax increases than communities without Wal-Marts, and where non-competing businesses in Wal-Mart communities experienced significant benefits while competing businesses experienced substantial revenue losses. On an industry level, Wal-Mart's use of information and communication technologies, combined with automation and centralization of warehousing as well as the scale of their retailing operations, has resulted in industry changes that have made many previous industry operations obsolete or unrecognizable.

KEY WORDS Retailing, operational innovation, economic impact

IMPLICATIONS
Marketers should not underestimate the significance of the array of Wal-Mart effects on firm and industry practices (particularly in the retail industry), as well as local and national economies. The success of the innovations introduced by Wal-Mart, combined with the scale of their operations, continues to put considerable pressure on firms to find ways to reduce their costs and to meet customer expectations of a firm providing offerings at prices that move continually lower. While Wal-Mart effects to particular firms depend on the extent that firms are or are not direct competitors with Wal-Mart, marketers should seek to understand

and anticipate such effects in preparation for future competitive moves (operationally or geographically) by the firm.

APPLICATION AREAS AND FURTHER READINGS

Retail Marketing

McGee, J. (1995). 'Local Merchants' Response to Wal-Mart,' *Proceedings of the National Small Business Institute Directors' Association.*

McGee, J. E., and Peterson, M. (2000). 'Surviving "W-Day": An Assessment of the Impact of Wal-Mart's Invasion of Small Town Retailing Communities,' *Proceedings of the USASBE/SBIDA National Conference,* 131–135.

BIBLIOGRAPHY

Fishman, Charles (2006). 'The Wal-Mart Effect and a Decent Society: Who Knew Shopping Was So Important?' *Academy of Management Perspectives,* 20(3), 6–25.

Fishman, Charles (2006). *The Wal-Mart Effect: How the World's Most Powerful Company Really Works—and How it's Transforming the American Economy.* London: The Penguin Press.

■ Walras' law

DESCRIPTION

An economic principle of general equilibrium that states that, for a given number of markets, if all but one are observed to be in equilibrium, then the last one must also be in equilibrium because there cannot be a net excess of supply or demand for the goods, including money.

KEY INSIGHTS

Developed by Leon Walras in the late 1800s, Walras' law says that markets cannot be in a one-sided disequilibrium (with disequibrium being where the quantity demanded is not equal to the quantity supplied at the going price). Thus, the law asserts that if there is disequilibrium in a market such as the labor market, there must also be disequilbrium in another market such as in the market demand for goods.

KEY WORDS Economics, general equilibrium

IMPLICATIONS

Marketers seeking to create advanced economic models of markets may benefit from a greater understanding of the principles and concepts associated with Walras' law. Whether modeling markets where there is a single good or multiple goods, the market equilibrium implications of Walras' law may provide the modeler with an important basis for subsequent model development that may ultimately assist decision makers in evaluating policies and practices influencing both markets and industries.

APPLICATION AREAS AND FURTHER READINGS

Marketing Modeling

Berkovec, James (1985). 'New Car Sales and Used Car Stocks: A Model of the Automobile Market,' *RAND Journal of Economics,* 16(2), Summer, 195–214.

Antras, P. (2005). 'Incomplete Contracts and the Product Cycle,' *American Economic Review,* 95, 1054–1073.

Chambers, Robert G., and Pick, Daniel H. (1994). 'Marketing Orders as Nontariff Trade Barriers,' *American Journal of Agricultural Economics,* 76(1), February, 47–54.

BIBLIOGRAPHY
Pingle, Mark (1994). *Walras' Law, Pareto Efficiency, and Intermediation in Overlapping Generations' Economies*. Ames, Ia.: Dept. of Economics, Iowa State University.

■ want

DESCRIPTION
A personal feeling of desire for something.

KEY INSIGHTS
Beyond the many needs of individuals (see **need**), individuals also have many wants, which may include, for example, favorite foods, stylish clothes, and internet connectivity. While the nature and scope of wants clearly varies from individual to individual, it can also be said that most individuals have an insatiable appetite for wants. Because most individuals are restricted in their ability to obtain their wants as a result of personal resource limitations, individuals must ultimately prioritize their wants. That which a consumer wants may, of course, be influenced by any number of factors, including the values, attitudes, and behaviors of family, friends, and individuals in broader society. As such, much of marketing is aimed at understanding the various factors influencing the strength of consumer wants and developing appropriate marketing approaches in response.

KEY WORD Desire

IMPLICATIONS
A significant part of marketing involves the identification of consumer wants and the factors that influence such wants. Building on such knowledge is often considered to be essential in developing effective marketing strategies and tactics for the provision of any offering that is to be the focus of an individual's desire.

APPLICATION AREAS AND FURTHER READINGS
Marketing Strategy
Firat, A. F., and Shultz, C. J. (1997). 'From Segmentation to Fragmentation: Markets and Marketing Strategy in the Postmodern Era II,' *European Journal of Marketing*, 31(3–4), 183–207.

Services Marketing
Pieters, R., Bottschen, G., and Thelen, E. (1998). 'Customer Desire Expectations about Service Employees: An Analysis of Hierarchical Relations,' *Psychology and Marketing*, 15(8), 755–774.

Consumer Behavior
Cross, G. (2002). 'Valves of Desire: A Historian's Perspective on Parents, Children, and Marketing,' *Journal of Consumer Research*, 29, December, 441–447.

Social Marketing
O'Shaughnessy, J., and O'Shaughnessy, N. J. (2002). 'Marketing, the Consumer Society and Hedonism,' *European Journal of Marketing*, 36(5–6), 524–547.

BIBLIOGRAPHY
Gagnier, Regenia (2000). *The Insatiability of Human Wants: Economics and Aesthetics in Market Society*. Chicago: University of Chicago Press.

■ warm/cold effect

DESCRIPTION

The tendency for the perception of a warm/cold personality trait of an individual to have an overwhelming effect on the formation of an impression of the individual's personality and expectations for associated behaviors.

KEY INSIGHTS

Pioneering research on the warm/cold effect by Asch (1946) and Kelley (1950) has determined that individuals' impressions of the personality of another individual can be significantly altered merely by describing the individual as either 'warm' or 'cold' when the warm/cold trait is included with other personality trait descriptions such as intelligent, industrious, and skilful. The broader term for the phenomenon is *trait centrality*, where such traits are observed to have a profound effect on impression formation in comparison to the contributing effects of other personality trait descriptions. In particular, observed traits descriptions that individuals associate with the 'warm' trait include popular, sociable, humorous, and happy. On the other hand, the 'cold' trait description is associated with a lack of such traits and, instead, associations with traits including restrained, persistent, and serious. The effect is explained in terms of the trait's centrality, where such traits possess the property of centrality as a result of being highly correlated with other personality traits in individual evaluators' implicit theories of personality.

KEY WORDS Personality, impression formation, trait centrality

IMPLICATIONS

Research on the warm/cold effect and trait centrality suggests that it is important for marketers to recognize that impressions of personality along the lines of a single trait such as warm/cold can have a significant effect on customer expectations and satisfaction with a service. For example, research by Widmeyer and Loy (1988) demonstrates how teaching effectiveness perceptions and expectations can be influenced by perceptions of the warm/cold personality trait among teachers. As such, any marketer involved in the development, delivery, and evaluation of a service offering where individual personality has a prominent role in the service should seek to understand better how customer perceptions of the service provider's personality may ultimately influence consumer expectations and satisfaction with the service.

APPLICATION AREAS AND FURTHER READINGS

Marketing Education

Widmeyer, W. Neil, and Loy, John W. (1988). 'When You're Hot, You're Hot! Warm-Cold Effects in First-Impressions of Persons and Teaching Effectiveness,' *Journal of Educational Psychology*, 80(1), 118–121.

Babad, Elisha, Kaplowitz, Henry, and Darley, John (1999). 'A "Classic" Revisited: Students' Immediate and Delayed Evaluations of a Warm/Cold Instructor,' *Social Psychology of Education*, 3(1–2), March, 81–102.

BIBLIOGRAPHY
Asch, S. E. (1946). 'Forming Impressions of Personality,' *Journal of Abnormal and Social Psychology*, 41, 258–290.
Kelley, H. H. (1950). 'The Warm–Cold Variable in First Impressions of Persons,' *Journal of Personality*, 18, 431–439.

■ Web marketing

(also called cybermarketing, cyberspace marketing, interactive marketing, internet marketing, internet-centric marketing, new economy marketing, online marketing, Web-based marketing, Web-centric marketing, World Wide Web marketing, or WWW marketing)

DESCRIPTION
Marketing focusing on the use of a large-scale, hypermedia-based computer network of internet sites enabling functionality including text, hypertext links, graphics, sound, and animation.

KEY INSIGHTS
Developed in 1989 at the CERN research institute in Switzerland, the World Wide Web (or Web or WWW) is a hypertext-based distributed information system that has subsequently been widely adopted by countless marketers and consumers worldwide. As such, the World Wide Web is a vast collection of interconnected documents and other resources that is accessible via the internet, which is itself a collection of interconnected computer networks. Approaches to marketing via the web are wide-ranging and may consist of simple text-based informational advertising to highly sophisticated, interactive, multi-media marketing aimed at encouraging frequent and regular customer participation. Web-based marketing is characterized by its potential for considerable audience reach as well as richness of content.

Marketing strategies and tactics for use of the Web continue to develop at a rapid pace. For example, many firms find it highly beneficial for their business to be found readily when searched for using any number of online search engines. Such a concern has led to developments in *search engine marketing*, which is a marketing approach involving the use of search engine capabilities to reach prospective customers, where the aim is to appear as high as possible on the list of a search engine's search results (e.g. on the first page) when consumers use any number of relevant key words related to the firm or its offerings. Search engine marketing may also involve initiatives by the firm to appear in 'sponsored' search results as a result of payment to search engine organizations.

While the terms internet marketing, online marketing, and Web marketing are often used interchangeably in marketing practice, *online marketing* may be viewed as the broadest term in terms of its scope, as it can be viewed as encompassing marketing via stand-alone computer connections to marketing via the internet to that which emphasizes the use of the many advanced features of the World Wide Web. As internet marketing as a term is used far more often in practice than Web marketing to convey any of a range of online marketing approaches, internet marketing has become synonymous with online marketing despite differences in any strict definitions. (See **online Marketing**.)

KEY WORDS **Online marketing**, hypermedia computer network

IMPLICATIONS
Increasingly, marketing via the Web is an imperative for firms competing in most markets today. Such a strategic approach, whether used alone or in combination with other forms of marketing, can enable the firm to remain accessible to current and potential customers around the clock and to individuals and organizations increasingly independent of geography—assuming, of course, that such individuals and organizations have access to and are able to use it. Customers flying on EasyJet, for example, have to find a computer to access the company's website in order to rebook an Easyjet flight that is cancelled—even though they are still at the airport and within easy reach of the company's personnel.

APPLICATION AREAS AND FURTHER READINGS
Marketing Strategy
Sharma, A., and Sheth, J. (2004). 'Web-Based Marketing: The Coming Revolution in Marketing Thought and Strategy,' *Journal of Business Research*, 57, 696–702.
Lederer, A. L., Mirchandani, D. A., and Sims, K. (2001). 'The Search for Strategic Advantage from the World Wide Web,' *International Journal of Electronic Commerce*, 5(4), 117–134.
Lynn, G. S., Lipp, S. M., Akgun, A. E., and Cortez, A. (2002). 'Factors Impacting the Adoption and Effectiveness of the World Wide Web in Marketing,' *Industrial Marketing Management*, 31(1), January, 35–49.

BIBLIOGRAPHY
Shapiro, Carl, and Varian, Hal R. (1999). *Information Rules*. Boston: Harvard Business School Press.
Turban, Ephraim (2006). *Electronic Commerce: A Managerial Perspective*. Upper Saddle River, NJ: Pearson Prentice Hall.

☐ **Web-based marketing** *see* online marketing; Web marketing
☐ **Web-centric marketing** *see* online marketing; Web marketing
☐ **Weber's law** *see* Weber–Fechner law

■ Weber–Fechner law

(also called Weber–Fechner's law, Fechner's law, Weber's law, or Weber–Fechner theory)

DESCRIPTION
The thesis that a just noticeable difference in a stimulus is proportional to the magnitude or intensity of the original stimulus.

KEY INSIGHTS
Based on pioneering research by Ernst Weber in 1834 on perceptions of change in stimuli and subsequent development in collaboration

with Gustav Fechner (Fechner 1964), the relationship between physical magnitudes of stimuli and their perceived intensity was developed and quantified. In studying such relationships, Fechner concluded, 'In order that the intensity of a sensation may increase in arithmetical progression, the stimulus must increase in geometrical progression.' Such a conclusion has since formed the basis of the Weber–Fechner law.

Sensory perceptions of weight, vision (brightness), and sound, among other areas, have since been the subject of considerable research examination, where the relationship between stimulus and perception is typically observed to be logarithmic. In particular, research on perception of stimuli finds that the *just noticeable difference* (abbreviated *JND*), or *differential threshold*, which is the smallest detectable change or difference in a sensory input that is perceivable by an individual, is a constant fraction of the level of stimulation. Marketing researchers have subsequently examined the law for its usefulness to understand pricing perception for, among other topics, different magnitudes of pricing and price comparisons in relation to reference prices as well as consumer perceptions of other sensory stimuli, and have found the law's predicted relationships to be consistent with research findings in many markting-related areas.

KEY WORDS Stimuli, perception, detectable change

IMPLICATIONS

Marketers seeking to understand better how and to what extent consumers may perceive pricing levels and pricing changes may benefit from a greater knowledge of the relationships indicated by the Weber–Fechner law. Ultimately, consumer responses to pricing strategies and tactics may be a function of relationships between stimuli and perception that are predicted by the Weber–Fechner law. Similarly, consumer responses to promotions and other marketing stimuli may also be potentially understood better by examining such stimuli in terms of consumer perceptions and the relationships expected given the Weber–Fechner law and the just noticeable difference (JND) or differential threshold concept.

APPLICATION AREAS AND FURTHER READINGS
Pricing

Miranda, M. J. (2001). 'The Influence of Price Reductions on Shoppers' Reference Price and Reservation Price when Upgrading to Premium Brands,' *Journal of Targeting Measurement and Analysis for Marketing*, 10(1), 42–54.

Skouras, T., Avlonitis, G. J., and Indounas, K. A. (2005). 'Economics and Marketing on Pricing: How and Why do they Differ?' *Journal of Product and Brand Management*, 14(6), 362–374.

Monroe, K. B., and Lee, A. Y. (1999). 'Remembering Versus Knowing: Issues in Buyers' Processing of Price Information,' *Journal of the Academy of Marketing Science*, 27(2), 207–225.

Monroe, Kent B. (1973). 'Buyers' Subjective Perceptions of Price,' *Journal of Marketing Research*, 10(1), February, 70–80.

Monroe, Kent B. (1971). 'The Information Content of Prices: A Preliminary Model for Estimating Buyer Response,' *Management Science*, 17(8), Application Series, April, B519–B532.

Promotion
Ailawadi, K. L., and Neslin, S. A. (1998). 'The Effect of Promotion on Consumption: Buying More and Consuming it Faster,' *Journal of Marketing Research*, 35(3), 390–398.

BIBLIOGRAPHY
Fechner, G. T. (1964). *Elemente der Psychophysik* (Elements of Psychophysics). Amsterdam: E. J. Bonset. (Original work published 1860.)
Weber, E. H. (1996). 'On Touch and on the Sense of Touch and Common Sensibility,' in H. E. Ross and D. J. Murray (eds. and trans.), *E. H. Weber on the Tactile Senses,* 2nd edn.), Hove: Erlbaum.
Cooper, P. (1969). 'Subjective Economics: Factors in a Psychology of Spending,' in B. Taylor and G. Wills (eds.), *Pricing Strategy.* London: Staples, 112–121.

■ wheel of retailing theory

(also called the wheel of retailing or the wheel of retailing hypothesis)

DESCRIPTION
A theory of change among retail institutions putting forth the view that retail institutions follow a consistent and predictable cycle of evolution in the way they compete strategically in the retail environment.

KEY INSIGHTS
Developed in pioneering research by McNair (1957) and Hollander (1960), wheel of retailing theory proposes that retail institutions evolve systematically. In particular, the theory argues that new retailers are able to gain a foothold in the retail market and compete successfully with existing retailers by offering lower prices that are achievable as a result of productivity gains and certain reductions in customer service. As such firms become established, however, there is a tendency for them to lose their competitive edge as a result of their raising prices, moving up-market in their product mixes and in the customers they wish to attract, and increasing levels of customer service. Such actions, however, result in strategic problems for the firms as new, low-priced retailers attack the firms from below.

KEY WORDS Retailing, evolution, institutional change

IMPLICATIONS
The wheel of retailing theory and its associated concepts can potentially help strategic marketers to understand, explain, and predict better how particular retail organizations may evolve given their particular stage of evolutionary development. While it may be difficult to identify exactly when retail organizations may undergo certain evolutionary changes, the theory is nevertheless useful in supporting analyses of one's own retail organization as well as competitor organizations in an effort to identify predictable evolutionary paths.

APPLICATION AREAS AND FURTHER READINGS
Retail Marketing
Brown, Stephen (1991). 'Variations on a Marketing Enigma: The Wheel of Retailing Theory,' *Journal of Marketing Management*, 7(2), 131–155.
Izraeli, D. (1973). 'The Three Wheels of Retailing: A Theoretical Note,' *European Journal of Marketing*, 7(1), 70–74.

BIBLIOGRAPHY
Hollander, Stanley C. (1960). 'The Wheel of Retailing,' *Journal of Marketing*, 24, July, 37–42.
McNair, M. (1957). 'Significant Trends and Developments in the Postwar Period,' in A. Smith (ed.), *Competitive Distribution in a Free High Level Economy and its Implications for the University*. Pittsburgh: University of Pittsburgh Press, 1–25.

☐ **white goods** *see* goods

■ **wholesale marketing**

DESCRIPTION
Marketing involving the sale of offerings intended for resale and where customers may be retailers or other marketing intermediaries.

KEY INSIGHTS
While wholesale marketing is most often associated with the sale of offerings to retailers for subsequent resale to consumers, it may also involve the provision of the firm's offerings to any number of marketing intermediaries or business organizations who may also be wholesalers themselves. Thus, the firm's customers may be industrial, institutional, commercial, and professional organizations. Wholesalers may also act as agents or brokers facilitating exchanges among such organizations. A common practice in wholesale marketing is to supply goods to customers in relatively large quantities and at bulk prices, where such customers, in turn, offer them to their customers in smaller quantities and at marked-up prices. Wholesale marketing may add value to a firm's offerings in any number of ways including providing storage for the firm's customers, sorting, repacking, and redistributing offerings, and delivering offerings to the firm's customers. Marketing communication methods may vary as well, although sales promotions and personal selling are common approaches in wholesale marketing.

KEY WORD Reselling

IMPLICATIONS
As wholesale marketing can involve interactions with any number of channel members, marketers involved in wholesale marketing may benefit from a greater knowledge of wholesale channel strategies as well as approaches for establishing effective relationships wth channel members. Understanding, too, the range of opportunities a wholesaler has to provide value-added services can further benefit the wholesale marketer seeking to enhance firm profitability.

APPLICATION AREAS AND FURTHER READINGS

Marketing Strategy

Hanson, J. C., and Rada, D. J. (1992). 'Developing a Wholesale Marketing Strategy for Produce in the Mid-Atlantic Region,' *Informational Series No. 209201*, Department of Agricultural and Resource Economics, University of Maryland at College Park.

Cadilhon, J. J., Fearne, A., Hughes, D., and Moustier, P. (2003). 'Wholesale Markets and Food Distribution in Europe: New Strategies for Old Functions,' *Discussion Paper no 2, Centre for Food Chain Research*, Imperial College, London.

Marketing Management

Lusch, Robert F., and Brown, James (1996). 'Interdependency, Contracting, and Relational Behavior in Marketing Channels,' *Journal of Marketing*, 60, October, 19–38.

Retail Marketing

Balderston, E. (1956). 'Assortment Choice in Wholesale and Retail Marketing,' *Journal of Marketing*, 21, October, 175-183.

Marketing Research

Kent, W. E., Meyer, R. A., and Reddam, T. M. (1987). 'Reassessing Wholesaler Marketing Strategies: The Role of Travel Research,' *Journal of Travel Research*, 25(3), 31-33.

BIBLIOGRAPHY

Eggland, Steven A. (1984). *Wholesale Marketing*. Austin, Tex.: Extension Instruction and Materials Center, Div. of Continuing Education, University of Texas.

Roe, Robert G. (1969). 'Short Course in Wholesaling,' *Journal of Marketing*, 33(3), 102-103.

☐ **wikimarketing** *see* online marketing

■ willingness to pay

DESCRIPTION

The maximum amount a consumer would pay for an offering based on the consumer's perception of the offering's value.

KEY INSIGHTS

Willingness to pay (or WTP) for an offering, being an indicator of the offering's perceived value by a consumer, can be viewed as the consumer's valuation of the gross benefits the consumer perceives in the offering, quantified in monetary terms. In marketing research, WTP can be a practical measure of the strength of a brand as it is indicative of consumers' attachment to the branded offering.

KEY WORDS Perceived value, product worth

IMPLICATIONS

Willingness to pay is an important consideration in research into the demand for a wide range of offerings and consumer products in particular. Marketers should seek to understand better consumers' willingness to pay for their offerings in an effort to manage the demand of such offerings through means not only including pricing but other areas of marketing that are able to enhance and communicate value that is to be perceived by customers.

APPLICATION AREAS AND FURTHER READINGS

Marketing Research
Cameron, T. A., and James, M. D. (1987). 'Estimating Willingness to Pay from Survey Data: An Alternative Pre-Test-Market Evaluation Procedure,' *Journal of Marketing Research*, 24, 389–395.

Services Marketing
Goett, A., Hudson, K., and Train, K. (2000). 'Consumers' Choice among Retail Energy Suppliers: The Willingnes-to-Pay for Service Attributes,' *Energy Journal*, 21, 1–28.

Retail Marketing
Krystallis, A., and Chryssohoidis, G. (2005). 'Consumers' Willingness to Pay for Organic Food: Factors that Affect it and Variation per Organic Product Type,' *British Food Journal*, 107(5), 320–343.

Consumer Behavior
Prelec, Drazen, and Simester, Duncan (2001). 'Always Leave Home without it: A Further Investigation of the Credit-Card Effect on Willingness to Pay,' *Marketing Letters*, 12(1), February, 5–12.

BIBLIOGRAPHY
Wertenbroch, K., and Skiera, B. (2002). 'Measuring Consumers' Willingness to Pay at the Point of Purchase,' *Journal of Marketing Research*, 39, May, 228–241.

☐ **window of opportunity** *see* strategic window

■ **winner's curse**

DESCRIPTION
The tendency for the highest bid at an auction to exceed the true market value of the item or lot being auctioned.

KEY INSIGHTS
Originally discussed by Capen, Clapp, and Campbell (1971) and subsequently developed in research by Thaler (1992), the winner's curse phenomenon arises when bidders' estimates of the true market value of an auctioned item (or lot) are unreliable as a result of incomplete information and when each bidder independently estimates the value of the item before bidding. In such circumstances, some bidders will underestimate the item's value while others will overestimate its value. While the average bid for an auctioned item is often less than its true market value, reflecting risk averseness among bidders, the bidder overestimating the item's true market value to the greatest extent among all bidders becomes the victim of the winner's curse. In general, the severity of the winner's curse increases as the number of bidders at an auction increases. When an auctioned item is sought for its private value, however, as when a bidder desires an object of art to complete his or her art collection, the winner's curse is not said to apply as private valuation is more important to the bidder than market valuation. Bidders seeking to avoid the winner's curse tend to make efforts to revise downward their ex ante estimations of an item's value to explicitly take into account the effect of the winner's curse.

KEY WORDS Auctions, valuation, bidding

IMPLICATIONS

Marketers involved in auction bidding should seek to understand the extent the winner's curse phenomenon may occur as a result of incomplete information concerning an item's value and knowledge of the number of an auction's participants. Marketers may then more judiciously make efforts to avoid the winner's curse by revising their ex ante value estimates downward as one possible practice. On the other hand, marketers running auctions should seek to understand the extent that a consumer participating in an auction may become a victim of the winner's curse and, while contributing positively to auction profitability, how such an outcome may influence the consumers' subsequent auction participation and bidding behaviors.

APPLICATION AREAS AND FURTHER READINGS

Auctions

Samuelson, W., and Bazerman, Max H. (1985). 'Negotiation under the Winner's Curse,' in V. Smith (ed.), *Research in Experimental Economics*, vol. iii. Greenwich, Conn.: JAI Press.

Ferris, Kenneth R., and Pécherot Petitt, Barbara S. (2002). *Valuation: Avoiding the Winners Curse*. Upper Saddle River, NJ: Prentice-Hall, Inc.

Chua, Clare, and Luk, Peter (2005). 'Be a Winner Not a Loser: Experimental Evidence of Winner's Curse,' *Marketing Review*, 5(4), Winter, 303–314.

BIBLIOGRAPHY

Capen, E. C., Clapp, R. V., and Campbell, W. M. (1971). 'Competitive Bidding in High-Risk Situations,' *Journal of Petroleum Technology*, June, 641–653.

Thaler, Richard (1988). 'Anomalies: The Winner's Curse,' *Journal of Economic Perspectives*, 2(1), 191–202.

Thaler, Richard (1992). *The Winner's Curse*. New York: The Free Press.

☐ **wireless marketing** *see* mobile marketing

☐ **word-of-mouse marketing** *see* viral marketing

■ word-of-mouth communication

DESCRIPTION

Communication by and among consumers about particular product or service offerings, promotions, firms, or markets that is generally informal and frequently person to person.

KEY INSIGHTS

Word-of-mouth (or WoM) communication among consumers regarding a particular product or service offering, promotion, firm, or market typically involves verbal and informal person-to-person communication. However, the scope of word-of-mouth communication also includes communication by electronic means such as e-mail, blogs, and message boards on the World Wide Web. Such communication may emphasize users' experiences with products or services, opinions of them, recommendations, or it may consist solely of unbiased information. Word-of-mouth communication may be characterized as being positive/negative,

favorable/unfavorable, or indifferent. Positive word-of-mouth communication can be viewed as the addition of a free flow of information which
augments the flow of information provided by advertising. Negative
word-of-mouth communication may take many forms including communication of unsatisfactory experiences or adverse rumors about a brand,
offering, firm, or industry.

KEY WORDS Verbal communication, informal communication

IMPLICATIONS
Knowledge of the type of information communicated via word of mouth
is often considered important to marketers since, for many products
and services, negative word-of-mouth communication is more common
than positive communication. In addition, since unfavorable information
tends to carry more weight than favorable information among prospective consumers for many products and services, marketing managers
should strive to actively monitor as well as influence both the type and
level of word-of-mouth communication.

APPLICATION AREAS AND FURTHER READINGS
Services Marketing
Mangold, W. G., Miller, F., and Brockway, G. R. (1999). 'Word-of-Mouth Communi-
  cation in the Service Marketplace,' *Journal of Services Marketing*, 13(1), 73–89.
Harrison-Walker, L. Jean (2001). 'The Measurement of Word-of-Mouth Communi-
  cation and an Investigation of Service Quality and Customer Commitment as
  Potential Antecedents,' *Journal of Service Research*, 4(1), 60–75.

Marketing Research
Godes, D., and Mayzlin, D. (2004). 'Using Online Conversations to Study Word-of-
  Mouth Communication,' *Marketing Science*, 23(4), 545–560.

BIBLIOGRAPHY
Ellison, G., and Fudenberg, D. (1995). 'Word-of-Mouth Communication and Social
  Learning,' *Quarterly Journal of Economics*, 110, 93–126.
Engel, James F., Kegerreis, Robert J., and Blackwell, Roger D. (1969). 'Word-of-
  Mouth Communication by the Innovator,' *Journal of Marketing*, 33(3), July, 15–19.

■ word-of-mouth effect

DESCRIPTION
Any effect resulting from word-of-mouth communication among consumers.

KEY INSIGHTS
The effects of word-of-mouth communication may be positive, negative,
or neutral depending on its magnitude and content. The effects may also
be limited to a particular brand, product, service, promotion, or firm but
may also encompass entire industries or markets. The strategic importance of word-of-mouth communication effects may also vary, where,
for some firms and some products (e.g. a local manufacturer of a new
popcorn snack), its positive effect is counted upon as the sole means to
spread awareness and interest in the product, while for other firms and
products (e.g. Coca-Cola) its positive effect may be dwarfed by ongoing
advertising by the firm.

KEY WORDS Informal communication effects

IMPLICATIONS
Marketing strategists often have an opportunity to create and leverage positive word-of-mouth communication for new offerings or promotions to achieve significant effects on the awareness, interest, evaluation, and/or purchase of a particular offering, where word of mouth can be generated either to augment other marketing communication approaches or to substitute for them. At the same time, marketers should seek to understand how and to what extent possible negative word-of-mouth communication may be generated through a strategy relying upon the approach and be prepared to weather responses that are unexpectedly negative.

APPLICATION AREAS AND FURTHER READINGS
Marketing Strategy
Mahajan, Vijay, Muller, Eitan, and Kerin, Roger A. (1984). 'Introduction Strategy for New Products with Positive and Negative Word-of-Mouth,' *Management Science*, 30(12), December, 1389–1404.
Grewal, Rajdeep, Cline, Thomas W., and Davies, Antony (2003). 'Early-Entrant Advantage, Word-of-Mouth Communication, Brand Similarity, and the Consumer Decision-Making Process,' *Journal of Consumer Psychology*, 13(3), October, 187–197.

Marketing Modeling
Bemmaor, Albert C. (1994). 'Modeling the Diffusion of New Durable Goods: Word-of-Mouth Effect versus Consumer Heterogeneity,' in Gilles Laurent, Gary L. Lilien, and Bernard Pras (eds.), *Research Traditions in Marketing*. Boston: Kluwer Academic, 201–223.

Services Marketing
Wangenheim, Florian V., and Bayón, Tomás (2004). 'The Effect of Word of Mouth on Services Switching: Measurement and Moderating Variables,' *European Journal of Marketing*, 38(9–10), September, 1173–1185.

BIBLIOGRAPHY
Robertson, Thomas S. (1971). *Innovative Behavior and Communication*. New York: Holt, Rinehart & Winston.

■ word-of-mouth marketing

(also called buzz marketing, grassroots marketing, peer-to-peer marketing, person-to-person marketing, evangelism marketing, or referral marketing)

DESCRIPTION
An approach aimed at leveraging the use of personal recommendations and referrals in the marketplace as a major basis for the firm's marketing efforts and where a desirable effect is a marketplace buzz, or intense and interactive word-of-mouth communication in the marketplace.

KEY INSIGHTS
A word-of-mouth marketing approach often involves identifying and cultivating opinion leaders for the firm's offerings and encouraging them

to spread positive information about the offering to others. While buzz marketing is frequently used interchangeably with word-of-mouth marketing, a similar but little-used term is that of *evangelism marketing*, which may be viewed as a somewhat more extreme version of word-of-mouth marketing characterized by a marketing emphasis on developing customers with exceptionally strong convictions in the firm's offerings—to such an extent that such customers actively and voluntarily persuade others to adopt the offerings. As a word-of-mouth marketing approach benefits from source credibility and may involve little marketing expenditure, the approach is considered to be valuable by many marketers. A variation of word-of-mouth marketing is viral marketing, which makes use of the internet for its effectiveness (see **viral marketing**).

KEY WORDS Verbal communication, informal communication

IMPLICATIONS
As the intent of marketers using word-of-mouth marketing is to produce highly beneficial and dramatic word-of-mouth effects (see **word-of-mouth effect**) through word-of-mouth communication (see **word-of-mouth communication**), marketers should seek to understand better how and to what extent such effects may be produced by the firm's efforts relative to its particular product offerings in order to leverage such knowledge in the firm's strategies and tactics. For example, a firm's word-of-mouth marketing strategy may involve use of traditional informal communication channels as well as communication via the internet.

APPLICATION AREAS AND FURTHER READINGS
Marketing Strategy
Rosen, Emanuel (2000). *The Anatomy of Buzz: How to Create Word of Mouth Marketing.* New York: Doubleday.

Consumer Behavior
Goldenberg, J., Libai, B., and Muller, E. (2001). 'Talk of the Network: A Complex Systems Look at the Underlying Process of Word-of-Mouth,' *Marketing Letters*, 12(3), 211–224.

BIBLIOGRAPHY
Dichter, Ernst (1966). 'How Word-of-Mouth Marketing Works,' *Harvard Business Review*, 44 (6), 148.

☐ **World Wide Web marketing** *see* online marketing; Web marketing
☐ **worldwide marketing** *see* global marketing
☐ **WWW marketing** *see* online marketing; Web marketing

X

■ X, theory

DESCRIPTION
A theory of human motivation that views individuals as inherently lazy and selfish.

KEY INSIGHTS
Developed as one of two competing theories by McGregor (1960), with the other theory being theory Y (see **Y, theory**), theory X views individuals as uninterested in work and eager to avoid responsibility. Based upon a pessimistic view of human nature, the theory provides a basis for a set of management practices for workforce motivation that includes the use of a more authoritarian management style, close supervision, and comprehensive controls where there is a threat of punishment for undesirable behaviors. Organizations adopting a theory X perspective are generally command-and-control organizations, where compliance is achieved through a combination of employee rewards and punishments. While many employee behaviors and corresponding management practices are not as extreme as those characterized by theory X, the theory nevertheless is influential in facilitating managements' understanding of the scope and range of management practice.

KEY WORDS Employee motivation, management practice

IMPLICATIONS
While many managers and employees discount the extreme views advocated by theory X, understanding the perspective can be beneficial to evaluate current and desired marketing management practices in an organization. Whether a marketing manager is seeking to evaluate a prospective organization with which to work or manage the firm's marketing workforce, greater knowledge of the theory can help in identifying and understanding pessimistic management perceptions of employees at the very least.

APPLICATION AREAS AND FURTHER READINGS
Marketing Management
Sirgy, M. Joseph (1991). 'Quality-of-Life Studies in Marketing and Management: An Overview,' *Journal of Business and Psychology*, 6(1), September, 3-7.
Buijs, J. (1998). 'Viewpoint: Towards a New Theory X,' *Creativity and Innovation Management*, 7(1), 17-22.

International Marketing
Herbig, P., and Genestre, A. (1997). 'International Motivational Differences,' *Management Decision*, 35(7-8), 562-569.

BIBLIOGRAPHY
McGregor, Douglas (1960). *The Human Side of Enterprise*. New York: McGraw-Hill.
McGregor, Douglas (1966). *Leadership and Motivation*. Cambridge, Mass.: MIT Press.

☐ **X-generation** see generational marketing

■ x-inefficiency

(also called x-[in]efficiency or the theory of x-inefficiency)

DESCRIPTION
Inefficiency in a firm arising when the average cost of producing a product at a particular level of output exceeds the lowest possible average cost of producing that output.

KEY INSIGHTS
Developed in pioneering research by Leibenstein (1966), x-inefficiency, or the theory of x-inefficiency, contrasts with x-efficiency (or allocative economic efficiency) where price equals marginal cost. While owners of firms seek to maximize profits, x-inefficiencies may arise when management practices of firms conflict with such a goal (e.g. where management practices are aimed at increasing salaries, departmental power, etc.) and where the result is that the firm produces at an average cost above the average total cost where price equals marginal cost.

KEY WORDS Economic efficiency, production costs, price

IMPLICATIONS
In highly competitive industries, the survival of a firm may be jeopardized if it is x-inefficient. Marketing managers must therefore be aware of the pursuit and implementation of management practices that are likely to result in excessive costs that ultimately become the source of x-inefficiency.

APPLICATION AREAS AND FURTHER READINGS
Marketing Strategy
Stigler, George J. (1976). 'The Xistence of X-Efficiency,' *American Economic Review*, 66(1), March, 213–216.
Lang, Mahlon G. (1980). 'Marketing Alternatives and Resource Allocation: Case Studies of Collective Bargaining,' *American Journal of Agricultural Economics*, 62(4), November, 760–765.
Tefula, Moses (2002). *The Implications of X-Inefficiency on the Banking Sector in Africa*. Manchester: Institute for Development Policy and Management, University of Manchester.
Anderson, R. I., Fok, R., Zumpano, L. V., and Elder, H. W. (1998). 'The Efficiency of Franchising in the Residential Real Estate Brokerage Market,' *Journal of Consumer Marketing*, 15(4), 386–396.

BIBLIOGRAPHY
Leibenstein, Harvey (1966). 'Allocative Efficiency and X-Efficiency,' *American Economic Review*, 56, 392–415.

Y

■ Y, theory

DESCRIPTION

A theory of human motivation that views individuals as innately productive and cooperative.

KEY INSIGHTS

Developed as one of two competing theories by McGregor (1960), with the other theory being theory X (see **X, theory**), theory Y views individuals as motivated, ambitious, and eager to accept responsibility and exercise self-control and self-direction. Based upon an optimistic view of human nature, the theory provides a basis for a set of management practices for workforce motivation that includes striving to remove barriers that prevent workers from reaching their full potential and providing conditions that give employees freedom to be their best. While most employee behaviors and corresponding management practices do not reach such an extreme as that characterized by theory Y, the theory nevertheless is influential through its incorporation into other management theories, practices, and styles which can be described in many other ways including hard vs. soft and tough vs. lenient. Organizations characterized as theory Y organizations, for example, can be described as relatively loose and free, where control is achieved through voluntary compliance that is gained through persuasion and affiliation.

KEY WORDS Employee motivation, management practice

IMPLICATIONS

Marketing managers involved in the development and implementation of management practices that seek to make the most of employees' full potential may benefit from an understanding of the principles and concepts associated with theory Y. While the theory Y view is characteristically extreme, an understanding of theory nevertheless enables the marketer to assess better its positive contribution to the development of beneficial marketing management practice.

APPLICATION AREAS AND FURTHER READINGS

Marketing Strategy
Urban, Glen L. (2003). 'The Trust Imperative,' *MIT Sloan Working Paper*, No. 4302-03, March. Available at SSRN: **http://ssrn.com/abstract=400421.**

Marketing Management
Willmott, H. (1993). 'Strength is Ignorance; Slavery is Freedom: Managing Culture in Modern Organizations,' *Journal of Management Studies* (Oxford), 30(4), 515–552.

International Marketing
Oh, Tai K. (1976). 'Theory Y in the People's Republic of China,' *California Management Review*, 19(2), Winter, 77.

BIBLIOGRAPHY
McGregor, Douglas (1960). *The Human Side of Enterprise*. New York: McGraw-Hill.
McGregor, Douglas (1966). *Leadership and Motivation*. Cambridge, Mass.: MIT Press.

☐ Y-generation *see* generational marketing
☐ yellow goods *see* goods

■ Yerkes–Dodson law

DESCRIPTION
A theoretical inverted U-shaped relationship between an individual's cognitive arousal and his or her task performance, where the individual's task performance is highest at medium levels of arousal and lowest at both low and high levels of cognitive arousal.

KEY INSIGHTS
Developed in pioneering research by Yerkes and Dodson (1908), the Yerkes–Dodson law relates an individual's cognitive arousal to his or her task performance and proposes that medium intensity stimulation provides an optimum level of arousal for the fastest and most effective learning by the individual. Drawing upon research in neuroscience and biopsychology, the law posits that too little stimulation results in a lack of motivation to perform a task, whereas too much stimulation results in distraction. The relationship proposed by the Yerkes–Dodson law, which is generally supported by research in marketing and psychology, suggests that two different processes influence task performance, the first being an energizing effect of cognitive arousal and the second being arousal's negative, stress-inducing effect. Low arousal levels make it difficult for an individual to distinguish between relevant and irrelevant information, leading to information overload and a lack of response by an individual. Medium levels of arousal, on the other hand, enable an individual to ignore irrelevant information and focus better on the task at hand, while higher levels of arousal can lead to over-sensitization by an individual where the individual disregards relevant as well as irrelevant information.

KEY WORDS Marketing stimuli, cognitive arousal, task performance

IMPLICATIONS
Marketers involved in presenting consumers with stimuli for inducing cognitive arousal as a means to encourage particular consumer actions can benefit from the communication principles suggested by the Yerkes-Dodson law. In particular, the law suggests that marketers should strive to avoid overwhelming consumers with relevant stimuli and information in marketing communications (e.g. sales pitches, advertising) as well as

underwhelming them with information providing insufficient motivations for action, if the aim is to provide optimal levels of marketing stimuli to induce desired consumer actions.

APPLICATION AREAS AND FURTHER READINGS

Marketing Communications

Day, Rong-Fuh, Shyi, Gary C.-W., and Wang, Jyun-Cheng (2006). 'The Effect of Flash Banners on Multiattribute Decision Making: Distractor or Source of Arousal?' *Psychology and Marketing*, 23(5), 369–382.

Tavassoli, N. T., Shultz, C. J., and Fitzsimons, G. J. (1995). 'Program Involvement: Are Moderate Levels Best for Ad Memory and Attitude toward the Ad?' *Journal of Advertising Research*, 35(5), 61–72.

Services Marketing

Singh, J., Goolsby, J. R., and Rhoads, G. K. (1994). 'Behavioral and Psychological Consequences of Boundary Spanning: Burnout for Customer Service Representatives,' *Journal of Marketing Research*, 31(4), 558–569.

BIBLIOGRAPHY

Yerkes, R. M., and Dodson, J. D. (1908). 'The Relation of Strength of Stimulus to Rapidity of Habit-Formation,' *Journal of Comparative Neurological Psychology*, 18, 459–482.

Broadhurst, P. L. (1957). 'Emotionality and the Yerkes–Dodson Law,' *Journal of Experimental Psychology*, 54, 345–352.

Broadhurst, P. L. (1959). 'The Interaction of Task Difficulty and Motivation: The Yerkes–Dodson Law Revisited,' *Acta Psychologica*, 16, 321–338.

Z

▪ Z, theory

DESCRIPTION
An approach to human resource management that emphasizes the adoption and integration of a 'Japanese' style of management and associated management practices.

KEY INSIGHTS
Developed by Ouchi (1981), who builds upon concepts developed and subsequently published by Deming (1986), theory Z is based on the premise that employees consider work as something that is natural and can be satisfying to the extent it meets their work-related psychological needs. In adopting a theory Z perspective, organizations therefore strive to develop employee loyalty through total concern for the person. Employment security and stable career prospects are key characteristics of theory Z organizations. A theory Z management approach emphasizes employee involvement in decision making, seeks to develop employee team spirit, recognizes employee contributions, and aims to develop mutual employee–management respect. In addition, while control systems may be implicit and informal, there is also an emphasis on the use of explicit and formal measures for evaluation.

KEY WORDS Employee motivation, management practice

IMPLICATIONS
While many organizations may find it challenging to adopt fully a management style based on theory Z, knowledge of the theory and its supporting concepts can be invaluable to marketing managers seeking to understand the many possible benefits as well as costs stemming from its implementation. At the very least, understanding better the theory and its principles can provide marketing managers with a basis of comparison for alternative managerial approaches as well as guidance for gradually transforming their organizations in ways that enable greater long-term effectiveness.

APPLICATION AREAS AND FURTHER READINGS
Marketing Strategy
Kotler, P., and Fahy, L. (1985). *The New Competition: What Theory Z Didn't Tell You about Marketing.* Englewood Cliffs, NJ: Prentice-Hall.

Marketing Management
England, G. W. (1983). 'Japanese and American Management: Theory Z and beyond,' *Journal of International Business Studies*, 14, Fall, 131–141.

Lazer, William, Murata, Shoji, and Kosaka, Hiroshi (1985). 'Japanese Marketing: Towards a Better Understanding,' *Journal of Marketing*, 49(2), Spring, 69–81.
Sullivan, J. J. (1983). 'A Critique of Theory Z,' *Academy of Management Review*, 8, 132–142.

BIBLIOGRAPHY
Ouchi, William G. (1981). *Theory Z: How American Business Can Meet the Japanese Challenge*. Reading, Mass.: Addison-Wesley.
Deming, W. Edwards (1986). *Out of the Crisis*. Cambridge, Mass.: MIT Press.

☐ **Z-generation** *see* generational marketing

☐ **zero-sum game** *see* game theory

☐ **zone pricing** *see* pricing strategies

Select Bibliography

Beyond the specific bibliographies presented for each of the terms in this dictionary, the following is a more general bibliography that may be beneficial for further reference and reading:

Bennett, Peter D. (ed.) (1995). *Dictionary of Marketing Terms*. Chicago: NTC Business Books.

Black, John (1997). *A Dictionary of Economics*. Oxford: Oxford University Press.

Colman, Andrew M. (2001). *A Dictionary of Psychology*. Oxford: Oxford University Press.

Heery, Edmund, and Noon, Mike (2001). *A Dictionary of Human Resource Management*. Oxford: Oxford University Press.

Marshall, Gordon (ed.) (1998). *A Dictionary of Sociology*. Oxford: Oxford University Press.

Mercer, David (1999). *Marketing: The Encyclopedic Dictionary*. Malden, Mass.: Blackwell Publishers, Inc.

Pallister, John, and Isaacs, Alan (ed.) (2002). *A Dictionary of Business*. Oxford: Oxford University Press.

Pearce, David W. (ed.) (1989). *The MIT Dictionary of Modern Economics*, 3rd edn. Cambridge, Mass.: The MIT Press.

Vogt, W. Paul (1993). *Dictionary of Statistics and Methodology*. London: Sage Publications, Inc.

www.wikipedia.com

Classification of Key Terms

The following lists categorize all the dictionary entries as laws, theories, concepts, and effects. Sub-categorizations are also provided. For an explanation of these categories, please see the Introduction.

1. Laws (along with principles and rules)
2. Theories (along with hypotheses, models, paradigms, and paradoxes)
3. Concepts (along with marketing approaches and techniques)
4. Effects (along with biases, fallacies and errors, phenomena, and syndromes)

---

1. Laws (along with principles and rules)

LAWS
averages, law of
comparative advantage, law of
comparative judgment, law of
demand, law of
diminishing marginal utility, law of
diminishing returns, law of
effect, law of
Engel's law
exchange, law of
exercise, law of
experience, law of *see* **experience curve effect**
first law of marketing *see* **marketing, laws of**
forgetting law *see* **forgetting curve**
forgetting, law of *see* **forgetting curve**
Goodhart's law
Gresham's law
heavy half, law of the *see* **Pareto principle**
Hick's law
increasing opportunity cost, law of *see* **diminishing returns, law of**
Jost's law *see* **forgetting curve**
large numbers, law of

law(s) of . . . *see specific entries, e.g.*
diminishing returns, law of
Little's law
marketing, laws of
Merkel's law *see* **Hick's law**
Metcalfe's law
Moore's law
Murphy's law
one price, law of
Pareto's law *see* **Pareto principle**
Parkinson's law
parsimony, law of
personal exploitation, law of *see* **least interest, principle of**
power law of forgetting
price, law of one *see* **one price, law of**
primacy, law of
Reilly's law *see* **retail gravitation, law of**
retail gravitation, law of
service, laws of
supply and demand, law of
supply, law of
variable proportions, law of *see*
diminishing returns, law of
Walras' law

Weber–Fechner law
Weber's law *see* **Weber–Fechner law**
Yerkes–Dodson law

PRINCIPLES
accelerator principle
eighty-twenty principle *see* **Pareto principle**
exclusion principle
iceberg principle
least effort, principle of
least interest, principle of
locality, principle of
marketing, principles of
Pareto principle

Peter principle
principle(s) of... *see specific entries, e.g.* least effort, principle of
recency principle

RULES
eighty-twenty rule *see* **Pareto principle**
marketing, rules of
recency rule *see* **recency effect**
rule(s) of... *see specific entries, e.g.* **ten percent, rule of**
sundown rule *see* **marketing, rules of**
ten foot rule *see* **marketing, rules of**
ten percent, rule of

---

2. Theories (along with hypotheses, models, paradigms, and paradoxes)

THEORIES
accordion theory *see* **retail accordion theory**
achievement motivation theory
adaptation-level theory
adoption theory
advertising theory
agency theory
AL theory *see* **adaptation-level theory**
arbitrage pricing theory
assimilation-contrast theory
attitudes, functional theory of
attribution theory
balance theory
bargaining theory
Bayesian decision theory
behavioral decision theory
behavioral theory of the firm *see* **firm, theory of the**
capture theory
catastrophe theory
central place theory
change, E and O theories of *see* **E and O theories of change**
chaos theory
characteristics theory
clubs, theory of
cluster theory
cognitive consistency theory
cognitive theory

communication-information processing theory
complexity theory
congruity theory
construal-level theory
consumer behavior, theory of
consumer choice, characteristics theory of *see* **characteristics theory**
consumer demand theory
consumer satisfaction theory
contingency theory
contingency theory of management accounting
cooperative game theory *see* **game theory**
Darwinian evolution theory
decision theory
demand, characteristics theory of *see* **characteristics theory**
dialectic process theory
drive theory of social facilitation
E and O theories of change
E, theory *see* **E and O theories of change**
economic theory of clubs *see* **clubs, theory of**
equity theory
ERG theory
exchange theory
expectancy theory

expectancy-value theory *see*
  expectancy theory
expected utility theory
field theory
firm, behavioral theories of the *see*
  firm, theory of the
firm, managerial theories of the *see*
  firm, theory of the
firm, theory of the
functional theory of attitudes *see*
  attitudes, functional theory of
fuzzy set theory
game theory
general systems theory *see* **systems
  theory**
generalizability theory
gestalt theory
goods-characteristics theory *see*
  characteristics theory
gravity theory
greater fool theory
Herzberg's theory of
  motivation
hierarchy of needs theory
information processing theory
information systems theory
inoculation theory
internalization theory
item response theory
job characteristics theory
Lancaster's characteristics theory *see*
  characteristics theory
latent trait theory *see* **item response
  theory**
learning theory
leisure class, theory of the *see*
  conspicuous consumption
Lewin's field theory *see* **field
  theory**
location theory
management theory
managerial theories of the firm *see*
  firm, theory of the
marketing, theories of
Maslow's theory of motivation or need
  hierarchy *see* **hierarchy of needs
  theory**
motivation, Herzberg's theory of *see*
  Herzberg's theory of motivation
natural selection theory *see* **Darwinian
  evolution theory**

need hierarchy theory *see* **hierarchy of
  needs theory**
network theory
non-cooperative game theory *see* **game
  theory**
O, theory *see* **E and O theories of
  change**
options theory
organization theory
personal construct theory
planned behavior, theory of
population ecology theory
portfolio theory
price theory
product characteristics theory *see*
  characteristics theory
prospect theory
psychoanalytic theory
queuing theory
random-walk theory
rational choice theory
reader-response theory
real options theory *see* **options
  theory**
reasoned action, theory of
resource dependency theory
retail accordion theory
retail location theory *see* **location
  theory**
self-actualization, Maslow's theory of
  see **hierarchy of needs theory**
self-perception theory
set theory
small group theory
social cognitive theory
social exchange theory
social identity theory
social learning theory
stakeholder theory
subcultural theory
subjective expected utility theory
symbolic interaction theory
systems theory
temperament theory
theory of/theories of... *see specific
  entries, e.g.* **marketing, theories of**
theory... *see specific entries, e.g.* X, theory
transaction cost theory
trickle down theory
upper echelons theory
utility theory

value, characteristics theory of *see*
   characteristics theory
waiting line theory *see* **queuing theory**
wheel of retailing theory
X, theory
Y, theory
Z, theory

HYPOTHESES
efficient market hypothesis
just world hypothesis

MODELS
Dirichlet model

elaboration likelihood model
expectation-disconfirmation model
hierarchy of effects model *see*
   hierarchy of effects

PARADIGMS
OLI paradigm *see* **eclectic paradigm**
Churchill's paradigm
Dunning's eclectic paradigm *see*
   eclectic paradigm
eclectic paradigm

PARADOXES
Icarus paradox

---

3. Concepts (along with marketing approaches and techniques)

CONCEPTS
a priori validity *see* **validity**
absolute cost advantage
absorptive capacity
accessibility *see* **segmentation**
   viability
acquiescence response set
action *see* **buyer influence/readiness**
actionability *see* **segmentation**
   viability
actor–observer difference
actual product *see* **product levels**
adaptation
adaptive strategy
administered VMS *see* **channel**
   arrangement
adopter categories
adoption *see* **adoption process**
adoption process
adverse selection
affect
affordable method *see* **promotion**
   budget setting methods
age segmentation *see* **segmentation**
agglomeration economies
AIDA *see* **buyer influence/readiness**
AIDCA *see* **buyer influence/readiness**
alternative evaluation *see* **buyer**
   decision process
anchoring and adjustment
Ansoff matrix *see* **product-market**
   investment strategies
approach *see* **selling process**

approach–avoidance conflict
asset *see* **strategic asset**
attention *see* **buyer**
   influence/readiness
augmented product *see* **product levels**
awareness *see* **adoption process;**
   buyer influence/readiness
baby boomer *see* **generational**
   marketing
backward integration *see* **integration**
balanced scorecard
barriers to entry *see* **entry barriers**
base-rate fallacy
basing-point pricing strategy *see*
   pricing strategies
Baumol's cost disease
BCG growth-share Matrix *see* **product**
   portfolio analysis
behavioral segmentation *see*
   segmentation
benchmarking
benefit segmentation *see*
   segmentation
benefits
better mousetrap fallacy
bias
blaming the victim
bliss point
Boston Consulting Group matrix (or
   Boston matrix) *see* **product portfolio**
   analysis
boundary spanning
bounded rationality

vertical integration *see*
**product-market investment
strategies**
vertical marketing system *see* **channel
arrangement**
VMS *see* **channel arrangement**
want
white goods *see* **goods**
willingness to pay
window of opportunity *see* **strategic
window**
winner's curse
word-of-mouth communication
X-generation *see* **generational
marketing**
X-inefficiency
yellow goods *see* **goods**
Y-generation *see* **generational
marketing**
zero-sum game *see* **game theory**
Z-generation *see* **generational
marketing**
zone pricing *see* **pricing strategies**

MARKETING APPROACHES
above-the-line marketing
affiliate marketing
affinity marketing
ambient marketing *see* **out-of-home
marketing**
ambush marketing
antimarketing
B2B marketing *see*
business-to-business marketing
B2C marketing *see* **consumer
marketing**
below-the-line marketing
bespoke marketing
blog marketing
bottom-up marketing
brick(s)-and-click(s) marketing *see entry*
at **online marketing**
brick(s)-and-mortar marketing *see entry*
at **online marketing**
business marketing *see*
business-to-business marketing
business-to-business marketing
business-to-consumer marketing *see*
consumer marketing
buzz marketing *see* **word-of-mouth
marketing**

by-the-book marketing *see* **traditional
marketing**
cause marketing *see* **cause-related
marketing**
cause-related marketing
celebrity marketing
cell phone marketing *see* **mobile
marketing**
click(s)-and-brick(s) marketing *see entry*
at **online marketing**
click(s)-and-mortar marketing *see entry*
at **online marketing**
collaborative marketing
comarketing *see* **cooperative
marketing**
commercial marketing
comparative marketing
concentrated marketing *see* **niche
marketing**
concurrent marketing
confusion marketing
consumer marketing
consumer-oriented marketing *see*
enlightened marketing
contrarian marketing *see*
unconventional marketing
convergence marketing
cooperative marketing
copycat marketing *see* **me-too
marketing**
corporate marketing
counter-marketing
cross-cultural marketing
cross-marketing *see* **cooperative
marketing**
cultural marketing *see* **multicultural
marketing**
custom marketing *see* **one-to-one
marketing**
customer-centric marketing *see*
customer-oriented marketing
customer experience marketing *see*
experiential marketing
customer-oriented marketing
customer relationship marketing *see*
relationship marketing
customer value marketing *see*
value-based marketing
customized marketing *see* **one-to-one
marketing**

local marketing
location marketing *see* **place marketing**
loyalty marketing
macromarketing
mail marketing *see* **direct marketing**
many-to-many marketing *see* **affiliate marketing**
markets-of-one marketing *see* **one-to-one marketing**
mass marketing
mass media marketing *see* **mass marketing**
matrix marketing *see* **network marketing**
megamarketing
me-too marketing
micromarketing
minority marketing *see* **multicultural marketing**
mission-based marketing *see* **non-profit marketing**
m-marketing *see* **mobile marketing**
mobile marketing
mobile phone marketing *see* **mobile marketing**
multicultural marketing
multi-level marketing *see* **network marketing**
multimarketing *see* **hybrid marketing**
network marketing
new economy marketing *see* **online marketing, Web marketing**
niche marketing
non-profit marketing
non-profit sector marketing *see* **non-profit marketing**
not-for-profit marketing *see* **non-profit marketing**
offensive marketing
offline marketing *see entry at* **online marketing**
one-to-many marketing *see* **traditional marketing**
one-to-one marketing
online marketing
on-the-edge marketing *see* **unconventional marketing**
OOH marketing *see* **out-of-home marketing**
opt-in marketing *see* **permission marketing**

opt-out marketing *see* **permission marketing**
organizational marketing *see* **business-to-business marketing**
out-of-home marketing
outbound marketing
outdoor marketing *see* **out-of-home marketing**
parity marketing *see* **me-too marketing**
partner marketing *see* **affiliate marketing**
partnership marketing *see* **cooperative marketing**
pay-for-performance marketing *see* **affiliate marketing**
pay-per-click marketing *see* **affiliate marketing**
peer-to-peer marketing *see* **word-of-mouth marketing**
performance-based marketing *see* **affiliate marketing**
permission marketing
person marketing *see* **celebrity marketing**
personal marketing *see* **one-to-one marketing**
personalized marketing *see* **one-to-one marketing**
person-to-person marketing *see* **word-of-mouth marketing**
place-based marketing *see* **out-of-home marketing**
place marketing
point-of-purchase marketing
point-of-sale marketing
postal marketing *see* **direct marketing**
precision marketing
private sector marketing *see* **commercial marketing**
product marketing
public sector marketing *see* **government marketing**
pull marketing
push marketing
radical marketing *see* **unconventional marketing**
reciprocal marketing *see* **cooperative marketing**
referral marketing *see* **word-of-mouth marketing; affiliate marketing**

World Wide Web marketing *see* **Web marketing; online marketing**
worldwide marketing *see* **global marketing**
WWW marketing *see* **Web marketing; online marketing**

door-in-the-face technique
foot-in-the-door technique
low-ball technique
rejection-then-retreat technique *see* **door-in-the-face technique**

---

4. Effects (along with biases, fallacies and errors, phenomena, and syndromes)

advertising wearout effect
anchoring effect
ancient mariner effect
announcement effect
audience effect
Averch–Johnson effect
backwash effects
bandwagon effect
Barnum effect
basement effect *see* **floor effect**
Baumol effect *see* **Baumol's cost disease**
boomerang effect
butterfly effect
bystander effect
carry over effect
ceiling effect
certainty effect
cohort effect
common ratio effect
context effect
contrast effect
country of origin effect
Crespi effect *see* **elation effect**
customer volume effect *see* **loyalty effect**
delayed response effect *see* **lagged effect**
distinctiveness effect *see* **von Restorff effect**
division of labor effect
domino effect
double jeopardy effect
edge effect *see* **serial position effect**
elation effect
end effect *see* **serial position effect**
endowment effect
even price effect
experience curve effect
experimenter effect
experimenter expectancy effect
false consensus effect
fan effect
floor effect
Forer effect *see* **Barnum effect**
framing effect
free rider effect
gain–loss effect
halo effect
Hawthorne effect
hierarchy of effects
hockey stick effect
honeymoon effect
horns and halo effect *see* **halo effect**
I-knew-it-all-along effect *see* **hindsight bias**
imitation effect
income effect
innovation effect
isolation effect
John Henry effect
lagged effect
lagged response *see* **lagged effect**
learning curve effect
loyalty effect
loyalty ripple effect
market share effect
mere exposure effect
mood effect
network effect
nine effect *see* **odd price effect**
odd price effect
order effect

order of entry effect *see* **market entry timing**
outlier effect
overconfidence effect
passing stranger effect *see* **ancient mariner effect**
placebo effect
placement effect *see* **order effect**
Pollyanna effect
price effect
primacy effect
profit-per-customer effect *see* **loyalty effect**
Pygmalion effect
ratchet effect
rebound effect
recency effect
red queen effect
repetition effect
reputation effect
Restorff effect *see* **von Restorff effect**
Ringelmann effect *see* **social loafing**
ripple effect
Rosencrantz and Guildenstern effect *see* **approach–avoidance conflict**
Rosenthal effect *see* **experimenter expectancy effect**
serial position effect
shared-cost effect
sleeper effect
snob effect
snowball effect
spillover effect
substitute awareness effect

substitution effect
testing effect
unique value effect
variety effect
Veblen effect *see* **goods**
volume effect *see* **loyalty effect**
von Restorff effect
Wal-Mart effect
warm/cold effect
word-of-mouth effect

BIASES
common method bias
confirmation bias
hindsight bias
late response bias *see* **bias**
non-response bias *see* **bias**
sequence bias *see* **bias**

FALLACIES AND ERRORS
Concorde fallacy *see* **sunk cost fallacy**
conjunction fallacy
fallacy of composition
fallacy of misplaced concreteness
fundamental attribution error
gambler's fallacy
sunk cost fallacy

PHENOMENA
Asch phemonenon
cocktail party phenomenon

SYNDROMES
me-too syndrome *see* **me-too marketing**
NIH syndrome *see* **new product development**
not invented here syndrome *see* **new product development**

Lightning Source UK Ltd.
Milton Keynes UK
UKOW05f0719140417
299102UK00015B/149/P